THE NEW TESTAMENT
An Expanded Translation

by KENNETH S. WUEST

Teacher Emeritus of New Testament Greek
The Moody Bible Institute

William B. Eerdmans Publishing Company
Grand Rapids, Michigan

The New Testament: An Expanded Translation by Kenneth S. Wuest.
© Copyright Wm. B. Eerdmans Publishing Co. 1961. All rights reserved.

Library of Congress catalog card number 61-17398

ISBN 0-8028-0882-4

Reprinted 2004

CONTENTS

Preface

THIS translation of the New Testament, unlike the standard translations such as the Authorized Version of 1611 and the American Revised Version of 1901, uses as many English words as are necessary to bring out the richness, force, and clarity of the Greek text. The result is what I have called an expanded translation. It is intended as a companion to, or commentary on, the standard translations, and as such it complements them in several important respects.

(1) So far as a due regard for good English order will allow, this expanded translation follows the Greek order of words in a sentence. It places the emphasis where the inspired writer put it, and brings out the style of the original. Thus, for example, according to the Authorized Version (A.V.), John says, "If we say that we have no sin, we deceive ourselves" (I John 1:8). This expanded translation has, "If we say that we do not have a sinful nature, ourselves we are deceiving." In the A.V. Satan says, "All these things will I give thee if thou wilt fall down and worship me" (Matt. 4:9). The Greek order of words, as well as their meaning, is, "These things, to you, all of them, I will give, if, having fallen down upon your knees and having touched the ground with your forehead in an expression of profound reverence, you would prostrate yourself in worship before me." In regard to style, an attempt has been made, for example, to bring out the abruptness of an exclamation or the severity of a rebuke. Thus, the A.V. has our Lord say to Satan, "Get thee behind me, Satan" (Matt. 16:23). The expanded translation offers, "Be gone under my authority, and keep on going, behind me, out of my sight, Satan." The A.V. has Jesus say, "Give place" (Matt. 9:24), a rather polite translation of the

Greek which demands, "Be clearing out of here so as to make room."

The translation here offered will undoubtedly often jar the reader who is used to the smoothness of the standard translations, but it is hoped that thus the reader's attention will be forcibly drawn to what he is reading.

(2) The translation attempts to bring out the full meaning of each Greek word. Some Greek words are so full of meaning that many English words are required to translate them adequately. For example, the A.V. has, "Be not conformed to this world: but be ye transformed" (Rom. 12:2). This expanded translation has, "Stop assuming an outward expression that does not come from within yourself and is not representative of what you are in your inner nature but is put on from the outside and patterned after this age, but change your outward expression to one that comes from within yourself and is representative of what you are in your inner nature." The A.V. has, ". . . that Christ may dwell in your hearts" (Eph. 3:17). The expanded translation has, ". . . in order that Christ might finally settle down and feel completely at home in your hearts." Compare the A.V. of Matthew 7:7, 8 with the following: "Keep on asking for something to be given and it shall be given you. Keep on seeking, and you shall find. Keep on reverently knocking, and it shall be opened to you. For everyone who keeps on asking for something to be given, keeps on receiving. And he who keeps on seeking, keeps on finding. And to him who keeps on reverently knocking, it shall be opened."

The Greek word translated "see" by the A.V. in Philippians 2:23 (". . . so soon as I shall see how it will go with me") says much about the character of Paul. It speaks of the act of a person who had up to a certain moment completely disregarded his own welfare in his concentration upon the welfare of others, and then had pulled his thoughts together sufficiently to look to his own interests. Paul was in prison, awaiting trial for his life. He was so concerned about the welfare of the churches that he had no thought about his own welfare. This expanded translation therefore offers: ". . . as soon as, having turned my attention from other things and having concentrated it upon my own circumstances, I shall have ascertained my position."

The Colossian heresy, in its attack upon the absolute deity of our Lord, states that the divine essence of deity is scattered among the angelic emanations from deity, and that our Lord possessed only a part of it. Paul answers, in the words of the A.V., "For it pleased the Father that in him should all fulness dwell" (1:19), and "For in him dwelleth all the fulness of the Godhead bodily" (2:9). The word "dwelleth" is *katoikeō,* made up of *oikeō,* "to live in a home, to be at home," and *kata,* whose root meaning is "down" and speaks of permanence. The expanded translation reads, ". . . because in Him [God] was well pleased that all the fullness be permanently at home" (1:19), and ". . . because in Him there is continuously and permanently at home all the fullness of absolute deity in bodily fashion" (2:9).

The apostle exhorts Timothy, "Preach the word" (4:2, A.V.). The noun form of the word "preach" is *kēryx.* It was used of the imperial herald, spokesman of Caesar Augustus, who when entering a town as a representative of the Emperor would make a public proclamation of the Emperor's message with such formality, gravity, and authority as must be heeded and obeyed. A full translation, therefore, of Paul's exhortation is: "Make a public proclamation of the Word with such formality, gravity, and authority as must be heeded and obeyed."

The word "sanctify" usually means to the student of the English Bible God's act of bringing a believer to a certain state of holiness in his life. But in Hebrews 10:14, for example, the Greek word used for "sanctify" is *hagiazō.* The basic idea in this word is the act of setting apart; it concerns position, not experience. Therefore this expanded translation has: ". . . for by one offering He has brought to completion forever those who are set apart for God and His service."

(3) Distinctions between Greek synonyms are brought out. In the conversation between our Lord and Peter in John 21:15-18, Jesus' first two questions are here translated, "Do you have a devotional love for me called out of your heart by my precious-

ness to you, a love which impels you to sacrifice yourself for me?" and His third question as, "Do you have a friendly feeling and affection for me?" Peter's three replies are given as, "You know I have a friendly feeling and affection for you." Thus may be seen the connection between the conversation and Jesus' declaration that Peter would indeed exhibit a devotional love for the Lord Jesus by dying as a martyr for His sake.

In Galatians 1:6, 7 Paul writes: "I marvel that ye are so soon removed from him that called you into the grace of Christ unto another gospel which is not another." The two Greek words translated "another" are, in their order, *heteros* and *allos*. The first means "another of a different kind," whereas the second means "another of the same kind." To obtain clarity this expanded translation has: ". . . to a message of good news diametrically opposed to the gospel, which message is not an alternative gospel." The Judaizer's message was both different from the message Paul preached and also diametrically opposed to it. Therefore, Paul declares, the Judaizer's message is not an alternative gospel.

(4) The force of the negative *mē* is carried over into translation. In Greek questions, the use of *mē* implies a negative answer. Thus Jesus' question to the Twelve becomes even more pointed: "And as for you. you are not desiring to be going away, are you?" (John 6:67). And Nicodemus' questions reveal his attempt to teach the great Teacher: "How is a man able to be born, being an old man? He is not able a second time to enter the womb of his mother and be born, is he?" (John 3:4).

(5) In this expanded translation the action found in the Greek tenses is carried over into English. The perfect tense, for example, speaks of an action completed in the past time which has present, and in some contexts permanent, results. The A.V. has, "By grace are ye saved" (Eph. 2:8). The expanded translation offers, "By the grace have you been saved completely, with the result that you are in a state of salvation which persists through present time." The A.V. reports our Lord as saying, "It is written" (Matt. 4:4). This translation has, "It has been written and is at present on record."

PREFACE

In Philippians 3:12 Paul says that he is not yet perfect, namely, spiritually mature. In 3:15 he includes himself with those who are perfect. The explanation of this apparent contradiction is brought out clearly in the expanded translation as follows: In 3:12 Paul uses the perfect tense. He denies the fact that he has been brought to the place of absolute spiritual maturity by the Holy Spirit, a place where there is no more possibility of growth and where it is impossible to sin. In 3:15 Paul uses the verb of being as a noun. Here he speaks of relative spiritual maturity, where there is room for growth in the Christian life. The translation therefore of the two passages is here given this way: "Not that I . . . have now already been brought to that place of absolute spiritual maturity beyond which there is no progress" (3:12), and "As many therefore as are spiritually mature [in a relative sense] . . ." (3:15).

The imperfect tense, which in Greek speaks of progressive action going on in past time, incomplete, is here translated so as to bring out more fully the meaning of a passage. For example, the A.V., speaking of the Jews who came to John's baptism, renders, "They came and were baptized" (John 3:23). The expanded translation has, "They kept on coming in a steady procession and were being baptized."

The expanded translation also distinguishes between the tenses within the modes of Greek verbs. Thus Romans 6:1 and 6:15 become, respectively, "Shall we continue to sin habitually?" and, "Shall we sin occasionally?". Thus, too, John 4:13, 14 is rendered more accurately: "Everyone who keeps on drinking of this water shall thirst again. But whoever takes a drink of the water which I shall give him, shall positively not thirst, no, never." By way of further example, it may be pointed out that the present imperative with the negative *mē* is clearly distinguished. Thus Paul said, "Stop having fellowship with the unfruitful works of darkness" (Eph. 5:11), not, "have no fellowship" (A.V.). Instances could be multiplied to show that in this expanded translation the tenses and modes of Greek verbs are rendered more accurately than in the standard translations.

(6) The translation here offered points up the significance of

the use of personal pronouns in the Greek text. In Greek the person of a verb is indicated in the ending of the verb, and therefore a pronoun is not needed. When a pronoun is used in conjunction with a verb, therefore, it is used for emphasis or contrast. Thus John 10:11, where a pronoun is used, is here translated: "I alone am the good shepherd." First John 2:2 becomes "He himself is a propitiation for our sins." And such distinctions as the one made by Jesus to the Samaritan woman (John 4:22) are made clear: "As for you, you all worship that which you are not knowing. As for us, we worship that which we know."

(7) The presence or absence of the definite article is noted in this expanded translation. The presence of the Greek article identifies, its absence qualifies. Thus "God is love" (I John 4:8) becomes "God as to His nature is love"; and "God is a spirit" (John 4:24), "God as to His nature is spirit." In both these instances the article is absent from the Greek text. In James 2:14 the article is present but its significance is not brought out, for example, by the A.V.: "What doth it profit, my brethren, though a man say he hath faith, and have not works? Can faith save him?" The Greek is really stronger: "Faith cannot save him, can it?" The clear teaching is that faith alone cannot save an individual. But did not Paul teach justification by faith alone without works? The clue to the explanation is the appearance of the Greek article before "faith." The Greek article was originally derived from the demonstrative pronoun, and it retains some demonstrative force. Thus this expanded translation has: "The aforementioned faith cannot save him, can it?" That is, the faith which does not issue in good works cannot save him, can it? The Galatian heresy is therefore not taught by James.

The Authorized Version of Hebrews 5:8 reads: "Though he were a Son, yet learned he obedience by the things which he suffered." But all believers are sons of God, and they learn obedience by the things which they suffer. The expanded translation brings out the fact that the word "Son" is without the definite article, which indicates qualification: "Though He was

Son [of God] by nature. . . ." The point is that in spite of the fact that He is the omniscient God, in His humanity He learned experientially what it was to obey.

A similar difficulty is presented by the A.V. of I Peter 3:1: "Likewise, ye wives, be in subjection to your own husbands; that, if any obey not the word, they also may without the word be won by the conversation of the wives." The second use of "word" here is open to misunderstanding. Some reader might think that the husbands are to be won "without the Word of God." The solution to the difficulty is in the fact that there is no definite article before the second use of "word." Peter exhorts the wives to live a Christian life in witness to their husbands, part of their witness being obedience to them, and so win them "without a word," that is, without further talking, which their husbands might consider nagging, but by example. Thus the expanded translation reads: "In like manner, wives, put yourselves in subjection to your own husbands with implicit obedience, in order that even though certain ones obstinately refuse to be persuaded by the Word and are therefore disobedient to it, they may through the manner of life of the wives without a word [from the wives] be gained."

(8) The distinction between the conditional particle of a hypothetical condition and that of a fulfilled condition is noted in this translation. Take, for example, Satan's words, "If thou be the Son of God, command that these stones be made bread" (Matt. 4:3, A.V.). In this translation Satan appears to present a hypothetical case, as if he were not sure that the Lord Jesus was the Son of God. But the conditional particle is *ei,* which introduces a fulfilled condition. This expanded translation therefore translates: "In view of the fact that you are Son of God by virtue of your participation in the divine essence of deity. . . ."

(9) It is hoped that this expanded translation will give the reader a clearer understanding of certain words used in previous translations. Some of these words are not the translation of the Greek word but its transliteration. Take, for example, the word "blasphemy" in the phrase "the blasphemy against the Holy

Ghost." This word is not itself an English word but merely a word formed by substituting English letters for Greek. Therefore the translation here given renders the famous phrase thus: "impious and reproachful speech injurious to the divine majesty of the Holy Ghost." Another example is Romans 6:3 ("baptized into Jesus Christ"), where "baptized" is a transliteration rather than a translation. The translation here given is: "placed in Jesus Christ."

The A.V. speaks of the angel of the church of Ephesus (Rev. 2:1). The Greek word for "angel" is *aggelos,* "a messenger." The word "angel" is not the translation of the Greek word, only its English spelling. In the translation here given the word "messenger" has been used where the individual is a human being, and "angel" where the individual is a created intelligence of another order of being, a heavenly being. In Revelation 2:1 the "angel" of the church of Ephesus was a human being, perhaps a representative of that local assembly to John, or the pastor of the church. Incidentally, the word "church" (A.V.) is *ekklēsia.* The simple verb form is *kaleō,* "to call." When preceded by the preposition *ek,* "out of," its meaning is "to call out of." The word was used of a called-out group of people, a regularly summoned political body, an assemblage, a gathering, a meeting, the Christian congregation, the meeting of the local church. Hence in this expanded translation the word "assembly" has been used in place of "church."

Other words used in previous translations are no longer in use (for example, "wot," "froward," "trow"), or have changed meaning. An example of the latter is the word "conversation." Today this word means speech between two or more individuals. But the A.V. uses it to translate two Greek words, both of which mean something quite different. The first is *anastrophē,* the general term meaning "manner of life, conduct, behavior," and the second is *politeia,* "the manner of life of a citizen as related to the commonwealth in which he lives." Paul uses this latter, specialized term in Philippians 1:27 because the city of Philippi was a Roman colony and its citizens were people who possessed the privileges and responsibilities of Roman citizenship. Paul uses the term to point out to the Philippians their heavenly citizenship with its privileges and responsibilities. The A.V. has, "Only let your conversation be as it becometh the gospel of Christ"; the expanded translation offers: "Only [since my only reason for remaining on earth is for your pioneer advance in the Christian life], see to it that you recognize your responsibility as citizens [of heaven] and put yourselves to the absolute necessity of performing the duties devolving upon you in that position, doing this in a manner which weighs as much as the good news concerning the Christ."

The reader is cautioned against thinking that this translation is full of interpretation and paraphrase. The translator has held very closely to the earliest and most accurate Greek texts. In isolated instances he has found it necessary to include interpretation or paraphrase in order to bring out clearly a very difficult passage. The following are a few examples: "His perspiration became like great drops of blood [by reason of the fact that His blood burst through the ruptured walls of the capillaries, the latter caused by His agony, coloring the perspiration and enlarging the drops]" (Luke 22:44). The interpretative material is in brackets. In places where interpretation is given in a word or a few words, no brackets occur. Such an instance is found where the word "Name" is used in connection with our Lord. Paul says, "Wherefore God also hath highly exalted Him and given Him THE NAME [the definite article is used in the Greek], that at THE NAME of Jesus every knee should bow" (Phil. 2:9). That name is not Jesus. The latter designation was given Him at His birth. Paul is speaking here of His exaltation consequent upon His humiliation. The expression, "The Name," is one found in the Old Testament, and refers there to all that God is in His attributes, character, majesty, and glory. All of that was placed upon the shoulders of the Man Christ Jesus at His exaltation, although in His deity He possessed it from eternity. Thus, when Jesus says, "Whatsoever you shall ask the Father in my Name, He will do it" (John 16:23), He means, "Whatever you shall request of the Father, He will give it to you in view of all that I am in His estimation." In some instances, therefore, instead of offering the translation "in my Name" we have interpreted, "in view of all that the Lord Jesus is in His Person and work."

For the word "full" when used in connection with the fulness of the Spirit, the word "controlled" is used, for that is what the word means in such a context. For instance, "Jesus being full of the Holy Ghost" (Luke 4:1, A.V.) becomes "Jesus, in the control of the Holy Spirit." The word "master," used of the Lord Jesus so often, is the translation of three different Greek words: *didaskalos,* "a teacher"; "Rabbi," which is a Hebrew word meaning "teacher"; and *epistates,* "a superintendent or overseer." The word "master" was used in the latter instance of one who had power or authority over men and things. This translation offers "teacher" for *didaskalos,* "Rabbi," which means "teacher" where that word is found, and "master" as the rendering of the other word.

For the Greek word *kurios,* translated "Lord" for the most part by the A.V., this expanded translation uses its meaning of "Sir" where a person addresses the Lord Jesus but has no conception of His deity; "master" where the speaker intends to recognize His power and authority but not His lordship or deity; and has reserved the word "Lord" where the speaker recognizes His full deity. The pronoun of the third person, "his," is always capitalized where His deity is recognized by the speaker. But where it is not, as in the case of the Pharisees, the word is kept in lower case for the purpose of reflecting correctly the attitude of the speaker. Again, the forms "thee" and "thou" are not used, even when God is addressed. The German has its ordinary and polite forms of address in *du* and *sie,* the first familiar and the second reverential and deferential, but neither the Aramaic nor the Greek has such forms.

Paragraph divisions in this expanded translation are made with a view to helping the reader to interpret the contents of a verse within its context. The paragraphs group together the larger units of thought. The conventional division according to chapter and verse has been replaced by division according to meaning, although chapter numbers are indicated in the top

PREFACE

margin and verse numbers in the outside margin of each page.

In the effort to capture the meanings of some Greek words and transfer them to the English language, *Webster's Unabridged Dictionary* was frequently used. If a reader should wish to know the meaning of any English word here used, that is the dictionary he should consult.

In places the reader will find that words, phrases, and· sometimes entire sentences which appear in the A.V. do not appear here. This is explained by the fact that the Nestle text upon which this translation is based, is itself based on more accurate manuscripts than those available in 1611. Large sections, such as John 8:1-11 and Mark 16:9-20, which are disputed by some scholars, have been left in this new translation.

In preparing this translation of the Greek New Testament, I have used the following Greek sources and I readily acknowledge with gratitude the aid I have received from them; *Expositor's Greek Testament,* W. R. Nicoll, editor; *Word Studies in the New Testament* by M. R. Vincent; *The Greek Testament,* Henry Alford, editor; *Word Pictures in the New Testament* by A. T. Robertson; *Greek-English Lexicon* by J. H. Thayer; *Vocabulary of the Greek Testament* by Moulton and Milligan; *Biblico-Theological Lexicon of New Testament Greek* by Hermann Cremer; *Greek-English Lexicon* by Liddell and Scott; *A Greek-English Lexicon of the New Testament and Other Early Christian Literature* by W. Bauer, translated by W. F. Arndt and F. W. Gingrich; *New Testament Synonyms* by R. C. Trench; *Acts* by R. J. Knowling; *Romans* by James Denney; *I Corinthians* by G. G. Findlay, *II Corinthians* by J. H. Bernard; *Galatians* by Frederic Rendall; *Ephesians* by S. D. F. Salmond; *A Grammar of the Greek New Testament in the Light of Historical Research* by A. T. Robertson; *A Manual Grammar of the Greek New Testament* by Dana and Mantey; *Light from the Ancient East* by Adolf Deissmann.

THE GOSPELS

A book of the lineage of Jesus Christ, son of David, son of Abraham.

Abraham begat Isaac, and Isaac begat Jacob, and Jacob **2-6**
begat Judas and his brethren, and Judas begat Phares
and Zara of Thamar, and Phares begat Esrom, and
Esrom begat Aram, and Aram begat Aminadab, and
Aminadab begat Naasson, and Naasson begat Salmon,
and Salmon begat Boes of Rachab, and Boes begat Obed
of Ruth, and Obed begat Jesse, and Jesse begat David the
king.

And David begat Solomon of her who had been the **6-16**
wife of Urias, and Solomon begat Roboam, and Roboam
begat Abia, and Abia begat Asaph, and Asaph begat
Jehoshaphat, and Jehoshaphat begat Joram, and Joram
begat Ozias, and Ozias begat Joatham, and Joatham
begat Achaz, and Achaz begat Ezekias, and Ezekias begat
Manasses, and Manasses begat Amon, and Amon begat
Josias, and Josias begat Jechonias and his brethren in
the time of the deportation to Babylon. And after the
deportation to Babylon Jechonias begat Salathiel, and
Salathiel begat Zorobabel, and Zorobabel begat Abiud,
and Abiud begat Eliakim, and Eliakim begat Azor, and
Azor begat Sadok, and Sadok begat Achim, and Achim
begat Eliud, and Eliud begat Eleazar, and Eleazar begat
Matthan, and Matthan begat Jacob, and Jacob begat
Joseph the husband of Mary out from whom [feminine
relative pronoun, singular number, referring to Mary
only] was born Jesus, He who is called Christ.

Therefore all the successive members of the genealogy **17**
from Abraham until David are fourteen members, and
from David until the deportation to Babylon, fourteen
members, and from the deportation to Babylon until the
Christ, fourteen members.

Now the birth of Jesus Christ was thus. After His **18-21**
mother Mary was promised in marriage to Joseph, before
they came together as husband and wife, she was found
to be pregnant, the source of that pregnancy being the
Holy Spirit. However, Joseph, her husband, being a
conscientious, law-abiding man and yet not proposing to

make her a public example, after mature consideration desired to dismiss her secretly. And after he had turned these things over in his mind, behold, an angel of the Lord appeared to him in a dream, saying, Joseph, son of David, do not be afraid to join to yourself Mary, your wife, for that which was begotten in her is as to its source from the Holy Spirit. And she shall give birth to a son, and you shall call His name Jesus, for He himself will save His people from their sins.

22-25   Now, all this has taken place in order that there might be fulfilled that which was spoken by the Lord through the prophet, saying, Behold, the virgin shall be with child, and she shall give birth to a son, and they shall call His name Emmanuel (which being interpreted is, With us is God). And Joseph, having awakened from his sleep, did as the angel of the Lord commanded him. And he took to himself his wife, and lived in absolute continence with her until she gave birth to a son. And he called His name Jesus.

1-6   Now, Jesus having been born in Bethlehem of Judaea in the days of Herod, the king, behold, learned men from the eastern regions, the lands of the sun-rising, made their way to Jerusalem, saying, Where is he who was born king of the Jews? for we saw his star at its rising, and we came to pay homage to him. And the king, Herod, having heard, was stirred up and irritated, and all Jerusalem with him; and gathering together all the chief priests of the people and the men of the people learned in the sacred scriptures, he went to inquiring of them where the Christ should be born. And they said to him, In Bethlehem of Judaea, for thus it has been written through the prophet and is on record: And, as for you, Bethlehem, land of Judaea, by no means are you least among the leaders of Judaea, for out from you shall come one who governs, such a one as will shepherd my people Israel.

7-12   Then Herod, having called the learned men secretly, ascertained accurately from them the length of time since the star's appearance, and sending them to Bethlehem he said, Having proceeded on your way, conduct an exhaustive and accurate investigation concerning the child, and after you discover that for which you are seeking, bring back the news to me in order that I also, having come, may render homage to him. And having heard the king, they proceeded on their way. And behold, the star which they saw in its rising kept on going before them until, having come, it stood above where the young child was. And having seen the star, they rejoiced with great joy, exceedingly. And having come into the house, they saw the young child with Mary, His mother, and having fallen down, they prostrated themselves in homage before Him. And having opened their treasure-chests, they brought to Him gifts, gold, and frankincense, and myrrh. And having been warned in a dream not to return to Herod, by another road they went back to their country.

Now, after they had returned, behold, an angel of the **13-15** Lord appears in a dream to Joseph, saying, Having arisen, take at once under your care the young child and His mother and be fleeing into Egypt, and be there until I tell you. For Herod is about to be seeking the young child to destroy Him. And having arisen, he took the young child and His mother under his care by night and withdrew to Egypt. And he was there until the death of Herod, in order that there might be fulfilled that which was spoken by the Lord through the prophet, saying, Out of Egypt I called my Son.

Then Herod, having seen that he was deceived by the **16-18** learned men, became greatly incensed, and having sent off those appointed to fulfill his wishes, he put out of the way all the male children, those in Bethlehem and in all its surrounding territory from two years and under, according to the time which he carefully ascertained from the learned men. Then there was fulfilled that which was spoken through Jeremiah the prophet, saying, A voice in Rama was heard, lamentation and great wailing; Rachel weeping audibly for her children; and she desired not to be comforted, because they are not.

19-23   But Herod having died, behold, an angel of the Lord appeared in a dream to Joseph in Egypt, saying, Having arisen, take the young child and His mother under your care and be proceeding into the land of Israel, for those who seek the life of the young child have died. And having arisen, he took the young child and His mother under his care and went to the land of Israel. However, having heard that Archelaus was reigning as king in Judaea instead of his father, Herod, he was afraid to go there. And having been warned in a dream, he withdrew into the regions of Galilee. And having come, he established his home in a city called Nazareth, in order that there might be fulfilled that which was spoken through the prophets, A Nazarene shall He be called.

1-3   Now, in those days there makes his public appearance John the Baptizer, making a public proclamation with that formality, gravity, and authority which must be listened to and obeyed, in the uninhabited region of Judaea, saying, Be having a change of mind which issues in regret and a change of conduct, for there has come near and is imminent the kingdom of heaven. For this man is He who was spoken of through Isaiah, the prophet, saying, A voice of One shouting out in the uninhabited region, Make ready at once the Lord's road. Be making straight and level His paths.

4-12   Now, John himself was in the habit of wearing his outer garment made from camel's hair, and a leather belt around his loins. And his diet was composed of locusts and wild honey. Then there proceeded out to him in a steady stream, Jerusalem and all Judaea and all the surrounding country about the Jordan. And they were being immersed in the Jordan river by him while making a public confession of their sins. But, having seen many of the Pharisees and Sadducees coming to the baptism, he said to them, Offspring of vipers, who gave you a private, confidential hint that you should be fleeing from the wrath about to break at any moment? Produce therefore fruit weighing as much as the repentance you profess. And do not think to be saying within yourselves, A father we have, Abraham; for I am saying to you that

6

God is able out of these stones as source material to raise up children to Abraham. And already the axe has been placed at the root of the trees and lies there ready for use. Therefore, every tree which is not producing fruit which is good is being cut out and is being thrown into fire. As for myself, I indeed immerse you in water because of repentance. But He who is coming after me is mightier than I, whose sandals I am not worthy to carry. He himself will baptize you in the sphere of and by means of the Holy Spirit and fire, whose winnowing fork is in His hand. And He will thoroughly cleanse His threshing-floor and will gather His wheat into the granary. But the chaff He will burn with fire unquenchable.

Then comes Jesus from Galilee up to the Jordan to **13-17** John for the purpose of being immersed by him. But he kept on trying to hinder Him, saying, As for myself, I have need by you to be immersed, and as for you, are you coming to me? But answering, Jesus said to him, Permit it at this time, for thus is it fitting for us to fulfill all righteousness. Then he acceded to His wishes. And Jesus, having been immersed, immediately went up from the water, and behold, the heavens were opened, and He saw God's Spirit descending in a form like that of a dove coming upon Him. And behold, a voice out of heaven, saying, This is my Son, the beloved One, in whom I take pleasure.

Then Jesus was led up into the uninhabited region **1-4** for the purpose of being put to the test by the devil, that test being in the form of a solicitation to do evil. And having fasted forty days and forty nights, after this He became hungry. And having come, facing Him, he who puts to the test by his solicitation to do evil said to Him, In view of the fact that you are Son of God by virtue of your participation in the divine essence of deity, speak, to the end that these stones become loaves of bread. But answering He said, It has been written and is at present on record, Not upon the basis of bread only shall the individual live, but upon the basis of every word proceeding out of God's mouth.

5-7   Then the devil takes Him with himself into the city set apart for the worship and service of God, and he caused Him to stand upon the wing of the temple, and says to Him, Since you are Son of God by virtue of your participation in the divine essence of deity, hurl yourself down, for it has been written and at present is on record, To His angels He will give a charge concerning you, and upon their hands they will take you up lest at any time you strike your foot against a stone. Jesus said to him, On the other hand, It has been written and at present is on record, You shall not put the Lord your God to an all-out test.

8-11   Again the devil takes Him with himself into a mountain, exceedingly lofty, and he shows to Him all the kingdoms of the world system and their glory. And he said to Him, These things, to you, all of them, I will give, if, having fallen down upon your knees and having touched the ground with your forehead in an expression of profound reverence, you would prostrate yourself in worship before me. Then Jesus says to him, Be gone, and keep on going, Satan, for it has been written and at present is on record, The Lord your God you shall worship, and to Him only you shall render sacred service. Then the devil leaves Him, and behold, angels came and went to ministering to Him.

12-17   Now, Jesus, having heard that John was delivered up to prison, withdrew into Galilee. And having abandoned Nazareth, having come, He established His permanent home in Capernaum which is beside the sea in the regions of Zabulon and Nephthalim, in order that there might be fulfilled that which was spoken through Isaiah the prophet, saying, Land of Zabulon and land of Nephthalim, road of the sea, beyond the Jordan, Galilee of the Gentiles. The people sitting in darkness saw great light, and with reference to those sitting in the region and shadow of death, light arose to them. From that time on, Jesus began to be making a public proclamation as a herald with that formality, gravity, and authority as must be listened to and obeyed, and to be saying, Be repenting, for the kingdom of heaven has drawn near and is imminent.

And walking about along the shore of the sea of Galilee, **18-20**
He saw two brothers, Simon, the one commonly called
Peter, and Andrew his brother, throwing a casting-net
into the sea, for they were fishermen. And He says
to them, Come here; after me; and I will make you
fishers of men. And they immediately let go the nets
and joined Him as His disciples. And having gone on
from there, He saw two other brothers, James the son
of Zebedee and John his brother, in the boat with Zebedee
their father, getting their nets ready for use. And He
called them. And immediately leaving the boat and
their father, they joined Him as His disciples.

And He was going around in the whole of Galilee, **21-25**
teaching in their synagogues and making a public proclamation of the good news regarding the kingdom, and
healing all chronic and serious disease and all occasional
illness among the people. And the report concerning
Him went off into the whole of Syria. And they brought
to Him all those who were in a miserable condition
physically, suffering with various kinds of chronic and
serious ailments and acute pains, and those who were
demonized and epileptic and paralytic, and He healed
them. And there followed with Him great multitudes
from Galilee and Decapolis and Jerusalem and Judaea
and beyond the Jordan.

And having seen the multitudes, He went up into the **1-12**
mountain. And when He had seated Himself, His pupils
came to Him. And having opened His mouth He went
to teaching them, saying, Spiritually prosperous are the
destitute and helpless in the realm of the spirit, because
theirs is the kingdom of heaven. Spiritually prosperous
are those who are mourning, because they themselves shall
be encouraged and strengthened by consolation. Spiritually prosperous are those who are meek, because they
themselves shall inherit the earth. Spiritually prosperous
are those hungering and thirsting for righteousness, because they themselves shall be filled so as to be completely

satisfied. Spiritually prosperous are those who are merciful, because they themselves shall be the objects of mercy. Spiritually prosperous are those who are pure in the sphere of the heart, because they themselves shall see God. Spiritually prosperous are those who make peace, because they themselves shall be called sons of God. Spiritually prosperous are those who have been persecuted on account of righteousness, because theirs is the kingdom of heaven. Spiritually prosperous are you whenever they shall revile you and persecute you and say every pernicious thing against you, speaking deliberate falsehoods on account of me. Be rejoicing and exult exceedingly, because your reward is great in heaven. For in this manner they persecuted the prophets who were before you.

13-16   As for you, you are the salt of the earth. But if the salt loses its pungency, by what means can its saltness be restored? For not even one thing is it of use any longer, except, having been thrown out, to be trampled under foot by men. As for you, you are the light of the world. A city is not able to be hidden, situated on top of a mountain. Neither do they light a lamp and place it under the bushel but upon the lamp stand, and it gives light to all those who are in the house. In the same manner let your light shine before men in order that they may see your good works and in order that they may glorify your Father who is in heaven.

17-20   Do not begin to suppose that I came to destroy the law or the prophets. I did not come to destroy but to fulfill. For assuredly I am saying to you, until the heaven and the earth pass away, not one smallest letter nor smallest letter-marking shall pass away from the law until all comes to pass. Whoever therefore shall deprive of authority one of these least commandments and shall teach men so, shall be called least in the kingdom of heaven. But whoever shall do and teach them, this man shall be called great in the kingdom of heaven. For I am saying to you, unless your righteousness excels that of the men learned in the sacred scriptures and that of the Pharisees, not in any case will you enter the kingdom of heaven.

You heard that it was said by those of a previous time, **21, 22**
You shall not commit murder, and whoever commits
murder shall be subject to the judgment. But, as for
myself, I am saying to you that everyone who is provoked to anger against his brother shall be subject to the
judgment. Moreover, whoever says to his brother, Raca,
that is, you senseless empty-head, shall be liable to the
Sanhedrin. But whoever shall say, *Mōre,* that is, you
imprudent man without forethought or wisdom, shall be
liable to the hell of fire.

Therefore, if you bring your gift to the altar of whole **23-26**
burnt-offerings and there you remember that your brother
has something against you, leave there your gift before
the altar of whole burnt-offerings and be going away.
First be reconciled to your brother, and then, having
come, be offering your gift. Be friendly and well-dis-
posed toward your opponent in a suit at law, quickly while
you are with him in the road, lest at any time the
opponent deliver you over to the judge and the judge
to the officer, and into prison you are thrown. Assuredly,
I am saying to you, you will not in any case come out
from there until you have paid off the last farthing.

You heard that it was said, You shall not commit **27-30**
adultery. But as for myself, I am saying to you, Everyone who is looking at a woman in order to indulge his
sexual passion for her, already committed adultery with
her in his heart. So then, if your eye, the right one,
causes you to stumble, root it out and throw it from you,
for it is to your profit that one of your members perish
and not that your whole body be thrown into hell. And
if your right hand causes you to stumble, cut it out
and throw it from you, for it is to your profit that one of
your members perish and that not your whole body go
off into hell.

Moreover, it was said, Whoever dismisses his wife, let **31, 32**
him give her a bill of divorce. But, as for myself, I am
saying to you, Everyone who dismisses his wife except in
a case of unchastity, causes her to commit adultery, and

whoever marries her who has been dismissed, commits adultery.

33-37   Again, you heard that it was said by those of a previous time, You shall not perjure yourself but you shall discharge your oaths with reference to the Lord. But I say to you, Do not put yourself under oath at all, neither by heaven, because it is the throne of God, nor by the earth, because it is the footstool of His feet, neither by Jerusalem, because it is the city of the great King. Neither put yourself under oath by your head, because you are not able to make one hair white or black, but let your word be, Yes, Yes, No, No; and that which is more than these things is of the evil which is in active opposition to the good.

38-48   You heard that it was said, An eye in substitution for an eye, a tooth in substitution for a tooth. But as for myself, I am saying to you, Do not set yourself against the evil which is in active opposition to the good, but whoever slaps you on the right cheek, turn to him also the other. And to the one who desires to summon you to be put on trial and have judgment passed upon you for the purpose of taking away your under-garment, yield up your outergarment also. And whoever commandeers your services as a courier for a mile, be going off with him two miles. To the one asking you for something, give, and from the one who desires to borrow money from you at interest, do not turn away. You heard that it was said, You shall love your friend and hate the one who is hostile to you, hates you, and opposes you. But, as for myself, I am saying to you, be loving with a divine, self-sacrificial love those who are hostile to you and hate and oppose you, and be praying for those who are persecuting you, in order that you may become sons of your Father in heaven, because His sun He causes to shine on those who are actively opposed to that which is good and upon those who are good, and causes it to rain on those who are fair and equitable in their dealings with others and on those who are not. For if you are loving those who are loving you, what reward are you having? Are not even the collectors of taxes doing the same? And if you greet with deference and respect your brethren only, what more are you doing? Are not even the pagan Gentiles doing the same? Therefore, as for you, you shall be those who are complete in your character, even as your Father in heaven is complete in His being.

Moreover, be holding your mind on the matter of not practicing your correctness of thinking, feeling, and acting before men in order to be attentively viewed by them as a spectacular performer. Otherwise, a reward you do not have in the presence of your Father in heaven. Therefore, whenever you are practicing the virtues of mercy or beneficence, do not sound a trumpet before you as the actors on the stage of life do in the synagogues and in the streets in order that they may be held in honor by men. Assuredly, I am saying to you, they have their reward and the receipt for the same in full. But while you are practicing the virtues of mercy or beneficence, do not allow your left hand to know what your right hand is doing, in order that your mercy or beneficence may be in secret. And your Father who sees in secret will reward you. **1-4**

And whenever you are praying you shall not be as the actors on the stage of life, because they are fond of praying in the synagogues and while standing at the corners of avenues in order that they may be seen by men. Assuredly, I am saying to you, They have their reward and the receipt for the same in full. But, as for you, whenever you are praying, enter into your secret and well-guarded place, and having closed your door, pray to your Father in secret. And your Father who sees in secret will reward you. Moreover, when praying, do not repeat the same thing over and over as the pagans do, for they think that they will be heard because of their multiplicity of words. Therefore, do not be like them, for your Father knows the things you have need of before you ask Him for them. **5-8**

Therefore, as for you, in this manner be praying: Our Father who is in heaven, let your Name be venerated, let your kingdom come, let your will be done, as in **9-13** heaven, so on earth. Our bread, that for the coming day, give us today. And forgive us the moral obligations we owe, even as also, as for us, we have forgiven those morally obligated to us. And do not lead us into the place of testing where a solicitation to do evil would tempt us to sin, but deliver us from the Pernicious One.

14-18 For, if you forgive men their trespasses, your heavenly Father will also forgive you. But if you do not forgive men, neither will your Father forgive your trespasses. Moreover, whenever you are fasting, stop being like the actors on the stage of life, of a sad and gloomy countenance, for they mask their faces in order that they may appear to men as those who are fasting. Assuredly, I am saying to you, they have their reward and the receipt for the same in full. But as for you, when fasting, massage your head with olive oil and wash your face, in order that you may not appear to men to be fasting but to your Father who observes in the sphere of the secret, and your Father who observes in the sphere of the secret will reward you.

19-21 Stop accumulating treasures upon the earth for yourselves, where the clothes-moth and corrosion destroy and where thieves break in and steal. But be accumulating treasures in heaven where neither a clothes-moth nor corrosion destroys and where thieves do not break in nor steal, for where your treasure is, there will also be your heart.

22-24 The lamp of the body is the eye. If therefore your eye be in single focus, pure, sound, your whole body will be well lighted. But if your eye be diseased, your whole body will be full of darkness. If therefore the light which is in you is darkness, the darkness, how great. No one is able to be habitually serving two masters, for either he will hate the one and the other one of a different kind he will love, or one he will hold to firmly as against the other, and the other one of a different kind he will disdain. You are not able to be rendering a slave's obedience to God and to a passion for accumulating wealth.

On this account I am saying to you, Stop worrying   25-34
about your life, what you shall eat, or what you shall
drink, and about your body, with what you will clothe
yourself. Is not the life more than food and the body
more than clothing? Consider the birds of the heaven.
They are not sowing seed, nor reaping, nor even are they
collecting into granaries. And yet your heavenly Father is
feeding them. As for you, do you not surpass them? Moreover, who is there of you who by worrying is able to put to
his stature eighteen inches? And concerning clothing, why
are you worrying? Consider well the lilies of the field,
and learn thoroughly in what way they grow. They are
not laboring to the point of exhaustion nor even are they
spinning. But I am saying to you, Not even Solomon in
all of his glory clothed himself as one of these. And in
view of the fact that the herbage of the field, which is in
existence today and tomorrow is thrown into a furnace,
God thus clothes, will He not the sooner clothe you, you
of little faith? Therefore, stop worrying, saying, What
shall we eat? or, What shall we drink? or, With what
shall we clothe ourselves? For all these things the pagan
Gentiles are diligently seeking. For your heavenly
Father knows that you are in constant need of all these
things. But be seeking first the kingdom and His righteousness, and these things, all of them, shall be added to
you. Therefore, do not begin to worry about tomorrow,
for the next day will take care of its own interests. Sufficient to the day is its trouble.

Stop pronouncing censorious criticism, in order that   1-5
you may not be the object of censorious criticism, for with
that judgment by which you are judging, you will be
judged, and with that standard of judgment with which
you are judging, by that standard will judgment be passed
on you. And why do you contemplate the splinter of
wood in the eye of your brother and do not put your mind
upon the log in your own eye? Or, how is it that you
will say to your brother, Permit me to draw out the
splinter from your eye, and, behold, the log is in your eye?
O actor on the stage of life, draw out first from your eye

the log, and then you will see clearly to draw out the splinter from the eye of your brother.

6   Do not give that which is holy to the dogs, neither throw your pearls before the hogs lest perchance they trample them under their feet and having turned, lacerate you.

7-12   Keep on asking for something to be given and it shall be given you. Keep on seeking, and you shall find. Keep on reverently knocking, and it shall be opened to you. For everyone who keeps on asking for something to be given, keeps on receiving. And he who keeps on seeking, keeps on finding. And to him who keeps on reverently knocking, it shall be opened. Or, who is there of you, a man, who, should his son ask for a loaf of bread; he will not give him a stone, will he? Or, should he also ask for a fish; he will not give him a snake, will he? Therefore, as for you, in view of the fact that though being those who are evil, actively opposed to that which is good, you know how to be constantly giving good gifts to your children, how much more shall your Father who is in heaven give good things to those who ask Him for them? Therefore, all things whatever you may be desiring men to be doing to you, in the same manner also, as for you, you be doing to them, for this is the law and the prophets.

13, 14   Enter through the narrow gate, because broad is the gate and spacious is the road, the one that leads away to ruin and everlasting misery. And many there are who are constantly entering through it. Because narrow is the gate and compressed is the road, the one which leads away into the life, and few there are who are finding it.

15-20   Constantly be guarding yourself against the false prophets, men who are of such a character as to be coming to you with sheep-like outward expressions, but in their inner being they are rapacious wolves. By their fruits you will clearly recognize them. They do not gather up grapes from bramble bushes or figs from a prickly wild plant, the thistle, do they? In the same manner every intrinsically good tree produces beautiful fruits, but a rotten tree produces fruits which are rotten to the core. An intrinsically good tree is not able to produce rotten fruits, neither is a rotten tree able to produce beautiful fruit. Every tree which is not producing beautiful fruit is customarily cut out and is thrown into the fire. So then, by their fruits you will clearly recognize them.

Not everyone who keeps on saying to me, Lord, Lord, **21-23** shall enter into the kingdom of heaven, but he who keeps on doing that which my Father who is in heaven has determined shall be done. Many shall say to me in that day, Lord, Lord, did we not in your Name prophesy, and in your Name cast out demons, and in your Name perform many miracles which demonstrated the power of God? And then I will declare in a public announcement to them, I never came to know you experientially. Be going away from me, you who are working the lawlessness.

Therefore, everyone who is of such a character as to **24-27** be habitually hearing these words of mine and habitually doing them, shall be likened to an intelligent man who is of such a nature that he built his house upon the rocky cliff. And the violent rainstorm came down and the torrents came, and the winds blew and rushed upon and beat against that house, and it did not fall, for it had been built upon the rocky cliff as its foundation and was firmly established upon it. And everyone who is hearing these words of mine and is not habitually doing them shall be likened to an imprudent man without forethought or wisdom who was of such a character that he built his house upon the sandy ground. And the violent rainstorm came down and the torrents came, and the winds blew and rushed upon and beat against that house, and it fell, and its downfall was great.

And it came to pass that when Jesus brought these **28, 29** words to a close, the crowds were struck with astonishment to the point of the loss of self-control by His teaching, for He was teaching them in the manner of one who possesses authority, and not in the manner of their men learned in the sacred writings.

1-4   And having come down from the mountain, great crowds followed with Him. And behold, a leper having come, fell upon his knees and touched the ground with his forehead in an expression of profound reverence before Him, saying, Master, in the event that you may be having a heartfelt desire, you are able to cleanse me. And having stretched out His hand He touched him saying, I am desiring it from all my heart. Be cleansed at once. And immediately his leprosy was cured by being cleansed away. And Jesus says to him, See to it, do not tell even one person, but be going away, show yourself at once as evidence to the priest, and offer the gift which Moses enjoined, as a testimony to them.

5-13   And having entered Capernaum, there came to Him the commander of a hundred soldiers, pleading with Him and saying, Sir, my servant is bedridden at my home, a paralytic, being constantly tormented, terribly. He says to him, I, having come, will heal him. But the commander of a hundred soldiers answering said, Sir, I am not worthy that you should come under my roof, but only speak a word and my servant will be healed. For I also am a man under authority, yet having under myself soldiers, and I say to this one, Be proceeding, and he proceeds, and to another, Be coming, and he comes, and to my slave, Do this at once, and he does it. Now, Jesus having heard, marvelled and said to those who were following with Him, Assuredly, I am saying to you, In the case of not even one person did I find such great faith in Israel. Moreover I am saying to you, Many from the east and from the west shall come and recline at the banqueting table with Abraham and Isaac and Jacob in the kingdom of heaven. But the sons of the kingdom shall be thrown into the darkness, that darkness which is outside of the King's banqueting house. There, in that place, there shall be the audible weeping and lamentation and the gnashing of the teeth. And Jesus said to the commander of a hundred soldiers, Be going on your way. In the manner in which you believed, let it become to you. And the servant was healed in that hour.

And having come into Peter's home, Jesus saw Peter's **14-17**
mother-in-law bedridden and burning with a fever. And
He touched her hand and the fever left her. And she
arose and went to serving Him a meal. Now, evening
having come, they brought to Him many who were possessed with demons. And He ejected the spirits by a
word. And all those who were ill He healed, in order
that there might be fulfilled that which was spoken
through Isaiah the prophet saying, He himself took away
our infirmities and carried off our diseases.

Now, Jesus having seen a crowd around Him, gave **18-22**
orders to go off to the other side. And having approached, one of those men learned in the sacred scriptures said to Him, Teacher, I will follow with you as a
disciple wherever you may be departing. And Jesus says
to him, The foxes always have burrows and the birds of
heaven always have roosting places, but the Son of Man
does not have where to recline His head. And another
of His pupils said to Him, Master, permit me first to go
off and bury my father. But Jesus says to him, Start
following with me as my disciple and continue to do so
as a habit of life, and allow the dead to bury their
own dead.

And after He had gone on board the boat, His disciples **23-27**
accompanied Him. And behold, a great storm arose in
the sea, an earthquake of the sea, its waters stirred to
their depths, so that the boat was so covered with the
waves that it was hidden. But He himself was sleeping.
And having come to Him, they aroused Him from His
sleep, saying, Lord, save us at once, we are perishing.
And He says to them, Why are you such timid ones,
men of little faith? Then having arisen, He rebuked
the winds and the sea, and there came a great calm.
But the men marvelled, saying, What manner of exotic
man is this that even the winds and the sea are obedient
to him?

And when He had come to the other side into the **28-34**
country of the Gadarenes, there met Him two demon-
possessed men coming out of the tombs, exceedingly fierce

and savage, so that a person is not strong enough and thus able to pass by along that road. And behold, they called aloud, saying, What bond of fellowship is there between us and you, O Son of God? Did you come to this place to torment us before the appointed time? Now, there was at a distance from them a herd of many hogs feeding. And the demons went to begging Him, saying, Since you are ejecting us, send us off into the herd of hogs. And He said to them, Be gone, and keep on going. And they, having come out, went off into the hogs. And behold, the entire herd started forward impetuously down the precipice into the sea. And they died in the waters. And those grazing them fled, and having gone into the city they reported all things and the things concerning those possessed with demons. And behold, the entire city went out to meet Jesus, and having seen Him, they begged Him to get out of their boundaries.

1-8   And having gone on board the boat, He crossed over and entered His own city. And behold, they were bringing to Him a paralytic lying prostrate on a couch. And having seen their faith, Jesus said to the paralytic, Courage, child, and continue to be courageous; your sins are being forgiven. And behold, certain of those men learned in the sacred scriptures said in themselves, This fellow is guilty of impious and reproachful speech injurious to the divine majesty of deity. And Jesus knowing their thoughts said, Why are you thinking pernicious things in your hearts? For which is easier, to say, Your sins are being forgiven, or to say, Be arising and start walking and keep on walking? But in order that you may know that the Son of Man possesses authority on the earth to be forgiving sins — then He says to the paralytic, Be arising. Pick up and carry away your couch, and be going off into your home. And having arisen, he went off to his home. And the crowds having seen, became afraid and glorified God who gave authority such as this to men.

9-13   And passing along from there, Jesus saw a man seated at his desk in the custom's office, a collector of export and import duties, called Matthew. And He says to him, Start following with me as my disciple and consider it a permanent appointment. And having arisen, he followed with Him as His disciple. And it came to pass that He was reclining at the dinner table in the house. And behold, many tax collectors and other sinners stained with certain vices or crimes having come, were feasting together with Jesus and His disciples. And having seen this, the Pharisees were saying to His disciples, For what reason with the tax collectors and men stained with such vices and crimes is your teacher eating? And having heard this, He said, No need do those have who are in sound health, of a doctor, but those who are ill; having gone on your way, learn what is meant, Mercy I am desiring, and not a sacrifice offered on an altar. For I did not come to call men righteous in character but those who are sinners by nature.

Then there come to Him the disciples of John, saying, **14-17** As for us, what is the reason why we and the Pharisees are observing fasts, but your disciples are not doing so? And Jesus said to them, The sons of the nuptials, companions of the bridegroom, are not able to be mourning while the bridegroom is with them, are they? But days will come when the bridegroom shall be taken away from them, and then they shall fast. Moreover, no one puts a patch made of cloth which has not been pre-treated upon a worn-out garment, for the patch which fills it tears away from the garment, and the rent becomes worse. Neither do they put just-made wine into worn-out wineskins. Otherwise, the wineskins burst and the wine is poured out and the wineskins are ruined. But they put just-made wine into wineskins new in quality, and both are preserved from perishing.

While He was saying these things to them, behold, **18-26** there came one, a ruler, and fell upon his knees and touched the ground with his forehead in an expression of profound reverence before Him, saying, My daughter just now died. But, having come, lay your hand upon her, and she shall live. And having arisen, Jesus followed with him, also His disciples. And behold, a woman suffering with a flow of blood twelve years, having come behind Him, touched the fringe of His outer garment, for she was saying within herself, If I only touch his garment, I shall be made whole. And Jesus, having turned around and having seen her, said, Cheerful courage, daughter, be having it constantly. Your faith has saved you and the cure is permanent. No relapse into your former condition. And the woman was restored to health from that hour. And Jesus, having come into the house of the ruler, and having seen the flute-players and the crowd wailing tumultuously, kept on saying, Be clearing out of here so as to make room, for the little girl did not die but is sleeping. And they looked down their noses at Him and went to laughing. But when the crowd was put out, having entered, He grasped her hand firmly, and the little girl was raised up. And this report went out throughout that land.

27-31   And as Jesus was passing by from there, two blind men followed with Him, shouting out and saying, Sympathize with our misery and help us, son of David. And after He had gone into the house, the blind men came to Him. And Jesus says to them, Do you believe that I am able to do this? They say to Him, Yes, Master. Then He touched their eyes, saying, According to your faith let it become to you. And their eyes were opened. And Jesus sternly charged them with earnest admonition, saying, Be seeing to it, let no one be knowing this. But they, having gone out, blazed abroad His fame throughout the whole of that land.

32-34   And as they were going out, behold, they brought to Him one who was dumb, being possessed by a demon. And the demon, having been ejected, the dumb man broke his silence and spoke. And the crowds marvelled, saying, Never yet was it thus seen in Israel. But the Pharisees were saying, By the ruler of the demons he is ejecting the demons.

35-38   And Jesus was going about all the cities and the villages, teaching in their synagogues and making a public proclamation of the good news concerning the kingdom, and healing every disease and every sickness. And having seen the crowds He was moved with compassion concerning them because they were exhausted by their troubles and their long, aimless wanderings, and had thrown themselves to the ground in an utterly prostrate condition as sheep not having a shepherd. Then He says to His disciples, The harvest indeed is great, but the workers, few. Therefore, beseech the Lord of the harvest to thrust out workers into His harvest.

And having called to Himself His twelve disciples, **1-4** He gave them authority over unclean spirits to be ejecting them and to be healing every disease and every sickness. Now, these are the names of the twelve who were sent off as ambassadors with credentials to fulfill a certain mission; first, Simon, the one called Peter, and Andrew his brother, and James the son of Zebedee and John his brother, Philip and Bartholomew, Thomas, and Matthew the tax collector, James the son of Alphaeus, and Thaddaeus, Simon the Canaanite, and Judas, the Iscariot, who also betrayed Him.

These twelve Jesus sent off on a mission, having given **5-10** them a charge, saying, Into the road of the Gentiles do not go forth. And into a city of the Samaritans do not go. But be going on your way rather to the sheep of the house of Israel, sheep who have been neglected and have lost their way and are now wandering about without guidance. Moreover, as you go, make a public proclamation with such formality, gravity, and authority as must be listened to and obeyed, saying, The kingdom of heaven has come near and is imminent. Be healing those who are sick. Be raising the dead. Lepers be cleansing. Demons be ejecting. In a gratuitous manner you received, in a gratuitous manner give. Do not begin to acquire for yourselves gold nor even silver nor even brass for your money-belt, nor even a beggar's collecting-bag for the road, nor even two undergarments nor even sandals nor even a walking stick, for the workman is worthy of his sustenance.

And in whatever city or village you enter, inquire care- **11-15** fully who in it is suitable, and there stay as a guest until whatever time you may depart. And while entering the house, pay it your due respects. And if the house is suitable, let your peace come upon it. But if it is not suitable, let your peace turn back to you. And whoever does not receive you, or heed your words, while going forth out of that house or city, shake out the dust of your feet, considering them as heathen whose dust would defile you. Assuredly, I am saying to you, it will be more endurable for the land of Sodom and Gomorrha in the day of judgment than for that city.

16   Behold, it is I who am sending you on a mission as sheep in the midst of wolves. Consequently, become those who are wary as snakes and guileless as doves.

17-23   Moreover, be constantly on your guard against the aforementioned men, for they shall deliver you over into the power of judicial tribunals, and in their synagogue courts of justice they shall scourge you. And before governors and even before kings you shall be brought on account of me, resulting in a testimony to them and to the Gentiles. However, whenever they deliver you up, do not begin to be concerned about the manner in which or what you shall speak, for it shall be given you in that hour what you shall say, for, as for you, you are not the ones who are speaking, but the Spirit of your Father who is speaking in you. Moreover, a brother shall deliver a brother up to death, and a father a child. And children shall rise up against parents for their own advantage and put them to death. And you shall be hated by all on account of my Name. But he who has persevered to the end, this one shall be kept safe and sound and rescued from danger and destruction. Moreover, whenever they are persecuting you in this city, be fleeing to one of a different character, for, assuredly, I am saying to you, you positively will not finish the cities of Israel until the Son of Man comes.

24-28   A pupil is not above the teacher nor even a slave above his master. It is sufficient for the pupil to be exactly like his teacher, and the slave exactly like his master. Since they surnamed the master of the house Beezeboul, how much more those under the control of the master of the house. Do not begin to fear them, for there is not even one thing that has been covered up which shall not be uncovered, and secret which shall not be made known. That which I am speaking to you in the privacy of darkness, speak in the light of a public disclosure, and that which you are hearing in the ear, publicly proclaim on the housetops. And stop fearing those who kill the body but do not have the power to kill the soul. But rather be fearing him who has power to bring both soul and body to the condition of utter ruin and everlasting misery in hell.

Are not two little sparrows sold for a penny? Yet **29-31** one of them shall not fall upon the ground without the will or the intervention of your Father. Moreover, also your hairs, the ones of your head, all of them, have been counted and the result tabulated. Therefore, stop fearing. As for you, you are of more importance than many sparrows.

Everyone therefore who is of such a character that he **32-XI 1** will confess me before men in the realization of and in testimony to his oneness with me, I also will confess him before my Father who is in heaven in the realization of and testimony to my oneness with him. But whoever is of such a nature that he will deny me before men, I also will deny him before my Father who is in heaven. Do not suppose that I came with the result that my coming would throw peace suddenly upon the earth. I did not come with the result that my coming would throw peace, but a sword. For I came with the result that my coming puts a man at variance with his father, and a daughter against her mother, and the newly married wife against her mother-in-law, and the enemies of a man shall be those of his household. He who has an affection for father or mother above that which he has for me, is not worthy of me. And he who has an affection for son or daughter above that which he has for me, is not worthy of me. And he who does not take his cross and take the same road with me which I take, is not worthy of me. He who has found his soul-life, shall ruin and render it useless, and he who has passed a sentence of death upon his soul-life for my sake shall find it. He who receives

you receives me, and he who receives me receives Him
who sent me on a mission. He who receives a prophet in
the name of a prophet shall receive a prophet's reward.
And he who receives a righteous man in the name of a
righteous man shall receive a righteous man's reward.
And whoever shall give one of these lesser ones in their
station in life a drink of cool water in the name of a
pupil, assuredly I am saying to you, he shall positively
not lose his reward. And it came to pass that when Jesus
finished giving detailed orders to the twelve disciples,
He went away from that place for the purpose of teaching
and of making a public proclamation in their cities with
that formality, gravity, and authority which must be
listened to and obeyed.

2-10   Now John, having heard in the prison the works of
the Christ, having sent through the intermediate agency
of his pupils, said to Him, As for you, are you He, the
One who is the coming One, or should we be looking for
another Messiah of a different character? And Jesus
answering said to them, Having gone on your way, take
word back to John concerning the things you are hearing
and seeing. Blind people are recovering their sight,
and lame people are walking about, lepers are being
cleansed, and deaf people are hearing, and dead people are
being raised up, and poor people are being given good
news. And spiritually prosperous is he whoever does
not find in me that of which he disapproves and that which
hinders him from acknowledging my authority. And
while these were going on their way, Jesus began to be
saying to the crowds concerning John, What did you go
out into the uninhabited place to be contemplating as a
spectacle? A reed being agitated by wind? Well, then,
what did you go out to see? A man clothed in the soft
garments of luxury and effeminacy? Behold, those
accustomed to wearing the garments of luxury are in the
homes of the kings. Well then, why did you go out? To
see a prophet? Yes, I am saying to you, and more than
a prophet. This is he concerning whom it has been written and the record is extant today, Behold, as for myself,
I send my messenger ahead of you who will make ready
your road before you.

Assuredly, I am saying to you, There has not arisen among those born of women a greater one than John the Baptizer. However, the person of most humble station in the kingdom of heaven is greater than he. Indeed, from the days of John the Baptizer until this moment, the kingdom of heaven is being taken by storm, and the strong and forceful ones claim it for themselves eagerly, for all the prophets and the law prophesied until John. And assuming that you would be disposed to receive the following favorably — he himself is Elijah, he who is about to come. He who has ears, let him be hearing. **11-15**

But to what shall I liken this breed of men? It is similar to children who are seated in the market places who are calling to a group of a different character, saying, We played the flute for you and you did not dance. We mourned and you did not beat your breast for grief. For there came John, not eating nor drinking, and they are saying, He has a demon. There came the Son of Man, eating and drinking, and they are saying, Behold, a man who is a glutton and given to wine, one who associates familiarly with tax collectors and sinners stained with vice and crime. And yet this aforementioned wisdom was shown to be such as it should be, righteous, this demonstration having its source in its works. **16-19**

Then He began to be reproaching the cities in which the most of His miracles, demonstrations of the power of God, were done, because they did not repent. Woe to you, Chorazin, woe to you, Bethsaida, because, if in Tyre and Sidon there had been done the miracles of God's power which were done in you, they would in that case long ago have repented in sackcloth and ashes. Nevertheless, I am saying to you, for Tyre and Sidon it shall be more endurable in the day of judgment than for you. And as for you, Capernaum, you will not be exalted as far as heaven, will you? You will be caused to descend even to the depths of misery and disgrace in the unseen world, because, if in Sodom there had been done the miracles demonstrating divine power which were done in you, it would in that case have remained until this **20-24** day. Nevertheless, I am saying to you, For the land of Sodom it will be more endurable in the day of judgment than for you.

25-27   At that epochal, strategic moment of time, Jesus answering said, I render praise to you, Father, Lord of the heaven and the earth, in joyful acknowledgment and concurrence of the fact that you hid these things from the wise and understanding ones, and revealed them to those who are untaught. Even so, Father, because thus it was your good pleasure. All things to me were delivered by my Father, and no one has a full and experiential knowledge of the Son except the Father, neither does anyone have a full and experiential knowledge of the Father except the Son, and he, whoever he may be, to whom the Son desires to reveal Him.

28-30   Come here to me, all who are growing weary to the point of exhaustion, and who have been loaded with burdens and are bending beneath their weight, and I alone will cause you to cease from your labor and take away your burdens and thus refresh you with rest. Take at once my yoke upon you and learn from me, because I am meek and lowly in heart, and you will find cessation from labor and refreshment for your souls, for my yoke is mild and pleasant, and my load is light in weight.

1-8   At that epochal and strategic time Jesus proceeded on the sabbath through the grain fields. And His disciples were hungry and began to be picking off the grain and to be eating it. Now, the Pharisees, having seen this, said to Him, Behold, your disciples are doing that which is not lawful to be habitually done on a sabbath. But He said to them, Have you not read what David did when he was hungry and those with him, how he went into the house of God, and the loaves of bread which were set forth they ate, which it was not lawful for him to eat, neither for those with him, except for the priests alone? Or, have you not read in the law that on the sabbath the priests in the temple desecrate the sabbath and are guiltless? However, I am saying to you, Something greater than the temple is in this place. Moreover, if you had known what this means, I desire mercy and not altar sacrifice, you would not in that case have pronounced guilty those who are guiltless, for the Son of Man is Lord of the sabbath.

And having gone away from that place, He went into their synagogue. And behold, there was a man there having a hand shrunken and wasted. And they asked Him, saying, Is it lawful on the sabbath to heal? in order that they might bring an accusation against Him in court. But He said to them, What man shall there be of you who shall have one sheep, and if this would fall on the sabbath into a pit, would he not get a grip on it and lift it out? Therefore, how much better is a man than a sheep. Wherefore, it is lawful on the sabbath to be doing good. Then He says to the man, Extend your hand at once. And he extended it, and it was restored to its former state of soundness as the other one. But the Pharisees, having gone out, consulted together against Him, how they might destroy Him.

9-14

Now, when Jesus came to know it, He withdrew from there, and many people followed with Him. And He healed them all. And He charged them sharply that they should not make Him known; in order that there might be fulfilled that which was spoken through the intermediate agency of Isaiah the prophet, saying, Behold, my servant whom I chose, my beloved, in whom my soul takes pleasure. I will place my Spirit upon Him, and an equitable administration of justice He will announce to the Gentiles. He will not wrangle nor even shout, neither will anyone hear His voice in the streets. A reed that has been completely crushed He will not break, and a dimly burning lamp wick He shall not quench until He will have caused the equitable administration of justice to move straight on to its intended goal resulting in victory. And in His Name will the Gentiles hopefully trust.

15-21

Then there was brought to Him one possessed with a demon, blind and dumb. And He healed him, so that the one who was dumb spoke and saw. And all the common people were beside themselves with astonishment, and kept on saying, This man, is he perchance the son of

22-32

David? But the Pharisees having heard, said, This fellow is not ejecting the demons except by means of Beezeboul, ruler of the demons. And knowing their thoughts, He said to them, Every kingdom split up into factions, at variance with itself, is reduced to naught, and every city or house split up into factions, at variance with itself, shall not stand. And, assuming that Satan is ejecting Satan, he was at variance with himself. How is it possible then for his kingdom to stand? And assuming for the moment that I by means of Beezeboul am ejecting the demons, your sons, by means of whom are they ejecting them? For this reason they themselves shall be your judges. But since by means of God's Spirit I am ejecting the demons, surely then the kingdom of God has come upon you unexpectedly. Or, how is a person able to enter the house of the strong man and carry off by force his household furnishings, unless he first binds the strong man, and then he will plunder his house? He who is not with me is against me, and he who is not gathering with me is scattering. On this account I am saying to you, Every sin and malicious slander shall be forgiven men, but the aforementioned impious and reproachful speech injurious to the divine majesty of the Spirit shall not be forgiven. And whoever speaks a word against the Son of Man, it shall be forgiven him. But whoever speaks against the Holy Spirit, it shall not be forgiven him, neither in this age nor in the one about to come.

33-37   Either declare the tree good and its fruit good, or declare the tree rotten and its fruit rotten, for by its fruit is the tree known. O progeny of vipers who are such by nature, how is it possible that you are able to be speaking good things, being by nature pernicious individuals, for out of that which fills the heart the mouth is accustomed to speak? The good man out of his good treasure-house brings out good things, and the pernicious man out of his pernicious treasure-house brings out pernicious things. Moreover, I am saying to you, Every word which men shall speak which has no legitimate work, which is inoperative and thus morally useless and unprofitable, they shall give account of at the day of judgment, for by your words you shall be justified, and by your words shall you be condemned.

Then certain of those learned in the sacred scriptures **38-42** and certain of the Pharisees answered Him saying, Teacher, we are desiring to see an attesting miracle from you. But He answering said to them, A pernicious and adulterous breed is always hankering after an attesting miracle. And an attesting miracle shall not be given it except the attesting miracle of Jonah, the prophet, for just as Jonah was in the gullet of the sea-monster three days and three nights, thus shall the Son of Man be in the heart of the earth three days and three nights. Men, Ninevites, shall arise in the judgment with this breed of men and shall condemn it, because they repented as a result of the proclamation of Jonah, and behold, something more than Jonah is here. A queen of the south shall rise up in the judgment with this breed of men and shall condemn it, because she came from the frontiers of the earth to hear Solomon's wisdom, and behold, something more than Solomon is here.

Now, whenever the unclean spirit goes out of the man, **43-45** he travels through arid places seeking a cessation of his circumstances, and as a result, tranquility, and he does not find it. Then he says, Into my home I will return from where I went out. And, having come, he finds it unoccupied and swept clean and fully decorated. Then he proceeds and takes with him seven other spirits more pernicious than himself, and having entered, he makes his permanent home there. And the last circumstances of that man become worse than the first ones. Thus shall it be also with respect to this breed of men, this pernicious breed.

While He was still speaking to the crowds, behold, His **46-50** mother and His brethren had taken their stand outside, seeking to speak to Him. And someone said to Him, Behold, your mother and your brethren are standing outside, seeking to speak to you. And answering He said to the one speaking to Him, Who is my mother, and who are my brethren? And having stretched out His hand toward those who were His pupils, He said, Behold, my mother and my brethren, for he who is of such a nature that he does the will of my Father who is in heaven, that very person is my brother and sister and mother.

1, 2   On that day, Jesus having come out of the house, was sitting at the seashore. And there gathered together to Him great crowds so that He went on board a boat in order that He might have a place where He could be seated. And the whole crowd had taken a position on the beach and was standing there.

3-6   And He spoke to them many things in the form of illustrations by using the familiar in nature or human life which would explain unfamiliar truths of the spiritual life, saying, Behold, the sower went out for the purpose of sowing seed. And in his sowing, some on the one hand fell beside the footpath, and, having come, the birds ate it up. Other seed on the other hand fell upon the shallow ground where the rock layers were near the surface, where it was not having much earth. And immediately it sprang up because it did not have depth of earth, and the sun having arisen, it was burnt with the heat, and because it was not having rootage, it withered away.

7-9   But still other seed fell among the seeds of thorns, and the thorns came up and choked them off. But still other seed fell upon the ground which was good, and kept on producing fruit, some on the one hand, one hundred per cent, some on the other hand, sixty per cent, and still some other, thirty per cent. He who has ears, let him be hearing.

10-15   And having come, the disciples said to Him, Why are you speaking to them by means of illustrations? And answering, He said, To you it has been given to come to know experientially the hidden truths now revealed and intelligible of the kingdom of heaven, with the result that you now know them, but to those it has not been given, with the result that at present they are ignorant of them. For, whoever is of such a nature as to have, it shall be given to him and he shall have an abundance. But whoever is of such a nature that he does not have, even that which he does have shall be taken away from him. On this account by means of illustrations I am speaking to them, because while seeing they are not seeing, and while hearing they are not hearing, neither are they understanding. And in them the prophecy of Isaiah is in process of fulfillment, the one which says, By means of the sense of hearing you shall hear and by no means shall you understand. And while you are seeing, you shall see and positively not perceive, for the heart of this people was rendered dull and callous, and with their ears they heard with difficulty, and their eyes they shut lest at any time they should see with their eyes, and with their ears hear, and with their heart understand, and turn back, and I should heal them.

But spiritually prosperous are your eyes because they see, and your ears because they hear; for assuredly, I am saying to you, Many prophets and righteous men passionately desired to see the things which you are seeing and did not see them, and to hear the things which you are hearing, and did not hear them. As for you, therefore, hear the illlustration of the one who sows seed. While everyone is listening and not comprehending the word of the kingdom, there comes the Pernicious One and snatches away that which was sown in his heart. This man is he who was sown as seed alongside the footpath. And he who was sown upon the shallow ground where the rock layers were near the surface, this man is the one who hears the word and immediately with joy receives it. And he does not have rootage in himself, but is by nature a temporizer, and the pressure of circumstances having come, and persecution because of the Word, immediately he sees in it that of which he disapproves and which hinders him from acknowledging its authority. And he who was sown as seed into the midst of the thorns, this is he who hears the Word, and the worries of this age and the deceitfulness of its wealth combine to utterly choke the Word, and he becomes unfruitful. But he who was sown as seed upon the good ground, this is he who hears the Word and understands it, who is

16-23

such a one as bears fruit and produces, in the case of
one on the one hand, one hundred per cent, and in the
case of another on the other hand, sixty per cent, and
in the case of still another, thirty per cent.

24-30   Another illustration He set before them, saying, The
kingdom of heaven is likened to a man who sows good
seed in his field. But while men were sleeping, his
enemy came and went to sowing bastard wheat over and
in the midst of the wheat, and went off. And when
the wheat stalk put forth leaves and produced fruit, then
also the bastard wheat came to light and became evident.
And the slaves of the master of the house having come,
they said to him, Master, did you not sow good seed in
your field? From where therefore does it have bastard
wheat? And he said to them, A man, an enemy, did this.
And the slaves say to him, Do you desire therefore,
having gone off, that we should gather them up? But he
said, No, lest when you are gathering up the bastard
wheat, you uproot at the same time with it the wheat.
Permit both to grow together until the harvest, and in
the strategic season of the harvest I will say to the
harvesters, Gather first the bastard wheat and bind it
into bundles for the purpose of burning it, but the wheat
gather together into my granary.

31-35   Another illustration He set before them, saying, The
kingdom of heaven is like a grain of mustard seed, which,
a man having taken, sowed in his field, which indeed is
the smallest of all the seeds, but when it is grown, it
is greater than the garden-herbs and grows to the shape
and size of a tree, so that the birds of the heaven come
and roost in its branches.

     Another illustration He gave them. The kingdom
of heaven is like yeast which a woman having taken,
mixed with three measures of wheat flour until the whole
of it was permeated by the yeast. These things, all of
them, Jesus spoke in the form of illustrations to the
crowds, and apart from an illustration He spoke not even
one thing to them, in order that there might be fulfilled
that which was spoken through the intermediate agency
of the prophet, saying, I will open my mouth in the

form of illustrations. I will utter things which have been kept secret from the time when the foundations of the universe were laid.

Then, having sent the crowds away, He came into the house. And His disciples came to Him, saying, Make thoroughly clear at once to us the illustration of the bastard wheat of the field. And answering He said, He who sows the good seed is the Son of Man. Moreover, the field is the world, and the good seed, these are the sons of the kingdom. But the bastard wheat represents the sons of the Pernicious One; and the enemy, the one who sowed it, is the devil. And the harvest is the consummation of the age, and the harvesters are angels. Even as therefore the bastard wheat is gathered and is burned in the fire, thus shall it be at the consummation of the age. The Son of Man shall send His angels on a mission, and they shall gather out of His kingdom all those who create stumbling blocks for others and those who make a practice of lawlessness, and they shall throw them into the furnace of fire. There, in that place, there shall be the lamentation and the gnashing of the teeth. Then those who are righteous, like the sun when it bursts through the clouds which have hidden it, shall shine forth through the world of evil, dissipating the darkness of sin which has obscured the good and veiled the true glory of their righteousness, in the kingdom of their Father. He who has ears to be hearing, let him be hearing. *36-43*

The kingdom of heaven is like a treasure which has been hidden in the field, which, after a man has found it, he hid, and in his joy goes off and sells as much as he possesses, and buys that field. Again, the kingdom of heaven is like a travelling merchant-buyer seeking beautiful pearls; and having found one pearl of great value, having gone off, sold all, as much as he was possessing, having staked all that he had in one business venture which would either make or break him, and purchased it in the market place. Again, the kingdom of heaven is like a drag-net which was thrown into the sea and which gathered some fish out of every species, which when it was filled, having drawn it up upon the beach, and having *44-52* seated themselves, they gathered up the good ones into receptacles, but the worthless they threw away. Thus shall it be in the consummation of the age. The angels shall go out and shall separate those who are pernicious out from the midst of those who are righteous, and shall throw them into the furnace of fire. There, in that place, there shall be the lamentation and the gnashing of the teeth. Have you understood all these things? They say to Him, Yes. And He said to them, Because of this, every man learned in the sacred scriptures who has accepted the precepts and instructions with reference to the kingdom of heaven is like a man who is a master of a house, who is of such a character that he dispenses with hearty enjoyment out of his treasure-house, things new as to quality and also things mellowed with age by reason of use.

53-58   And it came to pass that when Jesus finished these illustrations, He, soldier-like, broke up camp and departed from that place. And having come into His home town, He went to teaching them in their synagogue so that they were flabbergasted and were saying, What is the source of this wisdom and these miracles? Is not this the son of the carpenter? Is not his mother called Mary, and his brothers, James and Joses, and Simon and Judas? And his sisters, are they not all with us? From what source then does this fellow have all these things? And they saw in Him that of which they disapproved and that which hindered them from acknowledging His authority. But Jesus said to them, A prophet is not without a correct evaluation of his worth with a corresponding deference and respect which is his due, except in his own country and in his own house. And He did not perform there many miracles because of their unbelief.

1-12   At that epochal, strategic time, Herod, the tetrarch, came to hear the report about Jesus, and said to his servants, This is John the Baptizer. He himself was raised from the dead, and because of this the demonstrations of miraculous power are operative in him; for Herod, having seized John, bound him and put him away in prison for the sake of Herodias, the wife of Philip his brother, for

John had been saying to him, It is not lawful for you
to have her. And though desiring to put him to death,
he feared the people, because they were holding him to
be a prophet. Now, Herod's birthday having come, the
daughter of Herodias performed a rapid-motion, leaping,
lewd dance in their midst and pleased Herod, because of
which he put himself under oath, and acknowledging the
obligation he incurred thereby, promised to give her whatever she would ask. And she, having been previously
high-pressured to action by her mother, says. Give me
at once, right here, on the spot, upon a dish, the head
of John the Baptizer. And though having been put to
grief, the king, yet because of the oaths under which he
had put himself and because of those who were reclining
at the banquet table with him, issued the order for it
to be given. And having sent the executioner, he beheaded John in the prison. And his head was brought
upon a dish, and it was given to the young woman. And
she brought it to her mother. And his disciples having
come, took up the body and buried it, and having gone,
they brought word to Jesus.

And Jesus, having heard, withdrew from there by boat **13-21**
to an uninhabited place apart. And the crowds, having
heard this, followed Him by the land route from the cities.
And having come forth, He saw a vast multitude, and He
was moved with compassion for them, and He healed
their sick ones. And evening having come, the disciples
came to Him, saying, Uninhabited is the place, and the
hour already is advanced. Therefore dismiss the crowds
in order that, having gone off into the villages, they might
buy for themselves provisions in the market places. But
Jesus said to them, There is no necessity for them to go
away. As for you, you give them at once something to
eat. But they say to Him, We do not have here anything
except five loaves and two fish. And He said, Be bringing them here to me. And having commanded the
crowds to recline upon the grass, having received the five
loaves and two fish, having looked up to heaven, He asked
the blessing, and having broken them He gave the loaves
to the disciples, and the disciples to the crowds. And

they ate, all of them, and were all filled to their complete satisfaction. And they carried off with them the broken pieces which were left over — twelve full wicker baskets. And those eating were men, about five thousand, apart from women and children.

22-36   And immediately He compelled the disciples to board the boat and precede Him to the other side, so that in the meantime He could dismiss the crowds. And having sent the crowds away, He went up into the mountain in private for the purpose of praying. Now, evening having come, He was there alone. And the boat already was distant from the land many furlongs, being tossed by the waves, for the wind was against them. Now, during the fourth watch of the night He came to them, making His way upon the sea. But the disciples having seen Him walking directly upon the sea, His sandals in contact with the water, were terrified, saying, It is a phantasm, and they cried aloud for fear. And immediately Jesus spoke to them, saying, Be having courage. It is I. Stop fearing. And answering Him, Peter said, O Lord. Since it is you, command me to come to you on the waves. And He said, Come at once. And having come down from the boat, Peter made his way upon the waves and came towards Jesus. But seeing the wind, he became afraid, and beginning to be sinking, he cried aloud, saying, O Lord, save me quickly. And immediately Jesus, having stretched out His hand, seized him, and says to him, O you of little faith. Why did you waver? And after they had gone up into the boat, the wind grew weary of blowing and sank away. And those in the boat fell upon their knees in profound reverence and worshipped Him, saying, Truly, Son of God by nature you are. And having crossed over, they came to the land of Gennesaret. And the men of that place, having received knowledge of Him, sent word into the whole of that surrounding territory, and they brought to Him all those who were sick, and kept on begging Him that they might only touch the fringe of His outer garment. And as many as touched it were made whole.

Then there come to Jesus from Jerusalem Pharisees and men learned in the sacred writings, saying, Why do those who follow your teachings sidestep the precepts which the elders received from previous generations and have handed down to us to be delivered to our successors; for they do not wash their hands in that traditionally ceremonial fashion whenever they eat bread? And answering, He said to them, As for you, why are you also sidestepping the commandment of God because of the precepts handed down to you? For God said, Be placing a correct evaluation upon your father and your mother, and be according them the reverence and veneration due them, and, He who calls down curses upon father or mother, let him come to his end by death. But as for you, you are saying, Whoever says to his father or mother, It is a gift dedicated to God, whatever it may be by means of which you might derive help from me, he will positively not pay due reverence and respect to his father and his mother. In short, you deprived the Word of God of its force and authority because of your precepts which were handed down to you from your fathers. Actors on the stage of life that you are, playing a role of that which you are not, most admirably and with consummate finesse did Isaiah prophesy concerning you, saying, This people places a correct evaluation upon me with their lips, and with lip service accords me all due reverence and veneration, but their heart holds back at a great distance from me. But in vain are they worshipping me, teaching precepts which by nature are commandments of mankind.

And having called the crowd to himself, He said to them, Be hearing and be understanding. Not that which enters the mouth renders a man ceremonially unclean, but that which proceeds out of the mouth, this defiles the man. Then the disciples, having come, say to Him, Do you know that the Pharisees, having heard the aforementioned word, took violent exception to it, finding in it that of which they disapproved and that which hinders them from acknowledging your authority? But answering, He said, Every cultivated plant which my heavenly Father did not plant shall be pulled up by the roots. Let them alone.

Blind leaders are they of the blind. And if a blind person
is leading a blind person, both shall fall into the ditch.
And Peter answering said to Him, Explain the illustration
to us. And He said, And as for you, are you even yet
devoid of understanding? Do you not understand that
everything which enters the mouth passes into the intestines and is ejected into that which is provided as a
receptacle for it? But the things which proceed out of the
mouth come out of the heart, and those things defile
the man; for out of the heart come pernicious reasonings,
murders, adulteries, fornications, thefts, false testimonies,
malicious slanders. These are the things which defile the
man. But to eat with hands which have not been washed
ceremonially, does not defile the man.

21-28   And having gone out from that place, Jesus withdrew
into the country around Tyre and Sidon. And behold,
a woman, a Canaanite from those regions, having come,
cried out, saying, Have pity upon me quickly, O Sir, son
of David. My daughter is badly demonized. But He
did not answer her a word. And His disciples having
come, kept on begging Him, saying, Send her off, because
she is crying out after us. But He answering said, I was
not sent off on a mission except to the sheep, the perishing ones that belong to the house of Israel. And having
come, she fell upon her knees and touched her forehead
to the ground in profound reverence before Him, saying,
Sir, be helping me. But answering, He said, It is not a
fitting thing to take the bread which belongs to the children and throw it to their little pet dogs. But she said,
Yes, indeed, Sir, for also the little pet dogs are accustomed
to eat from the little morsels which fall from the table
of their masters. Then answering, Jesus said to her,
O woman, great is your faith. Let it become to you as
you desire. And her daughter was healed from that
hour.

29-31   And having passed over from that place, Jesus went
to the shore of the sea of Galilee. And having gone up
into the mountain, He was sitting there. And there came
to Him large crowds having with them those who were
lame, maimed, blind, dumb, and many others having ill-

nesses of a different nature, and they flung them to the
ground at His feet. And He healed them, so that the
crowd marvelled, seeing those who had been dumb speaking, and those who had been maimed whole, and those who
had been lame walking about, and those who had been
blind, seeing. And they glorified the God of Israel.

And Jesus having called His disciples to himself, said,   **32-39**
I am moved with compassion for the crowd, because already they are remaining with me three days, and they
do not have anything to eat; and to dismiss them, not
having eaten, I do not desire to do that, lest they at any
time faint along the road. And the disciples say to Him,
From what place in this uninhabited region should we
have so many loaves of bread as to satisfy such a crowd?
And Jesus says to them, How many loaves do you have?
And they said, Seven, and a few little fish. And having
commanded the crowd to recline upon the ground, He
took the seven loaves and the fish, and having offered the
blessing, He broke them and kept on giving them to the
disciples, and the disciples to the crowds. And they ate,
all of them, and were completely satisfied. And the sur-
plus of the broken pieces of food they took away, seven
full reed baskets. And those eating were four thousand
men, apart from women and children. And having sent
off the crowds, He went on board the boat and came to
the regions of Magadan.

And having come, the Pharisees and Sadducees, put-   **1-4**
ting Him to the test, demanded that He furnish them
for their observation an attesting miracle having its source
in heaven. But He answering said to them, Evening
having come, you are accustomed to say, Fair weather,
for the sky is reddening, and in the morning, Today,
stormy, for the sky is reddening and is becoming covered
with clouds. You possess indeed an understanding based
upon experience, to pass a discriminating judgment upon
the face of the sky, but on the other hand, with reference
to the attesting miracles of the epochal, strategic periods
of time, are you not able to pass a discriminating judgment? A pernicious and adulterous breed of men is constantly craving an attesting miracle, and an attesting

miracle shall not be given it except the attesting miracle of Jonah. And having left them, He went off.

5-12   And the disciples, having come to the other side, completely forgot to take loaves of bread. And Jesus said to them, Be taking heed to and be guarding yourselves against the yeast of the Pharisees and Sadducees. And they were reasoning among themselves, saying, It is because we did not take loaves of bread. And Jesus having come to know this, said, Why are you reasoning among yourselves, you of little faith? Is it because you do not have loaves of bread? Are you not yet understanding nor even remembering the five loaves of the five thousand, and how many baskets you took away, nor even the seven loaves of the four thousand, and how many baskets you took away? How is it that you are not understanding that I did not speak to you concerning loaves of bread? But be guarding yourselves against the yeast of the Pharisees and Sadducees. Then they understood that He did not speak regarding the guarding of one's self against the yeast that pertained to loaves of bread but against the teaching of the Pharisees and Sadducees.

13-20   Now, Jesus having come into the districts adjacent to Caesarea Philippi, was asking His disciples, saying, Who do men say that the Son of Man is? And they said, Some, indeed, John the Baptizer, but others, Elijah, and still others, Jeremiah, or one of the prophets. He says to them, But as for you, who do you say that I am? And answering, Simon Peter said, As for you, you are the Christ, the Son of God, the living God. And answering, Jesus said to him, Spiritually prosperous are you, Simon Barjona, because flesh and blood did not reveal this to you but my Father who is in heaven. Moreover, as for myself, I also am saying to you, You are Rock [*petros,* masculine in gender, a detached but large fragment of rock], and upon this massive rock [*petra,* feminine in gender, feminine demonstrative pronoun cannot go back to masculine *petros; petra,* a rocky peak, a massive rock] I will build my Church. And the councils of the unseen world shall not overpower it. I shall give to you the keys of the kingdom of heaven; and

whatever you bind on earth [forbid to be done], shall have
been already bound [forbidden to be done] in heaven;
and whatever you loose on earth [permit to be done],
shall have already been loosed in heaven [permitted to
be done]. Then He admonished the disciples sharply
that they should tell not even one person that He himself
is the Christ.

From that time on Jesus began to be showing His dis- **21-23**
ciples that it was a necessity in the nature of the case for
Him to go off to Jerusalem and to suffer many things
from the elders and the chief priests and the men learned
in the scriptures, and to be killed and on the third day
to be raised up. And having taken Him to himself apart
privately, Peter began to be rebuking Him, saying, May
mercy be shown to you, Lord. This shall positively not
be to you. And, having turned around, He [with His
back turned to Peter and Satan] said to Peter, Be
gone under my authority, and keep on going, behind me,
out of my sight, Satan. A stumbling-block you are to
me, because you do not have a mind for the things of
God but for the things of men.

Then Jesus said to His disciples, If anyone is desiring **24-27**
to come after me, let him forget self and lose sight of his
own interests, and let him pick up his cross and carry it,
and let him be taking the same road with me that I travel,
for whoever is desiring to save his soul-life shall ruin it,
but whoever will pass a sentence of death upon his soul-
life for my sake, shall find it. For what will a man be
profited if he gain the whole world but forfeit his soul-life.
Or, what shall a man give as an exchange for his soul-life?
For the Son of Man is about to be coming in the glory of
His Father with His angels, and then He shall recompense to each one according to his manner of acting.

Assuredly, I am saying to you, There are certain ones **28-XVII 8**
of those standing here who are of such a nature that they
shall not experience death until such time as they see the
Son of Man coming in His kingdom. And after six days
Jesus takes with himself Peter and James and John
his brother, and He brings them up into a mountain,

a lofty one, in private. And the manner of His outward expression was changed before them, that expression coming from and being representative of His inner being. And His face took on a different appearance so that it shone like the sun, and His outer garments became white like its light. And behold, there appeared to them Moses and Elijah talking with Him. And Peter, volunteering his judgment, said to Jesus, Lord, it is an excellent thing for us to be here. On the assumption that you are desiring it, I will make here three booths of leafy branches, for you one, and for Moses one, and for Elijah one. While he was still speaking, behold, a cloud composed of light enveloped them with brightness. And, behold there came a voice out of the cloud, saying, This is my Son, the Beloved, in whom I take pleasure. Be hearing Him. And the disciples, having heard, fell abruptly upon their face and were exceedingly afraid. And Jesus came, and having touched them, said, Arise at once and stop being afraid. And having lifted up their eyes, they saw not even one person except Jesus himself only.

9-13   And while they were coming down out of the mountain, Jesus commanded them, saying, To not even one person tell the spectacle until the Son of Man is raised out from among those who are dead. And His disciples asked Him, saying, Why then do those learned in the sacred scriptures say that it is a necessity in the nature of the case for Elijah to come first? And He answering said, Elijah indeed comes and will restore all things to their former state. Moreover, I am saying to you, Elijah already came, and they did not recognize him. But they did to him as many things as they desired. In the same manner also the Son of Man is about to be suffering at their hands. Then the disciples understood that concerning John the Baptizer He spoke to them.

14-18   And after they had come to the crowd, a man came to Him, falling upon his knees before Him and saying, Sir, have mercy upon my son because he is an epileptic, and he is in a miserable condition. For, often he falls into the fire and often into the water. And I brought him to your disciples and they were not able to heal him. And Jesus answering, said, O unbelieving breed of men, and men who have been morally distorted and twisted, how long shall I be with you? How long will I bear with you? Be bringing him to me here. And Jesus rebuked him, and there came out of him the demon. And the boy was healed from that hour.

Then the disciples having come to Jesus in private said, **19, 20** As for us, why were we not able to eject it? And He says to them, Because of the littleness of your faith. For, assuredly I am saying to you, If you are having faith as a grain of mustard seed, you will say to this mountain, Remove hence to that place, and it shall remove. And not even one thing will be impossible to you.

Now, while they were assembling in Galilee, Jesus **22-27** said to them, The Son of Man is about to be betrayed into men's hands, and they will kill Him, and on the third day He will be raised up. And they grieved exceedingly.

And after they had come to Capernaum, those who receive the half-shekel temple tax came to Peter and said, Your teacher, does he not pay a half-shekel temple tax? He says, Yes. And after Peter had come into the house, Jesus spoke to him before he could get a word in edgeways, saying, What do you think, Simon? The kings of the earth, from whom are they accustomed to receive import and export duties and a tax? from their sons or from those who do not belong to their families? And Peter having said, From those not of their families, Jesus said to him, So then, the sons are exempt. However, in order that they may not find something in us of which they would disapprove, having proceeded to the sea, throw in a fishhook, and the first fish that comes up, seize at once, and having opened its mouth, you will find a shekel. Having taken that, give it at once to them for me and you.

During that hour the disciples came to Jesus, saying, **1-6** Who then is greatest in the kingdom of heaven? And having called to himself a little child, He stood it in their midst and said, Assuredly, I am saying to you, Unless you reverse your present trend of thought and become as the little children, in no case shall you enter the kingdom of heaven. Therefore, he who is of such a nature as to humble himself like this little child, esteeming himself small inasmuch as he is so, thus thinking truly, and because truly, therefore humbly of himself, this person is the greatest in the kingdom of heaven. And whoever shall receive one such little child in my Name, me he receives. But whoever causes one of these little ones who believe in me to stumble, it would be to his profit that a millstone were hung about his neck and that he be drowned in the depth of the sea.

7-10   Woe to the world because of the stumbling-blocks, for it is inevitable that stumbling-blocks come, but woe to the man through whom the stumbling-block comes. Now, assuming that your hand or your foot causes you to stumble, cut it out at once and throw it from you. It is better for you to enter life disabled or lame, than having two hands or two feet, to be thrown into the fire which is everlasting. And, assuming that your eye causes you to stumble, root it out at once and throw it from you. It is better for you to enter life deprived of one eye, than having two eyes, to be thrown into the hell of fire. Be taking heed. Do not begin to underestimate the value of one of these little ones, for I am saying to you, Their angels in heaven are always contemplating the face of my Father who is in heaven.

11-14   What do you think? If there should come into the possession of a certain man one hundred sheep, and one of them should be enticed to roam about and go astray, would he not leave the ninety-nine upon the mountain, and having gone on his way, go to seeking the one that is roaming about? And if it should come to pass that he finds it, assuredly I am saying to you, he rejoices over it more than over the ninety-nine that have not been enticed to roam about and go astray. Thus, there is not a desire in the presence of your Father who is in heaven that one of these little ones perish.

15-17   Moreover, if your brother should commit an act of sin, be going, show him his sin with a view to convicting him of it and bringing about a confession between you and him alone. If he hears you, you won your brother over. But if he does not hear you, take with you one or two besides, in order that upon the basis of the mouth of two witnesses or three, every word may be established. And if he is unwilling to hear them, tell the assembly. And if he also is unwilling to hear the assembly, let him be to you as the pagan Gentile and the tax collector.

Assuredly, I am saying to you, Whatever you forbid on earth, shall have already been forbidden in heaven. And whatever you permit on earth, shall have already been permitted in heaven. Again, assuredly I am saying to you, If two of you upon the earth are in agreement, concerning every matter of which they ask that something be given it shall become theirs from the presence of my Father who is in heaven. For where there are two or three who have been joined together into my Name with the result that I am the common object of their faith, there I am in their midst. **18-20**

Then, having come, Peter said to Him, Lord, how often shall my brother sin against me and I shall forgive him; up to seven times? Jesus says to him, I do not say to you, Up to seven times, but up to seventy times seven. Therefore, the kingdom of heaven is likened to a man, a king, who desired to settle accounts with his slaves. And while he was beginning to compute the accounts, one was brought to him who owed him about twelve million dollars. And not having that by which to discharge the debt, the master commanded that he be sold, also the wife and the children and whatever he had, and that the debt be discharged. Then the slave, having fallen upon his knees, was touching the ground with his forehead in an expression of profound reverence before him, saying, Be patient with me, mild and slow in requiring payment, and I will pay back all to you. And being moved with compassion, the master of that slave released him and cancelled the debt. **21-27**

But having gone out, that slave found one of his fellow-slaves who owed him about twenty dollars. And having **28-31** seized him, he went to strangling him and wringing his neck, saying, Settle up at once, since you are owing me something. Then, having fallen down, his fellow-slave kept on begging him, saying, Be patient with me, mild and slow in requiring payment, and I will pay you. However, he was not willing, but having gone off, he threw him into prison until he would pay back that which he was owing. Then when his fellow-slaves had seen the things which had taken place, they were greatly affected by sorrow, and having come, they made entirely clear to their master all the things which took place.

32-35   Then his master, having called him, says to him, Slave, pernicious one, I cancelled for you that entire debt, seeing that you begged me to do so. Ought not you also in view of the very necessity imposed by these circumstances, to have shown mercy to your fellow-slave, just as I also was merciful to you? And having been aroused to the point of a justifiable anger, his master handed him over to the torturers until such time as he would pay back all that he owed him. Thus also my Father who is in heaven will do to you if you do not forgive, each one, his brother from your hearts.

1, 2   And it came to pass when Jesus brought to a close these discourses, that He went away from Galilee and came into the borders of Judaea across the Jordan. And large crowds followed with Him, and He healed them there.

3-12   And there came to Him Pharisees, putting Him to the test and saying, Is it lawful for one to dismiss his wife for every cause? And answering, He said, Have you not read, The Creator from the beginning, a male and a female He made them, and said, On this account a man shall forsake his father and his mother and shall be joined to his wife, and they shall be, the two, one flesh, insomuch that no longer are they two, but one flesh? Therefore, that which God once for all yoked together, let man not be separating. They say to Him, Why then did Moses command to give her a bill of divorce and dismiss her? He says to them, Moses, on account of the hardness of your heart permitted you to dismiss your wives. But

48

from the beginning it [namely, the right of divorce] has not been thus, right down to the present moment, and as a result it continues to be at variance with the original enactment. Moreover, I am saying to you, Whoever dismisses his wife for any other cause than fornication, and marries another, is committing adultery. His disciples say to Him, Since the matter is thus with reference to the man's aforementioned reason in the case of his wife, it is not expedient to marry. And He said to them, Not all receive with the understanding this word, but those to whom it has been given to receive it, for there are those of such a nature as to be eunuchs who were born thus from the mother's womb. And there are those of such a nature as to have been made eunuchs by men. And there are those of such a nature as to have constituted themselves eunuchs for the sake of the kingdom of heaven. He who is able to receive this with understanding, let him be receiving it.

Then there were brought to Him little children in **13-15** order that He might lay His hands upon them and pray. And the disciples rebuked them. But Jesus said, Permit the children, and stop forbidding them, to come to me, for of such as these is the kingdom of heaven. And having laid His hands on them, He departed from that place.

And behold, one having come to Him said, Teacher, **16-22** what good thing should I do in order that I might acquire life eternal? And He said to him, Why are you asking me concerning that aforementioned good thing? One there is who is good. But since you are desiring to enter the life, be keeping with a jealous solicitude the commandments. He says to Him, What sort of commandments? And Jesus said, You shall not commit murder; you shall not commit adultery; you shall not steal; you shall not bear false witness; be setting a correct evaluation upon your father and mother and be treating them with the reverence and love which is their due; and, you shall love with a divine and self-sacrificial love your neighbor in the same manner as yourself. The youth says to Him, These things, all of them, I took care not to violate and have observed. What is it that I still am lacking? Jesus said to him, Since you are desiring to be in a state where there is nothing wanting that is necessary to completeness, be going on your way, sell your belongings, and give at once to those who are poor, and you shall have treasure in heaven, and come, be taking with me the same road that I take. But having heard the aforementioned word, the youth went off, being grieved, for he had many possessions.

23-26   And Jesus said to His disciples, Assuredly, I am saying to you, A wealthy man with difficulty shall enter the kingdom of heaven. And again I am saying to you, It is easier for a camel to go into and through the eye of a sewing needle than for a rich man to enter the kingdom of God. And the disciples having heard this were for a time beside themselves with amazement, exceedingly so, saying, Who then is able to be saved? And Jesus, having turned His eyes upon them and having considered them, said to them, In the presence of men, as men look at this, it is impossible. But in the presence of God, as He looks at this, all things are possible.

27-30   Then answering, Peter said to Him, behold, as for us, we abandoned all things once for all and took the same road with you that you are taking. What then shall there be for us? And Jesus said to them, Assuredly, I am saying to you, As for you, you who took the same road with me which I am traveling; at the time when all things shall be restored to their pristine glory, when the Son of Man shall have taken his seat upon the throne of His glory, you yourselves also shall seat yourselves upon twelve thrones, judging the twelve tribes of Israel. And everyone whoever is of such a nature as to have abandoned houses or brothers or sisters or father or mother or children or farms for the sake of my Name, shall receive many times as much, and shall inherit life eternal. Moreover, many who are first shall be those who are last, and those who are last shall be those who are first.

1-7   For instance, the kingdom of heaven is like a man, a master of a house, who was of such a nature that he went out early in the morning to hire for himself workers for his vineyard. And having agreed with the workers upon the basis of a denarius for the day, he sent them off into his vineyard to fulfill the task assigned to them. And having gone out about the third hour, he saw others who had taken their stand in the market place and who were unemployed. And to them he said, As for you, you also be going into the vineyard, and whatever is fair, I will give you. And they went off. And again having gone out about the sixth and ninth hour he did the same thing. And about the eleventh hour, having gone out, he found others who had taken their stand and were standing there, and he says to them, Why have you stood here the whole day as unemployed men? They say to him, Because, as for us, nobody hired us for himself. He says to them, As for you, be also going into the vineyard.

Now, evening having come, the master of the vineyard **8-16** says to his manager, Call the workers at once and give them their pay, beginning with the last ones to those who were first. And having come, those who were hired about the eleventh hour received a denarius. And having come, those who were the first ones supposed that they would receive more. Yet they themselves also received a denarius. And having received it, they kept discontentedly grumbling and complaining against the master of the house, muttering in a low undertone, saying, These who were last worked one hour, and you made them equal to us who bore the burden of the day and its scorching heat. But answering one of them he said, My good friend. I am not treating you unjustly. Did you not agree with me for a denarius? Take that which is yours and be going on your way. Moreover, it is my pleasure to give to this last one as I also gave to you. Is it not lawful for me to do that which I desire to do with those things which are mine? Or is your eye pernicious because I in contradistinction to you am generous? Thus, those who are last shall be those who are the first ones, and those who are the first ones shall be the last ones.

17-19   Now Jesus, about to be going up to Jerusalem, took the Twelve with himself privately. And on the road He said to them, Behold. We are going up to Jerusalem, and the Son of Man shall be delivered up treacherously into the hands of the chief priests and the men learned in the sacred scriptures. And they shall condemn Him to death, and they shall deliver Him into the hands of the Gentiles to mock and to scourge and to crucify. And on the third day He shall be raised up.

20-23   Then there came to Him the mother of the sons of Zebedee with her sons, falling upon her knees and touching the ground with her forehead in an expression of profound reverence, and begging something from Him. And He said to her, What are you desiring? She says to Him, Speak with the voice of authority and cause that these, my two sons, may be seated, one on your right hand and one on your left in your kingdom. And Jesus answering said, You two are not knowing what you are asking for yourselves. Are you both able to drink the cup which I alone am about to be drinking? They say to Him, We are able. He says to them, My cup you both shall indeed drink. But to be seated on my right hand and on my left, this is not mine to give, but it is for those for whom it has been prepared and is at present reserved by my Father.

24-28   And the ten having heard this, were angrily indignant concerning the two brothers. But Jesus, having called them to himself, said, You know that the rulers of the Gentiles lord it over them, and those who are great play the tyrant and domineer over them. It is not thus among you. But whoever among you desires to become great, he shall be your servant. And whoever among you desires to have the position of preeminence, he shall be your slave; just as the Son of Man did not come to be served but to serve and to give His life as a ransom in exchange for and instead of many.

29-34   And as they were proceeding out from Jericho, a large crowd followed with Him. And behold, two blind men sitting at the side of the road having heard that Jesus was passing by, cried out with a loud voice, saying, Lord, sympathize with our misery and help us, son of David. But the crowd charged them sharply that they should be quiet. But they cried out the more, saying, Lord, sympathize with our misery and help us, son of David. And Jesus, having come to a stop, stood still, called them and said, What do you desire that I should do for you? They say to Him, Lord, that our eyes may be opened. And Jesus, having been moved with compassion, touched their eyes, and immediately they received their sight and followed with Him.

And when they came near to Jerusalem and came to Bethphage, to the Mount of Olivet, then Jesus sent two disciples on a mission, saying to them, Be going on your way to the village, the one opposite you, and immediately you shall find a donkey which has been securely tied, and a colt with her. Having untied them, bring them at once to me. And if anyone should say anything to you, you shall say, The Lord is having need of them. And immediately he will send them. Now this took place in order that there might be fulfilled that which was spoken through the intermediate agency of the prophet, saying, Tell the daughter of Sion, Behold! Your king comes to you, meek, and riding upon a donkey, even upon a colt, the male offspring of a beast of burden.

1-5

And the disciples, having proceeded and having done even as Jesus appointed them, brought the donkey and the colt. And they placed upon them their outer garments. And He took His seat upon them [the garments]. And the majority of those composing the crowd spread their own outer garments in the road, and others kept on cutting branches from the trees and kept on spreading them in the road. And the crowds, those going on ahead of Him and those following, kept on calling out aloud, saying, Hosanna [Save, we pray thee] to the son of David. Let the One who comes in the Name of the Lord be eulogized. Hosanna in the highest regions. And after He entered Jerusalem, the whole city was stirred, saying, Who is this? And the crowds kept on

6-11

saying, This is the prophet Jesus, the one from Nazareth of Galilee.

12-17   And Jesus went into the temple and threw out all those who were selling and buying in the temple; and the tables of the money-changers He overturned and the seats of those who sold the doves, and He said to them, It has been written and is on record, My house shall be called a house of prayer. But as for you, you are making it a cave belonging to robbers. And there came to him in the temple blind people, and those who were maimed, and He healed them. And the chief priests and the men learned in the sacred scriptures having seen the marvellous things which He did and the little boys crying out in the temple and saying, Hosanna to the son of David, were indignant, and said to Him, Are you hearing what these are saying? And Jesus says to them, Yes. Did you never read, Out of the mouth of infants, even those who are nursing at the breast, you brought to perfection praise for yourself? And having left them He went outside of the city to Bethany, and He lodged there.

18-22   Now, in the morning, while returning to the city, He felt hungry. And having seen a lone fig tree by the road, He went to it, and found nothing in it except only leaves. And He says to it, No longer shall fruit come from you, positively not forever. And instantly the fig tree wasted away. And the disciples, having seen, started to marvel, saying, How did the fig tree so quickly waste away? But Jesus answering said to them, Assuredly I am saying to you, If you are having faith, and are not doubting, not only will you do that which was done to the fig tree, but even if you say to this mountain, Be lifted up and be thrown into the sea, it shall come to pass. And all things whatever you shall ask in prayer, believing, you shall receive.

23-27   And after He came into the temple, the chief priests and the elders of the people came to Him while He was teaching, saying, By what sort of authority are you doing these things? And who gave you this authority? And Jesus answering said to them, As for you, I also will ask you one question, which if you tell me, I also will tell you by what sort of authority I am doing these things. The baptism of John, from where was it, from heaven or from men? And they were deliberating among themselves, saying, If we say, From heaven, he will say to us, Why then did you not believe it? But if we say, From men, we fear the common people, for all hold John as a prophet. And answering, they said to Jesus, We do not have any positive knowledge about this. And He himself said to them, As for myself, neither am I telling you by what sort of authority I am doing these things.

But what do you think? A man had two children. **28-32**
Having come to the first one he said, Child, be going, be working today in my vineyard. And answering, he said, I shall, Sir, and did not go. And having come to the second, he spoke in like manner. And he answering said, I have no desire to do so; but later, having regretted his action, he went. Who of the two fulfilled the desire of the father? They say, The latter. Jesus says to them, Assuredly, I am saying to you, the tax collectors and the harlots are preceding you into the kingdom of God. For John came to you within the sphere of a course of conduct characterized by righteousness, and you did not believe him. But the tax collectors and the harlots believed him. But as for you, having seen this, you did not even regret your action later in order that you might believe him.

Hear another illustration of the same kind. There was **33-39**
a man, master of a house, one who planted a vineyard and set a hedge about it, and dug a wine press in it, and built a tower, and rented it to vine dressers, and went away to foreign parts. And when the season of the fruits drew near, he sent off his slaves on a mission to the vine dressers for the purpose of receiving his fruits. And the vine dressers, having seized his slaves, thrashed one and killed another, and stoned another. Again he sent off on a mission other slaves, more than the first ones, and they treated them in the same manner. And lastly, he sent off his son on a mission to them, saying, They will reverence my son. But the vine dressers, having

seen the son, said among themselves, This is the heir. Come now. Let us be killing him and we shall have his inheritance. And having seized him, they threw him outside of the vineyard and killed him.

40-42   Therefore, when the master of the vineyard comes, what should he do to those vine dressers? They say to Him, Wicked men, he will cause them to perish in utter ruin, and he will rent the vineyard to other vine dressers who are of such a character that they will deliver to him the fruits in their seasons. Jesus says to them, Did you never read in the scriptures, A stone which those who were building rejected after having put it to the test for the purpose of approving it should it meet their specifications, this became head of the corner. From the presence of the Lord this came to be, and it is marvellous in our eyes?

43-46   On this account I am saying to you, The kingdom of God shall be taken away from you and shall be given to a nation bringing forth its fruits. And he who has fallen upon this stone shall be broken to pieces. But upon whomever it shall fall, it will scatter him as dust. And the chief priests and the Pharisees, having heard His illustrations, came to understand that He was speaking concerning them, and yet while desiring to seize Him, they feared the common people since they were holding Him for a prophet.

1-6   And answering, Jesus spoke again to them by way of illustrations, saying, The kingdom of heaven is like a man, a king, one who made a marriage feast for his son. And he sent off his slaves on a mission to call those who had been already given their invitations to the wedding feast. But they were not desiring to come. Again he sent off other slaves on a mission, saying, Tell those who have been invited, Behold, my luncheon I have made ready, my steers and the specially grain-fed and fattened animals I have slaughtered, and all things are ready. Come to the marriage feast. But they treated the invitation with indifference and went off, one to his own farm, and another to his trading. And the rest, having seized his slaves, treated them shamefully and killed them.

And the king was provoked to anger, and having sent   7-10
his soldiers, destroyed those murderers and burned their
city. Then he says to his slaves, The wedding feast is
indeed ready, but those who have been invited were not
worthy. Be proceeding therefore to the main streets, and
as many as you find, invite at once to the marriage feast.
And those slaves, having gone forth into the main streets,
gathered together all whom they found, both those who
were pernicious and those who were good. And the wedding dining hall was filled with those reclining at the
banquet tables.

And the king, having come in for the purpose of con-   11-14
templating those reclining at table, saw there a man
who had not clothed himself with a wedding garment.
And he says to him, My good friend, in what way did you
enter here, not having a wedding garment? And he
became speechless. Then the king said to the servants,
Bind his hands and feet and throw him out into the darkness which is outside. There, in that place, there shall
be the audible weeping and the gnashing of the teeth;
for many are invited ones but few are chosen-out ones.

Then the Pharisees having proceeded, took counsel   15-22
with one another in order that they might ensnare Him in
His discourse. And they sent off on a mission to Him
their students with the Herodians, saying, Teacher, we
know positively that you are true, and that the way of God
in the sphere of the truth you are teaching, and that you
do not kowtow to anyone, for you do not show partiality
to anyone because of his standing or appearance. Therefore, tell us, what do you think? Is it lawful to pay a
tax to Caesar or not? But Jesus, having perceived their
perniciousness, said, Why are you putting me to the test,
you actors on the stage of life, playing the role of something you are not? Show me the legal coin used to pay
taxes. And they brought to Him a denarius. And He
says to them, This derived likeness and the title belong
to whom? They say, Caesar. Then He says to them,
Give back therefore to Caesar the things which belong
to Caesar; and the things which belong to God, pay

back to God. And having heard this, they marvelled, and having left Him, they went off.

23-33   On that very day there came to Him Sadducees, saying, There is not a resurrection. And they put a question to Him, saying, Teacher, Moses said, If a man should die not having children, his brother shall marry his wife and cause offspring to be born to his brother. Now, there were with us seven brothers. And the first one, having married, died, and not having children, left his wife to his brother. Likewise also the second and the third, even to the seventh. And last of all, the woman died. In the resurrection therefore, whose wife shall she be of the seven, for all had her? And answering, Jesus said to them, You are in error, not knowing the scriptures nor the power of God, for in the resurrection they neither marry nor do they give themselves in marriage, but are like angels in heaven. But with reference to the resurrection of those who are dead, did you not read that which was spoken to you by God, saying, I am the God of Abraham, and the God of Isaac, and the God of Jacob? He is not the God of dead people but of living people. And having heard this, the common people were being driven out of their self-control with astonishment at His teaching.

34-40   Now, the Pharisees, having heard that He had muzzled the Sadducees, were gathered in full agreement with one another. And one of them, an interpreter and teacher of the Mosaic law, put a question to Him, putting Him on trial: Teacher, which kind of commandment is of such a character as to be a great one in the law? And He said to him, You shall love the Lord your God with your whole heart and your whole soul and your whole mind. This is the great and first commandment. A second one is like it. You shall love your neighbor in the same manner as you do yourself. Within the scope of these two commandments are suspended the whole law and the prophets.

41-46   Now the Pharisees, having been gathered together, Jesus asked them, saying, What do you think concerning the Christ? Whose son is He? They say to Him,

The son of David. He says to them, How is it possible then that David by means of the Spirit calls Him Lord, saying, The Lord said to my Lord, Be seated on my right hand until I place your enemies under your feet? Since therefore David calls Him Lord, how is it possible that He is his son? And no one was able to answer Him a word, neither dared anyone from that day onward ask Him anything.

Then Jesus spoke to the crowds and to His disciples, saying, The men learned in the scriptures and the Pharisees occupy the professorial chairs of authoritative teachers whose responsibility it is to interpret Moses. All things therefore as many as they say to you, do, and as a habit of life with a solicitous care observe, but stop doing according to their works, for they are always discoursing and not doing. Moreover, they are always binding together burdensome burdens and placing them upon the shoulders of men, but they themselves are not willing to remove them with their finger. Furthermore, all their works they do with ostentation for the purpose of being contemplated in the admiring glances of men, for they make broad their amulets and enlarge the tassles of their garments. Moreover, they are fond of the most prominent places at the dinners, and the chief seats in the synagogues, and of being accorded deferential respect and regard when they are greeted in the market places, and to be called by men, Rabbi. But as for you, do not seek to be called Rabbi, for One is your Teacher, and all you are brethren. And do not begin to call anyone your father upon the earth, for One is your Father, He who is in heaven. And do not be called Master and Guide, because one is your Master and Guide, the Christ. But he who is greatest among you shall be your servant. And whoever shall exalt himself shall be humbled, and whoever shall humble himself shall be exalted. *1-12*

But woe to you, men learned in the scriptures and Pharisees, actors on the stage of life, playing the role of something which you are not, because you bar the entrance into the kingdom of heaven before men, for, as for you, you are not entering, neither are you permitting those who *13-15*

are desiring to enter, to go in. Woe to you, men learned
in the scriptures and Pharisees, actors on the stage of life,
playing the role of something which you are not, because
you circle the sea and the land for the purpose of making
one convert, and when he becomes such, you make him
twofold more a son of hell than yourselves.

16-22   Woe to you, blind guides who are saying, Whoever puts
himself under oath by the inner sanctuary of the temple,
the oath is not binding. But whoever puts himself under
oath by the gold of the inner sanctuary, the oath is binding
upon him. Impious, godless morons and spiritually blind
ones, for which is greater, the gold or the inner sanctuary
which sets apart the gold to be used for the service of
God? And whoever puts himself under oath by the
altar of whole burnt-offerings, the oath is not binding,
but whoever puts himself under oath by the gift which
is upon it, the oath is binding upon him. Spiritually blind
ones, for which is greater, the gift or the altar of whole
burnt-offerings which sets apart the gift for the service of
God? Therefore, he who puts himself under oath by the
altar of whole burnt-offerings swears by it, and by all
things which are on it. And he who puts himself under
oath by the inner sanctuary, swears by it, and by the One
who is in permanent residence in it. And he who puts himself under oath of heaven, swears by the throne of God and
by the One seated upon it.

23, 24   Woe to you, men learned in the scriptures and Pharisees, actors on the stage of life, playing the role of that
which you are not, because you pay a tenth of sweet-
smelling garden-mint and dill seed and caraway seed,
and have omitted the weightier matters of the law, the
equitable administration of justice, and the mercy, and the
fidelity. And these things you were obligated as a necessity in the nature of the case to have done, and not to have
omitted those others. Blind guides, who by a filtering
process strain out the wine-gnat, yet gulp down the camel.

25, 26   Woe to you, men learned in the scriptures and Pharisees, actors on the stage of life, playing the role of that
which you are not, for you cleanse the outside of the cup
and the dish, but inside they are filled with rapacity and

lack of self-control. Blind Pharisee, cleanse first the inside of the cup in order that also the outside might become clean.

Woe to you, men learned in the scriptures and Phari-   **27, 28**
sees, actors on the stage of life playing the role of that which you are not, for you are like graves whose plastered coverings have been thoroughly whitewashed, which are of such a nature that on the one hand, the outsides appear beautiful, but on the other hand, their insides are full of dead men's bones and every uncleanness. In the same manner also, as for you, you on the one hand appear to men, righteous men outwardly, but on the other hand, you are full of the acting of an actor playing the role of that which he is not, and of lawlessness.

Woe to you, men learned in the sacred scriptures and   **29-31**
Pharisees, actors in the stage of life, playing the role of that which you are not, because you are building the tombs of the prophets and adorning the sepulchral monuments of the righteous, and you are saying, If we had lived in the days of our fathers, we would in that case not have been partners with them in the blood of the prophets. Therefore you are testifying against yourselves that you are by nature sons of those who killed the prophets.

And, as for you, add to that which is lacking in the   **32,33**
measuring unit containing the sins of your fathers, and thus fill it up. Snakes, progeny of vipers, how is it possible that you may escape the judgment of hell?

On this account, behold, I am sending to you prophets   **34-36**
and wise men and men learned in the scriptures, and some of them you will kill and crucify, and some of them you will scourge in your synagogues and persecute from city to city, in order that there may come upon you all of the righteous blood which is being shed upon the earth, from the blood of Abel the righteous one to the blood of Zacharias son of Barachias whom you murdered between the inner sanctuary and the altar of whole burnt-offerings. Assuredly, I am saying to you, All these things shall come upon this breed of men.

O Jerusalem, Jerusalem, the city which is in the habit   **37-39**
of killing the prophets and of stoning those sent to it on

a mission, how often did I long to gather to myself your children even as a bird gathers her brood of young ones under her wings, and you did not desire it. Behold, your house is left to you, abandoned to its own resources, for I am saying to you, you shall positively not see me from this time on until you shall say, Let the one who comes in the Name of the Lord be eulogized.

1, 2   And Jesus, having gone out from the temple, was proceeding on His way. And His disciples came to Him for the purpose of bidding Him look at the buildings of the temple. And answering He said to them, Do you not see all these things? Assuredly, I am saying to you, there shall positively not be left in this place a stone upon a stone which shall not be thrown down.

3-8   And as He was sitting upon the mount of Olivet, the disciples came to Him privately saying, Tell us, when shall these things be? And what shall be the attesting miracle which will indicate your coming and the consummation of the age? And answering, Jesus said to them, Be constantly seeing to it that no one leads you astray, for many shall come in my Name, saying, As for myself, I am the Christ, and shall lead many astray. Moreover, you are destined to be hearing of wars and reports of wars. Look! Stop being alarmed, for it is necessary in the nature of the case for these things to come to be, but not yet is the end. For there shall rise up nation against nation and kingdom against kingdom, and there shall be famines and earthquakes in various places. And all these are a beginning of excruciating sufferings.

9-14   Then they shall deliver you up to affliction, and they shall kill you, and you shall be hated by all the Gentile nations because of my Name. And then many shall begin to distrust and desert those whom they ought to trust and obey, and shall betray one another and hate one another. And many false prophets shall arise and lead many astray. And because of the multiplication of lawlessness, the love of the many shall grow cold. But he who has persevered to the end, this man shall be preserved from destruction. And there shall be proclaimed this good news of the kingdom in the whole Roman empire [the future revived empire] for a testimony to all the Gentile nations, and then shall the end come.

Therefore, whenever you see the object of religious nausea and loathing who has to do with the desolation, which person was spoken of through Daniel the prophet, standing in the holy place, he who reads, let him understand. Then those who are in Judaea, let them be fleeing into the mountains, he who is on the house-top, let him not descend to snatch the things out of his house, and he who is in the field, let him not turn back to snatch his outer garment. But woe to those with child and to those who nurse their young in those days. Moreover, pray that your flight may not be in winter, neither on a sabbath day, for then there shall be great tribulation such as has not occurred from the beginning of the universe until now, nor shall it ever be. And if those days had not been curtailed, all flesh would not be saved from destruction. But for the sake of the chosen-out ones, those days shall be curtailed.

15-22

Then, if anyone says to you, Behold, here is the Christ, or there, do not begin to believe him. For there shall arise false Christs and false prophets and shall produce great attesting miracles and miracles that arouse amazement, so as to deceive if that were possible, which it is not, even the chosen-out ones. Behold! I have told you ahead of time. If therefore they say to you, Behold, in the uninhabited region he is, do not go forth. Behold, in the secret rooms, do not begin to believe it, for just as the lightning comes out from the east and is seen even to the west, thus shall be the personal advent of the Son of Man, for wherever the corpse might be, in that place the carrion birds will be gathered together.

23-28

Now, immediately after the tribulation of those days, the sun shall be darkened, and the moon shall not give its light, and the meteors shall fall from the heaven, and the natural powers that control the heavenly bodies shall be disorganized. And then shall be seen the attesting miracle of the Son of Man in heaven. And then all the

29-31

people of the earth shall beat their breasts in anguish, and they shall see the Son of Man coming with the clouds of heaven with power and great glory. And He shall send on a mission His angels with a great trumpet, and they shall gather together in one place His chosen-out ones from the four winds, from the uttermost parts of heaven to the other.

32-36 Now, from the fig tree learn at once the illustrated lesson it has for you. Whenever its branch already becomes tender and puts forth its leaves, you know that the summer is near. Thus also, as for you, whenever you see all these things, you know that He is near, at the doors. Assuredly, I am saying to you, This nation shall by no means pass away until all these things take place. The heaven and the earth will pass away, but my words will positively not pass away. But concerning that day and hour no one knows, not even the angels of heaven nor even the Son, but only the Father.

37-42 For just as the days of Noah, thus shall it be at the time of the advent of the Son of Man. For as in those days before the deluge they were eating and drinking, marrying and giving in marriage, until the day Noah entered the ark, and they did not know until the deluge came and snatched them all away. Thus shall it also be at the time of the advent of the Son of Man. Then there shall be two in the field. One shall be taken and one shall be left. Two women shall be grinding at the mill. One shall be taken and one shall be left. Therefore, be constantly on the watch, because you do not know on what sort of a day your Lord is coming.

43, 44 But that thing you know, that if the master of the house had known during what period of the night when he should be on guard, the thief was coming, he would in that case have been on guard and would not have permitted his house to be broken into. On this account, as for you also, become those who are ready, because at an hour you do not think, the Son of Man comes.

45-51 Who then is a faithful slave and a judicious one whom the master appointed over his household slaves for the purpose of giving them their sustenance at the regularly appointed time? In a state of true well-being is that slave whom, his master having come, will find so doing. Assuredly, I am saying to you, over all his possessions he will appoint him. But if that evil slave should say in his heart, My master is delaying his coming, and shall begin to be beating his fellow-slaves, and to eat and drink with those who are drunken, the master of that slave will come on a day when he is not expecting him and at an hour which he does not know, and he shall scourge him severely and shall appoint his part with the actors on the stage of life who play the role of that which they are not. There, in that place, shall be the lamentation and the gnashing of the teeth.

Then the kingdom of heaven shall be likened to ten **1-13** virgins of such a nature as to have taken their torches and to have gone forth to meet the bridegroom. Now, five of them were without forethought or wisdom, and five were prudent, for those without forethought and wisdom, having taken their torches, did not take with themselves oil, but those who were prudent took oil in the receptacles with their torches. And while the bridegroom was delaying his coming, they all dropped off to sleep and went on slumbering. And at midnight there has come an outcry, Behold, the bridegroom. Be going forth to meet him. Then all those virgins arose and started to put their own torches in order. And those without forethought and wisdom said to those who were prudent, Give us at once some of your oil, because our torches are going out. And those who were prudent answered, saying, No, lest perchance there should not be by any means enough for us and you. Rather be going to those who sell, and buy for yourselves. And while they were going to buy, the bridegroom came, and those who were prepared went in with him to the wedding, and the door was closed. And later there come also the rest of the virgins saying, Sir, Sir, open at once to us. And answering he said, Assuredly, I am saying to you, I do not know you. Be ever on the watch therefore, because you do not know the day, neither the hour.

14, 15   It is just as a man about to go abroad who called his own slaves and gave his possessions to them with the responsibility of caring for and managing them. And to one, indeed, he gave a sum of money, five talents, and to another, a sum of money, two talents, and to still another, a sum of money, one talent, to each one in the measure of his own inherent ability; and went abroad.

16-30   Immediately, the one who had received the five talents proceeded, having taken them, and traded in them and made a profit of five others. Likewise, he who had received the two made a profit of two others. But he who had received one, having gone off, digged in the earth and hid his master's money. Now, after a long time, the master of those slaves comes and settles up accounts with them. And he who had received the five talents brought five other talents, saying, Master, five talents you gave into my keeping. See. I made a profit of five other talents. His master said to him, Excellent, good and faithful slave. Over a few things you were faithful. I will make you ruler over many. Enter into the joy of your master. And he who had received two talents said, Master, two talents you gave into my keeping. See. I made a profit of two other talents. His master said, Excellent, good and faithful slave. Over a few things you were faithful. Over many things I will make you a ruler. Enter into the joy of your master. And the one also who had received the one talent having come, said, Master, I have come to know you by experience that you are a hard man by nature, reaping where you did not sow, and gathering from where you did not winnow. And becoming afraid and having gone off, I hid your talent in the earth. See, you are having that which is yours. And his master answering said to him, Pernicious slave and slothful. Did you know that I am in the habit of reaping where I did not sow, and of gathering from where I did not winnow? Therefore it was a necessity in the nature of the case for you to have deposited my money with the bankers, and I having come, would receive back my money with interest. Take therefore from him the talent and give it at once to the one who has the ten talents, for to the one who has shall be given, and he shall be furnished with a superfluity, and he who does not have, even that which he has shall be taken from him. And the good-for-nothing slave throw out into the darkness, that which is outside. There, in that place, there shall be the lamentation and the gnashing of the teeth.

Now, when the Son of Man comes in His glory, and all the angels with Him, then He shall sit upon His throne of glory. And there shall be gathered before Him all the Gentile nations. And He shall separate them from one another even as the shepherd separates the sheep from the young goats. And He shall stand the sheep on His right hand and the young goats on His left. Then shall the King say to those on His right hand, Come, my Father's blessed ones. Inherit the kingdom which has been prepared for you from the foundation of the universe; for I was hungry and you gave me to eat, I was thirsty, and you gave me to drink, I was a stranger and you received me hospitably, naked and you clothed me, I was sick and you looked after me, in prison I was and you came to me.

31-36

Then the righteous ones shall answer Him, saying, Lord, when did we see you hungering and feed you, or thirsting and give you drink? And when did we see you a stranger and hospitably received you, or naked, and clothed you? And when did we see you sick or in prison and we came to you? And answering, the King shall say to them, Assuredly, I am saying to you, in so far as you did this to one of these my brethren, to the least, to me you did it. Then shall He say to those on His left hand, Be proceeding from me, you who have been doomed, into the fire, the everlasting fire which has been prepared and is in readiness for the devil and his angels; for I was hungry and you did not give me food, I was thirsty and you did not give me drink, a stranger I was, and you did not receive me hospitably, naked and you did not clothe me, sick and in prison and you did not look after me. Then they themselves shall also answer

37-46

Him, saying, Lord, when did we see you hungering or thirsting, or a stranger or naked or sick or in prison and did not relieve your necessities? Then He shall answer them, saying, Assuredly, I am saying to you, in so far as you did not do it to one of these least ones, neither did you do it to me. And these shall go off into everlasting punishment, but the righteous ones into life eternal.

1-5   And it came to pass when Jesus had finished all these discourses, He said to His disciples, You know that after two days occurs the passover, and the Son of Man is being betrayed to be crucified. Then were gathered together the chief priests and the elders of the people in the uncovered courtyard of the house belonging to the chief priest who is called Caiaphas, and they deliberated with one another with a view to seizing Jesus by craftiness and killing Him. But they were saying, Not during the feast, lest there arise an uproar among the people.

6-13   Now, when Jesus was in Bethany, in the home of Simon the leper, there came to Him a woman having an alabaster cruse of scented ointment of great value, and poured it down over His head as He reclined at the table partaking of a meal. And the disciples having seen this were indignant, saying, To what purpose is this dead loss? For it was possible for this to be sold for much and the proceeds given to poor people. And Jesus having come to know this said to them, Why are you causing the woman trouble? for a munificent service she did for me; for the poor people you always have with you, but me you are not always having. For, having poured this ointment upon my body, she did it to prepare me for my entombment. Assuredly, I am saying to you, wherever this gospel may be proclaimed in the whole world, there shall also be told this which this woman did as a memorial of her.

14-16   Then one of the Twelve, the one called Judas Iscariot, having proceeded, said to the chief priests, What are you willing to give me, and I will hand Him over to you? And they weighed out for him thirty pieces of silver.

And from then on he was seeking an auspicious time to betray Him.

Now, on the first day of bread baked without yeast, the disciples came to Jesus saying, Where are you desiring that we make ready for you to eat the passover? And He said, Be going into the city to a certain individual and say to him, The Teacher says, My critical, epoch-making time is near. I am observing the passover at your home with my disciples. And the disciples did as Jesus had arranged with them and made ready the passover. **17-19**

Now, evening having come, He was reclining at table with the twelve disciples. And while they were eating He said, Assuredly, I am saying to you, One of you shall betray me. And being grieved exceedingly, they began to be saying to Him one after the other, Surely, I am not the one, perchance, am I, Lord? And He answering said, He who dipped his hand with me in the dish, this man shall betray me. On the one hand, the Son of Man goes just as it stands written concerning Him, but on the other hand, woe to that man through whose agency the Son of Man is being betrayed. It would have been profitable for him if that man had not been born. And answering, Judas, the one betraying Him said, Surely, I am not the one, perchance, am I, Rabbi? He says to him, As for you, you said it. **20-25**

And while they were eating, Jesus having taken bread and having asked the blessing, broke it, and having given it to the disciples said, Take at once. Eat at once. This is my body. And having taken a cup, and having offered thanks for it, He gave it to them, saying, Drink of it, all of you, for this is my blood of the testament which in behalf of many is being poured out for the putting away of sins. And I am saying to you, I will positively not from now on drink of this product of the vine until that day when I drink it new in quality with you in the kingdom of my Father. And after they had sung a hymn, they went out into the mount of Olivet. **26-30**

31-35   Then Jesus says to them, As for you, all of you will find that of which you disapprove in relation to me and which hinders you from acknowledging me, thus finding in me an occasion for your stumbling on this night, for it stands written, I will cut down the shepherd and the sheep of the flock shall be scattered. And after I am raised up, I will go before you into Galilee. And Peter answering said to Him, Assuming that all will find an occasion of stumbling in you, as for myself, I will never find an occasion of stumbling in you. Jesus said to him, Assuredly, I am saying to you, on this night, before a rooster crows, three times you will deny me. Peter says to Him, Even if it would be a necessity in the nature of the case for me to die with you, I will positively not deny you. In the same way all the disciples spoke.

36-41   Then comes Jesus with them to a place called Gethsemane and says to the disciples, Sit down while I myself, having gone off to that place, will engage in prayer. And having taken with Him Peter and the two sons of Zebedee, He began to be affected with grief and to be distressed. Then He says to them, My soul is encircled and overwhelmed with grief, so much so that I am very close to dying. Remain here and be watching with me. And having gone forward a little He fell upon His face praying, and saying, My Father, if it is possible, let this cup pass from me. Nevertheless, not as I desire, but as you desire. And He comes to the disciples and finds them dropping off to sleep. And He says to Peter, Is it thus? Did you not have strength to watch one hour with me? Be ever watching and be ever praying lest you enter a place of testing where a solicitation to do evil may be the occasion which will lead to an act of sin. The spirit on the one hand is willing, but on the other hand, the flesh is weak.

42-46   Again a second time, having gone away, He prayed, saying, My Father, if it is not possible that this pass by except I drink it, let your will be done. And having come, again He found them sleeping, for their eyes had become weighed down with sleep. And having left them again and having gone away, He prayed a third time, saying again the same word. Then He comes to the disciples and says to them, Keep on sleeping now, and keep on taking your rest. Behold, the hour has been drawing near and has arrived, and the Son of Man is being betrayed into the hands of sinners. Be arising. Let us be going. Behold! He who is betraying me has drawn near and is now present.

And while He was still speaking, behold, Judas, one **47-56** of the Twelve came, and with him a large crowd with swords and cudgels from the chief priests and elders of the people. Moreover, he who was betraying Him gave them a token, saying, Whomever I shall kiss, it is He himself. Seize Him and hold Him fast. And immediately, having come to Jesus, he said, Hail, Rabbi, and he embraced Him and kissed Him tenderly and again and again. And Jesus said to him, Comrade! Upon the basis of a comrade are you present? Then, having come, they laid their hands upon Jesus and seized Him. And behold, one of those with Jesus having stretched out his hand, drew his sword and struck the slave of the chief priest and cut off his ear. Then Jesus says to him, Return your sword into its place, for all who have taken the sword shall perish by the sword. Or do you think that I am not able to call on my Father, and He shall provide me this moment with more than twelve legions [approximately 84,000] of angels? How then would the scriptures be fulfilled, because thus it is a necessity in the nature of the case for it to come to pass? In that hour Jesus said to the crowds, As against a robber you came forth with swords and cudgels to seize me? Daily I customarily sat in the temple, teaching, and you did not seize me. But all this has come to pass in order that the scriptures of the prophets might be fulfilled. Then the disciples, all of them, having forsaken Him, took to flight.

And those who seized Jesus led Him away to Caiaphas, **57-62** the chief priest, where the men learned in the scriptures and the elders were assembled. And Peter was following Him at a distance, even to the uncovered courtyard of the house belonging to the chief priest. And having gone

inside, he was sitting with the officers to see the end.
And the chief priests and the whole council were seeking
false witness against Jesus in order that they might put
Him to death, and they did not find it, though many false
witnesses came. But at last two having come, said, This
man said, I am able to destroy the inner sanctuary of God
and after three days to build it. And the chief priest
having arisen, said to Him, Are you answering not even
one thing? What is it that these are witnessing against
you? But Jesus maintained His silence.

63-68   And the chief priest said to Him, I am placing you
under oath by the living God that you tell us whether
you are the Christ, the Son of God. Jesus says to Him,
As for you, you said it. Nay. More. I am saying to
you, hereafter you shall see the Son of Man seated at
the right hand of the power and coming with the clouds
of heaven. Then the chief priest tore apart his outer
robes, saying, He has by contemptuous speech intentionally
come short of the reverence due to God. What need do
we yet have of witnesses? See. Now you heard His
contemptuous speech with reference to God. What do
you think? And they answering said, He is worthy of
death. Then they spit in His face and pummeled Him,
and they slapped His face, saying, Declare to us by
divine revelation, you Christ, who is it who struck you
with the fist?

69-75   Now, Peter was sitting outside in the open courtyard.
And there came to him one, a young female slave, saying,
And as for you, you were with Jesus, the one from Galilee.
But he denied before all saying, I do not know what you
are saying. And after going out into the porch, another
female slave saw him and says to those in that place,
This fellow was with Jesus, the one from Nazareth.
And again he denied, putting himself · under oath, I do
not know the man. And after a little while those standing there, having come up, said to Peter, Of a truth, as for
you, you also are one of them, for your dialect gives you
away. Then he began to be calling divine curses down upon
himself and putting himself under oath, saying, I do not
know the man. And immediately a rooster crowed. And

Peter was reminded of the word of Jesus who had said, Before a rooster crows, three times you will deny me. And having gone outside he wept loudly and bitterly.

Now, when morning came, all the chief priests and the elders of the people held a consultation with respect to Jesus in order to put him to death. And after binding Him they led Him away and delivered Him to the custody of Pilate the governor. **1, 2**

Then Judas, the one who had betrayed Him, having seen that He was condemned, remorseful because of what he had done, returned the thirty silver coins to the chief priests and elders, saying, I sinned, having betrayed innocent blood. But they said, What is that to us? As for you, you see to that. And having hurled the pieces of silver into the inner sanctuary, he withdrew, and having gone off, he hanged himself. But the chief priests, having taken the silver coins, said, It is not legal to put them into the sacred treasury, since it is the price of blood. And having held a consultation, they purchased with them the plot of ground where the potter dug his clay, as a burial place for the strangers, on which account that field was called a field of blood to the present time. Then was fulfilled that which was spoken through the intermediate agency of Jeremiah the prophet, saying, And they took the thirty silver coins, the evaluation of the One who has been valued, whom they of the sons of Israel valued, and gave them for the field where the potter dug his clay, according as the Lord appointed me. **3-10**

Now, Jesus was stood before the governor. And the governor asked Him, saying, As for you, are you the king of the Jews? And Jesus said, As for you, you said it. And while He was being accused by the chief priests and elders, He answered not even one thing. Then Pilate says to Him, Are you not hearing how many things they are bearing witness to against you? And He answered him not even one word, so that the governor marvelled greatly. **11-14**

Now, at the feast the governor according to custom released one to the crowd, a prisoner whom they were **15-19** desiring. And they were holding then a prisoner, a notorious one called Barabbas. Therefore after they had been gathered together, Pilate said to them, Whom are you desiring that I release to you, Barabbas, or Jesus, the one called Christ? For he knew that because of envy they had delivered Him into his custody. Now, while he was seated on the official bench of a judge, his wife sent to him, saying, Have not even one thing to do with proceedings against that just man, for I suffered many things today in a dream because of him.

20-26   But the chief priests and the elders persuaded the crowds that they should ask for that man Barabbas and that they should destroy Jesus. And answering, the governor said to them, Whom are you desiring of the two that I should release to you? And they said, That man Barabbas. Pilate says to them, What then shall I do with Jesus, the one called Christ? They say, all of them, Let him be crucified. And he said, Why, what evil did he do? And they kept on shouting beyond measure, saying, Let him be crucified at once. And Pilate, having seen that he could effect nothing, but that rather an uproar was created, having taken water, washed his hands in the sight of the crowd, saying, I am innocent of the blood of this man. As for you, you see to it. And all the crowd answering said, His blood be upon us and upon our children. Then he released to them Barabbas, and having scourged Jesus, he handed Him over to be crucified.

27-32   Then the soldiers of the governor, having taken Jesus with them into their barracks, gathered together before Him the whole detachment of soldiers stationed at the palace of the governor. And having stripped Him of all His clothing, they threw around Him a scarlet military cloak, and having woven a victor's crown composed of thorns, they placed it upon His head, and a staff made of a reed in His right hand. And having fallen upon their knees in a mock expression of reverence and honor before Him, they mocked Him, saying, Hail, King of the Jews. And having spit on Him they took the staff and kept on striking Him on the head with it. And when they had mocked Him, they took off from Him the military cloak and put on Him His garments. And they led Him away to crucify Him. And as they were going they found a man, a Cyrenian, his name, Simon. This man they commandeered that he might pick up and carry His cross.

And having come to a place called Golgotha, which is called a place of a skull, they gave Him to drink wine mixed with gall, a stupefying drink to deaden the pain of crucifixion. And having tasted it, He was not willing to drink it. And having crucified Him, they distributed His garments among themselves, casting a lot. And seating themselves they maintained a guard over Him there. And they put above His head His accusation which had been written, THIS IS JESUS, THE KING OF THE JEWS. **33-37**

Then there are being crucified with Him two robbers, one on the right and one on the left. And those passing by reviled Him, wagging their heads and saying, You who destroy the inner sanctuary and in three days build it, save yourself. Since you are Son of God by nature, also come down from the cross. In the same manner the chief priests mocking with the men learned in the scriptures and the elders, kept on saying, Others he saved. Himself he is not able to save. Israel's King he is. Let him now come down from the cross and we will believe on him. He rested his complete confidence upon God. Let Him now rescue him, assuming that He has a desire for him, for he said, Of God I am Son. Moreover, the robbers who were crucified with Him reviled Him with same. **38-44**

Now, from the sixth hour there came a darkness over all the land until the ninth hour. And about the ninth hour Jesus cried out with a great voice, saying, Eli, Eli, lama sabachthani, that is, O my God, O my God, why did you let me down? Now, certain ones of those standing there, having heard, were saying, Elijah this one calls. And immediately, one of them having run and having taken a sponge, having filled it with a mixture of sour wine and water which the soldiers drink, affixed it **45-49** to a reed and offered Him a drink. And the rest said, Hold off. Let us see whether Elijah comes to save him.

50-56   And Jesus, having again cried with a great voice, dismissed the spirit. And, behold, the curtain of the inner sanctuary was torn in two from the top to the bottom, and the earth was caused to tremble by reason of an earthquake, and the massive rocks were split into pieces. And the tombs were opened and many bodies of the saints who have fallen asleep were raised up, and having come out of the tombs after His resurrection they went into the holy city and appeared to many. And the captain of a hundred soldiers and those with him who were guarding Jesus, having seen the earthquake and the things which had taken place, were exceedingly afraid, saying, Of a truth, Son of God was this man. Moreover, there were there many women carefully observing the details from a distance, such as followed with Jesus from Galilee, ministering to Him the necessities of life, among whom was Mary, the Magdalene, and Mary the mother of James and Joses, and the mother of the sons of Zebedee.

57-61   Now, evening having come, there came a man, a wealthy one, of Arimathaea, his name Joseph, who also himself had become a disciple of Jesus. This man, having gone to Pilate, asked as a favor for the body of Jesus. Then Pilate commanded that it should be delivered to him. And having taken the body, Joseph wrapped it in clean linen cloth and laid it in his tomb which he cut in the rock and in which no corpse had ever been placed, and having rolled a great stone against the door of the tomb, he went away. And Mary, the Magdalene, and the other Mary were there, sitting before the tomb.

62-66   Now, on the next day, which was of such a nature as to be the day after the preparation, the chief priests and the Pharisees were gathered together to Pilate, saying, Sir, we have just been reminded that that deceiver said while still living, After three days I am being raised up. Therefore issue a command at once that the tomb be made secure until the third day, lest at some time or other the disciples having come, steal him and say to the people,

He was raised from the dead, and the last error shall be worse than the first. Pilate said to them, You have a guard. Be going on your way. Be making it as secure as you know how. And having proceeded, they made the tomb secure, having sealed the stone in the presence of the guard.

Now, the sabbath having passed, as it was growing **1-4** light toward the first day of the week, there came Mary, the Magdalene, and the other Mary, to inspect the tomb. And behold, there occurred a great earthquake, for an angel of the Lord having descended out of heaven and having come, rolled away the stone, and sat upon it. And his external appearance was as lightning, and his clothing white as snow, and because of their fear of him, the soldiers who were on guard were thrown into an uncontrollable trembling, and became as dead men.

And the angel answering said to the women, As for **5-10** you, stop being afraid, for I know that Jesus, He who has been crucified, you are seeking. He is not here, for He was raised up just as He said. Come here. See the place where He was lying. And having proceeded quickly on your way, tell His disciples, He was raised from the dead, and behold, He goes before you into Galilee. There you shall see Him. See, I told you. And having quickly gone away from the tomb with fear and great joy, they ran to bring word to His disciples. And behold, Jesus met them, saying, Be rejoicing. And having come to Him, they took hold of His feet and prostrated themselves upon the ground in worship before Him. Then Jesus says to them, Stop fearing. Be going and tell my brethren to go off into Galilee, and there they shall see me.

Now, while they were going on their way, behold, **11-15** certain ones belonging to the guard of soldiers having gone into the city, gave a report to the chief priests of all the things which occurred. And having assembled with the elders and having held a consultation, they gave a sufficient amount of money to the soldiers, saying, Say that his disciples having come by night took him away by

stealth while we were sleeping. And if this should come
to a hearing before the governor, as for us, we will persuade him, and as for you, we will render you free from
anxiety. And they, having taken the money, did as they
were taught. And this report was circulated among the
Jews until this day.

16-20   Now, the eleven disciples went on their way to Galilee,
to the mountain where Jesus had appointed them. And
having seen Him, they worshipped Him, prostrating
themselves on the ground before Him. But some doubted.
And Jesus, having come, spoke to them, saying, There
was given to me all authority in heaven and upon earth.
Having gone on your way therefore, teach all the nations,
making them your pupils, baptizing them into the Name
of the Father and of the Son and of the Holy Spirit,
teaching them to be attending to carefully, holding firmly
to, and observing all, whatever things I enjoined upon
you. And behold, as for myself, with you I am all the
days until the consummation of the age.

The beginning of the good news concerning Jesus **1-3**
Christ, Son of God, according as it stands written in
Isaiah the prophet: Behold, I send my messenger on a
mission before your face who will make ready your road,
a voice of One shouting out in the uninhabited place, Prepare the Lord's road. Straight and level be constantly
making His paths.

There came upon the human scene, John the Baptizer, **4-8**
in the uninhabited region, making a public proclamation
with that formality, gravity, and authority which must
be heeded and obeyed, of a baptism which had to do
with a change of mind relative to the previous life an
individual lived, this baptism being in view of the fact
that sins are put away. And there kept on proceeding out
to him in a steady stream all the Judaean region and all
the people of Jerusalem. And they were being baptized by
him in the Jordan river as they were confessing their
sins. And there was this John, clothed habitually in a
camel's hair garment, a leather belt about his loins, his
diet locusts and wild honey. And he made a proclamation, saying, There comes He who is mightier than I
after me, the thong of whose sandals I am not worthy
to stoop down and unloose. As for myself, I baptized
you by means of water. But He himself will baptize you
by means of the Holy Spirit.

And it came to pass in those days that Jesus came from **9-11**
Nazareth of Galilee and was baptized in the Jordan by
John. And immediately, while He was coming up out
of the water, He saw the heavens being rent asunder and
the Spirit in the form of a dove descending upon Him.
And a voice came out from within heaven, As for you,
you are my Son, the beloved one; in you I am well
pleased.

And immediately the Spirit thrusts Him out into the **12-15**
uninhabited place. And He was in the uninhabited
region forty days, being constantly put to the test, being
solicited to do evil by Satan; and He was with the wild
beasts; and the angels were constantly ministering to
Him. And after John was put in prison, Jesus came into

Galilee, making a public proclamation with that formality, gravity, and authority which must be heeded and obeyed of the good news of God, and saying, The time has been fulfilled with the present result that the present moment is epochal in its significance, and the kingdom of God has drawn near and is imminent. Be having a change of mind regarding your former life, and be putting your faith in the good news.

16-20 And while He was walking along the sea of Galilee, He saw Simon and Andrew the brother of Simon, casting their net about in the sea; for they were fishermen. And Jesus said to them, Come, after me, and I will make you to become fishers of men. And immediately, having put away their nets, they followed with Him as His disciples. And having gone on a little further, He saw James the son of Zebedee and John his brother, and they were in the boat mending their nets. And immediately He called them. And having left their father Zebedee in the boat with the employees, they went off after Him.

21-24 And they go into Capernaum. And immediately on the sabbath, having entered the synagogue, He went to teaching. And they were completely amazed at His teaching, for He was teaching them as one who possesses authority, and not as the men learned in the sacred scriptures. And immediately, there was in their synagogue a man with a spirit, an unclean one. And he cried out, saying, What is there in common between us and you, Jesus, Nazarene? You came to destroy us. I know you who you are, the Holy One of God.

25-28 And Jesus rebuked him, the rebuke not resulting in any conviction or confession of sin, saying, Shut your mouth and come out of him at once. And when the unclean spirit had torn him with convulsions, he screeched with a loud voice and came out of him. And they were all amazed, so that they kept on inquiring and demanding of one another, saying, What is this? Fresh teaching backed by authority. And the unclean spirits He commands, and they obey Him. And there went out the report concerning Him immediately throughout the whole region of Galilee.

And immediately, having come out of the synagogue, they entered the house of Simon and Andrew, with James and John. And Simon's mother-in-law had been bedridden for sometime, burning up with fever. And immediately they speak to Him concerning her. And having come, He went to lifting her up, having taken hold of her hand. And the fever left her, and she went to serving them.

29-31

And evening having come, when the sun had gone down, they kept on carrying in a steady procession to Him all those having ailments, and those who were demonized. And all the city was gathered together, seated, and facing the door. And He healed many who were afflicted with various kinds of diseases, and demons, many of them, He ejected, and He kept on refusing the demons permission to be speaking, because they knew Him.

32-34

And in the last watch of the night between three and six, in the early part of the watch while it was still somewhat dark, He arose and went out, and went off into a deserted place, and was there praying. And Simon and those with him hunted Him out. And they found Him and say to Him, All are seeking for you. And He says to them, Let us be going elsewhere into the nearby country towns in order that also there I may preach. For this purpose I came out. And He went preaching in their synagogues all over Galilee and casting out the demons.

35-39

And there comes to Him a leper, begging Him and kneeling, saying to Him, If you are willing, you have power to cleanse me. And having been moved with compassion, having stretched out His hand, He touched him and says to him, I desire it. Be cleansed at once. And immediately the leprosy left him completely, and he was cleansed.

40-42

And sternly charging him, He immediately thrust him out, and says to him, See to it that you say nothing to anyone, but go, show yourself as evidence to the priest, and present that offering with reference to your cleansing which Moses commanded for a testimony to them. But

43-45

having gone out, he began to be proclaiming in public a great deal and to be blazing abroad the account, so that no longer was He able to enter a city, but was outside in uninhabited places. And they kept on coming to Him from everywhere.

1-5   And having again entered Capernaum, after some days He was heard of as being at home. And there were gathered together many, so that no longer was there room to receive them, not even at the door; and He was talking to them about the Word. And they come, bearing to Him a paralytic who had been picked up and was being carried by four men. And not being able to bring the paralytic to a place before Him because of the crowd, they took off the surface of the roof where He was, and having dug through, they lowered the pallet upon which the paralytic was lying prostrate. And having seen their faith, Jesus says to the paralytic, Child, your sins are put away.

6-12   Now, there were certain of the men learned in the sacred scriptures sitting there and reasoning in their hearts, Why is this fellow speaking in this manner? He is by contemptuous speech coming short of the reverence due to God. Who is able to put away sins except one person, God? And immediately, Jesus having become fully aware in his inner being that in this manner they were reasoning within themselves, says to them, Why are you reasoning these things in your hearts? Which of the two is easier, to say to the paralytic, Your sins are put away; or to say, Be arising and pick up your pallet at once and carry it away, and start walking and keep on walking? But in order that you may have absolute knowledge of the fact that the Son of Man possesses authority to forgive sins on the earth, — He says to the paralytic, To you I say, Be arising, pick up your pallet at once, and be going away into your home. And he arose, and immediately, having picked up his pallet, went out before all of them, so that all were astonished, and were glorifying God, saying, In this manner, never have we seen it.

And He went out again along the seashore. And all the crowd kept on coming to Him, and He went to teaching them. And as He was passing by He saw Levi, the son of Alphaeus, sitting at the tax collector's desk. And He says to him, Start following with me, and continue to do so as a habit of life. And having arisen, he followed with Him. And it comes to pass that, as He was dining in his house, many tax collectors and sinners stained with vice and crime were dining with Jesus and His disciples, for there were many, and they were following with Him. **13-15**

And the men learned in the sacred scriptures belonging to the sect of the Pharisees, having seen that He was eating with the sinners and tax collectors, were saying to His disciples, With the tax collectors and the sinners stained with vice and crime is he eating? And having heard, Jesus says to them, No need do they have who are strong, for a doctor, but those who are ill. I did not come to call righteous ones but sinners. **16, 17**

And John's disciples and those of the Pharisees were observing a fast. And they come and say to Him, Why are John's disciples and the disciples of the Pharisees fasting, but your disciples are not fasting? And Jesus said to them, The sons of the bridechamber are not able to be fasting while the bridegroom is with them, are they? As long as they are having the bridegroom with them, they are not able to be fasting. But there shall come days when there shall be taken away from them the bridegroom, and then they shall fast in that day. No one sews a patch consisting of cloth which has not been pre-shrunk upon a worn-out garment. Otherwise that which fills it up takes away from it, the new from the worn-out, and the tear becomes worse. And no one puts newly-made wine into worn-out wineskins. Otherwise, the wine will burst the wineskins, and the wine and the wineskins are destroyed. But newly-made wine is put into wineskins which are just beginning to be used. **18-22**

And it came to pass that on the sabbath He was proceeding along a path through the fields of grain. **23-28**

And His disciples began to be making their way, picking off the grains as they were going along. And the Pharisees kept on saying to Him, Observe that, will you. Why are they doing on the sabbath that which is not lawful? And He says to them, You have read, have you not, what David did when he was having need and was hungry, he himself and those with him, how he entered the house of God when Abiathar was high priest, and the loaves that were set forth, he ate, which are not permitted to be eaten except by the priests, and he gave also to those who were with him? And He was saying to them, The sabbath for the sake of man came into being, and not man for the sake of the sabbath. So that the Son of Man is Lord even of the sabbath.

1-5 And He again entered a synagogue. And there was there in that place a man whose one hand had withered. And they kept on spying upon Him closely, whether He would on the sabbath heal him, in order that they might bring a formal accusation against Him before a tribunal. And He says to the man having the withered hand, Be arising in the midst of everybody around you. And He says to them, Is it lawful on the sabbath to do good or to do evil, to save life or to kill? But they kept on being quiet. And having looked round about on them with a righteous indignation, being grieved at the callousness of their hearts, He says to the man, Stretch out your hand at once. And he stretched it out. And his hand was restored to its former state.

6-8 And having gone out, the Pharisees at once with the Herodians were giving counsel against Him, in order that they might destroy Him. And Jesus with His disciples withdrew to the sea, and a vast multitude from Galilee followed. And from Judaea, and from Jerusalem, and from Idumaea and across the Jordan, and about Tyre and Sidon a vast multitude, hearing constantly of such great things which He was continually doing, came to Him.

9-12 And He spoke to His disciples to the effect that they should always keep a small boat in readiness for Him because of the crowd, in order that they might not crush

Him, for He healed many, so that as a result, they kept on jostling Him in order that they might touch Him, as many as were having a distressing bodily disease. And the spirits, the unclean ones, when they set eyes on Him, kept on falling prostrate before Him, and kept on crying out with a loud voice, saying, As for you, you are the Son of God. And He kept on rebuking them and charging them under penalty that they should not make Him known.

And He goes up into the mountain and calls for himself and to himself those whom He himself was desiring, and they went off to Him. And He appointed twelve in order that they might constantly be with Him, and in order that He might send them forth as ambassadors with credentials, representing Him, to accomplish a certain task, that of making a proclamation with such formality, gravity, and authority as must be heeded and obeyed, being equipped with delegated authority to be casting out the demons. **13-15**

And He appointed the Twelve, and added to Simon's name, the name Peter; and James the son of Zebedee, and John the brother of James, He surnamed Boanerges, which is, sons of thunder; and Andrew and Philip, and Bartholomew, and Matthew, and Thomas, and James the son of Alphaeus, and Thaddaeus, and Simon the Canaanite, and Judas Iscariot who also handed Him over. **16-19**

And He comes home. And there comes together again the multitude, so that they are not able even to eat bread. And having heard, those nearest to Him among His kinsfolk went out for the purpose of taking Him by force, for they were saying, He is out of His mind. **19-21**

And the men learned in the sacred scriptures, the ones from Jerusalem, having come down, kept on saying, He has Beezeboul, and by means of the ruler of the demons He is casting out the demons. And having called them to himself, He was speaking to them in the form of illustrations: How is Satan able to be casting out Satan? And if a kingdom be divided against itself, that kingdom is not able to stand. And if a house be divided against itself, that house will not be able to stand. And assum- **22-27** ing that Satan arose against himself and is divided, he is not able to stand but has an end. But no one is able, having entered the house of the strong man, thoroughly to ransack his equipment, unless first he binds the strong man, and then he will thoroughly plunder his house.

28-30   Assuredly I am saying to you, All sins shall be forgiven the sons of men, and all malicious misrepresentations, as many as they use to defame, but whoever maliciously misrepresents the Holy Spirit never has forgiveness, but he is guilty of an everlasting sin: because they kept on saying, He has an unclean spirit.

31-35   And there come His mother and His brethren, and standing outside, they sent to Him, calling Him. And a crowd was sitting in a circle around Him, and they say to Him, Behold, your mother and your brothers and your sisters outside are seeking you. And answering them He says, Who is my mother and my brethren? And having looked round about upon those sitting in a circle around Him, He says, Behold, my mother and my brethren. Whoever does the will of God, this one is my brother and sister and mother.

1-9   And again He began teaching along the seashore. And there gathers together to Him a crowd, the largest one up to that time, so that He entered a ship in order to occupy a place on the sea. And the whole crowd was on the land facing toward the sea. And He was teaching them many things by means of illustrations, and was saying to them in His teaching, Be listening. Give attention to this. The sower went out to sow. And it came to pass that while he was sowing, some indeed fell alongside the road, and the birds came and ate it up. And other seed fell upon ground full of rocks, where it was not having much earth. And immediately it sprang up because it was not having any depth of earth. And when the sun arose, it was burnt, and because it did not possess rootage, it withered. And other seed fell into the midst of thorns and the thorns sprang up and utterly choked it, and it did not give fruit. And other seeds fell on ground that was good, and it kept on yielding fruit, growing up and increasing, and it kept on bearing, up to thirty-fold and to sixty, and to one hundred. And He was saying, He who has ears to be hearing, let him be hearing.

And as soon as He was alone, those about Him, with the Twelve, went to asking Him concerning the illustrations. And He was saying to them, To you the mystery of the kingdom of God has been given, and it is in your possession. But to those who are outside, in the form of illustrations are all the things given, in order that seeing they may be seeing and may not perceive, and hearing, they may be hearing and may not understand, lest haply they turn again and it should be forgiven them. And He says to them, Do you not understand this illustration? Then how is it possible that you will understand all the illustrations? The sower sows the Word. And these are those alongside the road where the Word is being sown; and whenever they hear, immediately there comes Satan and snatches away by force the Word which has been sown in them. And these are, on the same principle of interpretation, those who are being sown on ground full of rocks, who, whenever they hear the Word, immediately with joy receive it; and they do not have rootage in themselves, but last only for a time; after that, affliction or persecution having come because of the Word, immediately they are displeased, indignant, resentful. And others are those who are being sown in the midst of the thorns. These are those who heard the Word, and the anxieties of the present age, and the deceitfulness of wealth, and the passionate desires with reference to the rest of the things not in these categories entering in, choke the Word, and it becomes unfruitful. And those are they which were sown on ground that is good, which are of such a nature as hear the Word and receive it, and bear fruit, some thirty-fold, some sixty, and some one hundred.

And He was saying to them, The lamp does not come, does it, in order to be placed under the peck measure or under the reclining couch? Does it not come in order to be placed upon the lampstand? For there is not anything which is hidden, except it be in order that it might be

10-20

21-25

made known, nor has anything become hidden but in order that it might come into full view. Assuming that a person has ears to be hearing, let him be hearing. And He was saying to them, Keep ever a watchful eye on what you are hearing. In the measure by which you are measuring, it will be measured to you; and it will be measured to you not only according to that measure, but there will be some added on top of that. For he who has, it shall be given to him. And he who does not have, even that which he has shall be taken away from him.

26-29   And He was saying, In this manner is the kingdom of God, as if a man should throw the seed upon the earth, and should be sleeping and arising night and day, and the seed should be sprouting and lengthening; how, he does not himself know. The earth bears fruit spontaneously, first, herbage, then a covering for the grain, then the fully-developed grain in its covering. And whenever the fruit permits, immediately, he sends forth the sickle, because the harvest stands ready.

30-34   And He was saying, In what way shall we liken the kingdom of God or by what illustration shall we set it forth? It is like a grain of mustard seed, which when it is planted in the earth, is less than all the seeds which are upon the earth; and when it is sown, it grows up and becomes greater than all of the herbs, and puts out great branches, so that the birds of the heaven are able to find shelter under its shadow. And by means of many illustrations of this kind He was speaking to them the Word as they were able to be understanding. But without an illustration He was not in the habit of speaking to them; but in private, He was in the habit of fully explaining all things to those pupils who were peculiarly His own.

35-41   And He says to them on that day, evening having come, Let us go over to the other side. And having dismissed the crowd, they take Him under their care just as He was, in the boat, and there were other boats with Him. And there arises a great windstorm of hurricane proportions, and the waves kept on beating into the boat, so that already it was being filled. And He himself was in the stern of the boat, sleeping on the steersman's leather cushion. And they arouse Him from sleep and say to Him, Teacher, is it not a concern to you that we are perishing? And having awakened, He rebuked the wind and said to the sea, Be getting calm; hush up and stay that way. And the wind ceased its raging, and there was a great calm. And He said to them, Why are you such timid, fearful ones? How is it that you do not have faith? And they feared a great fear, and were saying to one another, Who then is this person, that even the wind and the sea obey him?

And they came across the sea into the country of the Gerasenes. And having come out of the boat, immediately there met him out of the tombs a man with an unclean spirit who had settled down there, making his home in the tombs; and no longer was anyone able to bind him, not even with manacles, because he often was securely bound with shackles and manacles, and the manacles were snapped in two by him, and the shackles crushed together, and no one had sufficient strength to restrain him. And throughout all the night and the day, in the tombs and in the mountains, he was continually screaming and shrieking, and was constantly lacerating himself all over with stones. And having seen Jesus from a distance, he ran and prostrated himself on the ground before Him, and he cried out with a great voice, and says, What is there in common between me and you, Jesus, you Son of the most high God? I adjure you, by God, don't begin to torment me. For He was saying to him, Come out of the man, unclean spirit. And He kept on asking him, What is your name? And he says to Him, Legion is my name, because we are many. And he kept on pleading much with Him to the effect that He should not send them off outside of the country.

1-10

Now, there was there near the mountain, a herd of hogs feeding, a great herd. And they begged Him, saying, Send us at once into the hogs in order that we may enter them. And He gave them permission. And having gone out, the unclean spirits entered the hogs, and the herd rushed impetuously down the steep place into the

11-17

sea, about two thousand, and were drowned one after another in the sea. And those feeding them fled and brought away tidings into the city and into the farms. And they came for the purpose of seeing what it was that had taken place. And they come to Jesus and view with a critical, searching eye the demoniac sitting, clothed and in control of himself, the one who had had the legion. And they became afraid. And those who saw, related fully and in detail to them how it happened to the demoniac and concerning the hogs. And they began to be begging Him to go away from their boundaries.

18-20   And while He was going on board the boat, the one who had been demon-possessed kept on begging Him for permission to be with Him. And He did not permit him, but says to him, Be going into your home, to your own relatives, and bring back tidings to them of such great things which the Lord has done for you, and of the fact that He had a sympathy for you which issued in action in your behalf. And he went off and began proclaiming publicly in the Decapolis such great things which Jesus did for him. And all were marvelling.

21-29   And when Jesus had crossed over in the boat again to the other side, a great crowd was gathered together after Him, and He was at the seashore. And there comes one of the synagogue rulers, by name, Jairus; and having seen Him, he falls at His feet, and begs Him earnestly, saying, My little daughter is at the point of death. Come, place your hands upon her in order that she might be healed and live. And He went off with him. And there kept on following with Him a large crowd, and they kept on pressing upon Him almost to the point of suffocation. And a woman having come who had a flow of blood for twelve years, and had endured much suffering under the hands of many doctors, and had spent all of the things which she had, and was not even one bit improved but rather grew worse, having heard the things concerning Jesus, having come in the crowd behind, touched His garment, for she kept saying, If I touch even His garments, I shall be made whole. And immediately there was dried up the fountain of her blood, and she suddenly came to feel in her body that she had been healed of her plague and was at that moment in a state of health.

And immediately, Jesus, having had a personal and **30-34** clear knowledge in himself of the experience of power going out of Him, having turned around in the crowd, was saying: Who touched me on my garments? And His disciples kept on saying to Him, You are seeing the crowd pressing hard around you from all sides; yet you are saying, Who touched me? And He kept on looking round about to see the woman who had done this. And the woman, fearing and trembling, knowing that which had been done for her, came and fell down before Him, and told Him all the truth. And He said to her, Daughter, your faith has saved you. Be going into a state of peace, and be continually sound in body, healed of your affliction.

While He was still speaking, they come from the home **35-43** of the ruler of the synagogue saying, Your daughter died. Why are you still bothering the Teacher? And Jesus overhearing the word being spoken, says to the ruler of the synagogue, Stop fearing, only be believing. And He did not permit anyone to follow with Him except Peter, and James, and John the brother of James. And they come into the home of the ruler of the synagogue, and He looks carefully and with an understanding eye at the tumult, and at those who were weeping audibly and at those who were wailing greatly. And having come in He says to them, Why are you wailing tumultuously and weeping? The little girl did not die, but is sleeping. And they went to laughing and jeering at Him. But after He himself had thrown them all out, He takes the father of the little girl and her mother and those with Him, and proceeds in where the little girl was. And having taken a strong grip on the hand of the little girl, He says to her, Talitha koum, which being interpreted is, Little girl, to you I say, be arising. And immediately the little girl stood up and went to walking about, for she was twelve years old. And they were amazed with a great amazement. And He charged them sternly that no one should know this. And He gave orders that she be given something to eat.

1-6   And He went out from there and comes into His own country. And His disciples follow with Him. And when the sabbath had come, He began to be teaching in the synagogue. And the many hearing were completely flabbergasted, saying, From where does this one get these things? And what wisdom is this which has been given to this fellow? Even such great exhibitions of supernatural power take place through the medium of His hands? Is not this the carpenter, the son of Mary, and brother of James, and Joses, and Jude, and Simon? And are not His sisters here with us? And they saw in Him that of which they disapproved and which kept them from acknowledging Him. And Jesus was saying to them, A prophet is not without a correct evaluation and the due respect and deference which that evaluation demands except in his own country and among his own kinsfolk and in his own home. And He was not able to do there even one work of power, except that He laid His hands on a few sickly ones and healed them. And He marvelled because of their unbelief. And He kept going around the villages in the encircling country, teaching.

7-13   And He calls to himself the Twelve. And He began to to be sending them forth as His ambassadors with credentials on a mission to represent Him, sending them forth two by two. And He was giving them authority over the unclean spirits. And He commanded them not to be taking even one thing for the road except only a walking stick, not bread, nor a begging-bag, nor money in their belt, but to wear sandals, and not to clothe themselves with two undergarments. And He was saying to them. Wherever you enter a home, there be abiding as a guest until you go out from there, and whatever place does not welcome you nor hear you, when you are going on your journey out from there, shake off the dust that is underneath your feet as a testimony against them. And having gone out, they made a proclamation to the effect that they should be repenting. And demons, many of them, they were casting out, and they were massaging with oil many who were sick, and were healing them.

And the king, Herod, heard, for His name became **14-20**
known, and they were saying that John the Baptizer
had been raised out from among those who were dead,
and because of this, the miraculous powers are operative
in him. But others kept on saying that He was Elijah.
But others were saying that He was a prophet like one
of the prophets. But Herod, having heard, kept on
saying, Him whom I decapitated, John, this man was
raised. For Herod himself, having commissioned an
official representative, apprehended this aforementioned
John and bound him in prison for the sake of Herodias,
the wife of Philip his brother, because he had married her;
for John had been saying to Herod, It is not lawful for
you to be having the wife of your brother. Therefore,
Herodias set herself against him and was desiring to kill
him. But she was unable to do so, for Herod was fearing
John, knowing him to be a man, righteous and holy; and
he kept him constantly out of harm's way, and, having
heard him often, he was in a continual state of perplexity,
and he was in the habit of hearing him with pleasure.

And a strategic day came, when Herod on his birthday **21-29**
made a supper for his great men, and his military com-
manders, and the chief men of Galilee. And the daughter
of Herodias herself, having entered and danced a rapid-
motion, leaping, lewd dance, it pleased Herod and those
who were dining with him. And the king said to the
young woman, Ask me at once whatever your heart desires, and I will give it to you. And he put himself
under oath to her: Whatever you ask me I will give
you, up to the half of my kingdom. And having gone
out, she said to her mother, What shall I ask for myself?
And she said, The head of John the Baptizer. And having come immediately with haste to the king, she made a
request for herself, saying, I desire that you give me at
once on a dish the head of John the Baptizer. And
though the king became exceedingly sorrowful, yet because of his oaths and because of those who were dining
with him, he did not desire to frustrate her. And immediately, the king, having sent off one of his body-
guards, issued the order to bring his head. And having

gone off, he beheaded him in the prison, and brought his head upon a dish and gave it to the young woman, and the young woman gave it to her mother. And having heard, his disciples came and took up his corpse and laid it in a tomb.

30, 31 And the missionaries gathered themselves together to Jesus and brought back news to Him of all things whatever they did and whatever they taught. And He says to them, Come here, as for you, yourselves, into the privacy of an uninhabited place, and rest yourselves a little. For there were those who were coming and those who were going, many of them, and not even was there an opportune time to eat.

32-44 And they went off in the boat to the privacy of an uninhabited place. And they saw them going away, and many understood, and on foot from all the cities they ran there with one another and preceded them. And having come out, He saw a large crowd, and He was moved with compassion for them because they were as sheep not having a shepherd. And He began teaching them many things. And when the day was already far gone, His disciples came to Him and were saying, Uninhabited is the place, and already the hour is late. Dismiss them in order that, having gone off to the neighboring farms and villages, they might purchase for themselves something to eat. And He anwering said to them, As for you, you give them to eat. And they say to Him, Having gone off, shall we purchase two hundred denarii worth of bread, and give them to eat? And He says to them, How many loaves do you have? Be going and see. And having found out, they say, Five, and two fish. And He commanded them to make all recline in open squares like oriental diners, upon the green grass. And they reclined in squares that looked like flower-garden plots, by hundreds and by fifties. And having taken the five loaves and the two fish, having looked up to heaven, He invoked a blessing, and broke the loaves, and kept on giving to the disciples in order that they might continue setting them beside them, and the two fish He divided to all. And all ate and were filled. And they took up twelve wicker baskets full of broken pieces, and from the fish. And those who had eaten the loaves were five thousand men.

And immediately, He constrained His disciples to go on board the boat and precede Him to the other side, to Bethsaida, while He himself dismisses the crowd. And having taken leave of them, He went off into the mountain to pray. And evening having come, the boat was in the middle of the sea and He himself alone upon the land. And having seen them constantly distressed in their rowing, for the wind was against them, sometime between three and six in the morning He comes to them walking directly on the sea. And He was desiring to go to their side. But having seen Him walking directly upon the sea, they supposed that it was an apparition. And they screamed, for they all saw Him and were agitated. But He immediately spoke with them; and He says to them, Be of good courage. It is I. Stop being afraid. And He went up to them into the boat, and the wind ceased its violence. And exceedingly beyond measure, in themselves they were amazed, for they did not reason upon the basis of the loaves. In fact, their heart was in a settled state of callousness. **45-52**

And having crossed over, they came to the land, to Gennesaret, and they cast anchor off shore. And when they had gone out of the boat, immediately, having recognized Him, they ran around throughout that whole countryside, and began to be carrying around on pallets those who were afflicted, where they were hearing that He was. And wherever He kept on proceeding, into villages, or into cities, or into farming districts, they laid those who were sick in the market places, and they kept on begging Him if they might touch even the fringe of His cloak. And as many as touched Him were being made whole. **53-56**

And there gather together to Him the Pharisees and certain ones of the men learned in the sacred scriptures who came from Jerusalem. And having seen certain ones of His pupils, that with unhallowed hands, that is, unwashed hands, were eating the loaves, they found fault, **1-5** for the Pharisees and all the Jews, unless they wash their hands meticulously in a ritualistic fashion, do not eat, habitually keeping, carefully and faithfully, that which was delivered from the elders to be observed. And from the market place, if they do not wash, they do not eat; and many other things there are which they received for the purpose of keeping, washing of cups and pint measures and copper vessels. Both the Pharisees and the men learned in the sacred scriptures went to asking Him, Why are not your pupils ordering their manner of living according to that which was delivered from the elders to be observed, but with unhallowed hands are eating their bread?

6-13   And He said to them, Well did Isaiah prophesy concerning you, the hypocrites, as it stands written: This people is constantly honoring me with their lips. But their heart holds at a great distance from me. But in vain are they worshipping me while they are teaching as doctrines, commandments of men. Having abandoned the commandment of God, you are carefully and faithfully keeping those things which men delivered to you to be observed. And He was saying to them, In a very beautiful way you are constantly making the commandment of God null and void in order that that which has been delivered to you for observance you may keep. For Moses said, Be paying due respect and reverence to your father and your mother. And the one who is constantly reviling father or mother, let him come to an end by death. But as for you, you are saying, If a man should say to his father or his mother, Korban, which is a gift, whatever from me you may be profited; no longer are you permitting him to do anything for his father or his mother. You are rendering void the authority of the Word of God by that which has been delivered to you to observe, which in turn you are delivering over to another to keep. And many things of this kind you are constantly doing.

14, 15   And having again called to himself the crowd, He was saying to them, Hear me, all, and understand. There is not even one thing that from the outside of the man, which entering him, is able to defile him. But the things proceeding out from the man are those that defile the man.

And when He entered into residence away from the crowd, His disciples went to asking Him about the illustration. And He says to them, In this manner also, as for you, are you without understanding? Do you not know that everything which from the outside enters into the man is not able to defile him, because it does not enter his heart but his intestines, and goes out into that which is designed to receive it? This He said making all the foods clean. And He was saying, That which is constantly proceeding out of the man, that thing defiles the man. For from within, out of the hearts of men are constantly proceeding the depraved thoughts, fornications, thefts, murders, adulteries, covetousness, perniciousness, deceit, wantonness, a malicious, mischief-working eye, malicious misrepresentation, pride, folly. All these pernicious things from within are constantly proceeding and are constantly defiling the man.

17-23

Now from there, having arisen, He went off into the region of Tyre. And having entered a home, He was desiring that not even one should know. And He was not able to be hidden. But immediately, a woman having heard about Him, whose little daughter had an unclean spirit, having come, fell at His feet. And the woman was a Gentile, a Syrophoenician as to her race. And she kept on begging Him to cast out the demon out of her little daughter. And He was saying to her, Let first the children be fed, for it is not right to take the bread of the children and to throw it to the little pet dogs. But she answered and says to Him, Yes, Sir, yet the little pet dogs under the table are constantly eating from the little morsels of the little children. And He said to her, Because of this word, be going; the demon is gone out of your daughter. And having gone off into her home, she found the little child lying quietly upon her couch and the demon gone out.

24-30

And again, having gone out of the region of Tyre, He went through Sidon to the sea of Galilee in the midst

31-37

of the region of Decapolis. And they bring to Him one who was deaf and who spoke with difficulty. And they beg Him to place upon him His hand. And having taken him away from the crowd, in private He put His fingers into his ears, and having spit, He touched his tongue. And having looked up into heaven, He groaned and says to him, Ephphatha, which is, Be opened. And his ears opened, and immediately that which bound his tongue was loosed, and he began to be enunciating correctly. And He in His own interest commanded them to be saying not even one thing. But the more He kept on commanding them, they themselves kept on proclaiming it publicly so much the more to a greater degree. And they were completely flabbergasted, and that in a super-abundant degree which itself was augmented by the addition of yet more astonishment, saying, He has done all things well. He makes both the deaf to be hearing and the dumb to be speaking.

1-9   In those days again, there being a great crowd, and they not having anything to eat, having called His disciples to Him, He says to them, My heart goes out to the crowd, because now for three days they are staying with me and they do not have anything to eat. And if I send them off fasting to their homes, they will faint along the road. And some of them are from a distance. And His disciples answered Him, How can it be that anyone will be able to satisfy these with loaves of bread here in the uninhabited region? And He went to asking them, How many loaves of bread do you have? And they said, Seven. And He commands the crowd to recline on the ground. And having taken the seven loaves of bread, having given thanks, He broke them, and kept on giving them to His disciples in order that they might keep on setting them forth. And they served the crowd. And they had a few little fish. And having prayed that God might bless them to their intended use, He directed them to set these also before them. And they ate and were satisfied. And they took up that which was left over of broken pieces, seven baskets. And there were about four thousand. And He sent them away.

And immediately, having gone on board the boat with **10-14**
His disciples, He went to the region of Dalmanoutha.
And there came out the Pharisees and began to be disputing with Him, demanding of Him an attesting miracle
from heaven, putting Him to the test. And having
groaned deeply in His spirit, He says, Why is this breed
of men seeking an attesting miracle? Positively I am
saying to you, There shall no attesting miracle be given
to this breed. And having sent them away, again having
embarked, He went off to the other side. And they
had completely forgotten to take loaves of bread, and
except for one loaf, they did not have any with them in
the boat.

And He repeatedly charged them, saying, Be taking **15-21**
heed. Constantly be keeping a discerning mind's eye upon,
and ever be on the lookout for the yeast of the Pharisees
and the yeast of Herod. And they kept on discussing among themselves, saying, Because we do not
have loaves of bread. And having come to know, He
says to them, Why are you reasoning as follows: Because
you do not have loaves of bread? Not yet are you per-
ceiving, nor even understanding? In a settled state of
callousness do you have your hearts? Having eyes, you
are not seeing, and having ears, you are not hearing?
And you are not remembering, when the five loaves I
broke among the five thousand, how many baskets full of
broken pieces did you take up? They say to Him, Twelve.
When the seven among four thousand, how many baskets
of broken pieces did you take up? And they say, Seven.
And He kept on repeating to them, Not yet are you understanding?

And they come into Bethsaida. And they bring to **22-26**
Him a blind man. And they beg Him to touch him.
And having taken the hand of the blind man, He brought
him outside of the village, and having spit upon his eyes,
having placed His hands upon him, He kept on asking
him, Do you possibly see anything? And having looked
up, he kept on saying, I see the men; as trees I see them
walking around. Then again He placed His hands upon
his eyes; and he looked steadfastly; and he was restored

to his former state; and he was seeing all things at a distance and clearly. And He sent him off to his home, saying, Do not even go into the town.

27-30 And He went out, Jesus and His disciples, into the villages of Caesarea Philippi. And along the road He kept on asking His disciples, saying to them, Who do men say that I am? And they told Him, saying, John the Baptizer, and others, Elijah, and others, one of the prophets. And He himself kept on questioning them, But as for you, who are you saying that I am? Answering, Peter says to Him, As for you, you are the Christ. And He strictly charged them that they should not tell even one person concerning Him.

31-33 And He began to be teaching them that it was necessary in the nature of the case for the Son of Man to suffer many things, and, after having been put to the test for the purpose of being approved should He meet the specifications, to be rejected by the elders and the chief priests and the men learned in the sacred scriptures, and to be put to death, and after three days to arise. And with utter plainness of speech He was speaking this aforementioned word. And having taken Him aside to himself, Peter began to be rebuking Him. But having wheeled around, and having looked on His disciples, He rebuked Peter, and says, Be gone under my authority and keep on going. Behind me, out of my sight, Satan, because you do not have a mind for the things of God but for the things of men.

34-38 And having called the crowd together with His disciples to himself, He said to them, If anyone is desiring to come after me as a follower of mine, let him at once begin to lose sight of himself and his own interests, and let him at once begin to take up his cross and carry it, and let him start taking the same road that I travel in company with me, and let him continue to do so moment by moment. For whoever would desire to save his soul-life, will lose it. But whoever will lose his soul-life for my sake and the gospel, will save it. For what shall it profit a man to gain the whole world and lose his soul?

For what shall a man give in exchange for his soul? For whoever is ashamed of me and my words in this generation which is adulterous and sinful, also the Son of Man shall be ashamed of him when He comes in the glory of His Father with the angels, the holy ones.

And He was saying to them, Assuredly, I am saying to you, there are certain ones of those standing here who are such as will not taste of death until they see the kingdom of God having come in power. And after six days, Jesus takes with Him Peter, and James, and John, and brings them up into a mountain, a high one, in private, alone. And the manner of His outward expression was changed before them, that outward expression coming from and being truly representative of His inner nature. And His garments became glittering ones, exceedingly white, such as a fuller on earth is not able thus to whiten. And there appeared to them Elijah and Moses, and they were holding a protracted conversation with Jesus. **1-4**

And Peter giving off his judgment, says to Jesus, Rabbi, it is an excellent thing for us to be here. And let us make three booths made of tree branches, for you one, and for Moses one, and for Elijah one; for he did not know what to give as his judgment, for they were terribly frightened. And there came a cloud which enveloped and surrounded them. And there came a voice out of the cloud, This is my Son, the dearly-beloved One! be constantly hearing Him. And suddenly, after they had looked round about, no longer did they see anyone but Jesus only with them. **5-8**

And while they were coming down out of the mountain, He charged them that they should narrate the things which they saw to not even one person, except when the Son of Man should arise out from amongst the dead. And the aforementioned matter they kept carefully and faithfully to themselves, all the while discussing with one another what that particular thing, namely, to arise out from amongst the dead, was. And they kept on putting the question to Him, saying, How is it that the men learned in the sacred scriptures are constantly saying **9-13**

that it is necessary in the nature of the case for Elijah
to come first? And He said to them, Elijah, it is true,
having come first, restores all things. And how it stands
written concerning the Son of Man, that He will suffer
many things and be set at naught. But I say to you that
indeed Elijah has come, and they did to him whatever
things they were desiring to do, even as it stands written
of him.

14-24   And having come to those who were following Him as
their teacher, they saw a great crowd around them, and
men learned in the sacred scriptures wrangling with them.
And immediately, the entire crowd, having seen Him,
was completely amazed, and running to Him, welcomed
Him. And He asked them, What is it that you are
discussing with them? And one of the crowd answered
Him, Teacher, I brought my son to you, who has a spirit
that has rendered him incapable of speech. And wherever
he takes possession of him, he throws him into convulsions, and he foams and grinds his teeth and falls
into a motionless stupor. And I spoke to your disciples
that they should cast him out, and they did not have the
power to do so. And answering them, He says, O unbelieving generation, how long shall I have to do with
you? How long must I bear with you? Be bringing him
to me. And they brought him to Him. And, having
seen Him, the spirit immediately threw him into a complete convulsion, and having fallen upon the ground, he
was being rolled and was foaming. And He asked his
father, How long is it that this came to him? And he
said, Since he was a little boy. And often also he threw
him into fire and into water in order that he might destroy
him. But if you are able to do anything, help us at once,
having had compassion upon us. And Jesus said to him,
As for those words of yours, If you are able: — all
things are possible to the one who believes. Immediately
having cried out, the father of the little boy was saying,
I am believing. Be helping my weakness of faith.

25-32   And Jesus, having seen that a crowd was gathering together on the run, rebuked the foul spirit, saying to him,
Dumb and deaf spirit, I order you, be coming out of him,

and no longer enter him. And after crying out and throwing him into severe convulsions, he came out. And he became as one who is dead, so that many were saying that he had died. But Jesus, having taken a strong grip of his hand, went to raising him up. And he stood up. And having entered into a house, His disciples kept on asking Him privately, As for us, why were we not able to cast him out? And He said to them, This kind is able to come out by nothing but prayer. And going out from there, they went on their way through Galilee. And He was not desirous that anyone should know it, for He was constantly teaching His disciples. And He was saying to them, The Son of Man is being betrayed into men's hands, and they will kill Him, and having been put to death, after three days He will arise. But they were not understanding the word. And they were fearing to ask Him.

And they came into Capernaum. And having come **33-41** in the house, He kept on asking them, What along the road were you disputing about? But they kept on being quiet, for with one another they had discussed along the road who was the greatest. And having sat down, He called the Twelve and says to them, If, as is the case, anyone is desiring to be first, let him be last of all and a servant of all. And having taken a little child, He stood him in their midst; and when He had taken him in His arms, He said to them, Whoever receives one of such little children in my Name, receives me. And whoever receives me, does not receive me but the One who sent me. John said to Him, Teacher, we saw a certain individual casting out demons in your Name who does not follow with us. And we kept on forbidding him because he was not following with us. But Jesus said, Stop forbidding him, for there is no one who will perform a miracle upon the basis of my Name who will also soon be able to speak ill of me, for whoever is not against us is in behalf of us. For whoever will give you to drink a cup of water in my Name because you belong to Christ, truly I am saying to you, he will positively not lose his reward.

42-50   And whoever will cause one of these little ones who believe to stumble, it is good for him rather if a millstone is hung around his neck and that he has been thrown into the sea. And if your hand causes you to stumble, cut it off at once. It is good for you to enter life maimed, rather than having two hands to go off into hell, into unquenchable fire. And if your foot causes you to stumble, cut if off at once. It is good for you to enter into life maimed, rather than having the two feet, to be thrown into hell. And if your eye causes you to stumble, throw it out at once. It is good for you to enter the kingdom of God one-eyed, rather than, having two eyes, to be thrown into hell where their worm does not come to its end in death and the fire is not quenched. For everyone will be salted with fire. Salt is good. But if the salt loses its pungency, with what will you restore the saltness to it? Be having salt in yourselves, and be being at peace with one another.

1-12   And from there, having arisen, He comes into the regions of Judaea and across the Jordan, and again crowds journeying along with Him come constantly to Him, and as was His custom, He again was constantly teaching them. And having come to Him, Pharisees kept on asking Him whether it is lawful for a man to dismiss a wife, putting Him to the test. And He answering, said to them, What did Moses command you? And they said, Moses permitted a writing of a bill of divorce and to dismiss her. And Jesus said to them, On account of your hardheartedness he wrote this commandment for you. But from creation's beginning, a male and a female He made them. On account of this a man shall leave behind his father and mother and the two shall become one flesh, so that no longer are they two but one flesh. That therefore which God yoked together, let no man separate. And in the house again the disciples kept on asking Him concerning this. And He says to them, Whoever puts away his wife and marries another woman commits adultery against her. And if she herself, having put away her husband, marries another man, she commits adultery.

And they kept on bringing to Him young children in   **13-16**
order that He might touch them. And His disciples kept
on rebuking them unjustly and without effect. But Jesus
having seen this, became indignant, and said to them,
Be permitting the little children to come to me. Stop
preventing them, for of such ones is the kingdom of God.
Truly, I am saying to you, Whoever does not receive the
kingdom of God in the same manner as a little child,
will positively not enter it. And having taken them up
in His arms, He kept on fervently blessing them, placing
His hands upon them.

And when He was going out into the road there came   **17-22**
one running toward Him, and having fallen on his knees
before Him was asking Him, Teacher, you who are
intrinsically good, what one act shall I do in order that I
might inherit life eternal? And Jesus said to him, Why do
you say that I am intrinsically good? No one is intrinsically good except One, God. The commandments you
know: Do not commit murder, do not commit adultery,
do not steal, do not bear false witness, do not defraud,
honor your father and mother. And he said to Him,
Teacher, these things, all of them, I carefully guarded
and obeyed from my boyhood. And Jesus, having fixed
His searching gaze upon him, fell in love with him, and
said to him, One thing you are lacking; go, whatever you
have sell at once and give at once to the poor, and you
will have treasure in heaven, and come, make a beginning
of following with me on the same road that I am taking,
and continue to do so. And he, saddening at the word,
went off, being grieved, for he was in possession of great
wealth.

And Jesus, having glanced swiftly around, says to His   **23-31**
disciples, How with difficulty will those who keep on holding on to wealth enter the kingdom of God. And the
disciples were astonished at His words. And Jesus
again answering, says to them, Children, how difficult
it is to enter the kingdom of God. It is easier for a
camel to go through the eye of the sewing needle than
for a wealthy man to enter the kingdom of God. And
beyond measure they were amazed, to the point of almost

losing their self-possession, saying to one another, Then who is able to be saved? After having swiftly glanced around them, Jesus says, With men, impossible, but not in the presence of God, for all things are possible in the presence of God. Peter began to be saying to Him, Behold, as for us, we abandoned all once for all and have followed with you, and this as a permanent thing. Jesus said, Truly I am saying to you, There is no one who abandoned house or brothers or sisters or mother or father or children or lands for my sake and for the sake of the gospel, but that he will receive one hundred times as much now at this time, houses, and brothers, and sisters, and mothers, and children, and lands, with persecutions, and in the age to come, life eternal. But many who are first shall be last, and the last ones, first.

32-34   And they were on the road, going up to Jerusalem. And Jesus was going on before them, and they were amazed. And those who were following along were fearing. And having taken again the Twelve, He began to be speaking to them concerning the things that were about to be converging upon Him. Behold! We are going up to Jerusalem, and the Son of Man shall be delivered up treacherously to the chief priests and to the men learned in the sacred scriptures, and they shall condemn Him to death and shall hand Him over to the Gentiles, and they shall deride Him and spit upon Him and scourge Him and kill Him, and after three days He shall rise again.

35-45   And there come to Him James and John, the sons of Zebedee, saying to Him, Teacher, we desire that whatever we ask you, you will do for us. And He said to them, What do you desire me to do for you? And they said to Him, Grant us at once that, one on your right hand and one on your left hand, we might sit down in your glory. But Jesus said to them, You do not know what you are asking for yourselves. Are you able to be drinking the cup which I am drinking, or with the immersion with which I am to be overwhelmed, are you able to be immersed? And they said to Him, We are able. And Jesus said to them, The cup which I drink, you will drink. And the immersion with which I am to be overwhelmed, with that immersion you will be overwhelmed. But the sitting on my right hand or my left is not mine to give. But it is for those for whom it has been prepared. And when the ten heard, they began to be indignant concerning the matter with reference to James and John, and kept it up. And having called them to himself, Jesus says to them, You know that those who are accounted as ruling over the Gentiles, rule with absolute power over them, and their great ones domineer over them. But not thus is it among you. But whoever desires to become great among you, he shall be slave of all. And whoever desires to be first among you, he shall be your slave. For even the Son of Man did not come to have service rendered Him but to render service and to give His life a ransom for many.

And they come into Jericho. And as He is proceeding out from Jericho, and His disciples and a sizable crowd, the son of Timaeus, Bartimaeus, blind, a beggar, was sitting as was his habit alongside the road. And having heard that it was Jesus, the Jesus from Nazareth, he began to be crying out and saying, Son of David, Jesus, have sympathy with me in my affliction and help me at once. And many kept on censuring him severely to the effect that he should become silent. But he kept on crying out all the more, Son of David, have sympathy with me in my affliction and help me at once. And having come to a standstill, Jesus said, Call him at once. And they call the blind man, saying to him, Be of good courage, be arising, he is calling you. And having thrown off his outer garment, having leaped up, he came to Jesus. And answering him, Jesus said, What are you desiring that I shall do for you? And the blind man said to Him, Rabboni, that I might recover my sight. And Jesus said to him, Be going on your way. Your faith has healed you perfectly. And immediately he recovered his sight and was following with Him on the road.

46-52

And when they were getting near Jerusalem, Bethphage and Bethany, at the Mount of Olivet, He sends two of His disciples on a mission, and says to them, Be going off into the village opposite you, and immediately upon

1-11

proceeding into it, you will find a colt securely tied, upon
which not even one man ever sat. Loose it at once and
be bringing it. And if anyone says to you, Why are you
doing this? say, The Lord is having need of it and forthwith will send it here again. And they went off and
found a colt tied securely to a door outside in the open
street, and they loose it. And certain of those who were
standing there went to saying to them, What are you
doing, loosing the colt? And they spoke to them even as
Jesus had said. And they gave them permission. And
they bring the colt to Jesus and throw upon it their outer
garments, and He sat upon it. And many spread their
garments into the road, and others, soft foliage, having
cut it out of the countryside. And those who went before
and those who followed kept on crying out, Hosanna,
praised be He who comes in the Name of the Lord.
Praised be the coming kingdom of our father David.
Hosanna in the highest. And He entered Jerusalem and
the temple. And after He had given all things a com-
prehensive inspection, it being already the evening hour,
He went out to Bethany with the Twelve.

12-14   And the next day, they having come out of and away
from Bethany, He became hungry. And having seen a
fig tree a long way off having leaves, He came, assuming
that He would find something on it. And having come to
it, He found not even one thing, except leaves. For it
was not the season of figs. And answering, He said to it,
Hereafter forever, from you no one eats fruit. And His
disciples were listening.

15-21   And they come into Jerusalem. And having entered
the temple, He began to be throwing out those who sold
and those who bought in the temple, and He threw down
the tables of the money-changers and the seats of those
who sold doves, and was not permitting anyone to carry
household gear through the temple. And He went to
teaching and was saying to them, Does it not stand written,
My house shall be called a house of prayer for all the
nations? But as for you, you have made it a den of
robbers. And the chief priests and the men learned in
the sacred scriptures heard. And they went to seeking

how they might destroy Him, for they were fearing Him; for the entire multitude was struck with astonishment at His teaching. And when evening came they were going forth out of the city. And passing by in the morning they saw the fig tree completely withered from the roots. And being reminded, Peter says to Him, Rabbi, see, the fig tree which you cursed is withered away.

And answering, Jesus says to them, Be constantly having faith in God. Truly, I am saying to you, Whoever says to this mountain, Be lifted up and be thrown into the sea, and does not doubt in his heart but believes that that which he says comes to pass, it shall be his. On this account I am saying to you, All things whatever you are praying and asking for, be believing that you received them, and they shall be yours. And whenever you are standing, praying, forgive, if you have anything against a certain person, in order that your Father also who is in heaven may forgive you your trespasses. **22-26**

And they come again into Jerusalem. And when He was walking about the temple, there come to Him the chief priests and the men learned in the sacred scriptures and the elders, and they kept on saying to Him, By what sort of delegated authority are you doing these things, or, who gave you this authority to be doing these things? And Jesus said to them, I will ask you concerning one point, and answer me, and I will tell you by what sort of delegated authority I am doing these things. The baptism of John, from heaven was it or from men? Answer me. And they were reasoning with themselves, saying, If we say, From heaven, he will say, Then, why did you not believe him? But if we say, From men, — they were fearing the people. For all were holding John actually to be a prophet. And answering Jesus, they say, We do not know. And Jesus says to them, Neither am I telling you by what sort of delegated authority I am doing these things. **27-33**

And He began to be speaking to them in the form of illustrations. A man planted a vineyard, and set a hedge about it, and digged a place for a wine-press, and built a tower, and let it out for his own advantage to vineyard **1-12**

men, and went away to foreign parts. And he sent off
to the vineyard men at the season a slave, in order that
from the vineyard men he might receive some of the fruit
of the vine. And having taken him, they beat him severely
and sent him off empty. And again he sent off to them
another slave. And that one they knocked about the head
and grossly insulted. And another he sent off. And
that one they killed, and many others; some, on the one
hand, beating severely, and others, on the other hand,
killing. Yet one he had, a son, a beloved one. He sent
him off last to them, saying, They will reverence my son.
But those vineyard men said to themselves, This is the
heir. Come. Let us be putting him to death, and ours
shall be the inheritance. And having taken him, they
killed him and threw him out of the vineyard. What will
the master of the vineyard do? He will come and destroy
the vineyard men, and will give the vineyard to others.
And did you not even read this scripture, A stone which
the builders rejected after having put it to the test for
the purpose of approving it, and finding that it did not
meet their specifications, this became the head of the
corner? From the Lord came this. And it is marvellous
in our eyes. And they were seeking to seize Him, but
were fearing the crowd, for they knew that with reference
to them He had given the illustration. And having left
Him, they went off.

13-17   And they sent to Him certain of the Pharisees and
of the Herodians with a commission to snare Him in a
statement. And having come, they say to Him, Teacher,
we know positively that you are true and that you do not
kowtow to anyone, for you do not pay regard to the outward appearance of men, but upon the basis of the truth
you are teaching the way of God. Is it permissible to
give poll tax to Caesar or not? Shall we give, or, shall
we not give? But He, knowing their hypocrisy, said
to them, Why are you putting me to the test? Be bringing me a denarius in order that I may see it. And they
brought one. And He says to them, This likeness and
title belong to whom? And they said to Him, To Caesar.
And Jesus said to them, The things belonging to Caesar

pay off to Caesar, and the things belonging to God, to God. And they were marvelling at Him.

And there come Sadducees to Him, that class which **18-27** says there is not a resurrection. And they kept on questioning Him, saying, Teacher, Moses wrote us, If a brother of a certain man should die, and should leave a wife and should not leave a child, his brother should take the wife and raise up offspring for his brother. There were seven brothers. And the first took a wife, and dying, did not leave offspring. And the second took her, and he died, not having left offspring. And the third likewise. And the seven did not leave any children. Last of all the woman died also. In the resurrection, when they are raised, of which of them shall she be wife, for the seven had her as wife? Jesus said to them, Is it not because of this that you err, namely, that you do not know the scriptures nor even the power of God? For when they arise out from among the dead, neither do they marry nor do they give in marriage, but are [in this respect] just as angels in heaven. But concerning the dead that they arise, did you not read in the book of Moses, at the bush how God spoke to him, saying, I am the God of Abraham, and the God of Isaac, and the God of Jacob? He is not a God of the dead but of the living. Greatly do you err.

And having come, one of the men learned in the sacred **28-34** scriptures having heard them questioning together, knowing that He had answered them well, asked Him, Of what sort is the first commandment of all? Jesus answered, The first is, Be hearing O Israel, the Lord our God is one Lord, and you shall love the Lord your God with your whole heart, and with your whole soul, and with your whole mind, and with your whole strength. The second is this, You shall love your neighbor as yourself. Greater than these, another commandment there is not. And the man learned in the sacred scriptures said to Him, Right! Well! Teacher, truthfully you said, He is One, and there is not another except Him. And to be loving Him with your whole heart, and with your whole understanding, and with your whole strength, and to be loving your neighbor as yourself, is much more than all the whole burnt-offerings and sacrifices. And Jesus, having seen him, that he answered intelligently, said to him, Not far are you from the kingdom of God. And no one any longer was daring to ask him a question.

35-40   And answering, Jesus was saying as He was teaching in the temple, How is it that the men learned in the sacred scriptures say that the Christ is David's son? David himself said by the Holy Spirit, The Lord said to my Lord, Be seated on my right hand until I make your enemies the footstool of your feet. David himself calls him Lord, and how can it be that He is his son? And the great crowd was hearing Him gladly. And in His teaching He was saying: Be constantly bewaring of the men learned in the sacred scriptures who are fond of parading about in stately robes, and are fond of reverential and deferential greetings in the market places, and the seats of honor in the synagogues, and the chief places at the feasts, those who devour the houses of widows and for a pretense make long prayers; these will receive greater condemnation.

41-44   And having sat down opposite the treasury, He was viewing with a discerning eye how the crowd throws money into the treasury. And many wealthy ones were throwing in much. And one having come, a poverty-stricken widow, threw in two very small brass coins which make a farthing. And having called His disciples to himself, He said to them, Truly, I am saying to you, This widow, and she, poverty-stricken, threw in more than all those who are throwing into the treasury, for they all threw in out of their abundance, but she out of her poverty threw in all, as much as she had, the whole of her life's necessities.

1-4   And while He was proceeding out of the temple, one of His disciples says to Him, Teacher, see what manner of stones and what manner of buildings. And Jesus said to him, Do you see these great buildings? There shall positively not be left a stone upon a stone which is not torn down. And being seated on the Mount of Olivet opposite the temple, there were asking Him privately

Peter and James and John and Andrew, Tell us, when will these things be, and what will be the attesting miracle which will indicate when these things, all of them, are about to be consummated?

And Jesus began to be saying to them, Keep ever watching lest someone lead you astray. Many will come in my Name, saying, I, in contradistinction to others, am he, and will lead many astray. And when you hear of wars and reports of wars, stop being terrified. It is necessary in the nature of the case for these things to take place. But not yet is the end. For there will rise up nation against nation and kingdom against kingdom. There shall be earthquakes in various places; there shall be famines. A beginning of intolerable anguish are these. But as for you, be constantly paying heed to yourselves. They will deliver you up to councils, and in synagogues you will be beaten, and before rulers and kings you will be placed for my sake, as a testimony to them. And to all the nations first is it necessary in the nature of the case for the gospel to be proclaimed. And whenever they may be leading you, delivering you up, do not continue to be anxious as to what you will say, but whatever will be given you in that hour, this be speaking. For, as for you, you are not the ones who are speaking, but the Holy Spirit. And a brother will deliver a brother to death, and a father, a child, and children will rise up against parents, and will cause them to be put to death. And you will be those who are being hated by all for my Name's sake. But he who has persevered to the end, this one shall be preserved from destruction.

5-13

But when you see the object of religious nausea and loathing who has to do with the desolation, standing where he ought not; the one who reads, let him understand; then those who are in Judaea, let them flee into the mountains; the one who is on the housetop, let him not go down, neither let him enter to take anything out of his house; and the one in the field, let him not turn back to take his garment. But woe to those who are with child, and to those who are nursing their young in those days. But pray that it may not be winter. For those

14-23

days will be characterized by tribulation such as has not
been from the beginning of the creation which God created
until this particular time, and will positively not be. And
unless the Lord had shortened the days, no flesh would
be saved. But for the sake of the chosen-out ones whom
He chose out for himself, He shortened the days. And
then, if anyone says to you, Look, here is the Christ;
look, there; stop believing him. Moreover, there shall
arise false Christs and false prophets, and they will perform attesting miracles and miracles that arouse amazement in order to be leading astray, if that were possible,
which it is not, the chosen-out ones. But, as for you,
be constantly taking heed. I have told you beforehand
all things.

24-27   But in those days, after that tribulation, the sun will be
darkened and the moon will not give its light, and the
meteors will be falling out of the heaven, and the natural
powers that control the heavenly bodies will be disorganized. And then they will see the Son of Man coming with clouds, with much power and glory. And then
He will send off the angels and will gather together His
chosen-out ones from the four winds, from the outermost border of the earth to the outermost border of
heaven.

28-37   Now, from the fig tree be learning the meaning of the
illustration. When already its branch becomes tender
and is putting out the leaves, you know from experience
that the summer is near. Thus also, as for you, when you
see these things coming into being, you know that He
is near, at the doors. Truly I am saying to you, This
race will positively not pass away until these things, all
of them, take place. The heaven and the earth will pass
away, but my words will not pass away. But concerning
that day or hour no one knows, not even the angels in
heaven nor even the Son, only the Father. Be constantly
taking heed, be constantly on the watch, for you do not
know when it is the strategic season. It is as a man gone
off to another country, having left his house, and having
given his slaves the authority, to each his work; and to
the doorkeeper he gave orders to be constantly alert and

watching. Therefore, be constantly alert and on the watch, for you do not know when the master of the house comes, whether at evening time, or at midnight, or at cockcrowing, or in the morning, lest having come unexpectedly, he find you slumbering. And that which I am saying to you, I am saying to all, Be constantly watchful and alert.

Now, it was the feasts of the passover and the loaves **1, 2** baked without yeast, after two days. And the chief priests and the men learned in the sacred scriptures were seeking how, having seized Him by craftiness, they might put Him to death. For they were saying, Not during the feast, lest at any time there be an uproar on the part of the people.

And while He was in Bethany in the house of Simon **3-9** the leper, as He was reclining at table, there came a woman having an alabaster cruse of ointment, nard, pure, very costly. Having broken the alabaster cruse, she was pouring its contents upon His head. Now, there were certain there who were moved with indignation among themselves. To what purpose has been this waste of the ointment? For it was possible to have sold the ointment for more than three hundred denarii and to have given these to the poor. And they bristled with indignation against her. And Jesus said, Let her alone. Why are you causing her trouble? A munificent service she rendered me. For the poor you always have with you, and whenever you desire, you are able to do them good; but me you are not always having. That which she had, she used. She took occasion beforehand to anoint my body for the entombment. And truly I am saying to you, Wherever the gospel may be proclaimed in the whole world, also that which she herself did will be spoken as a memorial of her.

And Judas Iscariot, the one of the Twelve, went off **10, 11** to the chief priests for the purpose of betraying Him to them. And they, having heard, rejoiced inwardly and promised to give him money. And he went to seeking how he might betray Him when the opportunity presented itself.

12-16   And on the first day of the feast of loaves baked without yeast, at which time it was the custom to kill the passover, His disciples say to Him, Where do you desire that we go and prepare in order that you may eat the passover? And He sends off two of His disciples, and says to them, Go into the city and there will meet you a man carrying an earthenware pitcher of water. Follow him, and wherever he enters, say to the master of the house, The Teacher says, Where is my guest-chamber where I may eat the passover with my disciples? And he himself will show you an upper room, large, in a state of readiness, prepared. And there make ready for us. And the disciples went out and came into the city, and found even as He told them. And they prepared the passover.

17-21   And evening having come, He comes with the Twelve. And while they were reclining at table and eating, Jesus said, Truly, I am saying to you, one of you will betray me, the one eating with me. They began to be grieved and to be saying to Him, one after another, It is not I, is it? And He said to them, One of the twelve, the one who dips with me into the deep dish. The Son of Man indeed goes even as it stands written concerning Him. But woe to that man through whose agency the Son of Man is betrayed. Good were it for him, if that man had not been born.

22-26   And while they were eating, having taken bread, having offered a blessing, He broke it and gave to them and said, Take. This is my body. And having taken a cup, having given thanks, He gave it to them, and all drank from it. And He said to them, This is my blood of the testament which is being poured out in behalf of many. Truly, I am saying to you, I will positively no longer drink of the product of the vine until that day when I drink it new in quality in the kingdom of God. And having sung a hymn, they went out into the Mount of Olivet.

27-31   And Jesus says to them, All of you will fall away, because it stands written, I will smite the shepherd and the sheep will be scattered. But after I have been raised

I will go before you into Galilee. But Peter said to Him, Even if all will fall away, certainly not I. And Jesus says to him, Truly, I am saying to you, that, as for you, today, on this night, before a rooster crows twice, three times you will deny me. And he kept on saying with more vehemence and iteration, If it should be necessary for me to die with you, I will positively not deny you. Moreover, in like manner also all kept on saying.

And they come into a place called Gethsemane: and **32-40** He says to His disciples, Sit here while I shall pray. And He takes with Him Peter and James and John. And He began to be thoroughly alarmed and distressed. And He says to them, My soul is encompassed with grief even to the point of death. Abide here and be watching. And having gone on ahead a little, He fell repeatedly upon the ground, and was praying that if it were possible, the hour might pass from Him. And He was saying, Abba, [namely] Father, all things are possible to you. Cause this cup to pass by and from me. But not what I desire, but what you desire. And He comes and finds them sleeping, and He says to Peter, Simon, are you sleeping? Did you not have strength to watch one hour? Be constantly watching and praying in order that you might not enter a place of testing that will present to you a solicitation to do evil. The spirit indeed is willing but the flesh is weak. And again, having gone off, He prayed, having said the same thing. And again, having come, He found them sleeping, for their eyes were heavy, and they did not know what they should answer Him.

And He comes the third time and says to them, Keep on **41-46** sleeping now and taking your rest. It is enough. The hour has come. Behold, the Son of Man is being betrayed into the hands of sinners. Be arising. Let us be going. Behold, the one who is betraying me has come near and is at hand. And immediately, while He was still speaking, there approaches Judas, one of the Twelve, and with him a crowd with swords and cudgels who came personally from the chief priests and the men learned in the sacred scriptures and the elders. Now, the one

betraying Him had given them a prearranged signal,
saying, Whomever I shall kiss, it is He himself. Seize
Him and lead Him away safely. And having come, im-
mediately approaching Him he says, Rabbi, and kissed
Him. And they laid their hands upon Him and seized
Him.

47-52 And a certain one of those who stood by, drawing
his sword, struck the slave of the high priest and took
off his ear. And answering, Jesus said to them, As
against a robber you came out with swords and cudgels
to seize me. Daily I was with you in the temple, teaching,
and you did not seize me. But the scriptures must be fulfilled. And having forsaken Him, they fled, all of them.
And a certain young man was following with Him who
had thrown a linen cloth around his nakedness. And they
seize him. And having left the linen cloth, he fled unclothed.

53-65 And they led Jesus off to the chief priest. And there
are gathered together all the chief priests and the elders
and the men learned in the sacred scriptures. And Peter
followed Him at a distance even into the uncovered courtyard of the house of the chief priest. And he was sitting
with the officers and warming himself at the fire. Now,
the chief priests and the entire council were seeking testimony against Jesus with a view to putting Him to
death; and they were not finding any, for many were
repeatedly bearing false testimony against Him, but
their testimonies were not in harmony. And certain,
having arisen, were bearing false testimony against
Him, saying, As for us, we heard him saying, As
for myself, I will destroy this temple which is made
with hands, and after a period of three days another
one made without hands I will build. And not even
in the way described did their testimony harmonize. And
having arisen, the chief priest in the midst questioned Jesus,
saying, Do you not answer even one thing? What is this
that these are testifying against you? But He kept on
maintaining His silence and answered not even one thing.
Again, the chief priest went to asking Him, and says to
Him, As for you, are you the Christ, the Son of the

Blessed? And Jesus said, As for myself, in contradistinction to all others, I AM. And you will see the Son of Man sitting on the right hand of the power and coming with the clouds of heaven. Then the chief priest, having torn apart his tunics, says, Why do we still have need of witnesses? You heard his blasphemy. What is your view? And they all condemned Him to be guilty of death. And certain ones began to be spitting upon Him and to be covering His face and to be pummelling Him and to be saying to Him, Prophesy. And the officers caught Him by blows with the flat of the hand.

And when Peter was down in the courtyard, there **66-72** comes one of the female slaves of the high priest, and having seen Peter warming himself, having gazed intently at him, she says, And as for you, with the one of Nazareth you were, that Jesus. But he denied, saying, Neither do I know nor do I understand what you are saying. And he went outside into the forecourt. And the female slave having seen him, began again to be saying to the bystanders, This man is one of them. But again he kept on denying. And a short time afterwards, again the bystanders were saying to Peter, Truly, one of them you are. In fact, you are a Galilaean. But he began to be putting himself under a divine curse, and to be putting himself under oath, I do not know this man concerning whom you are speaking. And immediately a second time a rooster crowed. And Peter was brought to a remembrance of the word as Jesus spoke it to him, Before a rooster crows twice, three times, me you will deny. And having put his thought upon it, he began to be weeping audibly.

And immediately at daybreak, the chief priests con- **1-5** voked a council with the elders and men learned in the sacred scriptures and the entire Sanhedrin; having bound Jesus they took Him away, and handed Him over to Pilate. And Pilate asked Him, As for you, are you the King of the Jews? And answering him He says, As for you, you are saying it. And the chief priests kept on accusing Him of many things. And Pilate again went to asking Him, saying, Are you not answering even one thing? See how many things there are of which they are accusing you. But Jesus still answered not even one thing, so that Pilate was in a state of amazement.

6-15   Now, at the feast, it was his custom to release to them one prisoner whom they would be desiring. And there was the one commonly known as Barabbas, who was in chains with those who had participated in an insurrection, those being of that class that had committed murder in the insurrection referred to. And, having gone up, the crowd began to be asking him to do just as he had always been accustomed to do for them. And Pilate answered them, saying, Are you desiring that I release to you the King of the Jews? for it was gradually dawning upon him that because of envy the chief priests had delivered Him up. And the chief priests stirred up the crowd that he should rather release Barabbas to them. But Pilate again answering, was saying to them, What then shall I do to him whom you are calling the King of the Jews? But they again cried, Crucify him at once. But Pilate was saying to them, Why, what evil did he do? But they cried out with an indescribable uproar, Crucify him at once. Then Pilate, desiring after reflection to satisfy the crowd, released Barabbas to them, and having scourged Jesus, delivered Him to be crucified.

16-23   And the soldiers led Him off into the courtyard which is the Praetorium, and they call together the entire band. And they clothe Him with a purple robe, and having woven together a victor's crown of thorns, they place it upon Him. And they began to be saluting Him, Hail, King of the Jews. And they kept on beating His head with a staff made of a reed, and they kept on spitting upon Him; and bowing their knees, they were doing obeisance to Him. And when they had mocked Him, they took off from Him the purple robe, and put on Him His garments. And they lead Him out in order that they may crucify Him. And they commandeer the services of a certain Simon of Cyrene who was passing by at the time, coming from the surrounding farmland, the father of Alexander and Rufus, in order that he might carry His cross. And they bring Him to the place, Golgotha, which interpreted is, a place of a skull. And they offered Him wine mixed with myrrh. But He did not receive it.

And they crucify Him and distribute His garments among themselves, throwing a lot upon them, who should take what. Now, it was the third hour, and they crucified Him. And there was the inscription of His accusation written above, THE KING OF THE JEWS. And with Him they crucify two robbers, one on His right and another on His left. **24-27**

And those passing by kept on reviling Him, wagging their heads and saying, Ah, the one who is destroying the inner sanctuary and building it in three days, save yourself, having coming down from the cross. In the same way also, the chief priests, mocking, were saying to one another with the men learned in the sacred scriptures, Others he saved, himself he is not able to save. The Christ, the King of Israel, let him come down now from the cross in order that we may see with discernment and believe. And those crucified with Him were reviling Him. And the sixth hour having come, a darkness came upon the whole land until the ninth hour. And at the ninth hour Jesus shouted with a loud voice, Eloi, Eloi, lama, sabachthani? which interpreted is, My God, My God, why did you let me down? And certain ones of those standing by, having heard, were saying, Behold, he is calling for Elijah. And, having run, a certain one, having filled a sponge with sour wine, having put it upon a reed, was giving Him a drink, saying, Hold off. Let us see whether Elijah comes to take him down. And Jesus, having cried with a loud voice, breathed out His life. And the curtain of the inner sanctuary was torn in two from the top to the bottom. And the centurion standing by opposite Him, having seen that thus He breathed out His life, said, Truly, this man, Son of God He was. Now, there were also women looking on carefully and with interest, viewing attentively from a distance, among whom also were Mary, the Magdalene, and Mary the mother of James the younger and of Joses, and Salome, who when He was in Galilee, were accustomed to follow with Him and minister to Him the necessities of life, **29-41** and many other women who came up with Him to Jerusalem.

42-47   And already evening had come. Since it was the time of making ready, which is the day before the sabbath, Joseph, the one from Arimathaea, having come, an honorable member of the council, who also himself was waiting for the kingdom of God, having taken courage, went in to Pilate and asked as a personal favor for the body of Jesus. But Pilate wondered whether He were already dead. And having called the centurion, he asked him if He had just died. And having come to know it from the centurion, he freely gave the corpse to Joseph. And having purchased fine linen in the market place, having taken Him down, he wrapped Him with the fine linen and placed Him in a tomb which had been hewn out of rock, and rolled a large stone against the door of the tomb. And Mary, the Magdalene, and Mary the mother of Joses were attentively observing where He was laid.

1-8   And the sabbath being past, Mary, the Magdalene, and the mother of James, and Salome, purchased aromatic spices in order that, having come, they might anoint Him. And very early in the morning of the first day of the week they come to the tomb, the sun having risen. And they kept on saying among themselves, Who will roll away for us the stone out of the door of the tomb? And, having looked up, they saw clearly that the stone had been rolled back, for it was exceedingly great. And having entered the tomb, they saw a young man sitting on the right, clothed in a long stately garment, white. And they were utterly amazed. And he says to them, Stop being utterly amazed. Jesus you are seeking, the Jesus of Nazareth, the One who has been crucified. He was raised. He is not here. See the place where they laid Him. But be going; say to His disciples and to Peter, He is going before you into Galilee. There you will see Him just as He told you. And having gone, they fled from the tomb, for there had come upon them trembling and astonishment: and they said not even one thing to anyone, for they were afraid.

Now, having risen early, on the first day of the week, He appeared first to Mary, the Magdalene, from whom He had cast seven demons. That one, having proceeded, brought word to those who had been with Him, who were mourning and were weeping audibly. And those, having heard that He lives and was seen by her, disbelieved. And after these things, to two of them while they were walking He appeared in a different outward appearance as they were proceeding into the country. And those having gone off, brought word to the rest. Neither did those believe them. And afterward He appeared to the eleven themselves as they were reclining at table, and He reproached their disbelief and hardness of heart because they did not believe those who viewed Him attentively after He was raised. And He said to them, Having proceeded into all the world, make a public proclamation of the good news to the whole creation. The one who believes and is baptized, will be saved, but the one who disbelieves will be condemned. And these attesting miracles will accompany those who believe these things. In my Name they will cast out demons. In new languages they will speak. Snakes they will pick up. And if they drink anything deadly, it will positively not harm them. Upon the sick they will lay hands, and they will recover. So then the Lord Jesus, after He had spoken to them, was received up into heaven, and sat on the right hand of God. And those having gone forth, preached everywhere, the Lord working with them, and confirming the Word through the attesting miracles which accompanied them.

Since it is well known and a fact of importance that **1-4** many have undertaken to draw up in its historical sequence a narrative of events concerning which there has been a wide diffusion of knowledge among us, even as they delivered them to us for safekeeping, those who from the beginning were personal witnesses of and ministered the Word, it seemed good to me also, having traced the course of all things from the beginning in the minutest detail, to write to you in a consecutive order, Your Excellency, Theophilus, in order that you may come to have a full and accurate experiential knowledge concerning the undoubted truth of the matters in which you were instructed.

There arose in the days of Herod, king of Judaea, a **5-7** certain priest named Zacharias, of the class of priests whose time of service was designated by the name Abia. And his wife was of the daughters of Aaron, and her name was Elizabeth. And they were righteous, both of them, in the sight of God, ordering their lives within the sphere of all the commandments and ordinances of the Lord, blameless. And they did not have a child because Elizabeth was sterile, and both were advanced in age.

And it came to pass that while he was discharging his **8-17** duties as priest in the fixed succession of his appointed time of service before God according to the custom of the office of the priest, as a result of casting lots it fell to his lot to burn incense, having gone into the inner sanctuary of the Lord. And the whole multitude of the people was praying outside at the hour of the burning of the incense. And there appeared to him an angel of the Lord standing at the right side of the altar of incense. And having seen him, Zacharias became troubled, and fear fell upon him. And the angel said to him, Stop fearing, Zacharias, because your petition was heard, and your wife Elizabeth shall bear you a son, and you shall call his name John. And you shall have joy and gladness, and many shall rejoice because of his birth, for he shall be great in the Lord's sight, and wine and intoxicating beverage he will positively not drink. And he shall be controlled by the Holy Spirit while yet in his mother's womb.

And many of the sons of Israel he shall turn back to the Lord their God. And he himself will go forward in His sight, in the spirit and power of Elijah, to turn back paternal hearts to offspring, and the uncompliant, in the sphere of the prudence of those who are righteous, to make ready for the Lord a people which has been placed in the right spiritual state.

18-25   And Zacharias said to the angel, In accordance with what fact will I know this? for, as for myself, I am an aged man, and my wife is advanced in her years. And the angel answering said to him, As for myself, I am Gabriel who stands in the presence of God, and I was sent on a mission to speak to you and bring you good news of these things. And behold, you shall be continually silent and not able to speak until the day when these things take place because you did not believe my words, words of such a nature that they will be fulfilled in their appointed and strategic time. And the people were looking for Zacharias and were marvelling at his delay in the inner sanctuary. And having come out, he was not able to speak to them, and they perceived that he had seen a vision in the inner sanctuary. And he himself kept on making signs to them and was remaining speechless. And it came to pass that when the days of his sacred service were fulfilled, he went off to his home. And after these days, Elizabeth his wife conceived, and she kept herself at home in seclusion for five months, saying, In this manner to me the Lord has done in the days when He looked upon me to take away my reproach among men.

26-33   Now, in the sixth month there was sent on a mission from God the angel Gabriel to a city of Galilee named Nazareth, to a virgin promised in marriage to a man named Joseph, of the house of David. And the name of the virgin was Mary. And having come to her, he said, Be rejoicing because you have been encompassed with favor. The Lord is with you. But she was greatly agitated by reason of the word, and began reasoning what sort of an exotic greeting this might be. And the angel said to her, Stop fearing, Mary, for you found favor in the presence of God. And behold: you shall conceive in your womb and you shall give birth to a son, and you shall call His name Jesus. This One shall be great, and Son of the Most High shall He be called, and God, the Lord, shall give to Him the throne of David His father, and He shall reign as King over the house of Jacob forever and of His kingdom there shall not be an end.

But Mary said to the angel, How shall this be possible, **34-38** since I do not have an experiential knowledge of a man? And the angel answering said to her, The Holy Spirit shall come upon you, and the power of the Most High shall overshadow you. Wherefore also the holy thing which is being begotten shall be called Son of God. And behold, Elizabeth, your kinswoman, also herself conceived a son in her old age, and this is the sixth month with her who is called sterile, for in the presence of God no word shall be impossible. And Mary said, Behold, the Lord's bondslave. May it happen to me according to your word. And the angel departed from her.

And having arisen, Mary in these days went on her way **39-45** into the hill country with haste into a city of Judah. And she entered the home of Zacharias and greeted Elizabeth. And it came to pass that when Elizabeth heard the greeting of Mary, the child leaped in her womb, and Elizabeth was controlled by the Holy Spirit and lifted up her voice with a great outcry and said, As for you, you have been blessed among women, and the fruit of your womb has been blessed. And how can this be to me that the mother of my Lord should come to me? For behold, when the sound of your greeting came to my ears, the child leaped in extreme joy in my womb. And spiritually prosperous is she who believed, because there shall be a fulfillment of the things which have been told her from the Lord.

And Mary said, My soul is extolling my Lord, and **46-49** my spirit exultingly rejoiced in God my Saviour, because He had regard for the humble position of His bondslave. For behold, from this time forth as particularized by this great event in my life, all the generations shall speak of me as spiritually prosperous, enriched by the blessings of God, because He who is mighty did great things to me; and holy is His Name.

50-56 And His mercy is to those who fear Him to generations and generations. He brought about strength with His arm. He dispersed those who with contempt and haughtiness hold themselves as above others in the intellectual insight and moral understanding of their heart. He deposed potentates from their thrones and exalted those who are in a humble position in life. He filled those who are hungry with good things, and those who are wealthy He sent away empty. He laid hold of Israel, His servant, with a view to helping him, calling to remembrance His mercy even as He spoke to our fathers, to Abraham and to his offspring forever. And Mary remained with her as her guest for about three months, and returned to her home.

57-64 Now, to Elizabeth there was fulfilled the time of her delivery, and she gave birth to a son. And the neighbors and her relatives heard that the Lord had lavished His mercy upon her, and they rejoiced with her. And it came to pass that on the eighth day they came to circumcise the recently born infant. And they were intending to call him by the name of his father Zacharias. But his mother, answering said, By no means, but he shall be called John. And they said to her, There is no one of your relatives who is called by this name. And they were making signs to his father to the following effect — What would he wish him to be called? And having asked for a writing-tablet he wrote, saying, His name is John. And all wondered. And his mouth was opened instantly and his tongue loosed. And he began speaking, praising God.

65-75 And there came upon all those who lived around them a fear. And in the entire hill country of Judaea all these matters were continuously being talked over. And all who heard these things laid them up in their heart, saying, What then shall this newly-born infant come to, for indeed the Lord's hand was with him? And Zacharias his father was controlled by the Holy Spirit and spoke by divine inspiration, saying, Eulogized be the Lord God of Israel, for He looked upon in order to help and effected a redemption for His people, and raised up a horn of salvation for us in the house of David His servant, even as He spoke through the mouth of His holy prophets from of old, deliverance from our enemies and from the hand of all those who hate us, to show mercy to our fathers and to remember His holy covenant, an oath which He swore to Abraham our father, to the effect that He would grant us that without fear, having been delivered out of the hand of our enemies, we might render sacred service to Him in holiness and righteousness before Him during all our days.

And as for you, moreover, child, a prophet of the Most **76-80** High shall you be called, for you shall precede the Lord as His herald in His presence and sight to make ready His roads, to give a knowledge of salvation to His people in the putting away of their sins through the merciful compassions of our God, in the sphere of which compassions the Light rising in the east from on high shall come to look upon us and render us help, to bring light to those who sit in darkness and in the shadow of death, to direct our feet into the road of peace. And the child kept on growing strong in spirit, and was in the uninhabited regions until the day of his official presentation to Israel.

Now, it came to pass in those days that there was **1-7** promulgated a decree from Caesar Augustus that the entire Roman empire should have its census taken. This census was the first one taken while Cyrenius was governor of Syria. And all were proceeding on their way to be enrolled in the census, each one into his own city. Now there went up also Joseph from Galilee, out of the city of Nazareth to Judaea, into the city of David which by reason of its character is called Bethlehem, because he was of the house and ancestry of David, to enroll himself with Mary, she who had been promised as his wife, who was pregnant. And it came to pass that while they were there the days were completed that she should give birth

to a child. And she gave birth to a son, her first-born.
And she wrapped Him in cloth bands and laid Him down
in a feeding-trough because there was not a place for them
in the caravansary.

8-14　　　And there were shepherds in that very region bivouacking in the fields under the open sky, and guarding their
flock during the appointed night watches. And an angel
of the Lord took his stand at their side, and the glory
of the Lord shone round about them, and they feared a
great fear. And the angel said to them, Stop being afraid.
For behold, I am bringing you good tidings of great joy,
which joy is of such a nature that it shall pertain to all
the people, because there was born to you today a Saviour
who is Christ, the Lord, in the city of David. And this
shall be an unusual and distinguishing token of identification for you; you shall find a new-born infant which has
been wrapped in cloth bands, and is lying in a feeding-
trough. And suddenly there was with the angel a multitude of the army of heaven, praising God and saying,
Glory in the highest places to God, and upon earth peace
among men of good will.

15-20　　　And it came to pass that when the angels went away
from them into heaven, the shepherds kept on saying to
one another, Let us go at once, even to Bethlehem, and
let us see this thing which has come to pass which the
Lord made known to us. And they came, having hast-
ened, and after searching, they located not only Mary and
Joseph, but also the new-born infant lying in the feeding-
trough. And having seen this, they made known concerning the word which was spoken to them about this little
child. And all those who heard marvelled concerning
the things which were spoken by the shepherds to them.
But Mary kept on continually guarding all these words
in her heart and bringing them together for the purpose
of considering them in their total import. And the shepherds returned, glorifying and praising God for all the
things which they heard and saw just as it was told
to them.

21-24　　　And when eight days were completed at the end of
which period He was to be circumcised, His name also

was called Jesus, which was so designated by the angel before He was conceived in the womb. And when the days of their purification according to the law of Moses were completed, they brought Him up to Jerusalem to dedicate Him to the Lord, even as it stands written in the law of the Lord, Every first-born male child shall be called separated to the Lord to be exclusively His, and to offer a sacrifice according to that which has been spoken in the law of the Lord, A pair of turtledoves or two young pigeons.

And behold, there was a man in Jerusalem whose name **25-35** was Simeon, and this man was righteous and one who reverenced God and was pious, looking expectantly toward that which will afford comfort and refreshment for Israel. And the Holy Spirit was upon him. And it had been revealed to him by the Holy Spirit in answer to prayer, and to this revelation he was holding fast, that he would not see death before he had seen the Lord's Christ. And he went in the control of the Spirit into the outer temple. And when the parents brought in the child Jesus to do for Him according to the established custom of the law, he himself also gladly received Him into his arms, and he eulogized God and said, As things now are, you are releasing your bondslave, Master, according to your word, in peace, because my eyes saw your salvation which you prepared before the face of all the peoples, a light for a revelation to the Gentiles and for the glory of your people, Israel. And His father and mother were marvelling at the things which were spoken concerning Him. And Simeon blessed them and said to Mary His mother, Behold, this One is destined for the falling and the rising of many in Israel and for a miraculous attestation, assent to which is being constantly refused. And moreover, through your soul there shall pass a sword in order that the deliberations of many hearts may be uncovered.

And there was Anna, a prophetess, a daughter of **36-38** Phanuel, of the tribe of Aser. This woman, well advanced in years, having lived with her husband seven years from the time of her state as a virgin and she herself a widow eighty-four years, did not leave the temple, rendering sacred service to God with fastings and petitions night and day. And at that very hour coming up and standing by, she kept on giving thanks to God and kept on speaking concerning Him to all who were expectantly looking toward the redemption of Jerusalem.

39, 40 And when they completed all the things according to the law of the Lord, they returned to Galilee to their own city of Nazareth. And the little child kept on growing and kept on increasing in strength, being constantly suffused with wisdom. And God's grace was upon Him.

41-52 Now, His parents customarily went to Jerusalem each year for the feast of the passover. And when He was twelve years old, they went up in accordance with the custom of the feast. And having completed their stay during the days of the feast, while they were returning, Jesus, the boy, lingered behind in Jerusalem. And His parents did not know of it, but supposing Him to be in the company of their road-companions, went a day's journey along the road. And they conducted an intensive search for Him among their relatives and acquaintances, and not having found Him, they returned to Jerusalem, searching diligently for Him. And it came to pass after three days they found Him in the outbuildings of the temple, sitting in the midst of the teachers, both hearing them and asking them questions. And all who were listening to Him were astounded to the point of a mental imbalance at His grasp and comprehension, and His ability to give them answers which exhibited a discriminating private judgment. And having seen Him, they were struck with astonishment to the point of a loss of self-control. And His mother said to Him, My child, why did you treat us in this manner? Behold. Your father and I are searching constantly for you, being in anguish. And He said to them, Why is it that you were searching for me? Had you not known that it is necessary in the nature of the case for me to be occupied in the things of my Father? However, they themselves did not understand that which He said to them. And He went down with them, and came to Nazareth and subjected himself in constant obedience to them. And His mother carefully guarded all these words in her heart, pondering over them and comparing them with one another. And Jesus kept on hewing a pioneer path ahead, making steady progress in wisdom and maturity and in favor in the presence of God and with men.

Now, in the fifteenth year of the rule of Tiberius Caesar, when Pontius Pilate was governor of Judaea, and Herod governor of the tetrarchy of Galilee, and Philip his brother governor of the tetrarchy of Ituraea and of the region of Trachonitis, and Lysanius governor of the tetrarchy of Abilene, at the time when Annas and Caiaphas were chief priests, there came a word from God to John the son of Zacharias in the uninhabited region. And he went into all the country around the Jordan making a public proclamation with such formality, gravity, and authority as must be listened to and obeyed, announcing a baptism that had to do with repentance, this baptism, a testimony because of the putting away of sins, as it stands written in the book of the words of Isaiah the prophet, A voice of one shouting in the uninhabited region, Make ready the Lord's road. Be making His paths straight. Every ravine shall be filled and every mountain and hill shall be brought low. And the crooked places shall be straight, and the rough roads shall be smooth. And all flesh shall see the salvation of God. **1-6**

Then he kept on saying to the crowds which were proceeding out to him in a steady stream in order to be baptized by him, Offspring of vipers, who gave you a private, confidential hint that you should flee from the divine and righteous wrath against sin and sinners which is about to break at any moment? Therefore, produce fruits which weigh as much as the repentance you profess. And do not begin to be saying within yourselves, As father, we have Abraham, for I am saying to you, God is able out of these stones as source material to raise up children to Abraham. And moreover, already the ax is lying at the root of the trees. Therefore, every tree which is not producing good fruit is being cut out and is being thrown into the fire. **7-9**

10-14   And the crowds kept on inquiring of him, saying,
What therefore shall we do? And answering, he went
to saying to them, He who has two undergarments,
let him share one with him who does not have any, and
he who has foods, let him be doing the same. Moreover
there came also tax collectors to be baptized, and they
said to him, Teacher, what shall we do? And he said
to them, Be exacting no more than that which has been
prescribed for you. Moreover, soldiers in service also
kept on inquiring of him, saying, As for us, what shall
we also be doing? And he said to them, Extort nothing
from any man by violence; neither blackmail anyone,
and be satisfied with your provision-money.

15-20   And since the people were in a state of expectancy, and
all men were reasoning in their hearts concerning John
whether perchance he could possibly be the Christ, John
answered saying to all, As for myself, I baptize you by
means of water. But there comes He who is mightier
than I, the thong of whose sandals I am not worthy to
untie. He himself shall baptize you by means of the
Holy Spirit and by means of fire, whose winnowing-
shovel is in His hand for the purpose of thoroughly cleansing His threshing-floor and of gathering the wheat into
His granary. But the chaff He will burn up completely
in fire that is unquenchable. Now, many and various
things, as he was exhorting, he brought as good news to
the people. But Herod the tetrarch, being rebuked
effectually by him concerning Herodias the wife of his
brother, and concerning all the pernicious things Herod
did, added also this to them all, that he confined John
in prison.

21, 22   Now, it came to pass that at the time when all the
people were baptized, Jesus also was baptized, and while
He was praying, the heaven was opened, and the Holy
Spirit in a form like that of a dove descended upon Him,
and a voice came out of heaven, As for you, you are my
Son, the beloved one, in whom I take pleasure.

23-38   And Jesus himself when beginning His ministry was
about thirty years of age, being a son, as was supposed,

of Joseph who was the son of Heli, who was the son of
Matthat, who was the son of Levi, who was the son of
Melchi, who was the son of Janna, who was the son of
Joseph, who was the son of Mattathias, who was the son
of Amos, who was the son of Naum, who was the son
of Esli, who was the son of Nagge, who was the son
of Maath, who was the son of Mattathias, who was the
son of Semei, who was the son of Joseph, who was the
son of Juda, who was the son of Joanna, who was the
son of Rhesa, who was the son of Zorobabel, who was the
son of Salathiel, who was the son of Neri, who was the
son of Melchi, who was the son of Addi, who was the
son of Cosam, who was the son of Elmodam, who was
the son of Er, who was the son of Jose, who was the son
of Eliezer, who was the son of Jorim, who was the son
of Matthat, who was the son of Levi, who was the son
of Simeon, who was the son of Juda, who was the son of
Joseph, who was the son of Jonan, who was the son of
Eliakim, who was the son of Melea, who was the son of
Menan, who was the son of Mattatha, who was the son of
Nathan, who was the son of David, who was the son of Jesse, who was the son of Obed, who was the son of Booz, who
was the son of Salmon, who was the son of Naasson, who
was the son of Aminadab, who was the son of Admin, who
was the son of Arni, who was the son of Esrom, who
was the son of Phares, who was the son of Juda, who
was the son of Jacob, who was the son of Isaac, who
was the son of Abraham, who was the son of Thara, who
was the son of Nachor, who was the son of Saruch, who
was the son of Ragau, who was the son of Phalec, who
was the son of Heber, who was the son of Sala, who
was the son of Cainan, who was the son of Arphaxad, who
was the son of Sem, who was the son of Noe, who
was the son of Lamech, who was the son of Mathusala, who
was the son of Enoch, who was the son of Jared, who
was the son of Maleleel, who was the son of Cainan, who
was the son of Enos, who was the son of Seth, who
was the son of Adam, who was the son of God.

And Jesus, in the control of the Holy Spirit, returned
from the Jordan and was continually being led by the
Spirit in the uninhabited region, for forty days being

1-8

constantly put to the test by the devil as he solicited Him to sin. And He ate not even one thing during those days, and they having been brought to an end, He became hungry. Then the devil said to Him, In view of the fact that you are Son of God by virtue of your possession of the divine essence, speak to this stone to the effect that it will become a loaf of bread. And Jesus answered him, It has been written and is now on record, The individual person shall not live on bread alone. And taking Him up, he exposed to His eyes all the kingdoms of the Roman empire in a moment of time. And the devil said to Him, To you I will give this authority, all of it, and its glory, because to me it has been given and is now in my possession, and to whomever I desire, I give it. As for you therefore, if you will fall upon your knees before me and touch the ground with your forehead as an expression of profound and reverential worship, all shall be yours. And Jesus answering said to him, It has been written and is at present on record, You shall worship the Lord your God, and to Him only you shall render sacred service.

9-15   And he brought Him into Jerusalem, and stood Him upon the wing of the temple, and said to Him, In view of the fact that you are Son of God by virtue of your participation in the divine essence, hurl yourself down from this place, for it has been written and at present is on record, To His angels He shall give a charge concerning you, to carefully guard you, and also, In their hands they shall lift you up and carry you lest at any time you strike your foot against a stone. And Jesus answering said to him, It has been said and is at present on record, You shall not put the Lord your God to an all-out test. And having completed every test and solicitation to sin, the devil stood off from Him until a more propitious time. And Jesus returned in the power of the Spirit into Galilee. And a report went out through the whole of the surrounding countryside concerning Him. And He himself was teaching in their synagogues, being extolled by all.

And He came to Nazareth where He had been brought   16-19
up. And He went according to His custom on the day
of the sabbath into the synagogue and arose to read.
And there was given Him the scroll of the prophet
Isaiah. . And having unrolled the scroll, He found the
place where it stood written, The Lord's Spirit is upon
me because He anointed me, to announce good news to
the poor. He has sent me on a mission to proclaim release
to those held captive and recovery of sight to those who
are blind, to send away in release those who are broken
by calamity, to herald forth that epochal period of time
which the Lord has chosen and in which He takes
pleasure.

And having rolled up the scroll and having given it   20-30
back to the attending officer, He sat down. And the eyes
of all in the synagogue were gazing with a fixed attention upon Him. And He began to be saying to them,
Today this scripture has been fulfilled in your hearing
and stands fulfilled as an accomplished and finished fact.
And all were bearing witness to Him and marvelling
at the words marked by a charming graciousness which
were constantly proceeding out of His mouth; and they
kept on saying, Is not this man Joseph's son? And He
said to them, Doubtless, you will quote to me this
proverb; Physician, heal yourself. As many things, whatever we heard took place in Capernaum, begin to do
at once here in your own native city. But He said,
Assuredly I am saying to you, not one prophet is favorably received in his own native country. Moreover, I
am saying to you in truth, Many widows there were in
the days of Elijah in Israel, when the sky was shut up
for three years and six months, when there came a great
famine over all the land, and to not even one of them
was Elijah sent except to Sarepta, a city of Sidon, to a
woman who was a widow. And many lepers there were
in Israel in the time of Elisha the prophet, and not even
one of them was cleansed except Naaman the Syrian.
And all in the synagogue were filled with a rage which
boiled over in a sudden and angry outburst upon hearing
these things, and having arisen, they threw Him outside

of the city and led Him to an out-jutting cliff of the
mountain upon which their city stood built, so that they
might hurl Him headlong down the precipice. But He
himself, having passed through their midst, proceeded on
His way.

31-37   And He went down to Capernaum, a city of Galilee.
And He was teaching them on the sabbath. And they
were struck with astonishment to the point of a mental
imbalance by reason of His teaching, because His discourse was characterized by authority. And in the
synagogue there was a man having a spirit of an unclean
demon. And he raised a cry from the depths of his
throat in a great voice. Ha! What is there between us
and you, Jesus, Nazarene? Did you come to destroy us?
I know you, who you are, the Holy One of God. And
Jesus rebuked him, which rebuke elicited no acknowledgment of guilt or repentance, saying, Your mouth be
muzzled, and come out of him at once. And the demon,
having violently hurled him to the ground into the midst,
came out of him and did not injure him in any possible
way. And an amazement mingled with terror came upon
all. And they kept on speaking one with another, saying,
What is this word, because by authority and power he
marshalls the unclean spirits under his command and they
come out? And there kept on proceeding forth a re-
sounding report concerning Him to every place in the
surrounding countryside.

38, 39   And having arisen from the teacher's chair in the
synagogue, He went into the home of Simon. Now,
the mother-in-law of Simon had been afflicted for some
time with a chronic fever, a severe one. And they made
request of Him in her behalf. And having taken His
stand over her, He rebuked the fever, and it left her.
And instantly, having stood up, she served food and drink
to them.

40-44   Now, when the sun was setting, all, as many as had
those who were sick with various kinds of diseases,
chronic cases, brought them to Him. And having laid
His hands upon one after another separately, He healed
them. And there also came out demons from many,

shouting out and saying, As for you, you are the Son of God. And rebuking them with a rebuke that did not elicit an acknowledgment of guilt or repentance, He was not permitting them to be speaking, because they knew Him to be the Christ. And day having come, having gone out, He proceeded into a deserted place. And the crowds kept on searching for Him diligently. And they came to Him, and kept on attempting to hinder Him from going away from them. But He said to them, Also to other cities it is necessary in the nature of the case for me to bring the good news of the kingdom of God, because to this end I was commissioned. And He kept on preaching in the synagogues of Judaea.

And it came to pass that while the people crowded up   1-11
against him and were listening to the word of God, that He himself took His stand beside the lake of Gennesaret. And He saw two boats which had been moored along the lake. But the fishermen, having disembarked, were cleaning their nets. And having gone on board one of the boats, which was Simon's, He requested him to put out a little from the shore. And having sat down He went to teaching the crowds out of the boat. Now, when He had ceased speaking, He said to Simon, Put out into deep water and let down your nets for a catch. And answering, Simon said, Master, through the entire night having worked to the point of exhaustion, we took not even one thing. Nevertheless, at your word I will let down the nets. And having done this, they enclosed a great number of fish, and their nets were torn apart. And they made signs to their partners in the other boat to come and lend them a hand. And they came, and they filled both of the boats so that they began to be sinking. Now Simon Peter, having seen this, fell down at Jesus' knees, saying, Depart from me at once because I am a man, a sinner, Master. For amazement took possession of him and of all who were with him because of the catch of fish which they took, and likewise also James and John, the sons of Zebedee, who were partners with Simon. And Jesus said to Simon, Stop fearing. From this moment as characterized by what

has just taken place, you shall be catching men alive. And having brought the boats to the shore, having abandoned all, they followed Him as His disciples.

12-16   And it came to pass that while He was in one of the cities, behold, a man full of leprosy. And having seen Jesus, having fallen upon his face, he begged Him, saying, Sir, if you have the desire in your heart, you are able to cleanse me. And having stretched forth His hand, He touched him, saying at the same time, My heart desires it. Be cleansed at once. And instantly the leprosy left him. And He himself ordered him to tell not even one person, but: Having gone off, exhibit yourself as evidence to the priest, and offer a sacrifice in recognition of your cleansing as Moses appointed before, for a testimony to them. But there went abroad rather the word concerning Him, and many crowds kept on coming together to be hearing and to be healed of their infirmities. But He himself was withdrawing in the deserted regions and was praying.

17-26   And it came to pass that on one of the days He himself was teaching. And there were sitting there Pharisees and teachers and interpreters of the Mosaic law, those who had come out of every village of Galilee and Judaea and out of Jerusalem. And the Lord's power was with Him for the purpose of healing. And behold, there were some men carrying upon a couch a man who was afflicted with paralysis. And they went to seeking how they might bring him in and place him before Him. And not having discovered by what sort of a way they might bring him in because of the crowd, having gone up upon the housetop, through the clay tiles they let him down with his couch into the midst before Jesus. And having seen their faith He said, Man, your sins have been forgiven you. And the men learned in the scriptures and the Pharisees began to be deliberating, saying, Who is this fellow who is speaking impious and reproachful things injurious to the divine majesty of God? Who is able to forgive sins but God alone? Now, Jesus having come to understand their deliberations, answering, said to them, Why are you deliberating in your hearts? Which is easier, to say, Your sins have been forgiven you, or to say, Be arising and start walking and keep on walking? But, in order that you may know that the Son of Man has authority on the earth to be forgiving sins, He said to the one afflicted with paralysis, To you I am saying, be arising, and having snatched up your couch, be proceeding on your way to your home. And instantly, having stood up before them, having snatched up that upon which he had been lying prostrate, he went off to his home, glorifying God. And amazement to the point of being beside themselves, seized upon all, and they kept on glorifying God. And they were filled with fear, saying, We saw things contrary to received opinion today, uncommon, unexpected, such as are ordinarily incredible.

And after these things He went forth, and He saw a **27-32** collector of internal revenue named Levi seated at his desk in the collector's office, and he attentively contemplated him. And He said to him, Come and join me as one of my disciples, and consider it a permanent appointment. And having abandoned all and having arisen, he joined Him as His permanent disciple. And Levi gave a great reception for Him in his home. And there was a large crowd of tax collectors and others of a like nature who were reclining at table with them. And the Pharisees and their men learned in the scriptures went to grumbling in a low undertone, conferring secretly together and discontentedly complaining to His disciples, saying, For what reason with the tax collectors and sinners stained with vice and crime are you all eating and drinking? And Jesus answering said to them, Those who are sound in body do not have need of a doctor but those who are in a miserable condition so far as their health is concerned. I have not come to call righteous persons but sinners to repentance.

And they said to Him, The disciples of John are in **33-35** the habit of fasting often, and they are habitually offering up petitions for themselves, likewise also do those of the Pharisees the same, but yours are eating and drinking. And Jesus said to them, You are not able to make the friends of the bridegroom, whose duty it is to provide for the celebration of the nuptials, to fast while the bridegroom is with them, are you? But there shall come days of such a nature, even whenever the bridegroom is taken away from them. Then they shall fast in those days.

36-39   And He was also giving them an illustration: No one having torn a patch from a garment new and fresh in quality and use, puts it upon an old worn-out garment. Otherwise, he will both tear the new garment, and the patch from the new garment will not match the old, worn-out one. And no one puts just-made wine into worn-out wineskins. Otherwise the just-made wine will burst the wineskins and it itself will be spilled out and the wineskins will be destroyed. But freshly-made wine must be put into wineskins new in point of use. And no one having partaken of fully-aged wine has a desire for wine which has just been made, for he says, The fully-aged is pleasant.

1-5   Now it came to pass that on a sabbath He was making His way through fields which had been sown to crops. And His disciples were picking and eating the ears of grain, rubbing them in their hands in order to break them up into smaller pieces. And certain of the Pharisees said, Why are you all doing that which is not lawful on the sabbath? And answering, Jesus said to them, Have you not read even this which David did when he himself was hungry and those with him, how he entered the house of God, and having taken the loaves of bread which were set forth, he ate and gave to those with him, which loaves of bread it is not lawful to eat except only for the priests? And He was saying to them, The Son of Man is Lord of the sabbath.

6-11   And it came to pass that on another sabbath He entered the synagogue and went to teaching. And there was a man there, and his hand, the right one, was shrunk and wasted. And the men learned in the sacred scriptures and the Pharisees were standing by on guard, carefully observing for themselves whether on the sabbath He is going to be healing, in order that they might find some accusation which they could prefer against Him in court. But He himself knew their reasonings and said to the man having the shrunken hand, Be arising, and stand in the midst. And having arisen, he stood. And Jesus said to them, I will put a question to you. Is it lawful on the sabbath to do good or to do evil, to save a life or to destroy it? And having looked round about on them all, He said to him, Stretch out your hand at once. And he did so, and his hand was restored to its former state. But they themselves were filled with a senseless rage akin to insanity, and kept on conferring with one another with regard to what they might do to Jesus.

And it came to pass in these days that He went forth into the mountain to be praying, and He was spending the entire night in this aforementioned prayer to God. And when it became day, He called those who were His pupils, and from them He selected twelve whom He also named ambassadors to be sent on a mission with credentials; Simon whom He also called Peter, and Andrew his brother, and James and John and Philip and Bartholomew, and Matthew and Thomas, and James the son of Alphaeus, and Simon the one called Zelotes, and Judas the brother of James, and Judas Iscariot who became a traitor. And having gone down with them, He stood on a level place. And a great crowd of His pupils, and a large multitude of the people from all Judaea and Jerusalem and the seacoast of Tyre and Sidon who came to hear Him and to be healed of their diseases, and those who were troubled with unclean spirits, were being healed. And the entire crowd was constantly seeking to be touching Him, because power from His presence was constantly going forth and was healing all. ₁₂₋₁₉

And He himself, having lifted up His eyes on His disciples, was saying, Spiritually prosperous are the poor, because yours is the kingdom of God. Spiritually prosperous are those who are hungering now, because your desire shall be satisfied. Spiritually prosperous ₂₀₋₂₃

are those who are now weeping audibly, because you shall laugh. Spiritually prosperous are you when men shall hate you and snub you as a disreputable character and revile you and contemptuously reject your name as pernicious on account of the Son of Man. Rejoice in that day and leap for joy, for behold, your reward is great in heaven, for in the same manner their fathers were in the habit of doing to the prophets.

24-34   But woe to you who are abounding in material resources, because you have that solace and cheer which comes from a prosperous state of things and have nothing left to desire. Woe to you who are satiated now, because you shall hunger. Woe to you who are laughing now, because you shall mourn and weep audibly. Woe to you when all men speak well of you, for in the same manner their fathers were accustomed to do to the false prophets. But I am saying to you who are hearing, Be loving your enemies with a divine and sacrificial love, be handsomely and fairly doing good to those who are hating you, be invoking blessings upon those who are calling down curses upon you, be praying for those who are treating you abusively. To the one who is striking you upon the jaw, be offering him also the other side of your jaw. And from the one who takes away your outer garment do not even withhold your under garment. Keep on giving to everyone who keeps on asking you, and from the one who takes away the things you possess, stop asking for their return. And even as you are desiring that men should be doing to you, be doing in the same way to them. And assuming that you are loving those who are loving you, what sort of a recompense is yours? for even sinners considered as a class of individuals, also are in the habit of loving those who are loving them. In fact, if you are doing good to those who are doing good to you, what kind of graciousness is yours? Even sinners considered as a class of individuals are constantly doing the same. And if you lend money at interest to those from whom you hope to receive, what kind of graciousness is yours? Even sinners are in the habit of lending money at interest to sinners in order that they may get back the equivalents.

But be loving your enemies and be doing good and be **35-38** lending money at interest, despairing of no one's ability to pay back the loan with interest, and your reward shall be great, and you shall be sons of the Most High, because He himself is benevolent to those who are ungrateful and those who are pernicious. Be becoming compassionate, even as your Father is compassionate. And stop judging in a censorious manner, and you shall positively not be the object of censorious judgment. And stop condemning, and you shall positively not be condemned. Be setting free, and you shall be set free. Be constantly giving, and it shall be given you, a generous measure that has been pressed down hard and which has been shaken thoroughly and which is running over shall they give into the pouch of your outer garment, for with the measure by which you are accustomed to measure, it shall be measured to you again.

Now, He also gave them an illustration. A blind **39-42** person is not able to be leading a blind person, is he? Will not both surely fall into a ditch? A pupil is not above the teacher. But everyone who has been completely equipped shall be as his teacher. And why are you looking at the tiny splinter of wood in the eye of your brother, but the log in your own eye you do not consider attentively? How can you be saying to your brother, Brother, allow me to draw out the tiny splinter of wood, the one in your eye, when you yourself do not see the log in your eye? Actor on the stage of life, playing a role of something that you are not, first draw the log out of your eye and then you shall see clearly in order to draw out the tiny splinter of wood that is in the eye of your brother.

For there is not a good tree that brings forth rotten fruit, **43-45** nor on the other hand, does a rotten tree produce good fruit. In fact, each tree is known by its own unique fruit. Certainly, they do not from rough, prickly shrubs gather figs, nor from a thorny bush do they gather a ripe cluster of grapes. A good man out of the good treasure of his heart brings forth that which is good, and the pernicious man out of the perniciousness of his heart brings forth that which is pernicious; for out of the abundance of the heart the mouth is accustomed to be speaking.

46-VII 1 But why are you calling me, Lord, Lord, and are not doing the things which I am saying? Everyone who comes to me and is hearing my words and is putting them into practice, I will show you to whom he is like. He is like a man who is building a house, who dug and went deep and laid a foundation upon the solid rock. And a flood having come, the river dashed against that house, and it was not strong enough to shake it because it was built securely. But he who heard and did not do is like a man who built a house upon the ground without a foundation, against which the river dashed, and immediately it collapsed, and the ruin of that house was great. After He ended all His words in the hearing of the people, He entered Capernaum.

2-10 Now, a slave of a certain captain of a hundred soldiers, being sick, was at the point of death, one who was highly prized by him. And having heard concerning Jesus, he sent on a mission to Him elders of the Jews, asking Him to come and bring his slave safely through his illness. And having come into the presence of Jesus, they began to beg Him earnestly, saying, He is worthy for whom you should do this, for he loves our nation, and he himself built our synagogue for us. Now Jesus was going on His way with them, and already He being not far distant from the house, the captain of a hundred soldiers sent friends, saying to Him, Sir, do not continue to put yourself out for me, for I am not worthy that you should come under my roof, neither on this account did I judge myself worthy to come to you, but speak the word, even — Let my servant be healed at once, for I also am a man whose position in life places him under the constant authority of others, having at the same time soldiers

under me. And I say to this one, Go at once, and he
goes, and to another, Be coming, and he comes, and
to my slave, Do this and be quick about it, and he does
it. And Jesus, having heard these things, marvelled
at him, and having turned completely around to the
crowd itself which was following with Him, said, I
am saying to you, not even in Israel did I find such
great faith. And having returned to the house, those
who had been sent found the slave to be in good health.

And it came to pass soon after, that He went on His   **11-17**
way into a city called Nain, and His disciples were
going along with Him, also a large crowd. Now, when
He drew near the gate of the city, behold, there was
being carried out one who had died, an only son of his
mother. And this woman was a widow, and a sizable
crowd from the city was with her. And the Lord having seen her, was moved with compassion for her and
said to her, Stop weeping. And having approached,
He touched the coffin, and those who were carrying
it came to a standstill, and He said, Young man, to you
I am saying, arise at once. And the dead man sat
up and began to be speaking. And He gave him to his
mother. And fear took hold of all, and they glorified
God, saying, A prophet, a great one, has arisen among
us, and God has looked upon His people and has come
to their aid. And this word went out in the whole of
Judaea concerning Him and in every place in the surrounding territory.

And his pupils brought word to John concerning all   **18-23**
these things. And having called to himself a certain
two of his pupils, John sent them to the Lord, saying,
As for you, are you the One who is coming, or are we
to be looking for another? And having approached
Him the men said to Him, John the Baptizer sent us
off on a mission to you, saying, As for you, are you
the One who is coming, or are we to be looking for
another? In that hour He healed many of chronic
diseases and of acute, distressing illnesses and of pernicious spirits, and to many blind people He gave as a
free, gracious, joy-giving gift the restoration of their

eyesight. And answering He said to them, Having gone on your way, report to John the things which you saw and heard, blind people are recovering their sight, crippled ones are walking about, lepers are being cleansed, and those who are not able to hear are hearing, dead people are being raised up, poor people are being given the good news. And spiritually prosperous is he whoever does not find in me that of which he disapproves and which hinders him from acknowledging my authority.

24-29 And John's messengers having gone off, He began to be saying to the crowds concerning John, What did you come out into the uninhabited region to be gazing at, a reed being agitated by wind? But what did you come out to see, a man clothed in garments soft to the touch? Behold. Those who are clothed in gorgeous apparel and live in luxury are in royal palaces. But what did you come out to see, a prophet? Yes, I am saying to you, and something more excellent than a prophet. This man is he concerning whom it has been written and the record is extant today, Behold, I am sending off on a mission my messenger before your face who will make ready your road before you. I am saying to you, a greater among those born of women than John there is no one. But he who is comparatively little in the kingdom of God is greater than he. And both the entire people, having heard, and the tax collectors, having been baptized, declared God to have been right in the case of John's baptism.

30-35 But the Pharisees and the interpreters and teachers of the Mosaic law by rejecting the counsel of God thwarted its purpose and rendered it inefficacious with reference to themselves, not having been baptized by him. Therefore, to what shall I compare the men of this breed, and they are those who resemble whom? They are those who resemble little children sitting in a market place and calling to one another, who say, We played the flute for you and you did not dance. We lamented and you did not weep. For John the Baptizer has arrived on the scene neither eating bread nor drinking wine, and you are saying, He has a demon. The Son of Man has come on the scene eating and drinking, and you are saying, Behold, a man who is a glutton and given to wine, a comrade of tax collectors and sinners stained with vice and crime. And wisdom is wont to be vindicated by all her children.

Now a certain one of the Pharisees was asking Him **36-38** to dine with him. And having come into the home of the Pharisee, He reclined at the dinner table. And behold, there was a woman of the city who was in character a sinner stained with vice, and having come to know that He was taking dinner in the home of the Pharisee, having brought an alabaster cruse of a fragrant ointment, she stood behind Him beside His feet, weeping audibly. With her tears falling like rain she began to be wetting His feet, and she dried them with the hairs of her head. And she kissed His feet tenderly again and again, and began applying the fragrant ointment.

But the Pharisee, the one who had invited Him, said **39-50** in himself, saying, This fellow, if he were a prophet, would in that case have known who and what sort of a woman is touching him, that she is a vile sinner. And answering, Jesus said to him, Simon, I have something to say to you. Indeed, Teacher, he said, Say it. There were two debtors who were obligated to a certain moneylender. The one was owing five hundred denarii, and the other, fifty. Since they did not have the funds with which to repay him, he graciously forgave both. Therefore, who of them will love him more? Answering, Simon said, I assume, the one whom he so graciously forgave the more. And He said to him, You judged correctly, And having turned around to the woman, to Simon He said, Do you see this woman? I entered your home, and water to me to wash the dust from my feet you did not give, but this woman with her tears wet my feet and with her hair wiped them dry. A kiss you did not give me, but this woman from the time I entered has not ceased to kiss my feet tenderly and again and again. With common oil you did not anoint my head, but this woman with fragrant ointment massaged my feet. Wherefore I am saying to you, Forgiven are her sins which are many, because she loved much. Yes, to whom little is forgiven, little does he love. And He said to her, Your sins are forgiven. And those at the table with Him began to be saying among themselves, Who is this fellow who even forgives sins? And He said to the woman, Your faith has saved you. Be going away into a state of peace.

1-3   And it came to pass soon afterwards that He himself also continued to go up and down throughout city and village making a proclamation as a herald does with that formality, gravity, and authority as must be listened to and obeyed and giving out the good news of the kingdom of God, and with Him, the Twelve, and certain women who had been healed from spirits that were pernicious and from infirmities, Mary, the one called Magdalene, from whom demons, seven of them, had gone out, and Joanna, wife of Chuza, Herod's overseer, and Susanna, and others, many of them, who were of such a nature that they kept on supplying them with food and the other necessities of life out of their possessions.

4-8   And a vast crowd of people gathering together, even of those who kept on journeying to Him from city after city, He spoke in the form of an illustration, bringing spiritual truth by means of an analogy drawn from their every day life. There went out the sower for the purpose of sowing his seed. And as he was sowing, some fell alongside the road, and it was trampled under foot, and the birds of the heavens ate it up. And other seed fell upon the rock. And having commenced to grow, it dried up because it was not having moisture. And other seed fell in the midst of the seeds of thorns. And the thorns having grown up together with it, choked it. And other seed fell upon ground which was good, and having commenced growing, it produced fruit, one hundred per cent. Saying these things, He cried aloud, He who has ears to be hearing, let him be hearing.

9-15   And His disciples went to asking Him what this illustration might be. And He said, To you it has been given to come to know the mysteries of the kingdom of God, but to the rest in the form of illustrations, in order that seeing, they may not be seeing, and hearing, they may not be understanding. Now, the illustration is this. The seed is the word of God. And those alongside the road are those who heard. Then comes the devil and snatches the word from their heart lest having believed they should be saved. And those upon the rock are those who when they hear, with joy receive the word, and these do not have rootage, who for a season believe, yet during a season when they are being tested by trials, stand aloof. And that which fell into the thorns, these are those who heard, and under the pressure of anxieties and wealth and pleasure of a materialistic life as they go on their way, are being choked, and they are not bringing fruit to maturity. But that in the good ground, these are the ones who are of such a nature that in a noble and virtuous heart, having heard the word, are holding it fast and are bearing fruit in patience.

But no one, having lighted a lamp, covers it with a **16-18** hollow household utensil or places it down under a couch, but puts it upon a lampstand, in order that those entering may be seeing the light. For there is not anything which is concealed that shall not become known, nor even that which is hidden which shall not positively be made known, and come out into clear view. Therefore, be ever exercising watchful care how you are hearing, for whoever may be having, it shall be given to him, and whoever is not having, even that which he appears to be having, shall be taken away from him.

Then there came near to Him His mother and brothers **19-21** and sisters. Yet they were unable to contact Him because of the crowd. And it was told Him, Your mother and your brothers and sisters have taken their stand outside, desiring to see you. But answering, He said to them, My mother and my brothers and sisters are these who the word of God are hearing and doing.

Now, it came to pass on one of the days that both He **22-25** himself went on board a boat and His disciples, and He said to them, Let us cross over to the other side of the lake. And they put out to sea. And as they were sailing He fell to sleep. And there came down a whirlwind on the lake, breaking forth out of black thunderclouds in furious gusts, with floods of rain, throwing everything topsy-turvy, and they were filling, and were beginning to be in danger. And having come to Him they awakened Him abruptly, saying, Master, Master, we are perishing. And having been thoroughly awakened, He rebuked the wind and the turbulence of the water, and they ceased, and there came a calm. And He said to them, Where is your faith? But they having become afraid, marvelled, saying to one another, Who then is this, because even the winds He marshalls under His orders, and the water, and they, recognizing His authority, are obeying Him.

26-34   And they put in at the country of the Gerasenes which is opposite Galilee. And after He had disembarked, there met Him a certain man out of the city having demons who for a long time had not put on himself any clothing, and he was not living in a house but in the tombs. And having seen Jesus, and raising a cry from the depths of his throat, he prostrated himself before Him and with a great voice said, What is there in common between me and you, Jesus, Son of God, the Most High God? I beg of you, do not begin to torment me; for He was commanding the unclean spirit to go out of the man. For often he had seized him by force and carried him away. And he was put in chains, with his hands and feet shackled, being constantly guarded. And breaking the bands apart, he was being driven by the demon into the deserted regions. And Jesus asked him, What is your name? And he said, Legion; because many demons had entered him. And they kept on begging Him not to order them to go off into the bottomless abyss. Now, there was there a large herd of hogs feeding on the mountain. And they begged Him to permit them to go into them. And He gave them permission. And the demons, having gone out of the man, went into the hogs. And the herd started forward impetuously down the precipice into the lake and was drowned. And those who were feeding them, when they saw that which had taken place, ran from the scene and brought back word into the city and into the country.

Then they went out to see that which had taken place. **35-39** And they came to Jesus and found the man out from whom the demons had gone seated and clothed and in his right mind beside the feet of Jesus. And they became afraid. And those who had seen what happened reported to them how the one who was demonized was healed. And the entire population of the surrounding territory of Gerasa begged Him to go away from them, because they were beginning to be seized by a great fear. And He himself having gone on board the boat, returned. But the man out from whom the demons had gone kept on begging Him for permission to be with Him. But He dismissed him, saying, Return to your home, and be relating as many things as God did for you. And he went off throughout the whole city, proclaiming openly as many things as Jesus did.

Now, when Jesus returned, the people welcomed Him, **40-48** for they were all waiting for Him. And behold, there came a man named Jairus. And this man was a leader of the synagogue. And having fallen at Jesus' feet, he went to begging Him to come to his home, because he had an only daughter about twelve years of age, and this daughter was dying. And as He was going, the crowds were suffocating Him. And a woman afflicted with a flow of blood twelve years which was of such a nature that it could not be healed by anyone, having come from behind Him, touched the tassel of His outer garment hanging over His shoulder. And immediately the flow of her blood stopped. And Jesus said, Who is the one who touched me? And when all were denying, Peter said, Master, the crowds are pressing in on you and crushing you. But Jesus said, Someone touched me, for, as for myself, I have come to recognize experientially that power has gone out from me. And the woman, having seen that she was not hidden, trembling, came and having fallen down before Him, made known openly before all the people the reason why she touched Him, and how she was immediately healed. And He said to her, Daughter, your faith has restored you to health. Be going on your way into the realm of tranquillity.

49-56   While He was yet speaking, a certain one comes from the home of the leader of the synagogue, saying, She has died, your daughter. No longer keep on disturbing the Teacher. But Jesus, having heard, said to him, Stop fearing. Only believe at once, and she shall be brought back to life. And having entered the house, He did not permit any to go in with Him except Peter and John and James and the father of the little girl and her mother. And all were weeping audibly and beating their breasts with grief and mourning and bewailing her. But He said, Stop weeping. She did not die but is sleeping. And they looked down their noses at Him and kept on laughing at Him, knowing that she had died. But He himself, having taken a firm grip of her hand, called out, saying, Little girl, be arising. And her spirit returned, and she stood up immediately. And He ordered that she be given something to eat at once. And the parents were beside themselves with astonishment. But He charged them to tell not even one person that which had taken place.

1-6   Then, having called together the Twelve, He gave them power and authority over all the demons, and over diseases, to be healing them. And He sent them off on a mission to be heralding forth the kingdom of God with that formality, gravity, and authority which must be listened to and obeyed, and to be healing. And He said to them, Take not even one thing for your journey along the road, neither a walking stick nor a begging-bag, nor bread, nor money, nor have two undergarments apiece. And into whatever home you enter, there be remaining as a house guest, and from there be going out. And as many as may not be welcoming you as a guest, when leaving that city, be shaking off the dust from your feet which you have raised and which has settled upon them, as a witness against them. And going forth, they kept on going through the villages, village by village, proclaiming the good news and healing everywhere.

7-9   Now Herod the tetrarch came to hear of all the things taking place. And he was in a state of utter perplexity because of the fact that it was being said by certain ones that John had arisen out from amongst those who were dead, but by certain others that Elijah had appeared, also by others that a certain one of the early prophets had arisen. Now Herod said, As for myself, John I beheaded. But who is this concerning whom I am hearing such things? And he kept on endeavoring to see Him.

And those sent on a mission as His ambassadors with credentials, having returned, related in detail to Him as many things as they did. And having taken them with himself He withdrew in private to a city called Bethsaida. And the crowds having come to know it, followed with Him. And having welcomed them, He went to speaking to them concerning the kingdom of God, and He continued healing those who had need of healing. But the day began to decline. Now the Twelve having come, said to Him, Dismiss the crowd in order that, having gone on their way into the encircling villages and farms, they may put up for the night and lay in a stock of provisions, because here we are in an uninhabited place. But He said to them, You at once give them something to eat. But they said, There are among us not more than five loaves of bread and two fish, unless, we having proceeded, should purchase eatables in the market place for all this people; for there were about five thousand men alone.

10-14

And He said to His disciples, At once make them recline as they do at home at the dinner table, in dinner-parties, about fifty to a group. And they did so, and made them recline, all of them. And having taken the five loaves of bread and two fish, having looked up to heaven, He asked the blessing upon them and broke them in pieces and kept on giving them to the disciples to set beside the crowd. And they ate and all were filled to their complete satisfaction. And there was taken up that which remained over to them, of broken pieces, twelve baskets.

14-17

And it came to pass while He was praying apart, His disciples were with Him. And He asked them, saying, Who are the crowds saying that I am? And answering they said, John the Baptizer, but others, Elijah, but still

18-22

others, that one of the early prophets arose. But He said to them, But as for you, who are you saying that I am? And Peter answering said, The Anointed One of God. And having solemnly charged them under penalty, He ordered them to be telling this to not even one person, saying, It is a necessity in the nature of the case for the Son of Man to suffer many things and be repudiated by the elders and the chief priests and those learned in the sacred scriptures after they had put Him to the test for the purpose of approving Him as Messiah and had found that He did not meet their specifications, and to be put to death and on the third day to be raised.

23-26   And He was saying to all, Assuming that anyone desires to come after me as a follower of mine, let him disregard his own interests, and let him at once and once for all pick up and carry his cross day after day, and let him take the same road with me that I take as a habit of life. For whoever desires to save his soul-life, shall ruin it. But whoever will declare a sentence of death upon his soul-life for my sake, this one shall save it. For how is a man profited, having acquired the whole world but having ruined or forfeited himself. For whoever is ashamed of me and of my words, of this one the Son of Man shall be ashamed whenever He comes in His glory and that of the Father and that of the holy angels.

27-36   But I am saying to you, truly, there are certain ones of those standing here who will positively not experience death until they see the kingdom of God. And it came to pass after these words, about eight days, having taken with himself Peter and John and James, He went up into the mountain to pray. And it came to pass that while He was praying, the appearance of His face took on a different expression, and His apparel was white, as with the brilliance of lightning flashing. And behold, men, two of them, were talking with Him, who were of such a character as to be Moses and Elijah, who, having been caused to appear, surrounded with a heavenly brightness, were speaking of His exodus which He was about to be carrying into effect in Jerusalem. But Peter and those with him having been overcome by sleep, were in a state of deep slumber. But having become fully awake, they saw His glory and the two men who were standing with Him. And it came to pass that while they were departing from him, Peter said to Jesus, Master, it is an excellent thing for us to be here. I propose that we make three booths constructed of the leafy branches of trees, one for you, and one for Moses, and one for Elijah, not understanding that which he was saying. And while he was saying these things, there came a cloud, and it began to be surrounding and enveloping them with brightness. But they feared while they entered the cloud. And a voice came out of the cloud saying, This is my Son, He who has been chosen out for myself and who is my Chosen One. Be hearing Him. And at the coming of the voice, Jesus was found alone. And they themselves maintained a silence, and to not even one person did they report in those days anything concerning the things they had seen.

Now, it came to pass on the next day, they having come **37-43** down from the mountain, that a large crowd met Him. And behold, a man from the crowd shouted out, saying, Teacher. I beg you to look with pitying regard upon my son with a view to giving him aid, because he is my only child. And behold, a spirit takes him, and he suddenly cries out aloud, and he throws him into convulsions accompanied by foaming at the mouth, and with difficulty leaves him, disrupting his body functions and shattering his strength. And I begged your disciples to eject him, and they were not able. And answering, Jesus said, O unbelieving breed of men, and perverted. Until when shall I be with you and bear with you? Bring your son here to me at once. And while he was yet coming to Him, the demon threw him into convulsions and disrupted his body functions and shattered his strength. Then Jesus rebuked the unclean spirit and healed the little boy and gave him back to his father. And all were beside themselves with astonishment at the majesty of God.

And while they were marvelling at all the things He **43-45** was doing, He said to His disciples, As for you, put these words at once into your ears for your own good, for the Son of Man is about to be delivered into men's hands.

But they were not understanding this word, and it had been concealed from them in order that they might not understand it. And they were fearing to ask Him concerning this word.

46-50   Now, there arose among them a discussion, the point of which was — who would be the one of their number who is greatest. Then Jesus, knowing the reasoning of their heart, laying hold of a little child, stood it beside himself and said to them, Whoever takes this little child into his family in order to bring it up and educate it in my Name, me he receives. And whoever welcomes me, welcomes the One who sent me on a mission. For he who is least among you, this one is great. And answering, John said, Master, we saw a certain individual who in your Name is ejecting demons, and we were trying to hinder him, because he is not following along with us. But Jesus said to him, Stop hindering him, for he who is not against you is on your behalf.

51-56   Now, it came to pass when the days were being fulfilled with reference to his being taken up, that He himself set His face steadfastly to be proceeding to Jerusalem. And He sent messengers on a mission before His face. And having gone on their way, they entered a village of the Samaritans to make ready for Him. And they did not afford Him a hospitable welcome because His face was toward Jerusalem as He journeyed along. And the disciples, James and John, having seen this, said, Lord, do you desire that we speak to the end that fire comes down from heaven and consumes them? But having turned around, He rebuked them, the rebuke however being ineffectual. And they went on their way to another village.

57-62   And as they were journeying along the road, a certain man said to Him, I will follow with you as your disciple wherever you may go. And Jesus said to him, The foxes always have dens and the birds of heaven always have roosting places, but the Son of Man does not have where to lay His head. And He said to another, Start following with me as my disciple and keep on doing so as a habit of life. But he said, Permit me first, having gone, to bury my father. But He said to him, Leave those who are dead to bury their own dead, but as for you, having gone off, be announcing everywhere the kingdom of God. And another also said, I will follow with you as your disciple, Lord, but first permit me to say farewell to those in my home. But Jesus said to him, No one having put his hand to a plough and looking to the things he left behind, is fit for the kingdom of God.

Now, after these things, the Lord appointed seventy **1-12** others, and sent them on a mission two by two before His face into every city and place where He himself was about to come. And He was saying to them, The harvest indeed is great, but the workers are few. Pray therefore the Lord of the harvest to thrust out workers into His harvest. Be going on your way. Behold, I am sending you on a mission as lambs in the midst of wolves. Do not keep on carrying a purse nor a begging-bag like the pagan priest, nor sandals. And do not accost anyone along the road, engaging in a long, protracted, oriental greeting. Moreover, into whatever home you enter, first be saying, Peace to this home. And if there is in that place a son of peace, your peace shall rest upon him. But if not, it shall return to you. Moreover, in that very house be abiding as a guest, eating and drinking the things they set before you, for the workman is worthy of pay. Do not have the habit of changing your place of abode from one home to another. And into whatever city you are entering, and they are welcoming you, be eating the things set before you, and be healing those in it who are ill, and be saying to them, The kingdom of God has come near to you and is at hand. And into whatever city you go and they are not welcoming you, having gone out into its broad, open streets, say, Even the dust of your city which cleaves to us upon our feet we are wiping off against you, nevertheless, be knowing this, that there has come near the kingdom of God and it is now imminent. I am saying to you, For Sodom in that day it shall be more endurable than for that city.

Woe to you, Chorazin, woe to you, Bethsaida, because, **13-16** had in Tyre and Sidon been done the miracles demonstrating God's power which were done in you, long ago in that case would they have repented, sitting in a garment made of dark, coarse cloth woven from goat's hair and worn by penitents, and covered by ashes, a sign of voluntary humiliation. But for Tyre and Sidon it shall be more endurable in the judgment than for you. And as for you, Capernaum, you shall not be exalted to heaven, shall you? Down to the depths of misery and disgrace in the unseen world you shall go. He who hears you, hears me. And he who is rejecting you is rejecting me, and he who is rejecting me is rejecting the One who sent me on a mission.

17-20   And the seventy returned with joy, saying, Lord, even the demons are marshalling themselves under our orders in your Name. And He said to them, I was beholding with a calm, intent, continuous contemplation Satan having fallen in one fell swoop from heaven like lightning. Behold, I have given you the authority to advance by setting foot upon snakes and scorpions, and over all the power of the enemy, and nothing will in any case harm you. Nevertheless, in this do not continue to rejoice, namely, because the spirits marshall themselves in subjection under your orders, but be rejoicing that your names have been written in heaven and are on permanent record up there.

21-24   At that very hour He rejoiced exceedingly, this rejoicing being energized by the Holy Spirit, and said, I give praise to you, openly and from the heart, Father, Lord of heaven and earth, because you hid these things from the wise and the learned, and uncovered them to the untaught. Yes, Father, because it was your good pleasure and you willed it so. All things to me were delivered by my Father, and no one knows who the Son is except the Father, and who the Father is except the Son, and he to whom the Son desires to reveal Him. And having turned around to the disciples, in private He said, Spiritually prosperous are the eyes that are seeing the things which you are seeing, for I am saying to you, Many prophets and kings desired to see the things which you are seeing and did not see them, and to hear the things which you are hearing and did not hear them.

And behold. A certain interpreter and teacher of the Mosaic law stood to his feet, putting Him to the test, saying, Teacher, by having done what shall I inherit life eternal? And He said to him, In the law what has been written and is on record? In what way do you read it? And answering, he said, You shall love the Lord your God with your whole heart and with your whole soul and with your whole strength and with your whole mind, and your neighbor as yourself. And He said to him, You answered correctly. Be doing this and you shall live. But he, desiring to show himself to be righteous, such as he wished himself to be considered, said to Jesus, And who is my neighbor? **25-29**

Having picked up the substance of his interrogation, Jesus said in answer, A certain man was going down from Jerusalem to Jericho and fell into the midst of bandits who surrounded him, and having stripped him of his clothing and having laid blows upon him, went off, having left him half-dead. Now, by a coincidence of circumstances, a certain priest was going down along that road, and having seen him, came alongside and then went to the opposite side of the road. And likewise also a Levite, having come down to the place and having seen him, came alongside and then went to the opposite side of the road. But a certain Samaritan as he journeyed, came down upon him, and having seen him, was moved with compassion for him. And having come to him, he bound up his wounds, pouring upon them soothing oil and disinfecting wine, and having set him upon his own private beast of burden, he brought him to a caravansary and took care of him. And on the approach of the next day, having taken out two silver coins, he gave them to the innkeeper and said, Take care of him, and as for myself, whatever you spend in addition, when I return, I will recompense you. **30-35**

Who of these three does it seem to you proved to be a neighbor to the one who fell into the midst of the bandits? And he said, The one who showed mercy upon him. Then Jesus said to him, Be going on your way, and as for you, you be doing likewise. **36, 37**

38-42   Now, as they were going on their way, He himself
entered a certain village. And a certain woman named
Martha welcomed Him as a guest into her home. And
she had a sister called Mary, who also having seated
herself beside the Lord's feet, was listening to His
word. But Martha was going around in circles, over-
occupied with preparing the meal. And bursting in
upon Jesus she assumed a stance over Him and said,
Lord, is it not a concern to you that my sister has
let me down to be preparing the meal alone? Speak
therefore to her at once that she take hold and do her
part with me. And answering, the Lord said to her,
Martha, Martha, you are worried and excited about
many things, but of few things there is need, or of one,
for Mary chose out for herself the good portion, which
is of such a nature that it shall not hastily be snatched
away from her.

1-4   And it came to pass while He was praying in a certain place that when He ceased, a certain one of His
pupils said to Him, Lord, teach us to be praying even
as also John taught his pupils. And He said to them,
When you pray, be saying, Father, cause your Name to
be set apart as sacred and the object of veneration. Your
kingdom, cause that it should come. Our bread for the
coming day be giving us daily. And forgive us our sins
even as we ourselves also are in the habit of forgiving
everyone who is indebted to us. And do not bring us into
the place of testing where the circumstances in which we
are tested may lead on to the place where we are solicited
to do evil.

5-13   And He said to them, Who is there of you who shall
have a friend, and shall go to him at midnight and say
to him, Friend, lend me at once and because of our
friendship three loaves of bread, since now a friend of
mine has come suddenly to my hearth from his journey
and I do not have that which I shall place beside him.
And that one from within, answering shall say, Stop
furnishing me with troubles. Already my door has been
closed with the result that it is shut for the night, and
my children are with me in our bed. I am not able

to get up and give to you. I am saying to you, though he will not give to him, having arisen, because of being his friend, yet on account of his persistence, having arisen, he will give him as many as he is needing. And as for myself, I am saying to you, Keep on asking for something to be given, and it shall be given you. Keep on seeking and you shall find. Keep on reverently knocking, and it shall be opened to you. For everyone who keeps on asking for something to be given, keeps on receiving, and he that keeps on seeking, keeps on finding, and to the one who keeps on reverently knocking, it shall be opened. Moreover, who of you, the father, should the son ask him for a fish, he will not give him a snake instead of a fish, will he? or should he also ask for an egg, will he give him a scorpion? Therefore, as for you, since you who are pernicious know how to be giving good gifts to your children, how much more will your Father who is in heaven give the Holy Spirit to those who ask Him for Him to be given.

And He was in the process of ejecting a demon, and **14-23** it was one that rendered the one demonized unable to speak. And it came to pass that the demon having been ejected, the one who could not speak broke his silence and uttered words. And the crowds marvelled. But certain ones from among them said, By means of Beezeboul, the ruler of the demons, he is ejecting the demons. And others putting Him to the test kept on demanding an attesting miracle out of heaven from Him. But He himself, knowing their thoughts and the intents and purposes back of them, said to them, Every kingdom having been divided against itself in opposing factions is reduced to a state of ruin, and a home divided against itself in opposing factions, falls. Moreover, assuming also that Satan was divided against himself, how is it possible that his kingdom shall be made to stand, because you are saying that by means of Beezeboul I am ejecting the demons? But, as for myself, assuming for the moment that by means of Beezeboul I am ejecting the demons, your sons, by whom are they ejecting them? Upon this basis they themselves shall be your critics. But since by means of the finger of God, I, in contradistinction to them, am actually ejecting the demons, accordingly the kingdom of God came upon you sooner than you expected. When the strong man, having fully armed himself from head to foot, is guarding his own homestead, his possessions are safe. But when a stronger man than he having come upon him, overcomes him, he takes away his complete armor [shield, sword, lance, helmet, greaves, and breastplate] upon which he had fully placed his confidence, and distributes among others his booty. He who is not with me is against me. And he who is not gathering with me, is scattering.

24-28   When the unclean spirit makes his exit from the man, he goes through places devoid of water, seeking a temporary respite, and not finding any, he says, I will return into the house from where I came out. And having come, he finds it broom-swept and in a present state of cleanliness, also having been put in order and decorated. Then proceeding, he also takes with himself other spirits more pernicious than himself, seven of them, and having entered, they take up their permanent residence there. And the last state of that man becomes worse than the first. Now it came to pass while He was saying these things, a certain woman in the crowd having lifted up her voice said to Him, Blessed is the womb which bore you and the breasts from which you drew milk. But He himself said, Rather, spiritually prosperous are those who are hearing the word of God and are exercising care to observe and not violate it.

29-32   And while the people were gathering together in throngs, He began to be saying, This breed of men is a pernicious breed. It is constantly demanding an attesting miracle, and an attesting miracle shall not be given to it except the attesting miracle of Jonah, for just as Jonah became a supernatural proof to the Ninevites of the fact that his message was from God, thus also shall the Son of Man be to this breed of men. A queen of the south shall arise in the judgment with the men of this breed and shall condemn them, because she came out of the remotest frontiers of the earth for the purpose of hearing Solomon's wisdom, and behold something more than Solomon is here. Men, Ninevites, shall arise in the judgment with this breed of men and shall condemn it, because they repented as a result of Jonah's proclamation, and behold, something more than Jonah is here.

No one, having lit a lamp, puts it in a cellar or under the grain-measure but upon the lampstand, in order that those who are entering from time to time may see the light. The lamp of the body is the eye. When your eye is in single focus, sound, and fulfilling its function, also your whole body is well lighted. But when it is pernicious, also your body is full of darkness. Be constantly scrutinizing yourself therefore lest the light which is in you is darkness. Therefore, assuming that your whole body is well lighted, not having any part full of darkness, the whole shall be full of light as when the lamp by its bright shining illuminates you.

33-36

Now, as He spoke, a Pharisee asks Him to take breakfast with him. And having gone in, He reclined at the breakfast table. But the Pharisee, having taken notice, wondered that He had not first before the breakfast observed the ceremonial washing of the hands before meals which was traditional amongst the Jews. But the Lord said to him, Now, since you are intent upon observing the requirements of your tradition, as for you, the Pharisees, the outside of the cup and of the dish you are in the habit of cleansing, but your inner part is full of plunder and perniciousness. Stupid men. Did not He that made that which is outside also make that which is inside? Rather, the things which are inside give as alms, and behold, all things are clean to you.

37-41

But woe to you, the Pharisees, because you pay a tenth of sweet-smelling garden-mint and that strong smelling plant with yellow flowers and bitter leaves, and every garden-herb, and you are neglecting the equitable administration of justice and the love of God. Now, these things it has constantly been a necessity in the nature of the case to do and those things not to leave off.

42-44

Woe to you, the Pharisees, because you highly prize a place on the bench first in importance in the synagogues, one that faces the audience and which is only for the authoritative teachers of Moses' law and other eminent personages, and are unwilling to forego a place there, and you highly prize the deferential greetings in the market places in which the people pay their respects to you as to an exalted personage. Woe to you, because you are as the tombs which because not whitewashed are indistinct, which defile the passerby who is ignorant of their whereabouts, and men going about their daily business, walking above them, do not know it.

45-48 And answering, a certain one of the interpreters and teachers of the Mosaic law says to Him, Teacher, saying these things, you are also according us outrageous treatment and a positive insult. But He said, Also, as for you in distinction to the Pharisees, to you who are interpreters and teachers of the Mosaic law, woe to you, because you load men with burdens, precepts hard to obey and irksome, and you yourselves will not touch these burdens with one of your fingers. Woe to you, for you build the sepulchral monuments of the prophets, and your fathers killed them. Consequently you are witnesses and give your full approval to the works of your fathers, because they themselves on the one hand killed them, and you on the other hand are building their memorials.

49-52 On this account also the wisdom of God said, I will send on a mission to them prophets and ambassadors, and some of them they will kill and persecute, in order that there may be required the blood of all the prophets which has been shed since the foundation of the universe by this breed of men, from the blood of Abel to the blood of Zachariah, the one who perished between the altar of burnt-offering and the sanctuary. Yes, I am saying to you, it shall be required of this breed of men. As for you, woe to you, the interpreters and teachers of the Mosaic law, because you took away the key to the knowledge. You yourselves did not go in, and those who are trying to enter, you prevented from doing so.

And after He had gone out from there, the men learned **53, 54**
in the sacred scriptures and the Pharisees began to set
themselves against Him with a vengeance, and to be
plying Him with questions so as to entice Him to give
answers to questions to which He would have no opportunity to give consideration beforehand, concerning many
things, preparing a trap for Him in order to catch something out of His mouth.

In these circumstances, many thousands of the people **1-7**
having gathered together in one place so that they
trampled one another under foot, He began to be saying
to His disciples first, Be constantly on your guard
against the yeast which is of such a nature as to be in
character the acting of a player on the stage assuming
a role of that which he is not, the yeast of the Pharisees.
Moreover, there is not even one thing which has been
completely covered up with the result that it is in a
state of concealment which shall not be uncovered, and
hidden which shall not be made known, because as many
things as in the darkness you spoke, in the light shall
be heard. And that which to the ear you spoke in the
secret and well-guarded places, shall be proclaimed upon
the housetops. But I am saying to you, you who are
my friends, do not become afraid of those who are
killing the body and after these things do not have
anything more that they can do. But I will warn you
whom to fear. Fear the one who, after he kills, has
authority to throw into the hell. Verily, I am saying
to you, this one fear. Are not five little sparrows sold
for one cent? And one of them has not been forgotten
in the watch-care of God. In fact, even the hairs of your
head, all of them, have been counted, and their number
is tabulated on a permanent record. Stop fearing. You
surpass in importance many little sparrows.

Moreover I am saying to you, everyone whoever shall **8-10**
declare openly and freely his oneness with me before
men, also shall the Son of Man openly and freely declare
His oneness with him before the angels of God. But
the one who disowned me before men, shall be disowned
before the angels of God. And everyone who speaks

a word against the Son of Man, it shall be forgiven him. But to the one who by contemptuous speech intentionally comes short of the reverence due the Holy Spirit, there shall not be extended forgiveness.

11, 12   And whenever they bring you to the synagogues and to magistrates and authorities, do not begin to be troubled how or what your verbal defense shall be, or what you shall say, for the Holy Spirit shall teach you in that very hour the things that are necessary in the nature of the case to speak.

13-15   Now, a certain person in the crowd said to Him, Teacher, speak to my brother that he divide the inheritance with me. But He said to him, Man, who constituted me a judge or a divider over you? And He said to them, Take heed and be guarding yourself from every kind of greedy desire for more, because not in the sphere of that which is in superabundance enjoyed by anyone is his life to be found, from the source of his possessions.

16-21   And He told them an illustrative story, saying, The land of a certain wealthy man was fertile and produced large crops. And he kept on revolving the matter within himself, saying, What shall I do, because I do not have a place where I shall gather together my crops? And he said, This I shall do. I will pull down my storehouses and I will build greater ones, and I will gather together there all the grain and my good things. And I shall say to my soul, Soul, you have many good things laid up for many years. Be taking it easy. Eat. Drink. Keep on being merry. And God said to him, Senseless, stupid, foolish man. On this night your soul they are demanding from you. Now, the things which you prepared, whose shall they be? Thus is it in the case of the one who hoards up treasure for himself and is not rich with a view to that which God considers true riches.

22-40   And He said to His disciples, On this account I am saying to you, Stop worrying about your life, what you shall eat, and about your body, what you shall put on,

for the soul is more than food and the body than clothing. Consider attentively the ravens, that they neither
sow nor reap, for which there is neither a storehouse
nor a granary. And God feeds them. As for you, of
how much more importance are you than the birds.
Moreover, who of you by worrying is able to add one
foot and a half to his height? Since therefore you are
not even able to do that which is least, why are you
worrying about the rest? Consider attentively the lilies,
how they neither are spinning nor weaving. Yet I am
saying to you, not even Solomon in all his glory clothed
himself as one of these. Moreover, in view of the fact
that God in this manner clothes the herbage in the field
which exists today and tomorrow is thrown into the
furnace, how much more you, little-faith-ones. And as
for you, stop striving after what you shall eat and what
you shall drink, also stop wavering between hope and
fear, living in suspense, since for these things, all of
them, the nations of the world system are seeking.
Moreover your Father knows that you have need of
these things. But you be continually seeking His kingdom, and these things will be added to you. Stop fearing, little flock; because your Father chose to give you
the kingdom. Sell your possessions and give alms.
Provide for yourselves money-bags which do not de-
teriorate with use, a treasure which is unfailing, in
the heavens, where a thief does not draw near nor even a
clothes-moth destroys, for where your treasure is, there
also your heart shall be. See to it that your garments
are fastened about yourself with a belt, and the lamps,
that they are burning constantly. And as for you, be
like men looking for their own master when he should
return from the marriage feast, in order that, having
come and knocked, immediately they might open to him.
In a prosperous and goodly state are those slaves, who,
the master having come, he will find in an alert state of
mind. Assuredly, I am saying to you, He will fasten his
garments about himself with a belt and will cause them
to recline at the table and having come, will serve them
food and drink. And if during the second or the third
period in which a guard was stationed to watch, he

would come and find them thus, in a prosperous and goodly state are those slaves. Moreover, be knowing this, that, assuming that the house master would know at what sort of an hour the thief is coming, he would in that case not have permitted his house to be broken into. And as for you, be becoming those who are always ready, because the Son of Man comes in an hour at which you are not thinking.

41-46 Then Peter said, Lord, to us are you giving this illustration or also to all? And the Lord said, Who then is the steward who is trustworthy, the prudent one, whom the master will appoint over his corps of household servants to be giving them at the proper time their portion of food? That slave is in a prosperous and goodly state, whom, his master having come, will find so doing. Of a truth, I am saying to you, he will give him the responsibility over all his possessions. But should that slave say in his heart, My master is delaying his coming, and shall begin to be beating the men and women slaves, moreover also to be eating and drinking and to be in a state of intoxication, the master of that slave will come on a day when he was not looking for him, and at an hour which he does not know, and will severely scourge him and will appoint him his part with those who are untrustworthy.

47, 48 Now, that slave who knew the will of his master and did not make the necessary preparations or do his will, will be beaten with many stripes. But he that did not know, and did things worthy of blows, will be beaten with few stripes, for to everyone to whom much was given, much shall be required from him, and to whom much was entrusted, more they will ask.

49-53 Fire I came to throw upon the earth, and how much I wish that it were already set blazing. Moreover, I have an immersion by which I will be overwhelmed, and how am I being hard pressed from every side until it be consummated. Are you thinking that peace I have come forth to bestow upon the earth? Not at all, I am saying to you, but rather dissension, for from this particular time on there shall be five in one home at variance with one another, three against two and two against three.   They shall be divided against one another, a father against a son and a son against a father, a mother against a daughter and a daughter against a mother, a mother-in-law against her daughter-in-law, and a daughter-in-law against her mother-in-law.

And He was saying also to the crowds, Whenever   **54-59** you see a cloud arising out of the west, immediately you say, A violent rain accompanied by high wind with thunder and lightning is coming.   And so it happens. And when a south wind is blowing, you say, Heat there will be.   And it takes place.   Actors on the stage of life, playing the role of that which you are not, the face of the earth and of the heaven you know how to evaluate and interpret.   But this strategic, epochal period of time, how is it that you are not evaluating and interpreting it?   And why, even by your own inherent ability, are you not deciding as to that which is right? For while you are going with your opponent in a suit at law to the magistrate, on the road endeavor to be released from him, lest at any time he drag you forcibly to the judge, and the judge hand you over to the officer of the law whose business it is to inflict punishment, and this officer throw you into prison.   I am saying to you, you will positively not go out from that place until you have paid the very last penny.

Now, there were present at that very season, epochal   **1-5** in its significance, certain ones who brought word to Him concerning the Galilaeans whose blood Pilate had mixed with their sacrifices.   And answering, He said to them. Are you thinking that these Galilaeans were greater sinners in comparison to all the Galilaeans, because they have suffered these things?   Not at all, I am saying to you, but unless you are repenting, you all will likewise perish.   Or, those eighteen, upon whom the tower in Siloam fell and killed them, are you thinking that they themselves were greater offenders in comparison to all the men who were residents of Jerusalem?   Not at all,

I am saying to you, but unless you repent, you all will
likewise perish.

6-9   Now, He was presenting this illustration. A certain
man was in possession of a fig tree, one already planted
in his vineyard. And he came seeking fruit on it, and
did not find any. Then he said to the vine-dresser,
Look. It is three years from the time I came seeking
fruit on this fig tree, and I am not finding any. Cut it
out at once. Why also is it exhausting the ground?
But answering, he says to him, Master, let it alone also
for this year until I dig around it and throw in manure.
And if it indeed produces fruit after that, but if not, you
will cut it out.

10-17   And He was doing some teaching in one of the synagogues on the sabbath day. And behold. A woman
had a spirit that caused an infirmity eighteen years and
was completely bent together by a curvature of the
spine, and was not able to raise herself up at all. And
having seen her, Jesus called her and said to her,
Woman, you have been released from your infirmity,
and the cure is permanent. And He placed His hands
on her. And immediately she was restored to an erect
position. And she glorified God. But the ruler of the
synagogue answering, being indignant that on the sabbath Jesus had healed, was saying to the crowd, Six days
there are during which it is right and proper to accomplish things. In them therefore you should come and
be healed, and not on the day of the sabbath. But the
Lord answered him and said, Actors on the stage of life,
playing the role of that which you are not, does not each
one of you on the sabbath release his ox or his donkey
from the feeding-trough and lead it off to give it a drink?
And this woman, being a daughter of Abraham, whom
Satan bound, just think of it, eighteen years, was it not a
necessity in the nature of the case that she be released
from this binding restriction on the sabbath? And while
He was saying these things, all those who had opposed
Him blushed for shame. And the entire crowd went to
rejoicing because of all the glorious things which were
being done by Him.

Then He was saying, To what is the kingdom of God similar, and to what shall I liken it? It is like a grain of mustard seed which a man having taken, threw into his garden. And it grew and became as large as a tree. And the birds of the heaven roosted in its branches. And again He said, To what shall I liken the kingdom of God? It is like yeast which a woman having taken, hid in three measures of wheat flour until the whole of it was permeated by the yeast. **18-21**

And He went on His journey through the cities and villages, teaching and making His way toward Jerusalem. And a certain one said to Him, Lord, are they few in number, those who are being saved? And He said to them, Be endeavoring with a strenuous zeal to enter through the narrow door, because many, I am saying to you, will seek to enter and will not be able from the time when the master of the house arises and slams the door fast, and you begin to have taken your stand outside and to be knocking on the door, saying, Lord, open to us at once. And answering he will say to you, I do not know you nor from where you are. Then you will begin to be saying, We ate in your presence and drank, and in our streets you taught. And he shall speak, saying to you, I do not know from where you are. Depart at once from me, all workers of unrighteousness. There, in that place, there shall be the audible weeping and the gnashing of the teeth, when you shall see Abraham and Isaac and Jacob and all the prophets in the kingdom of God, but you being thrown outside. And they shall come from east and west and north and south, and shall feast in the kingdom of God. And behold. There are last ones who shall be those who are first, and there are first ones who shall be those who are last. **22-30**

In that very hour there came certain Pharisees saying to Him, Get out at once and be going away from here, because Herod is desiring to kill you. And He said to them, Having gone on your way, say to this fox, Behold, I am ejecting demons and am perfecting cures today and tomorrow, and on the third day I am being perfected. Nevertheless, it is a necessity in the nature of the case for me **31-35** to be proceeding, today and tomorrow and the next day, because it is contrary to all practice that a prophet perish elsewhere than in Jerusalem. O Jerusalem, Jerusalem, the one that habitually kills the prophets and stones those sent on a mission to it, how often did I desire to gather together in one place your children, even as a hen gathers her own brood under her wings, and you did not desire it. Behold, your home is being left to itself, abandoned to its own resources. Moreover, I am saying to you, you will positively not see me until the time comes when you shall say, Eulogized be the One who comes in the Name of the Lord.

1-6   And it came to pass that as He went into a house of a certain one of the rulers, a Pharisee, to eat bread on a sabbath, they themselves also were watching Him assiduously from a position of vantage. And behold, there was a certain man before Him who had the dropsy. And Jesus answering spoke to the teachers and interpreters of the Mosaic law and to the Pharisees, saying, Is it lawful on the sabbath to heal or is it not? But they were silent. And having taken hold of him, He healed him and dismissed him, and to them he said, Who of you having a son or an ox, and it shall fall into a cistern, will not also immediately pull it up on the sabbath day? And they were not able to meet His argument with reference to these things.

7-11   And He was giving an illustration to those who had been invited, while He was concentrating on how they were choosing out for themselves the chief places at the table, saying to them, Whenever you are invited by a certain individual to a wedding, do not begin to take the chief place at the table, lest a more honorable one than you has been invited by him, and having come, he who invited you and him will say to you, Give this man a place, and then you begin with shame to take the last place. But whenever you are invited, proceeding, take the last place, in order that when he who has invited you say to you, Friend, come up higher. Then there shall be honor conferred upon you before all who are at the table with you; because everyone who exalts himself shall be reduced to a rank below those who are honored, and he who places himself in a lower rank in life, shall be elevated to a place where he is honored.

Moreover, He also went to saying to the one who had invited Him, Whenever you give a breakfast or a dinner, stop calling your friends and your brethren and your relatives and your wealthy neighbors, lest also they themselves invite you in turn and you are reimbursed. But whenever you give a banquet, be calling the poor, the disabled, the lame, the blind, and you shall be in a spiritually prosperous state of soul, because they do not have the wherewithal to reimburse you, for your reimbursement shall come at the time of the resurrection of the just. And a certain one of those dining with Him having heard these things said to Him, Spiritually prosperous is the one who is of such a nature that he eats bread in the kingdom of God. **12-15**

And He said to him, A certain man was making a great dinner, and he invited many. And he sent off his slave on a mission at the hour of the dinner to say to those who had been invited, Be coming, because already it is prepared. And they all began in concert to beg off. The first said to him, A farm I bought, and it is necessary for me, having gone, to see it. I beg of you, please, have me excused. And another said, Five yoke of oxen I bought, and I am on my way to examine them for my approval. I beg of you, please, have me excused. And another said, A wife I married, and because of this I am not able to come. **16-20**

And the slave, having come, reported to his master these things. Then, becoming angry, the master of the house said to his slave, Go out quickly into the broad avenues and narrow lanes of the city, and the poor and disabled and blind and lame bring in here. And the slave said, Master, It has been done, that which you commanded, and still there is room. And the master said to the slave, Go out at once into the country roads and the footpaths alongside the hedges, and compel them to come in, in order that my home may be filled, for I am **21-24** saying to you that not one of those men who have been invited will taste my dinner.

25-30   Now, many crowds were journeying along with Him. And having turned around, He said to them, If anyone comes to me and does not hate his father and mother and wife and children and brothers and sisters in the event that they become hindrances to his supreme love for me, yes, moreover also his own life in the same manner, he is not able to be my disciple. And whoever is not taking up and carrying his own cross and coming after me, is not able to be my disciple. For, who is there of you, desiring to build a tower, does not first, having seated himself, compute the expense, whether he has sufficient resources for its completion, lest perchance, having laid the foundation and not being able to complete it entirely, all who examine it with a view to carefully observing its details should begin to be mocking, saying, This man began building operations and did not have sufficient resources to complete them entirely?

31-35   Or, what king on his way to an open encounter with another king in war, having seated himself, does not first take counsel with himself whether he is able with ten thousand to go to meet the one who is coming against him with twenty thousand? In the event that he does not think himself able to do so, while he is still a great way off, having sent an ambassador, he requests details looking towards peace. Therefore, in the same manner, everyone of you who does not in self-renunciation bid farewell to all his possessions, is not able to be my disciple. Therefore, the salt is excellent in its nature and characteristics, and therefore well adapted to the purpose for which it is in existence. But if also the salt lose its strength and flavor, by what means shall it be restored to its original state? Neither for the land nor for the manure pile is it fit. They throw it outside. He who has ears to be hearing, let him be hearing.

1-7   Now, all the tax collectors and those sinners stained with certain vices and crimes were continually crowding close to Him for the purpose of hearing Him. And the

Pharisees and those learned in the sacred scriptures went to grumbling in a low undertone muttering, conferring secretly with one another and discontentedly complaining, saying, This fellow is giving sinners access to himself and his companionship and is eating with them. And He gave them this illustration, saying, What man of you having one hundred sheep and having lost one of them, does not leave behind the ninety-nine in the pasture and go after the one which has been lost until he finds it? And having found it, he lays it upon his shoulders rejoicing and having come to his home he calls together the friends and the neighbors, saying to them, Rejoice with me, because I found my sheep, the one that was lost. I am saying to you, Thus there shall be joy in heaven over one sinner who repents rather than over ninety-nine righteous persons who are of such a nature that they do not have need of repentance.

Or, what woman having ten silver coins, if she lose **8-10** one, does not light a lamp and sweep the house with a broom and seek carefully until she finds it? And having found it, she calls together her women friends and her women neighbors, saying, Rejoice with me because I found the silver coin which I lost. Thus, I am saying to you, joy arises in the presence of the angels of God over one sinner who repents.

And He said, A certain man had two sons. And the **11-20** younger of them said to the father, Father, give me directly the share of the estate which falls to me. And he distributed to them his wealth. And not many days afterward the younger son, having put all his resources into one lump sum, left his own country to go to a far away place. And there he squandered his resources, living an abandoned, dissolute life. And having squandered all, there came a mighty famine in that country, and he himself began to be in want. And having proceeded, he forced himself upon one of the citizens of that country who was unwilling to hire him and only took him after persistent entreaty. And he sent him into his fields to be feeding hogs. And he was longing to fill his stomach with some of the carob-pods which the hogs were eating. And no one was giving to him. And, having come to his senses, he said, How many employees of my father have more bread than they can eat, and, as for myself, I am perishing here with hunger. Having pulled up stakes, I shall go on my way to my father and I shall say to him, Father, I sinned against heaven and in your sight. No longer am I worthy to be called a son of yours. Make me at once as one of your employees. And, having put things in readiness for his journey, he went to his own father.

20-24 And while he was yet a long distance away, his father saw him and was moved with compassion, and having run, he fell on his neck and tenderly kissed him again and again. And the son said to him, Father, I sinned against heaven and in your sight. No longer am I worthy to be called your son. But the father said to his slaves, Quick. Bring out at once a festive stately robe, one of the best quality, and put it on him. And put at once a ring on his hand and sandals on his feet. And be bringing the calf, that one which we have been fattening for just such an occasion of rejoicing as this. Slaughter it at once, and, having eaten, let us be merry, because this son of mine was dead and has been restored to a correct life. He was lost and has been found. And they began to be merry.

25-30 Now, his son, the elder one, was in the field. And when coming, he drew near the house, and heard music played by a number of musicians in concert, and the sound of people dancing a circular dance on the lawn. And having called to himself one of the servants, he began to inquire what these things might be. And he said to him, Your brother has arrived, and your father slaughtered the calf, that one we have been fattening for just such an occasion of rejoicing as this, because he has gotten him back safe and sound. But he flew into a rage that was the explosive outlet of a long-time resentment against his brother, a resentment that had been smouldering in his breast. And he was not willing to come in. Then his father, having come out, went to pleading with him. And answering he said to his father,

Look. So many years I am slaving for you, and never did I neglect your order. And to me you have never given even a young goat in order that with my friends I might make merry. But when this son of yours, the one who went through your money with harlots, came, you slaughtered for him the fatted calf.

But he said to him, Child, as for you, always with me you are, and all my things are yours. Now, to make merry and to rejoice was a necessity in the nature of the case, because this brother of yours was dead and is alive, and has been lost and has been found.

31, 32

Now He was also saying to the disciples, A certain man was continuing in his employ a manager of his estate, and this man was maliciously accused to him from a hostile source of wasting his possessions. And having called him, he said to him, What is this I hear concerning you? Render an account at once of the way you have been managing my estate, for you cannot any longer function as my manager. Then the estate-manager said within himself, What shall I do, because my master is taking away the position of estate-manager from me? To become one who earns his living by digging, I am not strong enough. To become a beggar I am ashamed. I have it — what I shall do, in order that when I am put out of the position of estate-manager, they may receive me into their own homes. And having called to himself one at a time, each of those who owed his own master money, he went to saying to the first, How much are you owing my master? And he said, One hundred measures of oil. And he said to him, Take at once your contract showing your indebtedness and sit down quickly and write fifty. Then he said to another, Now, as for you, how much are you owing? And he said, One hundred measures of wheat. He says to him, Take at once your contract showing your indebtedness and write eighty. And the master praised the estate-manager whose character was that of one who violates both law and justice with impunity, because he acted shrewdly with his own best interests in mind, this praise being in view of the fact that the sons of the spirit of this age are shrewder

1-13

in their dealings with their own kind than the sons of the light. And, as for myself, I am saying to you, Make for yourselves friends by means of the use of the riches which are the object and desire of the unrighteous world in order that when they [the riches] fail, they [the friends you have made by your generosity] may welcome you into everlasting dwelling-places. He who is faithful in a very little and therefore can be relied upon, is faithful also in much and can be relied upon there. And he who violates law and justice in a very little thing does the same also in regard to much. Since you therefore were not faithful in the use of the riches which are the object and desire of the unrighteous world, who will entrust you with that wealth which is genuine? And in view of the fact that you were not faithful in the use of that which belongs to another person, who will give you that wealth which is your own? Not one household slave is able to keep on rendering a slave's service to two masters, for either the one he will hate and the other he will love, or to one he will hold firmly, and the other he will despise. You are not able to keep on serving God and riches.

14-18   Now the Pharisees, being money lovers, were listening to all these things, and they were turning up the nose and making a hook of it on which to suspend Him as an object of ridicule. And He said to them, As for you, you are those who declare yourselves to be righteous before men. But God knows your hearts, since that which among men is considered to be of an exalted nature is in the sight of God an object of moral and religious nausea and loathing. The law and the prophets were until John. Since that time the good news of the kingdom of God is being proclaimed, and everyone with the utmost earnestness and effort is pressing into it for his share in it. Moreover, it is easier for heaven and earth to perish than for the minutest part of the law to fail. Everyone who dismisses his wife and marries another commits adultery. And he who marries her who has been dismissed from a husband commits adultery.

Now, there was a certain rich man. And he was in **19-21**
the habit of clothing himself in purple and fine linen,
living luxuriously and in magnificent style every day.
And a certain beggar named Lazarus had been flung
down carelessly at his gateway and was still there, full
of ulcerated sores and eagerly desiring to be fed with
those things which fell from time to time from the table
of the rich man. Yes, even the dogs coming, went to
licking his sores.

And it came to pass that the beggar died and was **22-24**
carried off by the angels to become a partaker of blessedness with Abraham in paradise. And the rich man also
died and was entombed. And in the unseen world of
departed human beings, having lifted up his eyes, being
in torments, he sees Abraham afar off, and Lazarus
enjoying the blessedness of paradise with him. And
he himself cried out and said, Father Abraham, be
sympathetic towards my misery and do something for
me at once, and send Lazarus directly in order that he
may dip the tip of his finger in water and cool off my
tongue, because I am in anguish in this flame.

And Abraham said, Child, remember that you received **25-31**
back your good things in your life, and Lazarus likewise
the evil things. But now in this place he is being refreshed and cheered, but as for you, you are in anguish.
And in all these regions, between us and all of you a
chasm, a great one, has been placed permanently in order
that those who desire to cross over hence to you may
not be able to do so, and that they may not pass over
to us from that place. Then he said, I beg you, therefore, father, to send him to the home of my father, for
I have five brethren, in order that he might testify to
them, to the end that they themselves also may not come
into this place of torment. But Abraham says, They
have Moses and the prophets. Let them hear them. But
he said, By no means, father Abraham, but if someone
from those who are dead would come to them, they will
repent. But he said to him, Since Moses and the prophets
they are not hearing, not even if someone out from

amongst those who are dead should arise, will they be persuaded.

1-6   And He said to His disciples, It cannot be admitted that the stumbling blocks will not come. But woe to the person through whose agency they come. It is profitable for him if a millstone is hung around his neck and he has been hurled into the sea, than that he would cause one of these little ones to stumble. Be taking heed to yourselves. If your brother commits an act of sin, reprove him at once. And if he repents, forgive him. And if he commits a sin against you seven times a day, and seven times returns to you saying, I repent, forgive him. And the apostles said to the Lord, Increase our faith. And the Lord said, If you had faith like a grain of mustard seed, you would in that case say to this sycamine tree, Be pulled up by the roots and be planted in the sea, and it would obey you.

7-10   Now, who of you having a slave who is plowing or tending a flock of sheep, who having come out of the field will say to him, Having arrived, go at once and have your meal? But will he not rather say to him, Prepare at once something in order that I may have my dinner, and having properly attired yourself for serving me, wait on me until I eat and drink, and after these things you will eat and drink? He does not thank the slave because he did the things which were commanded, does he? Thus also, as for you, whenever you do all the things which have been commanded you, say, We are slaves who, because we have done nothing more than that which was commanded us, are not deserving of any meritorious mention. We have done that which we ought to have done.

11-19   And it came to pass that as He was proceeding on His way to Jerusalem, He also himself was going through the midst of Samaria and Galilee. And as He was entering a certain village there met Him ten lepers, men, who stood at a distance, and they themselves raised their voice, saying, Jesus, Master, you who have power and authority, be sympathetic with our affliction and do something to help us. And having seen them He said to them, Having gone on your way, show yourselves as proof to the priests. And it came to pass that while they were going, they were cleansed. And one of them, having seen that he was healed, returned with a loud voice, glorifying God, and fell on his face at His feet, expressing his gratitude to Him. And he himself was a Samaritan. And answering, Jesus said, Were not the ten cleansed? But the nine, where are they? Were they not found returning to give glory to God except this foreigner? And He said to him, Having arisen, be going on your way. Your faith has restored your body to soundness of health.

And having been asked by the Pharisees when the **20-27** kingdom of God comes, He answered them and said, The kingdom of God does not come in such a manner that one can carefully observe its approach. Neither shall they say, Look, here or there, for, see, the kingdom of God is in your midst. And He said to the disciples, Days of such a nature shall come when you shall have a passionate longing to see one of the days of the Son of Man and shall not see it. And they shall say to you, Look! There, in that place. Look! Here. Do not follow him as a leader nor run after him, for just as the lightning flashes from one part under heaven and shines to the other part under heaven, so shall the Son of Man be in His day. But first it is necessary in the nature of the case for Him to suffer many things, and after having been put to the test for the purpose of approving Him should He meet the specifications prescribed, to be rejected by this generation because He does not meet its requirements. And just as it was in Noah's days, so it shall be also in the days of the Son of Man. They were eating, they were drinking, they were marrying, they were being given in marriage, until the day when Noah entered the ark. And there came the deluge and destroyed all.

Likewise, it was so in Lot's days. They were eating, **28-37** they were drinking, they were buying, they were selling, they were planting, they were building. But the day on which Lot went out from Sodom, it rained fire and brimstone from heaven and destroyed all the inhabitants. According to the same pattern shall it be on the day when the Son of Man is being revealed. On that day, he who shall be on the housetop and his household possessions in his house, let him not come down to take them away. And he who is in the field, likewise, let him not return to the things which he left behind. Be remembering Lot's wife. Whoever shall seek to preserve his life shall lose it, and whoever shall lose it, shall preserve it alive. I am saying to you, on this night there shall be two in one bed. The one shall be taken and the other shall be left. There shall be two women grinding at the same place. The one shall be taken and the other left. And answering they say to Him, Where, Lord? And He said to them, Where the carcass is, there also the birds which feed on putrefied flesh will be gathered together.

1-8   And He was giving them an illustration which had for its teaching point that it is a necessity in the nature of the case for them at all times to be praying and not to be losing courage, saying, A certain judge there was in a certain city. God he did not fear, and man he did not respect. Now, there was a widow in that city, and she kept on coming to him at recurring intervals, saying, Protect me by an equitable administration of justice from my opponent in a lawsuit. And he kept on being unwilling to do so for a considerable time. However, afterward he said in himself, Although God I do not fear or man respect, at least because this widow is continually furnishing me trouble I will see that justice is done her in order that lest by her continual coming finally she may be assaulting me. And the Lord said, Hear what the unjust judge is saying. And God, shall He not most assuredly accomplish the vindication of His chosen-out ones who are crying aloud to Him day and night, exacting justice in their behalf, even though He is longsuffering in their case [that of the enemies of His chosen-out ones]. I am saying to you, He will exact justice in their behalf speedily. Yet, the Son of Man having come, will He find the aforementioned kind of faith on the earth [a faith which keeps on pleading in prayer such as that exemplified by the persistance of the widow with regard to the judge]?

And He gave this illustration also to certain ones who had come to a settled conclusion as a result of a finished process of persuasive reasoning, that upon the basis of their own worthiness and merit they were righteous individuals, and who utterly despised the rest of mankind. Two men went up to the temple to pray, the one a Pharisee, and the other, a man of a different character, a tax collector. The Pharisee, having assumed a stance, was uttering these things in prayer to himself: O God, I am constantly grateful to you that I am not even as the rest of mankind, extortioners, unjust, adulterers, or even as this fellow, the tax collector. I fast twice a week. I pay a tenth of all my income whatever it might be. But the tax collector having come to a stand at a distance, was unwilling even to lift up his eyes to heaven but kept on beating his breast, saying, O God, justify me the sinner upon the basis of an expiatory sacrifice which satisfies the demands of divine justice and makes possible the just bestowal of righteousness on the basis of justice satisfied. I am saying to you, this man went down to his home having been justified and declared righteous rather than that one, for everyone who exalts himself shall be brought down to the place where he recognizes his moral littleness and guilt. But he who esteems himself small, inasmuch as he is so, and thinks truly, and therefore, humbly of himself, shall be raised to a place of honor.

And they kept on bringing to Him even their infants that He might touch them. Now, the disciples having seen this, kept on rebuking them. But Jesus called them [the infants] to himself, saying, Permit the little children to come to me and stop preventing them, for of such as these is the kingdom of God. Assuredly, I am saying to you, whoever does not receive the kingdom of God in the same manner as a little child does, shall absolutely not enter it.

And a certain ruler put a question to Him saying, Teacher, you who are intrinsically good, by having done what single act shall I inherit life eternal? And Jesus said to him, Why are you calling me intrinsically good? No one is intrinsically good except one, namely, God. The commandments you know. You shall not commit adultery, you shall not commit murder, you shall not steal, you shall not bear false witness. Evaluate your father and mother correctly and treat them with the respect and love which is their due. And he said, These things, all of them I took care not to violate but jealously guarded since my boyhood. And Jesus, having heard this, said to him, There is still one thing you are lacking. All things, as many as you possess, sell at once and distribute immediately to poor people, and you shall have treasure in heaven, and come, take the same road with me that I am traveling. But having heard these things, he became very sad for he was very wealthy. And Jesus having seen him said, How with difficulty are those possessing wealth entering the kingdom of God, for it is easier for a camel to enter and go through the eye of a surgeon's needle than for a wealthy person to enter the kingdom of God. And they who heard, said, And who is able to be saved? And He said, The things impossible with men are possible with God. Then Peter said, Look. As for us, having abandoned all our own private possessions, we became your followers, travelling the same road with you that you are taking. And He said to them, Assuredly, I am saying to you, There is no one who has abandoned house or wife or brethren or parents or children for the sake of the kingdom of God, who will not receive how many times as much at this time, and in the age to come life eternal.

31-34   Then, having taken along with himself the Twelve, He said to them, Behold, we are going up to Jerusalem, and there shall be fulfilled all the things which have been written through the intermediate agency of the prophets and are thus on record with reference to the Son of Man. For He shall be delivered to the Gentiles and shall be mocked and shamefully treated and spit upon, and after scourging Him, they shall put Him to death, and on the third day He shall arise again. And they themselves understood none of these things. And this word was completely hidden from them, and they were not having a comprehension of the things which were being spoken.

Now, it came to pass that as He was nearing Jericho, **35-43**
that a certain blind man was seated at the side of the road,
begging. And having heard the crowd going through he
kept on inquiring what this could be. And they reported
to him, Jesus, the one from Nazareth, is passing by. And
he shouted out at once, saying, Jesus, son of David, look
with sympathy upon my affliction and help me. And
those who were approaching in the front of the procession
went to rebuking him to the effect that he should become quiet. But he himself cried out much more, Son
of David, look with sympathy on my affliction and help
me. And Jesus, having come to a standstill, commanded
him to be brought to Him. And after he had come near,
He asked him, What do you desire that I do for you?
And he said, Lord, that I may see again. And Jesus
said to him, Recover your sight at once. Your faith has
healed you. And immediately he recovered his sight and
began following with Him, glorifying God. And all the
people having seen it, gave praise to God.

And having entered, He was passing through Jericho. **1-10**
And, behold, there was a man called by the name of
Zacchaeus. And he himself was the collector of internal
revenue for the district, having other tax collectors under
his supervision. And he himself was wealthy. And he
was endeavoring to see who Jesus was. And he was not
able to do so because of the crowd, for he was small as
to stature. And having run on ahead, he went up a syca-
more tree in order that he might see Him, because He was
about to pass through that way. And as He came to the
place, Jesus having looked up, said to him, Zacchaeus,
hurry, come down at once, for today at your home it is
a necessity in the nature of the case for me to be a guest.
And he came down in a hurry and welcomed Him as his
guest, rejoicing. And having seen this, they all went to
grumbling in undertone mutterings with one another,
discontentedly complaining, saying that He had gone in to
be the house-guest of a man who was a notorious sinner.
And Zacchaeus, having come to a standstill, said to the
Lord, Behold, half of my possessions, Lord, I now give
at once to the poor. And since I have wrongfully exacted

something from some individual, I now restore at once four times as much. And Jesus said to him, Today salvation came to this home, because he himself is also a son of Abraham, for the Son of Man came to seek and to save that which has been lost.

11-14   And while they were listening to these things, in addition to what has just been said, He gave an illustration because He was near Jerusalem and they supposed that the kingdom of God would immediately make its appearance. He said therefore, A certain man of noble blood and social position, fit for a kingly throne, went off to a distant country to receive for himself a kingdom and to return. And having called his own ten slaves, he gave them ten pounds in money, and said to them, Engage in some business enterprise until I return. But his fellow-citizens hated him and sent after him an accredited governmental representative, saying, We do not desire this man to reign as king over us.

15-27   And it came to pass that on his return after having received the kingdom, he ordered that these slaves be called to him to whom he had given the money, in order that he might come to know who had gained what in his business enterprise. And the first one approached, saying, Master, your pound by having been invested in a business project has earned ten pounds in addition. And he said to him, Well done, you good slave. Because in a small thing you were faithful, be having authority over ten cities. And the second one came saying, Your pound, master, brought in a return of five pounds. And he said to this one, And as for you, be over five cities. And the other came, saying, Master, look, your pound, which I have been holding, waiting for you in a handkerchief. For I have been constantly fearing you because you are an austere man. You are in the habit of appropriating that which you did not deposit and reaping that which you did not sow. He says to him, Out of your mouth I will judge you, pernicious slave. Did you know that I was an austere man, appropriating that which I did not deposit, and reaping that which I did not sow? And why did you not deposit my money with the bank, and I,

having come, would have required it with interest? And
to those who were standing there he said, Take at once
from him the pound and give it to the one who has the
ten pounds. And they said to him, Master, he has ten
pounds. I am saying to you, To everyone who has shall
be given, and from the one who does not have shall be
taken even that which he was. But these enemies of mine
who did not desire that I reign as king over them, bring
here at once and slaughter them before me by slashing
their throats.

And having said these things, He kept on proceeding **28-40**
on His way ahead, ascending the slope to Jerusalem. And
it came to pass as He neared Bethphage and Bethany at
the mount called Olivet, that He sent two of the disciples
on a mission, saying, Be going into the village opposite,
in which as you are entering, you will find a colt securely
tied, upon which no man ever yet sat. And having loosed
it, bring it. And if anyone asks you, Why are you loosing
it? say as follows, The Lord is having need of it.
And having gone off, those who were sent on the mission
found it to be just as He had told them. Now, while
they were untying the colt, its masters said to them,
Why are you untying the colt? And they said, The
Lord is having need of it. And they brought it to Jesus,
and having placed their outer garments upon the colt, they
had Jesus mount it. And as He was proceeding on His
way, they spread their own garments in the road. And
as He was now nearing the descent of the mount of Olivet,
the entire multitude of the disciples began, as they were
rejoicing, to be praising God with a loud voice for all the
miracles demonstrating the power of God which they had
seen, saying, Let the one who comes be eulogized, the
King, in the name of the Lord, in heaven peace, and glory
in the highest. And certain ones of the Pharisees in the
crowd said to Him, Teacher, rebuke your disciples at
once. And answering, He said, I am saying to you, If
these should be silent, the stones will cry out.

And as He came near, having caught sight of the city, **41-48**
He burst into tears, weeping audibly over it, saying, If
you had known in this day, even you, the things tending

toward your peace. But now they have been hidden from your eyes. For there shall come days of such a character upon you when your enemies shall both throw up a rampart before you and encircle you and exert pressure on you from every side. And they shall raze your city to the ground, both you and your children in you, and shall not leave stone upon stone in you, because you did not recognize the strategic, epochal season of God's gracious overseeing care and offer of help. And having gone into the temple, He began to be throwing out those who were selling, saying to them, It has been written and is at present on record, And my house shall be a house of prayer. But as for you, you made it a robber's cave. And He was teaching daily in the temple. And the chief priests and the men learned in the sacred scriptures and the leaders of the people were seeking to destroy Him, and they were not finding the particular thing which they might do, for all the people hearing Him were clinging closely to Him, hanging on His words.

1-8   And it came to pass that on one of the days while He was teaching the people in the temple and proclaiming the good news of the gospel, the chief priests and the men learned in the sacred scriptures with the elders came upon Him suddenly and stood up against Him, and addressed Him, saying to Him, Tell us at once by what sort of authority you are constantly doing these things, or who is the one who gave you this authority? And answering He said to them, As for myself, I also shall ask you concerning a matter, and you tell me at once. The baptism of John, out of heaven was it or did it find its source in men? And they conferred together saying, If we say, Out of heaven, he will say, Why did you not believe him? But if we say, From men as a source, all the people will stone us to death, for they have come to a settled persuasion that John was a prophet. And they answered that they did not know where it originated. And Jesus said to them, As for myself, neither am I telling you by what sort of authority I am doing these things.

9-18   Then He began to be giving to the people this illustration. A man planted a vineyard and let it out as an investment to vine-dressers, and went away to foreign parts for a considerable time. And at the fruit season he sent a slave on a mission to the vine-dressers, in order that they might give him part of the fruit of the vineyard. But the vine-dressers, having given him a thrashing, sent him away empty. In addition to this, he sent another slave. And also that one, having thrashed him and treated him shamefully, they sent away empty. In addition to the foregoing efforts, he sent a third. And also this one, having wounded him, they threw out. Now, the master of the vineyard said, What shall I do? I will send my son, the beloved one. I should think that they will reverence this one. But having seen him, the vine-dressers deliberated with one another, saying, This is the heir. Let us kill him off, in order that the inheritance may become ours. And having thrown him out of the vineyard, they killed him. Therefore, what will the master of the vineyard do to them? He will come and destroy these vine-dressers and will give the vineyard to others. And having heard this they said, May such a thing not occur. And having looked at them with a piercing gaze He said, What then is this which has been written and is at present on record, A stone which the builders put to the test for the purpose of approving should it meet their specifications, and which was rejected because it did not, this became the cornerstone? Everyone who falls upon that stone shall be shattered. But upon whomever it may fall, it will grind him to powder.

And the men learned in the sacred scriptures and the chief priests sought to lay hands on Him that very hour. Yet they feared the people, for they knew that He used this illustration with reference to themselves. And having watched for their opportunity, they sent off on a mission men whom they hired to entrap Him by crafty words, men who would act the part of upright and honest men, in order that they might catch hold of His discourse if they could get a grip anywhere, with the end in view of delivering him to the power and the authority of the governor. And they asked Him, saying, Teacher, we know positively that when you speak and teach you al-   **19-26** ways say the right thing, and that you do not evaluate a person on the basis of his appearance or personality, but in your teaching you are impartial to all. In fact, you teach that course of thought, feeling, and action prescribed and approved by God. Are we permitted to pay a tax to Caesar or not? And having recognized their knavery and cunning craftiness, He said to them, Produce at once a denarius for me. It has whose image and inscription? And they said, Caesar's. And He said to them, Therefore, discharge your obligations to Caesar in the things which belong to him, and to God, in the things which are His. And they were not able to catch hold of His utterance in the presence of the people, and having marvelled at His answer, they lapsed into silence.

27-33   Then certain of the Sadducees having come, being those who declare themselves as against the idea that there is a resurrection, put . a question to Him, saying, Teacher, Moses wrote for us, If a brother of a certain individual die who has a wife, and this man would be childless, his brother should take his wife and produce offspring for his brother. Now there were seven brothers. And the first took a wife and died childless. And the second and the third took her, and in the same manner also the seven, and did not leave children behind, and died. Finally, the woman died also. The woman therefore in the resurrection becomes the wife of which one of them, for the seven had her as wife?

34-38   And Jesus said to them, The sons of this present existence marry and are given in marriage, but those who have been deemed worthy to obtain that age and the resurrection out from among those who are dead, neither marry nor are given in marriage. For neither are they any longer able to die, for they are equal to the angels, and are sons of God, being sons of the resurrection. Now that the dead are raised, even Moses indicated at the bush when he calls the Lord the God of Abraham and the God of Isaac and the God of Jacob. Now God He is, not of dead people but of those who are alive, for all live with respect to Him.

39-44   Then certain of the men learned in the sacred scriptures answering said, Teacher, you spoke excellently; for no longer did they have the daring to be asking Him even one thing. And He said to them, How do they say that the Christ is David's son? for David himself says in the Book of Psalms, The Lord said to my Lord, Be seated at my right hand until I set your enemies down as the footstool of your feet. David therefore calls Him Lord. How yet is He his son?

Then, while all the people were listening, He said to the disciples, Be guarding yourselves against the men learned in the sacred scriptures who take delight in promenading in long stately robes and are fond of deferential greetings in the market places and the exalted places of honor in the synagogues occupied by those of eminent rank or influence such as teachers and judges, and the chief places at banquets, who forcibly expropriate the homes of widows and as a pretense pray long prayers, These shall receive a severer, heavier judgment.   **45-47**

And having looked up He saw those who were throwing their gifts into the treasury, wealthy men. And He saw a certain widow who was in need throwing therein two very small copper coins. And He said, Truly, I am saying to you, this widow who is poor threw in more than all of them, for all these out of their superfluous funds threw in their gifts, but she herself, out of that which she possessed and which did not meet her need in the necessities of life, threw in all that she had with which to sustain life.   **1-4**

And while certain ones were speaking of the temple, that it had been adorned with beautiful stones and gifts consecrated and laid up in it, He said, These things which you are looking at and attentively considering, days shall come of such a nature that in them there shall not be left stone upon stone which shall not be loosened from its place and thrown down. Then they asked Him, saying, Teacher, when therefore shall these things be? And what attesting miracle will indicate when these things are about to take place? And He said, Ever be keeping a watchful eye upon yourselves lest you be led astray, for many shall come in my Name saying, I am he, and, The strategic, epochal time has drawn near and is now present.   **5-11**

Do not begin to go after them. Moreover, whenever you hear of wars, disturbances, and disorders, do not begin to be terrified, for it is a necessity in the nature of the case for these things to take place first. But the end is not immediately. Then He was saying to them, There shall rise nation against nation and kingdom against kingdom. Earthquakes, great ones, and in various places, pestilences and famines there shall be, also things that will terrify, and great attesting miracles from heaven.

12-19   But before all these things, they shall lay their hands on you and persecute you, delivering you to the custody of synagogues and prisons, leading you away for trial, prison, and punishment before kings and governors on account of all that I am in my Person. This will eventuate in your advantage since testimony will be borne to your credit and honor. Resolve once for all therefore in your hearts not to meditate beforehand what legal defense you shall offer with reference to the charges preferred against you, for, as for myself, I shall give you a delivery and wisdom which all those who are putting themselves in opposition to you will not be able to withstand nor refute. And you shall be betrayed both by parents and brethren and relatives and friends. And some of you they shall put to death. And you shall be those who are being continually hated by all because of all that I am. But there shall positively not a hair of your head perish. In the sphere of your steadfastness, constancy, and endurance you shall win for yourselves your lives.

20-24   Now, when you see Jerusalem being encircled by armies, then recognize the fact that its desolation is imminent. Then those in Judaea, let them be fleeing into the mountains, and those in the midst of it, let them be departing out of it, and those in the fields, let them not go into it, because these are days when full justice shall be meted out in order that all the things which stand written may be fulfilled. Woe to those who are pregnant and to those who are nursing their young in those days, for there shall be great distress upon the earth, and wrath upon this people, and they shall fall by the edge of the sword and shall be led away captive into all the nations, and Jerusalem shall be under the heel of the conquering Gentiles until the period of Gentile dominion has run its course.

And there shall be attesting miracles in the realm of the sun and moon and stars, and upon the earth, national distress in the midst of perplexity, sea and billows roaring, men fainting because of fear and expectation of the things that are coming upon the Roman empire [revived], for the natural powers that regulate the heavenly bodies shall be disorganized. And then shall they see the Son of Man coming in a cloud with power and much glory. Now, when these things are beginning to take place, be elated and lift up your heads, because your deliverance is imminent.   **25-28**

And He gave them an illustration. Behold the fig tree and all the trees. When they now put forth their leaves, observing this, you yourselves understand that now the summer is at hand. Thus also as for you. When you see these things taking place, you know that the kingdom of God is imminent. Assuredly I am saying to you, This race shall positively not pass away until all takes place. The heaven and the earth shall pass away, but my words shall positively not pass away.   **29-33**

But be taking heed to yourselves lest at any time your hearts are weighed down with drunken nausea and intoxication and the anxieties pertaining to the affairs of this life, and that day bursts in upon you unexpectedly, for as a snare it shall come upon all those who are living on the face of all the earth. But be circumspect, attentive, ready, in every season being in prayer, in order that you may have sufficient strength to be escaping all these things which are about to take place, and to stand before the Son of Man.   **34-36**

Now, during the days, He was teaching in the temple, but during the nights, going out, He was in the habit of bivouacking in the mount called Olivet. And all the people kept on arising early in the morning and coming to Him in the temple to be hearing Him.   **37, 38**

Now, there was drawing near the feast of bread baked without yeast, which is called Passover. And the chief   **1-6** priests and the men learned in the sacred scriptures were seeking the solution to their problem as to the particular, efficient method of putting Him out of the way, for they were fearing the people. Then Satan entered Judas, the one called Iscariot, who was one among the number constituting the Twelve. And having gone off, he conferred with the chief priests and the captains with reference to the particular method he might use in betraying Him to them. And they were glad and made an agreement with him to give him money. And he promised and went to seeking an opportune time to betray Him to them in the absence of the people.

7-13   Then came the day of bread baked without yeast, during which it was necessary for the paschal lamb to be sacrificed. And He sent off Peter and John on a mission, saying, Having gone on your way, make ready for us the paschal lamb in order that we may eat. And they said to Him, Where do you desire that we make preparations? And He said to them, Behold. After you have entered the city, a man will meet you carrying an earthenware jar of water. Follow him into the house into which he goes. And you shall say to the master of the house, The Teacher says to you, Where is the guest-room where I shall eat the passover with my disciples? And that one will show you a large upper room completely furnished. There make preparations. And having gone off, they found things just as He had told them, and they made ready the passover feast.

14-20   And when the hour came, He reclined at table and the apostles with Him. And He said to them, With an intense desire I desired to eat this passover with you before I suffer, for I say to you, I will positively not any longer eat the same until the time when it is fulfilled in the kingdom of God. And having taken a cup, having given thanks, He said, Take this and divide it among yourselves, for I say to you, I will positively not drink of the product of the vine from this particular moment as characterized by this passover feast until that time when the kingdom of God shall come. And having taken bread, having given thanks, He broke it and gave to them, saying, This is my body which is being given on behalf of you. This keep on doing in my memory. And the cup likewise He took after they had supper, saying, This cup is the testament which is new in quality, constituted so by means of my blood which is being poured out in your behalf.

But behold. The hand of the one now engaged in **21-23** betraying me is with me on the table. For, indeed, the Son of Man is proceeding according to that which has been irrevocably determined. But woe to that man through whose intermediate agency He is being betrayed. And they themselves began to be discussing among themselves which one of them it would be who was about to be doing this.

Now, there arose also an eager contention among them **24-27** as to who of them gave the impression of being greatest. And He said to them, The kings of the Gentiles exercise lordship over them, and those who exercise authority over them are called Benefactors. Now as for you, it is not thus. But he who is greatest among you, let him become as the younger one. And he who exercises the office of leadership, let him become as he who serves. For, who is greater, the one who reclines at the dinner table or the one who serves? Is it not the one who reclines at the dinner table? Now, as for myself, in your midst I am as the one who serves.

Now, as for you, you are those who have remained with **28-30** me through my trials and testings. And as for myself, I am appointing for you a kingdom just as my Father appointed one for me, in order that you may be eating and drinking at my table in my kingdom, and you shall be on thrones judging the twelve tribes of Israel.

Simon, Simon, behold, Satan by asking obtained you **31-34** and your fellow disciples for himself and from my power to his, in order that he may shake you in a sieve as grain is sifted, by an inward agitation, trying your faith to the verge of overthrow. But as for myself, I made petition concerning you that your faith should not be totally eclipsed. And as for you, when you have returned to your original position with respect to your faith, stabilize your brethren. But he said to Him, Lord, with you I am ready to proceed both to prison and to death. And He said, I am saying to you, Peter, a rooster shall not crow this day until three times you will deny that you know me.

35-38   And He said to them, When I sent you off on a mission without a purse and a begging-bag and sandals, you did not lack anything, did you? And they said, Not one thing. And He said to them, But now, he who has a purse, let him take it, likewise also a begging-bag, and he who does not have a sword, let him sell his outer garment and buy one, for I am saying to you that it is a necessity in the nature of the case for this which has been written and is at present on record to be fulfilled in me, namely this, And with violators of the law He was accounted; for indeed the things which have to do with me are at present having a consummation. And they said, Lord, see. Here are two swords. And He said to them, It is sufficient.

39-46   And having gone out, He proceeded according to His custom to the mount of Olivet. And the disciples also followed with Him. And having come to the place, He said to them, Keep continually praying that you will not enter the place where testing will be so severe that it will lead to solicitation to do evil under which you will fall. And He himself tore himself away from them to a distance of about a stone's throw. And having fallen upon His knees, He was praying, saying, Father, if you are willing, remove this cup from me. Nevertheless, not my desire but yours, let it keep on being done. And there appeared to Him an angel from heaven, strengthening Him. And having entered a state of severe mental and emotional struggle to the point of agony, He was praying more earnestly. And His perspiration became like great drops of blood [by reason of the fact that His blood burst through the ruptured walls of the capillaries, the latter caused by His agony, coloring the perspiration and enlarging the drops] continually falling down upon the ground. And having arisen from His prayer, having come to the disciples, He found them sleeping because of their sorrow. And He said to them, Why are you sleeping? Having arisen, be praying in order that you may not enter into a place of testing which would subject you to a solicitation to do evil.

While He was still speaking, behold, a crowd, and the **47-53** one called Judas, one of the Twelve, was proceeding before them, and he drew near to Jesus to kiss Him. And Jesus said to him, Judas, with a kiss are you betraying the Son of Man? And those around Him, having seen that which would follow, said, Lord, shall we strike with the sword? And a certain one of them struck the slave of the chief priest and took off his ear, the right one. And, answering, Jesus said, Be permitting me to do what I wish to do up to this point. And having touched the ear, He healed him. Then Jesus said to the chief priests and captains of the temple and elders who had come to Him, As against a robber did you come forth with swords and cudgels? Daily I was with you in the temple, and you did not stretch out your hands against me. But this is your hour, and this is your delegated authority, and the power of the darkness.

Then having taken Him along, they led Him and **54-62** brought Him into the house of the chief priest. And Peter was following at a distance. And after they had made a good fire in the center of the uncovered courtyard of the house and had seated themselves together, Peter was settling down in their midst. And having seen him seated facing the light, a certain young female slave fixed her searching gaze upon him and said, This man was with him also. But he denied, saying, I do not know Him, woman. And after a little while, another having seen him, said, And as for you, you are one of them. But Peter said, Man, I am not. And about an hour intervening, another certain one asserts confidently, saying, Of a truth, this man also was with him, for indeed he is a Galilaean. But Peter said, Man, I do not know what you are saying. And immediately, while he was still speaking, a rooster crowed. And the Lord having turned around, fixed His gaze on Peter, and Peter remembered the word of the Lord how He said to him, Before a rooster crows, today you shall deny me three times. And having gone outside, he burst into tears and wept audibly and bitterly.

63-65   And the men who were holding Him fast went to mocking Him while they were beating Him. And having blindfolded Him, they were asking Him, saying, Declare by divine revelation who it is who struck you? And many other things, speaking contemptuously and irreverently of God and of sacred things, they were saying to Him.

66-71   And when day dawned, the assembly of the elders of the people, both chief priests and men learned in the sacred scriptures came together and brought Him into their council, saying, As for you, assuming that you are the Christ, tell us. But He said to them, If I tell you, you will positively not believe. And if I put a question to you, you will positively not answer. But from this time forth as characterized by what is taking place right now and in contrast to it, the case shall be as follows: The Son of Man shall be seated on the right hand of the power of God. Then they all said, As for you therefore, you are the Son of God? And to them He said, As for you, you are saying that I am. And they said, What further need do we have of testimony for we ourselves heard it from his mouth?

1-12   And the entire number of them rose up and brought Him to Pilate. And they began to be accusing Him, saying, We found this fellow corrupting our nation and forbidding to pay taxes to Caesar, and saying that he himself is Christ, a king. Then Pilate asked Him, saying, As for you, are you the king of the Jews? And answering him He said, As for you, you are saying it. Then Pilate said to the chief priests and to the crowds, I find not even one thing blameworthy or punishable in this man. But they kept on growing more energetic and emphatic, saying, He is constantly stirring up the people, teaching throughout the whole of Judaea, and beginning with Galilee to this place. Now Pilate, having heard this asked whether the man was a Galilaean. And having come to know that He belonged to Herod's jurisdiction, he sent Him up to

Herod who also himself was in Jerusalem during these days. Now Herod, having seen Jesus, was much pleased, for he was for a considerable time desiring to see Him because of that which he was hearing about Him, and he was hoping to see some attesting miracle performed by Him. Then he kept on putting questions to Him in many words. But He himself answered him not even one thing. Now, the chief priests and the men learned in the sacred scriptures, having maneuvered themselves into position, were vehemently accusing Him. Then Herod with his soldiers, having treated Him with contempt and having mocked Him, threw about Him a brilliant robe, and sent Him back to Pilate. Now, Herod and Pilate became friends with one another that very day, for they had previously lived in a state of continuous enmity towards each other.

And Pilate, having called together the chief priests and **13-24** the rulers and the people, said to them, You brought to me this man as one who is stirring up the people, and behold, as for myself, having examined him thoroughly before you I found in this man not one bit of cause for blame concerning the things of which you brought accusation against him. Yes, moreover, not even Herod, for he sent him back to us. And behold, not even one thing worthy of death has been done by him. Therefore, having disciplined him by scourging, I will release him. But they kept on shouting in concert, saying, Take this fellow away, and release at once to us this Barabbas; who was such that because of a certain insurrection that took place in the city and for murder had been thrown into the prison. Then Pilate again called out to them, desiring to release Jesus. But they kept on calling out, saying, Be crucifying, be crucifying him. Then the third time he said to them, Why? What evil did this man do? Not even one cause of death did I find in him. Therefore, having disciplined him by scourging, I will release him. But they kept on pressing the issue in loud voices, demanding for themselves that He be crucified at once. And their voices began to be prevailing. So Pilate gave sentence that their demand should be put into effect. And he released the one who had been thrown into jail because of insurrection and murder, he whom they were demanding for themselves, and Jesus he handed over to their desire.

25-31   And when they had led Him away, having seized upon a certain Simon, a Cyrenian coming from the farming district, they placed upon him the cross to be carried by him after Jesus. And there was following with Him a large crowd of the people and of women who were beating the breast for grief and were lamenting Him. And Jesus having turned around and facing them said, Daughters of Jerusalem, do not continue weeping for me, but be weeping for yourselves and for your children, because, behold, days of such a character shall come in which they shall say, In a fortunate and goodly state are those who are sterile, and the wombs which did not bare, and the breasts which did not afford nourishment. Then they shall begin to be saying to the mountains, Fall upon us, and to the hills, cover us; because since they are doing these things in a green tree, what shall it be in a dry tree?

32-38   And two others, evil doers, also were being led with Him, to be put out of the way. And when they came to the place called a skull, there they crucified Him and the evildoers, one on the right hand and one on the left. And Jesus was saying, Father, forgive them, for they do not know what they are doing. And distributing His garments among themselves, they cast lots. And the people stood, looking attentively. And the rulers also went to turning up their noses at Him, sneering and scoffing, saying, Others he saved. Let him save himself, assuming that this fellow is the Christ of God, the Chosen One. And the soldiers also, approaching Him, mocked Him, offering Him sour wine and saying, As for you, assuming that you are the king of the Jews, save yourself. And there was also an inscription over Him, THE KING OF THE JEWS — THIS ONE.

39-43   Now, one of the evildoers who was suspended went to railing at Him, As for you, are you not the Christ? Save yourself and us. But answering, the other one rebuking him said, As for you, are you not fearing even God, since you are under the same condemnatory sentence, And as for us, we indeed are justly condemned, for we are receiving that which is befitting the things we did, but this man did nothing out of place. And he was saying to Jesus, Remember me when you come into your kingdom. And He said to him, Assuredly I to you am saying, Today with me you shall be in the paradise.

And it was now about the sixth hour. And a darkness **44-49** came over the whole land until the ninth hour. The sun's light failed, and the curtain of the inner sanctuary was torn into two parts down the center. And Jesus, crying out with a loud voice said, Father, into your hands I entrust my spirit. And having said this, He breathed out His life. Now, the captain of one hundred Roman soldiers having seen this that had taken place, glorified God saying, Truly this man was upright in character. And all the people who had gathered together because of this spectacle, viewing attentively the things that had taken place, beating their breasts for grief, were returning. And all those who knew Him had taken a stand at a distance, also women, the ones who followed with Him from Galilee, to see these things.

And behold, a man, by name, Joseph, being a member **50-56** of the council, a man good at heart and equitable in his dealings, this man had not given his consent to their counsel and deed. He was from Arimathaea, a city of the Jews, one who expectantly looked forward to the kingdom of God. This man, having gone in to Pilate asked as a personal favor for the body of Jesus. And having taken it down, he wound it in linen cloth. And he placed Him in a tomb cut out of stone, where no one had ever yet been lying. And the day was the day in which preparations were made for the coming sabbath. And the sabbath was beginning to dawn. And the women who had followed after, such as had come with Him from Galilee, viewed the tomb with attention and the manner in which the body had been laid. And having returned they prepared aromatics and ointments.

1-12   And during the sabbath they ceased from work according to the commandment, but on the first day of the week, as the dawn was just breaking, they came to the tomb, bearing the aromatics which they had prepared. Then they found the stone rolled away from the tomb, but having entered, they did not find the body of the Lord Jesus. And it came to pass that while they were in a quandary concerning this, behold, two men stood by them in apparel that flashed like lightning. And they having become fear-stricken and bowing their faces to the ground, they said to them, Why are you seeking the One who is living among those who are dead? He is not here. In fact, He was raised up. Remember how He spoke to you while He was yet in Galilee, saying that it was a necessity in the nature of the case for the Son of Man to be delivered into the hands of men who are sinners and be crucified and on the third day to arise again. And they remembered His words, and having returned from the tomb, they brought back tidings of all these things to the Eleven and to the rest. And there were Mary, the Magdalene, and Joanna, and Mary the mother of James: and the rest of the women with them were telling the apostles these things. And these words appeared in their sight as the wild talk of those in delirium or hysteria. And they refused to believe them. Then Peter, having arisen, ran to the tomb. And stooping down with body bent and with head bowed forwards for the purpose of a careful inspection, he sees the strips of linen cloth used for embalming the dead forsaken by the body. And he went off, wondering in himself at that which had come to pass.

13-27   And behold, two of them on that very day were proceeding on their way to a village which was about seven miles from Jerusalem, its name, Emmaus. And they themselves were conversing with one another concerning all these things which had converged upon one another. And it came to pass while they were conversing and discussing, Jesus himself having drawn near, was walking with them as they journeyed along. But their eyes were being restrained from recognizing Him. And He said to them, What are these words which you are tossing to and fro to one another in this animated, heated conversation as you are walking? And they came to a standstill, gloomy-countenanced. And answering, one by the name of Cleopas said to Him, As for you, are you the only temporary resident in Jerusalem and have not come to know about the things which have taken place in it in these days? And He said to them, What sort of things, And they said to Him, The things concerning Jesus of Nazareth, who was a man, a prophet mighty in deed and word in the sight of God and all the people, and how the chief priests and our rulers delivered Him to a judgment of death and crucified Him. But as for us, we were hoping that it was He who was about to be liberating Israel. But also with all these things it is the third day since these things took place. But also certain women of our number amazed us, having come to the tomb very early, and not having found His body, they came, saying that they had also seen an appearance of angels who said that He was living. And certain of those with us went off to the tomb and found it just as also the women had said, but Him they did not see. And He himself said to them, O dull of perception and slow of heart to be believing in all the things which the prophets spoke, was it not necessary in the nature of the case for the Christ to suffer these things and to enter His glory? And beginning from Moses and from all the prophets He interpreted to them in all the scriptures the things concerning himself.

And they drew near the village where they were going, **28-35** and He himself elected to go on. And they constrained Him by entreaties, saying, Stay with us as our guest, because it is toward eventide, and already the day has declined. And He went in with them to be their houseguest. And it came to pass as He was partaking of a meal with them, having taken the bread, He offered thanks, and having broken it, He was giving it back to them. And their eyes were opened, and they recognized Him. And He himself vanished from their sight. And they said to one another, Was not our heart continually burning within us as He was talking with us along the road, as He expounded to us the scriptures? And having arisen that very hour, they returned to Jerusalem, and found the Eleven assembled together and those with them, saying, The Lord was raised in reality and appeared to Simon. And they themselves kept on rehearsing the things along the road and how He was made known to them by the breaking of the bread.

36-45   And while they were saying these things, He himself stepped into their midst and stood there. But having become terrified and affrighted, they kept on thinking that they were seeing a spirit. And He said to them, Why are you in such a state of agitation, and why are reasonings arising in your heart? See my hands and my feet, that it is I myself. Handle me with a view to investigation and see, because a spirit does not have flesh and bones even as you see me having. And while they were yet disbelieving for joy and were wondering, He said to them, Do you have anything here that is eatable? And they handed Him a portion of broiled fish. And having taken it, He ate it in their presence. And He said to them, These are my words which I spoke to you while I was yet with you, that it was a necessity in the nature of the case for all the things which stand written in the law of Moses and in the prophets and psalms concerning me to be fulfilled. Then He opened their mind so that they might understand the scriptures.

46-53   And He said to them, Thus it has been written and is at present on record, that the Christ was to suffer and be raised out from among those who are dead on the third day, and that there is to be preached in His Name repentance with reference to the putting away of sins to all the nations, beginning at Jerusalem. And as for you, you are those who, having seen these things, are to testify concerning them. And behold! As for myself, I am sending forth the promise of my Father upon you. And as for you, you take up your residence in the city until you are endued with power from on high.

And He led them out as far as Bethany. And having lifted up His hands, He blessed them. And it came to pass that while He was blessing them, He withdrew from them. And they themselves returned to Jerusalem with great joy, and were continually in the temple, eulogizing God.

In the beginning the Word was existing. And the Word was in fellowship with God the Father. And the Word was as to His essence absolute deity. This Word was in the beginning in fellowship with God the Father. All things through His intermediate agency came into being, and without Him there came into being not even one thing which has come into existence. In Him life was existing. And this aforementioned life was the light of men. And the light in the darkness is constantly shining. And the darkness did not overwhelm it.

1-5

There suddenly appeared a man upon the human scene, sent off as an ambassador from God's presence, his name, John. This man came as a witness in order that he might bear testimony concerning the light to the end that all might believe through his intermediate agency. That man was not the light. But he came in order that he might bear witness concerning the light.

6-8

He, the aforementioned Word, was the light, the genuine light which enlightens spiritually every man as it comes into the universe. In the universe He was, and the universe through His intermediate agency came into existence, and the world of sinners did not have an experiential knowledge of Him.

9, 10

Into the midst of His own possessions He came, and His uniquely-owned people did not take Him to themselves. But as many as appropriated Him, He gave to them a legal right to become born-ones of God, to those who place their trust in His name, who, not out of a source of bloods, nor even out of a desire of the flesh, nor even out of a desire of a male individual, but out of God were born.

11-13

And the Word, entering a new mode of existence, became flesh, and lived in a tent [His physical body] among us. And we gazed with attentive and careful regard and spiritual perception at His glory, a glory such as that of a uniquely-begotten Son from the Father, full of grace and truth.

14

15-18   John is constantly bearing witness concerning Him and calls out aloud, saying, This One is He concerning whom I said, The One who comes after me was in existence before me because He preceded me, for out of His fulness as a source we all received, and grace in exchange for grace. Because the law through the intermediate agency of Moses was given, the aforementioned grace and the truth came through Jesus Christ. Absolute deity in its essence no one has ever yet seen. God uniquely-begotten, He who is in the bosom of the Father, that One fully explained deity.

19-23   And this is the testimony of John, when the Jews sent off to him on a mission out of Jerusalem, priests and Levites, in order that they might ask him, As for you, who are you? And he made a declaration and did not deny, and declared, As for myself, I am not the Christ. And they asked him, What then? As for you, Elijah, are you? And he says, I am not. The Prophet are you? And he answered, No. They said then to him, Who are you, in order that we may give an answer to those who sent us? What do you say concerning yourself? He said, As for myself, I am a voice of One crying out in the uninhabited region, Make straight the Lord's road, even as Isaiah the prophet said.

24-28   And those who were sent off on the mission were of the Pharisees. And they asked him and said to him, Why then are you baptizing since you are not the Christ, nor even Elijah, nor even the Prophet? John answered them saying, As for myself, I am baptizing by means of water. In your midst there stands He whom you are not knowing, He who comes after me, the thong of whose sandal I am not worthy to unloose. These things in Bethany across the Jordan took place where John was engaged in baptizing.

29-34   On the next day he sees Jesus coming towards him and says, Look! The Lamb of God who takes away the sin of the world. This is He concerning whom I said, After me there comes a Man who was in existence before me because He antedated me. And as for myself, I did not know Him in an absolute way, but in order that He might be made known to Israel, because of this I came baptizing by means of water. And John testified, saying, I have beheld the Spirit descending as a dove out of heaven, and He abode upon Him. And as for myself, I did not know Him in an absolute way. But He who sent me to be baptizing by means of water, that One said to me, Upon whomever you see the Spirit descending and abiding upon Him, this One is He who baptizes by means of the Holy Spirit. And as for myself, I have seen with discernment and have borne witness that this One is the Son of God, and this witness stands.

On the next day again John was standing, and of his **35-39** disciples, two. And having turned his eyes upon Jesus while He was walking about, he says, Look! The Lamb of God. And the two disciples heard him speaking, and they followed with Jesus as His disciples. Then Jesus, having turned around and having looked at them attentively as they were following, says to them, What are you seeking? And they said to Him, Rabbi [which having been interpreted is to say, Teacher], where are you dwelling? He says to them, Be coming and you shall see. They went therefore and saw where He was dwelling, and with Him they dwelt that day. The hour, it was about the tenth.

There was Andrew, the brother of Simon Peter, one **40-46** of the two who heard John speak and followed with Him. This one first finds his own brother Simon and says to him, We have found the Messiah [which is, having been interpreted, the Anointed One, Christ]. He brought him to Jesus. Having turned His eyes upon him, Jesus said, As for you, you are Simon the son of Jonas; as for you, you shall be called Kephas [which being interpreted is, Rock]. On the next day, He was desiring to go forth into Galilee, and He finds Philip. And Jesus says to him, Start following with me, and keep on doing so as a habit of life. Now, Philip was from Bethsaida, out of the city of Andrew and Peter. Philip finds Nathanael and says to him, Him concerning whom Moses wrote in the law, and concerning whom the prophets wrote, we have found, Jesus, son of Joseph, the one from Nazareth. And Nathanael said to him, Out of Nazareth is any good thing able to come? Philip says to him, Be coming and see.

47-51   Jesus saw Nathanael coming to Him and says concerning him, Behold, truly an Israelite, in whom guile does not exist. Nathanael says to Him, From what source do you have an experiential knowledge of me? Answered Jesus and said to him, Before Philip called you, while you were under the fig tree, I saw you. Nathanael answered him, Rabbi, as for you, you are the Son of God. As for you, King you are of Israel. Answered Jesus and said to him, Because I said to you that I saw you down under the fig tree, are you believing? Greater things than these you shall see. And He says to him, Most assuredly, I am saying to you, you shall see heaven opened and the angels of God ascending and descending upon the Son of Man.

1-5   And on the third day a marriage festival took place in Cana of Galilee, and the mother of Jesus was there. Now there were invited also Jesus and His disciples to the marriage festival. And the supply of wine having failed, the mother of Jesus says to Him, Wine they do not have. And Jesus says to her, What is that to me and to you, woman? Not yet has my hour arrived. His mother says to the waiters, Whatever He says to you, do it with dispatch.

6-8   Now, there were standing there stone water jars used for the ritualistic ablutions of the Jews, six of them, holding about eighteen or twenty-seven gallons. Jesus says to them, Fill the water jars at once with water. And they filled them even to the top. And He says to them, Draw it off now and be carrying it to the supervisor of the wedding feast. And they carried it.

9-11   Now, when the supervisor tasted the water which had become wine, and did not know from where it was, but the waiters knew, the ones who had drawn off the water, the supervisor calls the bridegroom and says to him,

Every man first puts out the good wine, and whenever they become satiated, that which is worse. As for you, you have safely guarded the good wine until now. This as a beginning of His attesting miracles Jesus performed in Cana of Galilee and displayed His glory. And His disciples believed on Him.

After this He went down to Capernaum, He himself **12-17** and His mother and brethren, and His disciples. And there they abode not many days. And the Passover Feast of the Jews was about to be observed. And Jesus went up to Jerusalem. And He found seated in the outer courts of the temple those who were in the habit of selling oxen and sheep and doves, and those who for a fee exchanged one type of money for another. And having made a scourge of small cords, all of them He ejected from the outer courts of the temple, also the sheep and the oxen, and poured out the small coins of the money-changers, and their tables He overturned, and to those who were selling the doves, He said, Take these things at once from this place, and stop making the house of my Father a market place. His disciples remembered that it stands written, The zeal of your house shall eat me up.

Then the Jews answered and said to Him, What **18-22** attesting miracle are you permitting us to be seeing, since you are doing these things? Answered Jesus and said to them, You destroy this inner sanctuary, and in three days I will raise it up. Then the Jews said to Him, In forty and six years there was built this sanctuary, and as for you, in three days you will raise it up? But that One was speaking concerning the inner sanctuary, the one which is His body. Then when He was raised up out from among those who are dead, His disciples remembered that this He was saying. And they believed the scripture and the word which Jesus spoke.

Now, when He was in Jerusalem at the Passover **23-25** Feast, many put their trust in His Name, carefully observing with a purposeful interest and a critical and a

discerning eye, His attesting miracles which He was
constantly performing. But Jesus himself was not entrusting himself to them because He possessed an experiential knowledge of all individuals, and because He
was in no need of anyone bearing testimony concerning
the individual person, for He himself was knowing experientially what was in the individual.

1-3   Now, there was a man of the Pharisees, Nicodemus
by name, an outstanding man in authority among the
Jews. This one came to Him in a night-time visit,
and said to him, Rabbi, we know positively that from
God you have come, a teacher; for no one is able to keep
on constantly performing these attesting miracles which
you are constantly performing, except God be with him.
Answered Jesus and said to him, Most assuredly, I am
saying to you, unless a person is born again, that second
birth having the same source as the first one, he is not
able to see the kingdom of God.

4-8   Nicodemus says to Him, How is a man able to be
born, being an old man? He is not able a second time
to enter the womb of his mother and be born, is he?
Answered Jesus, Most assuredly, I am saying to you,
unless a person is born out of water as a source, even
out of the Spirit as a source, he is not able to enter the
kingdom of God. That which has been born out of the
flesh is flesh and by nature, fleshly. And that which has
been born out of the Spirit, is spirit, and by nature,
spiritual. Do not begin to marvel that I said to you,
It is necessary in the nature of the case for all of you
to be born again, that second birth having the same
source as the first one. The wind blows where it desires
to blow. And its sound you hear. But you are not
knowing from where it is coming and where it is going.
So is everyone who has been born out of the Spirit as
a source.

9-11   Answered Nicodemus and said to Him, How are these
things able to come to pass? Answered Jesus and said to
him, As for you, are you the teacher of Israel, and do
not you have an experiential knowledge of these things?

Most assuredly, I am saying to you, that which we are knowing, we are speaking, and that which we have seen with discernment, to that we are bearing testimony, and our testimony all of you are not receiving.

Since I told you concerning the things which have to do with the earth, and you are not believing, how is it possible, if I tell you about the things which have to do with heaven, that you will believe? And no one has ascended into heaven except He who came down out from heaven, the Son of Man.

12, 13

And just as Moses elevated the snake in the uninhabited region, in like manner is it necessary in the nature of the case for the Son of Man to be lifted up, in order that everyone who places his trust in Him may be having life eternal. For in such a manner did God love the world, insomuch that His Son, the uniquely-begotten One, He gave, in order that everyone who places his trust in Him may not perish but may be having life eternal. For God did not send off His Son into the world in order that He might be judging the world, but in order that the world might be saved through Him.

14-17

He who places his trust in Him is not being judged. He who is not believing, has been judged already, and is as a result under judgment, because he has not put his trust in the Name of the uniquely-begotten Son of God, with the result that he is in a state of unbelief. And this is the judgment, that the light has come into the universe and is here, and men loved rather the darkness than the light, for their works were pernicious. For everyone who practices evil things hates the light, and does not come and face up to the light lest his works be effectually rebuked. But he who habitually does the truth comes and faces up to the light in order that his works might be clearly shown to have been produced by God.

18-21

After these things came Jesus and His disciples into the Judaean land. And there He was staying with them and was baptizing. Now, John was also engaged in baptizing in Aenon near Salem, because water, much of

22-24

it, was there. And they kept on coming in a steady procession and were being baptized, for not yet had John been thrown into the prison.

25-36 Then there arose a discussion on the part of John's disciples with a Jew concerning ceremonial purification. And they came to John and said to him, Rabbi, He who was with you across the Jordan, to whom you have borne witness, behold, this One is baptizing and all are going to Him. Answered John and said, A man is not able to be receiving even one thing unless it has been given to him out of heaven. As for you, you yourselves bear me witness that I said, As for myself, I am not the Christ but that I have been sent before that One. He who has the bride is the bridegroom. But the friend of the bridegroom, he who stands and hears him, with joy rejoices because of the voice of the bridegroom. This, therefore, my joy has been fulfilled. It is necessary in the nature of the case for that One to become constantly greater but for me constantly to be made less. He who comes from above is above all. He who is of the earth is of earthly origin and nature, and from the earth as a source he speaks. He who comes from heaven is above all. That which He has seen and heard, to this He bears testimony, and His testimony not even one receives. He who received His testimony has set his seal to this, that God is true, for He whom God sent off on a mission speaks the words of God, for not by measure does He give the Spirit. The Father loves the Son, and all things He has given into His hand. The one who places his trust in the Son has life eternal. But he who refuses to place his trust in the Son, being of such a nature that he refuses to be persuaded, shall not see life, but the wrath of God is abiding on him.

1-9 Then, when the Lord came to know that the Pharisees heard that Jesus was constantly making and baptizing more disciples than John, although Jesus himself was not baptizing but His disciples were, He abruptly went away from Judaea and went off again into Galilee. Now, it was necessary in the nature of the case for Him to be going through Samaria. He comes therefore to a city of Samaria called Sychar, near the small plot of ground which Jacob gave his son Joseph. Now, there was in that place a spring, the one which had belonged to Jacob. Then Jesus, having become wearied to the point of exhaustion by reason of His journey, was sitting thus at the spring. The hour was about the sixth. There comes a woman of Samaria to draw water. Jesus says to her, Give me to drink, for His disciples had gone off into the city in order that they might buy food in the market place. The Samaritan woman then says to Him, How is it that you being a Jew, are asking a drink from me, being a woman of Samaria, for Jews do not associate with Samaritans?

Answered Jesus and said to her, If you knew the **10-14** gratuitous gift of God, and who it is who is saying to you, Give me to drink, you would in that case have asked Him and He would have given to you water which is alive. She says to Him, Sir, you do not have anything with which to draw, and the well is deep. From where therefore do you have this water, this living water? As for you, you are not greater than our father Jacob who gave us the well, and he himself drank from it, and his sons and his cattle, are you? Answered Jesus and said to her, Everyone who keeps on drinking of this water shall thirst again. But whoever takes a drink of the water which I shall give him, shall positively not thirst, no, never, but the water which I shall give him shall become in him a spring of water gushing up into life eternal.

The woman says to Him, Sir, give me this water in **15-19** order that I may not continually be thirsty and keep on coming here to be drawing. He says to her, Be going on your way. Call your husband at once and come here. The woman answered and said, I do not have a husband. Jesus says to her, You aptly said, A husband I do not have, for five men you have had, and now he whom you have is not your husband. This truly you have said. The woman says to Him, Sir, as I am carefully observing you, I am coming to the place where I see that you are a prophet.

20-24   Our fathers in this mountain worshipped. And as for all of you, you all say that in Jerusalem is the place where it is necessary in the nature of the case to be worshipping. Jesus says to her, Be believing me, woman, there comes an hour when neither in this mountain nor in Jerusalem will you all worship the Father. As for you, you all worship that which you are not knowing. As for us, we worship that which we know, for the salvation is from the Jews as a source. But there comes an hour and it is now, when the genuine worshippers shall worship the Father in a spiritual sphere, and in the sphere of truth. For indeed, the Father is seeking such as these who worship Him. God as to His nature is spirit, and for those who are worshipping, it is necessary in the nature of the case to be worshipping in a spiritual sphere, and in the sphere of truth.

25-27   The woman says to Him, I know positively that Messiah comes, the One who is commonly called Christ. Whenever that One comes, He will make known to us all things. Jesus says to her, I am He, the one speaking to you. And at this juncture His disciples came and kept on wondering because with a woman He was speaking. However, no one said, What are you seeking? or, Why are you talking with her?

28-30   Thereupon, the woman abruptly discarded her water jar and went off into the city, and says to the men, Come here. See a man who told me all the things I did. Can this be the Christ? They went out of the city and proceeded in a steady stream toward Him.

31-34   In the meanwhile, His disciples kept on begging Him, saying, Rabbi, eat. But He said to them, As for myself, I have food to eat concerning which you have no knowledge. Then the disciples kept on saying to one another, No one brought Him anything to eat, did he? Jesus says to them, My food is to be doing the will of Him who sent me and to carry His work to completion.

35-38   As for you, are you not saying, There are yet four months and the harvest comes? Behold, I say to you, Lift up your eyes at once, and view attentively the fields, that they are white for harvest. Already the one who is reaping is receiving pay and is gathering together fruit for life eternal, in order that he who is sowing and he who is reaping may be rejoicing together. For in this is this aforementioned saying genuinely true, that there is one who sows and another who reaps. As for myself, I sent you to be reaping that with reference to which you have not labored. Others have labored, and as for you, you have entered into their labor.

Moreover, out of that city many of the Samaritans **39-42** believed on Him because of the report of the woman when she was bearing the following testimony, He told me all things which I did. Therefore, when the Samaritans came to Him, they kept on begging Him to abide with them. And He remained there two days. And many more believed because of His word and kept on saying to the woman, No longer because of your talk are we believing, for we ourselves have heard Him, and we know positively that this one is truly the Saviour of the world.

Now, after the two days He went out from there **43-45** into Galilee, for Jesus himself testified that a prophet in his own country is not correctly evaluated, and is therefore not treated with the respect and deference which is his due. When therefore He came into Galilee, the Galilaeans received Him in a friendly manner, having seen with a discerning eye all things as many as He did in Jerusalem at the feast, for they themselves also went to the feast.

He came then again into Cana of Galilee where He **46-49** made the water wine. And there was a certain one, a king's courtier, whose son was sick with a chronic ailment in Capernaum. This one, having heard that Jesus had come from Judaea into Galilee, went off at once to Him and commenced begging Him to come down at once and heal his son, for he was about to die. Then Jesus said to him, Unless you see attesting miracles and miracles that excite wonder, you will positively not believe. The king's courtier says to Him, Sir, come down at once before my little boy dies.

50-54   Jesus says to him, Be proceeding on your way. Your son is living. The man believed the word which Jesus spoke to him and proceeded on his way. And as he was now going down, his slaves met him, saying that his little boy was living. So he inquired the hour from them during which he was getting better. They said then to him, Yesterday, at the seventh hour the fever left him. Then the father knew that it was during that hour in which Jesus said to him, Your son is living. And he himself believed, and his whole house. Now, this again is a second attesting miracle Jesus performed, having come out of Judaea into Galilee.

1-4.   After these things there was a feast of the Jews, and Jesus went up to Jerusalem. Now, there is at Jerusalem at the sheep gate a pool which is called in Hebrew, Bethesda, having five covered porticoes. In these there was lying down a multitude of infirm people, of blind people, of crippled people, of those, the members of whose bodies were withered, waiting for the stirring up of the water, for an angel from time to time was accustomed to descend into the pool, and he stirred up the water. Then the first one who stepped in after the stirring up of the water was cured of whatever disease had gotten possession of him and was holding him down.

5-9   Now there was there a certain man who had spent thirty-eight years in his infirm condition. Jesus, having seen this one lying prostrate, and knowing that for a long time already he had been in that condition, says to him, Do you have a longing to become well? The man who was infirm answered Him, Sir, a man I do not have in order that whenever the waters are stirred up, he might throw me at once into the pool. But during the time I am coming, another steps down before me. Jesus says to him, Be arising. Snatch up your pallet, and start walking and keep on walking. And immediately the man became well. And he snatched up his pallet and went to walking about.

Now, there was a sabbath on that day. Therefore the Jews kept on saying to the man who had been healed, It is sabbath, and it is not lawful for you to pick up your pallet and carry it. But he answered them, He who made me well, that one said to me, Snatch up your pallet and start walking and keep on walking. They asked him, Who is the man who said to you, Snatch up your pallet and be walking? But the one who was healed did not know who it was, for Jesus had withdrawn, a crowd being in the place. **9-13**

After these things Jesus found him in the temple and said to him, Behold, you have become well. Do not go on sinning any longer lest something worse happen to you. The man went off and told the Jews that it was Jesus who made him well. And on account of this the Jews went to persecuting Jesus, because these things He was doing on the sabbath. But He answered them, My Father keeps on working until now, and as for myself, I also am continually working. On this account therefore the Jews kept on seeking the more to kill Him off, because not only was He continually breaking the sabbath, but also because He was saying that God was His privately owned, unique Father, a Father in a way in which no one else had Him for a Father, making himself equal with the deity. **14-18**

Accordingly, Jesus answered and was saying to them, Most assuredly, I am saying to you, The Son is not able to be doing by himself anything except that which He is seeing the Father doing; for whatever things that One is doing, these things also the Son in like manner is doing. For the Father is fond of the Son and is constantly showing Him all things which He himself is doing. And greater works than these will He show Him in order that you may be marvelling. For even as the Father raises the dead and makes them alive, thus also the Son makes alive whom He desires to. For not even does the Father judge anyone but has given the judgment wholly to the Son, in order that all may be honoring the Son just as they are honoring the Father. He who is not honoring the Son is not honoring the Father who sent Him. **19-23**

24-27 Most assuredly, I am saying to you, He who habitually
hears my word and is believing the One who sent me has
life eternal, and into judgment he does not come, but
has been permanently transferred out from the sphere
of death into the life. Most assuredly, I am saying to
you, There comes an hour and now is, when the dead
shall hear the voice of the Son of God, and those having
heard, shall live. For as the Father has life in himself,
so also He gave to the Son to be having life in himself.
And authority He gave Him to be executing judgment
because He is a son of man.

28-32 Stop marvelling at this, because there comes an hour
in which all who are in the tombs shall hear His voice
and shall come out, those who did the good things to a
resurrection of life, those who practiced the evil things,
to a resurrection of judgment. As for myself, I am not
able to be doing even one thing by myself. Even as I hear,
I judge. And the judgment which is mine is a just one,
because I am not seeking the desire which is mine but the
desire of the One who sent me. If I alone testify concerning myself, [you say] my testimony is not true. There is
another who bears testimony concerning me, and I know
positively that the testimony which He gives concerning
me is true.

33-35 As for you, you have sent men on a mission to John,
and he has borne testimony to the truth. But as for
myself, not from the presence of man am I receiving
testimony. But these things I am speaking in order that
you might be saved. That one was the lamp which burns
and shines, and as for you, you became willing to rejoice
for an hour in his light.

36-38 But, as for myself, I have a witness greater than that
of John, for the works which the Father has given me
in order that I might bring them to a final consummation,
the works themselves which I am constantly performing,
they are bearing witness concerning me to the effect that
the Father has sent me on a mission. And He who sent
me, namely, the Father, that One has borne witness concerning me. Neither His voice have you ever heard
nor His form have you seen. And His word you do not

have abiding in you, because Him whom that One sent
on a mission, this One you are not believing.

You are always searching the scriptures, because, as   **39-44**
for you, you think that in them you are having life eternal.
And those are the ones which testify concerning me. And
yet you do not desire to come to me in order that you
may be having life. Laudation from men I do not accept.
Moreover, I have known you from experience, that the
love of God you do not have in yourselves. As for myself,
I have come in the Name of my Father, and you are not
receiving me. If another comes in his own private name,
that one you will receive. As for you, how are you able
to believe, habitually receiving laudation from one another,
and the praise which is from the presence of the only God
you are not seeking?

Stop thinking that, as for myself, I will bring an accusa-   **45-47**
tion against you before the Father. There is one who
accuses you, Moses, on whom you have placed your hope.
For, had you been believing Moses, in that case you
would have been believing me, for concerning me that
one wrote. But since the writings of that one you are
not believing, how is it possible that you will believe my
words?

After these things Jesus went off to the other side   **1-3**
of the sea of Galilee, of Tiberius. And there followed
with Him a great throng because they had been viewing
with a discerning eye the attesting miracles which He
was performing upon those who were sick. And Jesus
went up into the mountain, and there He was sitting with
His disciples.

And there was near the passover, the feast of the Jews.   **4-7**
Then Jesus, having lifted up His eyes and having looked
attentively at a great crowd coming toward Him, says
to Philip, From what place shall we buy loaves in order
that these may eat? However, this He was saying, putting him to the test, for He himself knew what He was
about to be doing. Answered Him Philip, Loaves worth
two hundred denarii are not sufficient for them in order
that each one might take a little.

8-11   One of His disciples, Andrew, the brother of Simon
Peter, says to Him, There is a little boy here who has
five barley loaves and two small fish. But these things,
what are they among so many? Jesus said, Make the men
sit down. Now there was much grass in the place. Then
the men sat down, the number about five thousand.
Then Jesus took the loaves, and having given thanks, He
distributed them to those who were seated; likewise also
from the fish, as much as they desired.

12-14   Now, when they were satisfied, He says to His disciples,
Gather up the broken pieces which remain over, in order
that nothing be lost. Then they gathered them together,
and they filled twelve wicker baskets with the broken
pieces of the five barley loaves which remained over to
those who had eaten. Then the men, having seen the
attesting miracle which He performed, began to say, This
man is truly the prophet who comes into the world.

15-21   Then Jesus, having perceived that they were about to
come and to be taking Him by force in order that they
might make Him King, withdrew again into the mountain
himself alone. Now, when evening came, His disciples
went down to the sea, and having gone on board a boat,
were going across the sea to Capernaum. And darkness
had already fallen and not yet had Jesus come to them.. The
sea, a great wind blowing, was rising. Then, having rowed
about twenty-five or thirty furlongs, they carefully watch
Jesus walking upon the surface of the sea and coming near
the boat. And they became afraid. But He says to them, It
is I. Stop fearing. Then they began to be willing to
receive Him into the boat. And immediately the boat
was at the land to which they had been going.

22-25   The next day, the crowd which had taken its stand
across the sea and was still standing there, saw that
another little boat was not there, except one, and that Jesus
did not enter the large boat with His disciples, but that His
disciples had gone away alone. Other little boats came
from Tiberius, near the place where they ate the bread
after the Lord had given thanks. When therefore the
crowd saw that Jesus was not there, nor even His disciples, they themselves went into the little boats and came

to Capernaum seeking Jesus. And having found Him across the sea, they said to Him, Rabbi, when have you come here?

Jesus answered them and said, Most assuredly, I am saying to you, You are seeking me, not because you saw attesting miracles, but because you ate of the loaves and were satisfyingly filled. Stop working for the food which perishes, but work for the food which abides for life eternal which the Son of Man will give you, for this One the Father sealed, even God. Then they said to Him, What are we to do as a habit of life in order that we may continually be working the works of God? Answered Jesus and said to them, This is the work of God, that you continually be believing on Him whom that One sent off on a mission.

26-29

They said then to Him, What therefore are you performing as an attesting miracle in order that we may come to see and believe you? What are you working? Our fathers ate the manna in the deserted region, even as it stands written, Bread out of heaven He gave them to eat. Then Jesus said to them, Most assuredly I am saying to you, It was not Moses who has given you the bread out of heaven; but my Father gives you the bread out of heaven, that which is genuine. For the bread of God is He who comes down out of heaven and gives life to the world.

30-33

They said therefore to Him, Lord, ever give us this bread. Jesus said to them, I alone, in contradistinction to all others, am the bread of the life. He who comes to me shall positively not become hungry, and he who places his trust in me shall positively never thirst. But I said to you that you have both seen me, yet are not believing. All that the Father gives to me shall come to me, and the one who comes to me I will positively not throw out into the outside, because I have come down from heaven, not in order that I might continually be doing my will, but the will of Him who sent me. And this is the will of Him who sent me, that all which He has given me I shall not lose anything of it, but shall raise it up on the last day. For this is the will of my Father,

34-40

that everyone who discerningly sees the Son and believes on Him may be having life eternal, and as for myself, I will raise him up at the last day.

41-46   Then the Jews went to grumbling concerning Him, discontentedly complaining in a low, undertone muttering, because He said, I alone am the bread which descended out of heaven. And they kept on saying, Is not this Jesus, the son of Joseph, whose father and mother we know? How now does he say, Out of heaven I have come down? Answered Jesus and said to them, Stop grumbling, conferring with one another secretly in undertone mutterings. No one is able to come to me unless the Father who sent me draw him. And as for myself, I will raise him up on the last day. It stands written in the prophets, And they shall all be those who are instructed by God. Everyone who has heard in the presence of and directly from the Father and has learned, comes to me. Not that anyone has discerningly seen the Father except He who is from the presence of God. This One has with discernment seen the Father.

47-51   Most assuredly I am saying to you, He who believes has life eternal. I alone, in contradistinction to all others, am the bread of the life. Your fathers ate the manna in the deserted region and they died. This is the bread which out of heaven descends, in order that a person may eat of it and not die. I alone am the bread, the living bread which out of heaven came down. If anyone eats of this bread, he shall live forever. And the bread indeed which I shall give is my flesh, given on behalf of the life of the world.

52-59   Therefore the Jews began wrangling with one another, saying, How is this man able to give us his flesh to eat? Then Jesus said to them, Most assuredly I am saying to you, Unless you eat the flesh of the Son of Man and drink His blood, you are not having life in yourselves. He who is eating my flesh and is drinking my blood is having life eternal, and I will raise him up on the last day, for my flesh is true food and my blood is true drink. He who keeps on eating my flesh and drinking my blood, in me is continually abiding and I in him. Even as the living Father sent me on a mission, and I live because of the Father, likewise he who is eating me, that one shall also live because of me. This is the bread which out of heaven descended; not even as the fathers ate and died. He who eats this bread shall live forever. These things He said in the synagogue as He was teaching in Capernaum.

Many of those who had been following His teaching and learning from Him having heard this, then said, Offensive and intolerable is this discourse. Who is able to be hearing it? And Jesus knowing in himself that His pupils were grumbling concerning this, said to them, Does this cause you to disapprove of me and hinder you from acknowledging my authority? What if then you would be seeing with discernment the Son of Man ascending where He was before? The Spirit is He who makes alive. The flesh is not of any use at all. The words which I have spoken to you, spirit are they and life. But there are certain of you who are not believing. For Jesus knew from the beginning who they were who were not believing, and who the one was who was betraying Him. And He was saying, Because of this I have told you that no one is able to come to me unless it has been given to him from the Father. As a result of this many of His pupils went away to the things they had left, and no longer with Him were they ordering their manner of life. **60-66**

Then Jesus said to the Twelve, And as for you, you are not desiring to be going away, are you? Answered Him Simon Peter, Lord, to whom shall we go away? Words of life eternal you have. And as for us, we have believed and still believe and have come to know and still know experientially that you are the Holy One of God. Jesus answered them, Have I not chosen you Twelve? And of you, one is a devil. Now, He was speaking of Judas, son of Simon Iscariot, for this one was on the point of betraying Him, one of the Twelve. **67-71**

And after these things Jesus was walking in Galilee, for He was not desiring in Judaea to be walking because the **1-9**

Jews were seeking to kill Him. Now, there was near
the feast of the Jews, the feast of tabernacles. Therefore, His brethren said to Him, Depart from this place
and, withdrawing yourself, be going away into Judaea in
order that also your pupils might carefully observe your
works which you are constantly doing, for no one is in
the habit of doing anything under cover and he himself is
boldly seeking publicity. Since you are constantly doing
these things, make yourself known to the world. For
not even were His brethren believing on Him. Then
Jesus says to them, My appointed time is not yet here, but
your time is always seasonable. The world is not able
to be hating you. But me it is hating because I alone
am testifying concerning it that its works are pernicious.
As for you, go up to the feast. As for myself, not yet
am I going up to this feast, because my appointed time
has not yet been consummated. And having said these
things to them, He remained in Galilee.

10-13   But when His brethren had gone up to the feast, then
He himself also went up, not publicly, but as it were, in
secret. Therefore, the Jews persistently sought for Him
at the feast and kept on saying, Where is that one? And
wrangling concerning Him there was, much of it, among
the crowds. Some on the one hand kept on saying, He
is a good man. But others on the other hand were saying,
No, but he is leading the crowd astray. However, no one
was talking openly concerning Him because of the fear
of the Jews.

14-18   And the feast being now at its midway point, Jesus
went up into the temple and went to teaching. Then the
Jews began marvelling, saying, How is it possible that
this man has a knowledge of formal education, not having learned, with the result that he is at present unedu-
cated? Then Jesus answered them and said, My teaching
is not mine in origin but belongs to the One who sent me.
If anyone is desiring to be doing His will, he shall know
experientially concerning the teaching, whether it is
out of God as a source or whether I am speaking from
myself as a source. The one who is speaking from himself as a source is seeking his own private glory. But

He who is seeking the glory of the One who sent him, this one is true, and unrighteousness in him is not.

Did not Moses give you the law? And yet not one **19-24** of you is carrying out the law. Why are you seeking to kill me? The crowd answered, You have a demon. Who is seeking to kill you? Answered Jesus and said to them, One work I did and all of you are marvelling. On this account Moses has given you circumcision, not because it is from Moses as a source but from the fathers, and yet on a sabbath you circumcise a man. Since a man receives circumcision on a sabbath in order that the law of Moses might not be broken, are you filled with bitter spleen against me because I made a man completely sound on a sabbath? Stop judging according to external appearance. But be judging the just judgment.

Then certain ones of those living in Jerusalem were **25-29** saying, Is not this one he whom they are seeking to kill? And look! He is speaking openly, and they are saying not even one thing to him. Can it be that those first in authority have come to know of a truth that this one is the Christ? Surely not. But this man, we know positively from where he is. Moreover, the Christ, whenever He comes, no one knows from where He is. Then Jesus spoke with a loud voice while He was teaching in the temple and saying, And yet you know me with a positive knowledge and with the same knowledge you know from where I am. And by my own volition I have not come. But He is genuine, He who sent me, whom, as for you, you do not know. As for myself, I know Him, because from His presence I am, and that One sent me on a mission.

Therefore they were seeking to apprehend Him. Yet **30-34** no one laid his hand upon Him because not yet had His hour come. But many out of the crowd believed on Him and were saying, The Christ, whenever He comes, surely, He will not at all do more attesting miracles than these which this man performed, will He? The Pharisees heard the crowd in an undertone conferring together with reference to these things concerning Him. And the chief priests and the Pharisees sent off officers charged with the responsibility of apprehending Him. Then Jesus said, Yet a little time with you I am, and I withdraw to Him who sent me. You shall seek me and you shall not find me. And where I am you are not able to come.

35, 36   Therefore, the Jews said among themselves, Where is this fellow about to be proceeding that we will not find him? He is not about to go to those dispersed among the Gentiles and to be teaching the Gentiles, is he? What is this word that he said, You shall seek me and shall not find me, and, Where I am, you are not able to come?

37-42   Now, on the last day, the great day of the feast, Jesus was standing, and He shouted out in a loud voice, saying, If anyone is thirsty, let him be coming to me and let him be drinking. He who believes on me, just as the scripture said, rivers out of his inmost being shall flow, of living water. But this He said concerning the Spirit whom those who believed on Him were about to be receiving, for not yet was the Spirit sent, because Jesus was not yet glorified. Certain ones therefore of the crowd, having heard these words, were saying, This man is truly the prophet. Others were saying, This man is the Christ. But some were saying, Why, the Christ does not come out of Galilee, does He? Did not the scripture say that out of the family of David and from Bethlehem, the village where David was, there comes the Christ?

43-52   Therefore, there arose a division in the crowd because of Him. Now, certain ones among them were desiring to apprehend Him. But no one laid hands upon Him. Then the officers came to the chief priests and Pharisees, and those said to them, Why did you not bring him? The officers answered, Never did a man speak in such a manner as this man is speaking. Then the Pharisees answered them, As for you, you also have not been led astray, have you? Not anyone among the rulers believed on him or among the Pharisees, has he? But this crowd which does not know the law is accursed. Nicodemus says to them, the one who came to Him in time past being one of them, Our law does not pass judgment on the man except it hear first from him and know what he is doing, does it? They answered and said to him, As for you, you are not also out of Galilee, are you? Search and see that out of Galilee a prophet does not arise.

And each one proceeded to his home, but Jesus went on His way to the mount of Olivet. But at daybreak He came again into the temple. And all the people kept on coming to Him in a steady stream. And having sat down, He went to teaching them. And the men learned in the sacred scriptures and the Pharisees bring to Him a woman who had been caught in adultery. And having stood her in the midst, they say to Him, Teacher, this woman was caught committing adultery, in the act.   **1-4**

Now, in the law Moses commanded us that such persons should be stoned. Therefore, as for you, what are you saying? But this they were saying, putting Him to the test, in order that they might be having ground upon which to be accusing Him. But Jesus, having stooped down, with His finger wrote on the ground. And while they were remaining, continuing to ask Him, having raised himself up, He said to them, He who is sinless among you, let him be the first to throw the stone upon her. And again having stooped down, He wrote on the ground. And they having heard and being convicted by their conscience began going out, one by one, starting with the eldest ones until the last ones. And Jesus was left behind alone and the woman standing in the midst. And Jesus, having raised himself up, and seeing no one except the woman, said to her, Woman, where are those accusers of yours? Did not one condemn you? And she said, Not one Sir. And Jesus said to her, As for myself, neither do I condemn you. Be proceeding and no longer go on sinning.   **5-11**

Then Jesus spoke again to them, saying, I alone, in contradistinction to all others, am the light of the world. He who habitually follows with me shall positively not order his behavior in the sphere of the darkness, but shall possess the light of the life. Then the Pharisees said to Him, As for you, you are bearing testimony concerning   **12-20**

yourself. Your testimony is not true. Answered Jesus
and said to them, Even if I am bearing testimony concerning myself, my testimony is true, because I know with
an absolute knowledge from where I came and where I
am departing. But as for you, you do not know from
where I come nor where I am going. As for you, according to the flesh you are in the habit of judging. As
for myself, I judge no one. And if indeed I am passing
judgment, the judgment which is mine is genuine, because
I am not alone, but I and He who sent me. And in the
law indeed which is yours, it stands written that the
testimony of two men is true. I am the One who bears
testimony concerning myself, and there testifies concerning me He who sent me, the Father. Then they were
saying to Him, Where is your father? Answered Jesus,
Neither do you know me nor my Father. If you had
known me, in that case also my Father you would have
known. These words He spoke in the treasury while
teaching in the temple. And no one laid hands on Him
because not yet had His hour come.

21-30   Therefore again He said to them, I will withdraw
and you shall seek me, and in your sin you shall die.
Where I am departing, as for you, you are not able to
come. Then the Jews were saying, Surely, he will not
by any chance kill himself, will he, because he is saying,
Where I am departing, you are not able to come? And
He was saying to them, As for you, from beneath you
are. As for myself, from above I am. As for you, of
this world you are. As for myself, I am not of this
world. Therefore I said to you, You shall die in your
sins, for if you do not believe that I AM, you shall die
in your sins. Therefore they were saying to Him, As for
you, who are you? Jesus said to them, I am essentially
that which I also am telling you. I have many things
to be saying and to be judging concerning you. But He
who sent me is true, and as for myself, the things which
I heard directly from Him, these things I am speaking
to the world. They did not understand that He was
speaking to them concerning the Father. Then Jesus
said, Whenever you lift up the Son of Man, then you

shall come to perceive that I AM, and that of myself I
do nothing, but even as the Father taught me, these things
I am speaking. And He who sent me is with me. He
did not leave me alone because I always am doing the
things that are pleasing to Him. While He was saying
these things many believed on Him.

Then Jesus was saying to the Jews who, having believed Him, were at the moment maintaining that attitude
of faith, As for you, if you remain in the word which is
mine, truly, my disciples you are. And you shall know
the truth in an experiential way, and the truth shall make
you free. They answered Him, Offspring of Abraham we
are, and we have never yet been in bondage to anyone.
How is it that you are saying, You shall become those
who are free? Answered them Jesus, Most assuredly,
I am saying to you, Everyone who habitually commits
sin is a slave of sin. But the slave does not abide in
the house forever. The Son abides forever. If therefore
the Son make you free, you shall be free individuals in
reality.

31-36

I know that you are Abraham's offspring. But you are
seeking to kill me, because the word which is mine is
not having free course in you. The things which I have
seen in the presence of my Father I am speaking. And
as for you, therefore, the things which you heard in the
presence of your father, you are doing. They answered
and said to Him, Our Father is Abraham. Jesus says
to them, If you were, according to your assumption,
children of Abraham, the works of Abraham you would
be doing. But now you are seeking to kill me, a man
who has spoken the truth to you which I heard from God.
This did not Abraham. As for you, you are doing the
works of your father. They said to Him, As for us, we
were not born of fornication. One Father we have,
God. Jesus said to them, If God had been your Father,
in that case you would have loved me, for I came forth
from God and am here, for I have not come of myself,
but that One sent me on a mission.

37-42

Why do you not understand the mode of speech which
is mine? Because you are not able to be hearing the

43-47

word which is mine. As for you, out from your father, the devil, you are, and the passionate cravings of your father you are desiring to be doing. That one was a manslayer from the beginning, and in the truth he did not maintain his standing, because truth does not exist in him. Whenever he is speaking the lie, out of the things which are his own private possessions he is speaking, because a liar he is and the father of it. But as for myself, because I am speaking the truth, you are not believing me. Who of you convicts me of sin? Since I am speaking truth, why are you not believing me? The one who is of God hears the words of God. On this account you are not hearing them, because you are not of God.

48-53   Answered the Jews and said to Him, Are we not expressing it beautifully when we say that you are a Samaritan, and that you have a demon? Jesus answered, As for myself, I do not have a demon, but I honor my Father, and as for you, you are dishonoring me. Moreover, I am not seeking my glory. There is One who seeks and judges. Most assuredly, I am saying to you, If anyone keeps my word, death he will never, positively not, look at with interest and attention. The Jews said to Him, Having come to know it perfectly before, we are now confirmed in our opinion that you have a demon. Abraham died, and the prophets. And as for you, you are saying, If a person keeps my word, he shall never, positively not, taste of death. As for you, you are not greater than our father Abraham who was such that he died, are you? And the prophets died. Whom are you making yourself?

54-59   Answered Jesus, If I glorify myself, my glory is nothing. There is my Father who glorifies me, concerning whom you are saying, He is our God. And you have not known Him in an experiential way, and do not know Him at present. But I know Him. And if I say that I do not know Him, I shall be like you, a liar. But I know Him, and His word I am keeping. Abraham, your father, rejoiced to see the day which is mine, and he saw it and was glad. Then the Jews said to Him, You are not yet fifty years old, and Abraham you have seen? Jesus said to them, Most assuredly I am saying to you, Before Abraham came into existence I AM. Then they took up stones to throw at Him. But Jesus hid himself and went out of the temple.

And passing by, He saw a man whose blindness originated from his birth. And His disciples asked Him, saying, Rabbi, who sinned, this man or his parents, with the result that he was born blind? Answered Jesus, Neither this man sinned nor his parents, but he was born blind in order that there might be openly shown the works of God in him. As for us, it is a necessity in the nature of the case for us to be doing the works of Him who sent me as long as it is day. There comes night when no one is able to be working. When I am in the world, I am to light the world.   **1-5**

Having said these things, He spat on the ground and made clay of the saliva, and placed the clay upon his eyes, and said to him, Be departing, wash in the pool of Siloam [which being interpreted means, having been sent off on a mission]. Therefore he went off and washed and came seeing. Therefore the neighbors and those who had formerly observed him carefully that he was a beggar were saying, Is not this man the one who customarily sat and begged? Some were saying, This is he. Others were saying, By no means, but he is like him. That one kept on saying, I am he. Then they began saying to him, How then were your eyes opened? That one answered, The man who is called Jesus made clay and spread it upon my eyes and said to me, Be departing to Siloam and wash. Therefore having gone off and having washed, I received my sight. And they said to him, Where is that man? He says, I do not know.   **6-12**

They bring him to the Pharisees, the once-blind man. Now, there was a sabbath on the day that Jesus made the clay and opened his eyes. Therefore the Pharisees again went to questioning him with reference to how he had received his sight. He said to them, He placed clay upon my eyes, and I washed, and I am seeing. Therefore certain of the Pharisees also were saying, This man is not   **13-17**

from God because he is not keeping the sabbath. Others
were saying, How is a man, a sinner, able to be performing
such attesting miracles as these? And there was a
division among them. Therefore they say to the blind
man again, As for you, what do you say concerning him
in view of the fact that he opened your eyes? And he
said, He is a prophet.

18-23   However, the Jews did not believe concerning him
that he was blind and had received his sight until which
time they called the parents of the man himself who had
received his sight, and they asked them saying, This
man, is he your son whom you say was born blind? How
then does he now see? Then his parents answered and
said, We know positively that this is our son and that
he was born blind. But how he now sees, we do not
know positively, or who opened his eyes we do not know
positively. Ask him. He has attained maturity. He
himself will speak in behalf of himself. These things said
his parents because they were fearing the Jews. For already the Jews had formed a compact to the effect that
if anyone should confess him as Christ, he would become
one who is excluded from the synagogue. Because of
this his parents said, He has attained maturity. Inquire
of him.

24-29   Then they called the man a second time who had been
blind and said to him, Give glory to God. As for us,
we know positively that this man is a sinner. Then that
one answered, Whether he is a sinner I do not know
positively. One thing I know positively. Having been
blind, now I am seeing. Then they said to him, What did
he do to you? How did he open your eyes? He answered
them, I told you already, and you did not hear. Why do
you desire again to be hearing it? As for you, you would
not also desire to become his disciples, would you? And
they railed upon him harshly with a scornful insolence
and said, As for you, a disciple you are of that fellow.
But as for us, of Moses we are disciples. As for us, we
know positively that God has spoken to Moses, but this
fellow, we do not know from where he is.

The man answered and said to them, Why, in this very
thing is the wonder, that you do not know from where
he is, and yet he opened my eyes. We know positively
that God does not hear sinners but if anyone be a wor-
shipper of God and His will is habitually doing, this
one He hears. From of old it has not been heard that
anyone opened the eyes of one who has been born blind.
Assuming that this man was not from God, he would not
be able to be doing anything. They answered and said
to him, As for you, in sins you were born, the whole of
you, and are you teaching us? And they threw him outside. Jesus heard that they had thrown him outside,
and having found him, He said, As for you, do you
believe on the Son of Man? Answered that one and said,
And who is he, Sir, in order that I may believe on him?
Jesus said to him, You have both seen Him and the One
talking with you, that One is He. And he said, I believe,
Lord. And he worshipped Him. And Jesus said, With
a view to judgment into this world I came, in order
that those who are not seeing may be seeing, and those
who are seeing might become those who are blind. Those
of the Pharisees who were with Him heard these things
and said to Him, We also are not blind ones, are we?
Jesus said to them, If you were blind ones, you would
in that case not have had sin. But now you are saying,
We are seeing. Your sin remains.

Most assuredly, I am saying to you, He who does not
go through the door into the walled-in enclosure for the
sheep, but climbs up from some other quarter, that one
is a thief and a robber. But he who enters through the
door is a shepherd of the sheep. To this one the doorkeeper opens. And the sheep hear his voice, and he
personally calls the sheep which are his private possession
by name and leads them out. Whenever he puts forth
all who are his very own, before them he proceeds, and
the sheep follow with him because they know his voice.
But one belonging to another flock they will positively not
follow, but will run away from him because they do not
know the voice of the others.

6-10   This illustration Jesus gave them. But those did not
understand what things they were which He was speaking
to them. Therefore Jesus said again, Most assuredly, I
am saying to you, I alone, in contradistinction to all
others, am the door belonging to the sheep. All, as many
as came before me, are thieves and robbers. But the sheep
did not listen to them. I alone am the door. By means
of me, if anyone enters, he shall be saved, and shall go in
and shall go out and shall find food. The thief does not
come except to steal and to kill and to destroy. I alone
came in order that they might be possessing life, and
that they might be possessing it in superabundance.

11-18   I alone am the shepherd, the good one. The shepherd,
the good one, lays down his life on behalf of and instead
of the sheep. The one who is a paid helper and not a
shepherd, whose very own the sheep are not, watches with
a discerning eye the wolf as he is coming, and sends away
the sheep and flees, because he is a paid helper and it is
not a concern to him regarding the sheep, and the wolf
snatches them and scatters them. I alone am the shepherd,
the good one. And I know by experience those that are
mine, and those that are mine know me by experience, just
as the Father knows me and I know the Father. And my
life I lay down on behalf of and instead of the sheep. And
other sheep I have which are not of this sheepfold. Those
also it is necessary in the nature of the case for me to lead,
and my voice they shall listen to, and there shall come
to be one flock, one shepherd. On this account my Father
loves me, because I lay down my life in order that again
I might take it. No one takes it from me, but I lay it
down myself. Authority I have to lay it down, and
authority I have again to take it. This commandment I
received from my Father.

19-21   A division again arose among the Jews because of these
words. And many of them were saying, A demon he has
and is raving mad. Why are you listening to him?
Others were saying, These words are not the words of
one demonized. A demon is not able to open eyes of
blind people, is he?

At that time there occurred the feast of the dedication **22-26** in Jerusalem. It was winter. And Jesus was walking around in the temple in the covered colonnade of Solomon. Then the Jews encircled Him and were saying to Him, How long are you holding us in suspense? As for you, assuming that you are the Christ, tell us plainly. Answered them Jesus, I told you and you are not believing. The works which I am constantly doing in the Name of my Father, these are bearing testimony concerning me. But as for you, you are not believing because you are not of the sheep which are mine.

The sheep which are mine are in the habit of listening **27-33** to my voice, and I know them by experience, and they take the same road that I take with me, and I give to them life eternal. And they shall positively not perish, never. And no one will snatch them by force out of my hand. My Father who gave them to me as a permanent gift is greater than all. And no one is able to be snatching them by force out of the hand of my Father. I and the Father are one in essence. Again the Jews picked up stones and brought them in order that they might stone Him. Jesus answered them, Many works I showed you as evidence, beautiful, noble works, from my Father. What is the character of that particular work among these on account of which you are purposing to stone me? The Jews answered Him, For a noble work we are not purposing to stone you, but for blasphemy, and because you, being a human being, are deifying yourself.

Jesus answered them, Does it not stand written in your **34-39** law, I said, You are gods? Since He called those gods to whom the word of God came — and the scripture is unable to be broken — concerning Him whom the Father consecrated and sent on a mission into the world, are you saying, You are blaspheming, because I said, By nature, Son of God I am? Assuming that I am not doing the works of my Father, stop believing me. But since I am doing the works, even if you are not believing me, the works be believing, in order that you may come to know by experience and continue knowing that in me the Father is and I in the Father. Thereupon they kept on seeking again to seize Him. And He went forth out of their hand.

40-42. And He went off again to the other side of the Jordan to the place where John at the first was baptizing. And He was dwelling there. And many came to Him and were saying, John did not perform even one attesting miracle. But all things, as many as John spoke concerning this one, were true. And many believed in Him there.

1-4 Now, there was a certain one sick, Lazarus from Bethany, from the village of Mary and Martha, her sister. Now, it was Mary, she who anointed the Lord with ointment and who wiped dry His feet with her hair, whose brother Lazarus was sick. Therefore, the sisters sent word to Him saying, Lord, behold, he of whom you are fond is sick. And Jesus, having heard, said, This sickness is not with reference to death but for the sake of the glory of God, in order that the Son of God might be glorified through it.

5-10 Now Jesus was loving Martha and her sister and Lazarus with a love divine in its essence and self-sacrificial in its nature. Therefore, when He heard that he was ill, at that time He remained in the place where He was, two days. Then after this He says to the disciples, Let us be going into Judaea again. The disciples say to Him, Rabbi, the Jews were but now seeking to stone you, and again are you going there? Answered Jesus, Are there not twelve hours of daytime? If a person is walking about in the day he does not stumble because the light of this world he sees. But if a person is walking about in the night, he stumbles, because the light just mentioned is not in him.

11-16 These things He said, and after this He says to them, Lazarus, our friend, has fallen asleep. But I am setting out in order that I may awaken him. Then the disciples said to Him, Lord, since he has fallen asleep he will recover. However, Jesus had spoken of his death. But those supposed that He was speaking of taking rest in sleep. Then therefore Jesus said to them plainly, Lazarus died. And I am rejoicing for your sakes that I was not there, in order that you may believe. But let us be going to him. Then Thomas, the one commonly called the twin, said to his fellow-disciples, Let us also be going in order that we may die with Him.

Then Jesus, having come, found that he had been already four days in the tomb. Now, Bethany was near Jerusalem, about two miles. And many of the Jews had come to Martha and Mary in order to console them concerning their brother. Then Martha, when she heard that Jesus is coming went and met Him. But Mary kept on sitting in the house. Then Martha said to Jesus, Lord, if you had been here, my brother in that case would not have died. And now I know positively that whatever you may ask God, God will give it to you. Jesus says to her, Your brother will arise. Martha says to Him, I know of a surety that he will arise in the resurrection on the last day. Jesus said to her, I myself am the resurrection and the life. He who believes in me, even if he die, shall live. And everyone who lives and believes on me shall positively never die. Do you believe this? She says to Him, Yes, Lord, as for myself, I have believed and do so now that you are the Christ, the Son of God, He who comes into this world. And having said this, she went off and secretly called Mary, her sister, saying, The Teacher is present and is calling for you. Now, when that one heard, she arises quickly and went on her way to Him. **17-29**

Now, Jesus had not yet come into the village, but was still in the place where Martha met Him. Therefore the Jews, those who were with her in the house and were consoling her, having seen Mary that she had arisen quickly and had gone out, followed her, supposing that she was going to the tomb in order to weep there. Then Mary, when she came where Jesus was, having seen Him, fell at His feet, saying to Him, Lord, if you had been here, in that case my brother would not have died. Then Jesus, when He saw her weeping audibly and the Jews who had come with her, weeping audibly, was moved with indignation in His spirit, and deeply **30-37** troubled himself, and said, Where have you laid him? They say to Him, Lord, be coming and see. Jesus burst into tears and wept silently. Then the Jews were saying, Behold, how fond He was of him. But certain ones of them said, Was not this man able, who opened the eyes of the one who was blind, to have caused that even this one should not die?

38-45   Jesus again moved with indignation in himself comes to the tomb. Now, it was a cave, and a stone was lying upon it. Jesus says, Remove the stone at once. The sister of the one who had died, Martha, says to Him, Lord, already there is an offensive odor, for it is four days. Jesus says to her, Did I not say to you that if you would believe, you will see the glory of God? Then they lifted up the stone and took it away. And Jesus lifted up His eyes and said, Father, I thank you because you heard me. Moreover, I knew positively that you always hear me. But on account of the crowd which is standing around, I spoke, in order that they may come to believe that you sent me on a mission. And having said these things, He shouted with a great voice, Lazarus, here, out. There came out the dead man, bound securely as to his feet and his hands with swathing-bands. And his face was bound around with a handkerchief. Jesus says to them, Untie him at once and permit him to be departing. Therefore, many of the Jews, those who had come to Mary and had viewed attentively that which He did, believed in Him.

46-53   But certain ones among them went off to the Pharisees and told them the things which Jesus did. Therefore the chief priests and the Pharisees convoked a council, and were saying, What are we doing, for this man is performing many attesting miracles? If we disregard him in this manner, all will believe in him, and the Romans will come and take away both our place and our nation. But a certain one of them, Caiaphas, being chief priest that year, said to them, As for you, you do not know even one thing, nor do you take into account the fact that it is to your interest that one man die on behalf of the people and that not the whole nation be destroyed.

But this from himself as a source he did not speak, but being chief priest that year he predicted that Jesus was about to be dying on behalf of the nation, and not on behalf of the nation only, but in order that also the children of God which have been scattered abroad He might gather together into one. Therefore from that day they took counsel together to be killing Him off.

Therefore Jesus no longer walked about openly among the Jews, but went off from there into the country near the uninhabited region, to a city called Ephraim, and there He dwelt with His disciples. Now, there was near the passover of the Jews, and many went up to Jerusalem out of the country before the passover in order that they might ceremonially purify themselves. Then they went to seeking Jesus, and were conversing with one another as they stood in the temple, What do you think? He certainly will not come to the feast, will he? Now, the chief priests and the Pharisees had given commandments to the effect that if anyone knows where He is, he should make it known in order that they might apprehend Him. **54-57**

Now Jesus, six days before the passover came to Bethany where Lazarus was, whom Jesus raised out from among the dead. So they made Him there a meal at eventide, supper. And Martha was serving, but Lazarus was one of those who were at the table with Him. Then Mary, having taken a pound of nard ointment, unadulterated, very valuable, spread it on the feet of Jesus, rubbed it in, and dried His feet with her hair. And the house was filled with the aroma of the ointment. **1-3**

Then Judas, the Iscariot, one of His disciples, the one who was about to be betraying Him, says, Why was not this ointment sold for three hundred denarii and given to poor people? But he said this, not because he was concerned about the poor, but because he was a pilferer, and holding the purse, purloined the things thrown in. Then Jesus said, Let her alone. It was in order that with a view to the day of the preparation of my body for entombment she might take care of it, for the poor always you have with you, but me you do not always have. **4-8**

9-11   Then the common people among the Jews learned that
He was there, and they came, not only because of Jesus,
but also in order that they might see Lazarus whom He
raised out from among the dead. But the chief priests took
counsel to kill Lazarus also, since many of the Jews
because of him went away and were believing in Jesus.

12-19   The next day the common people who came to the
feast, having heard that Jesus is coming into Jerusalem,
took the branches of the palm trees and went out with a
view to meeting Him. And they kept on shouting, Save
now. Let Him who comes in the name of the Lord, the
One who in times past has been eulogized, be regarded
as such at present, even the King of Israel. And Jesus,
having found a young donkey, sat upon it, even as it stands
written, Stop fearing, daughter of Sion. Behold, your
King is coming, seated upon a donkey's colt. These
things His disciples did not understand at the first, but
when Jesus was glorified, then they remembered that
these things had been written of Him and were on record,
and that these things they did to Him. Then the crowd
which was with Him when He called Lazarus out from
the tomb and raised him out from among the dead kept
on bearing testimony. On this account also the crowd
went and met Him, because they heard that He had performed this attesting miracle. Therefore the Pharisees
said to one another, Be considering that you are not doing
even one thing that would be of help to us. Look! The
world went away after him.

20-28   Now, there were some among those who went up,
Greeks, for the purpose of worshipping at the feast.
Then these went to Philip, the one from Bethsaida of
Galilee, and they were requesting him, saying, Sir, we
are desiring to see Jesus. Philip goes and tells Andrew.
Andrew goes and Philip, and they tell Jesus. And Jesus
answers them, saying, The hour has come and is here
in order that the Son of Man be glorified. Most assuredly,
I am saying to you, unless the grain of wheat, having fallen
into the earth, die, it itself remains alone. But if it die,
much fruit it bears. He who is fond of his soul-life, is
losing it. And he who is hating his soul-life in the sphere

of this world with a view to life eternal, is preserving it safe and unimpaired. If anyone habitually serves me, let him as a habit of life keep on following with me, and where I am, there also the servant who is mine shall be. If anyone is serving me, him will the Father honor. Now has my soul been troubled, with the result that it is in a state of agitation. And what shall I say? — Father, save me [in and through and] out of this hour. Certainly, on account of this I came to this hour. Father, glorify your Name.

Then there came a voice out of heaven, I both glorified it and will again glorify it. Then the crowd, the one standing by and hearing, was saying, Thunder has come to pass. Others were saying, An angel has spoken to him. Answered Jesus and said, Not on my account has this voice come, but for your sakes. Now is a judgment of this world. Now the ruler of this world will be thrown out, clean out. And as for myself, when I am lifted up out from underneath the earth, all men I will draw to myself. And this He was saying, indicating what sort of death He was about to be dying. Then the crowd answered Him, As for us, we heard out of the law that the Christ lives forever. And how is it that you are saying, It is a necessity in the nature of the case for the Son of Man to be lifted up? Who is this Son of Man? Therefore Jesus said to them, Yet a little time the light is among you. Be ordering your behavior according as you are having the light, in order that darkness may not overtake you. Indeed, he who is ordering his behavior within the sphere of the darkness just mentioned, does not know where he is departing. According as you are having the aforementioned light, be believing in the light in order that you may become sons of light. These things Jesus spoke, and having gone off, He was hidden from them. **28-36**

But in spite of the fact that He had performed so many attesting miracles before them, they kept on not believing on Him, in order that the word of Isaiah the prophet might be fulfilled who said, Lord, who believed our preaching? And the Lord's power, to whom was it revealed? On account of this they were not able to be believing, **37-43**

because again said Isaiah, He has blinded their eyes
with the present result that they are still blind, and He
hardened their heart, in order that they might not see
with their eyes and perceive with the heart and change
their mind and I should heal them.   These things said
Isaiah because he saw His glory, and he spoke concerning Him.   Yet, nevertheless, even from among the rulers
many believed on Him, but because of the Pharisees
they kept on not confessing in order that they might not
become those excluded from the synagogue, for they
deemed precious the good opinion of men rather than the
good opinion of God.

44-50   And Jesus called out aloud and said, He who believes
on me does not believe on me but on Him who sent me.
And he who is contemplating me with discernment, is
contemplating with discernment Him who sent me.   I,
in contradistinction to all others, have come a light into
the world, in order that everyone who places his trust
in me may not remain in the sphere of the darkness.
And if anyone hears my words and does not keep them,
I am not judging him, for I did not come to be judging
the world but in order that I might save the world.   He
who rejects me and does not receive my words has the
One who judges him.   The word which I spoke, that
will judge him on the last day, because, as for myself,
not from myself as a source did I speak, but He who sent
me, the Father himself, has given me a commandment
what I should say and what I should speak.   And I know
with a positive knowledge that His commandment is life
eternal.   Therefore, the things which I am speaking,
just as the Father has spoken to me, thus do I speak.

1-4   Now, before the feast of the passover, Jesus, since He
knew that His hour had come the purpose of which was
that He should pass over out of this world to the Father,
having loved with a divine, self-sacrificial love His
uniquely-owned ones, those in the world, He loved them
to the uttermost.   And supper being in progress, the
devil having already hurled into the heart of Judas Iscariot,
son of Simon, with a force so that it stayed there, to
betray Him, Jesus knowing that all things the Father gave

into His hands and that from God He had come and to God He was departing, arises from the supper and lays aside His outer garments, and having taken a towel, He bound it around himself.

Next, He throws water into the basin and began to be **5-11** washing the feet of the disciples and to be wiping them off with the towel with which He was girdled. So He comes to Simon Peter. He says to Him, You — my feet you are washing? Answered Jesus and said to him, That which I am doing, as for you, not now do you know with an absolute and complete knowledge, but you shall learn by experience after these things. Peter says to Him, You shall by no means wash my feet, no, never. Jesus answered him, If I do not wash you, you do not have a part with me. Simon Peter says to Him, Lord, not my feet only but also my hands and my head. Jesus says to him, He who has been bathed all over stays bathed, and does not have need except to wash his feet but is entirely clean. And, as for you, you are clean ones, but not all, for He knew the one who was betraying Him. On this account He said, Not all are clean ones.

Then when He had washed their feet and had taken **12-17** His outer garments and had taken His place at the table again, He said to them, Do you understand what I have done to you? You call me the Teacher and the Lord, and well do you say, for I am. Since therefore I, the Lord and the Teacher, washed your feet, you also have a moral obligation to be washing one another's feet, for I gave to you an example that just as I did to you, you also should be doing. Most assuredly, I am saying to you, A slave is not greater than his master, nor even one who is sent on a mission greater than the one who sent him. Since you know these things, spiritually prosperous ones you are if you are doing them.

Not concerning all of you am I speaking. I know **18-20** whom I selected; but in order that the scripture may be fulfilled; He who eats bread with me lifted up his heel against me. From now on, I am telling you before it comes to pass, in order that you might be believing whenever it comes to pass, that I AM. Most assuredly, I am saying to you, He who receives whomever I shall send, me he receives. And the one who receives me, receives Him who sent me.

21-30   Having said these things, Jesus was distressed in His spirit and testified and said, Most assuredly, I am saying to you, One of you shall betray me. The disciples kept on looking to one another, being at a loss concerning whom He was speaking. There was one of His disciples reclining on the bosom of Jesus whom Jesus loved. Therefore, Simon Peter nods to this one and says to him, Tell me who it is concerning whom He is speaking. That one, having leaned thus on the breast of Jesus, says to Him, Lord, who is it? Then Jesus answers, That one it is for whom I will dip the morsel and to whom I will give it. Then, having dipped the morsel, He takes it and gives it to Judas, son of Simon Iscariot. And after the morsel, then there entered into that one, Satan. Then Jesus says to him, That which you are doing, do at once, and more quickly. Now, no one of those at the table understood with reference to what He spoke this to him, for certain were thinking that since Judas held the purse, Jesus said to him, Purchase in the market what things we need for the feast, or, that he should give something to the poor. Then, having taken the morsel, that one went out immediately. And it was night.

31-35   Then, when he had gone out, Jesus says, Now is the Son of Man glorified, and God is glorified in Him. Since God is glorified in Him, God also will glorify Him in himself, and forthwith will glorify Him. Little children, yet a little while I am with you. You shall seek me. And even as I said to the Jews, Where I am departing you are not able to come, so now I am telling you. A commandment, a new one, I am giving you, that you should be constantly loving one another with a divine and self-sacrificial love; even as I loved you, you also be loving one another. In this all shall know that you are my disciples, if you constantly have love among one another.

36-38   Simon Peter says to Him, Lord, where are you departing? Answered Jesus, Where I am departing you are not able now to follow with me, but you shall follow later. Peter says to Him, Lord, why am I not able to follow you right now? My life on your behalf I will lay down. Answers Jesus, Your life on behalf of me you will lay down? Most assuredly, I am saying to you, A rooster shall positively not crow until you deny me three times.

Let not your heart continue to be agitated. Be put-   **1-4**
ting your trust in God. Also be putting your trust in me. In the house of my Father there are many dwelling places. Indeed, if it were not so, in that case I would have told you, for I go to prepare a place for you. And if I go and prepare a place for you, again I come and will receive you to myself in order that where I am also you may be. And where I am departing, you know the road.

Thomas says to Him, Lord, we do not know where   **5-10**
you are going; how is it possible for us to know the road? Jesus says to him, I alone, in contradistinction to all others, am the road and the truth and the life. No one comes to the Father except through me. If you had learned to know me through experience, in that case also my Father you would have come to know. From now on you are beginning to know Him, and have seen Him with discern-ment. Philip says to Him, Lord, show us the Father at once, and it is sufficient for us. Jesus says to Him, Such a long time I am with you, yet you have not come to have an experiential knowledge of me, Philip? He who has discerningly seen me has seen the Father with discernment. How is it that you, you are saying, Show us the Father at once? Do you not believe that I am in the Father and that the Father is in me? The words which I am speaking to you, not from myself as a source am I speaking. But the Father who in me is abiding, He is doing His works.

Be believing me, that I am in the Father and that the   **11-18**
Father is in me. But if not, because of the works them-selves be believing. Most assuredly, I am saying to you, he who believes in me, the works which I am constantly doing, also that one shall do. And greater than these shall he do because I am proceeding to the Father. And

whatever you may ask in my Name, this I will do, in order that the Father may be glorified in the Son. If you ask me anything in my Name, I will do it. If you are loving me with a divine and self-sacrificial love, the commandments which are mine you will keep. And as for myself, I will ask the Father, and another Counsellor of the same kind as I am He will give to you in order that He might be with you forever, the Spirit of the truth, whom the world is not able to receive because it does not see Him with discernment and does not know Him experientially. But, as for you, you know Him experientially, because by your side He dwells, and in you He shall be. I will not leave you behind, helpless. I come to you.

19-26   Yet a little while, and the world no longer sees me, but as for you, you see me. Because I live, also you shall live. In that day you shall know experientially that I am in my Father and you in me and I in you. He who has my commandments and habitually keeps them, that one is he who is loving me with a divine and self-sacrificial love. And he who is loving me thus, shall be loved with this same kind of love by my Father, and I shall love him with a divine and self-sacrificial love, and I shall disclose myself to him. Judas says to Him, not Iscariot, Lord, and what has come to pass that to us you are about to be disclosing yourself and not to the world? Answered Jesus and said to him, If anyone as a habit of life loves me with a divine and self-sacrificial love, my word he will keep, and my Father will love him, and to him we shall come, and an abiding place with him we shall make for ourselves. He who is not habitually loving me with a divine and self-sacrificial love, my words he is not keeping. And the word which you are hearing is not mine but belongs to Him who sent me, the Father. These things I have spoken to you while abiding with you. And the Counsellor, the Holy Spirit, whom the Father will send in my Name, that One will teach you all things and recall to your mind all things which I spoke to you.

27-31   Peace I am leaving behind for you. Peace which is mine I am giving to you. Not such as the world gives, do I give to you. Let not your heart continue to be agitated, neither let it continue to be fearful. You heard that I said to you, I am departing and I am coming to you. If you were loving me, you would in that case already have rejoiced that I am proceeding to the Father, for the Father is greater than I. And now I have told you before it comes to pass in order that whenever it does come to pass you may believe. Many things no longer will I speak with you, for there comes the ruler of the world; and in me he has nothing. But in order that the world may come to know experientially that I love the Father, and even as the Father commanded me, thus I am doing. Be arising. Let us be going from this place.

I, in contradistinction to anyone else, am the vine, the genuine vine, and my Father is the tiller of the soil. Every branch in me not bearing fruit He takes away. And every branch bearing fruit, He cleanses it in order that it may keep on bearing more fruit. As for you, already you are cleansed ones because of the word which I have spoken to you. Maintain a living communion with me, and I with you. Just as the branch is unable to be bearing fruit from itself as a source unless it remains in a living union with the vine, so neither you, unless you maintain a living communion with me.

1-4

As for myself, I am the vine. As for you, you are the branches. He who maintains a living communion with me and I with him, this one is bearing much fruit, because apart from me you are not able to be doing anything. If anyone is not maintaining a living communion with me, he was thrown outside as the branch is and was caused to wither. And they gather them and into the fire they throw them, and they are burned. If you maintain a living communion with me and my words are at home in you, I command you to ask, at once, something for yourself, whatever your heart desires, and it will become yours. In this my Father is glorified, namely, that you are bearing much fruit. So shall you become my disciples. Just as the Father loved me, I also loved you. Remain within the sphere of the love which is mine. If my commandments you keep, you will remain within the sphere of my love, just as I have kept the commandments of my

5-17

Father and am remaining within the sphere of His love. These things have I spoken to you that the joy which is mine may be in you, and that your joy may be filled full. This is the commandment which is mine, namely, that you should be loving one another with a divine and self-sacrificial love just at I loved you. Greater love than this no one has, namely, that anyone lay down his life on behalf of his friends. As for you, friends of mine you are, if you habitually do that which I am enjoining upon you. No longer do I call you slaves, because the slave does not have an instinctive perception of what his master is doing. But you I have called friends, because all things which I heard from my Father I made known to you. You did not make me the object of your choice for yourselves, but I selected you out for myself, and I appointed you in order that you might be going away and constantly bearing fruit, and that your fruit might be remaining, in order that whatever you might ask the Father in my Name, He may give it you. These things I am enjoining upon you, namely, that you should be loving one another with a divine and self-sacrificial love.

18-21   If, as is the case, the world is hating you, you know by experience that me it has hated and still does before it hated you. If out of the world you were, the world in that case would be fond of that which is its own private possession. But because out of the world you are not but I selected you for myself out of the world, on this account the world hates you. Be remembering the word which I spoke to you, A slave is not greater than his master. Since me they persecuted, also you will they persecute. Assuming that they kept my word, also yours they will keep. But these things, all of them, they will do to you on account of all that I am in my Person, because they do not know the One who sent me.

22-27   If I had not come and spoken to them, sin they would not have had. But now they do not have an excuse for their sin. He who hates me, hates my Father also. If I did not do the works among them which no other one did, sin they would not have had. But now they have both seen and hated both me and my Father, and they still maintain that attitude of hate. But — in order that the word which in their law stands written might be fulfilled: They hated me without just cause. Whenever the Counsellor comes whom I shall send to you from the presence of the Father, the Spirit of the truth who from the Father's presence proceeds, that One will testify concerning me. And you also are bearing testimony because from the beginning with me you are.

These things I have spoken to you in order that you may not be made to stumble. They will make you outcasts from the synagogue. In fact, there comes an hour that everyone who kills you will be of the opinion that he is offering a sacred service to God. And these things they will do because they did not come to know the Father nor me in an experiential manner. But these things I have spoken to you in order that whenever their hour comes, you might recall them to mind, that I told you. And these things to you from the beginning I did not tell, because I was continually with you. But now I am going away to Him who sent me, and yet not one of you is asking me, Where are you departing? But because these things I have spoken to you, grief has filled your heart and is now controlling it. **1-6**

But I am telling you the truth. It is advantageous for you that I go away. For if I do not go away, the Counsellor will positively not come to you. But if I depart, I will send Him to you. And having come, that One will convict the world with respect to sin, and with respect to righteousness, and with respect to judgment; with respect to sin on the one hand, because they are not believing on me; with respect to righteousness on the other hand, because to the Father I am going away and no longer are you seeing me; and with respect to judgment, because the ruler of this world has been judged and is now under judgment. **7-11**

I have yet many things to be saying to you, but you are not able to be bearing them now so far as your understanding and receiving of them is concerned. However, whenever that One comes, the Spirit of the truth, He will lead you into all the truth, for He will not speak from **12-15** himself as a source, but as many things as He hears He will speak, and the things that are coming He will make known to you. That One shall glorify me, because He shall take out from that which pertains to me and make it known to you. All things, as many as the Father has, are mine. On this account I said that He takes out from that which pertains to me and shall make it known to you.

16-22   A little while and no longer are you attentively contemplating me, and again a little while, and you shall look at me with a discerning sight. Therefore, some of His disciples said to one another, What is this which He is saying to us, A little while and no longer are you attentively contemplating me, and, Again a little while, and you shall look at me with a discerning sight? and, Because I am going away to the Father? Therefore they were saying, This, what is it that He is saying, The little while? We do not know with a positive knowledge what He is saying. Jesus perceived that they were desiring to be asking Him, and said to them, Concerning this are you inquiring of one another, that I said, A little while and no longer are you attentively contemplating me, and, Again a little while and you shall look at me with a discerning sight? Most assuredly, I am saying to you, You shall weep audibly, and you shall audibly lament, and the world shall rejoice. As for you, you shall be made to grieve, but your grief shall become joy. The woman, whenever she is about to bear, has grief, because her hour has come. But whenever she bears the child, no longer does she remember her anguish because of her joy that a man was born into the world. And, as for you, you therefore now are having grief. But again I shall see you, and your heart shall rejoice, and your joy no one will snatch away from you.

23-33   And in that day you shall ask me no question about anything. Most assuredly, I am saying to you, Whatever you shall request of the Father, He will give it to you in view of all that I am in His estimation. Up to this time you requested not even one thing in my Name. Be constantly making request, and you shall receive, in order that your joy, having been filled completely full, might persist in that state of fulness in present time. These things I have spoken to you by way of illustration in similes and comparisons. An hour comes when no longer in similes and comparisons will I speak to you, but plainly, without the use of similes and comparisons I will tell you concerning the Father. In that day in view of all that I am in His estimation you shall request something for yourselves, and I do not say to you that I will ask the Father in behalf of you, for the Father himself is fond of you because you have been fond of me and still are, and have believed that I from the presence of God came and still hold to that belief. I came out from the Father and have come into the universe. Again I leave the universe behind and proceed on my way to the Father. His disciples say, Behold, now in plainness of words are you speaking, and not with even one simile or comparison are you uttering your thoughts. Now we know positively that you know all things and that you do not have need that anyone keep on questioning you. By this we believe that from God you came forth. Jesus answered them, Do you just now believe? Behold, an hour comes, yes, it has come, that you shall be scattered, each one to the things he possesses, and me you will leave alone. And yet I am not alone, because the Father is with me. These things I have spoken to you in order that in me peace you may be having. In the world you are having tribulation. But be having courage. I have come off victorious over the world with a permanent victory.

These things spoke Jesus, and having lifted up His eyes to heaven, He said, Father, the hour has come. Glorify your Son in order that the Son may glorify you, even as you gave to Him authority over all flesh, in order that all that you have given Him as a permanent gift, He should give to them life eternal. And this is the eternal life, namely, that they might be having an experiential knowledge of you, the only genuine God, and of Him whom you sent on a mission, Jesus Christ. **1-3**

I glorified you on the earth, having carried through to completion that which you have given me to do. And now glorify me, Father, beside yourself, with the glory which I was constantly having with you before the universe **4-10** existed. I made known your Name to the men whom you gave me out of the world. They were yours, and you gave them to me, and your word they have held to firmly. Now, they have known that all things, as many as you have given to me are from you, because the words which you gave me, I have given them, and they themselves received them and recognized truly that from your presence I came forth, and they believed that you sent me on a mission. As for myself, I make request concerning them. Not concerning the world do I make request, but concerning those whom you have given me, because they are yours, and all things that are mine are yours, and the things that are yours are mine, and I stand glorified in them.

11-15 And as for myself, no longer am I in the world, but they themselves are in the world, and I am coming to you. O holy Father, maintain a watchful care over them in your Name, which you have given me, in order that they may be one even as we. When I was with them, I constantly maintained a watchful care over them in your Name, those whom you have given me, and I guarded them, and no one of them was lost except the son of perdition in order that the scripture might be fulfilled. And now to you I am coming, and these things I am speaking in the world in order that they may be constantly having the joy which is mine, which joy having been filled full may exist in the state of fulness in themselves. I have given them your word, and the world hated them, because they are not of the world even as I am not of the world. I do not ask that you should take them out of the world, but that you should guard them safely from the reach of the Pernicious One.

16-23 Of the world they are not, even as I am not of the world. Consecrate them in the sphere of the truth. The word which is yours is truth. Even as me you sent off on a mission into the world, so I sent off them on a mission into the world. And on behalf of them I am setting myself apart, in order that they themselves also, having been set apart for God in the sphere of the truth, may continually be in that state of consecration. But not concerning these only am I making request, but also concerning those who believe on me through their word, in order that all might be one, even as you, Father, are in me and I in you, in order that they themselves also might be in us, to the end that the world may be believing that you sent me on a mission. And as for myself, the glory which you have given me, I have given them, in order that they might be one even as we are one, I in them and you in me, in order that they, having been brought to the state of completeness with respect to oneness, may persist in that state of completeness, to the end that the world might be understanding that you sent me on a mission and that you loved them even as you loved me.

Father, that which you have given me as a permanent **24-26** gift, I desire that where I am, also those might be with me, in order that they might be continually beholding the glory which is mine, which you have given me because you loved me before the foundation of the universe. O, righteous Father, though the world did not know you, yet I knew you, and these knew that you sent me on a mission. And I made known to them your Name, and will make it known, in order that the love with which you loved me might be in them and I might be in them.

Having spoken these things, Jesus went out with His **1-11** disciples across the brook Kedron where there was a garden, into which He himself went, also His disciples. Moreover, also Judas, he who was betraying Him, knew the place, because frequently Jesus met there with His disciples. Then Judas, having taken the company of soldiers and officers from the chief priests and from the Pharisees, comes there with torches and lamps and weapons. Jesus therefore knowing all the things coming upon Him, went out and says to them, Whom are you seeking? They answered Him, Jesus, the one from Nazareth. He says to them, I am He. Now, Judas, the one betraying Him, was also standing with them. Then when He said to them, I am He, they went backward and fell to the ground. Therefore again He asked them, Whom are you seeking? And they said, Jesus, the one from Nazareth. Answered Jesus, I told you that I am He.   Therefore, since you are seeking me, permit these to be departing; in order that there might be fulfilled the word which He spoke, Those whom you have given me as a permanent gift, I lost not even one of them. Then Simon Peter, having a small sword, unsheathed it, and struck the slave of the chief priest and cut off his ear, the right one. And the slave's name was Malchus. Then Jesus said to Peter, Thrust the small sword into its sheath. The cup which the Father has given me, shall I not surely be drinking it?

12-18   Then the company of soldiers and the commander of the Roman cohort and the officers of the Jews seized Jesus and bound Him, and led Him to Annas first, for he was father-in-law of Caiaphas who was chief priest that year. Now, Caiaphas was the one who gave counsel to the Jews that it was expedient that one man die on behalf of the people. And there was following with Jesus, Simon Peter and another disciple. And that disciple was known to the chief priest, and he entered in with Jesus into the uncovered courtyard of the chief priest's house. But Peter was standing at the door, outside. Then the disciple, the other one, the one known to the chief priest, went out and spoke to the woman doorkeeper, and brought in Peter. Then the female slave, the one who had charge of the door, says to Peter, And as for you, you are not also one of this man's disciples, are you? That one says, I am not. Now, the slaves and the officers, having made a coal fire, had taken their stand there because it was cold, and they were warming themselves. Now, Peter also was with them, standing and warming himself.

19-27   Then the chief priest asked Jesus concerning His disciples and concerning His teaching. Jesus answered him, As for myself, I have spoken openly to the world. I at all times taught in a synagogue and in the temple where all the Jews habitually come together, and in secret I said nothing. Why are you asking me? Ask those who have heard what I said to them. Behold, these know the things which I said. Now, after He had said these things, one of the officers standing by gave Jesus a slap in the face, having said, In this manner are you answering the chief priest? Jesus answered him, Assuming that I spoke evil,

furnish testimony concerning the evil. But assuming that
I spoke well, why do you flay me? Then Annas sent
Him bound to Caiaphas, the chief priest. And there was
Simon Peter, standing and warming himself. Then they
said to him, And as for you, you are not also one of his
disciples, are you? That one denied and said, I am not.
One of the slaves of the chief priest, being a relative of
him whose ear Peter cut off, says, As for myself, did I
not see you in the garden with him? Then again Peter
denied, and immediately a rooster crowed.

Then they lead Jesus from Caiaphas into the palace of **28-32**
the governor. Now, it was early. And they themselves
did not enter into the palace in order that they might not
be defiled but might eat the passover. Therefore Pilate
went outside to them and says, What accusation are you
bringing against this man? They answered and said to
him, If this man were not an habitual evildoer, we would
not in that case have delivered him up to you. Then
Pilate said to them, As for you, you take him and according to your law judge him. The Jews said to him, It is
not legal for us to put anyone to death; in order that the
word of Jesus might be fulfilled which He spoke when He
was making known what kind of a death He was about to
be dying.

Then again Pilate entered his palace and called Jesus **33-40**
and said to Him, As for you, are you the King of the
Jews? Answered Jesus, As for you, of yourself are you
saying this, or did others say this to you concerning me?
Answered Pilate, As for myself, I am not a Jew, am I?
Your own nation and the chief priests delivered you
over to me. What did you do? Answered Jesus, The
kingdom which is mine is not of this world. If the kingdom which is mine were of this world, the servants who
are mine in that case would now be fighting in order that
I would not be delivered to the Jews. But now the kingdom which is mine is not from this place. Then Pilate
said to Him, Are you therefore not a king? Answered
Jesus, As for you, you are saying that I am a king.
I for this purpose have been born and for this purpose
have come into the universe, in order that I might bear

witness to the truth. Everyone who is of the truth hears
my voice. Pilate says to Him, What is truth? And
having said this he went out again to the Jews and says to
them, As for myself, I do not find a cause for accusation
in him, not one bit. But there is a custom with you that
one I should release to you at the passover. Therefore,
is it your reasoned desire that I should release to you the
King of the Jews? Then they shouted again saying, Not
this fellow, but the one known to you and us, that Barabbas. Now, the aforementioned Barabbas was a robber.

1-7   Then Pilate therefore took Jesus and scourged Him.
And the soldiers, having woven a victor's crown made of
thorns, placed it upon His head, and they threw around
Him a purple cloak. And they kept coming to Him and
saying, Hail, King of the Jews. And they kept on
giving Him cuffs with their hands. And Pilate went
outside again and says to them, Look! I am bringing
him out to you in order that you may come to know that
I do not find cause for accusation in him, not one bit.
Then Jesus came out wearing the thorny victor's crown
and the purple cloak. And he says to them, See, the
man. Then, when the chief priests and the officers saw
Him, they shouted, saying, Crucify, crucify him, at once.
Pilate says to them, As for you, you take him and crucify,
for, as for myself, I do not find cause for accusation in
him. The Jews answered him, As for us, we have a law,
and according to the law he is under moral obligation to
die, because he made himself Son of God, and that by
nature.

8-15   When therefore Pilate heard this word, he was made
the more afraid, and went into the palace again and says
to Jesus, As for you, from where are you? But Jesus
did not give him an answer. Therefore Pilate says to
Him, To me you are not speaking? Do you not know
that I have authority to release you and authority to
crucify you? Answered Jesus, You would not be having
authority over me, not one bit, except that it has been
given you from above. Because of this, he who handed
me over to you has the greater sin. Because of this Pilate
made repeated efforts to release Him. But the Jews

shouted, saying, If you release this fellow, you are not a friend of the Ceasar. Everyone who makes himself a king declares himself against the Caesar. Then Pilate, having heard these words, brought Jesus outside, and seated himself on a raised platform provided for a judge in a place called a mosaic pavement, and in Hebrew, Gabbatha. Now, it was the preparation for the passover. As to the hour, it was about the sixth. And he says to the Jews, See! Your king. Then those shouted out, Take him away. Take him away. Crucify him at once. Pilate says to them, Your king shall I crucify? The chief priests answered, We do not have a king except Caesar.

Then therefore he handed Him over to them in order   **16-22**
that He might be crucified. Then they took Jesus with them, and bearing the cross himself, He went out to the place called the place of a skull, which in Hebrew is called Golgotha, where they crucified Him, and with Him, two others, on either side one, and in the midst, Jesus. Moreover, Pilate also wrote a notice on a placard and placed it on the cross. And that which stood written was, JESUS, THE ONE FROM NAZARETH, THE KING OF THE JEWS. Therefore this placard many of the Jews read, because the place where Jesus was crucified was near the city. And it had been written in Hebrew, Latin, Greek. Then the chief priests of the Jews kept on saying to Pilate, Do not allow it to remain written, The King of the Jews, but, That man said, I am King of the Jews. Answered Pilate, That which I have written, stands written.

Then the soldiers, when they crucified Jesus, took His   **23-27**
outer garments and made four parts, to each soldier a part, also His undergarment. Now, the undergarment was without seam, woven from the top throughout. Therefore they said one to another, Let us not tear it, but let us cast lots for it, whose it shall be; in order that the scripture might be fulfilled, They distributed my outer garments among themselves and upon my clothing they cast a lot. The soldiers therefore did these things. Now, there were standing beside the cross of Jesus His mother, and His mother's sister, Mary the wife of Cleophas, and Mary,

the Magdalene. Then Jesus, having seen His mother and the disciple whom He was loving standing by, says to His mother, Woman, see, your son. Then He says to the disciple, See, your mother. And from that hour, the disciple just mentioned took her to his own home.

28-30   After this, Jesus knowing that all things had now been brought to a consummation and stood finished in order that the scripture might be fulfilled says, I am thirsty. A vessel was standing there full of sour wine. Then, after putting a sponge filled with sour wine around a hyssop reed, they put it to His mouth. Then when Jesus received the sour wine He said, It has been finished and stands complete. And having bowed His head, He delivered up the spirit.

31-37   Then the Jews, since it was a day of preparation, in order that the bodies might not remain on the cross on the sabbath, for it was an important sabbath, that sabbath, asked Pilate that their legs might be broken and that they might be carried away. Therefore the soldiers went and broke the legs of the first one and of the other one who was crucified with Him. But upon coming to Jesus, when they saw that He was already dead, they did not break His legs. But one of the soldiers with the head of a spear pierced His side, and there came out immediately blood and water. And he who has with discernment seen, and at present has that which he has seen in his mind's eye, has borne testimony, and his testimony is at present on record. And his testimony is genuine, and that one knows positively that he is speaking true things, in order that also you might be believing, for these things took place in order that the scripture might be fulfilled; A bone belonging to Him shall not be broken. And again, another scripture says, They shall look on Him whom they pierced.

38-42   Now, after these things, Joseph, the one from Arimathaea, being a disciple of Jesus, but one who had been so secretly because of fear of the Jews, asked Pilate that he might carry away the body of Jesus. And Pilate gave him permission. Then he went and carried away His body. Moreover, there came also Nicodemus, he who came to Him at the first in a night-time visit, bearing a mixture of myrrh and aloes, about one hundred pounds. Then they took the body of Jesus and bound it in linen cloths with perfumes, just as the custom is of the Jews to prepare a body for entombment. Now, there was in the place where He was crucified a garden, and in the garden a new tomb in which never yet had anyone been laid. In that place therefore, on account of the preparation of the Jews, because the tomb was near at hand, they laid Jesus.

Now, on the first day of the week, Mary, the Magdalene, **1-10** comes early while it is still dark to the tomb, and she sees the stone moved out of its place out of the tomb. Then she runs and comes to Simon Peter and to the other disciple of whom Jesus was fond and says to them, They took the Lord out of the tomb, and we do not know where they laid Him. Then Peter and the other disciple went out and were going on their way to the tomb. Now, the two were running together. And the other disciple was running ahead more swiftly than Peter and came first to the tomb, and having stooped down he sees at a glance the strips of linen cloth lying. However, he did not go in. Then comes also Simon Peter following him and entered the tomb. And he intently gazes upon the strips of linen cloth lying there and the handkerchief which had been upon His head, not lying with the strips of linen cloth, but apart, rolled up in one place. Then therefore went in also the other disciple who had come first to the tomb, and he saw and believed, for not yet did they know the scripture that it is a necessity in the nature of the case for Him to stand up [arise] out from among those who are dead. Then the disciples went off again to their own homes.

But Mary continued standing, facing the tomb, outside, **11-13** weeping audibly. Then as she was weeping, she stooped down and looked into the tomb, and she carefully observes two angels in brilliant white garments sitting, one facing the head and one facing the feet, where the body of Jesus had been lying. And those say to her, Woman, why are you weeping? She says to them, They took away my Lord, and I do not know where they laid Him.

14-18 Having said these things, she turned herself back and carefully observes Jesus standing, and she did not know that it was Jesus. Jesus says to her, Woman, why are you weeping? Whom are you seeking? That one, thinking that it was the gardener, says to Him, Sir, as for you, if you carried Him off, tell me at once where you laid Him, and, as for myself, I will carry Him off. Jesus says to her, Mary. That one, having turned around, says to Him in Hebrew, Rabboni, (which is to say, Teacher). Jesus says to her, Stop clinging to me, for not yet have I ascended to the Father, but be on your way to my brethren and say to them, I am ascending to my Father and your Father and my God and your God. Mary, the Magdalene, goes, announcing to the disciples, I have with discernment seen the Lord, and He is vivid in my mind's eye still, and these things He said to her.

19-23 Then when it was evening on that day, the first day of the week, the doors having been shut and at that time tightly closed where the disciples were because of fear of the Jews, Jesus came and stepped into their midst. And He says to them, Peace be to you. And having said this, He showed them both His hands and side. Then the disciples rejoiced, having seen the Lord. Then Jesus said to them again, Peace be to you. Even as the Father has sent me on a mission for which I still am responsible, I also am sending you. And having said this, He breathed on them and says to them, Receive at once the Holy Spirit. If the sins of any certain individuals you forgive, they have been previously forgiven them, with the present result that they are in a state of forgiveness. If the sins of any certain individuals you retain in not forgiving them, they have been previously retained and thus have not been forgiven, with the present result that they are retained and in a state of not being forgiven.

24-29 But Thomas, one of the Twelve, the one called the twin, was not with them when Jesus came. Therefore the other disciples were saying to him, We have with discernment seen the Lord and He is still vivid to us in our mind's eye. But he said to them, If I do not see the mark of the nails in His hands and put my finger into the place of the nails, and put my hand into His side, I will positively not believe. And after eight days again His disciples were within, and Thomas with them. There comes Jesus, the doors having been shut with the result that they were tightly closed at that time, and stepped into their midst and said, Peace be to you. Then He says to Thomas, Be reaching here your finger, and see my hands, and reach here your hand and put it into my side, and call a halt to your progressive state of unbelief, but become one who is believing. Answered Thomas and said to Him, My Lord and my God. Jesus says to him, Because you have seen me and at present have me within the range of your vision, you have believed, with the result that you are in a state of belief. Spiritually prosperous are those who, not having seen, yet believed.

Accordingly, many other attesting miracles did Jesus also perform in the sight of the disciples which have not been written in this book. But these have been written and are on record in order that you may be believing that Jesus is the Christ, the Son of God, and in order that believing, you may be having life in His Name.   **30, 31**

After these things Jesus again made himself visible to the disciples at the sea of Tiberias. And under these circumstances He disclosed himself to them. There were together Simon Peter, and Thomas, the one called the twin, and Nathanael, the one from Cana of Galilee, and the sons of Zebedee and others of His disciples, two of them. Simon Peter says to them, I am going off, breaking my former connections, to my former fishing business. They say to him, As for us, we are coming also to join you. They went out and went on board the boat, and during that night they caught not even one thing.   **1-3**

When day was now breaking, Jesus stood on the beach. However, the disciples did not know that it was Jesus. Then Jesus says to them, Boys still under instruction, you do not have anything to add to your bread, such as fish, have you? They answered Him, No. And He said to them, Throw the net on the right side of the boat at once and you will find. Therefore they threw it, and   **4-8** no longer did they have the strength to draw it because of the great number of fish. Then that disciple whom Jesus loved says to Peter, The Lord it is. Then Simon Peter, having heard that it was the Lord, put around himself his fisherman's linen blouse, for he was only partially clad, and threw himself into the sea. But the other disciples came in the little boat, for they were not far from the land, in fact, about three hundred feet, dragging the net full of fish.

9-11   Then when they had come off the boat out upon the shore, they see a charcoal fire there, and fish laid upon it, and bread. Jesus says to them, Bring at once some of the fish which you now caught. Simon Peter went up and drew the net to the land full of fish, great ones, one hundred fifty three. And yet there being so many, the net was not split.

12-14   Jesus says to them, Here, have breakfast. No one of the disciples was daring to inquire of Him, As for you, who are you? knowing that it was the Lord. Comes Jesus and takes the bread and gives it to them, and the fish in the same way. This already is a third time in which Jesus made himself visible to the disciples after He was raised out from among the dead.

15-19   Then when they had breakfasted, Jesus says to Simon Peter, Simon, son of Jonas, do you have a love for me called out of your heart by my preciousness to you, a devotional love that impels you to sacrifice yourself for me? Do you consider me more precious and thus love me more than these [fish]? He says to Him, Yes, Lord, as for you, you know positively that I have an emotional fondness for you. He says to him, Be feeding my little lambs. He says to him again a second time, Simon, son of Jonas, do you have a devotional love for me called out of your heart by my preciousness to you, a love that impels you to sacrifice yourself for me? He says to Him, Yes, Lord. As for you, you know positively that I have a friendly feeling for you. He says to him, Be shepherding my sheep. He says to him the third time, Simon, son of Jonas, do you have a friendly feeling and affection for me? Peter was grieved that He said to him the third time, Do you have a friendly feeling and affection for me? And he said to Him, Lord, as for you, all things you know positively. You know from experience that I have a friendly feeling and affection for you. Jesus says to him, Be feeding my sheep. Most assuredly, I am saying to you, When you were younger, you were accustomed to clothe yourself and to walk where you were desiring to walk. But when you grow old, you shall stretch out your hands, and another shall bind you around and carry you where you do not desire. And this He said, indicating by what kind of death he will glorify God. And having said this, He says to him, Be following with me.

Peter, having turned around, sees the disciple whom Jesus loved following, who also leaned back at the supper upon his breast and said, Lord, who is the one who is betraying you? Then Peter, having seen this one, says to Jesus, Lord, but this one — what? Jesus says to him, If I desire that he be remaining while I am coming, what is it to you? As for you, you be following with me. Therefore, this word went out to the brethren that that disciple does not die. But Jesus did not say to him that he would not die, but, If I desire that he be remaining while I am coming, what is it to you? **20-23**

This is the disciple who is bearing testimony concerning these things, and the one who wrote these things. And we know positively that his testimony is true. Now there are also many other things which Jesus did which are of such a nature that if they were written, each one, I do not suppose that the universe itself could contain the books that would be written. **24, 25**

THE ACTS OF THE APOSTLES

The first historical narrative indeed I produced concerning all things, O Theophilus, which Jesus began and continued both to be doing and to be teaching until the day in which He was taken up, having previously given a commandment to the apostles through the intermediate agency of the Holy Spirit, those apostles whom He had selected out for himself, to whom also He presented himself as one who was living after His suffering by many indubitable proofs through a period of forty days, being seen by them at successive intervals and speaking of the things concerning the kingdom of God. And being assembled together with them He charged them not to go away from Jerusalem, but to be waiting for the promise of the Father which you heard from me, because John indeed baptized by means of water, but as for you, by the agency of the Holy Spirit you will be baptized not many days from now.

1-5

Then indeed having assembled together, they went to asking Him, saying, Lord, at this time are you restoring to its former state the kingdom to Israel? He said to them, It is not yours to know the chronological events in the passing of time nor the strategic, epochal periods of time which the Father placed within the sphere of His own private authority. But you shall receive power of the kind which God has and exerts after the Holy Spirit has come upon you. And you shall be those who testify of what they have seen and experienced, my witnesses, both in Jerusalem and in all Judaea and in Samaria and to the end of the earth.

6-8

And having said these things, while they were looking, He was taken up, and a cloud came under Him in order to bear Him up on high out of their sight. And while they were looking with fixed and protracted attention up to heaven as He was proceeding on His way, behold, also two men in brilliant white apparel had taken their position alongside of them and were standing there, who also said, Men, Galilaeans, why have you taken your stand, looking up to heaven? This Jesus, He who was taken up from you into heaven, shall come in like manner as you saw Him proceeding into heaven.

9-11

12-14   Then they returned to Jerusalem from the mount called Olivet which is near Jerusalem a sabbath day's journey. And when they entered the city, they went up to the upper room where they had taken up their residence for the ensuing time, both Peter and John and James and Andrew, Philip and Thomas, Bartholomew and Matthew, James the son of Alphaeus, and Simon the Zealot, and Judas the brother of James. These all continued to give their persistent attention with absolute unanimity to prayer which was characterized by its definiteness of purpose, together with the women and Mary the mother of Jesus and with His brethren.

15-17   And in these days Peter having arisen in the midst of the brethren said (and there was a group of persons gathered together, about one hundred and twenty), Men, brothers, it was a necessity in the nature of the case for the scripture to be fulfilled which the Holy Spirit spoke on a previous occasion through David's mouth concerning Judas, the one who became guide to those who seized Jesus, for he was numbered among us and received his portion of this ministry.

18-20   Now, this man acquired a piece of ground, the purchase price having its source in wages obtained by wrongdoing, and having fallen flat on his face, he cracked open at the waist with a crashing noise and all his inner organs gushed out. And it became known to all the residents of Jerusalem, so that that piece of ground came to be called in their own language, Akeldamach, that is, a bloody piece of ground, for it stands written in the Book of Psalms, Let his place of abode become deserted, and let there not be he who establishes his permanent residence in it, and his office let another person of a different character take.

21-26   Therefore, it is a necessity in the nature of the case that of those men who have accompanied us during all the time the Lord Jesus went in and went out in our presence, beginning from the time of John's baptism until the day when He was taken up from us, there be one of these appointed as one who bears testimony with us that he was a personal witness of His resurrection. And they nominated two, Joseph, the one called Barsabas, who was surnamed Justus, and Matthias. And having prayed, they said, Lord, you who have an experiential knowledge of the hearts of all, appoint the one of these two whom you selected out to receive the place of this ministry and apostleship, from which ministry and apostleship Judas fell away to proceed to his own private, unique place. And they handed out lots to be placed in an urn with respect to them, and the lot fell to Matthias, and he was numbered with the eleven apostles.

And when the day of Pentecost was in process of being fulfilled, they were all together in the same place. And suddenly there came an echoing sound out of heaven as of a wind borne along violently. And it filled the whole house where they were sitting. And there appeared to them tongues that had the appearance of fire, these tongues being distributed among them, and one of these tongues took up a position upon each of them. And all were controlled by the Holy Spirit and began to be uttering words in languages different from their own native language and different from those spoken by the others, even as the Spirit kept giving them ability to speak forth, not in words of everyday speech but in words belonging to dignified and elevated discourse.

And there were in Jerusalem Jews who were in residence there, devout men who reverenced God, from all nations of those under heaven. Now, when this sound was heard, the multitude came together and was at a loss to understand this, because they were hearing each one of them uttering words in his own dialect. And they were astounded to the point of being beside themselves, and went to wondering, saying, Look. To be sure. Are not all these who are speaking Galilaeans? And as for us, how can it be possible that we are hearing each one in our own private dialect in which we were born, Parthians and Medes, and Elamites, and those who had taken up residence in Mesopotamia, and also in Judaea and Cappadocia, in Pontus and Asia, also in Phrygia and Pamphylia, in Egypt, and in the parts of Libya about Cyrene, also sojourners from Rome, both Jews and Gentile converts to Judaism, Cretes and Arabians, we are hearing them uttering in our languages the mighty works of God?

12, 13   And they were all astounded to the point of being beside themselves, and were wholly at a loss what to think, saying one to another, What does this desire to be? But others of a different class, mocking, were saying, They have been filled brimful with sweet wine with the result that they cannot hold any more.

14-18   But Peter having taken his stand with the eleven raised his voice and said to them in words which belonged to dignified and elevated discourse, Men of the Jewish race, and all those who are residents of Jerusalem, let this be known to you, and give ear to my words, for, as for you, these are not intoxicated as you suppose, for it is nine o'clock in the morning. But this is that which has been spoken through the intermediate agency of the prophet Joel and is on record, And it shall be in the last days, says God, that I will abundantly bestow my Spirit upon all flesh. And your sons shall speak forth by divine inspiration, also your daughters. And your young men shall see visions. And your old men shall dream with dreams. Yes, and upon men and women who are the slaves of others and yet belong to me, in those days I will abundantly bestow my Spirit and they shall speak by divine inspiration.

19-21   And I will bring forth miracles of a startling, amazement-awakening character in the heaven above and miracles upon the earth whose purpose it is to attest the workings and words of God, blood and fire and vapor of smoke. The sun shall be turned into darkness and the moon into blood before the day of the Lord comes, that great, conspicuous day. And it shall be that everyone whoever shall call upon the Name of the Lord shall be saved.

22-24   Men, Israelites. Hear these words at once. Jesus, the Nazarene, a man who has been demonstrated to you by God to be that which He claims to be, this demonstration taking the form of miracles that show the power of God, and miracles that are a startling, imposing, amazement-awakening portent, and miracles that have for their purpose the attestation of the divine mission of the one who performs them, which miracles God performed through His intermediate agency in your midst even as you yourselves know positively; this One, having been delivered up by the counsel of God which [in the council held by the Trinity] had decided upon His destiny, even by the foreordination of God which is that act fixing His destiny, by wicked hands you crucified and killed, whom God raised up, having loosed the pangs of death because it was not possible for Him to be mastered by it.

For David says concerning Him, I was beholding the Lord always before my face, because He is at my right hand in order that I might not be agitated and disturbed, thrown out of my sober and natural state of mind. On this account my heart was made glad and my tongue rejoiced exceedingly. Yes, moreover also my flesh shall still pitch its tent upon hope, there to rest, because you will not leave my soul surviving in that place in the unseen world reserved for the human dead. Neither will you permit your Holy One to see corruption. You made known to me the courses of thought, feeling, and action of life [that life, the eternal life given a believer in salvation]. You will fill me with joy with your countenance.

25-28

Men. Brothers. I may speak to you with utter freedom of speech concerning our progenitor David, that he came to his end in death and was entombed. And his sepulchral memorial is among us even to this day. Therefore, being a foreteller of future events, and knowing that God had sworn with an oath to him that from his offspring He would seat One upon his throne, he having seen this beforehand, spoke concerning the resurrection of the Christ [the Messiah], that neither was He left surviving in that place in the unseen world reserved for the human dead, nor did His flesh see corruption. This Jesus God raised up, whose witnesses we all are, bearing testimony to what we have seen and heard and learned concerning Him. Therefore, by the right hand of God exalted, and having received from the presence of the Father the promise of the Holy Spirit, He bestowed this which you are both seeing and hearing; for David did

29-36

not ascend into heaven, but he himself says, The Lord said to my Lord, Take your seat at my right hand until I make your enemies the footstool of your feet. Assuredly therefore, let the whole house of Israel be knowing that God made Him both Lord and Christ, this Jesus whom you crucified.

37-41   Now, having heard this, they were stung to the heart with poignant sorrow. And they said to Peter and the rest of the apostles, What shall we do, men, brothers? And Peter said to them, Have a change of mind, that change of mind being accompanied by abhorrence of and sorrow for your deed, and let each one of you be baptized upon the ground of your confession of belief in the sum total of all that Jesus Christ is in His glorious Person, this baptismal testimony being in relation to the fact that your sins have been put away, and you shall receive the gratuitous gift of the Holy Spirit, for to you is the promise and to your children and to all who are at a distance, as many as the Lord our God shall with a divine summons call to himself. And with many other words he solemnly affirmed, and kept on exhorting them, saying, Be saved from this perverse generation. Then those who received his word with approval were immersed. And there were added to their number on that day about three thousand souls.

42-47   And they were giving constant attention to the teaching of the apostles and to that which they held in common with them, and to the breaking of the bread and to the gatherings where prayers to God were offered. And a reverential fear came upon every soul. And many miracles that excited amazement and attesting miracles were performed by the apostles. And all those who believed were gathered together as a unit and were holding all things in joint-participation, and were selling their houses and lands and other possessions and kept on distributing them to all, according as anyone was having a need. And daily they continued to remain in the temple, in perfect unanimity, breaking bread at home, partaking of food together in gladness and simplicity of heart, praising God and having the good will of the people. And the Lord kept on adding to them daily those who were being saved.

Now Peter and John were going up into the temple **1-11**
at the hour of prayer, three o'clock in the afternoon. And
a certain man whose lameness was due to prenatal causes
was being carried, whom they were accustomed to place
daily at the door of the temple, the gate which is called
Beautiful, for the purpose of asking alms from those who
were entering the temple, who having seen Peter and
John about to go into the temple, went to asking for a
benefaction. And Peter having looked at him with a
piercing gaze together with John said, Look at once on
us. And he began to fix his attention on them, expecting
to receive something from them. Then Peter said, Silver
and gold coins I do not have, but that which I have, this
I give to you. In the Name of Jesus Christ the Nazarene,
start walking and keep on walking. And having firmly
grasped his right hand, he raised him up. And instantly
his feet and ankle bones were made strong. And leaping
up he stood and went to walking about. And he entered
the temple with them, walking about, leaping and
praising God. And all the people saw him walking about
and praising God. And they recognized him as being
the one who customarily sat at the Beautiful Gate of the
temple for alms. And they were filled with amazement
and were in a state of mental imbalance because of that
which had happened to him. And while he was holding
firmly to Peter and John, the entire crowd ran together
to them in the covered colonnade, the one called
Solomon's, completely flabbergasted.

And Peter, having seen this, answered the people; **12-16**
Men, Israelites, why are you marvelling at this, or why
are you fixing your attention upon us as though by means
of our own power or piety we have made him to be walking? The God of Abraham and Isaac and Jacob, the God
of our fathers glorified His servant, Jesus, whom you
indeed delivered up and denied before the face of Pilate
when it was that one's verdict to release Him. But, as for
you, you denied the Holy One and the Just One, and demanded a man who was a murderer to be granted to you
as a favor, and killed the Author of the life whom God
raised out from among those who are dead, of whom, as
for us, we are those who bear testimony to what we have

seen and heard and learned concerning Him. And upon
the ground of our faith in His Name, this man whom
you are attentively gazing at with a critical, discerning eye
and whom you positively identify as the person you
know — His Name made him strong, and the faith which
is exercised through Him gave to him this entire soundness in the sight of all of you.

17-21   And now brothers, I know positively that in ignorance you did it, even as also your chief men. But the
things which God announced fully beforehand through
the mouth of all the prophets that His Christ should suffer, He thus fulfilled. Therefore repent at once, instantly changing your attitude, and perform a right-about-
face in order that your sins may be obliterated, in order
that there may come epoch-making periods of spiritual
revival and refreshment from the presence of the Lord,
and in order that He may send off on a mission to you
Christ Jesus who has been appointed, this appointment
being in the interest of your well-being; whom it is a
necessity in the nature of the case for heaven indeed to
receive until times when all things will be restored to their
pristine glory, things regarding which God spoke through
the mouth of His holy prophets who lived in bygone
times.

22-26   Moses indeed said, A prophet from among your
brethren the Lord your God shall raise up for you who
is like me. Him you are to hear with reference to all
things whatever He may say to you. And it shall be that
every soul which is of such a nature that he will not hear
that prophet shall be utterly destroyed from among the
people. And indeed, all the prophets since Samuel, and
those who followed, one after another, as many as spoke,
also announced these days. As for you, you are the sons
of the prophets and of the covenant which God cove-
nanted with your fathers, saying to Abraham, And by
means of your race all the nations of the earth shall become the recipients of benefits. To you first, God, having raised up His Servant, sent Him on a mission to con-
fer benefits upon you in turning away each one of you
from your pernicious deeds.

And while they were speaking to the people, the
priests and the captain of the temple police and the Sadducees burst suddenly upon them and stood there in a
hostile attitude, being greatly displeased because they
were teaching the people and announcing in the case of
Jesus the resurrection from among the dead. And they
laid their hands upon them and placed them in custody
where they would be guarded until the next day, for it
was already evening. But many of those who heard the
Word believed. And the number of male individuals
came to be about five thousand.

And it came to pass on the next day that their rulers
and elders and men learned in the sacred scriptures were
gathered together in Jerusalem, also Annas the chief
priest and Caiaphas and John and Alexander, and as
many as were relatives of the chief priest. And having
stood them in their midst, they went to inquiring of them,
By what sort of power or by what manner of name did
you do this? Then Peter, being controlled by the Holy
Spirit, said to them, Rulers of the people and elders, as
for us, since we are being examined regarding a good
deed done to an infirm man, by what means this man has
been made whole, let it be known to you all and to all
the people of Israel, that by means of the Name of Jesus
Christ, the Nazarene, whom, as for you, you crucified,
whom God raised out from among those who are dead,
by means of this One this man stands in your presence
sound in body. This is the stone which was utterly despised and treated with contempt by you, the builders,
which has become the cornerstone. And there does not
exist in any other the salvation, for there is not even another name under heaven which has been given among
men by means of which we can be saved, the need for this
salvation being a necessity in the nature of the case. And
viewing with a practiced eye the free and fearless confidence of Peter and John as manifested in their uninhibited and unreserved manner of speaking, and comprehending the fact that they were without formal education and that they were not professional men but lay-
men, they began to wonder and kept on wondering, and
they began to recognize them as those who were with

Jesus. And seeing the man who was standing with them, the one who had been healed, they kept on having not even one thing to say against it.

15-18   But having ordered them to go off outside of the council, they went to conferring with one another, saying, What shall we do to these men? for that indeed a miracle which has for its purpose the attestation of the divine source of a message given by the one who performs the miracle, and one which is known, has been done through their agency, is known to all those who are residing in Jerusalem. And we are unable to deny it. But, in order that it may not be caused to spread the more among the people, let us with sternest threats forbid them to be speaking upon the basis of this name to even one of the people. And having called them, they commanded them not to be speaking at all nor to be teaching upon the basis of the Name of Jesus.

19-22   But Peter and John, answering, said to them, Whether it is right in the sight of God to be yielding obedience to you rather than to God, you be the judges, for, as for us, we are not able not to be speaking the things which we saw and heard. And having sternly threatened them in addition, they released them, finding not even one thing relative to the particular way in which they might punish them because of the people, for all glorified God for that which had taken place, for the man was more than forty years old upon whom this attesting miracle of healing had been wrought.

23-31   And having been released, they went to their own associates and reported as many things to them as the chief priests and the elders had said. And they having heard this, with one accord raised their voice to God and said, O Lord, absolute in power, you who made the heaven and the earth and the sea and all the things in them, who by the mouth of our father David your servant through the Holy Spirit said, Why did the Gentiles take on lofty airs and behave arrogantly, and the people devise futile things? The kings of the earth set themselves in array and the rulers formed a coalition to the same end, that of antagonism against the Lord and against His Anointed One,

for of a truth, there joined together in this city, against
your holy servant Jesus, whom you anointed, both Herod
and Pontius Pilate with the Gentiles and with the people
of Israel, to do as many things as your hand and counsel determined beforehand should come to pass. And as
to the present circumstances, Lord, look upon their threat-
enings and grant at once to your bondslaves the ability
to be speaking your word with all fearless confidence and
freedom of speech while you stretch out your hand to
heal, and grant that attesting miracles and miracles which
arouse wonder may be done through the Name of your
holy servant Jesus. And having prayed, the place in which
they were gathered was shaken. And they were all controlled by the Holy Spirit and went to speaking the word
of God with fearless confidence and freedom of speech.

And in the multitude of those who believed there was   **32-37**
one heart and soul. And not even one was saying that
anything of the things he possessed was his private property, but they had all things in common. And with great
power the apostles of the Lord were constantly giving
their testimony of the resurrection. And great grace was
upon all of them, for there was no one among them who
was in need, for as many as were possessors of lands
or houses, selling them, kept on bringing the equivalent
values of the things that were being sold and kept on placing them at the feet of the apostles, and distribution was
constantly being made to each one according as he was
having a need. And Joseph, who by the apostles was surnamed Barnabas, which latter name by interpretation
means Son of Encouragement, a Levite, of the land of
Cyprus, possessing a field, having sold it, brought the
money and placed it at the feet of the apostles.

But a certain man named Ananias with his wife Sap-   **1-6**
phira sold a possession and set apart part of it for himself, his wife also knowing of this together with him. And
having brought a certain part, he placed it at the feet of
the apostles. And Peter said, Ananias, how is it that Satan exercised control over your heart with the result
that you lied to the Holy Spirit and set apart for yourself a portion of the value of the land? While it remained,
did it not remain your own? And having sold it, was

it not under your authority? Why did you resolve upon this deed in your heart? You did not lie to men but to God. And Ananias, having heard these words, having fallen down, expired. And there came a great fear upon all those who heard. And having arisen, the younger men covered him with a shroud, and having carried him out, buried him.

7-11 Now, there elapsed an interval of about three hours, and his wife, not knowing of that which had taken place, entered. And Peter answered her, Tell me at once whether you both sold the land for so much? And she said, Yes, for so much. And Peter said to her, Why is it that it was agreed by both of you craftily to make trial of and put to the proof the Lord's Spirit [to see whether He would condone or condemn this act]? Behold, the feet of those who buried your husband are at the door, and they shall carry you out. And she fell down immediately at his feet and expired. And the younger men, having entered, found her dead. And having covered her with a shroud, they buried her with her husband. And there came a great fear upon the whole assembly and upon all who heard these things.

12-16 And by the hands of the apostles, attesting miracles and miracles which excite wonder and amazement, many of them, were constantly being performed among the people. And they were in perfect unanimity, all of them, in Solomon's covered colonnade. And of the rest, not even one was daring to be entering into fellowship with them, but the people were esteeming them highly. And those believing on the Lord were the more constantly being added to the number, crowds both of men and women, with the result that also into the streets they were carrying out those who were ill and placing them upon small couches for the sick and upon pallets in order that the shadow of Peter as he was coming might overshadow some of them. Moreover, there kept on congregating also the multitude of those from the environs of Jerusalem, carrying sick ones and those who were being troubled by unclean spirits; such as these were being healed, all of them.

Then having arisen, the chief priest and all those with **17-25**
him, the sect which is of the Sadducees, were filled with
jealousy. And they laid their hands upon the apostles and
put them in the public prison. But an angel of the Lord
during the night opened the doors of the prison, and
having brought them out said, Be going on your way,
and having taken a stand, be speaking in the temple to
the people all the words of this life. And having heard
that, they went about daybreak into the temple and began teaching. Now the chief priest and those with him,
having come, called together the Sanhedrin and all the
council of elders of the sons of Israel, and they sent to
the prison-house to have them brought. But the officers
having come, did not find them in the guard-house. And
having returned, they made an announcement, saying,
The prison-house we found to have been shut, and it was
locked, in a state of perfect security, and the guards
standing at the doors. But having opened them, we found
not one person inside. Now, when they heard these
words, the captain of the temple guard and the chief
priests continued to be entirely at a loss concerning them
as to what might become of this. Then a certain one
having come, brought word to them saying, Look. The
men whom you put in the prison are in the temple, standing there and teaching the people.

Then the captain, having gone with the officers, was **26-28**
bringing them without a show of force or violence, for
they were fearing the people lest they be stoned. And
having brought them, they stood them in the midst of
the council. And the chief priest questioned them, saying,
With a charge we commanded you not to be teaching in
the name of this fellow, and look, you have filled Jerusalem with your teaching, and purpose to bring upon us
the blood of this fellow.

Then, answering, Peter and the apostles said, It is a **29-32**
necessity in the nature of the case to be obeying God
rather than men. The God of our fathers raised up Jesus, whom, as for you, you killed, hanging Him upon a
cross. This One God exalted to His right hand as the
Chief Leader and the Saviour, to give repentance to Israel and the putting away of sins. And as for us, we are

those who are bearing testimony concerning these words, and so is the Holy Spirit whom God gave to those who obey Him.

33-36   Now when they heard this, their hearts were, as it were, sawn in two with vexation and rage. And they were consulting with one another with a view to killing them. Then there arose a certain one in the council, a Pharisee named Gamaliel, a teacher and interpreter of the law, held in honor by all the people. He ordered that the men be put outside for a brief period. And he said to them, Men, Israelites, be taking heed to yourselves with regard to what you are about to be doing to these men, for before these days there arose Theudas, saying that he was somebody, with whom a number of men, about four hundred, took sides, who was killed, and all, as many as obeyed him, were broken up and dispersed and came to nothing.

37-42   After this man there arose Judas of Galilee in the days of the census and drew away people after him. That one also perished, and all, as many as obeyed him, were scattered abroad. And with reference to the present things I am saying to you, stand off from these men and let them alone, because if this counsel or this work be of men, it will be overthrown. But assuming that it is of God, you are not able to destroy them, lest perchance you even be found to be those who are fighting God. And they permitted themselves to be persuaded by him. And having called the apostles, having beaten them, they ordered them not to be speaking in the Name of Jesus, and released them. They then went on their way rejoicing from the presence of the Sanhedrin, rejoicing that they were deemed worthy to be dishonored for the sake of the Name. And all through every day in the temple and at home they did not cease teaching and giving out the good news that the Christ is Jesus.

1-7   And in these days when the number of the disciples was multiplying, there arose a low, undertone murmuring of the Hellenists who were conferring together, secretly complaining against the Hebrews, the complaint being that their widows were being neglected in the daily provision of food. Then the Twelve, having called to themselves the entire number of the disciples, said, It is not fitting that we should neglect the word of God, to be occupied with the distribution of food. Now, look, brethren, for men from among yourselves who are accredited, seven of them, controlled by the Spirit and filled with broad and full intelligence whom we shall appoint over this business. But as for us, to prayer and the ministry of the Word we shall give constant attention. And the word pleased the entire multitude. And they selected out from their number Stephen, a man full of faith and controlled by the Holy Spirit, and Philip, and Prochorus, and Nicanor, and Timon, and Parmenes, and Nicolas, a proselyte from Antioch, whom they stood before the apostles, and they, having prayed, laid their hands upon them. And the word of God kept on increasing, and the number of the disciples in Jerusalem kept on multiplying greatly. And a large number of the priests were becoming obedient to the Faith.

And Stephen, full of grace and of power, was constantly performing great miracles among the people that aroused wonder and amazement, and miracles that had for their purpose the attestation of the message of the one performing the miracle as one that was inspired of God. Then there arose certain ones from the synagogue which is called the synagogue of the Libertines [those who had once been slaves but were set free by Rome], and certain ones from the synagogues of the Cyrenians and of the Alexandrians and from those of Cilicia and of Asia disputing with Stephen, and they continued to be unable to stand up against his wisdom and the Spirit by whom he was speaking. Then they secretly instructed and instigated men who said, We have heard him saying slanderous words against Moses and God. And they stirred up the people and the elders and the men learned in the sacred scriptures as a mass, and moved them to a concerted point of view, and having come upon him suddenly, they seized him and brought him to the council of the Sanhedrin, and presented false witnesses saying, This man does not cease from continually speaking words against this place which is holy and against the law, for

8-15

we have heard him saying that Jesus, the Nazarene, this fellow will destroy this place and will change the customs which Moses delivered to us to keep, and the recollection of this is still vivid in our memory. And all those sitting in the council, having gazed intently upon him, saw his face as if it were an angel's face.

1-7   Then the chief priest said, These things, are they factual, as has been stated? And he said, Men, brethren, and fathers, hear me. The God of the glory appeared to our father Abraham when he was in Mesopotamia, before he took up his residence in Charran and said to him, Come out of your country at once and away from your relatives and come into the country which I will indicate to you. Then, having come out of the country of the Chaldaeans, he took up his residence in Charran. And from that place, after his father died, He transferred him to this land in which you now are residing. And He did not give him an inheritance in it, nor even the space which a human foot covers. Yet He promised to give it to him as a permanent possession and to his offspring after him, this promise made at the time when he did not have a child. And God spoke to this effect, that his offspring shall be temporary residents in a foreign land belonging to another, and that they shall enslave his offspring and oppress them four hundred years. And the nation for which they will slave, as for myself, I will bring to the bar of justice and punish, God said. And after these things, they shall come out and render sacred service and worship to me in this place.

8-10   And He gave him a covenant, the rite of circumcision being its seal and sign. And thus he begat Isaac, and circumcised him on the eighth day. And Isaac begat Jacob, and Jacob begat the twelve progenitors of the twelve tribes. And these aforementioned founders, burning up with envy of Joseph, sold him into Egypt. But God was with him and delivered him out of all his tribulations. And He gave him favor and wisdom in the sight of Pharaoh, king of Egypt. And he appointed him governor over Egypt and his whole house.

Then there came a famine over the whole of Egypt   **11-16**
and Chanaan, and great affliction. And our fathers were
not finding fodder for their cattle. And when Jacob
heard that there were provisions in Egypt he sent off on
a mission our fathers first. And during their second visit
Joseph was made known to his brothers, and the identity of Joseph's nationality became evident to Pharaoh.
And Joseph having sent, summoned to himself Jacob his
father and all his relatives, seventy-five souls. And Jacob came down into Egypt, and he himself ended his
days, also our fathers, and were carried over to Sychem
and placed in the tomb which Abraham bought for a sum
of money from the sons of Emmor in Sychem.

But as the time of the promise which God had sworn   **17-21**
to Abraham was drawing near, the people increased and
multiplied in Egypt until there arose a king of a different
kind over Egypt who did not know Joseph. This one
dealt craftily against our nation and oppressed our fathers
so that they threw out their babies to the end that they
might not be preserved alive, during which time Moses
was born. And he was comely in the sight of God, and
was nourished in the house of his father three months.
And when he was thrown out the daughter of Pharaoh
took him up and nourished him for her own son.

And Moses was instructed in all the wisdom of the   **22-29**
Egyptians, and he was powerful in his words and deeds.
And when he was forty years old, it came into his heart
to pay a visit to his brethren, the sons of Israel, for the
purpose of acquainting himself with their needs and with
a view to helping them in their difficulties. And having
seen a certain one being ill treated, he defended him and
avenged the one who was being roughly treated, having
cut down the Egyptian. Now, he was supposing that his
brethren understood that God through his hand was giving them deliverance. But they did not understand. And
on the next day he appeared to them while they were
fighting and tried to reconcile them with a view to peace,
saying, Men, you are brothers. Why are you wronging
one another? But the one who was wronging his neighbor pushed him away, having said, Who constituted you
a ruler and an arbitrator over us? As for you, you are

not desiring to kill me even as you killed the Egyptian yesterday, are you? Then Moses fled at this word and became a temporary resident in the land of Madian where two sons were born to him.

30-41   And after forty years had passed by, there appeared to him in the uninhabited region of Mount Sinai an angel in a flaming fire of a bush. And Moses, having seen it, went to wondering at the spectacle. And as he was approaching it for the purpose of considering it attentively, the Lord's voice came, As for myself, I am the God of your fathers, the God of Abraham and Isaac and Jacob. But Moses becoming terrified, was not daring to attentively consider it. Then the Lord said to him, Take off your sandals at once from your feet, for the place upon which you have taken a stand is holy ground. I have surely seen the affliction of my people which are in Egypt, and I heard their groaning, and I came down to rescue them. And now, come. I will send you to Egypt. This Moses whom they denied, saying, Who constituted you a ruler and an arbitrator? this man God sent on a mission as both a ruler and a deliverer in cooperation with the angel who appeared to him in the bush. This one led them out, having performed miracles which arouse wonder and amazement and miracles whose purpose is that of attesting the divine source of the message and mission of the one who performed them, performing them in Egypt and at the Red Sea and in the uninhabited region for forty years. This is the aforementioned Moses, the one who said to the sons of Israel, A Prophet to you God will raise up from your brethren who is like me. This is he who was in the called-out assembly [called out of Egypt] in the uninhabited region with the angel who was speaking to him in Mount Sinai and with our fathers, who received the living, divine utterances to give to you, to whom our fathers were not desirous of becoming obedient, but thrust him away from themselves and turned back in their hearts to Egypt, having said to Aaron, Make us at once gods who will go before us. For this Moses who led us out of the land of Egypt, we do not have any positive knowledge as to what has happened to him. And they made a calf in those days and offered a sacrifice to the idol, and they kept on rejoicing in the works of their hands.

Then God turned His back upon them and delivered **42, 43** them up to be rendering religious service to the sun, moon, and stars of heaven, even as it stands written in the book of the prophets, You did not offer as sacrifices beasts slaughtered for sacrifice and sacrifices to me for forty years in the uninhabited region, house of Israel, did you? Yes, you raised up the tent of Moloch and the star of your god Remphan, the images which you made for the purpose of worshipping them. And I will cause you to be removed beyond Babylonia.

The tent of the testimony was for our fathers in the **44-47** uninhabited region even as He appointed when He was speaking to Moses that he should make it according to the pattern which he had seen, which tent also our fathers in their turn having received, brought in with Joshua when they entered the territory possessed by the Gentiles, whom God expelled from before our fathers until the days of David who found favor before God and asked as a personal favor that he be permitted to find a habitation for the house of the God of Jacob. But Solomon built Him a house.

Nevertheless, the Most High does not reside in things **48-53** made by hands, even as the prophet says, The heaven is my throne. The earth is the footstool for my feet. What sort of a house will you build me, says the Lord, or what is the place of my rest? Did not my hand make all these things? Stiffnecked, stubborn, headstrong, obstinate, and uncircumcised in heart and ears, as for you, incessantly do you strive against the Holy Spirit. As your fathers did, so also do you. Which of the prophets did not your fathers persecute? And they killed those who announced beforehand concerning the advent of the Just One, of whom, as for you, you now became the betrayers and the murderers, you who are of such a character as to have received the law as it was ordained by angels, and did not guard it so as not to violate it and to observe it.

And having heard these things they were cut to the **54-VIII 1** heart, and they began to gnash their teeth at him. And

Stephen being under the control of the Holy Spirit, having fixed his gaze into heaven, saw God's glory and Jesus standing at the right hand of God, and said, Behold, I see the heavens which have been opened, and the Son of Man standing on the right hand of God. And having cried out with a great voice, they covered their ears and rushed upon him in concert, and having thrown him outside of the city, they went to stoning him. And the witnesses put aside their outer garments beside the feet of a young man called Saul. And they kept on stoning Stephen as he was calling upon the Lord and saying, Lord Jesus, receive my spirit. And having knelt down, he cried with a great voice, Lord, do not place this sin against them. And having said this, he fell asleep. And Saul was together with the others approving of his death, taking pleasure with them in his death and applauding it.

1, 2   Then on that day there arose a persecution, a great one, against the assembly at Jerusalem. And all were scattered throughout the regions of Judaea and Samaria except the apostles. And men of piety and reverence toward God carried Stephen to his burial and made great lamentation over him, this lamentation accompanied by the beating of the breast.

3-8   But Saul kept on ravaging and devastating the Church, entering house after house, dragging both men and women by their feet along the street, consigning them to prison. Then those who were scattered abroad went about proclaiming the good news of the Word. And Philip, having gone down to the city of Samaria, proclaimed to them the Christ. And the people with one accord kept on giving heed to the things spoken by Philip, hearing them and seeing the attesting miracles which he was constantly doing, for in the case of many who had unclean spirits, the spirits came out shouting with a great voice. And many who were paralyzed and lame were healed. And there arose much joy in that city.

9-11   But there was a certain man whose name was Simon, who previous to this in the aforementioned city was practicing his magical arts in the form of charms and incantations and astounding the people of Samaria to the point of being beside themselves in a mental imbalance, saying that he was some great personage, to whom they were continually giving heed, all of them from the least to the greatest, saying, This man is the [impersonated] power of God, that power which is called great [since in him it is seen in an outstanding way]. And they kept on giving heed to him because for a considerable length of time he had rendered them beside themselves with amazement by means of his magical arts.

Now, when they believed Philip as he was proclaim- **12, 13**
ing the good news concerning the kingdom of God and the Name of Jesus Christ, they were being baptized, both men and women. Moreover Simon himself also believed, and having been baptized, continuing as an adherent of Philip, viewing with an interested and critical eye both the attesting miracles and also the great miracles which excited wonder as they were being performed, was being rendered beside himself with amazement.

Now, the apostles who were in Jerusalem, having **14-17**
heard that Samaria had received the word of God, sent on a mission to them Peter and John, who, after they had come down, prayed for them in order that they might receive the Holy Spirit, for not yet had He fallen upon any one of them, but they had been baptized only into the Name of the Lord Jesus. Then they laid their hands upon them and they received the Holy Spirit, one after another, as each one submitted to the laying on of the apostles' hands.

And Simon having seen that through the laying on **18-25**
of the hands of the apostles the Spirit was being given, offered them money, saying, Give to me also at once this authority in order that on whomsoever I lay my hands, he may be receiving the Holy Spirit. But Peter said to him, May your money accompany you in your destruction, because the gift of God you thought to acquire with money. You do not have a part nor a lot in this matter concerning which I am speaking, for your heart is not straightforward and sincere in the sight of God. Therefore repent at once of this your wickedness and beseech

the Lord if perhaps the purpose of your heart may be forgiven you, for I plainly see that you are in the gall of bitterness and in the bond of iniquity. Then Simon answering said, As for you, you beseech the Lord on my behalf in order that none of the things of which you have spoken may come upon me. Then after they had borne their testimony and had spoken the word of the Lord they proceeded on their return journey to Jerusalem and kept on proclaiming the good news in many villages of the Samaritans.

26, 27   And an angel of the Lord spoke to Philip, saying, Arise at once and be going on your way in a southerly direction along the road which goes down from Jerusalem to Gaza. This road is in an uninhabited region. And having arisen, he proceeded on his journey.

27-33   And behold. A man, an Ethiopian, a eunuch, a royal official of great authority serving under Candace, queen of the Ethiopians, who was in charge of all her treasure, who had gone to Jerusalem for the purpose of worshipping, was now returning and sitting in his chariot and reading the prophet Isaiah. And the Spirit said to Philip, Go towards this chariot at once and join yourself to it. And having run towards it, Philip heard him reading Isaiah the prophet. And he said, Do you really understand the things which you are reading? And he said, How am I able to unless someone guides me? And he urged Philip to come up and sit with him. Now, the contents of the scripture which he was reading were these: In the same manner as a sheep, to slaughter He was led. And in the same manner as a lamb before the one who is shearing it is without a sound, in the same manner He does not open His mouth. In His humiliation the equitable administration of justice due Him was denied Him. His nativity who shall set forth, for His life is taken from the earth?

34-40   And the eunuch answering Philip said, I beg of you, concerning whom is the prophet saying this, concerning himself or concerning some other person of a different character? And Philip opened his mouth and beginning from this scripture announced the good news to him concerning Jesus. And as they were proceeding along the road they came to a certain water, and the eunuch says, Look, water. What is there that hinders me from being baptized? And he gave orders for the chariot to stand still. And the two descended into the water, both Philip and the eunuch. And he baptized him. And when they came up out from the water, the Lord's Spirit caught away Philip, and the eunuch saw him no longer, and he proceeded along his road rejoicing. And Philip was discovered at Azotus. And passing through, he proclaimed the good news to all the cities until he came to Caesarea.

And Saul, still breathing in a personally produced atmosphere of threatening and slaughter against the disciples of the Lord, having gone to the chief priest, asked from him as a personal favor letters to Damascus, to the synagogues, in order that if he found certain ones who belonged to the Way [that characteristic course of conduct exemplified by believers in the Christ of Christianity], both men and women, he might bring them bound to Jerusalem. **1, 2**

And as he was proceeding on his journey he was drawing near to Damascus. And suddenly there flashed around him a light out of heaven. And having fallen upon the ground he heard a voice saying, Saul, Saul, why are you persecuting me? And he said, Who are you, Sir? And as for myself, I am Jehoshua, whom, as for yourself, you are persecuting. But arise at once and go into the city and it shall be told you that which is a necessity in the nature of the case for you to be doing. And the men who were journeying with him stood speechless, hearing indeed the voice as a sound only and not understanding the words, moreover not seeing anyone. And Saul arose from the ground, but having opened his eyes he was seeing nothing. And leading him by the hand, they brought him into Damascus. And he was three days without sight. And he did not eat nor did he drink. **3-9**

And there was a certain disciple in Damascus named Ananias. And the Lord said to him in a vision, Ananias. And he said, Behold, I am here, Lord. And the Lord said to him, Having arisen, proceed to the street called **10-14** the Straight Street, and inquire in the home of Judas for one whose name is Saul, a citizen of Tarsus; for behold, he is praying, and he saw a man whose name is Ananias who came and laid his hands upon him in order that he may recover his sight. And Ananias answered, Lord, I heard from many concerning this man, how many evil things he did to your saints in Jerusalem. And here he has delegated authority from the chief priests to bind all those who are calling on your Name.

15-19   But the Lord said to him, Be going on your way, because this man is a selected-out instrument of mine for the purpose of bearing my Name both before Gentiles and kings and the sons of Israel, for, as for myself, I will show him how many things it is necessary in the nature of the case for him to suffer on behalf of my Name. Then Ananias went off and entered the city. And having placed his hands upon him he said, Saul, brother, the Lord has sent me on a mission, Jehoshua, He who appeared to you on the road as you were coming, in order that you may recover your sight and be controlled by the Holy Spirit. And immediately there fell off from his eyes something having the appearance of incrustations. He recovered his sight, and having arisen, he was baptized, and having taken nourishment, he was strengthened.

19-21   Then he was with the disciples in Damascus for certain days. And immediately in the synagogues he proclaimed Jesus, his message being that this very person is the Son of God. And all those hearing continued to be amazed to the point of being beside themselves with wonder, and kept on saying, Is not this man he who made havoc among those who in Jerusalem are calling upon this Name, and who came here for this purpose, in order that having bound them he might bring them to the chief priests?

22-25   And Saul kept on being endued with power to a greater degree, and he bewildered Jews, those residing in Damascus, proving that this very person is the Christ. And when a considerable number of days had elapsed, the Jews consulted together with a view to putting him out of the way. But their plot became known to Saul. And they kept on watching the gates both day and night in order that they might make away with him. Then the disciples, having taken him at night, sent him down through [a window in] the wall, having lowered him in a large basket.

And having come to Jerusalem, he kept on trying to **26-31** keep company with the disciples. And all were fearing him, not believing that he was a disciple. But Barnabas, coming to his help, brought him to the apostles and related in detail to them how on the road he saw the Lord and that He spoke to him, and how in Damascus he spoke out boldly in the Name of Jesus. And he was with them, going in and going out in Jerusalem, speaking boldly in the Name of the Lord, and he kept on both speaking and disputing with the Jews who had adopted Greek culture. But they kept on attempting to make away with him. And the brethren, having come to know of this, brought him down to Caesarea and sent him forth to Tarsus on a mission. So then the Church throughout Judaea and Galilee and Samaria was in possession of unbroken tranquillity, being constantly built up and proceeding on its way in the fear of the Lord, and by means of the instrumentality of the exhortation and encouragement of the Holy Spirit was multiplied as to its membership.

Now, it came to pass that as Peter was passing **32-35** through all parts, he came down also to the saints who were residing in Lydda. And there he found a certain man named Aeneas who for eight years had been lying prostrate on his bed, he being completely paralyzed. And Peter said to him, Jesus Christ is healing you right now. Arise at once and immediately spread your bed out evenly for comfort, doing this for yourself. And immediately he arose. And all those who were residing in Lydda and Saron saw him, who were such as turned to the Lord.

Now, in Joppa there was a certain woman disciple **36, 37** named Tabitha, which name being interpreted is Dorcas, the name Dorcas meaning gazelle, the creature with the beautiful eyes. This woman was abounding in good works and in the giving of alms to the needy, in which activities she was constantly engaged. And it came to pass that in those days she became ill and died. And having bathed her, they placed her in a room in the upper part of the house.

38-43   Now, Lydda being near Joppa, the disciples having heard that Peter was there, sent two men on a mission to him with the following urgent request, Do not delay to come through to the place where we are. And Peter, having arisen, went with them, whom when he came, they brought up into the upper room. And all the widows stood by him weeping audibly and exhibiting the undergarments and the long flowing outer robes, as many as Dorcas was accustomed to make while she was with them. And Peter, having put them all outside and having kneeled down, prayed. And having turned to the corpse he said, Tabitha, arise at once. And she opened her eyes, and having seen Peter, she sat up. And having given her his hand, he raised her up to a standing position. And having called the saints and the widows, he presented her alive. And this became known throughout the whole of Joppa, and many believed on the Lord. And it came to pass that he was the guest in Joppa for a considerable length of time of a certain Simon, one who made his living by tanning hides.

1-6   Now, there was a certain man in Caesarea named Cornelius, a centurion from the military cohort which was called the Italian cohort, a pious man and one who feared God with all his household, who gave many alms to the Jewish people and who made supplication to God always. He saw in a vision clearly and distinctly, about three o'clock in the afternoon, an angel of God who came to him and said to him, Cornelius. And having fixed his gaze upon him and having become afraid, he said, What is it, Sir? And he said, Your prayers and your alms ascended as a memorial before God. And now send men at once to Joppa and fetch a certain Simon who is surnamed Peter. This man is being entertained as a house-guest by a certain individual, Simon, a tanner, whose house is on the seashore.

And when the angel who spoke to him had gone, hav-   7-16
ing called two of his household slaves and a pious soldier
who were numbered among those who were in continual
attendance upon him, and having narrated to them the
entire matter, he sent them off on a mission to Joppa.
Now on the next day as those were on their journey and
nearing the city, Peter went up to the house-top [the
oriental veranda which was used for meditation and
prayer] to engage in prayer, the time, about noon. And
he became very hungry and was desiring to eat. And
while they were preparing the meal, he entered into a
new experience, that of an individual whose attention
has been drawn to and concentrated upon one thing to
the degree that he might as well be outside of his body
so far as his physical senses registering anything is concerned. And he views with a critical eye heaven having
been opened and a certain container descending, this object being like a sheet, a great one, being let down to the
earth by means of four ropes attached to the four corners,
in which there were all kinds of four-footed animals and
reptiles of the earth and birds of the heaven. And there
came a voice to him, Having arisen, Peter, kill at once
and eat. But Peter said, By no means, Lord, because not
yet have I eaten anything which is unhallowed or unclean. And a voice spoke a second time to him, The
things which God cleansed, as for you, stop declaring
unhallowed. And this occurred three times. And immediately the container was taken up into heaven.

Now, while Peter was completely at a loss as to what   17-22
the vision which he saw might be, behold, the men who
were sent off on a mission by Cornelius, having made
diligent inquiry regarding the home of Simon, stood at
the gate, and having called, inquired whether Simon, the
one surnamed Peter, was staying there as a guest. And
while Peter was earnestly pondering in his mind the matter concerning the vision, the Spirit said, Behold, two
men are looking for you. But, having arisen, go down
at once and be going on your way with them without any
hesitation as to whether it is lawful or not, because, as
for myself, I have sent them on a mission. Then Peter,
having gone down to the men, said, Behold, as for my-

self, I am he for whom you are looking. What is the reason for your being here? And they said, Cornelius, a centurion, a man who is upright and who fears God and who is being highly recommended by the entire nation of the Jews, was divinely commanded by a holy angel to send for you to come to his home and to hear words from you.

23-27   Then he invited them in and extended to them the hospitality of the home. On the next day, having arisen, he went with them, and certain of the brethren of Joppa accompanied him. On the following day they entered Caesarea. Now, Cornelius was looking for them with eager expectation and hope, having called together his relatives and intimate friends. And when it came to pass that Peter entered, Cornelius having met him, having fallen at his feet, prostrated himself in an expression of profound respect. But Peter raised him up saying, Stand up. As for myself, I also am myself a man. And as he was conversing with him he entered and found many gathered together.

28, 29   And he said to them, As for you, you understand that it is a violation of established order for a man, a Jew, to enter into close relations with or come to a foreigner. And yet to me God showed that I am not to be calling any man unhallowed or unclean. Wherefore I also came without debating the issue, having previously been sent for. I am inquiring therefore, for what reason did you send for me?

30-33   And Cornelius said, Four days ago I was observing the afternoon prayer hour at three o'clock in my home, and behold, a man stood before me in brilliant apparel and said, Cornelius, your prayer was heard and your benefactions to others in need are held in remembrance as a memorial before God. Send therefore at once to Joppa and call here Simon who is surnamed Peter. This man is a house-guest in the seaside home of Simon, a tanner. I sent to you, and as for you, you have done well in coming. Now then, as for us, we all are present before God to hear all things which have been commanded you by the Lord.

And Peter, having opened his mouth, said, Of a truth **34-38**
I am in the process of comprehending the fact that God
does not show partiality to anyone because of his looks
or circumstances, but in every nation he who fears Him
and does uprightly is acceptable with Him. The word
which He sent to the sons of Israel, proclaiming as good
news peace through Jesus Christ, this One is Lord of all,
as for you, you know, which word went throughout the
whole of Judaea, beginning from Galilee after the time of
the baptism which John preached; Jesus, the one from
Nazareth, how God anointed Him with the Holy Spirit
and with power, who went about doing good and healing
all who were being oppressed by the devil, because God
was with Him.

And as for us, we are those who are bearing testi- **39-43**
mony to the things we saw, all those things He did both
in the land of the Jews and in Jerusalem, whom they also
killed and suspended on a cross. This One God raised up
on the third day and appointed that He should become
clearly identified, not to all the people, but to witnesses
who had been designated beforehand by God, to us, who
were such as ate and drank with Him after He arose from
the dead. And He charged us to make a proclamation to
the [Jewish] people and to bear testimony that this is
the One who was appointed by God to be the Judge of
the living and the dead. To this One all the prophets
bear testimony, that through His Name everyone who
places his trust in Him receives remission of the penalty
of sins.

While Peter was speaking these words, the Holy **44-48**
Spirit fell upon all those who were hearing the Word.
And the believers who belonged to the circumcision, as
many as came with Peter, were amazed to the point of
being beside themselves with consternation, because also
upon the Gentiles the gift of the Holy Spirit had been
bestowed with the result that now He was in their possession, for they were hearing them speaking by means
of languages [other than their own and not naturally
acquired], and extolling God. Then answered Peter, No
one can forbid the water in order that these may be baptized, who are such as received the Holy Spirit even as

also we, can he? Then he ordered that they be baptized in the Name of Jesus Christ. Then they asked him to be their guest for certain days.

1-10   Now, the apostles and the brethren who resided throughout Judaea heard that the Gentiles also received the word of God. And when Peter went up to Jerusalem those of the circumcision disputed with him saying, You went in to men who were uncircumcised and ate with them. And Peter having begun, went to expounding the matter in its sequence of events, saying, As for myself, I was in the city of Joppa praying, and I being in a state in which my attention was withdrawn from everything else and fixed on things divine, saw a vision, a certain container like a great sheet descending, being let down out of heaven by four great strips of cloth. And it came even to me, and having fastened my gaze upon it, I considered it attentively. And I saw the four-footed animals of the earth and the wild beasts and the birds of heaven. And I heard also a voice saying to me, Having arisen, Peter, kill at once and eat. And I said, By no means, Lord, because that which is unhallowed or unclean, never yet did it enter my mouth. But there answered a second time a voice out of heaven, The things which God cleansed, as for you, stop calling them unhallowed. And this was done three times. And all was drawn up again into heaven.

11-18   And behold. Immediately, three men had come to the house in which we were, sent on a mission from Caesarea to me. And the Spirit told me to go with them without even one bit of hesitation as to its propriety. Moreover, there came with me also these six brethren, and we entered into the house of the man. Then he reported to us how he saw the angel in his house stand and say, Send at once a mission to Joppa and bring back Simon, the one surnamed Peter, who will speak words to you by which, as for yourself, you shall be saved and everyone of your household. Now, when I began to be speaking, the Holy Spirit fell upon them even as upon us at the beginning. Then there was brought to my remembrance the word of the Lord how He was saying, John indeed baptized by means of water, but as for yourselves, you will be baptized by means of the Holy Spirit. Therefore, in view of the fact that God gave the equal gift to them as also to us who believed on the Lord Jesus Christ, as for myself, who was I that I would be able to hinder God? And having heard these things, they were silent and glorified God saying, Then also God gave repentance to the Gentiles resulting in life.

Therefore, those who were scattered abroad, scattered as seed by the distress and affliction which arose on account of Stephen, passed through the country as far as Phoenicia and Cyprus and Antioch, speaking the Word to nobody except only to Jews. Now, there were certain ones of these, men of Cyprus and Cyrene, being such as those who having come to Antioch, began speaking also to the Jews who had acquired Greek culture, announcing as glad tidings the Lord Jesus. And the Lord was with them, and a large number who believed, turned to the Lord.   19-21

Then the word concerning them reached the ears of the assembly at Jerusalem. And they sent off on a mission Barnabas to go as far as Antioch, who, having come and having seen the grace of God, rejoiced and went to exhorting all that with purpose of heart they should live in close fellowship with the Lord; for he was a good man and controlled by the Holy Spirit and full of faith. And there was added to the Lord many people. Then he went off to Tarsus for the purpose of hunting up Saul, and having found him, he brought him to Antioch. And it came to pass that even for a whole year they were gathered together with them in the assembly and taught many people. And the disciples were first given the name, Christian, at Antioch.   22-26

And in these days there came down from Jerusalem, prophets to Antioch. And having arisen, one of them, by name, Agabus, made known through the agency of the Holy Spirit that there was about to be a famine over the whole of the Roman empire, which occurred at the time of Claudias. And the disciples, according as any one of them was prospered, determined, each one of them, to send things which would minister to the needs of those   27-30 brethren who were residing in Judaea, which thing also they did, having sent them to the elders by the hand of Barnabas and Saul.

1-4   Now, at that strategic, significant period [in the growth of the Church and the success of the gospel message], Herod the king laid his hands upon certain of those who belonged to the Church for the purpose of maltreating them. And he put James, the brother of John, out of the way, beheading him with a sword. And having seen that it was a pleasing thing to the Jews, he proceeded to seize Peter also. Now, it was the days of bread baked without yeast. And having apprehended him, he put him in prison, having delivered him into the custody of sixteen soldiers who were to guard him constantly, purposing as the result of mature consideration after the passover to set him before the people for the purpose of being tried in their courts.

5-9   Therefore, on the one hand, Peter was continually guarded in the prison, but on the other hand, prayer was continually and earnestly being directed by the Church to God concerning him. Now, when Herod was about to bring him out, on that night Peter was slumbering between two soldiers, securely bound by two chains, and guards were at the door who were maintaining a constant watch. And behold, the Lord's angel came suddenly and stood by him, and a light shone in his cell. And having gently tapped Peter's side, he raised him up, saying, Arise quickly. And his chains fell off his hands. Then the angel said to him, Put on your belt and bind on your sandals. And he did this. And he said to him, Throw your outer garment around yourself and keep on following with me. And having gone out, he kept on following, and he did not know that it was true, namely, that which was taking place through the agency of the angel, but he was of the opinion that he was seeing a vision.

10   Now, after they had gone through the guards posted at the first and second stations, they came up against the iron gate which leads into the city, which opened to them automatically, and having gone out they went on along one street, and immediately the angel departed from him.

And Peter, having come to himself, said, Now I know **11-17** truly that the Lord dispatched His angel on a mission and delivered me out of Herod's hand and from every expectation of the people of the Jews. And having taken in his situation clearly, he went to the home of Mary the mother of John, the one surnamed Mark, where there were many who had come together and were praying. And after Peter had knocked on the door of the passageway, there came a female slave to answer the knock, her name, Rhoda. And having recognized the voice of Peter, in her joy she failed to open up the passageway, but having run in she announced that Peter was standing before the entrance. But they said to her, You are raving mad. But she strongly and consistently asserted that thus it was. But they kept on saying, It is his angel [his guardian angel, assuming his form and voice, a Jewish belief]. But Peter remained and kept on knocking. And having opened the door, they saw him and were beside themselves with astonishment. And having beckoned to them with his hand to keep quiet, he related in detail to them how the Lord had brought him out of the prison, and said, Report these things to James and the brethren. And having gone out, he proceeded to a different place.

Now, day having come, there was no small commo- **18,19** tion among the soldiers as to what then had become of Peter. And after Herod had made a careful search for him and did not find him, having questioned the guards, he ordered that they be led away to execution, and having gone down from Judaea to Caesarea, he spent some time there.

Now, Herod was having a violent quarrel with the **20-25** Tyreans and Sidonians that had lasted for some time. And they with one accord came to him, and having won the favor of Blastus, the king's chief valet, they kept on requesting peace, because their country received its supplies of food from the country of the king. And on an appointed day Herod, having arrayed himself in royal apparel, having seated himself upon the judgment seat, was making an address to them. And the people kept on shouting, The voice of a god and not of a man. And immediately an angel of the Lord afflicted him with a disease because he did not give God the glory. And having reached that stage in the disease where worms were eating him, he expired. But the word of God kept on growing and multiplying. And Barnabas and Saul returned from Jerusalem, and having completed their ministry, took with them John whose surname was Mark.

1-3   Now, there were in Antioch in the assembly which was there, prophets and teachers, as Barnabas and Simeon, the one called Niger, and Lucius and Cyrenian, Manaean who had been reared with Herod the tetrarch, and Saul. Now, as they were ministering to the Lord in sacred things and were fasting, the Holy Spirit said, Now, therefore, set apart for me at once Barnabas and Saul for the work to which I have called them to myself. Then, having fasted and prayed and having laid their hands upon them, they sent them away.

4-12   So then they themselves, having been sent out by the Holy Spirit, went down to Seleucia. And from there they sailed away to Cyprus, and having come to Salamis, they went to making the word of God known in the synagogues of the Jews. And they were also having John as their attendant and assistant. And having gone through the whole island until they came to Paphos, they found a certain man, one who practiced the magical arts, a false prophet, a Jew, his name, Bar-jesus, who was with the proconsul, Sergius Paulus, a man of understanding. This man having called Barnabas and Saul to himself, desired to hear the word of God. But Elymas the soothsayer [for thus is his name by interpretation, the wise one] kept on standing up against them, seeking to turn away the proconsul from the Faith. But Saul, who also is called Paul, controlled by the Holy Spirit, having fixed his gaze upon him, said, O full of every craftiness and every unscrupulousness, son of the devil. enemy of every righteousness, will you not cease perverting the right ways of the Lord? And now, behold, the Lord's hand is upon you, and you will be blind, not seeing the sun for a time. And immediately there fell upon him a dimness of the eyes and darkness. And walking about, he went to seeking someone to lead him by the hand. Then the proconsul, having seen that which had taken place, believed, being astonished to the point of a loss of self-control at the teaching of the Lord.

Now, having put out to sea from Paphos, Paul and his associates came to Perga of Pamphylia, but John having withdrawn from them, returned to Jerusalem. Then, they themselves having gone on through the country from Perga, came to Antioch, the Pisidian Antioch, and having gone into the synagogue on the day of the sabbath, seated themselves. And after the reading of the law and the prophets, the rulers of the synagogue sent to them saying, Men, brethren, if, as is the case, you have any word of exhortation to the people, you are invited to speak.

13-15

Then Paul, having arisen and having beckoned with his hand, said, Men, Israelites, and those who fear God [the latter, Gentile proselytes], give me your attention. The God of this people Israel selected out [from the rest of humanity] our fathers and exalted the people during their temporary residence in the land of Egypt, and with a high arm He brought them out of it, and for about forty years He tenderly cared for them in the uninhabited region, and having destroyed seven nations in the land of Canaan, He divided their land, distributing it by lot among them as an inheritance for about four hundred and fifty years. And after these things He gave them judges until Samuel the prophet.

16-20

And after this they requested a king, and God gave them Saul, the son of Kish, a man of the tribe of Benjamin, for forty years. And having deposed him, He raised up David for them as king, to whom He bore testimony and said, I found David, the son of Jesse, a man after my heart who will do all things which are my desires. Of this man, God from his family according to promise brought to Israel a Saviour, Jesus, John having previously heralded to all the people, Israel, before His entry upon His ministry, a baptism associated with repentance. And when John was finishing the course of his office [as herald], he kept on saying, What do you conjecture that I am? As for myself, I am not He. But behold.

21-25

There comes One after me, the sandals of whose feet
I am not worthy to unloose.

26-41   Men, brethren, sons of the family of Abraham and
those among you who fear God, to us the word of this
salvation was sent forth, for those who are residing in
Jerusalem and their rulers, having been ignorant of this
One and of the voices of the prophets which every sabbath are read, in condemning Him fulfilled this word,
and though not having found even one cause of death in
Him, they asked Pilate as a personal favor that He be
put out of the way. And when they fulfilled all the things
which stand written concerning Him, having taken Him
down from the cross, they laid Him in a tomb. But God
raised Him out from among the dead. He was seen for
many days by those who had come up with Him from
Galilee to Jerusalem, who now are as to their nature those
who are testifying to what they have seen of Him to the
people. And, as for us, we are bringing good news to you
of the promise which was made to our fathers, that God
has completely fulfilled this to our children, having raised
up Jesus [as the Messiah], as also in the second psalm
it stands written, As for you, you are my Son. As for
myself, today I have begotten you. Now that He raised
Him up from among those who are dead, no longer destined to return to corruption, thus has He spoken, and
the record is a permanent one, I will give to all of you
the holy things of David, the trustworthy things, because
also in another psalm He says, You will not appoint your
Holy One to see corruption, for indeed, David during his
own generation having ministered in the sphere of the
counsel of God, fell asleep [died], was buried with his
fathers, and saw corruption. But He whom God raised
up did not see corruption. Let it be known therefore to
you, men, brethren, that through this One to you is being
announced the putting away of sins, and from all things
from which you were not able by the law of Moses to
be justified, by this One everyone who believes is justified. Therefore, be bewaring lest there come upon you
that which has been spoken by the prophets and is on permanent record, Behold, you despisers, and you who wonder and perish, because as for myself, I am accomplishing

a work in your days, a work which you will by no means
believe if anyone keep on narrating it in full to you.

Now, as they were going out they kept on begging
that on the next sabbath these words might be preached
to them. Then after the congregation had dissolved,
many of the Jews and the proselytes who were worshipping followed with Paul and Barnabas who, speaking to
them, were urging them to be continuing in the grace of
God. And on the next sabbath almost the entire city
was gathered together to hear the word of God. Then the
Jews, having seen the crowds, became filled with jealousy
and went to speaking against the things which were being spoken by Paul, saying slanderous and evil things.
And having become bold, Paul and Barnabas said, To you
it was required in the nature of the case for the word of
God to be spoken first. Since now you are thrusting it
away from yourselves and are judging yourselves not
worthy of life eternal, behold, we are turning ourselves to
the Gentiles, for thus has the Lord commanded us; I
have appointed you as a light of Gentiles in order that
you may be for salvation to the end of the earth. Now,
the Gentiles hearing this were rejoicing and glorifying
the word of the Lord. And as many as had been appointed to life eternal believed. And the word of the Lord was
being carried in different directions and to different places
throughout the entire country. But the Jews urged on
the devout women, those of high position and the leading men of the city, and raised up persecution against
Paul and Barnabas, and threw them out of their boundaries. But having shaken off the dust of their feet against
them, they came to Iconium. And the disciples were
continually filled with joy and controlled by the Holy
Spirit.

And it came to pass in Iconium that they entered the
synagogue of the Jews together and spoke in such a manner that a large company of both Jews and Gentiles believed. But the Jews who were unwilling to be persuaded
and thus withheld belief, stirred up the minds of the Gentiles and rendered them antagonistic toward their brethren. So then for a long time they stayed there, speaking
boldly in reliance upon the Lord who bore testimony

42-52

1-7

upon the basis of His word to His grace by granting attesting miracles and miracles exciting wonder to be done constantly through their hands. But the population of the city was split up into factions, and some on the one hand were with the Jews and others on the other hand were with the apostles. Now, when there arose a hostile intention on the part of both Gentiles and Jews with their rulers to treat them in a shameful manner and to stone them, having become aware of it, they fled for refuge to the cities of Lycaonia, Lystra, and Derbe, and to the surrounding region, and there they were engaged in proclaiming the good news.

8-10   And a certain man who was without strength in his feet, his lameness having its source in a prenatal condition, who never yet had walked, was sitting there at Lystra. This man was listening to Paul speak, who, having fixed his gaze attentively upon him and having seen that he was having faith to be healed, said in a great voice, Stand upright upon your feet. And he leaped up with a single bound and went to walking about.

11-13   And the crowds having seen what Paul did, raised their voice in the language of Lycaonia saying, The gods, having assumed the likeness of men, came down to us. And they began calling Barnabas, Zeus, and Paul, Hermes, since he himself was the leader in the discourse. And the priest of Zeus, whose temple was before the city, having brought oxen and garlands to the gates, was desiring to offer sacrifice with the crowds.

14-18   But the apostles, Barnabas and Paul, having heard of this, having torn in two pieces their outer garments, leaped into the midst of the crowd, shouting out and saying, Men, why are you doing these things? And as for us, we are men who possess the same kind of feelings that you have, proclaiming the good news that you should turn from these things that are futile, ineffectual in accomplishing the purpose for which they were intended, to God who is alive, who made the heaven and the earth and the sea and all the things which are in them, who in the generations gone by permitted all the nations to be proceeding along their ways of life. And yet He did not leave himself without a witness in that He did good, giving to you rain from heaven and fruitful seasons, filling your hearts with food and good cheer. And saying these things they with difficulty restrained the crowds from offering sacrifice to them.

Then there arrived Jews from Antioch and Iconium, and having persuaded the crowds and having stoned Paul, they dragged him by his feet outside of the city, thinking that he had died. However, after the disciples had gathered around him, he arose suddenly and went into the city. And on the next day he went forth with Barnabas to Derbe. And proclaiming the good news in that city and having made many disciples through their teaching, they returned to Lystra and Iconium and Antioch, establishing and strengthening the souls of the disciples, exhorting them to be persevering in and holding true to the Faith, and exhorting them that it is a necessity in the nature of the case to enter the kingdom of God through many tribulations. **19-22**

And having appointed for them elders in every assembly, having prayed in connection with fasting, they commended them to the Lord on whom they had believed. And having gone throughout Pisidia, they came to Pamphylia, and having spoken the Word in Perga, they went down to Attalia, and from there they sailed away to Antioch, from which place they had been committed to the grace of God for the work which they fulfilled. And reaching their destination and gathering the assembly together, they went to reporting as many things as God had done in helping them, and that He opened to the Gentiles a door of faith. And they stayed with the disciples not a little time. **23-28**

And certain men having come down from Judaea began teaching the brethren, and these were their words, Unless you are circumcised after the custom of Moses, you are not able to be saved. And there having come no little discord and questioning to Paul and Barnabas as they faced them, they [the brethren] appointed Paul and Barnabas and certain others of them to go up to the apostles and elders at Jerusalem concerning this question in dis- **1-4** pute. They therefore having been furnished with the requisites for the journey by the assembly, proceeded on their way through Phoenicia and Samaria, narrating in full the turning of the Gentiles [from idolatry to God], and they were constantly giving great joy to all the brethren. And having come to Jerusalem, they were formally and cordially received by the assembly and the apostles and the elders, and they reported as many things as God had done in helping them.

5   But there suddenly rose up [among the assembled believers] certain ones from the religious sect of the Pharisees who believed, saying that it was a necessity in the nature of the case for them to be circumcised and to be commanding them to keep the law of Moses.

6-12   Both the apostles and the elders had come together for the purpose of looking into this matter. And after there had been much debate, Peter, having arisen, said to them, Men, brethren. As for you, you know that a good while ago God made a choice among us to the effect that through my mouth the Gentiles should hear the story of the good news and believe. And God who knows the hearts, bore attesting testimony to them by having given them the Holy Spirit even as also to us. And He made no distinction at all between both us and also you, in answer to their faith having cleansed their hearts. Now, therefore, why are you putting God on trial [to see whether He has committed an error or not] by putting a yoke upon the neck of the disciples which neither our fathers nor we were able to endure? But through the grace of the Lord Jesus we believe that we are saved in the like manner as also those. Then the entire group lapsed into silence and went to listening to Barnabas and Paul recounting in detail as many attesting miracles and miracles that excite wonder and amazement which God performed among the Gentiles through their intermediate agency.

13-18   And after they became silent, James answered, saying, Men, brethren, may I have your attention. Simeon related in detail how that God for the first time exercised His overseeing care in taking out from the Gentiles a people for His Name. And to this agree the words of the prophets, even as it has been written and as a result is on record, After these things I will return and I will build again the hut of David which has fallen down and now lies in ruins. And I will build again the things belonging to it which are lying about in utter ruin. And I will build it anew, in order that those left remaining of mankind may seek out the Lord, also all the Gentiles upon whom my Name has been pronounced, says the Lord who makes these things known from the beginning of the world.

Wherefore, as for myself, my judgment is that we are not to be troubling those from among the Gentiles who are turning to God, but that we write them to be holding themselves off from the pollutions of the idols and from fornication and from eating the flesh of an animal which was killed without the shedding of its blood, and from this blood; for Moses from the time of generations long past has those in every city who proclaim him, being read in the synagogues every sabbath.   **19-21**

Then it seemed good to the apostles and the elders together with the entire assembly to send men who had been selected out of their own number to Antioch with Paul and Barnabas, namely, Judas, the one called Barsabas, and Silas, men who exercised leadership among the brethren, writing through them as follows: The apostles and the elders, brethren, send greetings to those brethren who are of the Gentiles in Antioch and Syria and Cilicia. In view of the fact that we heard that certain ones of our number perplexed and disturbed you with words, throwing your souls into confusion, to whom we did not give any express injunctions, it seemed good to us, having arrived at a unanimous agreement, to send men who have been selected out from our number to you with our beloved Barnabas and Paul, men [Barnabas and Paul] who have jeopardized their lives on behalf of the Name of our Lord Jesus Christ. We have sent therefore Judas and Silas, and they themselves will report the same things verbally, for it seemed good to the Holy Spirit and to us to lay no greater burden upon you than these things which are necessary, that you abstain from eating the flesh of animals left over from the pagan sacrifices, and   **22-29** blood and the flesh of animals killed without the shedding of their blood, and from fornication, from which if you carefully keep yourselves, it shall be well with you. Farewell.

30-35   So they, having been sent off, went down to Antioch, and having gathered together the whole assembly, delivered the letter. And having read it, they burst into exultant joy because of the encouragement it brought them. And both Judas and Silas, also being prophets themselves, through much discourse exhorted the brethren and encouraged them besides. And having been there for some time, they were sent off with peace from the brethren to those who had sent them on the mission. But Paul and Barnabas continued their stay in Antioch with many others, teaching and giving out as good news the word of the Lord.

36-41   And after certain days Paul said to Barnabas, Now, therefore, retracing our steps, let us look in on our brethren for the purpose of seeing what they are in need of and supplying that need, city by city in which we publicly proclaimed the word of the Lord, observing how they are getting along. Now, Barnabas, after thinking the matter over, kept on insisting that they take along with them also John, the one called Mark. But Paul kept on considering it the part of wisdom with reference to this one who withdrew from them from Pamphylia and did not go with them to the work, not to be taking him. And there arose a sharp contention so that they separated from one another, and Barnabas having taken Mark with him, set sail for Cyprus. And Paul, having chosen Silas for himself, went forth, having been commended to the grace of the Lord by the brethren. And he went through Syria and Cilicia establishing the assemblies.

1-5   And he came also to Derbe and Lystra. And behold, a certain disciple was there named Timothy, a son of a Jewish woman who was a believer. However, his father was a Greek, he [Timothy] constantly being well recommended by the brethren in Lystra and Iconium. This one Paul desired to go forth with him. And having taken him, he circumcised him because of the Jews who were in those regions, for they all knew that his father was a Greek. And as they were proceeding through the cities they kept on delivering to them the decrees for them to be keeping which had been issued by the apostles and elders in Jerusalem. So then the assemblies were being strengthened with respect to the Faith and increased in number daily.

Then they passed through Phrygia and the Galatian region, having been forbidden by the Holy Spirit to speak the Word in Asia. And having come down to the borders of Mysia, by a trial-and-error method they kept on attempting to discover whether it was right to go to Bithynia. But the Spirit of Jesus did not permit them to do so. And having skirted Mysia they came down to Troas. **6-8**

And a vision appeared to Paul during the night. A certain man, a Macedonian, was standing and begging him and saying, Come over into Macedonia at once and give us aid. And when he had seen the vision, immediately we endeavored to go forth into Macedonia, concluding that God had called us to tell them the good news. **9, 10**

Then setting sail from Troas we ran a straight course before the wind to Samothracia, and on the morrow, to Neapolis. And from there we went to Philippi which was the first Macedonian city of the district, a [Roman] colony [its citizens, Roman citizens]. Now, we were in this city, staying certain days. And on the day of the sabbath we went outside the gate along the river bank where we supposed there was a place of prayer. And having seated ourselves, we went to speaking to the women who had come together. And a certain woman, by name Lydia, a seller of purple fabrics, from the city of Thyatira, who worshipped God, was listening, whose heart the Lord had opened up wide so that she kept her mind concentrated upon the things which were spoken by Paul. Now, when she was baptized and her household, she begged us, saying, Since you have judged me to be a believer on the Lord, having come into my home, be my guest for a while. And she, by her entreaties, persuaded us to accept her hospitality. **11-15**

16-18   And it came to pass that as we were proceeding to the place of prayer, a certain female slave possessing a spirit [a demon], a pythian spirit [associated with the demonology of the pagan Greek religions], encountered us, who was of such a nature that she provided her masters with a profitable business by acting as a seer and delivering prophecies and oracles. This woman, having followed after Paul and us, cried out saying, These men are slaves of God, the Most High God, such as are making known to you the way of salvation. And this she kept on doing many days. But Paul, thoroughly annoyed and indignant, was worn out, and having turned around to the spirit, said, I charge you in the Name of Jesus Christ to come out of her at once. And he came out that same hour.

19-24   Now, her masters, having seen that the hope of their gain had vanished, having seized Paul and Silas, dragged them by their heels into the market place to the civil rulers, and having brought them to the magistrates said, These men are causing a great deal of trouble in our city, being Jews, and are promulgating customs which it is not lawful for us to be receiving nor to be doing, since we are Romans. And the crowd rose up together against them, and the magistrates, having torn off their clothing, were issuing orders to be beating them with rods. And having inflicted many stripes upon them they threw them into prison, charging the jailer to be guarding them safely, who, having received such an order, threw them into the inner prison and made their feet secure in an instrument of torture having five holes, four for the wrists and ankles and one for the neck.

25-34   Now, about midnight Paul and Silas while they were praying were also singing praises to God, mingling petition with songs of praise, and the prisoners were listening to them, enjoying their singing. And suddenly there was an earthquake, a great one, so that the foundations of the prison were caused to totter. And all the doors were instantly opened, and the bonds of all were loosened. And the jailer, having been roused out of sleep and having seen the doors of the prison opened, having drawn

out his sword, was about to be killing himself, supposing
that the prisoners had escaped. But Paul shouted in a
loud voice, saying, Do not begin to do yourself one bit
of harm, for we are all here. Then, having asked for a
light, he sprang in, and having become terrified, fell down
before Paul and Silas, and having brought them outside,
said, Sirs, what is it necessary in the nature of the case
for me to keep on doing in order that I may be saved?
And they said, Put your trust at once and once for all
in the Lord Jesus, and as for yourself, you shall be saved,
also your household. And they spoke to him the word of
God together with all those in his home. And having
taken them in that same hour under his care, he bathed
their stripes, washing away the coagulated blood. And he
himself was immediately immersed and all those who belonged to him. And having brought them up into his
home, he put them at his own table and set food before
them. And he rejoiced, having believed in God with his
whole household.

And day having come, the magistrates sent the lictors **35, 36**
on a mission saying, Release those men at once. Then
the jailer reported these words to Paul, The magistrates
have sent men with a commission to release you. Therefore, now having gone out, be proceeding on your way
in peace.

But Paul said to them, Having beaten us publicly, we **37-40**
who are uncondemned, men who are Romans, they threw
us into prison. And, as for us, in secret are they now
thrusting us out? No indeed, but having come themselves,
let them bring us out. Then the lictors reported to the
magistrates these words. And they became afraid, having
heard that they were Romans. And having come, they
begged them, and having brought them out, they went to
asking them to go away from the city. And having come
out of the prison, they went to the home of Lydia, and
having seen the brethren, they encouraged them and went
off.

Now, after traveling through Amphipolis and Apol- **1-3**
lonia, they came to Thessalonica, where there was a synagogue of the Jews. And Paul according to his custom

went in to them, and for three sabbaths reasoned with them upon the basis and from the source of the scriptures, making these plain to the understanding and setting them forth as proof of the fact that it was a necessity in the nature of the case for the Christ [Messiah] to suffer and to be raised out from among the dead, and that this Man is the Christ [the Messiah], this Jesus whom, as for myself, I am proclaiming to you.

4-9   And certain of them were persuaded and were allotted [by God] to Paul and Silas [as disciples], a great multitude of the devout Greeks, and not a few women who were of the very first rank. But the Jews, motivated by jealousy, having taken to themselves certain pernicious men belonging to the loungers in the market place, and gathering a crowd, put the city in an uproar, and having attacked the house of Jason, they were seeking to bring them [Paul and Silas] before the people. But not having found them, they went to dragging Jason by the feet and certain brethren to the city officials, shouting, These who turned the Roman empire upside down, have arrived here also, whom Jason received as his guests. And these, all of them, are doing things contrary to Caesar's decrees, saying that there is another king of a different nature, Jesus. And they stirred up the people and the city officials hearing these things. And having put Jason and the rest under bond, they released them.

10-14   And the brethren immediately sent off both Paul and Silas by night to Berea, who, having arrived there, went into the synagogue of the Jews. Now, these were more noble-minded than those in Thessalonica, who were such that they received the Word with all readiness of mind, daily scrutinizing the scriptures whether these things were so. Many of them indeed therefore believed, and of the Greek women, the ones who were of rank, and of men not a few. But when the Jews of Thessalonica came to know that in Berea also the word of God was proclaimed by Paul, they went there also, stirring up and agitating the crowds. And then immediately the brethren sent Paul off to be proceeding as far as the sea. And both Silas and Timothy remained there.

Now, those who conducted Paul brought him up to   **15**
Athens. And having received a command for Silas and
Timothy to the effect that they should come to him as
quickly as possible, they went off.

Now, while Paul was waiting for them in Athens, his   **16-21**
spirit was constantly provoked and irritated in him, viewing with a critical eye the city which was full of idols.
Then indeed he went to reasoning in the synagogue of the
Jews and with the devout persons in the town square
which was used as the public forum every day with those
whom he happened to meet. And certain also of the Epi-
curean and Stoic philosophers kept on encountering him
for the purpose of disputing with him. And some went
to saying, What would he desire to be saying, granted he
was able to say anything, this ignorant plagiarist, picking
up scraps of information here and there, unrelated in his
own thinking and passing them off as the result of his
own mature thought? But others began saying, He seems
to be a proclaimer of foreign divinities; because he was
announcing as good news Jesus and His resurrection. And
having taken him, they brought him to the Court of Areopagus [the seat of the ancient and venerable Athenian
court which decided the most solemn questions connected
with religion], saying, May we come to know what this
teaching is, new as to its character, which you are pro-
pounding, for you are bringing certain startling and be-
wildering things to our ears? Therefore it is our reasoned desire that we come to know what the intent of
these things is. Now, all Athenians and the foreigners
residing there devoted their leisure time in not even one
other thing of a different character than to be telling or
listening to something that was newer in its nature.

Then Paul, having stood up in the midst of the Court   **22-31**
of Areopagus, said, Men, Athenians, my critical, understanding eye tells me that in all things you are more di-
vinity-fearing [than the rest of the Greeks]. For when
passing through [your city], looking attentively at the
objects of your worship, I found an altar upon which
was written, TO AN UNKNOWN GOD. That therefore which you are unknowingly worshipping, this, as
for myself, I am announcing to you. The God who made

the universe and all the things in it, this God being the natural Lord of heaven and earth, does not take up His residence in sanctuaries made by hands, neither is He served by the hands of mankind as though needing any certain thing in addition to what He already has, and this in view of the fact that He himself is constantly giving to all life and breath and all things. And He made out of one source material every nation of mankind to inhabit the entire surface of the earth, having marked out the limitations of strategic, epochal periods of time which have been appointed and the fixed boundaries of their occupancy, in order that they should be seeking this aforementioned God, if so then they will grope after Him and find Him, though He is not far from each one of us, for in Him we derive our life and have motion, as also certain of your poets have said, For of Him are we also offspring. Therefore, since we are the offspring of God, we are not under moral obligation to be thinking that this aforementioned Being possessing divine attributes is like gold or silver or stone, a carved work of art and of man's invention. Now, therefore, the times of ignorance God having allowed to pass unnoticed, with reference to the present set of circumstances He declares to men that everyone everywhere should be repenting, because He appointed a day in which He is about to be judging the inhabitants of the earth with an equitable administration of justice by means of a Man whom He appointed, furnishing a guarantee to all in that He raised Him out from among those who are dead.

32-34 And having heard of a resurrection out from among the dead, some began to mock, but others said, We will hear you concerning this yet again. Under these circumstances Paul went out from their midst. But certain men having clung to him, believed, among whom was Dionysius, one of the judges of the Court of Areopagus, and a woman named Damaris, and others with them.

1-3 After these things, having gone out of and away from Athens, he came to Corinth. And having found a certain Jew named Aquila, a man from Pontus recently having come from Italy, and Priscilla his wife, because Claudias had given orders that all the Jews were to be expelled from Rome, he went to them. And because he was of the same occupation, he lived at their home. And they were working at their occupation, for they were by trade makers of small, portable tents used by shepherds and travellers.

And he continued reasoning in the synagogue every **4-11** sabbath, and kept on trying to persuade both Jews and Greeks. Then, when both Silas and Timothy had come down from Macedonia, Paul was wholly occupied with and absorbed in the Word, solemnly affirming to the Jews that the Christ [the Messiah] is Jesus. But when they began to offer an organized and concerted opposition, and began to revile him, he, having shaken off his garments as an expression of extreme contempt for them and an expression of his refusal to have any further intercourse with them, said to them, Your blood be upon your head. As for myself, I am clean [from your blood, having discharged my duty with a clear conscience]. From this moment as particularized by what has just taken place, to the Gentiles I will go. And having removed from there he went into the house of a certain man whose name was Titus Justus, who revered God, whose home was next to the synagogue. And Crispus, the chief ruler of the synagogue, believed on the Lord with his entire household. And many of the Corinthians hearing, were believing and were being baptized. And the Lord said to Paul during the night through a vision, Stop being afraid, but continue to be speaking and do not begin to be silent, because, as for myself, I am with you, and not even one person will assault you to do you harm, for I have a large group of people in this city. And he took his seat there as a teacher for a year and six months, teaching the word of God.

Now, when Gallio was proconsul of Achaia, the Jews **12-17** made a concerted assault upon Paul and brought him to the place where legal cases were tried, saying, This fellow, by the means of persuasion, is stirring up the men to worship God in a manner contrary to the law. And when Paul was about to be opening his mouth, Gallio said to the Jews, If it were a matter of wrong-doing against someone or pernicious villainy, O Jews, reason would dictate that I should have borne patiently with you. But since it is a parcel of questions concerning a word and names and your own law, you yourselves be seeing to it. As for myself, a judge of these things I do not after mature consideration desire to be. And he drove them away from his judgment seat. Then they all, having seized Sosthenes, the chief ruler of the synagogue, began beating him before the judgment seat. And of these things, not even one was a concern to Gallio.

18-23   And Paul, having remained there yet a considerable length of time, having bidden the brethren farewell, started to sail to Syria, and with him Priscilla and Aquila, having cut his hair short after the manner of the shearing of a sheep, for he had been under a vow which he had taken upon himself. And he came down to Ephesus and left them there, and he himself, having gone into the synagogue, reasoned with the Jews. But when they went to asking him to remain a longer time, he did not consent to do so, but having bidden them farewell and having said, I will return again to you if God so desires it, he sailed from Ephesus. And having landed at Caesarea, having gone up [to Jerusalem] and having paid his respects to the assembly, he went down to Antioch. And having spent some time there, he went off, going through the region of Galatia and Phrygia in that order, stabilizing all the disciples.

24-28   And a certain Jew named Apollos, a native of the city of Alexandria, a learned and eloquent man, came down to Ephesus, being a powerful man in the scriptures. This man had been instructed in the way of the Lord, and being fervent in his spirit was speaking and teaching accurately the things concerning Jesus, knowing only John's baptism. And this man began to be speaking out boldly in the synagogue. Now, Priscilla and Aquila, having heard him, took him to themselves and expounded the way of God more accurately to him. And when he desired to go through into Achaia, the brethren wrote, encouraging the disciples to receive him, and he, having come, threw himself into the work with those who had believed through grace, giving them much help, for he argued the case down to a finish and conclusively refuted the Jews publicly, proving through the medium of the scriptures that the Christ [the Messiah] is Jesus.

Now, it came to pass that while Apollos was at Corinth, Paul having gone through the upper districts came to Ephesus. And having found certain disciples he said to them, The Holy Spirit, did you receive Him as a result of your initial act of faith? And they said to him, In fact, we did not hear that there was a Holy Spirit. And he said, Upon what basis then were you baptized? And they said, Upon the basis of John's baptism. Then Paul said, John baptized with a baptism that had to do with repentance, saying to the people that they should believe on the One who comes after him, that is, on Jesus. And having heard this they were baptized into the Name of the Lord Jesus. And after Paul had placed his hands upon them the Holy Spirit came upon them, and they began speaking in languages [other than their own and unacquired], and began to prophesy. And all the men were about twelve.

1-7

And having entered the synagogue, he kept on speaking boldly for three months, reasoning and persuading concerning the kingdom of God. But when some became stubborn and obstinate and were non-persuadable, speaking evil of the Way before the crowd, having withdrawn from them, he separated his disciples from them, daily reasoning in the school of Tyrannus. And this went on for two years, so that all those residing in Asia heard the word of the Lord, both Jews and Greeks. And God kept on performing miracles by the hand of Paul, miracles demonstrating the power of God, not the ordinary kind known to the apostles and completely different from the deeds of the Jewish exorcists, but uncommon, extraordinary ones, so that even to the sick were being brought from his body handkerchiefs and work aprons, and the diseases left them. And the spirits, the pernicious ones, proceeded out of them. Then certain also of the Jews who went from place to place employing a formula of conjuration to expel demons, attempted also to be naming over those who had pernicious spirits the Name of the Lord Jesus, saying, I adjure you by the Jesus whom Paul is proclaiming.

8-13

14-17 Now, there were seven sons of a certain Sceva, a Jew, a chief priest, doing this. And the pernicious spirit answering said to them, This Jesus I recognize and with this Paul I am acquainted. But as for you, who are you? And the man in whom the pernicious spirit was, having leaped upon them, having gained the mastery over them, overpowered them so that they fled out of that house with their clothing in shreds and having been wounded. And this became known both to all Jews and Gentiles, those residing in Ephesus. And fear fell upon all of them. And the Name of the Lord Jesus was being extolled and highly esteemed.

18-20 And many of those who were true believers kept on coming, openly confessing, and by fully declaring them, making a clean sweep of their practices. And a considerable number of those who practiced the magical arts, having brought their books together, kept on throwing book after book into the fire before all. And they added up their total cost and found it to be fifty thousand pieces of silver. So mightily did the word of the Lord keep on growing and gaining strength.

21, 22 When these things were fulfilled, Paul purposed in his spirit [his own mind], having gone through Macedonia and Achaia, to proceed on his way to Jerusalem, having said, After I have been there, it is a necessity in the nature of the case for me also to see Rome. Then, having sent on a mission into Macedonia two who were his aids, Timothy and Erastus, he himself stayed for a time in Asia.

23-27 And there arose at that strategic, epochal time no small tumult concerning the Way, for a certain individual, Demetrius by name, a silversmith, making miniature silver temples of Diana containing an image of the goddess, was furnishing no little business for the artisans, and having called them together also with the workmen of the associated trades, he said, Men, you know that from this occupation we have our wealth. And you are clearly seeing and hearing that not only in Ephesus but almost throughout all of Asia this fellow, Paul, having persuaded them, turned away a great number of people, saying that they are not gods, those being made by hands. Moreover, not only is our department of trade in danger of coming into disrepute, but also the temple of the great goddess Artemis is in danger of being considered as nothing and is destined also to be deprived of her magnificence, whom all of Asia and the Roman empire worships.

Moreover, also having heard these things, having become filled with a boiling rage, they kept on continuously crying out, saying, Great is Artemis of the Ephesians. And the city was filled with the confusion, and they rushed with one accord into the theatre, having seized Gaius and Aristarchus of Macedonia, Paul's travel companions. And when Paul was desiring to go into this great mass of people assembled in this public place, the disciples kept on forbidding him to do so. Moreover, also certain of the chief officers of Asia, wealthy men who supervised the Greek games and festivals, being his friends, having sent to him, kept on begging him not to take the risk of entering the theater. So then some kept on crying one thing and some another, for the assembly had been called together in an irregular way, and was as a result in a state of confusion, and the majority did not know on what account they had come together. Then they brought Alexander out of the crowd, the Jews thrusting him forward. And Alexander, having beckoned with his hand, was desiring to present his verbal defense to the people. But having come to recognize that he was a Jew, one voice arose from all for about two hours, crying, Great is Artemis of the Ephesians. Then the city recorder [the officer who drafted decrees, had charge of the city treasury, and had control of the town meeting], having quieted the people, said, Men, Ephesians, who is there then of men who does not know that the city of the Ephesians is warden of the temple of the great Artemis and of her heaven-fallen image? Therefore, these things being such that they are indisputable, it is needful for you to restrain yourselves and to be doing nothing rashly, for you brought these men here who are neither despoilers of temples nor those who have by contemptuous speech come short of the reverence due our goddess.

28-37

38-41   So then, if, as is the case, Demetrius and the craftsmen with him have a matter against anyone, court-meetings are now going on and there are proconsuls. Let them accuse one another. But if you are inquiring concerning anything of a nature further than accusations, it shall be decided in a legally constituted assembly. For indeed we are in danger of being called in question concerning this day's riot, there being not even one bit of cause for it, and with reference to it. We shall not be able to give an account concerning this disorderly riot. And having said these things, he dismissed the assembly.

1-5   And after the uproar ceased, Paul, having sent after the disciples to come to him, having exhorted them, having taken his leave of them, went off for the purpose of proceeding to Macedonia. And having passed through those parts and having exhorted them in much discourse, he went to Greece. And having spent three months there, a plot having been laid against him by the Jews as he was about to set sail for Syria, he became of the opinion that he should return through Macedonia. And there accompanied him Sopater, the son of Pyrrhus of Berea, and of the Thessalonians Aristarchus and Secundus; and Gaius of Derbe, and Timothy; and the Asians, Tychicus and Trophemus. And these having gone on ahead were waiting for us at Troas.

6-12   Now, as for us, we sailed away from Philippi after the days of bread baked without yeast, and came to them at Troas in five days, where we stayed seven days. And on the first day of the week, when we were gathered together to break bread, Paul was discoursing to them, about to go forth next day. And he prolonged his discourse until midnight. Now there were many oil lamps in the upper room where they were gathered together. And there was sitting on the window sill a certain young man named Eutychus, being gradually overcome by a deep sleep. While Paul was continuing his discourse longer, having finally been completely overcome by sleep, he [Eutychus] fell down from the third story and was picked up dead. And Paul, having gone down, fell upon him and having embraced him, said, All of you stop your wailing, for his life is in him. And having gone up and having broken the bread [of the Lord's Supper], and having eaten, and having communed with them for a long while until daybreak, thus he went off. And they brought the lad alive. And they were not a little comforted.

Now, as for us, having gone on ahead to the boat, **13-16** we set sail for Assos, there intending to pick up Paul, for he had ordered it so, intending himself to travel on foot. And when he was meeting us at Assos, having taken him on board, we came to Mitylene. And from there we set sail and on the next day arrived at a point opposite Chios. And on the following day we put in at Samos. And on the succeeding day we came to Miletus, for Paul had resolved to sail past Ephesus in order that he might not waste time in Asia, for he was hurrying on if it were possible for him to be at Jerusalem on the day of Pentecost.

And from Miletus, having sent to Ephesus, he called **17-21** the elders of the assembly to himself. Then, when they came to him, he said to them, As for you, you know that from the first day when I set foot in Asia, how I was with you in close association for the entire time, serving the Lord as His slave with every humility and with tears and trials which befell me by reason of the plots of the Jews; how I did not shrink from declaring to you anything that was profitable, and to teach you publicly and from house to house, testifying both to Jews and Greeks repentance toward God and faith in our Lord Jesus.

And now, behold, as for myself, having been com- **22-24** pletely bound in my spirit, I am proceeding to Jerusalem, not knowing the things that shall befall me in it, except that the Holy Spirit in city after city is bearing testimony to me, saying that bonds and afflictions are awaiting me. But I esteem my life of absolutely no account as precious to myself in order that I [like a Greek athlete] may finish my race, even the ministering work which I received from the presence of the Lord Jesus to bear testimony to the good news of the grace of God.

And now, behold, as for myself, I know positively **25-31** that as for you all, you shall no longer see my face, all of you among whom I went about proclaiming the kingdom. On this account I call you to bear witness on today's day to the fact that I am pure from the blood of all, for I did not shrink from declaring to you the entire counsel of God. Be constantly maintaining a careful watch over yourselves with a view to guarding yourselves, also do the same with respect to all the flock in which the Holy Spirit appointed you as spiritual overseers, shepherding the Church of God which He bought for himself through the agency of the blood, the blood which is His own unique blood, possessed by himself alone. As for myself, I know positively that after my departure [from you now] there shall enter in among you rapacious wolves, not sparing the flock. And from among yourselves there shall arise men mouthing things which have been distorted and corrupted for the purpose of drawing away the disciples after themselves. Therefore, be exercising the most punctilious care, remembering that for three years, night and day, I did not cease admonishing each one with tears.

32-38   And now, as to the present things, I commend you to the Lord and to the word of His grace which has power to build you up, and to give you the inheritance among all those who have been set apart for God. Not even one person's silver or gold or apparel did I covet. You yourselves know from experience that these hands ministered to my necessities and to the necessities of those with me. In all things I gave you an example, that in this manner, working to the point of exhaustion, it is a necessity in the nature of the case to lend a helping hand yourselves to those who are weak, helping them to help themselves in their difficulties, and to be remembering the words of the Lord Jesus, that He himself said, There is more spiritual prosperity in constantly giving than in constantly receiving. And having said these things, having kneeled upon his knees, together with them all, he prayed. And there was much audible weeping by all. They were crying like a child cries. And having fallen upon his neck, they kept on kissing him, one after another, being in anguish especially because of the word which he had spoken, that no longer would they affectionately be gazing upon Paul's face. And they were bringing him to the boat.

And it came to pass when we set sail, having torn   **1-6**
ourselves away from them, having run a straight course, we came to Cos, and the next day to Rhodes, and from there to Patara. And having found a boat crossing over to Phoenicia, having gone on board, we set sail. And having sighted Cyprus and having left it on the left hand, we sailed to Syria, and disembarked at Tyre, for there the boat was unloading its cargo. And after a search, having found the disciples, we remained there seven days, who were such that they kept on saying to Paul through the intermediate agency of the Spirit that he should not be setting foot in Jerusalem. And it came to pass that when we had fulfilled the days, having gone off, we were going on our way, all of them with wives and children accompanying us until we were out of the city. And having kneeled upon our knees on the beach, having prayed, and having said good-bye to one another, we went on board the boat. And those returned home again.

Now, as for us, when we had finished the voyage   **7-12**
from Tyre, we arrived at Ptolemais, and having greeted the brethren, we remained one day with them. And on the next day, having gone off, we came to Caesarea, and having entered the home of Philip the evangelist [the bringer of good news], he being one of the seven [deacons], we remained with him as his guests. This man had four daughters, virgins, exercising the gift of prophecy. Now, while we were remaining there many days, a certain man came down from Judaea, a prophet named Agabus. And having come to us and having taken the belt belonging to Paul, having bound his own feet and hands, he said, Thus says the Holy Spirit, The man who owns this belt, the Jews shall bind in the same manner and deliver him into the hands of the Gentiles. And when we heard these things, as for us, both we and those of that place, kept on begging him not to be setting foot in Jerusalem.

13-17   Then Paul answered, What are you doing, weeping audibly and breaking my heart? For, as for myself, I am holding myself in readiness on behalf of the Name of the Lord Jesus, not only to be bound but also to die in Jerusalem. And he not being persuaded, we lapsed into silence, having said, The will of the Lord, let it be done. And after these days, having packed our luggage, we went on our way up to Jerusalem. And there went also with us certain ones of the disciples from Caesarea, conducting us to a certain Mnason whose guests we were to be, a disciple of long standing. And when we came to Jerusalem, the brethren received us gladly.

18-21   Now, on the next day, Paul went in with us to James. And all the elders were present. And having greeted them he took them through the story of the things God did among the Gentiles through his ministry, rehearsing them one by one. And having heard these things, they glorified God and said to him, You see clearly, brother, how many thousands there are among the Jews of those who have believed. And all are zealous for the law. Now, they have been carefully instructed with reference to yourself that you are teaching all the Jews who live among the Gentiles to apostatize from Moses, saying that they are not to be circumcising their children, neither to order their manner of life after their customs.

22-26   What is it, therefore? They will certainly hear that you have come and are here. This, therefore, do at once, that which we tell you. There are with us four men who have a vow on them. Having taken these to yourself as associates, ceremonially purify yourself in association with them and pay their expenses incurred in taking this vow in order that they may shave their head. And all will know that the things in which they were instructed concerning you are nothing, but that you yourself also are ordering your behavior according to rule, keeping the law. Now, as concerning the Gentiles who have believed, as for us, we wrote, having come to the conclusion that they are to be keeping themselves both from animal flesh which had been sacrificed to idols, and from blood and from flesh of animals which had been killed in such a way that the blood had not been drained out, and from fornication. Then Paul, having taken the men to himself the next day, having purified himself ceremonially together with them, went on into the temple, declaring the fulfillment of the days of the purification, until the sacrifice was offered for each one of them.

Now, when the seven days were about to draw to a **27-36** close, the Jews from Asia having seen him in the temple, kept on throwing the entire crowd into confusion, and they laid their hands on him, crying out, Men, Israelites, be bringing aid. This is the man who is teaching all men everywhere against the people and the law and this place and, moreover, also brought Greeks into the temple and has profaned this holy place. For they had before seen Trophimus, the Ephesian, in the city with him, whom they supposed Paul brought into the temple. And the entire city was thrown into a commotion, and there occurred a running-together of the people, and having seized Paul, they were dragging him by the heels outside of the temple. And immediately the doors were closed. And as they were seeking to kill him, a report went up to the chiliarch who commanded the cohort that all Jerusalem was in confusion, who immediately having taken soldiers and centurions ran down to them. And having seen the chiliarch and the soldiers, they ceased beating Paul. Then, the chiliarch having come near, seized him and ordered that he be bound with two chains. And he went to inquiring who he might be and what he had done. And some in the crowd were shouting one thing and others something else. And when he was not able to come to know the particular thing that could be relied upon as the truth because of the confusion, he commanded that he [Paul] be brought into the barracks. And when he came upon the stairs things came to such a pass that he was being carried by the soldiers because of the violence of the people, for the great mass of people was following, crying out, Be doing away with him.

And as Paul was about to be brought into the bar-**37-XXII 2** racks he says to the chiliarch, Will you permit me to say something to you? And he said, Do you know Greek? As for you, are you not then the Egyptian, that one who

before these days stirred up to sedition and led out
into the uninhabited region four thousand men of the
Assassins? But Paul said, As for myself, I am indeed a
man, a Jew, of Tarsus, a city of Cilicia, a citizen of
no undistinguished city. And I beg of you, permit me
to speak to my people. And after he had given him
permission, Paul, having taken his stand on the stairs,
beckoned with his hand to the people. And a sustained
silence having come, he addressed them in the Hebrew
dialect, saying, Men, brethren, and fathers, hear my
defense which I am making to you just now. And having heard that in the Hebrew dialect he was addressing
them, they provided him all the more with silence.

2-5   And he said, As for myself, I am a man who is a
Jew, having been born in Tarsus of Cilicia, having been
brought up with reference to my education in this city,
at the feet of Gamaliel having been instructed in accordance with the strictness of the law received from the
fathers, being zealous for God even as all you are this
day. I who persecuted this Way to the extent of death,
binding and delivering to prison both men and women,
as also the chief priest bears me witness, also the elder-
ship of the Sanhedrin, from whom having also received
letters to the brethren, was journeying to Damascus for
the purpose of bringing those who were there in chains
to Jerusalem in order that they might be punished.

6-13   And it came to pass that as I was proceeding on my
journey and nearing Damascus, about noon, suddenly
out from heaven there flashed around me like lightning
a great light, and I fell to the ground and heard a voice
saying to me, Saul, Saul, why are you persecuting me?
And as for myself, I answered, Who are you, Sir? And
he said to me, As for myself, I am Jehoshua, the One from
Nazareth, whom you are persecuting. And those with
me saw indeed the light but did not hear the voice of
the One speaking to me so as to understand the words,
but heard it merely as a sound. And I said, What shall
I do, Lord? And the Lord said to me, Having arisen,
be going on your way into Damascus, and there it shall
be told you concerning all things which have been
appointed for you to do. And when the ability of look-

ing upon surrounding objects was taken away from me
because of that light and I was not seeing, being led by
the hand by those with me, I came into Damascus. And
a certain Ananias, a pious man who reverenced God
according to the law, being well recommended by all the
Jews who resided there, having come to me and standing
over me said to me, Saul, brother, look up at once and
recover your sight. And as for myself, I looked up to
him that very hour and recovered my sight.

And he said, The God of our fathers chose and **14-16**
appointed you to come to know experientially His will
and to see with discernment the One who is righteous
and to hear the voice of His mouth, because you shall
be one who bears testimony for Him to all men concerning the things you have seen and heard. And now,
why are you delaying? Having arisen, be baptized and
wash away your sins, having previously called upon His
Name.

And it came to pass that after I returned to Jeru- **17-21**
salem and while I was praying in the temple, I entered
into a new experience, that of having my mind drawn
off from surrounding objects and wholly fixed on things
divine, and I saw Him while He was saying to me,
Hurry, and at once get out of Jerusalem, quickly, because they will not accept your testimony concerning me.
And as for myself, I said, Lord, they themselves know
that I was continually imprisoning and beating in every
synagogue those who put their trust in you. And when
the blood of Stephen your witness was shed, the witness
who bore testimony to you by his death, I myself also was
standing by and exulting, and was guarding the clothes
of those who were putting him out of the way. And
He said to me, Be going on your way, because, as for
myself, to Gentiles afar off I will send you forth on a
mission.

And they kept on listening to him up to this word, **22-24**
and they raised their voice, saying, Be taking away
from the earth such a person, for it was not fitting
that he should live. And when they were crying out and
throwing off their garments and throwing dust into the

air, the chiliarch commanded that he should be brought
into the barracks of the soldiers, having said that he
should be given a judicial examination under the duress
of the torture inflicted by scourging, in order that he
might come to fully know the cause on account of which
they were continually shouting so against him.

25-30   And when they had stretched him out for the lashes,
Paul said to the centurion standing by, A man who is a
Roman and uncondemned, is it legal for you to be
scourging? And the centurion having heard this, having
gone to the chiliarch, brought this report saying, What
are you about to be doing, for this man is a Roman?
And having come, the chiliarch said to him, Be telling
me, as for you, a Roman are you? And he said, Yes.
And the chiliarch answered, As for myself, with a great
sum of money I procured this citizenship. But Paul said,
And as for myself, I am a Roman by heredity. Then
immediately they stood off from him, those who were
about to be examining him. And the chiliarch became
afraid, having come to know that he was a Roman and
because he had put him in chains. Now, on the next day,
desiring after mature consideration to come to know what
the particular thing was of which he was being accused
by the Jews, he unshackled him and commanded the chief
priests and the entire Sanhedrin to assemble. And having brought Paul down, he stood him before them.

1-5   And Paul, having riveted his gaze upon the Sanhedrin,
said, Men, brethren, as for myself, I have conducted
myself as a citizen [of God's commonwealth of Israel]
in all good conscience toward God up to this day. And
the chief priest, Ananias, ordered those standing by to
be striking him upon his mouth. Then Paul said to him,
To be striking you, God is about to be doing, you wall
that has been plastered over and white-washed with lime
[hypocrite that you are who conceals your malice under
an outward assumption of piety]. And as for you, being
what you are, are you sitting as a judge to be pronouncing judgment upon me according to the law, and contrary
to the law are you commanding me to be beaten? And
those standing by said, The chief priest of God, are you
heaping abuse on him? And Paul said, I did not know,

brethren, that he was a chief priest, for it has been written and is at present on record, Concerning the ruler of your people, you shall not speak evil.

Now, Paul having come to see that the one part were Sadducees and the other part Pharisees, cried out in the Sanhedrin, Men, brethren, as for myself, a Pharisee I am, a son of Pharisees. Concerning a hope even of a resurrection of dead people I am being judged. As he was saying this a dissension arose between the Pharisees and the Sadducees, and the crowd was split in two, for Sadducees say that there is not a resurrection, neither angel nor spirit, but Pharisees profess the both. And there arose a great clamor, and certain of the men learned in the sacred scriptures who were attached to the Pharisees, having arisen, went to fighting it out, saying, We do not find one bit of evil in this man. And what if a spirit spoke to him, or an angel? And a great dissension arising, the chiliarch having become afraid lest Paul should be torn in pieces by them, commanded the soldiers, having gone down, to take him by force from their midst, and to be bringing him into their barracks. And on the next night the Lord having taken His stand by Paul said, Be having a cheerful courage, for as you testified with reference to the things concerning me in Jerusalem, thus as for you, it is a necessity in the nature of the case also to testify in Rome.

6-11

And when day dawned the Jews having entered into a conspiracy, invoked God's curse upon themselves if they should violate their vow, saying that they would neither eat nor drink until that time in which they would kill Paul. And there were more than forty who entered this conspiracy. They, having come to the chief priests and the elders, said, We invoked God's curse upon ourselves should we violate our vow, declaring ourselves anathema should we do so, vowing to eat not even one thing until such time as we killed this Paul. Now, therefore, as for all of you, together with the Sanhedrin, suggest at once to the chiliarch that he bring him down to you as though you were about to be judging the things concerning him more accurately. And as for us, before he comes near, we are those who are in readiness to put him out of the way.

12-15

16-22   Now, the son of Paul's sister having heard of their ambush, having come and having entered the barracks, reported this to Paul. Then Paul, having called one of the centurions to him, said, Be taking this young man away to the chiliarch, for he has something to report to him. Then, having taken him, he brought him to the chiliarch and said, The prisoner Paul having called me to himself asked that I bring this young man to you who has something to say to you. Then the chiliarch, having taken him by his hand and having withdrawn, went to inquiring of him privately, What is it that you have to report to me? And he said, The Jews agreed among themselves to ask you to bring Paul down to the Sanhedrin tomorrow as though about to be inquiring more accurately concerning him. As for you, therefore, do not permit yourself to be persuaded by them, for there lie in ambush for him more than forty of their men, those who are such that they invoked God's curse upon themselves should they break their vow not to eat nor drink until such time as they have destroyed him. And now they are in readiness, looking for the promise from you. So then the chiliarch dismissed the young man, having charged him to tell not even one person these things which he had made plain to him.

23, 24   And having called to himself a certain two of the centurions, he said, Make ready at once two hundred heavily armed foot soldiers in order that they may proceed to Caesarea, and seventy soldiers of the cavalry unit, and two hundred lightly armed soldiers, about nine o'clock at night, and furnish them beasts of burden in order that having mounted Paul upon one they might bring him safely through to Felix the governor.

25-30   And he wrote a letter having this form: Claudias Lysias, to his Excellency, the governor Felix, greeting. This man, having been seized by the Jews and about to be put out of the way by them, having rushed in in the nick of time with my heavily armed legionnaires, I rescued, having learned that he was a Roman. And desiring to come to know fully the cause on account of which they were bringing a charge against him, I brought him down to the Sanhedrin, their council, whom I found to be accused

concerning questions of their law, but having not even
one thing worthy of death or bonds laid to his charge.
And when it was pointed out to me that there would be
a plot against the man, immediately I sent him to you,
having given orders also to his accusers to be telling before you what they have against him.

So then the soldiers, according to the order given **31-35**
them, having taken up Paul, brought him through a night
of travel [forty miles] to Antipatris. And on the next
day, having left the horsemen to be going with him, they
returned to their barracks, and they, having gone on to
Caesarea and having delivered the letter to the governor,
presented also Paul to him. And having read the letter,
he also asked as to what kind of a province [senatorial or
imperial] he came from. And having ascertained that
he was from Cilicia he said, I will hear fully and adju-
dicate your cause whenever also your accusers have come;
having previously ordered that he be put under guard in
the palace of Herod.

Now, after five days the chief priest with certain **1-4**
elders and a certain prosecuting attorney, Tertullus, came
down, who were such that they preferred charges before
the governor against Paul. And after he [Paul] was
called, Tertullus began to be accusing him, saying, In
view of the fact that we are obtaining much peace through
you, and evils are constantly being corrected and things
set right for our nation through your forethought in all
ways and in all places, we accept these, most illustrious
Felix, with all gratefulness. But in order that I may not
further cut in on your time and detain you [from your
beneficent reforms] I beg of you to hear us in your sweet
reasonableness, and we will be concise.

For we found this man to be a pest and a plague and **5-9**
an instigator of insurrections among all the Jews throughout the Roman empire, and a front-rank champion of
the heretical sect of the Nazarenes; who also attempted
to profane the temple, whom also we seized, whom you
will be able, having yourself conducted an investigation
concerning all these things, to come to know fully the

things of which, as for us, we are accusing him. And the Jews also joined in the charge, affirming that these things were so.

10-16   And Paul answered, the governor having nodded to him to be speaking, Knowing that for many years you have been a judge of this nation, I confidently present my defense with respect to the things concerning myself, you being able to understand that there are not more than twelve days since I went up to Jerusalem to worship. And neither in the temple did they find me disputing with any certain individual nor stirring up a crowd, nor even in the synagogues nor in the city; neither are they able to substantiate before you the charges concerning which they now are accusing me. But I confess this to you, that in accordance with the Way, which system of belief they call heresy, thus am I serving the God of my fathers, believing all things which stand written according to the law and those things in the prophets, having hope toward God, which hope they themselves also look for, that there shall be a resurrection of both the just and the unjust. And in this also I myself am constantly disciplining myself to be having a conscience which does not cause offense to God and to men at all times.

17-23   Now, after an interval of some years I came, having brought alms to my nation and [sacrificial] offerings, in the presenting of which offerings they found me ceremonially purified in the temple, not with a crowd nor with an uproar. But certain Jews from Asia, who ought to have been present before you and to be bringing accusation if they were having anything against me — Or, let these themselves tell what wrongdoing they found when I stood before the Sanhedrin, except concerning this one voice which, while standing among them, I cried aloud, Concerning a resurrection of dead people I am being judged today by you. Then Felix put them off by deferring the hearing and the deciding of the case, knowing more accurately the things concerning the Way, having said, When Lysias, the chiliarch comes down I will determine the things which pertain to you. He gave orders to the centurion that he should be kept under guard and that

he should relax the severe conditions of imprisonment
and make things easier for him, and that he should not
forbid any of his own people to be ministering to him.

Now, after certain days, Felix, having come [back]   **24-27**
with Drusilla his own wife who was a Jewess, sent for
Paul and heard him concerning his faith in Christ Jesus.
And while he was discoursing concerning righteousness
and self-control and the judgment which was about to
come, Felix, having become terrified, answered, Be proceeding on your way for the present, and having found
an opportune time, I will summon you; at the same time
also hoping that money will be given to him by Paul.
On this account also he kept on sending for him more
frequently and conversing with him. But after two years
had gone by, Felix was succeeded by Porcius Festus, and
desiring to ingratiate himself with the Jews, he left Paul
behind in shackles.

Then, Festus having come into his province, after   **1-6**
three days, went up to Jerusalem from Caesarea. And
the chief priests and the principal men among the Jews
laid legal and formal information against Paul before
him. And they kept on begging him, asking a personal
favor for themselves against him to the effect that he
would send for him to be brought to Jerusalem, all the
while preparing an ambush to put him out of the way
along the road. Now then, Festus answered that Paul
was kept in charge in Caesarea and that he himself would
proceed there shortly. Let those therefore among you,
he says, who are vested with power, having gone with
me, assuming that there is anything amiss in this man,
bring accusation against him. And having spent not more
than eight or ten days among them, having gone down
to Caesarea, on the next day having taken his place on
the judge's bench, he commanded Paul to be brought.

And after he had come down, the Jews who had come   **7, 8**
down from Jerusalem took up positions in a circle around
him, bringing against him many and weighty accusations
which they did not have the ability to prove by argument,
while Paul was saying in his defense, Neither against
the temple nor against Caesar did I sin in anything.

9-12   But Festus, desiring to ingratiate himself with the Jews, answering Paul, said, Are you willing, having gone up to Jerusalem, there to be judged concerning these things in my presence? Then Paul said, I have taken my stand before the judgment seat of Caesar, and here I stand where it is a necessity in the nature of the case for me to be judged. To Jews I have not done even one wrong thing, as also, as for yourself, you understand very well. Now, therefore, assuming for the moment that I am a wrongdoer or have committed anything worthy of death, I do not refuse to die. But since there does not exist even one thing of those things of which these accuse me, no one has the power to give me up as a favor to them. I lodge my appeal with Caesar. Then Festus, after he conferred with his council, answered, You lodged your appeal with Caesar. To Caesar you shall proceed.

13-21   Now, certain days having elapsed, Agrippa the king and Bernice arrived at Caesarea and paid their respects to Festus. And when they had spent many days there, Festus laid the things concerning Paul before the king, saying, There is a certain man who has been left behind by Felix in shackles, concerning whom when I was in Jerusalem the chief priests and the elders of the Jews informed me, requesting as a personal favor to themselves a condemnatory sentence against him, to whom I answered, It is not a custom with Romans to be giving up to another any man whom he may punish or put to death before the one who is accused have his accusers face to face and have opportunity to present a defense with reference to the accusation. Therefore, having assembled here without one bit of delay the next day, having sat down on the judge's bench, I commanded that the man be brought concerning whom after his accusers stood up, they brought not one accusation with reference to such pernicious things as I surmised, but they were having certain questions against him concerning their own religion and concerning a certain Jesus who was dead, whom Paul has kept on asserting is alive. And as for myself, being perplexed with reference to an inquiry concerning these things, I went to asking him if he would desire to be proceeding to Jerusalem and there be judged concerning these things. But since Paul had made his appeal to be reserved for the decision of The August One, I commanded that he be kept until I should send him up to Caesar.

Then Agrippa said to Festus, I myself also was wishing to hear the man. Tomorrow, he said, you shall hear him. Therefore, on the next day Agrippa having come, and Bernice, accompanied by much pomp, and having entered the court room, both with chiliarchs and the outstanding men of the city, and Festus having given the order, Paul was brought in. And Festus says, King Agrippa and all those men who are present with us, you see this man concerning whom the entire multitude of the Jews petitioned me both in Jerusalem and here, shouting that in accordance with the necessity in the nature of the case he ought no longer to be living. But as for myself, having learned that he had done nothing worthy of death, and that he himself had appealed to The August One, I determined to be sending him, concerning whom I do not have anything definite to write to my Lord. Because of this I brought him before you all, and especially before you, King Agrippa, in order that after the examination has taken place, I may have something to write; for it seems to me contrary to reason, sending a prisoner, and not indicating the charges against him.

Then Agrippa said to Paul, Permission is granted you to be speaking on behalf of yourself. Then Paul, having stretched out his hand, went to presenting his verbal defense. Concerning all things of which I am being accused by the Jews, King Agrippa, I have considered myself fortunate that I am about to be presenting my verbal defense today before you, since you are especially expert with reference both to all the customs and also questions regarding the Jews. On this account I beg of you to hear me patiently.

Now, therefore, the manner of life which was mine from youth, that which was from the beginning among my nation in Jerusalem, all Jews know, having previous knowledge of me from the very first, if they would be willing to be bearing testimony, that according to the sect

22-27

1-3

4-7

in our religious discipline which was most precise and rigorous in interpreting the Mosaic law and observing even its most minute precepts, I lived as a Pharisee. And now upon the basis of the hope of the promise made by our God to our fathers I stand here being judged, which promise our twelve tribes earnestly night and day rendering sacred service to God are hoping to arrive at, concerning which hope I am being accused by the Jews, O King.

8-11   Why is it being judged by you all an unbelievable thing that God raises dead individuals, as He has done? As for myself, verily, I was of the opinion that it was a necessity in the nature of the case for me to do many things against the Name of Jesus, the one from Nazareth, which also I did in Jerusalem, and many of the saints, as for myself, I shut up in prisons, having received the authority from the chief priests. And when they were being put to death I registered my vote against them. And often in every synagogue while punishing them I kept on attempting to compel them by contemptuous speech intentionally to come short of the reverence due to God, and possessing an insane fury against them beyond measure, I went to persecuting them even to foreign cities.

12-18   Being engaged in these things, while I was proceeding to Damascus with authority and a commission from the chief priests, at midday I saw along the road, O King, a light from heaven above the brilliance of the sun shining about me and those who were travelling with me. And after all of us had fallen down upon the ground, I heard a voice saying to me in the Hebrew dialect, Saul, Saul, why are you persecuting me? It is hard for you to be kicking against the goads. And as for myself, I said, Who are you, Sir? And the Lord said, As for myself, I am Jehoshua, whom, as for yourself, you are persecuting. But arise at once and stand upon your feet. For this purpose I appeared to you, to appoint you as one who ministers and as one who bears testimony both to the things you saw and to the things in which I will appear to you, delivering you from the people and the Gentiles, to whom, as for myself, I will send you on a mission to open their eyes that they may turn from darkness to light and from the authority of Satan to God, that they may receive forgiveness of sins and an inheritance among those who have been sanctified by faith which is in me.

Wherefore, O King Agrippa, I did not become disobedient to the heavenly vision, but both to those in Damascus first and in Jerusalem and in all the region of Judaea and to the Gentiles I kept on bringing word that they should be repenting and turning to God, doing works that weigh as much as the repentance they profess. **19, 20**

On account of these things the Jews, having made me a prisoner, were attempting to kill me. Therefore, having the help that is from God until this day, I stand testifying both to small and great, saying nothing except the things which the prophets and Moses said are destined to take place, that the Christ is to be a suffering Messiah, that He being the first to arise from the dead is destined to be proclaiming light to the people and to the Gentiles. **21-23**

And as he was saying these things in his defense, Festus says with a loud voice, You are going insane, Paul. Your vast learning is turning you around to insanity. But Paul says, I am not going insane, most illustrious Festus. But words of truth and soundness of mind am I uttering; for the King knows about these things before whom I also am speaking freely, for I am persuaded that none of these things is hidden from him, for this thing has not taken place in a secret place. Are you believing, King Agrippa, the prophets? I know positively that you are believing. But Agrippa says to Paul, With but [such] little persuasion you are attempting to make me a Christian. But Paul said, I am praying to God that whether by little or by much persuasion not only you but also all who are hearing me today would become such as even I am, except these chains. **24-29**

And the king arose and the governor and Bernice and those seated with them, and having withdrawn, they were speaking to one another, saying, Not even one thing worthy of death or bonds is this man doing. Then Agrip- **30-32** pa said to Festus, This man could have been released if he had not appealed to Caesar.

1-6   Now, when it was determined that we should sail away to Italy, they gave both Paul and certain other prisoners of a different type into the custody of a centurion named Julius, belonging to the Augustan military cohort. And having gone on board a ship of Adramyttium which was about to be sailing to places along the coast of Asia, we put to sea, there being with us Aristarchus, a Macedonian of Thessalonica. And on the next day we landed at Sidon. And Julius treated Paul kindly, giving him permission to go to his friends to receive care and attention. And having put out to sea from there we sailed under the sheltered protection of Cyprus because the winds were against us. And having sailed across both the sea which is off the coast of Cilicia and that which is off the coast of Pamphylia, we came down to Myra in Lycia. And having found there a ship of Alexandria sailing to Italy, he put us on board.

7, 8   And when we sailed slowly for a considerable number of days and with difficulty down along Cnidus, since the wind did not permit our straight course onwards, we sailed under the protective shelter of Crete off Cape Salmone, and with difficulty coasting along it we came to a certain place called Snug Harbors, which is near the city of Lasea.

9-13   Now, a considerable time having elapsed and the voyage already being dangerous and also because the fast already was past, Paul went to exhorting them, saying to them, Men, I perceive as the result of past experience and observation that the voyage is destined to be with injury and much loss, not only of the cargo and the ship but also of our lives. But the centurion allowed himself to be persuaded by the steersman and the skipper rather than by the things which were being spoken by Paul. And the harbor being unfit as a place in which to spend the winter, the majority gave it as their counsel to put out to sea from there, if somehow they might be able to reach Phenice and there to spend the winter, this being a harbor of Crete looking to the

northeast and southeast. And a south wind having blown
gently, thinking that they had obtained their purpose,
having hoisted their anchor, they sailed along Crete
close in shore.

Now, after no long time there beat down from it   **14-20**
[mountainous Crete] a wind of typhoon proportions
which is called Euraquilo. And the ship having been
caught by it and not able to face the wind, having given
up to it, we were carried along. And running under the
protective shelter of a certain island called Clauda, we
were with difficulty able to get possession of the little
boat, which, after they had hoisted it up [into the large
boat] they went to using things that would aid us, putting
chains around the hull of the ship to hold it together.
And fearing lest we veer from our course and be driven
against the shoals and rocks of the Syrtis, having taken
in some of the sails, we were in this manner being borne
along. And we being greatly beaten about by the storm,
on the next day they began to be throwing the cargo
overboard. And on the third day they threw out with
their own hands the furnishings of the ship. Now, when
neither sun nor stars were shining for many days, and
no small storm was pressing down upon us, all hope that
we would be saved, which hope was still clinging to us,
was at last being stripped away from us.

And when those on board had been long without   **21-26**
food, then Paul having taken his stand in their midst
said, Surely, O men, in view of the very necessity imposed by the circumstances, you should have taken my
advice and not have set sail from Crete and to have
incurred this harm and loss. And now I advise and exhort you to be of good courage, keeping up your spirits,
for there shall be a loss of not even one life among you,
but a loss of the ship, for there took a stand at my side
this night a messenger of the God whose I am and to
whom I render sacred service, saying, Stop fearing,
Paul. It is necessary in the nature of the case for you
to stand before Caesar. And behold, God has graciously
safeguarded for you all those who are sailing with you.
On which account be having courage, men, for I trust
God that it shall be in the manner as it has been told

me. However, it is a necessity in the nature of the case
for us to be driven into a certain island.

27-32   Now, when the fourteenth night came, as we were
being driven to and fro in the sea of Adria, about midnight, the sailors began to suspect that some land was
drawing near to them, and having let down the lead for
the purpose of finding out the depth of the water, they
discovered it to be about one hundred and twenty feet.
And after a little distance, having again taken a sounding,
they found ninety feet. And fearing lest we should be
driven somewhere against rocky places, having thrown
four anchors out of the back of the ship, they kept on
praying for day to come. Now, as the sailors were seeking to abandon ship and had lowered the small boat
under pretense of being about to be laying anchors out
of the front of the ship, Paul said to the centurion and
the soldiers, Unless these remain in the ship, as for you
all, you will not be able to be saved. Then the soldiers
cut off the ropes of the small boat and permitted it to
fall off.

33-38   Now, until that time at which it should become day,
Paul kept on exhorting all to take food, saying, This is
the fourteenth day in which you are looking ahead with
expectation, continuing to be without food, having taken
nothing. On which account I beg of you all, please, to
take food, for this is for your preservation, for not one
hair of your head shall perish. And having said these
things and having taken bread, he gave thanks to God
in the presence of all, and having broken it, he began
to be eating. Then all having taken courage, they themselves took food. There were two hundred and seventy-
six souls on the ship. And having eaten food to their
entire satisfaction, they began to lighten the ship by
throwing its cargo of grain into the sea.

39-41   Now, when day came, they attempted to recognize
the land but were unsuccessful, but they began to observe
a certain bay having a beach, and they were deliberating
with one another whether they would be able to drive
the boat into it. And having cast off the anchors they
left them in the sea, at the same time loosing the bands

of the rudders, and having spread the foresail to the wind they began to hold the ship's course steadily to the beach. And having come unexpectedly upon a reef against which the waves dashed on both sides, they ran the vessel aground. And the front of the ship struck, remained immovable, but the back of the ship began to break up by reason of the waves.

Now, the counsel of the soldiers was to kill the **42-44** prisoners lest anyone having swum out should escape. But the centurion desiring to bring Paul safely through kept them from their purpose and ordered those who were able to swim, having thrown themselves overboard, to get first to the land, and the rest, some on the one hand upon planks and some on the other hand on pieces of the ship. And in that way it came to pass that all came safely through to the land.

And having been brought safely through, then we **1-6** recognized at once that the island was called Melita. And the inhabitants who were such that they did not speak Greek nor did they possess Greek culture, showed us not the humane and kind treatment with which one meets ordinarily, but an uncommon, extraordinary, humane, and kindly treatment which was the expression of their natural affection for their fellow-man, for, having set fire to a heap of sticks, they took all of us to themselves because of the rain which, having come down upon us, was now a steady downpour and because of the cold. Now Paul, having gathered together a capacity load of dry sticks and having put them upon the fire, a viper having come out by reason of the heat fastened itself upon his hand. And when the inhabitants saw the poisonous creature dangling from his hand, they kept on saying to one another, No doubt this man is a murderer, whom, having been brought safely through out of the reach of the sea, the goddess of Justice did not permit to continue living. Now, therefore, having shaken off the creature into the fire, he suffered not even one bit of harm. Now they kept on expecting that he was about to swell up or to be falling down dead suddenly. But while they were expecting this for a long time and were seeing not even one thing of a harmful nature happening to him, having changed their minds, they went to saying that he was a god.

7-10   Now, in that place there were the estates of the chief man of the island who was named Publius, who received us hospitably and treated us in a kindly manner as his guests for three days. And it came to pass that the father of Publius was lying prostrate in the grip of an intermittent fever and dysentery, into whose presence Paul having come and having prayed, having laid his hands upon him, he healed him. Now, this having taken place, also the rest of those in the island who were in possession of infirmities came in a steady procession and were being healed, who also honored us with many honors, and when we sailed put on board the things of which we had need.

11-16   Now, after three months we put out to sea in a boat which had passed the winter in the island, a ship of Alexandria, upon the prow of which there were painted the figures of Castor and Pollux [tutelary deities of sailors]. And having landed at Syracuse, we remained there three days, from where having sailed by a circuitous course we came to Rhegium. And after one day a south wind having commenced blowing, we came on the second day to Puteoli, where having found brethren, we were urged to remain with them as their guests seven days. And in this manner we came to Rome. And from there the brethren, having heard of the things concerning us, came to meet us up to the Market of Appius and the Three Hotels, whom when Paul saw he thanked God and took courage. And when we entered Rome, Paul was given permission to live by himself with the soldier who guarded him.

17-19   And it came to pass after three days that Paul called together those first in prominence and authority among the Jews. And they having met together, he went to saying to them, As for myself, men, brethren, although not having done even one thing against the people or the customs of the fathers, yet I was delivered as a prisoner from Jerusalem into the hands of the Romans, who were such that after having examined me, desired to release me because there was not even one bit of blameworthiness in me deserving of death. But when the Jews were speaking against me, I was compelled to appeal to Caesar, not at all that I was having anything of which to accuse my nation.

Because of this reason therefore I exhorted you to see me and to speak with me, for on account of the hope of Israel I am bound around by this chain. And they said to him, As for us, neither did we receive a letter from Judaea concerning you, nor has any one of the brethren, having come, reported or spoken of any perniciousness concerning you. But we think it only right and proper that we hear from you personally the things which you are thinking, for indeed concerning this heresy, we know that everywhere it is being opposed.

20-22

And having mutually agreed with him as to the day, there came many to the place where he was staying, to whom he continued to give a detailed exposition, solemnly bearing testimony to the kingdom of God, persuading them concerning Jesus both from the Mosaic law and from the prophets, from early morning until evening. And some on the one hand were persuaded by the things, but others on the other hand persisted in their unbelief. And being at odds with one another, they rid themselves of Paul by going off after Paul had spoken a word, just one: Most fittingly and truly did the Holy Spirit speak through the intermediate agency of Isaiah the prophet to your fathers saying, Proceed at once to this people and say, By means of your sense of hearing you will hear and will positively not understand. And while seeing, you will see and will positively not perceive. For the heart of this people was made dull and callous, and with their ears they heard with difficulty, and their eyes they shut, lest at any time they might see with their eyes and hear with their ears and understand with their heart and return and I should heal them.

23-27

Let it become known to you therefore that to the Gentiles there has been sent this, the salvation of God, and they themselves will also hear it.

28

30, 31   And he lived two whole years in his own hired
dwelling. And he kept on receiving all those who came
to him, proclaiming the kingdom of God and teaching
the things concerning the Lord Jesus Christ with all
freedom of speech and fearless confidence, without
hindrance.

THE EPISTLES

Paul, a bondslave by nature belonging to Christ Jesus, an ambassador by divine summons, permanently separated to God's good news which He promised aforetime through the intermediate agency of His prophets in holy writings concerning His Son, who came from the ancestral line of David so far as His humanity is concerned, who was demonstrated in the sphere of power as Son of God so far as His divine essence was concerned by the resurrection of the dead, Jesus Christ our Lord; through whom we received grace and apostleship in order that there may be obedience to the Faith among all the Gentiles in behalf of His name, among whom you also are divinely summoned ones belonging to Jesus Christ, to all who are in Rome, God's loved ones, divinely summoned saints. Grace to you and peace from God our Father and our Lord Jesus Christ.

1-7

First, I am constantly thanking my God through Jesus Christ concerning all of you because your faith is constantly being spread abroad in the whole world; for my witness is God, to whom I render sacred service in my spirit in the good news concerning His Son, how unceasingly I am making mention of you always at my prayers, making supplication if somehow now at last I may be prospered in the will of God to come to you, for I long to see you in order that I may impart some spiritual gift to you resulting in your being stabilized, that is, moreover, that I may be strengthened by you through the mutual faith which is both yours and mine.

8-12

Moreover, I do not desire you to be ignorant, brethren, that often I proposed to myself to come to you, but I was prevented up to this time, in order that I might procure some fruit also among you even as also among the rest of the Gentiles. Both to Greeks and to those who do not possess Greek culture, both to wise and unwise, I am debtor in such a manner that to the extent of my ability I am eager to proclaim the good news also to you who are in Rome.

13-15

For I am not ashamed of the good news. For God's power it is, resulting in salvation to everyone who believes, to Jew first and also to Gentile, for God's righteous-

16-23

ness in it is revealed on the principle of faith to faith, even as it stands written, And the one who is just, on the principle of faith shall live. For there is revealed God's wrath from heaven upon every lack of reverence and upon every unrighteousness of men who in unrighteousness are holding down the truth. Because that which is knowable concerning God is plainly evident in them, for God made it clear to them; for the things concerning Him which are invisible since the creation of the universe are clearly seen, being understood by means of the things that are made, namely, His eternal power and divine Being, resulting in their being without a defense. Because, knowing God, not as God did they glorify Him, nor were they grateful, but they became futile in their reasonings, and their stupid heart was darkened. Asserting themselves to be wise, they became fools and exchanged the glory of the incorruptible God for a likeness of an image of corruptible man and of birds and of quadrupeds and of snakes.

24-27   On which account God delivered them over in the passionate cravings of their hearts to bestial profligacy which had for its purpose the dishonoring of their bodies among themselves; who were of such a character that they exchanged the truth of God for a lie and worshipped and rendered religious service to the creation rather than to the Creator who is to be eulogized forever. Amen. Because of this God gave them over to dishonorable passions, for even their females exchanged their natural use for that which is against nature. And likewise also the males, having put aside the natural use of the females, burned themselves out in their lustful appetite toward one another, males with males carrying to its ultimate conclusion that which is shameful, receiving in themselves that retribution which was a necessity in the nature of the case because of their deviation from the norm.

28-32   And even as after putting God to the test for the purpose of approving Him should He meet their specifications, and finding that He did not, they disapproved of holding Him in their full and precise knowledge, God gave them up to a mind that would not meet the test for that which a mind was meant, to practice those things which were not becoming or fitting; being filled with every unrighteousness, pernicious evil, avarice, malice, full of envy, murder, wrangling, guile, malicious craftiness; secret slanderers, backbiters; hateful to God, insolent, haughty; swaggerers, inventors of evil things; disobedient to parents, stupid, faithless, without natural affection, merciless; such are those who, knowing the judgment of God that these who practice such things are worthy of death, not only habitually do the same things but also take pleasure in those who practice them.

Therefore, you are without a defense, O man, every- **1-10** one who judges, for in that in which you are judging another, yourself you are condemning, for you who judge practice the same things. But we know that the judgment of God is according to truth against those who practice such things. And do you reason thus, O man, who judges those who practice such things, and are doing the same things, that as for you, you will escape the judgment of God? Or, the wealth of His kindness and forbearance and longsuffering are you treating with contempt, being ignorant that the goodness of God is leading you to repentance? But according to your obstinate and unrepentant heart you are storing up for yourself wrath in the day of wrath and revelation of the righteous judgment of God who recompenses each according to his works, to those on the one hand who by steadfastness of a good work seek glory and honor and incorruptibility, life eternal; but to those on the other hand who out of a factious spirit are both also non-persuadable with respect to the truth and persuadable with respect to unrighteousness, wrath and anger. Tribulation and anguish upon every soul of man who works out to a finish the evil, both upon the soul of a Jew first and also upon the soul of a Gentile, but glory and honor and peace to everyone who works out to a finish that which is good, both to a Jew first and also to a Gentile.

For there is not partiality in the presence of God. **11-13** For as many as without law sinned, without law shall also perish. And as many as in the sphere of law sinned, through law shall be condemned. For not those who are instructed in the law are righteous in the presence of God but those who are doers of the law shall be justified.

14-16   For whenever Gentiles, who do not have law, do habitually by nature the things of the law, these not having law, are a law to themselves, they being such that they show the work of the law written in their hearts, their conscience bearing joint-witness and their reasonings in the meanwhile accusing or also excusing one another in the day when God judges the hidden things of men according to my gospel through Jesus Christ.

17-24   Now, assuming, as for you, that you bear the name of Jew, and have a blind and mechanical reliance on the law, and boast in God, and have an experiential knowledge of His will, and after having put to the test for the purpose of approving the things that differ, and having found that they meet your specifications, you put your approval upon them, being instructed in a formal way in the law, you have persuaded yourself and have come to a settled conviction that you are a guide of the blind, a light of those in darkness, a corrector of those who are without reflection or intelligence, a teacher of the immature, having the rough sketch of the experiential knowledge of the truth in the law. Therefore, you who are constantly teaching another, are you not teaching yourself? You who are constantly preaching a person should not be stealing, are you stealing? You who are constantly saying that a person should not be committing adultery, are you committing adultery? You who are turning away constantly from idolatry as from a stench, are you robbing temples? You who are making your boast in the law, through your transgression of the law are you dishonoring God? For the Name of God because of you is reviled among the Gentiles, even as it stands written.

25-29   For, indeed, circumcision is profitable if you are making a practice of law, but if, on the other hand, you are a transgressor of law, your circumcision has become uncircumcision. Therefore, if the uncircumcision habitually guards the righteous requirements of the law, will not his uncircumcision be credited to his account for circumcision? And the uncircumcision which by nature is fulfilling the law will judge you who with the advantage of the letter and of circumcision are a transgressor of law. For, not he who is so in an outward fashion is a Jew, nor even that which is in an outward fashion in flesh is circumcision. But he who is so in the sphere of the inner man is a Jew, and circumcision is of the heart, in the sphere of the spirit, not in the sphere of the letter, concerning whom the praise is not from men but from God.

What pre-eminence or advantage is there therefore which the Jew possesses? Or, what profit is there in circumcision? Much every way, for, first of all, because they were entrusted with the divine utterances of God.   **1, 2**

Well then — if, as is the case, certain ones did not exercise faith? Their unbelief will not render the faithfulness of God ineffectual, will it? Let no one ever think such a thing. Let God be found veracious and every man a liar, even as it stands written, To the end that you may be acknowledged righteous in your words, and may come out victor when brought to trial.   **3, 4**

But in view of the fact that our unrighteousness establishes by proof God's righteousness, what shall we say? God is not unrighteous who inflicts wrath, is He? I am using a mode of speech drawn from human affairs. Away with the thought. Otherwise, how will it be possible for God to judge the world? Moreover, assuming that the truth of God by means of my lie became the more conspicuous, resulting in His glory, why then yet am I also being judged as a sinner? And not, as we were slanderously reported and even as certain are saying that we are saying, Let us do the evil things in order that there might come the good things; whose judgment is just.   **5-8**

What then? Are we better? Not in any way, for we previously brought a charge against both Jews and Gentiles that all are under sin; as it stands written, There is not a righteous person, not even one. There is not the one who understands; there is not the one who seeks out God. All turned aside; all to a man became useless. There is not the one who habitually does goodness; there is not as much as one. Their throat is a grave that stands   **9-18** open. With their tongues they continually were deceiving. Asps' poison is under their lips; whose mouth is full of imprecations and bitterness; their feet are swift to pour out blood. Destruction and misery are in their paths. The road of peace they did not know. There is not a fear of God before their eyes.

19, 20   But we know absolutely that whatever things the law says, it says to those within the sphere of the law, in order that every mouth may be closed up and the whole world may become liable to pay penalty to God. Wherefore, out of works of law there shall not be justified any flesh in His sight, for through law is a full knowledge of sin.

21-26   But now, apart from law, God's righteousness has been openly shown as in view, having witness borne to it by the law and the prophets; indeed, God's righteousness through faith in Jesus Christ to all who believe, for there is not a distinction, for all sinned and are falling short of the glory of God; being justified gratuitously by His grace through the redemption which is in Christ Jesus, whom God placed before the eyes of all as an expiatory satisfaction through faith in His blood for a proof of His righteousness in view of the pretermission of the sins previously committed, this pretermission being in the sphere of the forbearance of God, also for a proof of His righteousness at the present season, with a view to His being just and the justifier of the one whose faith is in Jesus.

27, 28   Where then is the glorying? It was once for all excluded. Through what kind of a law? Of the aforementioned works? Not at all, but through the law of faith, for our reasoned conclusion is that a man is justified by faith apart from works of law.

29-31   Or, of Jews only is He God? Is He not also of Gentiles? Yes, also of Gentiles, assuming that there is one God who will justify the circumcision out of a source of faith and the uncircumcision through the intermediary instrumentality of faith. Then are we making law of none effect through this aforementioned faith? Let not such a thing be considered. Certainly, we are establishing law.

What then shall we say that Abraham our forefather **1-8** found with reference to the flesh? For, assuming that Abraham was justified out of a source of works, he has ground for boasting, but not when facing God. For what does the scripture say? Now Abraham believed God, and it was put to his account, resulting in righteousness. Now, for the one who works with a definite result in view [his wages], the remuneration is not put down on his account as an undeserved, gratuitous gift, but as a legally contracted debt. But in the case of the one who does not work with a definite result in view [salvation] but who places his trust upon the One who justifies the person who is destitute of reverential awe towards God, there is put to his account his faith, resulting in righteousness, even as David also speaks of the spiritual prosperity of the man to whose account God puts righteousness apart from works: Spiritually prosperous are those whose lawlessnesses were put away and whose sins were covered. Spiritually prosperous is the man to whose account the Lord does not in any case put sin.

Therefore, does this spiritual prosperity come upon **9-12** the circumcised one or the uncircumcised one, for we say, There was put to Abraham's account his faith, resulting in righteousness? How then was it put to his account, at the time when he was circumcised or at the time when he was uncircumcised? Not in circumcision but in uncircumcision. And he received the attesting sign of circumcision as a seal of the righteous character of the faith which he had in his uncircumcision, resulting in his being the father of all who believe while in the state of uncircumcision, in order that there may be put to their account the righteousness; and the father of circumcision to these who are not of the circumcision only but to those who walk in the footsteps of the faith of our father Abraham when he was in uncircumcision.

For not through law was the promise made to Abra- **13-15** ham or to his offspring that he should be the heir of the world, but through a righteousness which pertains to faith. For, assuming that those who are of the law are heirs, the aforementioned faith has been voided with the result that it is permanently invalidated, and the aforementioned promise has been rendered inoperative with the result that it is in a state of permanent inoperation. For the law results in divine wrath. Now, where there is not law, neither is there transgression.

16-22   On account of this it is by faith, in order that it might be by grace, to the end that the promise might be something realized by all the offspring, not by that which is of the law only, but also by that which is of the faith of Abraham who is father of all of us; even as it stands written, A father of many nations I have established you permanently, before Him whom he believed, before God who makes alive those who are dead and calls the things that are not in existence as being in existence; who, being beyond hope, upon the basis of hope believed, in order that he might become father of many nations, according to that which has been spoken with finality, In this manner will your offspring be. And not being weak with respect to his faith, he attentively considered his own body permanently dead, he being about one hundred years old, also the deadness of Sarah's womb. Moreover, in view of the promise of God, he did not vacillate in the sphere of unbelief between two mutually exclusive expectations but was strengthened with respect to his faith, having given glory to God, and was fully persuaded that what He had promised with finality He was able also to do; wherefore also it was put down in his account, resulting in righteousness.

23-25   Now, it was not written for his sake alone, namely, that it was put to his account, but also for our sakes, to whose account it is to be put, to ours who place our faith upon the One who raised Jesus our Lord out from among the dead, who was delivered up because of our transgressions and was raised because of our justification.

1-5   Having therefore been justified by faith, peace we are having with God through our Lord Jesus Christ, through whom also our entree we have as a permanent possession into this unmerited favor in which we have been placed permanently, and rejoice upon the basis of hope of the glory of God. And not only this, but we also are exulting in our tribulations, knowing that this tribulation produces endurance, and this endurance, approvedness, and this approvedness, hope. And this hope does not disappoint, because the love of God has been poured out in our hearts and still floods them through the agency of the Holy Spirit who was given to us.

For when we were yet without strength, in a strategic **6-8** season Christ instead of and in behalf of those who do not have reverence for God and are devoid of piety died; for, very rarely in behalf of one of those individuals who is legally exact and precise in his observance of the customs and rules of the society in which he lives will anyone die, yet perhaps in behalf of the one who is generous in heart, always doing good to others, a person would even dare to die. But God is constantly proving His own love to us, because while we were yet sinners, Christ in behalf of us died.

Much more therefore, having been justified now by **9-11** His blood, we shall be saved through Him from the wrath. For though, while being enemies, we were reconciled to God through the death of His Son, much more, having been reconciled, we shall be saved by the life He possesses. And not only so, but we also rejoice in God through our Lord Jesus Christ, through whom now we received the reconciliation.

Wherefore, as through the intermediate agency of **12-14** one man the aforementioned sin entered the world, and through this sin, death; and thus into and throughout all mankind death entered, because all sinned. For until law, sin was in the world, but sin is not put to one's account, there being no law. But death reigned as king from Adam to Moses, even over those who did not sin in the likeness of the transgression of Adam, who is a type of the One who is to come.

But not as the transgression, thus also is the gratui- **15-17** tous favor. For since by the transgression of the one the many died, much more the grace of God and the gratuitous gift by grace which is of the one Man, Jesus Christ, to the many will abound. And not as through one who sinned, was the gift, for the judgment, on the one hand, was out of one transgression as a source, resulting in condemnation. But the gratuitous gift, on the other hand, was out of many transgressions as a source, resulting in justification. For in view of the fact that by means of the transgression of the one death reigned as king through that one, much more those who receive the abundance of grace and of the gift of righteousness, in life will reign as kings through the One, Jesus Christ.

18-21 So then, therefore, as through one act of transgression, to all men there resulted condemnation, thus also through one act of righteousness, to all men there resulted a righteous standing that had to do with life. For just as through the disobedience of the one man the many were constituted sinners, thus also through the obedience of the One, the many will be constituted righteous. Moreover, law entered in alongside in order that the transgression might be augmented. But where the sin was augmented, the grace superabounded with more added to that, in order that just as the aforementioned sin reigned as king in the sphere of death, thus also the aforementioned grace might reign as king through righteousness, resulting in eternal life through Jesus Christ our Lord.

1-4 What then shall we say? Shall we habitually sustain an attitude of dependence upon, yieldedness to, and cordiality with the sinful nature in order that grace may abound? May such a thing never occur. How is it possible for us, such persons as we are, who have been separated once for all from the sinful nature, any longer to live in its grip? Do you not know that all we who were placed in Christ Jesus, in His death were placed? We therefore were entombed with Him through this being placed in His death, in order that in the same manner as there was raised up Christ out from among those who are dead through the glory of the Father, thus also we by means of a new life imparted may order our behavior.

5-10 For in view of the fact that we are those who have become permanently united with Him with respect to the likeness of His death, certainly also we shall be those who as a logical result have become permanently united with Him with respect to the likeness of His resurrection, knowing this experientially, that our old [unregenerate] self was crucified once for all with Him in order that the physical body [heretofore] dominated by the sinful nature might be rendered inoperative [in that respect], with the result that no longer are we rendering a slave's habitual obedience to the sinful nature, for the one who died once for all stands in the position of a permanent relationship of freedom from the sinful nature. Now, in view of the fact that we died once for all with Christ, we believe that we shall also live by means of Him, knowing that Christ, having been raised up from among those who are dead, no longer dies. Death over Him no longer exercises lordship. For the death He died, He died with respect to our sinful nature once for all. But the life He lives, He lives with respect to God.

Thus, also, as for you, you be constantly counting upon the fact that, on the one hand, you are those who have been separated from the sinful nature, and, on the other, that you are living ones with respect to God in Christ Jesus. Stop therefore allowing the sinful nature to reign as king in your mortal body with a view to obeying it [the body] in its passionate cravings. Moreover, stop putting your members at the disposal of the sinful nature as weapons of unrighteousness, but by a once-for-all act and at once, put yourselves at the disposal of God as those who are actively alive out from among the dead, and put your members as weapons of righteousness at the disposal of God, for [then] the sinful nature will not exercise lordship over you, for you are not under law but under grace. **11-14**

What then? Shall we sin occasionally, because we are not under law but under grace? Away with the thought. Do you not know that to whom you put yourselves at the disposal of as slaves resulting in obedience, slaves you are to whom you render habitual obedience, whether slaves of the sinful nature resulting in death, or obedient slaves [of Christ] resulting in righteousness? But God be thanked, that [whereas] you were slaves of the evil nature, you obeyed out from the heart as a source a type **15-20** of teaching into which you were handed over. And having been set free once for all from the sinful nature, you were constituted slaves to righteousness. I am using an illustration drawn from human affairs because of the frailties of your humanity. For just as you placed your members as slaves at the disposal of uncleanness and lawlessness resulting in lawlessness, thus now place your members as slaves at the disposal of righteousness resulting in holiness. For, when you were slaves of the sinful nature, you were those who were free with respect to righteousness.

21-23   Therefore, what fruit were you having then, upon the basis of which things now you are ashamed? For the consummation of these things is death. But now, having been set free from the sinful nature and having been made bondslaves of God, you are having your fruit resulting in holiness, and the consummation, life eternal. For the subsistence pay which the sinful nature doles out is death. But the free gift of God is life eternal in Christ Jesus our Lord.

1-6   Or, are you ignorant, brethren, for I am speaking to those who have an experiential knowledge of law, that the law exercises lordship over the individual as long as he lives? For the woman subject to a husband is permanently bound by law to her husband during his lifetime. But if her husband dies she is released from the law of her husband. So then, while her husband is living, an adulteress she will be called if she is married to another man. But if her husband is dead, she is free from the law, so that she is not an adulteress, though being married to another man. So that, my brethren, as for you, you also were put to death with reference to the law through the intermediate agency of the body of Christ, resulting in your being married to another, to the One who was raised up from among the dead, in order that we might bear fruit to God. For when we were in the sphere of the sinful nature, the impulses of the sins which were through the law were operative in our members, resulting in the production of fruit with respect to death. But now we were discharged from the law, having died to that in which we were constantly being held down, insomuch that we are rendering habitually a slave's obedience in a sphere new in quality, that of the Spirit, and not in a sphere outworn as to usefulness, in a sphere of that which was put in writing.

What therefore shall we say? The law, is it sin? Away with the thought. Certainly I did not come into an experiential knowledge of sin except through the instrumentality of law, for I had not known evil desire except that the law kept on saying, You shall not desire evil. But the sinful nature, using the commandment as a fulcrum, brought about in me every kind of evil craving. For without law, the sinful nature was dead. But I was alive without law aforetime. But the commandment having come, the sinful nature regained its strength and vigor, and I died. And the commandment which was to life, this I found to be to death; for the sinful nature, using the commandment as a fulcrum, beguiled me and through it killed me. So that the law is holy, and the commandment holy, and righteous, and good. Therefore, that which is good, to me did it become death? Away with the thought. But the sinful nature, in order that it might become evident that it is sin, through that which is good [the commandment] brought about death in me, in order that the sinful nature [its impulses and workings] through the intermediate agency of the commandment may become exceedingly sinful. For we know that the law is spiritual. But as for myself, I am fleshly [being dominated by the sinful nature], permanently sold under the sinful nature. For that which I do, I do not understand. For that which I desire, this I do not practice. But that which I hate, this I am doing.

In view of the fact then that what I do not desire, this I do, I am in agreement with the law that it is good. And since the case stands thus, no longer is it I who do it, but the sinful nature which indwells me; for I know positively that there does not dwell in me, that is, in my flesh, good; for the being desirous is constantly with me; but the doing of the good, not; for that which I desire, good, I do not; but that which I do not desire, evil, this I practice. But in view of the fact that that

7-15

16-20

which I do not desire, this I do, no longer is it I who do it, but the sinful nature which indwells me does it.

21-23   I find therefore the law, that to me, always desirous of doing the good, to me, the evil is always present. For I rejoice in the law of God according to the inward man. But I see a different kind of a law in my members, waging war against the law of my mind, making me a prisoner of war to the law of the sinful nature which is in my members.

24, 25   Wretched man, I. Who shall deliver me out of the body of this death? Thanks be to God, through Jesus Christ our Lord. Therefore, I myself with my mind serve the law of God but with my flesh the law of sin.

1-4   Therefore, now, there is not even one bit of condemnation to those who are in Christ Jesus, for the law of the Spirit, that of the life in Christ Jesus, freed you once for all from the law of the sinful nature and of death. For that which is an impossibility for the law, because it was weak through the sinful nature, God having sent His Son in likeness of flesh of sin, and concerning sin, condemned sin in the sinful nature, in order that the righteous requirement of the law may be brought to completion in us who, not as dominated by the sinful nature are ordering our behavior but as dominated by the Spirit.

5-8   For those who are habitually dominated by the sinful nature put their minds on the things of the sinful nature, but those who are habitually dominated by the Spirit put their minds on the things of the Spirit. For to have the mind dominated by the sinful nature is death, but to have the mind dominated by the Spirit is life and peace; because the mind dominated by the sinful nature is hostile to God, for it does not marshall itself under the command of the law of God, neither is it able to. Moreover, those who are in the sphere of the sinful nature are not able to please God.

9-13   But, as for you, you are not in the sphere of the sinful nature but in the sphere of the Spirit, provided that the Spirit of God is in residence in you. But, assum-

ing that a person does not have Christ's Spirit, this one
does not belong to Him. But, assuming that Christ is
in you, on the one hand the body is dead on account of
sin, but on the other hand the [human] spirit is alive
on account of righteousness. And assuming that the
Spirit of the One who raised up Jesus out from among
the dead is in residence in you, He who raised from
among the dead Christ Jesus, will also make alive your
mortal bodies through the agency of the Spirit who is
resident in you. So then, brethren, we are those under
obligation, not to the sinful nature to live habitually
under the dominion of the sinful nature. For, assuming
that you are living habitually under the dominion of the
sinful nature, you are on the way to dying. But, assuming that by the Spirit you are habitually putting to death
the deeds of the body, you will live.

For as many as are being constantly led by God's **14-18**
Spirit, these are sons of God. For you did not receive
a spirit of slavery again with resulting fear, but you
received the Spirit who places you as adult sons, by
whom we cry out with deep emotion, Abba, [namely]
Father. The Spirit himself is constantly bearing joint-
testimony with our [human] spirit that we are God's
children, and since children, also heirs; on the one hand,
heirs of God, on the other, joint-heirs with Christ, provided that we are suffering with Him in order that we
also may be glorified together, for I have come to a
reasoned conclusion that the sufferings of the present
season are of no weight in comparison to the glory which
is about to be revealed upon us.

For the concentrated and undivided expectation of **19-25**
the creation is assiduously and patiently awaiting the
revelation of the sons of God; for the creation was subjected to futility, not voluntarily, but on account of the
One who put it under subjection upon the basis of the
hope that the creation itself also will be delivered from
the bondage of corruption into the liberty of the glory
of the children of God. For we know that the whole
creation groans and travails together up to this moment,
and not only, but we ourselves also who have the firstfruit of the Spirit, we ourselves also are groaning within

ourselves, assiduously and patiently waiting the full realization of our adult sonship at the time of the redemption of our body. For we were saved in the sphere of hope. But hope that has been seen is not hope, for that which a person sees, why does he hope for it? But if that which we do not see, we hope for, through patience we expectantly wait for it.

26, 27   And in like manner also the Spirit lends us a helping hand with reference to our weakness, for the particular thing that we should pray for according to what is necessary in the nature of the case, we do not know with an absolute knowledge; but the Spirit himself comes to our rescue by interceding with unutterable groanings. Moreover, He who is constantly searching our hearts knows what is the mind of the Spirit because, according to God, He continually makes intercession on behalf of the saints.

28-30   And we know with an absolute knowledge that for those who are loving God, all things are working together resulting in good, for those who are divinely-summoned ones according to His purpose. Because, those whom He foreordained He also marked out beforehand as those who were to be conformed to the derived image of His Son, with the result that He is firstborn among many brethren. Moreover, those whom He thus marked out beforehand, these He also summoned. And those whom He summoned, these He also justified. Moreover, those whom He justified, these He also glorified.

31-39   What then shall we say to these things? In view of the fact that God is on our behalf, who could be against us? Indeed, He who His own Son did not spare, but on behalf of us all delivered Him up, how is it possible that He shall not with Him in grace give us all things? Who shall bring a charge against God's chosen-out ones? God, the One who justifies? Who is the one who condemns? Christ Jesus, the One who died, yes, rather, who has been raised, who is on the right hand of God, who also is constantly interceding on our behalf? Who shall separate us from the love of Christ? Shall tribulation or distress or persecution or famine or nakedness or peril or sword? Even as it stands written, For your sake we are being put to death all the day long. We were accounted as sheep destined for slaughter. But in these things, all of them, we are coming off constantly with more than the victory through the One who loved us. For I have come through a process of persuasion to the settled conclusion that neither death nor life, nor angels, nor principalities, nor things present, nor things about to come, nor powers, nor height, nor depth, nor any other created thing will be able to separate us from the love of God which is in Christ Jesus our Lord.

Truth I speak in Christ. I am not lying, my conscience bearing joint-testimony with me in the Holy Spirit that I have a consuming grief, a great one, and intense anguish in my heart without a let-up. For I could wish that I myself were accursed from Christ on behalf of my brethren, my kindred according to the flesh, who in character are Israelites, who are possessors of the position of a son by having been placed as such, and of the glory, and of the covenants, and to whom was given the law, and who are possessors of the sacred service and the promises, of whom are the fathers, and out from whom is the Christ according to the flesh, the One who is above all, God eulogized forever. Amen.

1-5

But the case is not such as this, that the word of God is fallen powerless; for not all who are out of Israel, these are Israel, nor because they are offspring of Abraham are all children, but: In Isaac an offspring shall be named for you.

6, 7

That is, not the children of the flesh, these are children of God, but the children of the promise are counted for offspring; for the word of promise is this, According to this season I will come and there will be to Sarah a son. And not only, but also Rebecca, conceiving by one, Isaac, our father. For not yet having been born nor having practiced any good or evil, in order that the purpose of God dominated by an act of selecting out may abide, not out of a source of works, but out of the source of the One who calls, it was said to her,

8-13

The older shall serve the younger; even as it stands written, Jacob I loved, but Esau I hated.

14-18 What shall we say then? There is not unrighteousness with God, is there? Away with the thought. For to Moses He says; I will have mercy upon whomever I will have mercy, and I will have compassion on whomever I will have compassion. Therefore, then, it [this being the recipient of God's mercy] is not of the one who desires nor even runs, but of the One who is merciful, God. For the scripture says to Pharaoh, For this same purpose I raised you up, in order that I may demonstrate in you my power, and in order that there may be published everywhere my Name in all the earth. Therefore, then, upon whom He desires, He shows mercy; and whom He desires to harden, He hardens.

19-21 Then you will say to me, Why does He still persist in finding fault? For, with respect to His counsel, who has taken a permanent stand against it? O man, nay, surely, as for you, who are you who contradicts God? The moldable material shall not say to the one who molds it, Why did you make me thus, shall it? Or, does not the potter possess authority over the clay, out of the same lump to make, on the one hand, an instrument which is for honorable purposes and, on the other hand, one which is for dishonorable uses?

22-24 But if, as is the case, God desiring to demonstrate His wrath and to make known His power, endured with much long-suffering instruments of wrath fitted for destruction, and in order that He might make known the wealth of His glory upon instruments of mercy which were previously prepared for glory, even us whom He called, not only from among Jews but also from among Gentiles.

25-29 As also in Hosea He says, I will call those, not my people, my people, and those, not beloved, beloved. And it shall come to be that in the place where it was said to them, Not my people are you, there they shall be called sons of the living God. And Isaiah cries in anguish concerning Israel, If the number of the sons of Israel be as the sand of the sea, the remnant will be saved. For the Lord will execute His word upon the earth, finishing and cutting it short. And even as Isaiah said before, Except the Lord of Sabaoth had left us offspring, we would in that case have become even as Sodom and been made like Gomorrah.

What then shall we say? That Gentiles, the ones who do not earnestly endeavor to acquire righteousness, appropriated righteousness, in fact, a righteousness which is out of a source of faith. But Israel, earnestly endeavoring to acquire a law of righteousness, did not measure up to the law. Because of what? Because, not out of a source of faith but even as out of a source of works they sought to acquire it. They stumbled up against the stone which is a stumbling stone, even as it stands written, Behold, I place in Sion a stone, a stumbling stone, and a rock of offense. And the one who places his faith upon Him will not be put to shame. **30-33**

Brethren, the consuming desire of my heart and my supplication to God on behalf of them is with a view to their salvation. For I bear testimony to them that a zeal for God they have, but not according to a full and accurate knowledge. For, being ignorant of the righteousness of God and seeking to set up their own private righteousness, to the righteousness of God they have not subjected themselves. For the termination of the law is Christ for righteousness to everyone who believes. **1-4**

For Moses writes that the man who does the righteousness which is of the law shall live in its sphere. But the righteousness which is out of a source of faith speaks in this manner, Do not say in your heart, Who shall ascend into heaven? This, in its implications, is to bring Christ down. Or, Who shall descend into the abyss? This, in its implications, is to bring Christ up from among those who are dead. But what does it say? Near you the word is, in your mouth and in your heart. This is the word of the Faith which we are proclaiming. If you confess with your mouth Jesus as Lord and believe in your heart that God raised Him from among the dead, you will be saved. For with the heart faith is exercised resulting in righteousness, and with the mouth confession is made resulting in salvation. For the scripture says, Everyone who **5-13**

believes on Him shall not be put to shame. For there is
not a distinction between Jew and Greek. For the same
Lord is over all, constantly rich toward all those who call
upon Him. For whoever shall call upon the Name of the
Lord shall be saved.

14-17   How is it possible then that they shall call upon the
One in whom they did not believe? Moreover, how is it
possible that they will believe on the One concerning whom
they did not hear? And how is it possible that they shall
hear without one who proclaims? And how is it possible
that they shall make a proclamation except they be sent
on a mission? Even as it stands written, How beautiful
are the feet of those who bring good tidings of good
things. But not all lent an obedient ear to the good news.
For Isaiah says, Lord, who believed our message? So
then, faith is out of the source of that which is heard,
and that which is heard [the message] is through the
agency of the Word concerning Christ.

18-21   But I say, did they not hear? Most certainly. Into
all the earth their sound went out, and into the extremi-
ties of the inhabited earth, their words. But I say, Israel
did not fail to know, did it? First Moses says, I will
provoke you to jealousy by those who are no people, and
by a foolish people I will provoke you to anger. Moreover, Isaiah breaks out boldly and says, I was found by
those who are not seeking me. I was made manifest to
those who are not inquiring about me. But to Israel He
says, The whole day I stretched out my hands to a non-
persuasible and cantankerous people.

1-6   I say then, God did not repudiate His people, did He?
Far be the thought, for as for myself, I also am an
Israelite, the offspring of Abraham, of the tribe of Benjamin. God did not repudiate His people whom He foreordained. Or, do you not know absolutely in the case of
Elijah what the scripture says, how he pleads to God
against Israel? Lord, your prophets they killed. Your
altars they demolished. And as for myself, I was left
alone, and they are seeking my life. But what does the
divine answer say to him? I reserved for myself seven
thousand men who are of such a character that they did

not bow the knee to Baal. Therefore, thus also at this
present season a remnant according to a choice of grace
has come into being. But since it is by grace, no longer
is it out of a source of works. Otherwise no longer is
grace, grace.

What then? That which Israel is constantly seeking, **7-10**
this it did not obtain. But those chosen out obtained it.
And the rest were hardened, even as it stands written,
God gave them a spirit of insensibility, eyes for the purpose of not seeing, and ears for the purpose of not hearing, until this day. Even David says, Let their table become for a snare and a trap, and a stumbling block and
a just retribution to them. Let their eyes be darkened in
order that they may not see and in order that they may
always bow down their back.

I say then, Surely, they did not stumble so as to fall, **11-14**
did they? Away with the thought. But through the instrumentality of their fall salvation has come to the Gentiles with a view to provoking them [Israel] to jealousy.
But since their fall is the enrichment of the world, and
their defeat and loss the enrichment of the Gentiles, how
much more their fulness? But to you I am speaking, the
Gentiles. Inasmuch then, as for myself, as I am an
apostle of Gentiles, I do my ministry honor, if by any
means, possibly, I may provoke to jealousy those who are
my flesh, and save some of them.

For, in view of the fact that their repudiation results **15-22**
in the world's reconciliation, what will the receiving of
them result in if not in life from among the dead? Now,
in view of the fact that the firstfruit is holy, also the
lump, and since the root is holy, also the branches. Now,
since certain of the branches were broken off, and you,
being a wild olive, were grafted in among them and became joint-partaker with them of the root of the fatness
of the olive, stop boasting against the branches. But,
assuming that you are boasting, you are not sustaining the
root, but the root you. You will say then, Branches were
broken off in order that I might be grafted in. Well!
Because of their unbelief they were broken off. But, as
for you, by faith you stand. Stop having a superiority

complex, but be fearing; for in view of the fact that God did not spare the branches which were according to nature, neither will He spare you. Behold therefore God's benevolent kindness and His severity; on the one hand, upon those who fell, severity, and, on the other hand, upon you, God's benevolent kindness, upon the condition that you continue to remain in and abide by His benevolent kindness. Otherwise, also you will be cut out.

23-25   And, moreover, those also, if they do not remain in unbelief, will be grafted in, for God is able to again graft them in. For, as for you, in view of the fact that you were cut out of the olive tree which is wild by nature, and contrary to nature were grafted into the good olive tree, how much more will these who are according to nature be grafted into their own olive tree. For I do not desire you to be ignorant, brethren, concerning this mystery, in order that you may not be wise in yourselves, that hardening in part has come to Israel until the fulness of the Gentiles has come in.

26-32   And thus all Israel shall be saved, even as it stands written, There shall come out of Sion the Deliverer, and shall turn ungodliness from Jacob. And this to them is the covenant from me when I shall take away their sins. On the one hand, with reference to the gospel they are enemies for your sakes; on the other hand, with reference to the selected-out ones they are beloved ones for the fathers' sake; for the gifts in grace and the calling of God are with respect to a change of mind irrevocable. For, even as you formerly disbelieved God, yet now have been made recipients of mercy through the occasion of the unbelief of these, thus also these now have disbelieved in order that through the occasion of the mercy which is yours, they themselves also might now become the recipients of mercy, for God included all within the state of unbelief in order that He might have mercy upon all.

33-36   O the depth of the wealth and wisdom and knowledge of God. How unsearchable are His judgments, and how untraceable the paths He takes; for whoever knew the Lord's mind? or who became His counsellor? or who has previously given to Him and it will be recompensed to him? Because out from Him and through Him and for Him are all things. To Him be the glory forever. Amen.

I therefore beg of you, please, brethren, through the instrumentality of the aforementioned mercies of God, by a once-for-all presentation to place your bodies at the disposal of God, a sacrifice, a living one, a holy one, well-pleasing, your rational, sacred service, [rational, in that this service is performed by the exercise of the mind]. And stop assuming an outward expression that does not come from within you and is not representative of what you are in your inner being but is patterned after this age; but change your outward expression to one that comes from within and is representative of your inner being, by the renewing of your mind, resulting in your putting to the test what is the will of God, the good and well-pleasing and complete will, and having found that it meets specifications, place your approval upon it. **1, 2**

For I am saying through the grace which is given me, to everyone who is among you, not to be thinking more highly of himself, above that which the necessities in the nature of the case impose upon him to be thinking, but to be thinking with a view to a sensible appraisal of himself according as to each one God divided a measure of faith. For even as in one body we have many members but all the members do not have the same function, thus we, the many, are one body in Christ, and members severally one of another. **3-5**

Having therefore gifts differing according to the grace given us, whether that of prophecy, prophesy according to the proportion of faith; or serving, exercise that gift within the sphere of service; or teaching, within the sphere of teaching; or he who exhorts, within the sphere of exhortation; the one who distributes of his earthly possessions, in the sphere of an unostentatious simplicity; the one who is placed in a position of authority, with intense eagerness and effort; the one who shows mercy, with a joyous abandon. **6-8**

Love, let it be without hypocrisy. Look with loathing and horror upon that which is pernicious. Stick fast to that which is good. In the sphere of brotherly love have **9-18** a family affection for one another, vying with one another in showing honor; with respect to zeal, not lazy; fervent in the sphere of the Spirit, serving the Lord; rejoicing in the sphere of hope; patient in tribulation; with respect to prayer, persevering in it continually; with respect to the needs of the saints, being a sharer with them, eager for opportunities to show hospitality. Be constantly blessing those who are constantly persecuting you; be blessing and stop cursing. Be rejoicing with those who are rejoicing, and be weeping with those who are weeping; having the same mind towards one another, not setting your mind upon lofty things, but associating yourselves with lowly things and lowly people. Stop being those who are wise in their own opinion, requiting to no one evil in exchange for evil, taking thought in advance with regard to things that are seemly in the sight of all men. If it is possible so far as it depends upon you, with all men be living at peace.

19-21   Do not be avenging yourselves, beloved ones, but give place at once to the wrath, for it stands written, To me belongs punishment, I will repay, says the Lord. But, if your enemy is hungry, be feeding him. If he thirsts, be giving him to drink, for doing this, you will heap burning coals of fire upon his head. Stop being overcome by the evil, but be overcoming the evil by means of the good.

1-4   Let every soul put himself habitually in subjection to authorities who hold position over them, for there is not an authority except that ordained by God. Moreover, the existing authorities stand permanently ordained by God. So that the one who sets himself in array against the authority, against the ordinance of God has set himself, with the result that he is in a permanent position of antagonism against the ordinance. And those who resist shall receive for themselves judgment. For the rulers are not a terror to the good work but to the evil. Now, do you desire not to be afraid of the authority? Keep on doing the good, and you will have commendation from him, for he is God's servant to you for good. But if you are habitually doing that which is evil, be fearing, for not in vain is he wearing the sword, for he is God's servant, an executor of wrath upon the one who practices the evil.

On which account there is a necessity for putting one's self in subjection, not only because of wrath, but also because of conscience, for because of this you pay taxes; for God's public servants they are, continually giving their attention to this very thing. Deliver to all the debts due them to the one collecting the tax, the tax; to the one collecting the custom, the custom; to the one to whom the fear is due, the fear; to the one to whom the honor is due, the honor.

5-7

Stop owing even one person even one thing, except to be loving one another; for the one who is loving another, has fulfilled the law. For this, You shall not commit adultery, you shall not kill, you shall not steal, you shall not covet, and if there is any commandment of a different nature, in this word it is summed up, in this, You shall love your neighbor as yourself. The aforementioned love does not work evil to a neighbor. Therefore, love is the fulfilling of law. And this, knowing the strategic season, that it is an hour now for you to awake out of sleep, for now our salvation is nearer to us than when we believed. The night has long been on its way, and the day has arrived. Therefore, let us at once and once for all put off the works of the darkness, and let us at once and once for all clothe ourselves with the weapons of the light.

8-12

In the same manner as in the day let us order our behavior in a seemly fashion, not in carousals and drunkenness, not in sexual intercourse and a dissolute abandon, not in strife and jealousy. But clothe yourselves with the Lord Jesus Christ and stop making provision for the sinful nature with a view to a passionate craving.

13, 14

Now, to the one who is weak with respect to his faith, be giving a cordial welcome, not with a view to a critical analysis of his inward reasonings. One, on the one hand, has confidence that he may eat all things; but the one, on the other hand, who is weak, constantly eats vegetables. The one who eats, let him not be treating with contempt the one who does not eat; and the one who

1-4

does not eat, let him not be criticising the one who eats, for God received him. As for you, who are you who are judging another's household slave? To his own personal master he stands or falls. Indeed, he shall be made to stand, for the Lord has power to make him stand.

5-9   For, on the one hand, there is he who judges a day above another day. On the other hand, there is he who subjects every day to a scrutiny. Let each one in his own mind be fully assured. The one who has formed a judgment regarding the day, with reference to the Lord he judges it. And the one who eats, with reference to the Lord he eats, for he gives thanks to God. And the one who does not eat, with reference to the Lord does not eat, and he gives thanks to God. For no one lives with reference to himself, and no one with reference to himself dies. For, whether we are living, with reference to the Lord we are living. Whether we are dying, with reference to the Lord we are dying. Therefore, whether we are living or whether we are dying, we belong to the Lord; for to this end Christ both died and lived, in order that He might exercise lordship over both dead ones and living ones.

10-13   But as for you, why are you judging your brother? Or, as for you also, why are you treating your brother with contempt? For we all shall stand before the judgment seat of God. For it stands written, As I live, says the Lord, every knee shall bow to me, and every tongue shall confess to God. Therefore, then, each one of us shall give an account concerning himself to God. Therefore, no longer let us be judging one another. But be judging this rather, not to place a stumbling block before your brother, or a snare in which he may be entrapped.

14-18   For I know with an absolute knowledge and stand persuaded in the Lord Jesus that not even one thing is unhallowed in itself except it be to the one who reasons it out to be unhallowed. To that one it is unhallowed. For, if because of food your brother is made to grieve, no longer are you conducting yourself according to love. Stop ruining by your food that one on behalf of whom Christ died. Therefore, stop allowing your good to be spoken of in a reproachful and evil manner; for the kingdom of God is not eating and drinking, but righteousness and peace and joy in the sphere of the Holy Spirit; for the one who in this serves the Christ is well pleasing to God, and because having met the specifications is approved by men.

Accordingly, therefore, the things of peace let us be **19-21** eagerly and earnestly seeking after, and the things which edify, which edification is with a view to the edification of one another. Stop on account of food ruining the work of God. All things indeed are pure. But it is evil to the man who eats so as to be a stumbling block. It is good not to eat flesh, nor to drink wine, nor even anything by which your brother stumbles.

As for you, the faith which you have, be having to **22, 23** yourself in the sight of God. Spiritually prosperous is the one who does not judge himself in that which he has tested with a view to approving it should it meet specifications and, having found that it does, has placed his approval upon it. But the one who doubts, if he eats, stands condemned because not by faith did he eat. Moreover, everything which is not of faith is sin.

As for us, then, the strong ones, we have a moral **1-4** obligation to be bearing the infirmities of those who are not strong, and not to be pleasing ourselves. Each one of us, let him be pleasing his neighbor with a view to his good, resulting in his edification. For even the Christ did not please himself, but even as it stands written, The reproaches of those who reproached you fell upon me. For whatever things were written aforetime with a view to our learning were written, in order that through the patience and through the encouragement arising from the scriptures we might be having hope.

Now, the God of the patience and the encouragement **5-7** give to you to be thinking the same thing among one another according to Christ Jesus, in order that with one mind and one mouth you may keep on glorifying the God and Father of our Lord Jesus Christ. Wherefore, be receiving one another even as also the Christ received us, with a view to the glory of God.

8-12   For I am saying, Christ has become a servant to the circumcision on behalf of God's truth, resulting in the confirmation of the promises to the fathers and [resulting] in the Gentiles, on behalf of His mercy, glorifying God; even as it stands written, Because of this I will openly confess to you among the Gentiles and in your Name sing. And again he says, Rejoice, Gentiles, with His people. And again, Be extolling, all you Gentiles, the Lord. And let all the people extol Him. And again Isaiah says, There shall be a sprout out of the root of Jesse, even the One who arises to be a ruler of the Gentiles. Upon Him will the Gentiles place their hope.

13, 14   Now the God of the hope fill you with every joy and hope in the sphere of believing, resulting in your superabounding in the sphere of the hope by the power of the Holy Spirit. But I have reached a settled conviction, my brethren, even I myself, concerning you, that you yourselves also are full of goodness, having been filled completely full of every knowledge with the result that you are in an abiding state of fullness, able also to be admonishing one another.

15, 16   The more boldly indeed I write to you in some measure as recalling to your mind again because of the grace which was given to me from God, resulting in my being a servant of Christ Jesus in holy things to the Gentiles, exercising a sacred ministry in the good news of God in order that the offering of the Gentiles might be well pleasing, having been sanctified by the Holy Spirit.

17-21   I have therefore my glorifying in Christ Jesus with reference to the things which pertain to God. For I will not dare to be speaking concerning anything of the things which Christ did not bring about through my agency resulting in the obedience of the Gentiles, by word and deed, by the power of attesting miracles and miracles of an extraordinary character, by the power of the Holy Spirit: so that from Jerusalem and the environs of Illyricum I have fulfilled my commission of preaching the good news of the Christ. Indeed, in this manner I have been actuated by considerations of honor to be ambitious to announce the glad tidings not where Christ was named, in order that I would not be building upon a foundation belonging to another; but as it stands written, They shall see, those to whom there was not made an announcement concerning Him, and those who have not heard, they shall understand.

Wherefore, I also have been continually hindered by the many things in coming to you. But now no longer having opportunity in these parts, and having a passionate desire to come to you these many years, whenever I journey into Spain I am hoping to see you as I journey through, and by you to be furnished with the necessities of travel to that place, if first in part I may be fully satisfied with your fellowship.   **22-24**

But now I am going on my journey to Jerusalem, ministering to the saints. For it was the good pleasure of Macedonia and Achaia to make up a certain benefaction jointly contributed for the poor of the saints which are in Jerusalem; for it was their good pleasure, and their debtors they are. For in view of the fact that the Gentiles were fellow-partakers of their spiritual things, they are under moral obligation to minister to them in the sphere of things needed for the sustenance of the body, considering this material ministry as a sacred service. Then, having brought this to a successful termination and having secured to them this fruit, I will come through you into Spain. And I know positively that when coming to you, in the fulness of the blessing of Christ I will come.   **25-29**

But I beg of you, please, brethren, through our Lord Jesus Christ and through the love which is of the Spirit, contend vigorously with me in your prayers on my behalf to God, in order that I may be delivered from those who are non-persuasible in Judaea, and that my service which is for Jerusalem may become well pleasing to the saints, in order that in joy, having come to you through God's will, I may rest and refresh myself with you. Now, the God of the peace be with you all. Amen.   **30-33**

Now, I recommend to you, Phoebe, our sister, who is a deaconess of the assembly which is at Cenchrea, to the end that you take her to yourselves in the Lord in a   **1-5** manner which is fitting to the saints, and that you stand by her in whatever business she may have need of you, for verily, she herself became a benefactress of many, and of me myself. Greet Prisca and Aquila, my fellow-workers in Christ Jesus, who are such that on behalf of my life they laid down their necks, to whom I not only give thanks, but also all the assemblies of the Gentiles. Also, greet the assembly which meets in their home.

5-9   Greet Epaenetus, my well-beloved, who is the first-fruit of Asia with reference to Christ. Greet Marian who is such as to have labored with wearisome effort to the point of exhaustion on your behalf with reference to many things. Greet Andronicus and Junia, my fellow countrymen and my fellow prisoners who are of excellent reputation among the apostles, who also came in Christ before I did. Greet Amplias, my beloved in the Lord. Greet Urbane, our fellow helper in Christ, and Stachys, my beloved.

10-12   Greet Apelles, the one who, having been put to the test and having been found to meet the test, is approved in Christ. Greet those belonging to Aristobulus. Greet Herodion, my fellow countryman. Greet those belonging to Narcissus, those who are in the Lord. Greet Tryphena and Tryphosa, those who labored to the point of exhaustion in the Lord.

12-16   Greet Persis, the beloved who was such that she labored to the point of exhaustion with reference to many things in the Lord. Greet Rufus, the one selected out in the Lord, and his mother and mine. Greet Asyncritus, Philegon, Hermas, Patrobas, Hermes, and the brethren with them. Greet Philologus, and Julia, Nereus and his sister, and Olympas, and all the saints with them. Greet one another with a holy kiss. There greet you all the churches of Christ.

17-20   Now, I beg of you, please, brethren, be keeping a watchful eye ever open for those who are causing the divisions and the scandals which are contrary to the teaching that you learned, and be turning away from them. For they are such as are not rendering service as bond-slaves to our Lord Christ, but to their own stomachs;

and with smooth and plausible address, which simulates goodness, and with polished eulogies, are leading astray the hearts of the innocent; for your obedience has come to the ears of all. Because of you, therefore, I am rejoicing. But I desire you to be wise ones with reference to that which is good, and pure ones with reference to that which is evil. And the God of the peace will trample Satan under your feet soon. The grace of our Lord Jesus be with you.

There greet you Timothy, my co-worker, and Lucius, and Jason, and Sosipater, my countrymen. As for myself, I, Tertius, greet you in the Lord, the one who is putting this letter in writing. There greets you Gaius, my host and host of the whole assembly. There greet you Erastus, the manager of the city, and Quartus, the brother. Now, to the One who is of power to establish you according to my gospel, even the proclamation concerning Jesus Christ, according to the uncovering of the mystery which during eternal times has been kept in silence but now has been made known through prophetic writings according to the mandate of the eternal God, having been made known with a view to the obedience to the Faith among all nations, to God alone wise, through Jesus Christ, to Him [God alone wise] be the glory for ever and ever. Amen.

21-27

Paul, a divinely-summoned and divinely-appointed ambassador belonging to Christ Jesus, an ambassador by reason of God's determining will, and Sosthenes our brother, to the assembly of God which is at Corinth, to those who have been set apart for the worship and service of God, this act of setting apart having been accomplished by being placed in Christ Jesus and thus being in vital union with Him, consecrated ones, this consecration having been by divine appointment and summons, with all those who are calling upon the Name of our Lord Jesus Christ in every place, their Lord and ours. Grace to you and peace from God our Father and from the Lord Jesus Christ. **1-3**

I am thanking my God always concerning you, the cause of my thanksgiving being the grace of God which was given you in Christ Jesus. I mean that in everything you were made rich in Him, this wealth being in the form of every exuberant aptitude in proclaiming the Word and in the form of every kind of experiential knowledge, inasmuch as the testimony concerning the Christ was proved to be divinely-revealed truth and its reality was verified among you with the result that you are not feeling that you are trailing behind others in even one spiritual enablement for service while you are assiduously and patiently waiting for the appearance of our Lord Jesus Christ, who also will make you steadfast and constant even to the end, in character such that you cannot be called to account in the day of our Lord Jesus Christ. Faithful is God through whom you were divinely summoned into a joint-participation with His Son, Jesus Christ our Lord. **4-9**

Now, I beg of you, please, brethren, my appeal to you being enforced by the Name of our Lord Jesus Christ [that Name holding within its compass all that He is in His glorious Person and wonderful salvation], I beg of you, please, that all of you be speaking the same thing, and that there be no factions among you, but that the breaches in your fellowship caused by these factions having been healed, you may remain perfectly united in the sphere of the same mind and in the sphere of the same opinion. **10**

11-17 For it was made clear to me concerning you, my brethren, by members of Chloe's household, that there are wranglings among you. Now, what I mean is this; that each one of you is saying, As for myself, I am a follower of Paul; But as for myself, I am a follower of Apollos; But as for myself, I am a follower of Cephas; But as for myself, I am a follower of Christ. The Christ has been divided into various parts, with the present result that He lies there broken up into fragments which are distributed among you. Paul was not crucified on your behalf, was he, or, it was not into the name of Paul that you were baptized, was it? I am thankful that not even one of you did I baptize except Crispus and Gaius; lest anyone should say that into my name you were baptized. However, I also did baptize the household of Stephanas. Besides, I do not know positively whether I baptized any other person, for Christ did not send me on a mission to be a baptizer but to be a bringer of good news, not bringing this good news within the realm of philosophical discourse, lest the Cross of the Christ be emptied of its true significance and power.

18-25 For the story, that story concerning the Cross, is, on the one hand, to those who are perishing, foolishness, but to us, on the other hand, who are being saved, it is God's power. For it has been written and is at present on record, I will destroy the wisdom of those who are wise, and the discernment of those who have the ability to discern I will frustrate. Where is a philosopher, skilled in letters, cultivated, learned? Where is a man learned in the sacred scriptures? Where is a learned sophist of this age, fallacious reasoner that he is? Did not God prove foolish the wisdom of this world system? For, in view of the fact that, in the wisdom of God, the world system through its wisdom did not come to have an experiential knowledge of God, God saw fit through the aforementioned foolishness of the previously alluded-to proclamation to save those who believe, for, both, Jews are constantly demanding an attesting miracle and Greeks are constantly searching for wisdom. But as for us, we are proclaiming a Christ, one who has been crucified; to Jews, on the one hand, an offense, to Greeks, on the other hand, folly, but to those themselves who have been divinely summoned into salvation, both Jews and Greeks, Christ, God's power and God's wisdom, because that aforementioned folly of God is wiser than men and that aforementioned weakness of God is stronger than men.

For, take a good look at your divine summons [into salvation], brethren, that not many wise men according to human standards, not many men of dignity and power, not many who are of royal or aristocratic lineage are given that divine summons [into salvation], but God selected out for himself those individuals among the world of sinners characterized by the aforementioned foolishness, in order that He might put to confusion those who are wise. And those individuals among the world of sinners, characterized by weakness, God selected out for himself, in order that He might put to confusion those who are characterized by strength. And those individuals among the world of sinners, who are not of royal or noble ancestry but belong to the common people and those who are utterly despised, God selected out for himself, the aforementioned classes of individuals looked upon as nonentities, in order that He might deprive of force, influence, and power those who think themselves to be somewhat, to the end that humanity may not in a single instance boast in His presence. **26-29**

But as for you, out from Him as a source are you in Christ Jesus who became wisdom for us from God, both righteousness and sanctification and redemption, in order that even as it stands written, He who boasts, in the Lord let him be boasting. **30,31**

And as for myself, having come to you, brethren, I came, not having my message dominated by a transcendent rhetorical display or by philosophical subtlety when I was announcing to you the testimony of God, for, after weighing the issues, I decided not to know anything among you except Jesus Christ and this very One as crucified. And as for myself, when I faced you, I fell into a state of weakness and fear and much trembling. And my message and my preaching were not couched in **1-5** specious words of philosophy but were dependent for their efficacy upon a demonstration of the Spirit and of power, in order that your faith should not be resting in human philosophy but in God's power.

6-8 There is a wisdom, however, which we are in the habit of speaking among those who are spiritually mature, but not a wisdom of this present age or even a wisdom of the rulers of this age who are in the process of being liquidated. But we speak God's wisdom in the form of a mystery long hidden but now revealed and understandable, that wisdom which has been kept secret which God foreordained before the ages with a view to our glory, which wisdom not one of the rulers of this age has known in an experiential way, for had they known it, in that case they would not have crucified the Lord of the glory.

9-11 But even as it stands written, The things which eye did not see nor ear hear and which did not arise within an individual's heart, so many things as God prepared for those who love Him, for to us God the Father revealed them through the intermediate agency of His Spirit. For the Spirit is constantly exploring all things, even the deep things of God. For who is there of men who knows the things of the individual person except the [human] spirit of that aforementioned individual person which is in him? In the same manner also the things of God no one has known except the Spirit of God.

12, 13 But as for us, not the spirit of the world system did we receive but the Spirit who is of God in order that we might come to know the things which by God have been in grace bestowed upon us, which things also we put into words, not in words taught by human philosophy but in words taught by the Spirit, fitly joining together Spirit-revealed truths with Spirit-taught words.

14-16 But the unregenerate man of the highest intellectual attainments does not grant access to the things of the Spirit of God, for to him they are folly, and he is not able to come to know them because they are investigated in a spiritual realm. But the spiritual man investigates indeed all things, but he himself is not being probed by anyone. For who has come to know experientially the Lord's mind, he who will instruct Him? But as for us, Christ's mind we have.

As for myself, I also, brethren, was not able to speak to you as I would to those dominated by the Holy Spirit, but as I would to those dominated by the evil nature, as I would to those in Christ who are still immature spiritually. Milk I fed you, not solid food, for not yet were you able to assimilate the latter. In fact, not even yet at the present time are you able to do so. For, in so far as there are among you jealousy and strife, are you not those dominated by the evil nature, and are you not ordering your manner of life as an unsaved man would do? For whenever someone says, As for myself, I indeed am a follower of Paul, but another of a different character says, As for myself, I am a follower of Apollos, are you not mere men? What then is Apollos? And what is Paul? We are ministering servants through whose intermediate agency you believed, servants in each case in the manner as the Lord gave to each of us. As for myself, I planted, Apollos watered, but God has been causing that which was sown to grow. So that he who plants is not anything, nor he who waters, but God who causes things to grow.

1-7

Now, the one who plants and the one who waters are one. But each one of us will receive his specific pay appropriate to his specific work, for we are God's fellow workers. You are God's land under cultivation, God's edifice. According to the grace of God which was given to me, I as a skillful master builder laid a foundation, but another builds upon it. But let each one be taking heed how he builds upon it, for an alternative foundation no one is able to lay alongside of the one which is being laid, which foundation is a person, Jesus Christ.

8-11

Now, assuming that anyone builds upon the aforementioned foundation gold, silver, precious stones, wood, hay, stubble, the work of each person will become apparent, for the day will make it known, because it [the day] will be made clear as to its identity by means of one of its attributes, namely, fire. And the fire itself will put

12-15

each person's work to the test for the purpose of approving it should it meet the required specifications, the test being to determine what sort of work it is as to quality. Assuming that the work of anyone which he has built upon it [the foundation, Christ] endures in that it has met these specifications, he shall receive a reward. Assuming that the work of anyone will be burned up, he will incur a loss, but he himself shall be saved, but being saved thus, it will be as escaping destruction in the midst of the fire which burns up his works.

16, 17   Do you not all know that all of you are God's inner sanctuary and that the Spirit of God is making His home in you? If, as is the case, anyone morally corrupts the inner sanctuary of God, this person God will bring to the place of ruin, for the inner sanctuary of God is holy, of which holy character you are.

18-23   Let no one continue to be deceiving himself. If, as is the case, anyone among you thinks himself to be wise in the sphere of the things of this age, let him become a fool [in the estimation of this age] in order that he may become wise, for the wisdom of this world system is foolishness as God looks at it. For it has been written and is at present on record, He catches those who are wise in their false wisdom, and again, The Lord knows the reasonings of those who are wise, that they are futile reasonings. Wherefore, let no one continue to be boasting in men, for all things are yours, whether Paul or Apollos or Cephas or the existing order of material things or life or death or present things or things about to come, all belong to you, and as for you, you belong to Christ and Christ belongs to God.

1-5   In this manner let a man measure and classify us, as servants of Christ and as those who have been entrusted with the mysteries of God and their disposition. Under these circumstances it is further sought in stewards that a man be found to be faithful. But with me it is a very small thing that I am being put on trial by you by the [judicial] day of mankind. In fact, I do not even put myself on trial, for I am conscious of not even one thing against myself, but not by this means do I stand justified. Indeed, He who puts me on trial is the Lord. Wherefore, stop exercising censorious judgment with reference to anything before the epochal, strategic season, until that time whenever the Lord may come, who will both turn the light on the hidden things of the darkness and bring out into the open the counsels of the hearts. And then to each one there shall come his praise from God.

And these things, brethren, I referred to myself and Apollos, things true of the whole class [of servants of the Lord Jesus] to which we belong, doing this for your sakes, in order that you may learn from our example not to go beyond the things that stand written, to the end that you do not bear yourselves loftily, one on behalf of one individual [teacher] as against another of a different character. For who makes a distinction between you and others? And what do you have which you did not receive? But since also you received it, why are you boasting as though you did not receive it? Already have you become completely satiated with the result that your state of complete satisfaction persists through present time? Already did you become wealthy? Without us did you enter that new state of being in which you reign as kings? However, I wish indeed that you did reign as kings, in order that, as for us also, we might reign as kings with you, for it seems to me that God exhibited us, the apostles, as those who in the eyes of men are the most inferior in the scale of human existence, as men doomed to die, because we were exhibited as a spectacle to be gazed at and made sport of by the universe, both by angels and by men. As for us, fools are we on account of Christ. But as for you, you are members of the intelligentsia in your union with Christ. As for us, we are those who are frail and infirm. But as for all of you, you are those who are mighty. As for all of you, you are those who are illustrious, honorable, held in esteem by others. But as for us, we are those whom no one respects. To this very hour we are hungry and thirsty and scantily clothed and maltreated and, going from place to place, we have no fixed home, and we labor to the point of exhaustion, working at our trade [that of

6-13

tent making] with our own hands. When insulting abuse is being heaped upon us, we invoke blessings upon those who are mistreating us. When we are being persecuted, we patiently bear it. When we are publicly slandered, we pleadingly admonish — I beg of you, please. We have become in the estimation of the world as the filth discarded by humanity as the result of cleansing one's self, dirt scraped off of all things, to this very moment.

14-21   Not as shaming you am I writing these things, but as my children, beloved ones, I am warning and admonishing you, for if you may be having ten thousand tutors in Christ, yet not many fathers do you have, for in Christ Jesus through the gospel, as for myself, I begot you. I beg of you, please, therefore, be becoming imitators of me. For this very reason I sent to you Timothy, who is my child, a beloved one, and one in the Lord, who is trustworthy and can be depended upon, who will bring to your remembrance my ways which are in Christ Jesus, even as in every assembly everywhere I am teaching. Now, on the supposition that I am not coming to you, certain ones have an inflated ego. But I will come to you shortly if the Lord wills, and I will take cognizance, not of the speech of those with an inflated ego but of their power, for the kingdom of God is not in the sphere of speech but in that of power. What are you desiring? With a stick shall I come to you or in a love that has as its impelling motive the benefit of the one loved, the exercise of which love demands self-sacrifice, and in the spirit of meekness?

1-8   There is actually fornication reported to be among you, and this fornication of such a nature that it does not exist even among the Gentiles, that a certain person is possessing the wife of his father. And as for you, you have been guilty of an inflated ego and are at present in the same state. And ought you not to have rather gone into mourning, to the end that the one who has done this deed might be taken out of your midst? For, as for myself, I indeed, being absent in body but present in spirit, already handed down my sentence, and this sentence stands as though I were present concerning this one who thus did this thing. In the Name of the Lord Jesus, when you are gathered together, and my spirit, with the power of our Lord Jesus, my sentence is that you deliver such a one to Satan for the subjugation of the flesh [the evil nature], in order that the spirit might be saved in the day of the Lord. Your boasting [in the state of the local assembly] is not seemly or fitting. Do you not know with a positive assurance that a little yeast permeates and affects the entire bread dough with itself? Cleanse out completely, at once and once for all, the old yeast which is part of a world which has passed away for you and out from which you were saved, in order that you may be a fresh aggregation of individuals, even as you are without yeast. For, indeed, our Passover was slain, Christ. Wherefore, let us be keeping the feast, not with the yeast which has been relegated to a time that is past when we lived a life not for us today, neither with the yeast of malice and perniciousness, but with cakes permeated and affected by the yeast of an unadulterated life, having no admixture of evil in them, and having in them the yeast of truth.

I wrote to you in my letter not to be mingling in a **9-13** close and habitual intimacy with those who indulge in unlawful sexual intercourse. I did not altogether forbid you having dealings with the fornicators who are members of this world system [of evil] or with those who are covetous and rapacious, or with idolaters, since then you would be obliged to go out of the world of mankind. But now I am writing to you to urge you not to be mingling in a close and habitual intimacy — should anyone who is called a brother [Christian] be a fornicator or a covetous person or an idolater or a reviler or a drunkard or rapacious — with such a person not even to be eating. For what responsibility of mine is it to pass judgment upon those who are outside [the Church]? Indeed, those who are outside will God judge. Expel at once the pernicious person from among yourselves.

Is anyone of you who has a case against another dar- **1-8** ing to be going to law before those who are unrighteous and not before the saints? Or, do you not all know that the saints shall judge the world system [of evil]? And in view of the fact that the world system is being judged by you, are you those who are unfit to sit on the tribunal of a judge where trifling affairs are judged [forming courts yourselves to settle matters among yourselves]? Do you not know that we shall sit in judgment upon angels, to say nothing at all of judging the affairs of this life? Therefore, if you may be having courts [for the adjudication of your private matters], those who are least esteemed and of the most humble station in the local assembly, seat these on the judge's bench. I am saying this to you with a view to arousing your sense of shame. Is it thus, that you do not have one among you who is wise, who will be able to arbitrate between brother and brother? But brother goes to law with brother, and this before unbelievers. Nay! It is already a total [moral] defeat for you, having lawsuits with one another. Why do you not permit yourselves rather to be wronged? Why do you not permit yourselves rather to be defrauded? But, as for yourselves, you are committing wrong, and you are defrauding, and doing this to brethren.

9-11   Or do you not know that unrighteous individuals will not inherit God's kingdom? Stop being deceived; neither fornicators nor idolaters nor adulterers nor those who are of a voluptuous nature, given to the gratification of sensual, immoral appetites, neither men who are guilty of sexual intercourse with members of their own sex, nor thieves, nor those who are always greedy to have more than they possess, nor drunkards, nor revilers, nor extortioners, shall inherit God's kingdom. And these things you were, certain ones of you. But you bathed yourselves clean [from sin in the fountain filled with blood drawn from Immanuel's veins], but you were set apart for God, but you were made righteous in the Name of the Lord Jesus and by the Spirit of our God.

12-20   All [good] things are under my power of choice to be doing, but all things are not profitable. All things are under my power of choice, but I will not be brought under the power of any one of them. The various kinds of food are for the stomach, and the stomach is for these various kinds of food. But God will abolish both it and them. But the body is not for fornication but for the Lord, and the Lord is for the body. And God raised up the Lord and will also raise us up through His power. Do you not know that your bodies are members of Christ? Having taken then the members of Christ, shall I make them members of a harlot? Let not such a thing take place. Or, do you not know that he who joins himself with his harlot is one body [with her]? For they shall become, He says, these two, one flesh. But he who joins himself to the Lord is one spirit [with Him]. Be fleeing from fornication. Every act of sin which a man may do is outside of his body, but he who commits fornication is sinning against his own body. Or do you not know that your body is an inner sanctuary of the Holy Spirit, whom you have from God, and that you are not your own? For you were purchased at a price. Now therefore, glorify God in your body.

Now, with reference to the things concerning which you wrote. It is perfectly proper, honorable, morally befitting for a man to live in strict celibacy. But because of the fornications, let each man be having his own wife, and let each woman be having her own husband. Let the husband be rendering to his wife that which is due her, and also let the wife render to her husband that which is due him. The wife does not have authority over her own body, but her husband does. Likewise also the husband does not have authority over his own body, but the wife does. Do not continue to rob each other [by withholding yourselves from one another] except it be by mutual consent for a time in order that you may give yourselves to prayer, and that you may be united again, in order that Satan may not solicit you to sin because of your lack of self-control. But this I am saying by way of a concession [in view of your circumstances], not by way of an injunction. But I wish that all men were even as also I myself. But each one has his own spiritual gift from God, one, on the one hand, in one way, and the other, on the other hand, in another way. **1-7**

I say then to the unmarried men and to the widows that it is a right procedure for them if they remain as I also am. But assuming that they are not able to exercise self-control in the realm of the continent life, let them marry, for it is more advantageous to marry than to **8-14** continue to burn [with the heat of sexual passion]. But to those who have married I command, not I, but the Lord, that the wife should not depart from her husband, but and if she depart, let her also remain unmarried or let her be reconciled to her husband. And the husband, let him not be putting away his wife. And to the rest I myself speak, not the Lord. Assuming that a certain brother has a wife who is an unbeliever and she herself is content to live with him, let him not be putting her away. And the wife who is such that she has an unbelieving husband, and this husband is content to live with her, let her not be putting her husband away, for the husband who is an unbeliever has been sanctified by virtue of his association with his wife in her position as a saved individual [this sanctification being in the marriage relation, that marriage being declared holy by reason of the Christian standing of the wife]. And the unbelieving wife has been sanctified by virtue of her association with her husband. Otherwise your children would be unclean. But now they are holy.

15-24   But assuming that the unbelieving husband departs, let him be departing. A [Christian] brother or [Christian] sister is not in the position of a slave, namely, bound to the unbelieving husband or unbelieving wife in an indissoluble union in cases such as these; but God has called us [to live] in peace. For how do you know positively, O wife, whether you will save your husband, or, how do you know, husband, whether you will save your wife? Only, as the Lord has assigned to each one his lot [in life], as God has called each one, in that way let him be ordering his manner of life. And so in all the assemblies I am giving orders. Was any certain person divinely summoned [into salvation] when he was in a state of circumcision? Let him not have the marks of circumcision effaced. Has any certain person been divinely summoned [into salvation] when he was uncircumcised? Let him not be circumcised. This thing called circumcision is not anything, and this thing called uncircumcision is not anything, but keeping the commandments of God [is what counts]. Each one, in the circumstance in which he was divinely summoned [into salvation], in this let him be remaining. Were you divinely summoned when you were a slave? Let not that be a concern to you. But on the assumption also that you are able to become a free man, the rather take advantage of the opportunity, for the slave who was divinely summoned by the Lord is the Lord's freedman. Likewise, he who was divinely summoned when he was a freedman, is Christ's slave. At a price you were purchased. Do not go on becoming those who are subservient to men. Each one in the sphere in which he was divinely summoned, brethren, in this let him be remaining in the presence of God.

Now, concerning the virgins [unmarried women], an **25-28** injunction from the Lord I do not possess. But I am giving my reasoned judgment as one who is trustworthy by reason of the mercy shown him by the Lord. I consider therefore this to be salutary because of the necessity imposed by the present circumstances, that it is good for an individual to be just as he is. Have you been bound to a wife? Stop seeking to be loosed. Have you been loosed from a wife? Stop seeking a wife. But and if you marry, you did not sin. And if the virgin marry, she did not sin. However, such as these shall have tribulation in the sphere of one's physical existence [on earth]. But, as for myself, I would be sparing you.

But this I am saying, brethren, The strategic, epochal **29-31** period of time [in which we are living] has been shortened, that henceforth both those who have wives be as though not having wives, and those who are weeping be as though they are not weeping, and those who are rejoicing as though not rejoicing, and those who are purchasing in the market place as though they did not possess anything, and those who are making use of this world [the things of human existence] as not making excessive use of the same, for the temporary fashion of this world is passing away.

But I desire you to be without anxious cares. He **32-40** who is unmarried seeks to promote the interests of the things of the Lord, how he may please the Lord. But he who is married is concerned with the things of the world, how he may please his wife, and is distracted. Both the unmarried woman and the virgin seek to promote the interests of the things of the Lord in order that they may be set-apart ones to God and His service both with respect to the body and the spirit. But the woman who is married is concerned with the things of the world, how she may please her husband. But this I am saying for your own profit, not in order that I may throw a noose over you [that is, constrain you to obey my commands], but I am saying this in order that in a seemly manner you may assiduously serve the Lord without distraction. But, assuming that a certain man thinks that he is acting in an unseemly manner in the case of his virgin daughter, if she be past the bloom of youth, and it [a marriage] thus ought to take place, whatever he desires, let him be doing. He is not sinning. Let them [the daughter and the man she loves] marry. But he who stands firm in his heart, having no constraint upon him, but has authority concerning his own private desire, and has come to a settled decision to be keeping his own daughter in a state of virginity, shall do well. So that also he who gives his own virgin daughter in marriage is doing well, and he who does not do so will do better. A wife is bound as long as her husband may live. But if her husband dies, she is free to marry whomever she desires, only in the Lord. But she is in a state more conducive to her well-being if she remains as she is, in my judgment. However, I think, as for myself, I also have God's Spirit [in this, as well as my own judgment].

1-7   Now, concerning things sacrificed to idols, We know, [do you say?], because all of us are possessers of knowledge. The aforementioned knowledge inflates the ego, but the love [God's love produced in the heart] builds up [the Christian life]. Assuming that anyone thinks that he has come to know anything, not yet has he come to know in a manner in which it is a necessity in the nature of the case to know. Now, assuming that anyone loves God, this person is known by God. Therefore, concerning the act of eating things that have been sacrificed to idols, we know positively that an idol is a nonentity in the world and that there is no God but one. For, indeed, assuming that there are so-called gods, whether in heaven or on earth, even as there are gods many and lords many, yet to us there is one God, the Father, out from whom as a source are all things and we for Him, and one Lord Jesus Christ, through whose intermediate agency all things exist and we through Him. But not in all men is this knowledge. Now, certain ones by reason of their long association with the idol until the present moment, eat the things that had been previously sacrificed to the idol, as an idol-sacrifice, and their conscience, being weak, is polluted.

But food will not provide for us an entree to God. **8-13**
Neither if we do not eat do we fall short. Neither if we eat do we exceed [others]. But be taking heed that this right of yours does not possibly become a stumbling block to those who are weak. For if a certain one sees you, the one who has knowledge, reclining at a sacrificial banquet in the idol's temple, will not the conscience of the one who is weak be built up to the place where he will be eating the things sacrificed to idols? For the one who is weak, through your knowledge is being ruined [in his Christian life], your brother on account of whom Christ died. Moreover, sinning in this manner against your brethren and inflicting a blow on their conscience when it is weak, against Christ you are sinning; because of which very fact, since food makes my brother stumble, I will in no case eat animal flesh forever, in order that I may not make my brother stumble.

Am I not free? Am I not an apostle? Have I not **1-3**
seen the Lord with a discerning eye and at present have Him in my mind's eye? Are not you all my work in the Lord? Assuming that to others I am not an apostle, yet at least I am to you, for as for you all, you by virtue of your position in the Lord and your vital union with Him, are the seal which confirms and proves and authenticates my apostleship. This is my defense to those who are investigating me.

We [Paul] do not have the right to eat and drink **4-10**
[as guests of the local church], do we? [Your answer in the negative, which I expect, is ridiculous]. We do not

have a right to be supporting a wife who is a [Christian] sister [believer] as also the rest of the apostles and the brethren of the Lord and Cephas, have we? [Your negative answer again is wrong]. Or, as for myself only and Barnabas, do we not have a right not to be working? Who makes a military expedition at any time at his own private expense? Who plants a vineyard and does not eat its fruit? Or, who shepherds a flock and does not partake of the milk of his flock? I am not saying these things in accordance with the reasoning of mankind, am I? Or, the law, does it not say these things? for in Moses' law it has been written and is at present on record, You shall not muzzle an ox when he is threshing out the grain. Oxen are not a concern to God, are they? Or, on account of us is He assuredly saying it? For on our account it was written, that he who is ploughing ought to be ploughing in hope of partaking, and he who is threshing ought to be threshing in hope of partaking.

11-14   As for us, since we sowed spiritual things for you, is it a great thing if we shall reap from you the things which are needful to sustain our physical existence? Since others partake of this claim upon you, do not we the more? Nevertheless, we did not make use of this right of ours, but are putting up with all things in order that we may not cut off the onward progress of the good news concerning the Christ. Do you not know positively that those who are engaged in the work relative to the sacred things of the temple derive their sustenance from the things that come out of the temple, that those who are in constant attendance at the altar have a share with the altar [in the sacrifice placed upon it]? In the same manner also the Lord ordained that those who are proclaiming the good news should be deriving their living from the good news.

15-17   But as for myself, I have not made use of these things in even one instance, and at present continue the same policy. Moreover, I am not writing these things [concerning privileges] in order that in this manner it should be done in my case, for it were good for me rather to die than — no one shall nullify my boasting. For if I am preaching the good news, there is nothing for me to boast about, for a necessary compulsion is pressing down upon me, for woe to me if I do not proclaim the good news. For, assuming that I am doing this of my own volition, I have a recompense; but doing it without my own volition, a responsibility of administering [the propagation of the good news] has been entrusted to me and at present is the impelling motive that makes it impossible not to proclaim it.

What then is my remuneration? namely, that when **18-23** I am proclaiming the good news I may give out the good news without charge, with the end in view of not making full use of my right [to be supported financially by those to whom I minister] in the [proclaiming of the] good news. For, being free from all [not obligated to anyone because of not holding a salaried position] I made myself a slave to all in order that I may win the more [souls to the Lord Jesus]. And I became to the Jews as a Jew in order that I may win Jews; to those under law, as one under law, not being myself under law, in order that I may win those under law; to those who are without law [the Gentiles], as being without law, not being an outlaw with respect to God, but within the sphere of Christ's law, in order that I may win those who are without law. To those who are weak, I became as one who is weak, in order that I may win those who are weak. To all men I have become all things in order that I may by all means save some. And I am doing all things for the sake of the good news in order that I may become a joint-participant with others in it.

Do you not know that those who are running in a **24-27** race are indeed all running, but one receives the victor's award? Be running in such a manner as the one who won the race, in order that you may obtain the victor's award. Everyone who participates in the athletic games exercises constant self-control in all things, those, to be sure, in order that they may receive a perishable victor's garland of wild olive leaves to be worn as a crown of victory, but as for us [we engage in Christian service, exercising constant self-control to obtain] a victor's garland which is imperishable. As for myself, therefore, I so run, in no uncertain manner. I so swing my fists, **not** as one who, when fighting, misses his opponent, merely beating the air and not striking a straight blow which finds its target. But I beat my body black and blue and make it my abject slave lest somehow, when I have preached to others, I myself should be disqualified [from further Christian service].

1-5   For I do not desire you to be ignorant, brethren, that our fathers, all of them, were under the [Shekinah] cloud and all went through the sea. And all had themselves immersed, surrounded by the cloud [above] and the sea [on both sides], thus shut up to Moses [as their leader]. And all ate the same spiritual food and all drank the same spiritual drink, for they were drinking from a spiritual Rock that followed them, and the aforementioned Rock was the Christ. But not with the greater part of them was God pleased, for they [their dead bodies] were strewn along the ground in the uninhabited region.

6-13   Now, these things have been made examples for us to the end that we should not be those who have a passionate craving for evil things as also those had a passionate craving. Stop becoming idolaters as some of them were, even as it stands written, The people sat down to eat and drink and rose up to be giving way to hilarity. Neither let us be committing fornication even as certain of them committed fornication, and there fell in one day twenty-three thousand. Neither let us be putting the Lord to an all-out test, trying Him to the utmost, even as certain of them tried Him and by means of snakes were perishing day after day. Stop grumbling, discontentedly complaining, even as certain of them grumbled and kept on being destroyed one after another by the destroyer. Now, these things were happening to them from time to time by way of examples, and they were written for our admonition to whom the ends of the ages have come. So that he who thinks he stands, let him be taking heed lest he fall. A testing time or a temptation has not laid hold of you with the result that these have you in their grip, except those to which mankind is continually subject. But God is faithful who will not permit you to be tested nor tempted above that with which you are able to cope, but will, along with the testing time or temptation, also make a way out in order that you may be able to bear up under it.

Wherefore, my beloved ones, be fleeing from the idolatry. I am speaking as to men of good sense. As for you, you be judges of what I am saying.   **14, 15**

The cup of the blessing [which our Lord consecrated by giving thanks] which we consecrate with prayer, is it not a symbol of our joint-participation in the blood of the Christ? The bread which we break, is it not a symbol of our joint-participation in the body of Christ? Seeing that there is one loaf of bread, we, the many, are one body, for we all share with one another in eating from the one aforementioned loaf of bread. Be looking at Israel, the nation. Are not those who are eating the sacrifices joint-participants in the altar? Therefore, what am I asserting? That that which is sacrificed to idols is anything? Or that an idol is anything? What I am saying is that the things they sacrifice, to demons and not to a god they sacrifice. And I do not desire you to become joint-participants in offering sacrifices to demons. You are not able to be drinking the Lord's cup and the demons' cup. You are not able to be partaking together at the Lord's table and the demons' table. Or, are we provoking the Lord to anger? We are not stronger than He, are we?   **16-22**

All things are permissible but not all things are profitable or expedient. All things are permissible, but not all things promote growth in Christian character. Let no person be seeking his own good but that of the other person. Everything which is being sold in the meat market be eating, asking not even one question [whether the meat offered for sale is the residue of heathen sacrifices], doing this for the sake of your conscience, for the earth belongs to the Lord, and its fulness. On the assumption that anyone of those who are unbelievers invites you to be his guest, and you desire to be going, everything which is set before you be eating, asking not even one question for the sake of your conscience. But if anyone says to you, This has been offered in sacrifice to idols, stop eating of it in consideration for that one who   **23-30**

pointed it out to you and for the sake of his conscience.
I mean by conscience, not his own but that of the other
person, for to what [good] purpose is my liberty being
censured by another's conscience? As for myself, assuming that I partake with thankfulness, why am I being
evil spoken of unjustly because of that for which I am
giving thanks?

31-XI 1   Whether, therefore, you are eating or drinking or
whatever you are doing, be doing all to the glory of God.
Be becoming those who do not cause others to sin by your
mode of life, giving no occasion of stumbling both to
Jews and Gentiles and also the Church of God, even as
I also in all things accommodate myself to all, not seeking my own profit but the profit of the many, in order
that they might be saved. Become imitators of me, even
as I also am an imitator of Christ.

2-10   Now, I am praising you because [as you say] you
have kept me in your remembrance in all things and at
present still do have me in your thinking, even as also
you are holding fast to those things which were delivered to me to be handed down to you, which I also delivered to you to be passed on to succeeding generations.
Moreover, I desire you to know that the head of every
man is the Christ, and the woman's head is the man, and
the head of the Christ is God the Father. Every man
while praying or prophesying [giving out the word of
God in the public assembly, which word he received by
divine revelation] having a shawl hanging down over his
head [a Jewish and Roman custom] dishonors his head.
But every woman while praying or prophesying with
her head uncovered dishonors her head, for this would
be one and the same thing as if she had her head shaved.
For, assuming that a woman is uncovered, let her also
cut her hair close. But since it is dishonorable for a
woman to be shaven or have her hair cropped close, let
her put a shawl down over her head. For, indeed, a male
individual is morally obligated not to cover his head in
that manner since he is so constituted as to be the derived image and glory of God. But the woman is the
glory of a man. For a man is not out of a woman as a
source, but a woman out of a man. Assuredly, a man

was not created for the sake of the woman, but a woman for the sake of the man. On this account the woman is under moral obligation to be having a sign of [the man's] authority [over her] on her head because of the angels.

Nevertheless, neither is a woman [complete] apart **11-16** from a man, nor a man [complete] apart from a woman in the Lord, for even as the woman came out of the man as a source, thus also does the man owe his existence to the intermediate agency of the woman. But all things are out of God as a source. Come to a decision among yourselves. Is it seemly or fitting for a woman to be engaged in prayer to God not wearing the shawl hanging down over her head? Does not the innate sense of propriety itself based upon the objective difference in the constitution of things [the difference between the male and the female] teach you that if indeed a man allows his hair to grow long, it is a disgrace to him, but if a woman allows her hair to grow long, it is her glory? because her head of hair has been given to her for a permanent covering [answering in character to but not a substitute for the shawl]. If, as is the case, anyone presumes to be cantankerous [about the moral obligation of a woman to wear a head covering when engaged in public prayer in the assembly], as for us, we do not have such a custom [namely, that of a woman praying with uncovered head], neither do the assemblies of God.

Moreover, when giving you this charge, I am not **17-22** praising you, because you are not coming together [in the local assembly] for the better but for the worse. For indeed, first of all, when you come together in the assembly, I am hearing that divisions have their regular place among you, and I partly believe it, for it is a necessity in the nature of the case also for factions to be among you, in order that also those who have been put to the test and have met the specifications and have been approved might become identified as such among you. Therefore, when you come together to the same place, it is not possible to eat a supper the character of which is that it could be a supper designated as belonging to the Lord. For each one in the eating [of the supper] takes his own private supper beforehand. And one indeed is hungry and another is intoxicated. Do you not have houses for the eating and the drinking? Or, the Church of God are you despising, and are you making those ashamed who do not have the means [by which to buy food]? What shall I say to you? Shall I praise you? In this I am not praising you.

23-34   For, as for myself, I received by direct revelation from the presence of the Lord that which also I in turn passed on to you, that the Lord Jesus on the night during which He was being betrayed took bread, and having given thanks, He broke it and said, This is my body which is [given] on your behalf. This be doing with a view to remembering me. In like manner also He took the cup after the partaking of the food, saying, This cup is the covenant new in its nature, a covenant which is within the sphere of my blood. This be doing as often as you are drinking it, with a view to remembering me. For as often as you are eating this bread and drinking this cup, the death of the Lord you are proclaiming until that time whenever He may come. So that, whoever is eating the bread or drinking the cup of the Lord in an unworthy manner shall be guilty of the body and the blood of the Lord. But let an individual be putting himself to the test for the purpose of approving himself and finding that he meets the prescribed specifications, let him thus be eating of the bread and drinking of the cup. For the one who eats and drinks is eating and drinking so as to bring judgment upon himself if he does not properly evaluate the body. Because of this, among you are many who have infirmities and are in continued ill health, and a considerable number are sleeping [dead]. Now, if we properly evaluated and formed a right estimate of ourselves, in that case we would not be judged. But when we are being judged by the Lord, we are the subjects of a disciplinary judgment in order that we may not be condemned with the world. So that, my brethren, when you are coming together for the purpose of eating, be waiting for one another. In the event that anyone is hungry, let him be eating at home in order that you do not come together with the result that you will be judged.

And the other matters which remain I will dispose of whenever I come.

Now, concerning the spiritual gifts, brethren, I do not desire you to be ignorant. You all know that when you were Gentiles you were led astray to the idols, which do not have the faculty of speech, as on different occasions you would be led. Wherefore, I make known to you that no individual speaking by means of God's Spirit says, Jesus is anathema [accursed], and no person is able to say, Jesus is Lord, except by means of the Holy Spirit. Now, there are different distributions of spiritual gifts, these gifts being diverse from one another, but there is the same Spirit. And there are different distributions of various kinds of ministries, but the same Lord. And there are different distributions of divine energy motivating these gifts in their operation, but the same God who by His divine energy operates them all in their sphere. But to each one there is constantly being given the clearly seen operations of the Spirit with a view to the profit [of all].

1-7

For to one is given through the intermediate agency of the Spirit a word of wisdom, and to another a word of knowledge according to the same Spirit, to another faith by the same Spirit, and to another gifts of healing by the one Spirit, and to another the working of miracles, and to another the giving forth of divine revelations, and to another the correct evaluation of those individuals who give forth divine revelations, and to another various kinds of languages, and to another the interpretation of languages. But all these the one and same Spirit is by divine energy putting into operation, dividing to each one separately even as He desires.

8-11

For even as the body is one and has many members, and all the members of the body being many, are one body, thus also is the Christ, for indeed by means of one Spirit we all were placed into one body, whether Jews or Gentiles, whether slaves or free men. And we all were imbued with one Spirit. For, indeed, the body is not one but many members. If the foot should say, Because I am not a hand, I am not of the body; it is not there-

12-17

fore not of the body? And if the ear should say, Because I am not an eye, I am not of the body; it is not therefore not of the body? If the whole body were an eye, where would the hearing be? If the whole body were the hearing, where would the sense of smell be?

18-27   But now God placed the members, each one of them, in the body even as He desired. But if all were one member, where would the body be? But now, indeed, they are many members, but one body. And the eye is not able to say to the hand, I do not have need of you, or again, the head to say to the feet, I do not have need of you. No, much rather, the members of the body which seem to be more feeble, are necessary. And the members of the body which seem to be less honorable, upon these we bestow more abundant honor. And our uncomely members have more abundant comeliness. And our comely members have no need. But God compounded the body together, having given more abundant honor to the part which lacked, in order that there may not be division, but that the members should have the same solicitous concern about the welfare of one another. And whether one member suffers, all the members suffer with it, or one member is honored, all the members rejoice with it. And as for you, you are Christ's body and members individually.

28-31   And God indeed placed some for His own use in the Church, first apostles; second, prophets; third, teachers; then workers of miracles; then gifts of healing; also those whose ministry it is to help others; and administrators; and different languages. Not all are apostles, are they? Not all are prophets, are they? Not all are teachers, are they? Not all are workers of miracles, are they? Not all have gifts of healing, do they? Not all speak in languages, do they? Not all interpret, do they? But be constantly zealous after the greater spiritual gifts. And yet I point out a superexcellent way.

1-3   If in the languages of men I speak and the languages of the angels but do not have love [Greek word here used of God's love produced in the heart of the yielded saint by the Holy Spirit, a love that impels one to deny himself for the sake of the loved one], I have already become and at present am sounding brass or a clanging cymbal. And if I have the gift of uttering divine revelations and know all the mysteries and all the knowledge, and if I have all the faith so that I am able to keep on removing mountain after mountain, but am not possessing love, I am nothing. And if I use all my possessions to feed the poor, and if I deliver up my body [as a martyr] in order that I may glory, but do not have love, I am being profited in not even one thing.

Love meekly and patiently bears ill treatment from **4-8** others. Love is kind, gentle, benign, pervading and penetrating the whole nature, mellowing all which would have been harsh and austere; is not envious. Love does not brag, nor does it show itself off, is not ostentatious, does not have an inflated ego, does not act unbecomingly, does not seek after the things which are its own, is not irritated, provoked, exasperated, aroused to anger, does not take into account the evil [which it suffers], does not rejoice at the iniquity but rejoices with the truth, endures all things, believes all things, hopes all things, bears up under all things, not losing heart nor courage. Love never fails.

But whether there are utterances given by a person **8-13** consisting of divine revelations he has received, they shall cease; whether languages, they shall stop, whether knowledge, it shall be done away; for we know in a partial, fragmentary, incomplete way, and we utter divine revelations in the same way. But whenever that which is complete comes, that which is incomplete and fragmentary will be done away. When I was a child I was accustomed to speak as a child. I used to understand as a child. I was accustomed to reason as a child. When I have become a man and have the status of an adult, I have permanently put away the things of a child, for we are seeing now by means of a mirror obscurely, but then, face to face. Now I know only in a fragmentary fashion, but then I shall fully know even as also I was known. But now there remains faith, hope, love; these three. But the greatest of these is this previously mentioned love.

1-5   Be constantly pursuing this love, earnestly endeavoring to acquire it. Moreover, be earnestly desiring the spiritual gifts, and do this in order that you might more efficiently impart to others the divine revelations you have received. For the one who is uttering words in a tongue [a language not understood except through an interpreter] is not speaking to men but to God, for no one hears him so as to understand what he is saying. And he utters with his human spirit [as energized by the Holy Spirit] divine revelations not explained. But he who imparts divine revelations to men is speaking with the result of upbuilding the Christian life, and exhortation, and consolation. The one who utters words in a tongue builds himself up in his Christian life. But he who imparts divine revelations to others builds up the local assembly. Now I desire that all of you be speaking in tongues, but I prefer that you impart divine revelations to others which you have received. Moreover, greater is the one who imparts divine revelations to others than he who speaks in tongues, with this exception — that he interpret, in order that the local assembly might receive upbuilding.

6-11   But now, brethren, if I come to you speaking in tongues, what will it profit you unless I speak to you either in the form of a disclosure of the truth or in that of experiential knowledge or in that of an impartation of a divine revelation, or in that of teaching? Yet even in the case of lifeless things which give out a sound, whether it be a wind instrument or a harp, if it does not make a difference in the sounds, how will the music which is played by the wind instrument or the harp be understood? For if a military trumpet gives an indistinct sound, who shall put himself in readiness for war? Thus also in your case, if by means of the tongue you do not give a word which is clear and definite, how will that which is being spoken be understood? For you will [otherwise] be speaking into the air. So many kinds of voices [languages], it may be, exist in the world, and not one is without its particular significance. Therefore, if I do not know the meaning of the voice, I shall be to the one who is speaking a person who utters confused and unintelligible sounds, mere jargon, and the one who is speaking will be to me just such a person too.

Thus also, as for yourselves, since you are those who **12-17** are most eagerly desirous of spirits [spiritual powers], be desiring them in order that you may abound in them with a view to the building up of the local assembly. Therefore, let the one who speaks in a tongue be praying that he may be unfolding the meaning of what he is saying, for if I am praying in a tongue, my spirit [the human spirit as moved by the Holy Spirit] is praying, but my intellect confers no benefits upon others. How, therefore, does the matter stand? I will pray by means of my spirit. But I will pray also with the aid of my intellect. I will sing by means of my spirit. But I also will sing with the aid of my intellect. Else if you are uttering eulogies and praises [to God] by means of your spirit, how is it possible for the one who occupies the position of the unlearned to say the Amen to your act of giving thanks since he does not know what you are saying? For you indeed give thanks in an admirable way, but the other one is not built up in his Christian life.

I thank my God that I speak in tongues more than **18-22** you all, but in the church assembly I would rather speak five words with my understanding in order that I might instruct others than ten thousand words in a tongue. Brethren, stop becoming little children who need instruction in reasoning, but be infants in the sphere of malice, and in the sphere of the reasoning process be becoming those who are mature. In the law it stands written, By means of tongues of a different nature and by means of the lips of a foreigner I will speak to this people, and not even thus will they listen to me, says the Lord. So that the aforementioned tongues are for an attesting miracle, not to those who believe but to unbelievers. But the impartation of divine revelations on the part of those who receive them is not for the unbelievers but for those who believe.

If, therefore, the entire local assembly comes together **23-25** in one place, and all are speaking in tongues, and there enter the unlearned or the unbelievers, will they not say that you are raving mad? But if all impart divine revelations to others, and someone comes in who is an unbeliever or an unlearned person, he is brought under conviction [as to his sins] by all. He is put on trial and is the subject of an examination and a scrutiny by all. The secrets of his heart become evident, and thus, having fallen upon his face, he will worship God, proclaiming that God is among you indeed.

26-33   How, therefore, does the matter stand, brethren? Whenever you come together, each one has a song or psalm, has something he wishes to teach, has a divine revelation, has a tongue, has an interpretation. Let all things be done with a view to building up [the assembly]. Whether anyone speaks in a tongue, let it be two, or at the most three [at any single meeting], and one after another, in turn, and let one person be interpreting. But if there is no interpreter present, let him be maintaining his silence in the assembly and let him be speaking to himself and to God. Let those who impart to others the divine revelations they received, speak, two or three of them, and let the others evaluate their discourse. And if anything is revealed to another who is seated, let the first one be keeping silence, for you all can function thus as a prophet one by one in order that all may be learning and all may be encouraged. And the [human] spirits of those giving out a divine revelation are subject to the control of these prophets, for God is not a God of disorder but of harmony.

33-40   As in all the local assemblies of the saints, let the women be keeping silent, for they are not permitted to be speaking, but let them be putting themselves in the place of subjection and obedience, even as also the law says. Now, assuming that they are desirous of learning something, let them be asking their own husbands at home, for it is a disgrace for a woman to be speaking in the local assembly. Or is it from you that the word of God went forth? Or to you only did it reach? Assuming that anyone thinks that he is a prophet or spiritual, let him recognize that the things which I am writing to you are the Lord's commandment. But assuming that he is ignorant [of the fact that Paul is inspired], he is being disregarded. So that, my brethren, be desiring earnestly to be imparting to others divine revelations, and stop forbidding the speaking in tongues. But let all things be done in a seemly manner and in a right order.

Now, I am making known to you, brethren, the good **1-11** news which I brought as glad tidings to you, which also you took to yourselves, in which also you have taken a stand, through which you are being saved, in what word I announced it to you as glad tidings, assuming that you are holding it fast unless you believed in vain; for I delivered to you among the first things that which also I received, that Christ died on behalf of our sins according to the scriptures, and that He was entombed, and that He has been raised on the third day according to the scriptures, and that He appeared to Cephas, then to the Twelve. After that He appeared to more than five hundred brethren at one time, of whom the majority are remaining to the present time, but certain ones fell asleep. After that He appeared to James, then to all the apostles, and in the last of all His appearances, He appeared also to me, an unperfected, stillborn embryo. For, as for myself, I am the least of the apostles. I am not fit to be called an apostle because I persecuted the Church of God. But by the grace of God I am what I am. And His grace to me did not turn out in vain, but I labored to the point of exhaustion more abundantly than all of them; however, not I myself, but the grace of God which labored with me. Therefore, whether it were I or they, thus are we preaching and thus did you believe.

Now, in view of the fact that Christ is being preached **12-19** that He arose from among the dead, how are certain saying that there is not a resurrection of dead people? Now, assuming that there is no resurrection of dead people, neither has Christ been raised. And assuming that Christ has not been raised, then it follows that our preaching is futile, and futile also is your faith. Moreover, we shall also be discovered to be false witnesses of God because we testified with respect to God that He raised up His Christ, whom He did not raise up, assuming then that dead people are not being raised up. For assuming that dead people are not being raised up, neither has Christ been raised up. And assuming that Christ has not been raised, your faith is futile. You are still in your sins. Then also those who fell asleep in Christ perished. Assuming that in this life we have hoped only, we are of all men those who are most miserable and most to be pitied.

20-28   But now Christ has been raised out from among the dead, a firstfruit of those who have fallen asleep. For since through the agency of man death came, also through the agency of man comes a resurrection of the dead. For even as in Adam all die, so also in the Christ all shall be made alive, but each one in his proper rank, Christ, a firstfruit, afterwards those who belong to the Christ in His coming. Then comes the end, whenever He yields up the kingdom to God, even the Father, whenever He shall abolish all rule and authority and power. For it is a necessity in the nature of the case for Him to be ruling as King until that time when He will put all His enemies under His feet. As a last enemy, death is being abolished, for all things He put in subjection under His feet. But when He says that all things He has put in subjection, it is clear that He is excluded who put all things in subjection to Himself. But whenever all things are put under subjection to Him, then also the Son himself shall be in subjection to Him who subjected all things under Him in order that God the Father may be all in all.

29-34   Otherwise, what shall those do who are being baptized for the sake of those who are dead? Assuming that the dead are not actually raised up, why then are we being baptized for their sake? And as for us, why are we constantly in danger every hour? I am daily in danger of death by my glorying about you, brethren, which I have in Christ Jesus our Lord. If, as is the case, in the manner of men I fought with wild beasts at Ephesus, what profit comes to me? Assuming that dead people are not raised, let us eat and let us drink, for tomorrow we die. Stop being led astray. Evil companionships corrupt good morals. Return to soberness of mind in a righteous fashion and stop sinning, for certain ones possess an ignorance of God. I say this to your shame.

But a certain one will say, How are the dead raised **35-38**
up, and with what kind of a body do they come? Stupid
one, as for you, that which you sow is not made alive
unless it dies. And that which you sow, not the body
which shall come into being do you sow, but mere seed,
it may be of wheat or any of the rest of the seeds. But
God gives to it a body in accordance with that procedure
which He originally purposed, and to each of the seeds
its own peculiar body.

All flesh is not the same flesh, but there is indeed one **39-41**
flesh of men, and another of beasts, yet another of birds,
still another of fish. There are bodies for heavenly beings and bodies for those who dwell on the earth. But
indeed, the glory of the heavenly bodies is one thing, and
the glory of the earthly bodies is of a different kind.
There is one kind of glory of the sun, and another glory
of the moon, and another glory of the stars, for star
differs from star in glory.

Thus also is the resurrection of those who are dead. **42-50**
It [the body] is sown in corruption. It is raised in incorruption. It is sown in dishonor. It is raised in glory.
It is sown in weakness. It is raised in power. It is sown
a body which is a fit instrument by which the individual
can live a life in which the interests and activities of the
soul-life predominate. It is raised a body which is a fit
instrument by which the individual can live a life in
which the interests and activities of the human spirit
predominate. Since there is a soulical body, there is also
a spiritual body. And thus it stands written, The first
man Adam came into existence a living soul. The last
Adam became a life-giving spirit. But not first is the
spiritual, but the soulical, afterward the spiritual. The
first man is out of the earth as a source, made of earth.
The second Man is out of heaven as a source. As is the
dust of the earth in character, such are those who are of
earthly origin, and as is that which is heavenly in character, such also are those who are of heavenly origin.
And even as we bore the derived image of that which is
earthly, we shall also bear the derived image of that which
is heavenly. Now, this I am saying, brethren, that flesh

and blood are not able to inherit God's kingdom, neither will corruption inherit incorruption.

51-58   Behold, I am imparting to you a mystery. Not all shall sleep, but all shall be changed. In an instant of time so small that it cannot be divided into smaller units, in the blink of an eye, at the last trumpet, for a trumpet will sound, and the dead shall be raised incorruptible, and as for us, we shall be changed, for it is a necessity in the nature of the case for that which is corruptible to invest itself with incorruption, and that which is mortal to clothe itself with immortality. Now, whenever that which is corruptible shall invest itself with incorruption, and that which is mortal shall clothe itself with immortality, then will be brought to pass the word which stands written, Death has been swallowed up with the result that victory has been attained. Where, O death, is your victory? Where, O death, is your sting? The sting of death is sin, and the power of sin is the law. But thanks be to God who gives to us the victory through our Lord Jesus Christ. So that, my brethren beloved, keep on becoming steadfast, unmovable, always abounding in the work of the Lord, knowing that your fatiguing labor is not unproductive of results, as this labor is done in the Lord.

1-4   Now, concerning the collection of money which is for the saints, even as I gave orders to the local assemblies of Galatia, thus also as for you, you do the same. On every first day of the week let each one of you have the habit of putting aside at home whatever he may be prospered in, accumulating and keeping it in reserve, in order that when I may come, then there may not be any collections. And whenever I come, whomever you will approve after having put him to the test, these I will send to carry your bounty to Jerusalem. And if it [the gift] be sufficiently large so as to warrant me also going, they shall go with me.

5-9   Now, I shall come to you whenever I pass through Macedonia, for I am passing through Macedonia. And it may be that with you I will remain or even spend the winter, in order that as for you, you may furnish me with the requirements of travel wherever I may be going, for I do not desire to see you now while passing by on my journey, for I hope to remain with you a certain length of time, if the Lord permits me. However, I remain at Ephesus until Pentecost, for a door is opened to me, great and effectual, and there are many who are entrenched against me.

Now, if Timothy comes, be seeing to it that he is with you without fear, for he carries on the Lord's work as also I do. Therefore, let no one treat him as of no account, setting him at naught, but send him on his way in peace, seeing to it that he has the requisites for travel in order that he may come to me, for I am awaiting him with the brethren. Now, concerning Apollos our brother, I begged him much to come to you with the brethren, but it was not at all his desire to come at present, but he will come whenever he deems the opportunity auspicious. **10-12**

Be keeping a watchful eye ever open. Be standing fast in the Faith. Be showing yourselves to be men. Be mighty in strength. All that you are doing, let it be done in love. Now, I exhort you, brethren, you know the household of Stephanas, that it is a firstfruit of Achaia, and that they took upon themselves the responsibility of a ministering service to the saints, that you yourselves also put yourselves under the leadership of such as these and everyone who works with us and labors to the point of exhaustion. Now I rejoice at the coming of Stephanas and Fortunatus and Achaicus, because that which was lacking on your part, these filled up, for they refreshed my spirit and yours. Recognize, therefore, such as these for what they are. **13-18**

The local assemblies of Asia send greeting. Aquila and Priscilla send cordial greetings in the Lord together with the assembly that meets in their home. All the brethren send greetings to you all. Greet one another with a holy kiss. The greeting with my own hand — Paul. If anyone is not fond of the Lord, let him be anathema [a man accursed, devoted to the direst woes]. Maranatha [Our Lord comes]. The grace of the Lord Jesus be with you. My love be with you all in Christ Jesus. **19-24**

Paul, an ambassador belonging to Christ Jesus through the desire of God, and Timothy our brother, to the local assembly of God, the one which is in Corinth, together with the saints, all of them, who are in the whole of Achaia. Grace be to you and peace from God our Father and from the Lord Jesus Christ.

1, 2

Eulogized be the God and Father of our Lord Jesus Christ, the Father of compassionate mercies and a God of every consolation and encouragement, who consoles and encourages us in our every affliction and tribulation in order that we may be able to console and encourage those who are in any affliction or tribulation by means of the consolation and encouragement with which we ourselves are being consoled and encouraged by God. Because even as the sufferings of Christ [for righteousness' sake endured in the opposition of sinners to His ministry on earth] overflow to us, thus our consolation and encouragement [given to others] overflow through Christ. And if we are being hard pressed by reason of affliction, it is for the sake of your consolation, encouragement, deliverance, and preservation. If we are being consoled and encouraged, it is for the sake of your consolation and encouragement, which consolation and encouragement are operative in the patient enduring of the same sufferings which we also are suffering. And our hope for you is unshaken and constant, knowing that as you are joint-participants of the sufferings, thus also you shall be of the consolation and encouragement.

3-7

For we do not desire you to be ignorant, brethren, concerning our affliction which came to us in Asia, that we were weighed down beyond our power so that we despaired even of living. But we ourselves have had the answer of death in ourselves and at this time still have that experience, in order that we should not be trusting in ourselves but in the God who raises the dead; who delivered us out of so great a death and will deliver us, on whom we have placed our hope and right now still maintain that attitude of hope that also He will yet deliver us, you also helping together on our behalf by your supplication, in order that thanksgiving may be given

8-11

for the gracious mercy shown to us by reason of the many [who prayed for us].

12-14   For our glorying is this, the testimony of our conscience, that in the holiness, purity, and unsullied character of God, not in human wisdom but by God's grace we ordered our behavior in the world, and this was more abundantly evident to you. For, no other things are we writing to you but those things which you are reading or even acknowledge to be what they really are, and which I hope you will acknowledge to the end, as also certain ones of you acknowledged us for what we really are, that we are even as that in which you glory, and you are that in which we glory in the day of our Lord Jesus.

15-20   And having become fully persuaded of this I, after mature consideration, desired to come to you first, in order that you may be having a second bestowment of grace [by reason of my second visit to you], and to go through you [your city] into Macedonia, and again from Macedonia to come to you and be sent on my way to Judaea with the travel requisites for the journey. Therefore, having this desire, under these circumstances I did not exhibit fickleness of mind, did I? Or, the things which I purpose, do I purpose them in a merely human capacity, that there should be with me the yes, yes [today] and the no, no [tomorrow]? But as God is faithful, our word to you is not a yes and a no, for the Son of God, Christ Jesus, who among you was proclaimed by us, through me and Silvanus and Timothy, did not become yes and no, but in Him yes has become yes and remains so. For as many promises as are promises of God have become in Him yes and are a yes at present. Wherefore also through Him is the Amen to the glory of God through us.

21-24   Now, He who is constantly confirming us more firmly in our position in and union with Christ [in conforming us to His likeness] and who anointed us is God, who also placed His seal upon us and gave us the token payment guaranteeing the payment in full of our salvation, which token payment is the Spirit in our hearts. Moreover, as for myself, I call God as a witness against my soul [if I am speaking falsely] that to spare you, I did not come as yet to Corinth, not that we have lordship over your faith, but that we are co-workers in producing your joy; for by faith you stand.

But I decided this in my own interest and for my own sake, not to come again to you in grief. For, as for myself, if, as is the case, I cause you grief, who then is he who makes me joyful except the one who was made to grieve by me? And I wrote this very thing, lest, when I came, I should have grief from those whom it was a necessity in the nature of the case to be making to rejoice, having confidence in you all that my joy is the joy of all of you, for out of a source of much affliction and anguish of heart I wrote to you through many tears, not in order that you may be made to grieve, but in order that you may come to know experientially the sacrificial love which I have so abundantly for you. Now, if, as is the case, anyone has caused grief, he has not grieved me, but to some extent he has caused grief to you all, in order that I may not be exerting too much pressure upon you all. Sufficient to such a one is this punishment which was inflicted by the majority, so that on the contrary you should rather graciously grant forgiveness and encourage and strengthen him lest, possibly, such a person may be swallowed up with his excessive grief. Wherefore, I beg of you, please, that you confirm publicly and solemnly by a judicial decision your love for him.

1-8

For with this end in view I wrote in order that I may come to know by experience your approved character, this approval based upon the fact that you met the specifications laid down, whether you are those who are obedient in all things. Now, to whom you forgive anything, I also forgive, for also that which I myself have forgiven, if I have forgiven anything, for your sakes I have forgiven it in the presence of Christ, in order that no advantage may be gained over us by Satan, for we are not ignorant of his purposes. Now, having come to Troas for the purpose of preaching the good news of the Christ, and a door having been opened for me by the Lord, I have had no relaxation in my spirit because I did not find

9-17

Titus, my brother, but having bidden them farewell, I went off to Macedonia. Now, thanks be to God who always leads us in triumph in the Christ and makes known the aroma of the experiential knowledge of himself through us in every place, because a fragrance of Christ we are to God among those who are being saved and among those who are perishing, to the one, an odor proceeding from death resulting in death, and to the other, an aroma proceeding from life resulting in life. And who is sufficient for these things? For we are not as the many who are adulterating the word of God, but as of an unadulterated, unsullied purity of character, but as from God we are speaking in the sight of God in Christ.

1-3   Are we beginning again to be commending ourselves? Or, we do not need, as some, commendatory letters to you or commendatory letters from you, do we? As for you, you are our letter which has been permanently engraved in our hearts, and which is being known and read by all men. You are those who are openly shown to be a letter which exhibits Christ, this letter having been ministered [written] by us, not having been written with ink but by the Spirit of the living God, not on stone tablets but on tablets that are human hearts.

4-9   And such confidence are we having through the Christ towards God. Not that we are sufficient in ourselves to evaluate anything, this evaluation originating from ourselves, but our sufficiency has its source in God who also made us sufficient as those who minister a testament, new in quality, not of the letter [of the law] but of the Spirit, for the letter [of the law] kills, but the Spirit makes alive. Now, since the ministration of death which has been engraved by means of letters on stones was surrounded with glory so that the sons of Israel were not able to fix their gaze upon the face of Moses because of the glory of his face, which glory was of a transient nature, how shall not rather the ministration of the Spirit be surrounded with glory? For in view of the fact that the ministration of condemnation was glorious, by so much more will the ministration of righteousness superabound in the sphere of the glorious.

For even that which has been made glorious [the **10-18** ministration of death] has not [really] been made glorious in this respect, namely, on account of the glory [of the ministration of righteousness], which glory superabounds. For, since that which is passing away was with glory, by so much more that which remains is within the sphere of glory. Having therefore such a hope, we use great freedom and boldness of speech, and not even as Moses put a covering over his face to the end that the sons of Israel should not fix their gaze upon the termination of that which is passing away. But their minds were hardened, for to this very day the same covering remains at the reading of the testament whose usefulness is over, it not being revealed that it [the covering] is being done away in Christ. But even today, whenever Moses is being read, a covering lies upon their heart. However, whenever it [Israel] shall turn to the Lord, the covering is being taken away [by the one who turns to the Lord]. But the Lord is the Spirit and where the Spirit of the Lord is there is liberty. Now, as for us, we all, with uncovered face, reflecting as in a mirror the glory of the Lord, are having our outward expressions changed into the same image from one degree of glory to another according as this change of expression proceeds from the Lord, the Spirit, this outward expression coming from and being truly representative of our Lord.

Because of this, having this ministry [of the new **1-6** testament] even as we were made the objects of mercy [in its bestowal], we do not lose courage, but we have renounced the hidden things of shame, not ordering the manner of our lives in the sphere of craftiness, nor even adulterating the word of God [by an admixture of error], but by means of an open declaration of the truth commending ourselves to every variety of the conscience of men in the sight of God. But if also, as is the case, our gospel has been covered, in the case of those who are perishing it has been covered, in whom the god of this age blinded the minds of the unbelievers to the end that the light of the good news of the glory of the Christ who is the derived image of God should not dawn upon them, for we do not proclaim ourselves but Christ Jesus as Lord; but we proclaim ourselves as your slaves for the sake of Jesus, because the God who said, Out of darkness light shall shine, shined in our hearts, resulting in an illumination being given of the knowledge of the glory of God in the face of Christ.

7-15   But we have this treasure [the reflection of the light of the knowledge of the glory of God in the face of Christ] in earthenware containers, in order that the super-excellence of the power might be from God as a source and not from us. We are being hard pressed from every side, but we are not hemmed in. We are bewildered, not knowing which way to turn, but not utterly destitute of possible measures or resources. We are being persecuted, but not left in the lurch, not abandoned, not let down. We are being knocked down, but not destroyed, always bearing about in our body the dying of the Lord Jesus in order that the life of Jesus might be clearly and openly shown in our body, for, as for us, we who are living are perpetually being delivered over to death for Jesus' sake in order that the life of Jesus might be clearly and openly shown in our mortal body. So that death is opera-tive in us but the life is operative in you. But we have the same Spirit of faith [as the Psalmist] according as it has been written and is at present on record, I believed, wherefore I spoke. And as for us, we are believing, wherefore also we are speaking, knowing that He who raised up the Lord Jesus shall also raise us with Jesus and shall present us with you, for all things are for your sake in order that the grace having been multiplied through the intermediate agency of the many [in their prayers for me] may cause the thanksgiving to super-abound, resulting in the glory of God.

16-18   Wherefore, we are not losing courage. But and if, as is the case, our outward self is progressively decaying, yet our inward self is being changed into a new kind of life [fit for the new spiritual existence into which we have been ushered in salvation, and constantly being conformed to the image of the Lord Jesus] day by day. For our momentary light burden of affliction is working out for us more and more surpassingly an eternal, heavy weight of glory while we are not contemplating the things that are seen but the things which are not seen, for the things which are seen are temporary, but the things which are not seen are eternal.

For we know that if our house of this present tent-life on earth be taken down, a building from God we have, a house not made with hands, eternal in the heavens. For indeed, in this [tent] we are groaning, longing to be clothed in addition with our house which is from heaven, seeing that also, having been clothed, we shall not be found naked [a disembodied spirit]. For indeed, we being in this tent, are groaning, being weighed down, because we do not desire to be unclothed [divested of our mortal body] but clothed upon [invested with our heavenly body], in order that that which is mortal may be swallowed up by the life.

1-4

Now, He who by His working in us made us fit for this very thing [the change from mortality to life] is God, He who gave us the Spirit as a token payment in kind, guaranteeing to us the rest of our salvation. Being therefore always confident, and knowing that while we are in our natural home [for this earthly existence] in our body, we are living abroad, absent from [that home in heaven] the Lord, for through faith we are ordering our manner of life, not by something seen. Now, we are of good courage and well pleased rather to be away from our body as our home, and at home face to face with the Lord. Wherefore, we make it our aim, whether at home or living abroad, to be well pleasing to Him, for it is necessary in the nature of the case for all of us to be openly shown as to our true character before the judgment seat of Christ, in order that each one may receive [a recompense with respect to] the things which were practiced through the agency of our body, whether they were good or bad.

5-10

Knowing therefore the fear of the Lord, we are persuading men [of our sincerity and integrity], but to God we have been openly shown [as to our character], and I am hoping that we have been openly shown to be what we are in your consciences. We are not again commending ourselves to you, but [are writing these things] as

11-17

giving you a base of operations from which to glory about us, in order that you may be having this matter of glorying with which to answer those who are glorying in outward appearance and not in the heart [the inner man]. For, whether we were out of our mind, it was with respect to God; whether we are of sober mind, it is with respect to you. For the love which Christ has [for me] presses on me from all sides, holding me to one end and prohibiting me from considering any other, wrapping itself around me in tenderness, giving me an impelling motive, having brought me to this conclusion, namely, that One died on behalf of all, therefore all died, and that He also died on behalf of all in order that those who are living no longer are living for themselves but for the One who died on their behalf and instead of them, and was raised. So that, as for us, from this particular time onward, not even one individual do we know as judged upon the basis of human standards. Even though we [Paul in his unsaved state] have known Christ as judged by human standards, yet now no longer do we know Him as such. So that, assuming that anyone is in Christ, he is a creation new in quality. The antiquated, out-of-date things [which do not belong to the new life in Christ Jesus] have passed away. Behold, all things have become new in quality.

18-21　　　But the aforementioned all things are from God as a source, the One who reconciled us to himself through the intermediate agency of Christ and gave to us the ministry whose work is that of proclaiming the message of this reconciliation, namely, that absolute deity in Christ was reconciling the world [of sinners] to himself, not putting down on the liability side of their ledger their trespasses, and lodged in us the story of the reconciliation. Therefore, on behalf of Christ and in His place we are acting as ambassadors, as though God were saying, I beg of you, please, through us as His intermediate agents. We beg you in Christ's stead, Be reconciled at once to God. He who did not know sin in an experiential way, on behalf of us and instead of us, was made [the representative of] sin, in order that, as for us, we might become a righteousness of God in Him.

Moreover also, we, working together with God, beg of you not to receive the grace of God without any salutary results, for He says, In an epochal, strategic season, propitious in character, I hearkened to you, and in a day of salvation I ran to your cry and brought you aid. Behold, now is a propitious, epochal season, behold, now is a day of salvation. We are giving no occasion of stumbling to anyone in order that our ministering service may not be found with blot or blemish and thus be censored but in all things recommending ourselves as God's ministering servants should do: in much patience under trials, bearing up and not losing heart or courage; in afflictions, in calamity and straits, in distressing situations, in stripes inflicted by a beating with rods, in imprisonments, in the midst of political instability, in labors to the point of exhaustion, in sleeplessness at night, in hunger, in pureness, in knowledge, in long-suffering patience under ill treatment, in kindness marked by gentleness and graciousness, in the Holy Spirit, in a love devoid of hypocrisy, in the word of truth, in God's power, by means of the weapons of the righteousness [offensive weapons] on the right hand and [defensive weapons] on the left, by glory and dishonor, by slanderous report and good report, as those who are disseminating deceit and yet true, as being a nonentity, obscure, without proper credentials and yet fully recognized, as dying and behold we are living, as chastened yet not put to death, as sorrowful yet always rejoicing, as poor yet making many wealthy, as having not even one thing, yet possessing all things.

Our mouth stands open to you [we speak freely to you, we keep nothing back]. O Corinthians, our heart is broadened and enlarged [widened in its sympathy towards you]. You are not compressed nor narrowed down in us [you have ample space in our heart; we hold you within a great love], but you are compressed and narrowed down in your affections [you have tightened up in your affection for me]. Now, as a return in kind for my affections toward you, as to children I am speaking to you, you also be enlarged [make a large place in your heart for me].

14-VII 1   Stop being joined as with a yoke to unbelievers in a common state or endeavor which latter are of a character different from and diametrically opposed to the state of a child of God and any endeavor in which he may properly engage, for what partnership does righteousness have with lawlessness? Or, what does light have in common with darkness? And what harmony does Christ have with Belial? Or, what part does a believer have with an unbeliever? And what agreement does the inner sanctuary of God have with idols? For, as for us, we are an inner sanctuary of the living God, even as God said, I will dwell in them in fellowship with them as in a home and I will live my life in and through them. And I will be their God and they themselves will be my people. Wherefore, come out at once from their midst and separate yourselves at once, says the Lord, and stop touching that which is unclean. And, as for myself, I will receive you kindly and treat you with favor. And I will be to you a Father. And as for you, you will be to me sons and daughters, says the Lord Almighty. Having therefore these promises, beloved ones, let us cleanse ourselves from all contamination which may defile the flesh [the human body] and the [human] spirit, progressively accomplishing holiness in the fear of the Lord.

2-16   Make room in your hearts for us. We wronged no man. We corrupted no man. We took advantage of no man for the sake of gain. I am not saying this in the spirit of condemnation, for I have said before that you are in our hearts, to die together and to live together. Great is my boldness of speech toward you. Great is my glorying on your behalf. I have been completely filled with the encouragement. I am being caused to superabound with joy in all our tribulation, for even after we came into Macedonia our frail humanity experienced no relaxing from the oppression and tension of tribulation, but I was having pressure brought to bear upon me from every side, on the outside, contentions [with adversaries], within, fears. Nevertheless, He who encourages those who are downcast, encouraged us, our God, in the coming and personal presence of Titus, and not only in his coming and personal presence but also by the encouragement with which he was encouraged over you, bringing back tidings to us of your longing [to see me], your mourning [at the rebuke I sent you], your zeal on my behalf, so that I rejoiced yet more; for though I caused you grief by my letter, I do not regret it, though I did regret it, for I see that that letter caused you to grieve, though but for a season; I now am rejoicing, not because you were made to grieve but because you were made to grieve resulting in your repentance, for you were made to grieve in accordance with the will of God, in order that in not even one thing would you sustain injury or damage by reason of us, for the grief which is according to the will of God achieves a repentance which leads to salvation, a repentance which has no regret. But the grief which is exercised by the world in its outworking results in death. For, look. This very same thing, this being made to grieve in accordance with God's will, to what extent it produced earnestness in you, yes, verbal defense of yourselves, in fact, indignation, yes, fear, in fact, longing, yes, zeal, in fact, the meting out of disciplinary punishment. In everything you showed yourselves to be immaculate in the aforementioned matter. [They had cleared themselves from the guilt of connivance with the case of incest by disciplining the guilty brother.] Therefore also I wrote to you, not on account of the one who committed the wrong [the incestuous son] nor even on account of the one who was wronged [his father], but that your earnestness which was on our behalf might be openly shown among you in the sight of God. On this account we have been encouraged and comforted. And in addition to this encouragement and comfort of ours we rejoiced the more exceedingly at the joy of Titus because his spirit has been refreshed by all of you, for if, as is the case, I have boasted to him about you, I was not caused any disappointment, but as all things in the sphere of truth we spoke to you, thus also our boasting before Titus turned out to be truth. And his heart is more abundantly toward you while he recalls to himself the obedience of you all, as with fear and trembling you received him. I rejoice that in everything I am of good courage concerning you.

Moreover, we make known to you, brethren, the grace of God which has been given among the churches   **1-7** of Macedonia, that in the midst of a severe testing which was in the form of afflictions, the test being for the purpose of approving them in their reaction to trials, the superabundance of their joy and their poverty which went down to the depths, superabounded with the result of the plenitude of their liberality; because in the measure of their ability, I testify, and beyond their ability, voluntarily, with much exhortation they begged us as a favor that they might participate in the ministry to the saints, and not even as we expected but they gave themselves first to the Lord and to us by the will of God with the result that we exhorted Titus that, even as he made a beginning on a previous occasion, thus also he would complete in you this grace also. Moreover, even as in everything you superabound, in the realm of faith and a ready exposition [of the Word] and in knowledge, and in every earnestness, and in the divine and self-sacrificial love which, proceeding from you, has us as its object, in this grace [of giving] also be superabounding.

8-12   I am not speaking by way of commandment, but through the instrumentality of others I am putting to the test the genuineness of your own love with the intent that it will meet my specifications and have my approval put upon it. For you know by experience the grace of our Lord Jesus Christ, that He being wealthy, for your sakes became poor, in order that, as for you, by means of His poverty you might be made wealthy. And in this I am giving my judgment, for this is profitable for you, being such that you were the first to make a beginning, not only to so do, but also to be desirous of doing a year ago. And now complete the doing also, in order that, according as there was the eagerness to be desirous, thus also there may be the completion in accordance with your ability; for, assuming that the eagerness is present, it is acceptable according to that which a person might have, not according to that which he does not have.

13-15   For the collection [of money] is not being made in order that to others there might be relief from stress and strain and that pressure might be brought to bear upon you. But, out of fairness to all, at the present season your superfluity may be a supply for that which they lack, in order that their superfluity may become a supply for your lack, so that there might be an equitable arrangement in this matter, even as it stands written, He who gathered much had nothing over, and he who gathered the little, did not lack.

But thanks be to God who is constantly putting into **16-24** the heart of Titus the same earnest solicitude for you, because he indeed embraced our exhortation, and being more than ordinarily earnest, of his own accord went to you. And we sent together with him the brother whose praise in the [proclamation of the] good news is spread throughout all the assemblies, and not that only, but who also was chosen by the assemblies as our travel companion in the matter of this grace [their financial contributions for the poor saints at Jerusalem] which is being administered by us [this arrangement whereby two are responsible for the distribution of the money] with a view to the glory of the same Lord and our eagerness, arranging this for ourselves lest anyone find fault with us in this great liberality which is being ministered by us. For we take forethought to provide things, in their external appearance as well as in their intrinsic value, honest not only in the sight of the Lord but also in the sight of men. And we sent with them our brother whom we often proved to be earnest in many things, having put him to the test for that purpose, namely, to put our stamp of approval upon him, but now much more earnest by reason of his great confidence which he has in you. Whether you are asking concerning Titus, he is my colleague and fellow-worker with respect to you; whether concerning our brethren, they are missionaries of the assemblies, the glory of Christ. Wherefore, be demonstrating to them in the presence of the assemblies the evidence of your divine and self-sacrificial love and of our boasting concerning you.

For indeed, concerning the ministering to the saints, **1-4** it is superfluous for me to be writing to you, for I know positively of your earnestness concerning which I boast of you to the Macedonians, that Achaia has been prepared since a year ago; and your zeal stimulated the majority of them. But I am sending the brethren in order that our boasting which is concerning you may not be rendered futile in this respect [in the collecting of the money] so that, just as I was saying, you may be prepared lest by any means, if there come with me any of Macedonia and they find you unprepared, we — we do not say you — should be put to shame in this confidence.

5-9   Therefore I deemed it necessary to exhort the brethren that they should go before to you and make ready your liberal gift which was previously promised, that this might be ready beforehand, thus as a matter of generosity and not as a gift which a covetous spirit would withhold but gives grudgingly under pressure. But [although I am not pressing you to give] this [is true] — he who sows sparingly shall also reap sparingly, and he who sows in a beneficent, generous spirit, with a view to the blessing of the recipient, shall also reap blessings given in a beneficent, generous manner. Let each one give according as he has purposed in his heart, not out of an annoyed and troubled heart, nor because of necessity, for God loves a cheerful, ready giver. Moreover, God is powerful to make every grace superabound to you in order that, having always an all-sufficiency in all things, you may superabound to every good work, even as it stands written, He [the liberal person] scattered abroad, he gave to those who are poor, his righteousness abides forever.

10-15   Now, He, who supplies seed to the sower and bread for food, shall also supply and multiply your seed [your means of giving] and increase the fruits of your righteousness, you being enriched in everything resulting in all liberality which is of such a nature as to achieve through us thanksgiving to God, because the ministration of this sacred service is not only filling up the things which the saints are lacking, but also is superabounding in many thanksgivings to God, inasmuch as they [the saints in Judaea] through your approved character, which approval finds its basis in this ministration, are glorifying God for the obedience of your confession with respect to the good news regarding the Christ and the liberality of your contribution to them and to all, while they also, with petitions on your behalf, are longing after you because of the grace of God upon you which cannot be measured. Thanks be to God for His ineffable gift.

Now, I myself, Paul, beg of you, please, through the meekness and sweet reasonableness of the Christ, who indeed in personal appearance am [as some of you say by way of reproach] grovelling, slavish, mean-spirited [the pagan attitude towards the Christian grace of humility] among you, but being absent, am of good courage toward you, [however that may be], I beg of you, please, that when I am present, I may not be courageous with the confidence with which I am counting on myself to be bold toward certain who take account of us as ordering our behavior in accordance with mere human considerations. For, though we are ordering our behavior in the sphere of human experience, not in accordance with mere human considerations are we waging warfare [against evil], for the weapons of our warfare are not human but mighty in God's sight, resulting in the demolition of fortresses, demolishing reasonings and every haughty mental elevation which lifts itself up against the experiential knowledge [which we believers have] of God, and leading captive every thought into the obedience to the Christ, and being in readiness to discipline every careless, apathetic hearing of and disobedience to the Word [if there remain any still disobedient] when your obedience [to me and my apostolic authority] shall be fulfilled. You are in the habit of looking at external appearance. If, as is the case, anyone has fully persuaded himself that he is Christ's [belongs to a special party of which he has placed Christ at the head], let him be considering this again with himself, that just as he himself belongs to Christ, so also do we. For, even if I should boast somewhat more abundantly concerning our authority which the Lord gave me for your building up and not for your casting down, I shall not be put to shame, in order that I may not seem as if I would make you afraid by my letters, because his letters, indeed, they say, are weighty and powerful, but his bodily presence is weak and his discourse of no account. Let such a one [who makes comments such as the above] take into account this fact that the kind of person we are in our discourse through our letters when we are absent, such are we also in action when we are present. For we are not daring to judge ourselves worthy to be among nor compare ourselves with certain ones of those who are commending themselves. But they themselves, measuring and comparing themselves with themselves, are without understanding.

13-18   But, as for us, we will not boast without a proper standard of measurement but in accordance with the measure of the measuring rule which God apportioned to us as a measuring unit, one that reaches even up to you [Paul's divinely appointed field of service]. For we did not extend ourselves beyond the prescribed limit as though we did not reach as far as to you, for we came as far as to you in announcing the good news about the Christ, not boasting without a proper standard of measurement, namely, not in other men's labors, but having hope that as your faith grows, we may be increased [in our apostolic efficiency] among you in accordance with our measuring rule [apportioned to us in our apostolic labors], resulting in a superabundance [of fruit in service], with a view to proclaiming the good news in the regions beyond you, not boasting ourselves in another's field of activity with reference to the things made ready [in advance by others, namely, the Christian assemblies already founded by others]. But he who boasts, let him be boasting in the Lord, for not he who recommends himself, that one is accepted after having been put to the test, but he whom the Lord recommends, that one has His stamp of approval placed upon him, that approval being based upon the fact that the approved one has met the test satisfactorily.

1-6   Would that you would be patiently tolerant of me in a little foolishness [ironically of his enforced self-vindication and boasting]. But you are really patiently tolerant of me. For I am jealous over you with a godly jealousy, for I gave you in marriage to one husband that I might present you as a pure virgin to the Christ. But I fear, lest by any means, as the snake deceived Eve in his craftiness, your minds should be corrupted from your simplicity [single-hearted loyalty] and purity [uprightness of life] which you express towards Christ. For, indeed, if, as is the case, he who comes proclaims another person as Jesus than the one whom we proclaimed, or you receive a spirit different in nature from the one you received, or a message of good news different in character from that message you received, you are most beautifully tolerant of him. For I account myself as not being in even one thing inferior to these superfine apostles. But even if, as is the case, I am not a professional orator in the realm of discourse, yet I am not unlearned nor unskilled in the realm of knowledge, but in everything we made it [our knowledge of God's word] plain among all with a view to your benefit.

7-9   Or, did I commit a sin in humbling myself [in supporting myself making tents] in order that you might be exalted [in spiritual privileges] because I preached the good news of God to you without charge? I robbed other assemblies, having taken wages from them, accepting from them more than their share of my support in order to minister to you. And when I was present with you and was in want, I was not a burden to anyone, for that which I lacked, the brethren, having come from Macedonia, supplied. And in all things I kept myself from being a burden to you and will continue to keep myself thus.

10-15   As the truth concerning Christ is in me, this boasting [in my independence of financial support] shall not be stopped so far as it pertains to me in the regions of Achaia. Wherefore? Because I do not love you? God knows. Moreover, that which I do [refusing to accept financial help from you] I will also continue to do, in order that I may cut off the particular occasion [the opportunity for attacking me should I accept help] from those who desire an occasion, that in the matter of their boast [namely, that since they had apostolic rank they possessed the right to be financially supported] they may be found even as also we are. For such men as these are false apostles, crafty workers, changing their outward expression to one which does not come from within and is not representative of their inner character but is assumed from without, masquerading as Christ's apostles. And no marvel, for Satan himself changes his outward expression from one that comes from his inner nature and is representative of it, to one that is assumed from without and not representative of his inner being, masquerading as a messenger of light. Therefore it is no great thing if also, as is the case, his servants change their outward expression from one that comes from their inner nature and is representative of their inner character, to one that is assumed from without and not representative of their inner being, masquerading as servants of righteousness, whose end shall be according to their works.

16-20   I say again, let no man think me to be foolish. But even if you do, as is the case, yet receive me as foolish in order that I also [as well as they] may boast a little. That which I am saying, not after the pattern of the Lord am I speaking, but as in foolishness, in this confidence of boasting. Seeing that many are boasting in accordance with human standards and in human attainments, I also will boast, for you gladly tolerate those who are foolish, being wise yourselves. For you tolerate a man, if, as is the case, he brings you to the point of abject slavery; if a man strips you of your possessions [by greedily demanding maintenance]; if a man takes you captive; if a man exalts himself; if a man slaps you in the face.

21-28   I am speaking by way of disparagement [humbly of myself], as though, as for ourselves, we have been weak. And yet, whereinsoever a man is bold, I am speaking in foolishness, as for myself, I am bold also. Hebrews are they? I also. Israelites are they? I also. Offspring of Abraham are they? I also. Servants of Christ are they? I am speaking as one who is beside himself, I more [in a higher degree than they], in labors to the point of exhaustion more abundantly than they, in prisons more abundantly than they, in stripes inflicted by being whipped, beyond measure, in danger of death, often. From the Jews five times I received forty stripes less one. Three times I was beaten with rods. Once I was stoned. Three times I was shipwrecked. I have spent a night and a day in the sea. In journeyings often, in perils of rivers, in perils of robbers, in perils from those of my own race, in perils from the Gentiles, in perils in the city, in perils in an uninhabited region, in perils in the sea, in perils among false brethren, in labor and travail, in sleepless nights often, in hunger and thirst, in need of food often, in cold and in lack of sufficient clothing; apart from the things I just enumerated is this, the pressure, day after day, namely, my anxiety for all the assemblies.

Who is weak, and I am not weak? Who is being **29-33** made to stumble, and I am not indignant? Since it is a necessity in the nature of the case for me to boast, I will boast of the things that concern my weakness. The God and Father of our Lord Jesus knows, He who is the Eulogized One forever, that I am not lying. In Damascus the ethnarch under Aretas the king kept a constant guard over the city of the Damascenes in an effort to apprehend me, and through a window I was let down in a rope basket through [a window in] the wall and escaped out of his hands.

It is a necessity in the nature of the case for me to be **1-5** boasting, though it is not expedient [my opponents force me to do so], but I will come to visions and revelations of the Lord. I know a man in Christ, fourteen years ago, whether in the body I do not know positively, or out of the body I do not know positively — God knows — this man being of such a character that he was caught up to the third heaven. And I know such a man, whether in the body or apart from the body, I do not know — God knows — that he was caught up into Paradise and heard unspeakable words which it is not lawful for a man to utter. Concerning such a man as this I will boast, but concerning myself I will not boast except in my weaknesses.

For, if I should desire to boast, I shall not be fool- **6-10** ish, for I shall speak the truth. But I am abstaining [from boasting] lest any man consider me above that which he sees me to be or above that which he hears from me. And with respect to the superabundance of the revelations, in order that I may not be exalted overmuch, there was given to me a thorn in the flesh, a messenger of Satan, to the end that he might constantly maltreat me lest I be exalted overmuch. Concerning this three times I begged the Lord that he might depart from me. And He has said to me, and His declaration still stands, My grace is enough for you, for power is moment by moment coming to its full energy and complete operation in the sphere of weakness. Therefore, most gladly will I the rather boast in my weaknesses in order that the power of the Christ [like the Shekinah Glory in the Holy of Holies of the Tent of Meeting] may take up its residence in me [working within me and giving me help]. Wherefore I am well content in weaknesses, in insults, in necessities, in persecutions, and in circumstances under which I am subject to extreme pressure on behalf of Christ, for when I am weak, then I am filled with ability and power.

11, 12   I have become foolish and am so now [boasting thus]. As for you, you drove me to it. For as for myself, I ought to have been by you commended, which obligation on your part you have not fulfilled. [Had you done so, you would have saved me from boasting], for in not even one particular was I behind the superfine apostles, although I am nothing. Indeed, the miracles of the apostle, the purpose of which is to furnish credentials of that office, were fully performed among you in all patience, both by means of attesting miracles and miracles of a startling, imposing, amazement-wakening character, and miracles that demonstrate God's power.

13-18   For what is there in which you were treated in an inferior manner to the rest of the assemblies except that, as for myself, I myself did not burden you? Forgive me this wrong. Look! This is a third time I am ready to come to you, and I will not be a burden to you, for I am not seeking your possessions but you. For the children are under no moral obligation to be accumulating material resources for the parents, but the parents for the children. But as for myself, I will most gladly spend and be wholly spent for the sake of your souls. Assuming for the moment that I love you more abundantly [than I love other assemblies I have founded], am I being

loved less [than I am being loved by other assemblies]?
[Is that the way you are requiting my love?] But let
it be so. [Let the former matter be dismissed.] As for
myself, I did not saddle you with a burden. Nevertheless, [you say that] being crafty, I caught you [for my
own enrichment from the collection for the poor saints]
by means of a tricky bait. Of those whom I have sent
to you, there was not one through whom I took advantage
of you, was there? I exhorted Titus, and with him I
sent the brother. Titus did not take advantage of you in
anything, did he? Did we not order our behavior by
means of the same Spirit, and in the same footsteps?

For a long time you are thinking that it is to you I am **19-21**
presenting my verbal defense. In the sight of God in
Christ are we speaking. But all the things, beloved ones,
[which we are speaking] are for your upbuilding. For
I fear lest by any means, having come, I will find you
such as I desire you not to be, and as for myself, I will
be found by you such as you do not desire me to be [in-
dignant to the point of severity at your backsliding], lest
by any means there should be strife, jealousy, outbursts
of boiling rage, factions, defamation of character, secret
slanders, inflated egos, disorders, lest, having come again,
my God should humiliate me before you, and I should
grieve for many of those who have sinned previously and
did not repent of their uncleanness, and fornication, and
unbridled passionate craving which they committed.

This is a third time I am coming to you. Upon the **1-4**
basis of the mouth of two witnesses or three shall every
word be established. I have said previously, and I do
say beforehand, as when I was present the second time,
so now being absent, to those who sinned heretofore and
to all the rest, that if I come again I will not spare you,
since you are seeking a proof that Christ speaks in me,
He who is not weak in relation to you [as you think me
to be], but is powerful in your midst, for though He was
crucified in [the] weakness [of His humanity], yet He
lives by means of God's power. And as for ourselves,
we are weak [in company] with Him [as partaking of
frail humanity], but we shall live with respect to you together with Him through God's power.

5, 6   Be putting yourselves to the test whether you are in the Faith. Be putting yourselves to the test for the purpose of approving yourselves, and finding that you meet the specifications, put your approval upon yourselves. Or, do you yourselves not recognize that Jesus Christ is in you, unless you are those who are disapproved? But I hope that you shall come to know that, as for us, we are not disapproved.

7-10   Now, we are praying to God that you do not even one bit of evil, not, as for us, in order that we may appear as approved, but in order that, as for you, you may be doing that which is honorable, but as for us, in order that we may be as those who are disapproved, for we are not able to do anything against the truth, but for the truth. For, as for us, we rejoice when we are weak, but as for you, when you are strong. And for this we also pray, for your spiritual equipment. On this account I am writing these things when I am absent, in order that I may not deal sharply [with you] in accordance with the authority which the Lord gave me for building up and not for casting down.

11-13   Finally, brethren, be rejoicing. See to it that you are being spiritually equipped and adjusted. Be encouraged. Be of the same mind. Be living at peace. And the God of love and peace shall be with you. Greet one another with a holy kiss. All the saints send greeting to you.

14   The grace of the Lord Jesus Christ and the love of God and the partnership of the Holy Spirit be with you all.

Paul, an apostle, not from men nor even through the intermediate agency of man, but through Jesus Christ and God the Father who raised Him from among the dead, and all the brethren with me, to the assemblies of Galatia. Grace to you and peace from God our Father and from the Lord Jesus Christ who gave himself in behalf of our sins so that He might rescue us out from this present pernicious age according to the will of our God and Father, to whom be the glory for ever and ever. Amen.

1-5

I am marvelling that in such a manner suddenly you are becoming of another mind and deserting from Him who called you in the sphere of Christ's grace to a message of good news diametrically opposed to the gospel, which message is not an alternative gospel. Only, there are certain ones who are troubling your minds and are desiring to pervert the gospel of Christ. In fact, even if we or a messenger from heaven should preach a gospel to you which goes beyond that which we preached to you as good news, let him be accursed. Even as we have said on a previous occasion, indeed, now again I am saying, If, as is the case, anyone preaches a gospel to you which goes beyond that which you took so eagerly and hospitably to your hearts, let him be accursed. For, am I at this present moment seeking to win the favor of men rather than the approval of God? Or, am I making it my business to be constantly pleasing men? If I still were pleasing men, in that case Christ's bondslave I would not be.

6-10

For I make known to you, brethren, the message which was announced as good news by me, that it is not as to its nature, human. For, as for myself, neither did I receive it directly from man, nor was I taught it, but I received it through a revelation given me by Jesus Christ.

11, 12

For you heard of my manner of life aforetime in Judaism, that beyond measure I kept on continually persecuting the Church of God and continually bringing destruction upon it, and I was constantly blazing a pioneer path, outstripping in Judaism many of my own

13, 14

age in my race, being more exceedingly zealous of my ancestral traditions.

15-17   But when it was the good pleasure of the One who set me apart before I was born and called me by His grace to give me an inward revelation of His Son in order that I might proclaim Him as glad tidings among the Gentiles, immediately I did not put myself in communication with flesh and blood for the purpose of consultation; neither did I go up to Jerusalem to those who were apostles before me, but I went away into Arabia, and again returned to Damascus.

18-24   Then, after three years, I went up to Jerusalem to become acquainted with Cephas, and remained with him fifteen days. But another of the apostles I did not see except James the brother of our Lord. But the things which I am writing to you, behold, in the sight of God, I am not lying. Then I went into the regions of Syria and Cilicia, but remained personally unknown to the assemblies of Judaea which are in Christ. Indeed, they only kept on hearing, The one who used to persecute us at one time now is announcing the glad tidings of the Faith which at one time he was ravaging. And they were continually glorifying God [for that which they found] in me.

1-10   Then, after the space of fourteen years, again I went up to Jerusalem, accompanied by Barnabas, having taken along also Titus. And I went up in accordance with a revelation. And I laid before them for their consideration the gospel which I am preaching among the Gentiles, but privately to those of recognized eminence, lest by any means I should be running or had run in vain. But not even Titus who was with me, although he was a Gentile, was compelled to be circumcised. Now it was because of the false brethren who had been surreptitiously brought in, those of such a character that they sneaked in for the purpose of spying out our liberty which we are having in Christ Jesus, with the expectation of reducing us to abject slavery; to whom not even for an hour did we yield with reference to the particular voluntary submission demanded, in order that the truth of the gospel might abide for you. But to be something at the hands of those who were of repute, whatever they were aforetime, is of no importance to me. God accepts not man's person. For those who were of repute imposed nothing on me. But on the contrary, when they saw that I had been entrusted with [the responsibility of preaching] the gospel to the uncircumcised as Peter with [the responsibility of preaching] the gospel to the circumcised — for He who worked effectively for Peter with respect to his apostolate to the circumcision also worked effectively for me with respect to the Gentiles — and having come to perceive the grace which was given to me, James, and Cephas, and John, those who in reputation were looked upon as pillars, gave to me and Barnabas the right hand of fellowship, to the end that we should preach the gospel to the Gentiles and they themselves to the circumcision; only, that we should keep on remembering the poor, which very thing I have made a diligent and eager effort to do.

But when Cephas came to Antioch, to his face I **11-21** opposed him, because he stood condemned. For before certain from James came, with the Gentiles it was his habit to eat meals. But when they came he began gradually to draw himself back, and began slowly to effect a final separation, fearing those of the circumcision. And the rest of the Jews also played the hypocrite jointly with him, so that even Barnabas was swept along with their hypocrisy. But when I saw that they were not pursuing a straight-forward course in relation to the truth of the gospel, I said to Cephas in the presence of everybody, If you, being a Jew, habitually are living after the manner of the Gentiles, and not after that of the Jews, how is it that you are compelling the Gentiles to live after the Jewish manner? As for us, we are Jews by nature, and not sinners of Gentile origin; and knowing that a man is not justified by law works but only through faith in Christ Jesus, we also placed our trust in Christ Jesus, in order that we might be justified by faith in Christ and not by law works, because by law works there shall no flesh be justified. But if, as is the case, while seeking to be justified in Christ, we [Jews] ourselves also were found to be sinners, is Christ therefore a promoter of sin? Away with the thought; for if the things I tear down, these again I build up, I exhibit myself as a transgressor; for, as for myself, I through the intermediate agency of the law died to the law, in order that I might live with respect to God. With Christ I have been crucified, and it is no longer I who live, but there lives in me Christ. And that life which now I live in the sphere of the flesh, by faith I live it, which faith is in the Son of God who loved me and gave himself on my behalf. I do not thwart the efficacy of the grace of God. For if through law comes righteousness, then Christ died to no purpose.

1-9   O, unreflecting Galatians, who bewitched you, before whose eyes Jesus Christ was placarded publicly as the crucified One? This only am I desiring to learn from you. By means of law works did you receive the Spirit or by means of the message which proclaims faith? Are you so unreflecting? Having begun by means of the Spirit, now are you being brought to spiritual maturity by the flesh? So many things did you suffer in vain? If indeed they really were in vain? Therefore, the One who is constantly supplying the Spirit to you in bountiful measure, and constantly working miracles among you, by means of law works is He doing these things, or by means of the message which proclaims faith?

Just as Abraham believed God, and his act of faith was credited to him, resulting in his righteousness. You perceive, therefore, that those who are of faith, these are sons of Abraham. And the scripture, foreseeing that on a basis of faith God justifies the Gentiles, announced the good news beforehand to Abraham, namely, All the Gentiles shall be blessed in you. So that those who are believing ones are being blessed in company with believing Abraham.

10-14   For as many as are of the works of the law are under curse, for it stands written, Cursed is every one who is not remaining constantly in all things which stand written in the book of the law in order to do them. But that in a sphere of law no one is being justified in the sight of God is clear, because, The righteous man shall live by means of faith. And the law is not of faith; but the one who has done them shall live in them. Christ delivered us by the payment of ransom from the curse of the law by becoming a curse in behalf of us, because it stands written, Accursed is everyone who is suspended upon a tree, in order that to the Gentiles the blessing of Abraham might come in Jesus Christ, to the end that the promise of the Spirit we [Jew and Gentile] might receive through faith.

Brethren, what I have to say is in accordance with **15-18** common human practice. Even though it be a man's covenant, when it has finally been ratified, no man annuls it nor adds stipulations to it. Now to Abraham were made the promises, and to his Descendant. He does not say, And to the descendants, as in respect to many descendants, but in respect to one Descendant, and to your Descendant, who is Christ. This now is what I mean. A covenant previously established by God, the law which came after four hundred and thirty years does not render void with the result that the promise becomes inoperative, for if the inheritance is from law [as a method of divine dealing], no longer is it from promise [as a method of divine dealing]. But to Abraham, through the intermediate instrumentality of promise, God has in grace freely bestowed it.

What is then the significance of the law? For the **19-23** sake of transgressions it was added until there should come the Descendant to whom the promise was made, having been promulgated by angels through the instrumentality of the hand of a mediator. Now, the mediator is not a go-between representing the interests of one individual, but God is one individual. Is therefore the law against the promises of God? God forbid. For if a law had been given which was able to impart life, righteousness in that case would have been from the law. But the scripture shut up all under sin in order that the promise on the ground of faith in Jesus Christ might be given to those who believe. But before the aforementioned faith came, under law we were constantly being guarded, being shut up with a view to the faith about to be revealed.

24-29 So that the law became our guardian until Christ, in order that on the grounds of faith we might be justified; but this faith having come, no longer are we under the guardian, for all of you are God's sons through faith in Christ Jesus, for as many as were introduced into union with Christ, put on Christ. There is neither Jew nor Greek, there is neither slave nor free, there is neither male nor female. For you are all one in Christ Jesus. And since you are Christ's, then are you Abraham's descendants, heirs according to the promise.

1-7 Now I say, that as long as the heir is in his minority, he does not differ one bit from a slave, even though he is owner of all, but is under guardians and stewards until the time previously fixed by his father. In like manner, we also, when we were in our minority, were in a permanent state of servitude under the rudimentary first principles of mankind. But when there came the fulness of the time, God sent off His Son, woman-born, made subject to law, in order that He might deliver those under law to the end that we might be placed as adult sons. And because you are sons, God sent forth the Spirit of His Son into your hearts crying, Abba [namely], my Father. So that no longer are you a slave but a son, and since you are a son, you are also an heir through God.

8-11 But at that time, in fact, not knowing God, you were in a slave's bondage to the gods which are not gods by nature. But now having come to know God, indeed, rather having become known by God, how is it possible that you are turning back again to the weak and beggarly rudimentary principles to which you are again bent on being in bondage? Days you are scrupulously and religiously observing, and months, and seasons, and years. I am afraid about you lest perhaps in vain I have labored to the point of exhaustion for you.

12-20 Become as I am, because I also became as you were, brethren; I am beseeching you. You had done me no wrong. But you know that because of an infirmity of the flesh I preached the gospel to you on the occasion of my first visit. And the test to which you were subjected and which was in my flesh, you did not loathe nor utterly despise, but as a messenger of God you received me, as Christ Jesus. Where is therefore your spiritually prosperous state? For I bear witness to you that if it had been possible, you would have dug out your own eyes and given them to me. So then I have become your enemy because I am telling you the truth? They are zealously paying you court, but not honestly, desiring to isolate you in order that you might be paying court to them. But it is good to be zealously courted in a good thing at all times, and not only when I am present with you, my born ones, concerning whom I am again striving with intense effort and anguish until Christ be outwardly expressed in you. Moreover, I was wishing that I were present with you at this very moment and could thus change my tone, because I am perplexed about you.

Be telling me, you that are bent upon being under **21-31** law, are you not hearing the law? For it stands written, Abraham had two sons, one from the maidservant and one from the freewoman. But, on the one hand, the son of the maidservant was one born in the ordinary course of nature. On the other hand, the son of the freewoman was one born through the promise, which class of things is allegorical. For these are two covenants, one from Mount Sinai, begetting bondage, which is as to its nature classed as Hagar. Now this Hagar is Mount Sinai in Arabia, and corresponds to the Jerusalem which now is, for she is in bondage with her children. But the Jerusalem which is above is free, which is our Mother. For it stands written, Rejoice, barren woman who does not bear. Break forth and cry, you who do not travail, because more are the children of the desolate than of the one who has a husband. And, as for you, brethren, after the manner of Isaac are you children of promise. But just as then, he who was born according to the flesh was constantly persecuting him who was born according to the Spirit, so also now. But what does the scripture say? Throw out the maidservant and her son. For the son of the maidservant shall by no means inherit with the son of the freewoman. Therefore, brethren, we are children, not of a maidservant, but of the freewoman.

1-12   For this aforementioned freedom Christ set you free. Keep on standing firm therefore and stop being subject again to a yoke of bondage. Behold, I, Paul, am saying to you that if you persist in being circumcised, Christ will be advantageous to you in not even one thing, and I solemnly affirm again to every man who receives circumcision, that he is under obligation to do the whole law. You are without effect from Christ, such of you as in the sphere of the law are seeking your justification. You have lost your hold upon [sanctifying] grace. For, as for us, through the agency of the Spirit, on the ground of faith, a hoped-for righteousness we are eagerly awaiting, for in Christ Jesus neither circumcision is of any power nor uncircumcision, but faith coming to effective expression through love. You were running well. Who cut in on you and thus hindered you from obeying the truth? This persuasion is not from the One who calls you. A little yeast is permeating the whole lump. As for myself, I have come to a settled persuasion in the Lord with respect to you, namely, that you will take no other view than this. But the one who troubles you shall bear his judgment, whoever he is. And I, brethren, if I am still preaching circumcision, why am I in spite of this fact still being persecuted? Then the stumbling block of the Cross has been done away. I would that they who are upsetting you would even have themselves mutilated.

13-15   For, as for you, upon the basis of freedom you were called, brethren. Only do not turn your liberty into a base of operations for the evil nature, but through love keep on constantly serving one another, for the whole law in one utterance stands fully obeyed, namely, in this, Love your neighbor as you do yourself. But if, as is the case, you are biting and devouring one another, take heed lest you be consumed by one another.

16-21   But I say, Through the instrumentality of the Spirit habitually order your manner of life, and you will in no wise execute the passionate desire of the evil nature, for the evil nature constantly has a strong desire to suppress the Spirit, and the Spirit constantly has a strong desire to suppress the evil nature. And these are entrenched in an attitude of mutual opposition to one another so that you may not do the things that you desire to do. But if you are being led by the Spirit you are not under law. Now the works of the evil nature are well known, works of such a nature as, for example, fornication, uncleanness, wantonness, idolatry, witchcraft, enmities, strife, jealousy, angers, self-seekings, divisions, factions, envyings, drunkenness, carousings, and the things of such a nature which are like these things, respecting which things I am telling you beforehand even as I told you in advance, that those who are in the habit of practicing things of that nature shall not inherit the kingdom of God.

22-26   But the fruit of the Spirit is love, joy, peace, long-suffering, kindness, goodness, faithfulness, meekness, self-control. Against such things as these there is no law. And they who belong to Christ Jesus crucified the evil nature with its dispositions and cravings once for all. In view of the fact that we are being sustained in spiritual life by the Spirit, by means of the Spirit let us go on ordering our conduct. Let us stop becoming vain-glorious, provoking one another, envying one another.

1-5   Brethren, if, however, a man be overtaken in a sin, as for you who are the spiritual ones, be restoring such a one in a spirit of meekness, taking heed to yourself lest you also be tempted. One another's burdens be constantly bearing, and thus you will fully satisfy the requirements of the law of the Christ. For if anyone thinks himself to be something when he is nothing, he is deceiving himself. But his own work let each one put to the test and thus approve, and then with respect to himself alone will he have a ground for glorying, and not with respect to the other one [with whom he had compared himself], for each shall bear his own private burden.

6-10   Moreover, let the one who is being taught the Word constantly be holding fellowship with the one who is teaching in all good things. Stop leading yourselves astray. God is not being outwitted and evaded. For whatever a man is in the habit of sowing, this also will he reap; because the one who sows with a view to his own evil nature, from his evil nature as a source shall reap corruption. But the one who sows with a view to the Spirit, from the Spirit as a source shall reap life eternal. Let us not slacken our exertions by reason of the weariness that comes with prolonged effort in habitually doing that which is good. For in a season which in its character is appropriate, we shall reap if we do not become enfeebled through exhaustion and faint. So then, in like manner, let us be having opportunity, let us be working that which is good to all, but especially to those of the household of the Faith.

11-18　　You see with what large letters I am writing to you with my own hand. As many as desire to make a good outward appearance in the sphere of the flesh, these are trying to compel you to receive circumcision, their only motive being that they might not be persecuted by reason of the cross of Christ, for not even those who are circumcised are themselves keeping the law, but they desire you to be circumcised in order that in your flesh they may glory. For, as for me, far be it from me to be glorying except in the cross of our Lord Jesus Christ, through whom to me the world stands crucified and I to the world. For neither circumcision is anything, nor uncircumcision, but a new creation. And as many as by this rule are ordering their conduct, peace be upon them, and mercy, even upon the Israel of God. Henceforth, let no man furnish me trouble, for I bear branded the marks of the Lord Jesus in my body. The grace of our Lord Jesus Christ be with your spirit, brethren. Amen.

Paul, an ambassador of Christ Jesus through the will of God, to the saints, the ones who are [in Ephesus], namely, believing ones in Christ Jesus. Grace to you and peace from God our Father and the Lord Jesus Christ. **1, 2**

May the God and Father of our Lord Jesus Christ be eulogized, the One who conferred benefactions upon us in the sphere of every spiritual blessing in the heavenly places in Christ, even as He selected us out for himself in Him before the foundations of the universe were laid, to be holy ones and without blemish before His searching, penetrating gaze; in love having previously marked us out to be placed as adult sons through the intermediate agency of Jesus Christ for himself according to that which seemed good in His heart's desire, resulting in praise of the glory of His grace which He freely bestowed upon us in the Beloved, in whom we are having our redemption through His blood, the putting away of our trespasses according to the wealth of His grace which He caused to superabound to us in the sphere of every wisdom and understanding, having made known to us the mystery of His will according to that which seemed good to Him, which good thing He purposed in himself, with respect to an administration of the completion of the epochs of time to bring back again to their original state all things in the Christ, the things in the heavens and the things on the earth, in Him, in whom also we were made an inheritance, having been previously marked out according to the purpose of the One who operates all things according to the counsel of His will, with a view to our being to the praise of His glory who had previously placed our hope in the Christ, in whom also, as for you, having heard the word of the truth, the good news of your salvation, in whom also having believed, you were sealed with the Spirit of the promise, the Holy Spirit, who is the token payment of our inheritance guaranteeing the full payment of all, looking forward to the redemption of the possession which is being preserved with a view to the praise of His glory. **3-14**

On account of this, I also, having heard of the faith in the Lord Jesus which is among you and of your love **15-23** to all the saints, do not cease giving thanks for you as I constantly make mention of you in my prayers, that the God of our Lord Jesus Christ, the Father of the glory, might give to you a spirit of wisdom and revelation in the sphere of a full knowledge of Him, the eyes of your heart being in an enlightened state with a view to your knowing what is the hope of His calling, what is the wealth of the glory of His inheritance in the saints, and what is the superabounding greatness of His inherent power to us who are believing ones as measured by the operative energy of the manifested strength of His might, which might was operative in the Christ when He raised Him from among the dead and seated Him at His right hand in the heavenly places, over and above every government and authority and power and lordship and every name that is constantly being named, not only in this age, but also in the one about to come. And all things He put in subjection under His feet, and Him He gave as Head over all things to the Church, which is of such a nature as to be His body, the fulness of the One who constantly is filling all things with all things.

1-10   And you being dead with reference to your trespasses and sins, He made alive; in the sphere of which trespasses and sins at one time you ordered your behavior as dominated by the spirit of the age in this world system, as dominated by the leader of the authority of the lower atmosphere, the source also of the spirit that is now operating in the sons of the disobedience among whom also we all ordered our behavior in the sphere of the cravings of our evil nature, continually practicing the desires of our evil nature and of our thoughts, and were continually children of wrath by nature, as also the rest. But God, being wealthy in the sphere of mercy, because of His great love with which He loved us, and we, being dead with respect to our trespasses, made us alive together with the Christ; by grace have you been saved completely in past time, with the present result that you are in a state of salvation which persists through present time, and raised us with Him and seated us with Him in the heavenly places in Christ Jesus, in order that He might exhibit for His own glory in the ages that will pile themselves one upon another in continuous succession, the surpassing wealth of His grace in kindness to us in Christ Jesus. For by the grace have you been saved in time past completely, through faith, with the result that your salvation persists through present time; and this [salvation] is not from you as a source; of God it is the gift, not from a source of works, in order that no one might boast; for we are His handiwork, created in Christ Jesus with a view to good works which God prepared beforehand in order that within their sphere we may order our behavior.

On this account be remembering that at one time, **11-18** you, the Gentiles in the flesh, the ones habitually called uncircumcision by that which is called circumcision in the flesh made by hand, that you were at that time without a Messiah, alienated from the commonwealth of the Israel and strangers from the covenants of the promise, not having hope and without God in the world. But now in Christ Jesus you, who at one time were far off, have become near by the blood of the Christ. For He himself is our peace, the One who made the both one, having broken down the middle wall of the partition, the enmity, in His flesh having rendered inoperative the law of the commandments in ordinances, in order that the two He might create in himself, resulting in one new man, making peace, and in order that He might reconcile the both in one body to God through the Cross, having put to death the enmity by it, and having come, He proclaimed glad tidings of peace to you who were far off, and to you who were near, because through Him we have our entree, the both of us, by one Spirit into the presence of the Father.

Now then, no longer are you aliens and foreign so- **19-22** journers, but you are fellow citizens of the saints and householders of God, having been built up upon the foundation of the apostles and prophets, there being a chief cornerstone, Jesus Christ himself, in whom the whole building closely joined together grows into a holy inner sanctuary in the Lord, in whom also you are being built together into a permanent dwelling place of God by the Spirit.

1-7   On this account I, Paul, the prisoner of the Messiah, Jesus, on behalf of you, the Gentiles, assuming that you heard of the administration of the grace of God which was given to me for you, that by revelation there was made known to me the mystery even as I wrote above in brief, in accordance with which you are able when you read to understand my insight into the mystery of the Christ which in other and different generations was not made known to the sons of men as now it has been revealed to His holy apostles and prophets by the Spirit, that the Gentiles are fellow heirs, and belong jointly to the same body, and are fellow partakers of His promise in Christ Jesus, revealed through the good news of which I became one who ministers according to the gift of the grace of God, which grace was given to me according to the operative energy of His power.

8-12   To me, the one who is less than the least of all saints, there was given this grace, to the Gentiles to proclaim the good news of the incomprehensible wealth belonging to the Christ, and to bring to light what is the administration of the mystery which has been kept covered up from the beginning of the ages in the God who created all things, in order that there might be made known now to the principalities and powers in the heavenly places through the intermediate agency of the Church the much-variegated wisdom of God, according to the eternal purpose which He carried into effect in the Christ, Jesus our Lord, in whom we are having our freedom of speech and entree in perfect confidence through faith in Him.

13-19   Wherefore, I am asking in my own interest, that you do not lose heart by reason of my tribulations on your behalf which are of such a nature as to be your glory. On this account I bow my knees to the Father from whom every family in heaven and on earth is named, that He would grant to you according to the wealth of His glory, with power to be strengthened through the Spirit in the inward man, that the Christ might finally settle down and feel completely at home in your hearts through your faith; in love having been firmly rooted and grounded in order that you may be able to grasp with all the saints what is the breadth and width and height and depth, and to know experientially the love of the Christ which surpasses experiential knowledge in order that you may be filled up to the measure of all the fulness of God.

Now to the One who is able to do beyond all things, **20, 21** superabundantly beyond and over and above those things that we are asking for ourselves and considering, in the measure of the power which is operative in us, to Him be the glory in the Church and in Christ Jesus into all the generations of the age of the ages. Amen.

I beg of you, please, therefore, I, the prisoner in the **1-6** Lord, order your behavior in a manner worthy of the divine summons with which you were called, with every lowliness and meekness, with longsuffering, bearing with one another in love, doing your best to safeguard the unanimity of the Spirit in the bond of peace. There is one Body and one Spirit, even as also you were called in one hope of your calling, one Lord, one Faith, one placing into [the Body of Christ by the Holy Spirit], one God and Father of all, the One above all and through all and in all.

But to each one of us there was given the grace in the **7-16** measure of the gift of the Christ. Wherefore He says, Having ascended on high, He led away captive those taken captive and gave gifts to men. Now, the fact that He ascended, what is it except that also He descended into the nether parts of the earth? The One who descended himself is also the One who ascended above all the heavens, in order that He might fill all things. And He himself gave some, on the one hand, as apostles, and, on the other hand, as prophets, and still again some as bringers of good news, and finally, some as pastors who are also teachers, for the equipping of the saints for ministering work with a view to the building up of the Body of Christ, until we all attain to the unity of the Faith and of the experiential, full, and precise knowledge of the Son of God, to a spiritually mature man, to the measure of the stature of the fulness of the Christ, in order that we no longer may be immature ones, tossed to and fro and carried around in circles by every wind of teaching in the cunning adroitness of men, in craftiness which furthers the scheming deceitful art of error, but speaking the truth in love, may grow up into Him in all things, who is the Head, Christ, from whom all the Body constantly being joined closely together and constantly being knit together through every joint of supply according to the operative energy put forth to the capacity of each part, makes for increased growth of the Body resulting in the building up of itself in the sphere of love.

17-19   This, therefore, I am saying and solemnly declaring in the Lord, that no longer are you to be ordering your behavior as the Gentiles order their behavior in the futility of their mind, being those who have their understanding darkened, who have been alienated from the life of God through the ignorance which is in them, through the hardening of their hearts, who, being of such a nature as to have become callous, abandoned themselves to wantonness, resulting in a performing of every uncleanness in the sphere of greediness.

20-24   But as for you, not in this manner did you learn the Christ, since, indeed, as is the case, you heard and in Him were taught just as truth is in Jesus, that you have put off once for all with reference to your former manner of life the old self who is being corrupted according to the passionate desires of deceit; moreover, that you are being constantly renewed with reference to the spirit of your mind; and that you have put on once for all the new self who after God was created in righteousness and holiness of truth.

25-32   Wherefore, having put off the lie once for all, be speaking truth each with his neighbor, because we are members belonging to one another. Be constantly angry with a righteous indignation, and stop sinning. Do not allow the sun to go down upon your irritated, exasperated, embittered anger. And stop giving an occasion for acting [opportunity] to the devil. The one who is stealing, let him no longer be stealing, but rather let him be laboring, working with his own hands that which is good, in order that he may be having that wherewith to be sharing with the one who is having need. Every word that is rotten and unfit for use, out of your mouth let it not be proceeding, but whatever is good, suitable for edification with respect to the need, in order that it may impart grace to the hearers. And stop grieving the Spirit, the Holy Spirit of God, with whom you were sealed with a view to the day of redemption. All manner of harshness and violent outbreaks of wrath and anger and brawling and slanderous speech, let it be put away from you together with all manner of malice. And be becoming kind to one another, tenderhearted, forgiving each other even as and just as also God in Christ forgave you.

Be becoming therefore imitators of God, as children **1-6** beloved, and be ordering your behavior within the sphere of love, even as Christ also loved you and gave himself up in our behalf and in our stead as an offering and a sacrifice to God for an aroma of a sweet smell. But fornication and uncleanness, every kind of it, or covetousness, let it not be even named among you, just as it is befitting to saints, and obscenity and foolish talking or ribaldry, which things have not been seemly or fitting, but rather giving of thanks, for this you know absolutely and experientially, that every whoremonger or unclean person or covetous person, who is an idolator, does not have an inheritance in the kingdom of the Christ and of God. Let no one keep on deceiving you by means of empty words, for because of these things there comes the wrath of God upon the sons of the disobedience.

Stop therefore becoming joint-participants with them; **7-12** for you were at one time darkness, but now you are light in the Lord. As children of light be habitually conducting yourselves; for the fruit of this light is in the sphere of every beneficence and righteousness and truth, putting to the test and then approving what is well pleasing to the Lord. And stop having fellowship with the unfruitful works of this darkness, but rather be rebuking them so as to bring out confession and conviction, for concerning the things done in secret by them it is shameful to be speaking.

But all the aforementioned things, when they are re- **13-21** proved by the light, are made visibly plain, for everything that is being made plain is light. Wherefore He says, Be waking up, he who is sleeping, and arise from the dead, and there shall shine upon you the Christ. Be constantly taking heed therefore how accurately you are conducting yourselves, not as unwise ones but as wise ones, buying up for yourselves the opportune time, because the days are pernicious. On this account stop becoming those who are without reflection or intelligence, but be understanding what the will of the Lord is. And stop being intoxicated with wine, in which state of intoxication there is profligacy. But be constantly controlled by the Spirit, speaking to one another in psalms and hymns and spiritual songs, singing and making melody in your hearts to the Lord, giving thanks always concerning all things in the Name of our Lord Jesus Christ to God, even the Father, putting yourselves in subjection to one another in the fear of Christ.

22-33   The wives, be putting yourselves in subjection with implicit obedience to your own husbands as to the Lord, because a husband is head of the wife as the Christ is Head of the Church, He himself being the Saviour of the Body. Nevertheless, as the Church subjects itself in obedience to the Christ, in this manner also the wives should subject themselves in obedience to their husbands in all things. The husbands, be loving your wives with a love self-sacrificial in its nature, in the manner in which Christ also loved the Church and gave himself on behalf of it, in order that He might sanctify it, having cleansed it by the bath of water in the sphere of the Word, in order that He might himself present to himself the Church glorious, not having spot nor wrinkle nor any of such things, but in order that it might be holy and unblamable. In this manner ought also the husbands to love their wives as their own bodies. The one who loves his own wife loves himself, for no one ever yet hated his own flesh, but nourishes and cherishes it, even as the Christ, the Church, because members are we of His Body. Because of this a man shall leave behind his father and his mother and shall be joined to his wife, and the two shall become one flesh. This mystery is great. However, I am speaking with regard to Christ and the Church. Nevertheless, also as for you, let each one in this manner be loving his own wife as himself, and the wife, let her be continually treating her husband with deference and reverential obedience.

The children, be always obedient to your parents in the Lord, for this is a righteous thing. Be always honoring your father and your mother, which is a commandment of such a nature as to be the first commandment with a promise, in order that it may be well with you, and in order that you may live long upon the earth. And the fathers, stop provoking your children to anger, but be rearing them in the discipline and admonition of the Lord. The slaves, be constantly obedient to those who, according to the flesh, are your masters, with fear and trembling, in singleness of your heart as to the Christ, not in the way of eye service as men-pleasers, but as Christ's bondslaves, doing the will of God from the soul, with good will rendering a slave's service as to the Lord and not as to men, knowing that each one, whatever good he may do, this he will receive from the presence of the Lord, whether he is a slave or whether he is free. And the masters, be practicing the same things toward them, giving up your threatening, knowing that also their Master and yours is in heaven, and there is not partiality with Him.

1-9

Finally, be constantly strengthened in the Lord and in the active efficacy of the might that is inherent in Him. Clothe yourselves with the full armor of God to the end that you will be able to hold your ground against the strategems of the devil, because our wrestling is not against blood and flesh, but against the principalities, against the authorities, against the world rulers of this darkness, against spirit forces of perniciousness in the heavenly places. On this account, take to yourself, at once and once for all, the complete armor of God in order that you may be able to resist in the day, the pernicious day, and having achieved all things, to stand. Stand therefore, having girded your loins in the sphere of truth, and having clothed yourself with the breastplate of righteousness, and having sandalled your feet with a firm foundation of the good news of peace; in addition to all these, taking to yourselves the shield of faith by

10-20

means of which you will be able to quench all the fiery arrows of the pernicious one, and take the helmet of salvation, and the sword of the Spirit which is the word of God; through the instrumentality of every prayer and supplication for need, praying at every season by means of the Spirit, and maintaining a constant alertness in the same with every kind of unremitting care and supplication for all the saints, and on behalf of me, in order that there might be given me utterance in the opening of my mouth, in every fearless, confident freedom of speaking, to make known the mystery of the good news on behalf of which I am an ambassador in a chain, in order that in it I may speak with every fearless and confident freedom as it is necessary in the nature of the case for me to speak.

21-24   But in order that you also might come to know my circumstances, what I am doing, all things to you, Tychicus, the beloved brother and faithful ministering servant in the Lord, will make known, whom I am sending to you for this same purpose in order that you might come to know our circumstances and in order that he might encourage your hearts. Peace to the brethren and love with faith from God the Father and the Lord Jesus Christ. The grace be with all those who are loving our Lord Jesus Christ in sincerity.

Paul and Timothy, bondslaves by nature, the property of Christ Jesus, to all the consecrated and separated ones in Christ Jesus who are in Philippi, together with overseers and deacons. [Sanctifying] grace be to you and [tranquilizing] peace from God our Father and the Lord Jesus Christ.

I am constantly thanking my God for my whole remembrance of you, always in every prayer of mine making supplication for all of you with joy. I am thanking my God constantly for your joint-participation [with me] in the furtherance of the good news from the first day [when Lydia opened her home for the preaching of the Word] until this particular moment [as characterized by the gift which you have sent], having come to this settled and firm persuasion concerning this very thing, namely, that He who began in you a work which is good [their financial support of Paul] will bring it to a successful conclusion right up to the day of Christ Jesus.

Even as it is only just and right on my part to be constantly turning my mind in the direction of this very thing in behalf of all of you [namely, the completion of God's good work in you], because you are holding me in your heart both in my defense and in my confirmation of the good news, all of you being sharers with me in this grace, for my witness is God, how I long after all of you with the tenderheartednesses of Christ Jesus.

And this is the constant purport of my definite petitions, namely, that your love [divine and self-sacrificial in its nature as ministered to you by the Holy Spirit] yet more and more might overflow, but at the same time be kept within the guiding limitations of an accurate knowledge [of God's word] gained by experience, and those [guiding limitations] of every kind of sensitive moral and ethical tact, so that you may after putting them to the test [of God's word] recognize the true value of the finer distinctions involved in Christian conduct and thus sanction them, in order that you might be unadulterated [by evil] and thus pure and not a stumbling block in view of the day of Christ, having been filled full with the fruit of righteousness and continue in that condition of fullness, which fruit is through Jesus Christ, resulting in the glory and praise of God.

12, 13 Now, after mature consideration my desire is that you gain this knowledge from [my] experience, namely, that the things which are holding me down [those associated with my imprisonment] have come to result rather in the pioneer advance of the good news, so that it has become plainly recognized that my shackles are because of Christ, this recognition of their true meaning existing throughout the whole of the Praetorium Guard and among all the rest.

14-17 And the great majority of the brethren having come to a state of settled confidence in the Lord, having been influenced by the gentle persuasion of my shackles to take that step of confidence, are more abundantly bold, fearlessly breaking their silence and speaking the word of God. In fact, certain ones even because of envy and rivalry, but also certain others because of good will are proclaiming the Christ; some indeed out of a spirit of love, knowing that I am appointed for the defense of the good news, but others out of a partisan, self-seeking spirit are proclaiming Christ, not with pure, unadulterated motives, but insincerely, thinking to raise up additional afflictions to my already existing chains.

18 What is my feeling in view of these things? The only thing that follows is that in every manner, whether in pretense or in truth, whether insincerely or sincerely, Christ is being proclaimed. And in this I am rejoicing, and I will certainly continue to be rejoicing.

19-21 For I know positively that this [the fact that Christ is being proclaimed] shall result in deliverance and preservation for me [lest I become discouraged in and because of my imprisonment which restricts my opportunity to proclaim the good news] through your petition and through the full-proportioned support and aid of the Spirit of Jesus Christ. And this is exactly in accordance with my undivided and intense expectancy and hope, namely, that with respect to not even one thing shall I be put to shame [defeated], but in every boldness, courage, and fearlessness of uninhibited freedom of speech as always so also now, Christ shall be conspicuously and gloriously manifested in my body, whether through [a continued] life [on earth] or through [a martyr's] death, for, so far as I am concerned, to be living, both as to my very existence and my experience, [that is] Christ, and to have died, that would be a gain.

But if for me [continued] life in this physical existence   22-26
be my lot, this very thing [namely, continued life on earth] is that in which the fruit of my ministry will be involved and is the condition of that fruit being produced. Then what I shall prefer for myself I do not know. Rather, I am being held perpendicularly by an equal pull from the two [namely, my desire to remain on earth for further fruit-bearing and my desire to die and be with Christ], so that I am not able to incline towards either one, having the passionate desire towards striking my tent and being with Christ which is by far better, but still to remain in my physical body is more needful for your sakes. And having come to this settled conviction [namely, that to remain in my physical body is more needful for you] I know positively that I shall remain and continue with all of you for your pioneer advance [in the Christian life] and your joy in the Faith in order that your rejoicing may abound in Christ Jesus through me by reason of my personal presence with you again.

Only [since my only reason for remaining on earth   27
is for your pioneer advance in the Christian life], see to it that you recognize your responsibility as citizens [of heaven] and put yourselves to the absolute necessity of performing the duties devolving upon you in that position, doing this in a manner which weighs as much as the good news concerning the Christ, in order that, whether having come and having seen you, or whether being absent, I am hearing the things concerning you, namely, that you are standing firm in one spirit, holding your ground, with one soul contending as a team of athletes do, in perfect

co-operation with one another for the Faith [the Christian system of belief], namely, the good news.

28-30   And do not be terrified in even one thing by those who are entrenched in their opposition against you, which failure on your part to be frightened is an indication of such a nature as to present clear evidence to them of [their] utter destruction, also clear evidence of your salvation, and this [evidence] from God. And the reason why you should not be terrified is because to you that very thing was given graciously as a favor for the sake of Christ and in His behalf, not only to be believing on Him but also to be suffering for His sake and in His behalf, having the same struggle which you saw in me and now hear to be in me.

1-5   In view of the fact that there is a certain ground of appeal in Christ which exhorts, since there is a certain tender persuasion that comes from divine love, in view of the fact that there is a certain partnership on the part of the Spirit [in which the Spirit gives us aid in the living of our Christian life], since there are certain tenderheartednesses and compassions, fill full my joy by thinking the same thing, by having the same divine self-sacrificial love, being in heart-agreement, thinking the one thing, doing nothing impelled by a spirit of factiousness, nothing motivated by empty pride, but in lowliness of mind consider one another as excelling themselves, this estimation resting, not upon feelings nor sentiment but upon a due consideration of facts, not consulting each one his own interests only, but also each one the interests of others. This mind be constantly having in you.

6-8   [This is the mind] which is also in Christ Jesus, who has always been and at present continues to subsist in that mode of being in which He gives outward expression of His essential nature, that of absolute deity, which expression comes from and is truly representative of His inner being [that of absolute deity], and who did not after weighing the facts, consider it a treasure to be clutched and retained at all hazards, this being on an equality with deity [in the expression of the divine essence], but him-

self He emptied, himself He made void, having taken the
outward expression of a bondslave, which expression
comes from and is truly representative of His nature [as
deity], entering into a new state of existence, that of mankind. And being found to be in outward guise as man,
He stooped very low, having become obedient [to God
the Father] to the extent of death, even such a death as
that upon a cross.

Because of which voluntary act of supreme self-renun-　**9-11**
ciation God also supereminently exalted Him to the highest
rank and power, and graciously bestowed upon Him the
Name, the name which is above every name, in order
that in recognition of the Name [all which the Lord
Jesus is in His Person and work] which Jesus possesses,
every knee should bow, of things in heaven, of things on
earth, and of things under the earth, and in order that
every tongue should plainly and openly agree to the fact
that Jesus Christ is Lord, resulting in the glory of God
the Father.

Wherefore, my beloved ones, as you always obeyed,　**12, 13**
not as in my presence only, but now much more in my
absence, carry to its ultimate conclusion [likeness to the
Lord Jesus] your own salvation with a wholesome, serious
caution and trembling, for God is the One who is constantly putting forth His energy in you, both in the form
of your being desirous of and of your doing His good
pleasure.

All things be constantly doing without discontented and　**14-18**
secret mutterings and grumblings, and without discussions which carry an undertone of suspicion or doubt, to
the end that you may become those who are deserving of
no censure, free from fault or defect, and guileless in
their simplicity, God's children without blemish, in the
midst of a perverse and distorted generation among whom
you appear as luminaries in the world, holding forth the
word of life, to the end that I may have a ground for
glorying reserved for the day of Christ, this glorying
being because of the fact that I did not run in vain nor
did I labor to the point of exhaustion in vain. In fact, if

also I am being poured out as a libation upon the sacrifice and priestly service of your faith, I rejoice and continue to rejoice with you all. But as for you, you even be rejoicing in the same thing and continue to rejoice with me.

19-21   But I am hoping in the Lord Jesus quickly to send Timothy to you, in order that I also may be of good cheer, having come to know of your circumstances. For not even one do I have who is like-souled, one of such a character who would genuinely and with no secondary regard for himself be concerned about your circumstances. For one and all without exception are constantly seeking their own things, not the things of Christ Jesus.

22-24   But you know from experience his character which has been approved after having been tested, that as a child to a father, with me he served as a slave would do in the furtherance of the good news. This very one therefore I am hoping to send as soon as, having turned my attention from other things and having concentrated it upon my own circumstances, I shall have ascertained my position. But I have come to a settled conviction, which conviction is in the Lord, that I also myself shall come shortly.

25-27   But after weighing the facts, I considered it indispensable to send to you Epaphroditus, my brother and fellow worker and fellow soldier, but your ambassador, to whom you entrusted a mission, and who in a sacred way ministered to my need. For he was constantly yearning after all of you, and was in extreme anguish because you heard that he was ill. For truly he was ill, next door to death. But God had mercy upon him, and not upon him alone, but also on me, in order that I might not have sorrow upon sorrow.

28-30   With increased haste and diligence therefore I am sending him, in order that, having seen him again, you may recover your cheerfulness, and as for myself, my sorrow may be lessened. Receive him to yourselves, therefore, in the Lord with every joy, and hold such ones in honor. Value them highly, and deem them precious, because on account of the work of Christ he drew near to death, having recklessly exposed his life in order that he might supply that which was lacking in your sacred service to me.

As for the rest [of which I wish to say to you] my brethren, be constantly rejoicing in the Lord. To be writing the same things to you is not to me irksome or tedious, while for you it is safe. Keep a watchful eye ever upon the dogs. Keep a watchful eye ever upon the evil-workers. Keep a watchful eye ever upon those who are mutilated, doing this for the purpose of bewaring of and avoiding the same. For, as for us, we are the circumcision, those who by the Spirit of God are rendering sacred service and obedience, and who are exulting in Christ Jesus, and who have not come to a settled persuasion, trusting in the flesh [human worthiness and attainment]. 1-3

Although as for myself, I [as a Jew] could be having confidence also in the flesh. If, as is the case, anyone else presumes to have come to a settled persuasion, trusting in the flesh, I could occupy that place, and with more reason; eight days old in circumcision, my origin from Israelitish stock, belonging to the tribe of Benjamin, a Hebrew from true Hebrew parents [i.e., not a Hellenist], with reference to the law, a Pharisee, with regard to zeal, persecuting the Church, with reference to that kind of righteousness which is in the law, become blameless. 4-6

But whatever things were to me a gainful asset, these things I have considered a loss when it comes to my acquisition of Christ, and still so consider them. Yes, indeed, therefore, at least, even I am still setting all things down to be a loss for the sake of that which excels all others, my knowledge of Christ Jesus my Lord which I have gained through experience, for whose sake I have been caused to forfeit all things, and I am still counting them dung, in order that Christ I might gain, yes, in order that I might in the observation of others be discovered by them to be in Him, not having as my righteousness that righteousness which is of the law, but that righteousness which is through faith in Christ, that righteousness which is from God on the basis of faith. Yes, for His sake I 7-11 have been caused to forfeit all things, and I count them but dung, in order that I might come to know Him in an experiential way, and to come to know experientially the power of His resurrection and a joint-participation in His sufferings, being brought to the place where my life will radiate a likeness to His death, if by any means I might arrive at the goal, namely, the out-resurrection from among those who are dead.

12-14   Not that I already made acquisition or that I have now already been brought to that place of absolute spiritual maturity beyond which there is no progress, but I am pursuing onward if I may lay hold of that for which I have been laid hold of by Christ Jesus. Brethren, as for myself, as I look back upon my life and calmly draw a conclusion, I am not counting myself yet as one who has in an absolute and complete way laid hold [of that for which I have been laid hold of by Christ Jesus]; but one thing: I, in fact, am forgetting completely the things that are behind, and am stretching forward to the things that are in front; bearing down upon the goal, I am pursuing on for the prize of the call from above of God which is in Christ Jesus.

15-21   As many therefore as are spiritually mature [in a relative sense], let us be constantly of this mind. And if, as is the case, in anything you are differently minded, and that, in an evil sense, this also will God reveal to you. Only one thing, so far as we have come, let us keep our lives in the same path. Become imitators of me, brethren, and observe attentively those who conduct themselves in a manner which reflects the example which you have in us, for many are going about, concerning whom I often have been telling you, but now also tell you weeping, the enemies [they are] of the Cross of the Christ, whose end is utter destruction, whose god is their stomach, and that which they esteem to be their glory is their shame, who regard the things upon the earth. For the commonwealth of which we are citizens has its fixed location in heaven out from which we, with our attention withdrawn from all else, are eagerly waiting to welcome the Saviour, the

Lord Jesus Christ, and to receive Him to ourselves, who shall transform this body of ours which has been humiliated [by the presence of indwelling sin and by death and decay], so that it will be conformed to His body of His glory, this in accordance with the operation of Him who is able to bring into subjection to himself all things.

Therefore, my brethren, individually loved ones, and individually and passionately longed for, my joy and my victor's festal garland, thus be standing firm in the Lord, beloved ones. Euodia I exhort, please, and Syntyche, I exhort, please, to be of the same mind in the Lord. Even so, I make request of you also, you who are a genuine yokefellow in deed as well as in name [knowing how to work harmoniously with others], lend a hand with these women in their efforts at settling the differences which they have between themselves, women of such a character that in the good news they labored and contended in perfect co-operation with me as a team of athletes would, together also with Clement and the rest of my fellow workers whose names are in the book of life.   1-3

Be rejoicing in the Lord always. Again I say, Be rejoicing. Let your sweet reasonableness, your forbearance, your being satisfied with less than your due, become known to all men. The Lord is near [in that His coming may occur at any moment]. Stop worrying about even one thing, but in everything by prayer whose essence is that of worship and devotion and by supplication which is a cry for your personal needs, with thanksgiving let your requests for the things asked for be made known in the presence of God, and the peace of God which surpasses all power of comprehension shall mount guard over your hearts and minds in Christ Jesus.   4-7

Finally, brethren, whatever things have the character of truth, whatever things are worthy of reverence, whatever things are righteous, whatever things are pure, whatever things are lovely, whatever things are attractive, whatever excellence there is or fit object of praise, these things make the subject of careful reflection. The things also which you learned and received and heard and saw   8, 9 in me, these things habitually practice, and the God of peace shall be with you.

10-13   But I rejoiced in the Lord greatly that already once more you let your concern for my welfare blossom into activity again, in which matter you were all along thoughtful, but you never had an opportunity. It is not that I speak as regards a need, for, so far as I am concerned, I have come to learn, in the circumstances in which I am placed, to be independent of these and self-sufficient. I know in fact how to discipline myself in lowly circumstances. I know in fact how to conduct myself when I have more than enough. In everything and in all things I have learned the secret, both to be satiated and to be hungry, and to have more than enough and to lack. I am strong for all things in the One who constantly infuses strength in me.

14-19   All the same, you did a beautiful thing when you made yourselves fellow partakers with me in my tribulation. But you yourselves also know, Philippians, that at the beginning of the good news, when I went out from Macedonia, not even one assembly made itself a partner with me as regards an account of giving and receiving except you only, that even in Thessalonica more than once you sent to relieve my necessity. Not that it is my character to be ever seeking the gift, but I am seeking the fruit which is accumulating to your account. But I have all things to the full and overflowing. I have been filled completely full and at present am well supplied, having received at the hands of Epaphroditus the things from you, a fragrant aroma, a sacrifice acceptable, well-pleasing to God. But my God shall satisfy to the full your every need in accordance with His wealth in glory in Christ Jesus.

20-23   Now to God, even our Father, be the glory forever and ever. Amen. Greet every saint in Christ Jesus. The brethren with me send greeting to you. All the saints send greeting to you, especially those of Caesar's household. The grace of the Lord Jesus Christ be with your spirit, with all of you in this respect individually.

Paul, an ambassador of Christ Jesus through the will of God, and Timothy our brother, to the saints in Colossae, even the faithful brethren in Christ. [Sanctifying] grace to you and [tranquilizing] peace from God our Father.

I am giving thanks to God the Father of our Lord Jesus Christ concerning you, constantly offering petitions, having heard of your faith in Christ Jesus and of the divine, self-sacrificial love which you constantly have for all the saints because of the hope which is laid aside for you in heaven, concerning which you heard before in the word of the truth of the good news which is present with you even as also it is in all the world constantly bearing fruit and increasing, just as it is also among you from the day when you heard it and came to know experientially the grace of God in the sphere of truth; even as you learned from Epaphras, the beloved, our fellow bondslave, who is faithful on your behalf as a servant of Christ, who also declared to us your love in the sphere of the Spirit.

Because of this, we also, from the day we heard, do not cease on behalf of you offering our petitions and presenting our definite requests, that you might be filled with the advanced and perfect experiential knowledge of His will in the sphere of every kind of wisdom and intelligence which is spiritual, so that you may order your behavior worthily of the Lord with a view to pleasing Him in everything, in every work which is good constantly bearing fruit and increasing by means of the advanced and perfect experiential knowledge of God, by every enabling power being constantly strengthened in proportion to the manifested power of His glory, resulting in every patience and forbearance, with joy constantly giving thanks to the Father who qualified you for the portion of the share of the inheritance of the saints in the sphere of the light; who delivered us out of the tyrannical rule of the darkness and transferred us into the kingdom of the Son of His love, in whom we are having our liberation, procured by the payment of ransom, the putting away of our sins; who is a derived reproduction and manifestation of absolute deity, the invisible deity, who [the Son] has priority to and sovereignty over all creation, because in Him were created all things in the heavens and upon the earth, the visible things and the invisible ones, whether they are thrones or lordships or principalities or authorities. All things through Him as intermediate agent and with a view to Him stand created.

17-20   And He himself antedates all things, and all things in Him cohere. And He himself is the Head of His Body, the Church. He is the originator [i.e., the creator], the firstborn out from among the dead, in order that He might become in all things himself the One who is pre-eminent, because in Him [God] was well pleased that all the fullness be permanently at home. And [God was well pleased] through His agency to reconcile all things to himself, having concluded peace through the blood of His Cross, through Him, whether the things upon the earth or the things in the heavens.

21-23   And you who were at one time those who were in a settled state of alienation, and hostile with respect to your intents in the sphere of your works which were pernicious, yet now He reconciled in the body of His flesh through His death, in order that He might present you holy and without blemish and unchargeable before His searching and penetrating gaze; assuming indeed that you are adhering to the Faith, having been placed upon a foundation with the present result that you are on that foundation, firmly established, and that you are not being shifted away from your hope held out by the good news which you heard, that good news which was proclaimed in all creation which is under heaven, of which, I, Paul, became one who ministers.

24-29   I now am rejoicing in my sufferings on your behalf, and on my part am filling up the things lacking of the afflictions of the Christ in my flesh for the sake of His Body which is the Church, of which I became a servant according to the stewardship of God which was given to me for you, to fulfill the word of God, the mystery which has been kept hidden from the ages and from the generations, but now was made known to His saints, to whom God desired to make known in an experiential way what is the wealth of the glory of this mystery among the Gentiles, which is Christ in you, the hope of the glory, whom we are constantly announcing, admonishing every man and instructing every man in every wisdom in order that we may present every man spiritually mature in Christ Jesus, to which end also I am constantly laboring to the point of exhaustion, engaging in a contest in which I am controlled by His energy which operates in me in power.

For I desire you to know how great a conflict I am having in your behalf and in behalf of those in Laodicea, and as many as have not seen my face in the flesh, in order that their hearts may be encouraged, having been knit together in the sphere of love and resulting in all the wealth of the full assurance of the understanding, resulting in an advanced and perfect experiential knowledge of the mystery of God, Christ, in whom are all the hidden treasures of the wisdom and knowledge.

1-3

This I am saying in order that no one may be leading you astray by false reasoning in the sphere of specious discourse. For if, as is the case, I am in fact absent in my flesh, yet I am with you in my spirit, rejoicing and beholding your orderly array and the solid front of your faith in Christ. In the same manner, therefore, as you received the Christ, Jesus, the Lord, in Him be constantly ordering your behavior, having been rooted with the present result that you are firmly established, and constantly being built up in Him and constantly being established with reference to the Faith, even as you were instructed, abounding in it in the sphere of thanksgiving. Be ever on your guard lest there shall be someone who leads you astray through his philosophy, even futile deceit, which is according to the tradition of men, according to the rudimentary teachings of the world, and not according to Christ, because in Him there is continuously and permanently at home all the fullness of absolute deity in bodily fashion. And you are in Him, having been completely filled full with the present result that you are in

4-12

a state of fullness, in Him who is the Head of every principality and authority, in whom you were circumcised by a circumcision not effected by hand, in the putting off and away from yourselves the body of the flesh in the circumcision of Christ, having been entombed with Him in the placing into [Christ by the Holy Spirit], in which act of placing into [Christ] you were also raised with Him through your faith in the effectual working energy of the God who raised Him out from among the dead.

13-17   And you being dead with reference to your trespasses and the uncircumcision of your flesh, He gave life together with Him, having in grace forgiven you all your trespasses, having obliterated the hand-written document consisting of ordinances, the one [which was] against us, which was directly opposed to us, and He removed it out of the midst with the result that it is no longer there, having nailed it to the Cross; having stripped off and away from himself the principalities and authorities, He boldly made an example of them, leading them in a triumphal procession in it. Stop therefore allowing anyone to be sitting in judgment upon you in eating or drinking or in the matter of a feast day or a new moon, or a Sabbath day, which things are a shadow of those things about to come. But the body belongs to Christ.

18, 19   Let no one as a judge declare you unworthy of a reward, taking delight in a self-imposed humility and worship of the angels, scrutinizing minutely the things he has seen, being futilely puffed up by the mind of the flesh, and not holding fast the Head, out from whom all the body, through the instrumentality of the joints and ligaments being constantly supplied with nourishment and being constantly compacted together, increases with the increase wrought by God.

20-23   In view of the fact that you died with Christ from the rudimentary things of the world, why, as living in the world, are you subjecting yourselves to ordinances [such as], do not begin to touch, neither begin to taste, nor begin to handle, which things all are destined for corruption in their consumption; [ordinances] which are according to the precepts and teachings of men, which things as a class have a reputation for wisdom in a self-made, self-imposed worship and [an affected, hypocritical] humility and an unsparing and severe treatment of the body, [ordinances which are] not of any value as a remedy against the indulgence of the flesh?

In view of the fact, therefore, that you were raised with Christ, the things above be constantly seeking, where Christ is, on the right hand of God, seated. The things above be constantly setting your mind upon, not the things on the earth; for you died, and your life has been hidden with Christ in God. Whenever the Christ is made visible, our life, then also you with Him shall be manifested in glory.

1-4

By a once-for-all act, and at once, put to death your members which are upon the earth: fornication, impurity, depraved passion, wicked craving, and avarice which is of such a nature as to be idolatry; because of which things there comes the wrath of God; in the sphere of which things also you ordered your behavior at one time when you were living in them. But now put away once for all, and at once, also all these things: a habitual, revengeful anger, violent fits of anger, malignity, slander, obscene speech out of your mouth. Stop lying to one another, having stripped off and away from yourselves and for your own advantage the old, antiquated, outworn, decrepit, useless man [that person you were before you were saved] with his evil practices, and having clothed yourselves with the new man [the person you are after you are saved] who is constantly being renewed, with a resulting advanced and perfect experiential knowledge which is according to the image of the One who created him; in which state there cannot be Greek or Jew, circumcision or uncircumcision, Barbarian, Scythian, slave, or free man, but Christ is all things and in all things.

5-11

Put on therefore as your spiritual apparel, as chosen-out ones of God, saints and beloved ones, a heart of compassion, kindness, humility, considerateness, longsuffering, bearing with one another and forgiving one another

12-17

if anyone has a matter of complaint against anyone. Even as and in the degree that the Lord forgave you, in the same manner also you forgive. And upon all these, put on divine and self-sacrificial love which is a binding factor of completeness. And the peace of Christ, let it be acting as umpire in your hearts, into which also you were called in one body. And be constantly thankful persons. The word of Christ, let it be continually at home in you in abundance; with every wisdom teaching and admonishing each other by means of psalms, hymns, spiritual songs, with the grace singing in your hearts to God. And all, whatever you do in the sphere of word or deed, do all in the Name of the Lord Jesus, constantly giving thanks to God the Father through Him.

18-22   Wives, be constantly subjecting yourselves with implicit obedience to your husbands as you ought to do in the Lord. Husbands, be loving your wives with a divine love which impels you to deny yourselves for their benefit, and stop being bitter and harsh to them. Children, be obeying your parents in all things, for this is commendable in the Lord. Fathers, stop irritating your children, lest they become disheartened. Slaves, be constantly obedient in all things to your human masters, not with eye-service as men-pleasers, but with an undivided heart, fearing the Lord.

23-IV1   Whatever you are doing, from your soul do it diligently as to the Lord and not to men, knowing that from the Lord you will receive back the just recompense which consists of the inheritance. The [heavenly] Master, Christ, you are serving. For the one who is doing wrong will get back that which he did which is wrong. And there is no showing of partiality. Masters, that which is just and equitable be rendering on your part to your slaves, knowing that you also have a Master in heaven.

2-6   Be giving constant attention to prayer, constantly vigilant in it with thanksgiving, praying at the same time also for us, that God would open for us a door for the Word, that we may speak the mystery of the Christ, because of which [mystery] also I have been bound, in order that I may make it plain as it is necessary in the nature of the case for me to speak. In wisdom be ordering your behavior towards those on the outside, buying up for yourselves the strategic, opportune time. Your word, let it always be with graciousness, with salt thoroughly seasoned, to the end that you know how it is necessary in the nature of the case to answer everyone.

All the things that relate to me, Tychicus will make known to you, the beloved brother and faithful servant and my fellow bondslave in the Lord, whom I am sending to you for this same purpose, in order that you may come to know the things concerning us and in order that he may encourage your hearts; [sending him] with Onesimus the faithful and beloved brother who is one of you. All things to you they will make known, the things here. There greet you Aristarchus, my fellow prisoner, and Mark, the cousin of Barnabas, concerning whom you received orders; if he comes to you, receive him, and Joshua, the one called Justus, who are of the circumcision. These are my only fellow workers with respect to the kingdom of God who are of such a character as to have become a solace to me. **7-11**

There greets you Epaphras, the one who is one of your number, a bondslave of Christ Jesus, always contending on your behalf in his prayers, to the effect that you may stand fast, spiritually mature ones, and those who have been brought to the place of full assurance in everything willed by God; for I bear witness to him that he has much toil on your behalf and on behalf of those in Laodicea, and those in Hierapolis. There greet you Luke, the physician, the beloved one, and Demas. **12-14**

Greet the brethren in Laodicea, and Nymphas, and the [local] assembly [which meets] in her home. And when this letter is read in your presence, see to it that also it is read in the assembly of the Laodiceans, and the letter from Laodicea, see to it that you also read it. And say to Archippus, Be ever keeping a watchful eye upon the ministry which you received in the Lord, that you discharge it fully. The greeting by my hand, the hand of Paul. Be remembering my bonds. The grace be with you. **15-18**

Paul and Silvanus and Timothy to the [local] assembly of Thessalonians [which assembly is] in God the Father and the Lord Jesus Christ. [Sanctifying] grace to you and [tranquilizing] peace.

We are always giving thanks to God concerning all of you, making mention of you in our prayers, remembering unceasingly your work produced and characterized by the faith which is yours, and your toil motivated and characterized by your divine and self-sacrificial love, and your patient endurance under trials which finds its source in your hope which rests in our Lord Jesus Christ in the presence of our God, even the Father, since we know, brethren, that you who have always been loved by God and at the present time are the objects of His affection, are the subjects of the divine selection [in which God in sovereign grace selected you out for salvation], inasmuch as our message of good news came to you not only in the form of discourse but also in the sphere of power and of the Holy Spirit and in much certainty and assurance, even as you know positively what sort of men we showed ourselves to be among you for your sakes.

And as for you, you became imitators of us and of the Lord, having welcomed the Word while under much pressure of affliction which [act of welcoming] was accompanied by joy that had its source in the Holy Spirit, so that you became a pattern to all those who are believers in Macedonia and in Achaia. For from you there has been caused to sound forth in a loud, unmistakable proclamation the word of the Lord, the echo of which still rolls on with a great sound; not only in Macedonia and Achaia, but in every place your faith which is directed toward God has gone forth, so that we are not under any necessity to be saying a thing, for they themselves keep on reporting concerning you what kind of an entrance we had as we came to you, and how you turned around to God from your idols for the purpose of serving a living and genuine God as His bondslaves, and to be expectantly waiting for His Son from heaven, whom He raised out from among the dead, Jesus, the One who delivers us from the wrath which is coming.

1-4   For you yourselves know positively, brethren, our entrance which was into your midst, that it has not proved futile, the evidence of its success being still in existence, but although we had previously suffered and had been mistreated in an arrogant and spiteful manner as you know well in Philippi, we became bold in our God to speak to you the good news of God in the midst of much conflict. For our exhortation did not have its source in error nor even in immorality, nor even in deceit, but even as we have been approved by God as worthy of being entrusted with the good news, that approval being based upon the fact that we had met His requirements, thus are we speaking, not as pleasing men but as pleasing God who puts His approval upon our hearts after we have met the test to which He has subjected us.

5-8   For neither were we found using flattering discourse, even as you know assuredly, nor a pretext to cover up the desire to have more than one already has, God is witness, nor seeking glory from men, neither from you nor from others, when we might have stood on our dignity as Christ's ambassadors. But we became gentle in your midst, even as a nursing mother cherishes her own children. Thus having a kindly feeling for you, we constantly took delight in imparting to you not only the good news of God but also our own souls, because you became beloved ones to us.

9-12   For you remember, brethren, our fatiguing labor and hardship, night and day working at manual labor that we might not burden any of you while we proclaimed to you the good news of God. As for you, you are those who bear testimony to what you have seen, also God [who bears witness to what He has seen], how devoutly in a manner pleasing to God, how uprightly according to the standards set by God, how blamelessly we ordered our lives among you who are believers, even as you know how as a father exhorts and encourages his own children, exhorting and encouraging and bearing witness to each one of you, that you should be habitually ordering your behavior in a manner worthy of the God who summons you into His own kingdom and glory.

And on this account, as for us, we also are constantly **13-16**
giving thanks to God, and that unceasingly, because when
you appropriated to yourselves the word of the message
which came from us, even the word of God, you welcomed it, not as a word finding its source in men but as it
truly is, God's word which is being constantly set in operation in you who believe. For as for you, you became
imitators, brethren, of the assemblies of God which are
in Judaea in Christ Jesus, because as for you, you also
suffered the same things at the hands of your own countrymen even as also they themselves suffered at the hands
of the Jews, those who both killed the Lord Jesus and
the prophets, and drove us out, and are not pleasing God,
and are hostile to all men, forbidding us to tell the Gentiles that they [also] may be saved, with the result that
they fill up the measure of their sins always. And there
came upon them the wrath to the utmost.

But as for us, brethren, having been bereaved of you **17-20**
for a short season so far as our presence with you is
concerned, not in heart, we did our best all the more with
much desire to see your face. On this account we set our
heart on coming to you, indeed, I, Paul, not only once
but twice, but Satan cut in on us and by that means
thwarted us. For what is our hope or joy or victor's
laurel wreath of glorying? Are not even you yourselves
such in the presence of our Lord Jesus at His coming?
For as for you, you are our glory and joy.

Wherefore, being no longer able to bear it, we thought **1-4**
it good to be left behind in Athens alone, and we sent
Timothy, our brother and a ministering servant of God
in the good news of the Christ, with a view to stabilizing
and encouraging you concerning your faith, that is, that
no one be shaken or disturbed and caused to break down
in the midst of these afflictions, for you yourselves know
with a positive assurance that for this we are destined.
For also when we were with you, we kept on telling you
beforehand that we are destined to be suffering affliction,
even as also it came to pass and you know well.

5-8   Because of this, when I also could bear it no longer, I sent [him] that I might come to know your faith, lest by any means the tempter had solicited you to do evil and my labor would turn out to be in vain. But even now, Timothy having come to us from you also brought to us the good news of your faith and divine and self-sacrificial love, and that you have a kindly remembrance of us always, passionately desiring to see us even as we also are passionately desirous to see you, because of this we were encouraged, brethren, in your every distress and crushing affliction, this encouragement finding its source in your faith, because now we are [really] living, if, as for you, you are standing fast in the Lord.

9-13   For what thanks are we able to give back to God in return concerning you for all the joy with which we are rejoicing on account of you in the presence of our God, night and day asking in prayer quite beyond measure and as earnestly as possible that we might see your face and complete the things which are lacking in your faith? Now, our God and Father himself and our Lord Jesus direct our way to you. And as for you, the Lord cause you to increase and superabound in your divine and self-sacrificial love for one another and toward all, even as also we have this divine and self-sacrificial love for you, to the end that He might stabilize your hearts blameless in the sphere of holiness in the presence of our God and Father at the coming of our Lord Jesus with all His saints.

1-8   Finally, therefore, brethren, I request you and I beg of you, please, in the Lord Jesus, that even as you received from us the particular way in which it is necessary in the nature of the case for you to be ordering your behavior and to be striving to please God, even as also you are conducting yourselves, that you superabound yet more and more. For you know with a positive assurance what charges we gave you through the Lord Jesus, for this is the will of God, your being set apart [from sin to holiness], that you should hold yourselves off from fornication; that each one of you should know that he is to procure his own vessel [wife] in [personal] holiness and honor, not in the passion of an inordinate desire even as also the Gentiles do who do not know God, that no one be transgressing and defrauding his brother [Christian] in the aforementioned matter because the Lord is the One who inflicts punishment with reference to all these things, even as also we told you before and charged you. For God did not issue His divine summons [into salvation] to you for uncleanness but within the sphere of holiness. Therefore, he who rejects [this], not man is he rejecting but God who also gives His Holy Spirit to us.

Now, concerning brotherly affection you are not having any need that I should be writing to you, for as for you, you yourselves are those taught by God with a view to loving one another with a love that impels you to deny yourselves for the benefit of the one whom you love, for you also are doing the same with respect to all the brethren in the whole of Macedonia. Now, as for you, I beg of you, please, brethren, that you see to it that you continually are increasing more and more [in this love], that you make it your ambition to be living a quiet life, that you are cultivating the habit of attending to your own private affairs, and that you are working with your hands, even as I gave you a charge, in order that you may be conducting yourselves in a manner becoming to you [as children of God] toward those who are on the outside, in order that you may not be having need of anything.   **9-12**

Now, we do not wish you to be ignorant, brethren, concerning those who from time to time are falling asleep [dying], in order that you may not be mourning in the same manner as the rest who do not have a hope. For in view of the fact that we believe that Jesus died and arose, thus also will God bring with Him those who have fallen asleep through the intermediate agency of Jesus. For this we are saying to you by the Lord's word, that as for us who are living and are left behind until the coming of the Lord, we shall by no means precede those who fell asleep, because the Lord himself with a cry of command, with an archangel's voice, and with a call of a trumpet sounded at God's command, shall descend from heaven, and the dead in Christ shall be raised first, then as for us who are living and who are left behind, together   **13-18** with them we shall be snatched away forcibly in [masses of saints having the appearance of] clouds for a welcome-meeting with the Lord in the lower atmosphere. And thus always shall we be with the Lord. So that — be encouraging one another with these words.

1-3   But concerning the duration of the successive intervals of time and the epoch-making periods of time, brethren, you have no need that I should be writing to you, for you yourselves know positively that the day of the Lord comes in the same manner as a thief at night. When they are saying, Peace and safety, then comes sudden destruction upon them as birth-pains upon a woman with child. And they shall by no means escape.

4-11   But as for you, brethren, you are not in darkness, that the day shall come down upon you as a thief, for as for all of you, sons of light you are and sons of day. We are not of the night nor of darkness. So then, let us not go on sleeping as do the rest, but let us be constantly on the alert, and let us be mentally and spiritually well-balanced and self-controlled. For those who are sleeping, sleep in the night time, and those who are intoxicated, are intoxicated at night. But as for us who are of the day, let us be mentally and spiritually well-balanced and self-controlled, having clothed ourselves with a breastplate of faith and love, and for a helmet, a hope of salvation, because as for us, God did not appoint us to wrath but to obtain salvation through our Lord Jesus Christ who died for us in order that whether we are awake [alive] or asleep [dead] we might live together with Him. Wherefore, be encouraging one another and be building one another up, one believer the other believer, even as also you are doing.

12-15 Now, we request of you, brethren, that you recognize those for what they are and as entitled to the respect due them who work to the point of weariness among you and who are in authority over you in the Lord and admonish you, and be esteeming them most highly with a divine and self-sacrificial love because of their work. Be constantly at peace among yourselves. Now, we beg of you, please, brethren, be admonishing those who are rebellious, be encouraging the fainthearted, be a mainstay to those who are [spiritually] weak, be always patient toward all with that patience which endures ill-treatment meekly and without retaliation. Be seeing to it constantly that a person does not return evil in exchange for evil to anyone, but always be striving for that which is beneficial for one another and for all men.

Always be rejoicing. Be praying unceasingly. In **16-22** everything be giving thanks, for this is the will of God in Christ Jesus for you. Stop stifling and suppressing the Spirit. Stop counting as nothing divine revelations given in the local assembly by the one who receives them, but be putting all things to the test for the purpose of approving them, and finding that they meet the requirements, put your approval upon them. Be constantly holding fast that which is good. Be holding yourselves back from every form of perniciousness.

Now, may the God of peace himself consecrate you, **23-28** every part of each one of you, to His worship and service, and may your spirit and soul and body be preserved in their entirety blameless at the coming of our Lord Jesus Christ. Faithful is He who gives you the divine summons [into salvation], who also will do it. Brethren, be praying definitely for us. Greet all the brethren with an affectionate kiss. I adjure you by the Lord that the [foregoing] letter be read to all the brethren. The grace of our Lord Jesus Christ be with you.

Paul and Silvanus and Timothy, to the [local] assembly of Thessalonians in God our Father and in the Lord Jesus Christ. [Sanctifying] grace and [tranquilizing] peace from God the Father and from the Lord Jesus Christ.

We have a sense of personal obligation to be constantly thanking God at all times concerning you, brethren, even as it is fitting and proper [to do so], because your faith is growing wonderfully and the divine and self-sacrificial love of each one of you all for one another exists in great abundance, so that we ourselves take pride in and boast about you in the assemblies of God concerning your fortitude and faith in all of your persecutions and tribulations which you are enduring, which [fortitude and faith] are a plain indication of the equitable adjudication of God to the end that you are considered worthy of the kingdom of God for the sake of which you also are suffering, since it is just in the sight of God to return affliction to those who are afflicting you.

And to you who are being afflicted, there is a surcease from this stress and strain [due to your persecutions] in the relaxing anticipation of the revelation of the Lord Jesus from heaven with the angels of His power in a fire of flame, alloting full justice to those who do not know God and who do not obey the good news concerning our Lord Jesus, who are such that they shall pay the penalty of everlasting ruin and death in [their] separation from the presence of the Lord and from the glory of His power, whenever He comes to be glorified in His saints and to be marvelled at in all those who believed, because our testimony to you was believed on that day.

To which end also we are praying always for you, namely, that our God may count you worthy of the station in life to which He has called you, and fulfill every delight [you Thessalonian saints have] in goodness and every work that finds its source in faith with power, in order that the Name of our Lord Jesus may be glorified in you and you in Him, in accordance with the grace of our God, even the Lord Jesus Christ.

1, 2

3-6

7-10

11, 12

1-4   Now, I am requesting you, brethren, with regard to the coming and personal presence of our Lord Jesus Christ, even our being assembled together to Him, not soon to become unsettled, the source of this unsettled state being your minds, neither be thrown into confusion, either by a spirit [a believer in the Christian assembly claiming the authority of divine revelation and claiming to give the saints a word from God], or through a word [received personally] as from us or through a letter falsely alleged to be written by us, to the effect that the day of the Lord has come and is now present. Do not begin to allow anyone to lead you astray in any way, because that day shall not come except the aforementioned departure [of the Church to heaven] comes first and the man of the lawlessness is disclosed [in his true identity], the son of perdition, he who sets himself in opposition to and exalts himself above everyone and everything that is called a god or that is an object of worship, so that he seats himself in the inner sanctuary of God, proclaiming himself to be deity.

5-7   Do you not remember that while I was still with you I kept on telling you these things? And now you know with a positive assurance that which [namely, the departure of the Church, the saints being assembled together to the Lord] is preventing his being disclosed [as to his true identity] in his strategic, appointed time, for the mystery of the aforementioned lawlessness is now operating. Only He [the Holy Spirit] who is holding [the lawlessness] down, [will do so] until He goes out from the midst [of humanity].

8-12   And then shall the Lawless One be disclosed [in his true identity], whom the Lord Jesus shall slay with the breath of His mouth and render inoperative by the sudden appearance of His personal presence, the coming and presence of whom [the man of lawlessness] is according to the operation of Satan in the sphere of miracles demonstrating power and attesting miracles and miracles of a startling, imposing, amazement-wakening character which deceive, and whose coming and presence is in the sphere

of every kind of wicked deception geared to [the gullibility of] those who are perishing, [this gullibility being]
caused by the fact that they did not accept the love for
the truth to the end that they might be saved. And because of this God sends them a deluding influence resulting in their believing the lie, in order that they all might
be judged who did not believe the truth but took delight
in wickedness.

But as for us, we have a sense of moral obligation to **13, 14**
be giving thanks to God always concerning you, brethren
beloved by the Lord, because God from the beginning
chose you out [from the rest of mankind] for salvation,
this choice being within the sphere of the setting-apart
work of the Spirit and a belief of the truth, into which
[the setting-apart work of the Spirit and a belief in the
truth] also He summoned you through our good news,
resulting in your acquisition of the glory of our Lord
Jesus Christ.

So then, brethren, be constantly standing firmly, and **15**
be holding fast to the teachings which were delivered to
you to be passed on to others, which you were taught
either orally or through our letter.

Now, our Lord Jesus Christ himself and God our **16, 17**
Father who loved us and who gave us everlasting encouragement and a good hope, this gift having been given
us in [His] grace, encourage your hearts and stabilize
them in the sphere of every good work and word.

Finally, be praying, brethren, for us, to the end that **1-3**
the word of the Lord might be spreading rapidly and be
continually glorified, even as it is doing in your case, and
that we may be delivered from the men who act in an im-
proper and unbecoming manner and who are in active
opposition to that which is good; for all do not possess
the Faith [the Christian system of belief]. But the Lord
is faithful [in the sense of trustworthy and dependable],
who shall stabilize you and shall protect you from the
Pernicious One [Satan].

4, 5   Now, we have come to a settled persuasion in the Lord regarding you, that the things which we are commanding you are also doing and will continue to be doing. And the Lord direct your hearts into the love which God is as to His nature and into the endurance and fortitude of the Christ.

6-9   Now, we command you, brethren, in the Name of the Lord Jesus Christ, that you keep away from every brother [Christian] who orders his behavior in an insubordinate manner [having an insufficient inclination to disciplined work], and who does not order his behavior according to the teaching which you received and which was delivered by us for you to pass on to others. For you yourselves know perfectly well how it is a necessity in the nature of the case for you to emulate us, that we did not act in an insubordinate manner among you, neither did we eat bread at the hand of anyone gratis. But we engaged in manual labor for our livelihood in weariness and hardship night and day, in order that we might not be a burden to any one of you; not because we do not have a right [to be financially supported in our work by you] but in order that we might give ourselves to you as a pattern for you to emulate.

10-12   For even when we were with you, this we kept on charging you, that if, as is actually the case, anyone does not desire to work for his livelihood, let him not be eating. For we hear that certain ones are ordering their behavior in an insubordinate manner among you, not working for a living, but are busying themselves about everybody else's business. Now, these we command and exhort, we beg of them, please, in the Lord Jesus Christ, that in quietness they be working for their living and be eating their own bread.

13-15   But, as for you, brethren, do not become weary and lose heart in doing good. And, if, as is the case, anyone is not obeying our word in this letter, be taking special notice of this person and do not have any association with him, in order that he may be put to shame. Yet, stop considering him as an enemy but be admonishing and warning him as a brother [Christian].

Now, the Lord of the peace himself give you [that] 16-18 peace [which He himself has] always in every way. The Lord be with you all. The greeting [1:1, 2 was written] by my hand, the hand of Paul, which [circumstance, namely, that I wrote it personally, whereas the rest of the letter was dictated to a secretary] is the mark of genuineness in every letter. In this manner am I in the habit of writing. The grace of our Lord Jesus Christ be with you all.

Paul, an ambassador of Christ Jesus by command of   1, 2
God our Saviour and Christ Jesus our hope, to Timothy,
my genuine child in the Faith. [Sanctifying] grace, mercy,
[tranquilizing] peace, from God our Father and Christ
Jesus our Lord.

Just as I begged you to continue on in Ephesus when   3, 4
I was going into Macedonia in order that you might charge
certain ones not to be teaching things contrary to sound
doctrine, nor to be giving assent to fables and useless
genealogies which are of such a character as to provide
occasion for exhaustive investigations rather than a
[knowledge of the] administration of the things by which
God has provided for and prepared salvation, which
salvation must be embraced by faith.

Now, the objective which is the aim of the aforemen-   5-11
tioned charge is divine and self-sacrificial love out of a
heart which is pure, and a conscience which is good, and
a faith which is not assumed but real, from which things
certain having deviated, have turned off into talk which is
futile, desiring to be law teachers, though they neither
understand the things they are saying nor what kind of
things they are concerning which they speak so confidently. But we know that the law is good if a person uses
it properly, knowing this, that law is not enacted for a
law-abiding person, but for lawless ones and for unruly
ones, for those who are destitute of reverential awe
towards God and for sinners, for unholy ones and for
those who are irreligious, for those who ill-treat fathers
and ill-treat mothers, for manslayers, for whoremongers,
for sodomites, for slave dealers and kidnapers, for liars,
for perjurers, and if, as is the case, there is anything of
a different nature which is opposed to sound teaching,
according to the good news of the glory of the blessed
God with which I was entrusted.

I am constantly grateful to the One who endued me   12-17
with the necessary strength, Christ Jesus our Lord, because He deemed me trustworthy, having placed me in
service, though I was the very one who heretofore was a
reviler and a persecutor and an insolent, destructive per-

son. But I was shown mercy because, being ignorant, I acted in unbelief. Moreover, the grace of our Lord superabounded together with faith and love which is in Christ Jesus. Trustworthy is the word and worthy of unqualified acceptance, that Christ Jesus came into the world to save sinners, of whom I in contradistinction to anyone else am foremost. Moreover, on this account I was shown mercy, in order that in me first Jesus Christ might demonstrate all the long-suffering [which He has] as an example to those who were to be believing on Him for life eternal. Now, to the King of the Ages, the incorruptible, invisible, unique God, be honor and glory forever and ever. Amen.

18-20   This charge I am entrusting to you, son Timothy, in accordance with the prophetic intimations which were made long ago concerning you, to the effect that in their sphere you are to wage the good warfare, holding faith and a good conscience, which [latter] certain having thrust from themselves concerning the Faith, have suffered shipwreck, among whom are Hymenaeus and Alexander, whom I have delivered over to Satan in order that they may be taught not to be blaspheming.

1-7   I exhort therefore, first of all, that petitions be made continually for personal needs, prayers, intercessions, giving of thanks on behalf of all men, on behalf of kings and all those holding high positions, in order that a quiet and peaceful life we may be leading in every godliness and becoming deportment. This is good and acceptable in the sight of our Saviour God who desires that all men be saved and come to a precise and experiential knowledge of the truth, for there is one God, and one mediator between God and men, a Man, Christ Jesus, who gave himself as a ransom on behalf of all, the testimony of which is to be given in strategic seasons having a unique character of their own, to which [testimony] I was appointed an official herald and an ambassador; I am speaking truth, I am not lying; a teacher of Gentiles in faith and truth.

I desire, therefore, that the men [definite article before "men" and distinctive word for a male individual designating the man as leader and in authority in the church] be praying in every place, lifting up holy hands without anger or skeptical criticism. Likewise, I desire that women be adorning themselves in apparel that is fitting [to their sex and to their position as Christians], having along with this, modesty and sober-mindedness; not with braided hair, or gold, or pearls, or very costly garments, but with that which is fitting for a woman professing godliness, adorning themselves by means of good works. Let a woman be learning in silence with every subjection. Moreover, I do not permit a woman to be a teacher [in an official position exercising authority over the man in matters of Church doctrine or discipline], neither to exercise authority over a man, but to be in silence, for Adam first was molded, then Eve, and Adam was not deceived, but the woman, having been completely hoodwinked, has fallen into transgression. Yet she shall be saved [in the sense of sanctifying, salutary influences in her spiritual life through the pains of childbirth] in her childbearing if they continue in faith and love and holiness accompanied by sober-mindedness.

This is a trustworthy word. If a certain one is seeking the office of an overseer, he passionately desires a good work. It is necessary in the nature of the case, therefore, that the overseer be irreproachable, a one-wife kind of a man [that is, married only once], calm, dispassionate and circumspect, sober-minded, one whose life is in accord with the position he holds and which is an adornment to it, hospitable, a skilled teacher, not addicted to wine, not pugnacious but sweetly reasonable, being satisfied with less than his due, not contentious, not a lover of money, presiding over his own household in a beautiful manner, holding children within the sphere of implicit obedience, doing so with the strictest regard to propriety. Indeed, if a person does not know how to preside over his own household, how is it possible that he take care of God's assembly? [He must] not [be] a new convert, lest having his mind blinded by pride, he fall into the judgment of the devil. Moreover, it is a necessity in the nature of the case for him also to be having an excellent testimony from those on the outside, lest he fall into reproach and into the snare of the devil.

8-13   Deacons, in like manner [should] be grave and dignified, not double-tongued, not addicted to much wine, not greedy of gain, holding the mystery of the Faith in a pure conscience. And these moreover are to be first put to the test for the purpose of being approved, and then approved if they meet the specifications; then let them be serving as deacons, provided they are unaccused. Women, likewise [should be] grave and dignified, not slanderers, calm, dispassionate, and circumspect, faithful in all things. Let the deacons be one-wife sort of men [that is, married only once], ruling their children and their own households in a commendable way, for those who have ministered in the office of a deacon in a commendable manner acquire a good standing for themselves and much confidence in the sphere of faith which is in Christ Jesus.

14-16   These things to you I am writing, hoping to come to you quickly, but if I delay, in order that you may know how it is necessary in the nature of the case for men to be conducting themselves in God's house which is of such a nature as to be the living God's assembly, a pillar and support of the truth. And confessedly, great is the mystery of godliness; who [Christ Jesus, v. 13] was made visible in the sphere of flesh [His humanity], vindicated in the sphere of spirit [as to His deity], seen by angels, proclaimed among the nations, believed on in the world, taken up in glory.

1-5   But the Spirit says expressly that in the last strategic, epochal periods of time some will depart from the Faith, giving heed to spirits that lead one into error, and to teachings of demons, doing this through the hypocrisy of liars, branded in their own conscience, forbidding to marry, commanding abstinence from foods, which things God created for those to receive with thanksgiving who are believers and who have a precise and experiential knowledge of the truth; because every created thing of God is good, and not even one thing is to be rejected if it is received with thanksgiving, for it is consecrated through God's word and through prayer.

Constantly reminding the brethren of these things, you will be a good servant of Christ Jesus, continually nourishing yourself by means of the words of the Faith and of the good teaching which you have closely followed. But unhallowed and old wives' fictions be shunning. On the other hand, be exercising yourself with a view to piety toward God. For the aforementioned bodily exercise is of some small profit, but the aforementioned piety toward God is profitable with respect to all things, holding a promise of this present life and of that about to come. **6-8**

This is a trustworthy word and worthy of every acceptance, for with a view to this we are laboring to the point of exhaustion; yes, we are putting forth great efforts against opposition, because we have set our hope permanently upon the living God who is the Saviour of all men, especially of believers. These things be constantly commanding and teaching. **9-11**

Stop allowing anyone contemptuously to be pushing you aside because of your youth, but keep on becoming an example of the believers, in word, in behavior, in divine and self-sacrificial love, in faith, in purity. While I am coming, keep concentrating on the public reading [of the Word], on exhortation, and on teaching. Do not keep on neglecting the spiritual enduement which is in you, which was given to you through prophecy in connection with the imposition of the hands of the body of elders. Be diligently attending to these things; be constantly engrossed in them, in order that your progress may be evident to all. Keep on paying careful attention to yourself and to the teaching. Constantly stay by them, for in doing this you will both save yourself and those who hear you [from the false doctrines of demons, 4:1-3]. **12-16**

1, 2   Do not upbraid an elderly man, but entreat him gently as a father, younger men as brothers, older women as mothers, younger women as sisters, with the strictest regard to purity.

3-10   Be constantly showing filial reverence and respect to widows who are truly widows. But, as is the case, if a certain widow has children or grandchildren, let them be learning first to show filial reverence and respect to their own household, and to discharge their obligation relative to a recompense to their forebears, for this is acceptable in the sight of God. But the one who is a widow and has been left completely and permanently alone, has set her hope permanently on God, and continues constantly in petitions for her needs and in prayers night and day. But the one who lives luxuriously, lives while she is in the state of having died, with the result that she is dead. And these things constantly be commanding in order that they may be irreproachable. But if, as is the case, a certain one does not anticipate the needs of his own and provide for them, and especially for those of his own household, he has denied the Faith and is worse than an unbeliever. Do not continue to allow a widow to be enrolled who is less than sixty years old; she must be a one-husband sort of a woman [married only once], have testimony borne her in the matter of good works, if she reared children, if she showed hospitality to strangers, if she washed the saints' feet, if she succored those who were hard pressed by circumstances, if she persevered in every good work.

11-13   But younger widows refuse. For whenever they feel the impulses of sexual desire, thus becoming unruly with respect to Christ, they determine to marry, incurring [the reproachful] judgment [of their fellow Christians] because they have nullified their first faith. And at the same time they also learn to be idle, gadding about from house to house, and not only idle but tattlers, and those who pry into the private affairs of others, speaking the things which they ought not to speak.

Therefore, after mature consideration, I desire that the younger widows marry, be bearing children, be managing household affairs, affording not even one place of advantage from which the Adversary would be able to revile, for already certain ones have turned aside to Satan. If, as is the case, a certain person who is a believer has widows, let him be giving them assistance, and let not the assembly be burdened, in order that it may give assistance to those who are truly widows.

Let the elders that are ruling well be deemed deserving of double honor, especially those who are laboring with wearisome effort in the Word and in the teaching; for the scripture says, You should not muzzle an ox while he is treading out the corn, and, The worker is worthy of his pay. Against an elder do not receive a formal accusation before a tribunal, except it be upon the authority of two or three who bear testimony. Those [elders] who are sinning, in the presence of all be rebuking, in order that the rest may be having fear. I solemnly charge you in the presence of our God, even Christ Jesus, and the elect angels, that these things you are to guard without showing prejudice, doing not even one thing dominated by the spirit of partiality. Be laying hands hastily on not even one [elder, that is, do not reinstate a sinning elder hastily], neither be a partner in others' sins. Exercise a watchful care over yourself with respect to your present purity. Be no longer an exclusive water-drinker, but be using a little wine for the sake of your stomach and your frequent illnesses. The sins of certain men are openly manifest to all eyes, going ahead to judgment; and in the case of certain individuals, they follow after. Likewise, also the good works are openly manifest to all eyes, and those that are otherwise than manifest are not able to be hidden.

Let as many as are under the yoke as slaves consider their own absolute masters worthy of every respect in order that the Name of God and the teaching be not evil spoken of. And those who have believing masters, let them not be despising them because they are brothers [in

Christ], but rather be rendering them a slave's service because they are believers [Christians] and divinely loved ones [of God] who busy themselves in kindly service [to their slaves]. These things be constantly teaching and exhorting.

3-10　　　　If, as is the case, anyone is teaching things of a different nature and opposed to the things just mentioned, and does not give his assent to wholesome words, those of our Lord Jesus Christ, and to the teaching which is according to a godly piety, he is in a beclouded and stupid state of mind which is caused by pride, not doing any concentrated or reflective thinking in even one instance, but exercising a morbid curiosity about inquiries and quarrels about words, from which comes envy, strife, speech injurious to another's good name, malicious suspicions, protracted and wearying discussions of men corrupted in mind, and who have disinherited themselves of the truth, thinking that godly piety is a way of gain. But godly piety associated with an inward self-sufficiency which is its natural accompaniment is great gain; for not even one thing did we bring into this world, because not even one thing are we able to take out. And having food and clothing, by these we shall be fortified sufficiently; but they that after giving the matter mature consideration desire to be wealthy, fall into temptation and a snare and many foolish and hurtful cravings which are of such a nature as to drown men in destruction and perdition; for a root of all the evils is the fondness for money, which certain ones, bending their every effort to grasp, have been led astray from the Faith and have pierced themselves through with many consuming griefs.

11-16　　　　But, as for you, O man of God, these things be constantly fleeing. But be as constantly eagerly seeking to acquire righteousness, godly piety, faith, divine and self-sacrificial love, steadfastness, gentleness. Be constantly engaging in the contest of the Faith, which contest is marked by its beauty of technique. Take possession of the eternal life into a participation of which you were called and concerning which you gave testimony to your agreement with the good profession [you made] in the presence of many witnesses. I am giving you a charge in the presence of God who is constantly preserving in life all things, and Christ Jesus, the One who in His testimony before Pontius Pilate made the good profession, preserve this commandment intact, unsullied, irreproachable, until the glorious manifestation of our Lord Jesus Christ, which [glorious manifestation] He will expose to the eyes in strategic seasons having a unique character all their own, the One who is the blessed and only Sovereign [the One having all power], the King of those who are reigning as kings, and Lord of those who are ruling as lords, who alone has immortality, dwelling in unapproachable light, whom not even one in the human race has seen nor even is able to see, to whom be honor and power forever. Amen.

To those who are wealthy in the present age, be giving a charge not to continue to be high-minded, neither to have their hope set upon the uncertainty of wealth, but upon God, the One who is constantly offering us all things in a rich manner to enjoy; to be doing good, to be wealthy in the sphere of good works, to be liberal, sharers with others, laying away for themselves a good foundation with a view to the future, in order that they may lay hold of that which is truly life. **17-19**

O, Timothy, that which was committed to you, guard, turning away from unhallowed and empty mouthings and oppositions of the falsely named knowledge, which [knowledge] certain ones announcing, missed the mark concerning the Faith. The grace be with all of you. **20, 21**

Paul, an ambassador of Christ Jesus through the will of God, according to the promise of life which is in Christ Jesus, to Timothy, beloved child. [Sanctifying] grace, mercy, [tranquilizing] peace, from God the Father and Christ Jesus our Lord.

I constantly have a spirit of thanksgiving to God, to whom I am rendering sacred service from the time of my forebears with a pure conscience, as unceasingly I have you in my mind in my petitions for needs, night and day, greatly longing to see you, remembering your tears, in order that I may be filled with joy, having been reminded of the unhypocritical faith which is in you, which is of such a nature as to have been at home first in your grandmother Lois and in your mother Eunice, and concerning which I have come to a settled persuasion is at home in you also; for which cause I am reminding you to keep constantly blazing the gift of God which is in you through the imposition of my hands, for God did not give to us a spirit of fearfulness but of power and of a divine and self-sacrificial love and of a sound mind.

Therefore, do not begin to be ashamed of the testimony borne by our Lord, nor of me His prisoner, but be a partaker with me in my sufferings for the sake of the good news, [being a partaker of these sufferings] according to the power of God, the One who saved us and divinely summoned us in the sphere of a holy summons, not according to our works but according to His own private purpose and grace which [grace] was given us in Christ Jesus before the beginning of time, but has now been made known through the appearing of our Saviour, Christ Jesus, since He not only made of none effect the death, but also brought to light life and incorruption through the good news, with reference to which good news I was appointed a herald and an ambassador and a teacher; on which account I am also suffering these things. But I am not ashamed, for I know with an absolute knowledge the One in whom I have permanently placed my trust, and have come to a settled persuasion that He is of power to guard that which has been committed as a trust to me [his Christian service] with reference to that day.

13-15   Be holding fast the pattern of sound words which [words] from me personally you heard, in faith and love which is in Christ Jesus. That good thing which was committed in trust to you, guard through the Holy Spirit who indwells us. You know this, that there turned away from me all those in Asia, of whom there are Phygellus and Hermogenes.

16-18   The Lord grant mercy to the household of Onesiphorus, because he often refreshed me and was not ashamed of my handcuff, but when he was in Rome he sought me out with more than ordinary diligence and found me. The Lord grant to him to find mercy in the presence of and from the Lord in that day. And in how many things he served me in Ephesus, you know by experience better [than I].

1, 2   As for you, therefore, my child, be clothed with inward strength by the grace which is in Christ Jesus; and the things which you heard from me personally in the presence of many witnesses, these things commit as a trust to trustworthy men who are of such a character as to be capable of teaching others also.

3-6   Take your part with others in enduring hardships as a good soldier of Christ Jesus. No one when engaged in military service allows himself to become involved in civilian pursuits, in order that he may please the one who enlisted him as a soldier. And if a person contends in the athletic games, he is not crowned as the victor unless he engages in the athletic contest according to the prescribed rules. It is a necessity in the nature of the case that the tiller of the soil who labors with wearisome effort be the first to be partaking of the fruits.

7-14   Be grasping the meaning of that which I am saying, for the Lord will give you understanding in all things. Be remembering Jesus Christ raised out from among the dead, from the ancestry of David according to my gospel [good news], in which sphere of action I am suffering hardship to the extent of bonds as a malefactor. But the word of God has not been bound, with the present result that it is not shackled. Because of this I am enduring all things for the sake of the selected-out ones [those sovereignly selected from mankind for salvation], in order that they themselves also may obtain salvation which is in Christ Jesus, together with everlasting glory. Trustworthy is the word. For in view of the fact that we died with Him, we shall also live by means of Him. If we are persevering, we shall also reign as kings with Him. If we shall deny Him, that One also will deny us. If we are unfaithful, that One remains faithful, for to deny himself He is not able. These things constantly be reminding them, charging them in the presence of God not to be continually wrangling about empty and trifling matters, which results in not even one useful thing, since it ruins those who hear.

Bend your every effort to present yourself to God, **15-18** approved, a workman unashamed, expounding soundly the word of the truth. But with reference to unhallowed and empty discussions, give them a wide berth, for they will progress to more impiety towards God, and their word will spread as does cancer, of whom are Hymenaeus and Philetus, the very ones who are of such a character as to have deviated from the truth, saying that the resurrection already has taken place, and are overthrowing the faith of certain ones.

However, the immovable foundation of God has stood **19-21** and at present stands, having this seal, The Lord knows those who are His, and, Let those who name the Name of the Lord depart from every wickedness. Now, in a great house there are not only utensils of gold and of silver, but also of wood and of baked clay, also some which are highly prized and others which are treated with contempt. If, therefore, a person separate himself from these [the utensils held in contempt], he shall be a utensil highly prized, in a state of permanent separation, useful to the master, for every good work equipped.

The passions of youth be constantly fleeing from, but **22-26** be pursuing as constantly righteousness, faithfulness, divine and self-sacrificial love, peace, in company with those who are calling upon the Lord out of a pure heart. But stupid questionings, and questionings that come from an uninstructed and undisciplined mind be refusing, knowing that they constantly beget contentions. And the Lord's bondslave must not in the nature of the case quarrel but be gentle to all, skillful in teaching, forbearing, in meekness correcting those who set themselves in opposition, if perchance God may grant them repentance resulting in a precise, experiential knowledge of the truth, and that they may return to soberness out of the snare of the devil, having been held captive by him, [returning to soberness so as to serve] the will of that One [God].

1-5   This be constantly knowing, that in the last days difficult times will set in, for men shall be fond of themselves, fond of money, swaggerers, haughty, revilers, disobedient to parents, unthankful, unholy, without natural affection, implacable, slanderers, lacking self-control, savage, haters of that which is good, betrayers, headstrong, besotted with pride, fond of pleasure rather than having an affection for God, having a mere outward semblance of piety toward God but denying the power of the same. And these be constantly shunning.

6-9   For of these are those who by means of insinuation slink into houses and take captive the minds of silly women who have been in times past heavily laden with sins, and who are at present heavily loaded down with them, who are under the impelling urge of variegated, passionate desires, ever learning and never able to come to a precise and experiential knowledge of the truth. Now, in the same manner as Jannes and Jambres set themselves against Moses, so also these set themselves against the truth, men corrupted in mind; after having been put to the test, disapproved concerning the Faith. But they shall make no further progress, for their insane folly shall become evident to all, as also their folly [namely, that of Jannes and Jambres] became evident.

10-13   But as for you, you were attracted as a disciple to me because of my teaching, conduct, purpose, faith, longsuffering, divine and self-sacrificial love, patience, persecutions, afflictions such as came to me in Antioch, in Iconium, in Lystra, what manner of persecutions I endured; and out of them all the Lord delivered me. And all indeed who desire to be living a life of piety towards God in Christ Jesus shall be persecuted. But pernicious men and impostors shall go on from bad to worse, leading astray and being led astray.

But, as for you, be remaining as you are in the things 14-17 which you learned and have been assured of, knowing the persons from whom you personally learned them, and that from a very young child you know the sacred scriptures which are able to make you wise with respect to salvation through faith, that faith which is in Christ Jesus. Every scripture is God-breathed, and is profitable for teaching, for conviction, for improvement, for training with respect to righteousness, in order that the man of God may be complete, fitted out for every good work.

I solemnly charge you as one who is living in the 1-4 presence of our God, even Christ Jesus, the One who is on the point of judging the living and the dead, I solemnly charge you as not only living in His presence, but also by His appearing and His kingdom; make a public proclamation of the Word with such formality, gravity, and authority as must be heeded. Hold yourself in readiness for this proclamation when opportunity presents itself and when it does not; reprove so as to bring forth conviction and confession of guilt; rebuke sharply, severely, and with a suggestion of impending penalty. Pleadingly exhort, doing all this with that utmost self-restraint which does not hastily retaliate a wrong, and accompany this exhortation with the most painstaking instruction; for the time will come when they will not endure our wholesome doctrine in that they will hold themselves firmly against it, but, dominated by their own personal cravings, they, having ears that desire merely to be gratified, shall gather to themselves an accumulation of teachers. In fact, from the truth they shall also avert the ear, and [as a result] they shall receive a moral twist which will cause them to believe that which is fictitious.

5-8

But as for you, you be constantly in a sober mood, calm, collected, wakeful, alert in all things. Endure hardships. Let your work [as a pastor] be evangelistic in character. Your work of ministering fully perform in every detail, for, as for myself, my life's blood is already being poured out as a libation, and the strategic time of my departure is already present. The desperate, straining, agonizing contest marked by its beauty of technique, I like a wrestler have fought to the finish, and at present am resting in its victory. My race, I like a runner have finished, and at present am resting at the goal. The Faith committed to my care, I like a soldier have kept safely through everlasting vigilance, and have delivered it again to my Captain. Henceforth there is reserved for me the victor's laurel wreath of righteousness, which the Lord will award me on that day, the just Umpire [the umpire who is always fair and never makes a mistake], and not only to me but also to all those who have loved His appearing and as a result have their love fixed on it.

9-15

Do your best to come to me quickly, for Demas let me down, having set a high value upon this present age and thus has come to love it. And he set out for Thessalonica, Crescens for Galatia, Titus for Dalmatia. Luke alone is with me. Mark pick up and be bringing him with you, for he is profitable to me for ministering work. But Tychicus I sent off on a mission to Ephesus. My cloak which I left behind at Troas in the care of Carpus, when you are coming, be carrying along, and my papyrus rolls, especially my parchments. Alexander, the metal worker, showed me many instances of ill-treatment. The Lord shall pay him off in accordance with his evil works. And you also, with reference to him, be constantly guarding yourself, for he in an extraordinary manner set himself in opposition to our words.

16-18

During my self-defense at the preliminary trial, not even one person appeared in court, taking his stand at my side as a friend of mine, but all let me down. May it not be put to their account. But the Lord took His stand at my side to render all the assistance I needed, and clothed me with strength, in order that through me the public proclamation might be heralded abroad in full measure, and that all the Gentiles might hear. And I was drawn to His side out of the lion's mouth. The Lord will draw me to himself away from every pernicious work actively opposed to that which is good, and will keep me safe and sound for His kingdom, the heavenly one, to whom be the glory forever and forever. Amen.

Greet Prisca and Aquila and the household of One- **19-22** siphorus. Erastus remained in Corinth, but Trophimus, being ill, I left behind in Miletus. Do your best to come before winter. There greet you Eubulus and Pudens and Linus and Claudia and all the brethren. The Lord be with your spirit. The grace be with you.

Paul, God's bondslave and an ambassador of Jesus
Christ in accordance with the Faith [the Christian faith]
of God's chosen-out ones and a precise, experiential
knowledge of truth which is in accordance with piety
towards God, upon the basis of an expectation of life
eternal which God who cannot lie promised before eternal
times; but in His own private, strategic seasons He made
known His Word in a proclamation with which I was
entrusted in accordance with the commandment of God,
our Saviour; to Titus, a genuine child in accordance with
the Faith held in common [by us]. [Sanctifying] grace
and [tranquilizing] peace from God the Father and Christ
Jesus our Saviour.

1-4

On this account I left you behind temporarily in Crete,
in order that you should set right the things which remain
to be done, and appoint [as overseers] in every city [men
who are] elders, as I gave you a charge; if a certain man
is such that no charge can be brought against him, a one-
wife kind of a man [that is, married only once], having
children who are believers, who are not such as could be
charged with dissolute living or cannot be subjected to
control; for it is a necessity in the nature of the case
that the overseer be such that no charge can be brought
against him as God's superintendent; not self-willed, not
irascible, not addicted to wine, not pugnacious, not fond
of dishonest gain but fond of showing hospitality, fond of
that which is good, sober-minded, just, holy, self-controlled, holding fast, yes, more than that, paying attention
to the trustworthy Word in accordance with the teaching,
in order that he may be able both to be exhorting in the
teaching which is sound and to be convicting those who
are opposing [Christianity]. For there are many who are
refractory, futile talkers and deceivers, especially those of
the circumcision, whom it is a necessity in the nature of
the case to be reducing to silence, who are of such a
character as to disrupt whole families, teaching things
which they ought not for the sake of dishonest gain. A
certain one of them, a prophet of their very own, said,
Cretans by nature are incessant liars, evil beasts, idle
gluttons.

5-12

13-16   This testimony is true, for which cause be rebuking them severely in order that they may be sound in the Faith, not giving consent to Jewish myths and the commandments of men who are turning themselves away from the truth. All things are pure to those who are pure. But to those who are defiled and unbelieving, not even one thing is pure. But both their mind and conscience are defiled. God they confess that they know but in their works they deny, being abominable and nonpersuasible, and with reference to every good work, disapproved.

1-5   But as for you, be constantly speaking the things which are fitting to sound teaching: that aged men be temperate [in the use of wine], venerable, self-controlled, sound in the Faith, in the love, in the patience; aged women likewise, that they be worthy of reverence in their demeanor, not slanderers, not enslaved to much wine, teachers of that which is good, in order that they may train the young women to be fond of their husbands, to be fond of their children, to be discreet, chaste, workers at home, kind, in subjection to their own husbands with implicit obedience, in order that the word of God may not be reproachfully spoken of.

6-8   The young men likewise be exhorting to be exercising self-control; concerning all things showing yourself [to be] a pattern of good works; in the teaching [exhibiting] incorruptness, gravity, sound speech which cannot be censured, in order that the one who is an opponent may be ashamed, not having one evil thing to be saying concerning us.

9-15   Exhort slaves to be putting themselves in subjection to their own masters with implicit obedience in all things; to give them satisfaction, not crossing them, not pilfering, but showing the utmost trustworthiness, in order that the teaching of God our Saviour they may embellish with honor in all things; for the grace of God bringing salvation appeared to all men, instructing us that denying impiety and worldly cravings we should live discreetly and righteously and piously in the midst of this present age, expectantly looking for the prosperous expectation, even the appearing of the glory of our great God and Saviour, Jesus Christ, who gave himself on our behalf in order that He might set us free from every lawlessness and purify for himself a people of His own private possession, zealous of good works. These things be constantly speaking and exhorting; and be rebuking with every authority. Let no one be despising you.

Be constantly reminding them to put themselves in subjection with implicit obedience to rulers who have been delegated their authority, to be obedient, to be ready to every good work, to be speaking evil of not even one person, to abstain from being contentious, to be sweetly reasonable, satisfied with less than that which is due one, exhibiting every meekness to all men. For we were at one time also foolish, nonpersuasible, deceived, rendering a slave's obedience to variegated passionate cravings and pleasures, in malice and envy passing the time, detestable, hating one another. **1-3**

But when the kindness and fondness of God our Saviour toward man appeared, not by deeds of uprightness which we performed [in our unsaved state], but according to His mercy He saved us, through the washing of regeneration and the renewing of the Holy Spirit whom He bestowed upon us abundantly through our Saviour, Jesus Christ, in order that, having been justified by His grace, we might become heirs according to the expectation of life eternal. **4-7**

Trustworthy is the word. And concerning these things I desire you to be constantly strongly assertive, in order that those who have believed God may be taking careful thought to busy themselves constantly in good works. These things are good and profitable to men. But stupid questionings and genealogies and wranglings and contentions about laws be turning away from and be shunning, for they are without profit and are futile. A heretical person causing divisions, after one or two admonitions be rejecting, knowing that he that is of such a character has been perverted, and keeps on constantly sinning, being self-condemned. **8-11**

12-15   When I shall send Artemas to you or Tychicus, do your best to come to me at Nicopolis, for there I have determined to spend the winter. Zenas the lawyer, and Apollos, diligently set forward on their journey in order that not even one thing be lacking to them. And let those also who are ours learn to busy themselves constantly in good works for necessary needs in order that they may not be unfruitful. All those with me send greetings to you. Greet those who are fond of us in the Faith. The grace be with you all.

Paul, a prisoner of Jesus Christ, and Timothy the brother, to Philemon the beloved and our fellow worker, and to Apphia our sister [in Christ], and to Archippus our fellow-soldier, and to the [local] assembly which meets in your home. [Sanctifying] grace to you and [tranquilizing] peace from God our Father and from the Lord Jesus Christ.

1-3

I thank my God always, remembering you on the occasions of my seasons of prayer, hearing constantly of your love and faith, your faith which you have in the Lord Jesus and the divine and self-sacrificial love which you show towards all the saints, remembering you in my prayer-times, praying that the contribution of your faith, which faith you share in common with other believers, may [through the resultant love which you have for all the saints] become effective in the sphere of a full and perfect experiential knowledge of every good thing in us with a view to [the glory of] Christ.

4-6

I thank my God always, for I had much joy and encouragement on account of your divine and self-sacrificial love, because the hearts of the saints have been cheered and revived through you, brother, and the results of your love are still in evidence. For this reason, though I have much boldness in Christ to be commanding you [to do] your duty, because of [the Christian principle of] love I am rather [saying], I beg of you, please; being such a one as Paul an ambassador but now also a prisoner of Christ Jesus.

7-9

I am imploring you concerning my child [my born-one, my bairn], of whom I became the [spiritual] father while in prison — Onesimus, the one who was once useless to you, but now useful both to you and to me, whom I am sending back to you; it is he himself, that is, [in sending him back to you I am sending] my very heart; whom, as for myself, after mature consideration, I was of a mind to retain with me as a companion in order that in your stead he might keep on ministering to me in my imprisonment for the sake of the good news.

10-13

14-16   But I came to a decision in my heart to do nothing without your consent, in order that your goodness [to me] might not be as it were by compulsion but of your own free will. For perhaps on this account he was parted [from you] for a brief time in order that you might be possessing him fully and forever, no longer in the capacity of a slave, but above a slave, a brother [in Christ], a beloved one, beloved most of all by me, how much more than that by you, both in his human relationship [to you as your slave] and in [his spiritual relationship to] the Lord.

17-21   In view, therefore, of the fact that you hold me as a comrade and friend, one who has the same interests, feelings, and work, receive him into your fellowship as you would receive me. If, as is the case, he wronged you in anything, or owes you something, be charging this to my account. As for myself, I, Paul, append my own signature to this; as for myself, I will pay the damages; not to say to you [though you cannot fairly claim repayment from me] that you owe yourself also to me in addition [since I am your spiritual father in Christ]. Yes, [my] brother [in Christ], as for myself, grant me profit and joy from you in the Lord. Cheer my heart in Christ. Having come to a settled persuasion that you will grant my request, I am writing you, knowing that you will do even beyond the things I say.

22-25   And at the same time also, be putting in readiness a guest room for me, for I am expecting through your prayers to be granted to you.

There greet you Epaphras, my fellow prisoner in Christ Jesus; Mark, Aristarchus, Demas, Luke, my fellow workers. The grace of the Lord Jesus Christ be with your spirit.

In many parts and in different ways God in former times having spoken to the fathers by means of the prophets, in the last of these days spoke to us in One who by nature is [His] Son, whom He appointed heir of all things, through whom also He constituted the ages; who, being the out-raying [effulgence] of His glory and the exact reproduction of His essence, and sustaining, guiding, and propelling all things by the word of His power, having made purification of sins, sat down on the right hand of the Majesty on high; having become by so much superior to the angels as He has inherited a more excellent name than they.

1-4

For to which of the angels did He say at any time, Son of mine you are, I this day have begotten you? and again, I will be to Him as a Father, and He himself shall be to me as a Son? And whenever He shall have brought again the first-begotten into the inhabited earth, He says, And let all God's angels worship Him. And with reference to the angels He says, Who makes His angels spirits, and His servants a flame of fire. But with reference to the Son He says, Your throne, O God, is forever and ever. And the scepter of equity is the scepter of His kingdom. You loved righteousness and hated lawlessness. On this account there has anointed you, God, your God, with the oil of exultant joy above your associates.

5-9

And as for you, in the beginning, O Lord, you laid the foundation of the earth. And the works of your hands are the heavens. They themselves shall perish, but as for you, you remain permanently. And all these shall become old and worn out as a garment. And as a garment which one throws about oneself you will roll them up; as a garment also shall they be changed. But as for you, you are the same, and your years shall have no termination. But to which of the angels has He said at any time, Be sitting at my right hand until I set your enemies down as the footstool of your feet? Are not they all ministering spirits to render service, sent on a commission for the sake of those who are about to inherit salvation?

10-14

1-4   On this account it is a necessity in the nature of the case for us to give heed more abundantly to the things which we have heard lest at any time we should drift past them. For in view of the fact that the word spoken by angels was steadfast, and every over-stepping of the line and neglecting to hear received a just recompense of reward, how is it possible for us to escape if we neglect so great a salvation, which salvation is of such a character as to have begun to be spoken at the first by the Lord, and was confirmed to us by those who heard Him, God also bearing joint-testimony with them, both with attesting miracles and miracles of a startling, imposing, amazement-waking character, and with variegated miracles, and with distributions [of spiritual gifts] from the Holy Spirit according to His will?

5-9   For He did not give to angels the administration of the inhabited earth to come concerning which we are speaking. But one in a certain place testified, saying, What is man that you are mindful of him, or the son of man that you look upon him in order to come to his aid? You made him for a little time lower than angels; with glory and honor you crowned him. All things you put in subjection under his feet. For in that He put all things in subjection under him, He left not even one thing that is not put under him. But now we see not yet all things put under him. But Jesus, made for a little time lower than angels with the design that He by the grace of God should taste death for every man, we see crowned as victor with glory and honor because of the suffering of death.

10-13   For it was fitting for Him, for whose sake all things exist, and through whose agency all things came into existence, when bringing many sons into glory, to make complete [as to His Saviourhood] the originator of their salvation through sufferings. For both He who sets apart for God and His service, and those who are set apart for God and His service, are all out of one source, for which reason He is not ashamed to be calling them brethren, saying, I will declare your Name to my brethren, in the midst of the Church will I sing praise to you. And again,

I will put my trust in Him. And again, Behold, I and the children which God gave me.

Therefore, since the children share in common with **14-18** one another blood and flesh, He himself also partook with them in the same, in order that through the aforementioned death He might render inoperative the one having the dominion of death, that is, the devil, and effect the release of those, as many as who by reason of fear of death through the entire course of their lives were held in bondage. For, as is well known, He does not take hold of angels for the purpose of helping them, but of the offspring of Abraham He takes hold, with a view to succoring them. For this reason it was an obligation for Him in all things to be made like His brethren, in order that He might become a compassionate and faithful High Priest in things pertaining to God, with a view to offering that sacrifice for the sins of the people that would perfectly meet the demands of God's justice. For in that He suffered, having himself been tempted and put to the test, He is able to run to the cry of those who are being tempted and put to the test, and bring them aid.

Wherefore, brethren, set-apart ones for God and His **1-6** service, participants in the [effectual] summons from heaven [into salvation], consider attentively and thoughtfully the Ambassador and High Priest of our confession, Jesus, who is faithful to the One who appointed Him, as also Moses was in his whole house. For this One was counted worthy of more glory than Moses by so much as he who built it has more honor than the house, for every house is built and completely furnished by someone. But the one who built and completely furnished all things is God. And Moses verily was faithful in all his house as a ministering servant holding a position of dignity and confidence, for a testimony of those things which were to be spoken after his time; but Messiah as Son over His house; whose house are we if we hold fast the courageous, fearless confidence and the rejoicing of the hope firm to the end.

Wherefore, as the Holy Spirit says: Today, if His **7-11** voice you will hear, do not go on hardening your hearts

as in the rebellion, in the day of the putting to the test
in the wilderness, when your fathers put me on trial
[and] when they put me to the test for the purpose of
approving me should I meet the test, and saw my works
forty years. Because of this I was angry with this generation, and I said, Always are they being led astray in
their heart. And they themselves did not have an experiential knowledge of my paths. In conformity with which
fact I placed myself under oath in my anger. They shall
not enter my rest.

12-14   Take heed constantly, brethren, lest there be in any
one of you a heart perniciously evil with unbelief in standing aloof from the living God, but be constantly exhorting one another daily, so long as the aforementioned
Today is being announced, lest any of you be hardened
through the stratagem of this sin; for we have become
participators of Messiah and as a present result are participators of Him, [and that is shown] if we hold the
beginning of our assured expectation steadfast to the end.

15-IV 2   While it is being said, Today, if His voice you will
hear, stop hardening your hearts as in the rebellion. For
who, having heard, rebelled? But was it not all who came
out of Egypt through the aid of Moses? But with whom
was He angry forty years? Was it not with those who
sinned, whose dead bodies fell in the wilderness? And to
whom did He swear that they should not enter into His
rest but to those who were nonpersuasible? So we see
that they were not able to enter because of unbelief. Let
us therefore fear lest, a promise at any time being left behind and still remaining of entering into His rest, anyone
of you should think that he has fallen short of it or has
come too late. For, as for us also, to us [first-century
Jews] was the good news [of rest in Messiah] thoroughly
proclaimed, with the present result that we have it indelibly impressed on our minds, as well as the good news [of
rest in Canaan] thoroughly proclaimed to them [the generation which came out of Egypt], good news that was
indelibly impressed on their minds.

But the word of the report did not profit them, not **2-8** having become mixed together with faith in the case of those who heard. For we enter into this rest, we who believed, as He has said, As I swore in my anger, They shall certainly not enter into my rest, although the works from the foundation of the universe had come into being. For He has spoken in a certain place concerning the seventh day thus, And God rested on the seventh day from all His works. And in this place again, They shall certainly not enter my rest. Since, therefore, it remains over [from past times] that certain must enter into it, and they who were first the subjects of the proclamation of the glad tidings did not enter because of disobedience, again, a certain day He designates, Today, speaking by means of David after such a long time, just as it has been said before and is still on record, Today, if His voice you will hear, stop hardening your hearts. For if Joshua had given them rest, then would He not have spoken of another day afterward.

Therefore there remains over a rest for the people of **9-13** God, for the one who entered His rest also himself rested from his works, even as God rested from His own works. Let us give diligence, therefore, to enter that rest, lest anyone fall in the same example of disobedience; for actively alive is the word of God, and energetic, and sharper than any two-edged sword, going through even to the dividing of soul and spirit, and of joints and marrow, and is a sifter and analyzer of the reflections and conceptions of the heart. And there is not a thing created which is hidden from His sight. But all things are naked and laid bare to His eyes, to whom we must give account.

Having therefore a High Priest, a great One, One who **14-16** has gone through the heavens, Jesus the Son of God, let us be holding fast our confession. For we do not have a High Priest who is not able to enter experientially into a fellow feeling with our infirmities, but one who has been tempted and tested in all points like as we are, without sin. Let us be coming therefore with boldness to the throne of grace, in order that we may procure mercy and find grace for seasonable help.

1-4   For every high priest, since he is taken from among
men, on behalf of men is constituted as such with reference to the things which pertain to God, in order that he
may continually be offering both gifts and sacrifices for
sins, who is able to exercise moderate and tender judgment with respect to those who are ignorant [spiritually]
and with respect to those who are being led astray, since
also he himself is completely encircled with [spiritual]
weakness. And because of this [weakness] he is under a
moral obligation, just as with reference to the people, thus
also concerning his own sins, to be offering [sacrifice].
And not to himself does one take this honor, but being
called by God [he accepts it], even as also Aaron.

5-11   So also the Messiah did not glorify himself in becoming a high priest, but the One who said to Him, My Son
you are, I this day have begotten you [this One glorified
Him by constituting Him a high priest]. As He says
also in another place, You are a priest forever after the
order of Melchisedec; who [the Lord Jesus] in the days
of His flesh, offered up special, definite petitions for that
which He needed, and supplications, doing this with
strong cryings and tears to the One who was able to be
saving Him out from within death [i.e., to raise Him out
from the state of death] and was heard on account of
His godly fear. Though He was Son [of God] by nature,
yet He learned obedience from the things which He suffered, and having been brought to the place of completeness [as a Saviour, a High Priest], He became to all
those who obey Him, the One who brought into being
eternal salvation, designated by God a high priest after
the order of Melchisedec; concerning which [teaching,
namely, that the Lord Jesus is a high priest after the
order of Melchisedec] there is much that we can be saying, yet when it comes to the saying of it, one finds it
difficult to explain, because you have become those who
are in a settled state of sluggishness, yes, of stupidity, in
your apprehension of the same.

12-14   In fact, when at this time you are under moral obligation to be teachers by reason of the extent of time [you
have been under instruction], again you are in need of

someone to be teaching you what are the rudimentary things of the very beginning in the oracles of God, and have become and still are such as have need of milk, not of solid food. For everyone whose sole diet is milk, is inexperienced in a message which is righteous in quality, for he is a [spiritually] immature person. But solid food belongs to those who are [spiritually] mature, to those who on account of long usage have their powers of perception exercised to the point where they are able to discriminate between both that which is good in character and that which is evil.

Therefore, having put away once for all the beginning word of the Messiah [the first testament in animal blood, i.e., the Mosaic economy], let us be carried along to that which is complete [the new testament in Jesus' blood], not again laying down a foundation of repentance from dead works, and of faith toward God, of the teaching of ablutions, and of imposition of hands, of a resurrection of the dead, and of eternal judgment [doctrines of the Mosaic economy]. And this will we do if only God permits, for it is impossible in the case of those who have been once for all enlightened, and have both tasted of the heavenly gift and have become companions of the Holy Spirit [willingly being led along towards the act of faith in the pre-salvation work of the Holy Spirit], and tasted the good word of God, also the powers [miracles] of the age that is about to come, and have fallen away, again to be renewing them to repentance, crucifying to themselves the Son of God and putting Him to an open shame. For land which drank in the rain that comes often upon it and produces herbage suitable for those on whose account it is also tilled, partakes of a blessing from God. But if it brings forth thorns and thistles, it is rejected and almost cursed, and its end is burning. 1-8

But we have come to a settled persuasion concerning you, divinely loved ones, the things which are better and which are attached to a saved condition of life, even if we also thus speak. For God is not unjust to forget your work and the divine, self-sacrificial love which you exhibited toward His Name in that you ministered to the 9-16 saints and are continuing to minister. But we are strongly desirous that each one of you exhibit the same diligence which will develop your hope into full assurance until the end, in order that you may become not sluggish, but imitators of those who through faith and patience are now inheriting the promises. For when to Abraham God made promise, since He had no one greater by whom to swear, He swore by himself saying, Blessing, I will bless you, and multiplying, I will multiply you, and thus, having patiently endured, he obtained the promise. For men swear by the greater, and the oath which is for the purpose of confirmation is to them an end of every dispute.

17-20   In [accordance with] which God, more abundantly desirous of demonstrating to those who are inheritors of the promise the immutability of His counsel, interposed with an oath, in order that through the instrumentality of two immutable facts in which it is impossible for God to lie, we might be having a strong encouragement, we who fled for refuge for the purpose of laying fast hold of the hope which is lying before us, which [hope] we are having as an anchor of the soul both stable and steadfast and which anchor enters into the place within the veil, where a forerunner on behalf of us entered, Jesus, having become a High Priest forever after the order of Melchisedec.

1-3   For this Melchisedec, king of Salem, priest of God the Most High, who met Abraham returning from the slaughter of the kings, and blessed him, to whom also Abraham divided a tenth part of all; the first designation on the one hand being interpreted means king of righteousness, and then, on the other hand [he was] also king of Salem which is king of peace, fatherless, motherless, having no genealogy, having no beginning of days nor termination of life, but likened [in these respects in the historical record] to the Son of God, remains a priest continually.

4-10   Now, be giving careful consideration to how great this man was, to whom a tenth part the patriarch Abraham gave of the best part of the booty. And those indeed of the sons of Levi who received the office of priest have a commandment to be taking tithes of the people according to the law, and this [namely, the taking of tithes] from their brethren, even though they have come out of the loins of Abraham. But he who is not genealogically derived from them, has received tithes from Abraham, and the one who has the promises [Abraham] he blessed. Now, it is indisputable that the inferior person is blessed by the superior one. And here, on the one hand, men subject to death are receiving tithes, but there he [Melchisedec] receives them, concerning whom the testimony is that he is living. And so to speak, by the intermediate agency of Abraham also Levi who receives tithes, has paid tithes, for yet in the loins of his father he was when Melchisedec met him.

If indeed, therefore, completeness were through the Levitical priesthood, for the people upon its basis had the law laid down [to them], what need after that should there be of a priest of a different kind arising according to the order of Melchisedec and not being called after the order of Aaron? For there being a transfer of the priesthood [to another order], of necessity also of the law there is a transfer, for He concerning whom these things are being spoken pertained to a different kind of a tribe from which no one gave attendance at the altar. For it is known to all that out of Judah our Lord has arisen, with reference to which tribe, concerning priesthood, not even one thing did Moses say. And it is yet far more obvious that after the likeness of Melchisedec there arises a different kind of a priest, who was constituted [a priest], not according to the norm of a commandment belonging to the realm of human relations, but according to the power of an indissoluble life. For He testifies, As for you, a priest you are forever after the order of Melchisedec. **11-17**

For there is indeed a doing away with a preliminary commandment because of its weakness and unprofitableness, for not even one thing did the law bring to completion; but a bringing in to take its place of a better hope [does], by means of which we are drawing near to God. And inasmuch as not without an oath [was He made **18-22** priest] ; for indeed without an oath they have become priests, but this One with an oath through the agency of the One who says to Him, The Lord placed himself under oath and will not change His mind. As for you, a priest forever you are. By so much was Jesus made a guarantee of a better testament.

23-28   And they indeed have been made many priests in number, because they were hindered from continuing by reason of death. But this [priest], because He is abiding forever, has the priesthood which is untransferable, for which reason also He is able to be saving completely and forever those who come to God through Him, being always alive for the purpose of continually making intercession for them. For such a high priest was also fitting to us, holy, without guile, undefiled, having been separated from sinners and made higher than the heavens; He who does not have a daily need, even as the aforementioned high priests, first to be offering up sacrifices for their own personal sins, then for those of the people, for this He did once for all, having offered up himself [as a sacrifice] ; for the law constitutes men having infirmity high priests, but the word of the oath which was after the law, constitutes One who is in character Son [of God] a High Priest, who has been brought to a state of completion forever [through His sacrificial death].

1-6   Now, in the consideration of the things which are being spoken, this is the chief point: such a High Priest we possess, who took His seat on the right hand of the throne of the Majesty in the heavens, a ministering servant of the holy places, even those of the tent, the genuine one, which the Lord pitched, not man. For every high priest is appointed to offer up both gifts and sacrifices. Wherefore it is necessary that this one also be having that which He might offer. If indeed therefore He were on earth, in that case He would not be a priest, there being those who offer the gifts according to law, who are of such a character as serve the copy and representation of the heavenly things, even as Moses was divinely commanded when about to be completing the tent. For, See, He says, make all things according to the pattern which

was shown to you on the mountain. But now a more
excellent ministry He has obtained, by how much also
He is a mediator of a better testament, which is of such
a character as to have been enacted upon the basis of
better promises.

For if that first testament had been faultless, in that **7-13**
case there would not have been a constant searching out
of a place for a second. For, finding fault with them He
says, Behold, days come, says the Lord, and I will consummate with the house of Israel and the house of Judah
a testament new in quality, not according to the testament
which I made with their fathers in the day when I took
them by the hand to bring them out of the land of Egypt,
because they themselves did not continue true to my testament, and I disregarded them, says the Lord. Because
this is the testament which I will arrange with the house
of Israel after those days, says the Lord, giving my laws
into their mind, also upon their hearts I will write them.
And I will be to them God, and they themselves will be
to me a people. And in no wise shall each one teach his
fellow citizen and each one his brother, saying, Come
to know the Lord in an experiential way, because all shall
know me in an absolute way, from the least to the greatest
of them, because I will be merciful in the case of their
unrighteousnesses, and their sins I will in no wise remember anymore. In the fact that He says, New in quality,
He has permanently antiquated the first. Now, that which
is being antiquated and is waning in strength, is near to
the point of vanishing away.

Then indeed the first testament was having ordinances **1-5**
of divine service, and its sanctuary a sanctuary of the
earth. For a tent was constructed, the first in which was
both the lampstand and the table and the presentation of
the loaves of sacred bread, which [the tent] is of such
a character as to be called the Holy Place. And after the
second veil, a tent which is called the Holy of Holies,
having a golden censer and the ark of the testament over-
laid round about with gold, in which was a golden pot
having the manna, and the rod of Aaron, the one that
budded, and the tablets of the testament, and over it the

cherubim of glory overshadowing the mercy seat, concerning which things we cannot now speak in detail.

6-10   But these things having been thus arranged, into the first tent the priests enter continually, fulfilling the sacred service. But into the second, once a year, alone, the high priest entered, not without blood which he offers in behalf of himself and in behalf of the sins of ignorance of the people, the Holy Spirit all the while making this plain, that not yet was made actual the road into the Holiest while still the first tent had standing [i.e., remained a recognized institution], which [tent] was of such a nature as to be an explanation for the ensuing time, according to which both gifts and sacrifices are being offered which are not able to make complete the one who offers them so far as the conscience is concerned; which [the Levitical system] had its basis only in food and drink and various ceremonial ablutions, ordinances befitting human beings, enjoined until the season of bringing matters to a satisfactory state.

11-14   But Messiah having appeared upon the scene, a High Priest of good things realized, through the instrumentality of the greater and more complete tent not made by hands, that is to say, not of this creation, nor even through the intermediate instrumentality of the blood of goats and calves, but through that blood of His own, He entered once for all into the Holy of Holies, having found and procured eternal redemption. For if, as is the case, the blood of bulls and of goats, and the ashes of a heifer, sprinkling those who are in a state of [ceremonial] uncleanness, set that person apart with reference to the purity of the flesh, how much more shall the blood of the Messiah, who by virtue of the intermediate instrumentality of [His] eternal spirit [His divine essence as deity, thus by His own volition as a member of the Godhead] offered himself spotless to God, purge our conscience from dead works to the serving of the living God.

15-22   And because of this, of a testament new in quality He is mediator, in order that a death having taken place for the redemption of the transgressions under the first testament, those who have been divinely summoned [into salvation] might receive the promise of the eternal inheritance. For where a testament is, a death must of necessity be brought in, the death of the testator, for a testament is of force after men are dead, since it has no strength when the testator is living. From whence it follows that neither was the first testament inaugurated without blood. For after every commandment was spoken by Moses to all the people, he took the blood of calves and of goats, with water and scarlet wool, and hyssop, and sprinkled both the book itself and all the people, saying, This is the blood of the testament which God enjoined to you. Moreover, the tent and all the instruments of the service with blood he likewise sprinkled. And one may almost say that with blood all things are cleansed according to the law. And without bloodshedding there is no remission.

It was therefore necessary on the one hand that the   23-28
representations of the things in the heavens [the earthly tent] should be cleansed constantly with these [animal sacrifices], but on the other hand, the heavenly things themselves with better sacrifices than these [the blood of the Lord Jesus]. For not into holy places constructed by human hands did Messiah enter, which are the types of the genuine [holy places], but into heaven itself, now to be manifested before the face of God on behalf of us. Nor yet [did He enter] in order that He might be offering himself often, even as the high priest enters the holy places every year with blood belonging to another, since then it would have been a necessity in the nature of the case for Him to suffer often since the foundation of the universe. But now at this very time, once in the consummation of the ages, for the putting away of sin through His sacrifice has He been manifested. And inasmuch as it is appointed to men once to die, but after this judgment, thus also the Messiah once was offered for the purpose of bearing the sins of many; a second time apart from sin shall He be manifested to those who eagerly wait for Him [Israel], resulting in salvation.

For the law having a shadow of the good things about   1-7
to be, and not the image itself of the actual things, is

never able by means of the same sacrifices which they are
offering year after year, continually to make those who
come to it complete, since then would they not have ceased
to be offered, because the worshippers once cleansed
would not be having any longer even one compunction
of conscience with respect to sins? But in them [the
sacrifices] there was a calling to mind of sins year by
year, for it is impossible for the blood of bulls and of
goats to be taking away sins. Wherefore, when coming
into the world He says, Sacrifice and offering you did
not desire, but a body you prepared for me. In whole
burnt offerings also for sin you took no pleasure. Then
I said, Behold, I come, in the volume of the book it stands
written concerning me, to do your will, O God.

8-18   Above, when saying, Sacrifice and offering and whole
burnt offerings also for sin you did not desire nor even
have pleasure in, which were of such a nature as those
being offered according to law, then He said, Behold, I
come to do your will. He takes away the first [testament]
in order that He may establish the second [testament], by
means of which will [God's will that His Son should be
the sacrifice for sin] we stand permanently set apart for
God and His service through the offering of the body of
Jesus Christ once for all. And indeed every priest has
stood and continues to remain in that same position, day
by day performing his sacred service and often offering
the same sacrifices which are of such a nature that they
cannot take away sins. But this priest, having offered
one sacrifice for sins, sat down in perpetuity on the right
hand of God, from henceforth expecting until His enemies be set down as a footstool for His feet, for by one
offering He has brought to completion forever those who
are set apart for God and His service. Moreover, there
testifies also to us the Holy Spirit. For after having said,
This is the testament which I will make with them after
those days, the Lord says, I am putting my laws upon
their hearts, and upon their minds I will write them. And
their sins and their lawlessnesses I will positively not
remember any more. Now where a putting away of these
is, no longer is there an offering for sin.

Having therefore, brethren, confidence in the entering
into the Holy of Holies by the blood of Jesus, which
[entrance into] He inaugurated for us, a road freshly
slain and living, through the veil, namely, His flesh, and
having a Priest, a Great One, over the house of God, let
us keep on drawing near with a genuinely true heart in
full assurance of faith, having had our hearts sprinkled
from an evil conscience and having had our body washed
with pure water. Let us constantly be holding fast our
confession of the hope, doing so without wavering, for
faithful is He who promised. And let us constantly be
giving careful attention to one another for the purpose of
stimulating one another to divine and self-sacrificial love
and good works, not letting down on the assembling of
ourselves together, even as the custom of certain is, but
exhorting one another, and so much the more as you are
seeing the day drawing near.

19-25

For if we go on sinning willfully after having received
a full knowledge of the truth, no longer for sins does
there remain a sacrifice, but a certain fearful expectation
of judgment and fiery indignation which is about to be
devouring the adversaries. Anyone who has set aside
Moses' law, without mercy, upon the evidence of two or
three witnesses, dies. By how much do you think shall
he be thought worthy of sorer punishment who has
trodden under foot the Son of God, and has considered
the blood of the testament a common thing by which
[blood] he was set apart for God and His service, and
has insulted the Spirit of grace? For we know the One
who said, To me the meting out of full justice belongs.
I will recompense. And again, The Lord will judge His
people. It is a fearful thing to fall into the hands of the
living God.

26-31

But constantly be recalling the former days in which
after being enlightened, you remained steadfast throughout a great struggle consisting of sufferings, on the one
hand, this, while you were being publicly exposed to
reproach and affliction, and on the other hand, this, while
you made yourselves fellow partakers of those who experienced the same. For you both sympathized with those

32-39

in bonds and accepted with joy the plundering of your goods, knowing in yourselves that you have a better and an enduring possession. Do not throw away therefore your confidence which is of such a nature that it has great recompense of reward, for you have need of patience in order that, having done the will of God, you might receive the promise. For yet a little, a very little while, and He who comes will come and will not delay. Now, my righteous person shall live by faith. But if he draw back in fear, my soul shall have no pleasure in him. But as for us, we are not of the shrinking-back kind who draw back to perdition, but of the believing kind who believe to the end of the saving of the soul.

1-3   Now faith is the title deed of things hoped for, the proof of things which are not being seen. For by means of this [namely, faith] the elders had witness borne to them. By means of faith we perceive that the material universe and the God-appointed ages of time were equipped and fitted by God's word for the purpose for which they were intended, and it follows therefore that that which we see did not come into being out of that which is visible.

4   By faith Abel offered to God a more excellent sacrifice than Cain, through which [sacrifice] it was testified that he was righteous, God bearing witness to his gifts, and through it [the sacrifice], though he is dead, yet he speaks.

5, 6   By faith Enoch was conveyed to another place [namely, heaven], with the result that he did not see death, and he was not found because God had conveyed him to another place [heaven]. For before his removal [from earth to heaven] he had witness borne [to him], that testimony still being on record, to the effect that he pleased God. Now, without faith it is impossible to please Him at all. For he who comes to God must of the necessity in the nature of the case believe that He exists, that He also becomes a rewarder of those who diligently seek Him out.

By faith Noah, having been divinely warned con-   7
cerning the things not seen, with reverential care prepared an ark for the preservation of his household; by
means of which [faith] he condemned the world, and
became an heir of the righteousness which is according
to faith.

By faith Abraham, while he was being called, obeyed   8-12
to go out into a place which he was about to be receiving
as an inheritance, and he went out, not troubling his mind
as to where he was going. By faith he lived as a foreigner
without rights of citizenship in the land of the promise
as in a land not his own, having settled down to live in
tents with Isaac and Jacob, joint-heirs with him of the
promise, the same one, for he was constantly waiting for
and expecting the city having the foundations, the archi-
tect and builder of which is God. By faith Sarah herself
also received power as regards the deposition of seed, and
that when she was past age, because she considered Him
faithful who promised. And therefore there sprang from
one, and this one a dead man, even as the stars of the
heaven in multitude and as the sand beside the lip of the
sea [seashore] innumerable.

These all died dominated by faith, not having received   13-16
the promises, but having seen them afar off and greeted
them, also confessed that they were strangers, even those
who had settled down alongside of a pagan population
upon the earth. For they who say such things as these
declare plainly that they are seeking a fatherland. And
if indeed they had been remembering that country from
which they had gone out, in that case they would have
had constant opportunity to bend their way back again.
But now as the case stands, they are reaching out in their
desires for a better [country], that is, a heavenly one,
because of which God is not ashamed of them to be surnamed their God, for He prepared for them a city.

By faith Abraham offered up Isaac while being put to   17-19
the test; even he who received the promises, offered up
his uniquely begotten, with reference to whom it was said,
In Isaac shall your offspring be called, counting upon the

fact that God also was able to be raising him out from amongst the dead, because of which fact [namely, that Isaac only passed through the likeness of death] he also received him back in the form of a parable [i.e., not actually, for Isaac did not die].

20-22   By faith, and that concerning things to come, Isaac blessed Jacob and Esau. By faith Jacob, when dying, blessed each of the sons of Joseph, and worshipped [leaning] upon his staff. By faith Joseph, when coming near to the end of his life, remembered the exodus of the sons of Israel and so gave a command concerning his bones.

23-29   By faith Moses, having been born, was hid three months by his parents, because they saw that he was a comely child. And they did not fear the mandate of the king. By faith Moses, when he had grown up, refused to be called a son of Pharaoh's daughter, having chosen for himself rather to be suffering affliction with the people of God than to be having sin's enjoyments temporarily, since after weighing and comparing the facts in the case, he considered the reproach of the Messiah greater wealth than Egypt's treasures, for he looked away [from the treasures of Egypt] to the recompense. By faith he abandoned Egypt, not fearing the wrath of the king, for he was staunch and steadfast as seeing the Invisible One. By faith he instituted the passover and the sprinkling of the blood in order that the destroyer of the first-born should not touch them. By faith they passed through the Red Sea as through dry land, which the Egyptians having attempted, were drowned.

30, 31   By faith the walls of Jericho fell, having been encircled seven days. By faith Rahab the harlot did not perish with those who were disobedient, having received the spies with peace.

32-35   And what shall I say yet? For the time will fail me telling of Gideon, Barak, Samson, Jepthae, and both David and Samuel and the prophets, who through faith overcame kingdoms, wrought righteousness, obtained promises, stopped the mouths of lions, quenched the power of fire, escaped the edge of the sword, from weakness were made strong, became mighty in war, turned to flight armies of aliens. Women received by resurrection their dead, and others were tortured, not accepting the deliverance in order that they might obtain a better resurrection.

And still others received a trial of mockings and 36-39 scourgings, yes, moreover, of bonds and imprisonment. They were stoned, tested, sawn asunder; they died, slaughtered by the sword; they wandered around in sheepskins and goatskins; being destitute, hard pressed, maltreated, men of whom the world was not worthy, wandering over deserts and mountains, and in caves and holes of the earth. And these all, although they had witness borne to them through their faith, did not receive the promise, God having provided some better thing for us, in order that they without us should not be brought to completeness.

Therefore also, as for us, having so great a cloud of 1, 2 those who are bearing testimony [i.e., the heroes of faith of chapter 11] surrounding us, having put off and away from ourselves once for all every encumbrance and that sin which so deftly and cleverly places itself in an entangling way around us, with patience let us be running the race lying before us, looking off and away to Jesus, the originator and perfecter of this aforementioned faith, who instead of the joy then present with Him endured the Cross, despising the shame, and has sat down at the right hand of the throne of God.

For consider by way of comparison the One who has 3-8 endured opposition by sinners against himself, in order that you do not become weary, fainting in your souls. Not yet have you withstood to the extent of blood, struggling against sin. And you have completely forgotten the exhortation which is of such a nature as to speak to you as to sons, Son of mine, stop making light of the Lord's discipline, correction, and guidance. Stop fainting when you are being effectually rebuked by Him. For the one whom the Lord loves, He disciplines, corrects, and guides, and He scourges every son whom He receives and cherishes. It is for the purpose of discipline, correction, and guidance that you are enduring. As those who by nature are sons is God dealing with you. For what son is there whom the Father does not discipline, correct, and guide? But if you are without discipline, correction, and guidance, of which all [sons] have been made partakers, it follows therefore that you are bastards and not sons.

9-11   Furthermore, we have been having indeed fathers of our flesh as those who disciplined, corrected, and guided us, and we have been in the habit of giving them reverence. Shall we not much rather put ourselves in subjection to the Father of spirits and live? For on the one hand, they disciplined, corrected, and guided us for a few days upon the basis of that which seemed good to them, but He disciplines, corrects, and guides us for our profit, to the end that we might partake of His holiness. In fact, all discipline, correction, and guidance for the time being does not seem to be joyous but grievous; yet afterward it yields a return of the peaceable fruit of righteousness to those who have been exercised by it.

12-17   Wherefore, the hands which are relaxed and the knees which have become paralyzed, reinvigorate. And be making smooth paths for your feet, in order that that which is limping may not be wrenched out of joint, but rather that it be healed. Be eagerly seeking after peace with all, and holiness, without which [holiness] no one shall see the Lord, exercising oversight [over yourselves] lest anyone be falling away from the grace of God, lest any root of bitterness springing up be troubling you, and through this the many be defiled, lest there be a fornicator, or an irreligious person such as Esau, who in exchange for one bit of food gave up his birthright. For you know that also after that, when desiring to inherit the blessing, he was disqualified, for he did not find a place of repentance [room to repent], even though he sought it [place of repentance] with tears.

18-21   For you have not come to the mountain [Sinai] which might be touched, and that has been set on fire, and to blackness and darkness and tempest, and to a sound of a trumpet, and to a sound of uttered words, concerning which sound those who heard made supplication that there should not be spoken an additional word to them, for they could not bear that which was commanded. And if a wild beast touches the mountain, it shall be stoned. And so terrible was its appearance that Moses said, I am terrified and trembling.

But you have come to Mount Sion, even to the city   22-24
of the living God, heavenly Jerusalem, and to an innumerable multitude of angels, to a festal gathering, and to the assembly of the first-born who are enrolled in heaven, and to God the Judge of all, and to the spirits of just men who have been brought to completeness, and to Jesus, the mediator of a new testament, and to blood of sprinkling which speaks better things than the blood of Abel [i.e., the animal blood which he shed sacrificially].

Constantly be seeing to it that you do not disavow   25-29
Him who is speaking. For if, as is the case, those did not escape who disavowed [any personal relation to] Him that warned [them] upon earth, much rather shall not we escape who are turning away from the One who is speaking from heaven, whose voice then shook the earth. But now He has promised, this promise being on record, saying, Yet once [more] I will shake not only the earth but also the heaven. And this word, Yet once more, makes evident the transferring to a new basis the things that are shaken as of things made, in order that the things that are not shaken might remain [the present universe under the curse of sin changed to the perfect universe of the eternal conditions]. Wherefore, receiving a kingdom which cannot be shaken, let us be having grace, by means of which we might be serving God, well pleasing to Him, doing this with pious care and fear, for our God is a consuming fire.

Let the brotherly affection continue. Of hospitality do   1-4
not continue to be forgetful, for through this [namely, hospitality] some have shown hospitality to angels unawares. Be constantly mindful of those in bonds as

bound with them, of them who are suffering ill-treatment as also yourselves being in a body. Let your marriage be held in honor in all things, and thus let your marriage-bed be undefiled, for whoremongers and adulterers God will judge.

5, 6　　Let your manner of life be without love of money, being satisfied with your present circumstances. For He himself has said, and the statement is on record, I will not, I will not cease to sustain and uphold you. I will not, I will not, I will not let you down. So that, being of good courage, we are saying, The Lord is my helper. I will not fear. What shall man do to me?

7-14　　Be constantly remembering those ruling over you, especially as they are those who spoke to you the word of God, whose faith imitate as you closely observe the outcome of their manner of life. Jesus is Messiah, yesterday and today the same, and forever. Stop being carried away with variegated teachings and teachings foreign to Christianity in that they come from the pagan religions, for it is good when the heart is established by grace, not with foods, by means of which they who ordered their behavior in their sphere were not profited. We have an altar from which they have no right to eat who are serving the tent, for the bodies of those animals whose blood is brought into the Holy of Holies by the high priest concerning sin are burned outside the camp. Wherefore, also Jesus, in order that He might set apart for God and His service the people through His own blood, suffered outside the gate. Therefore, let us be going out to Him outside of the camp, bearing His reproach, for we do not have here an abiding city, but we are seeking that one which is to come.

15-17　　Through Him, therefore, let us be offering sacrifice of praise continually to God, that is, the fruit of lips which make confession of His Name. But to do good and to share with others do not keep on forgetting, for with such sacrifices God is well pleased. Keep constantly obeying your rulers, and constantly be submitting to them; for they themselves are constantly keeping watch over your souls, knowing that they are to give account, that they may do this with joy, not with lamentation, for this would be profitless to you.

Be praying for us, for we are persuaded that we have **18-21** a good conscience, desiring in all things to be conducting ourselves in a seemly manner. Moreover, I beg of you the more earnestly to do this in order that I may be restored to you more quickly. Now the God of peace, the One who brought up out from among the dead the Shepherd of the sheep, the Great One, in the blood of an eternal testament, our Lord Jesus, equip you in every good thing to do His will, doing that in you which is well pleasing in His sight through Jesus Christ, to whom be the glory forever and ever. Amen.

And I beg of you, please, brethren, patiently be per- **22-25** mitting the word of exhortation, for verily I am writing you in few words. Know that our brother Timothy has been released, with whom, if he come quickly, I will see you. Greet all those who have the rule over you, and all the saints. There greet you those from Italy. Grace be with you all.

James, a bondslave of God and of the Lord Jesus Christ, to the twelve tribes, those in the dispersion. Be constantly rejoicing. Consider it a matter for unadulterated joy [without any admixture of sorrow] whenever you fall into the midst of variegated trials which surround you, knowing experientially that the approving of your faith, that faith having been put to the test for the purpose of being approved, and having met the test, has been approved, [that this approving process] produces a patience which bears up and does not lose heart or courage under trials. But be allowing the aforementioned patience to be having its complete work in order that you may be spiritually mature and complete in every detail, lacking in nothing.

And if, as is the case, anyone of you [when undergoing these trials] is deficient in wisdom, let him keep on presenting his request in the presence of the giving God who gives to all with simplicity and without reserve [a pure, simple giving of good without admixture of evil or bitterness], and who does not [with the giving of the gift] reproach [the recipient with any manifestation of displeasure or regret], and it shall be given him. But let him be presenting his request in a trusting attitude, not in an expression of that hesitation which vacillates [between faith and unbelief and inclines toward unbelief], for the person who vacillates [between faith and unbelief] is like the surf of the sea, driven and tossed by the wind; for let not that individual be supposing that he shall receive anything from the presence of the Lord, [being] a dubious, undecided man, vacillating in all his ways.

Moreover, let the brother who is in lowly circumstances [poor and afflicted] be glorying in his exalted position [namely, in the midst of trials which teach him patience]. But the one who is wealthy, let him be glorying in his humiliation [brought on by his trials and resulting in his being reduced to the level of the man who is poor and afflicted], because as the flower of the grass he shall come to an end; for the sun arises with its scorching heat and the grass withers and its flower falls off and the beauty of its appearance is destroyed. So shall also the wealthy person fade away together with his undertakings.

12   Spiritually prosperous is the man who remains steadfast under trial, because after he has met the test and has been approved, he shall receive the crown, namely, that crown which has to do with the life [eternal life], which [crown] He promised to those who love Him.

13-15   Let no man be saying when he is being solicited to sin, By God I am being solicited to sin, for God is incapable of being solicited to sin, the source of the solicitations being evils, [such as soliciting man to sin], and He himself solicits no one to sin. But each one is being solicited to sin when he is taken in tow and enticed by his own craving. Then when the aforementioned craving has conceived, it gives birth to sin, and this sin when it is full grown brings forth death.

16-18   Stop being deceived, my brethren, beloved ones. Every good gift and every perfect gift is from above, coming down from the Father of the lights [the heavenly luminaries], with whom there can be no variableness nor shadow which is cast by the motion of turning [such as that cast by the movements of the heavenly bodies]. In accordance with His deliberate purpose He brought us into being by means of the word of truth, resulting in our being a kind of first fruits of His creatures.

19-21   You know, my brethren, beloved ones, [the aforementioned facts]. Now, let every person be quick to hear, slow to speak, slow with respect to anger, for a man's wrath does not bring about that which is righteous in God's sight. Wherefore, having put away every moral uncleanness and vulgarity and wickedness which is abounding, in meekness receive the implanted Word which is able to save your souls.

22-25   Moreover, keep on becoming doers of the Word and stop being hearers only, reasoning yourselves into a false premise and thus deceiving yourselves, because if, as is the case, anyone is a hearer of the Word and not a doer, this one is like a man attentively considering in a mirror the face with which he was born. For he took one look at himself and was off, and he immediately forgot what sort of a person he was. But he who with eagerness and concentration has pored over the perfect law, the law of liberty, and has continued in it, not having been a hearer who forgets but a doer who works, this person shall be prospered spiritually in his doing.

If, as is the case, anyone imagines himself to be religious, not holding in check his tongue [with bit and bridle], but is deceiving his own heart, this person's religion is worthless. Religion which is pure and undefiled in the sight of God, even the Father, is this: to look after orphans and widows in their affliction with a view to ascertaining their needs and supplying them, and to be keeping one's self unspotted from the world. **26, 27**

My brethren, stop holding your faith in our Lord Jesus Christ, the Lord of the glory, in connection with an act showing partiality [to anyone]. For if there comes into your synagogue [the meeting-place of Christian Jews] a man whose hand is conspicuously loaded with gold rings [and] in brightly shining clothing, and there comes in also a poor man in dirty clothing who is dependent upon others for support, and you look upon the one wearing the clothing which is brightly shining with respectful consideration, and say, As for you, be sitting down here in this place of honor, and say to the poor man, As for you, stand in that place or be sitting down beside my footstool, are you not divided in your own mind [expressing a doubt as to the requirements of the faith you have in the Lord Jesus], and have become judges with pernicious thoughts? **1-4**

Listen, my brethren, beloved ones. Did not God select out for himself those who are poor in the world's estimation to be wealthy in the sphere of faith and heirs of the kingdom which He promised to those who love Him? But as for you, you dishonored the poor man. **5-6a**

6b, 7   Do not those who are wealthy exploit, oppress, and dominate you, and they themselves drag you into lawcourts? Is it not they themselves who revile and defame the honorable name [Christian] which was given you?

8-11   If indeed you fulfill the royal law of the scripture, namely, You shall love with a divine and self-sacrificial love your neighbor as you love yourself, you are doing splendidly. But if, as is the case, you are showing partiality [to certain individuals], you are committing a sin, being effectually convicted by the law as transgressors. For whoever observes the whole law and yet stumbles in one point, he has become guilty of all [the commandments]. For He who said, Do not commit adultery, also said, Do not commit murder. Now if, as is the case, you are not committing adultery, but are committing murder, you have become a transgressor of the law.

12, 13   In this manner be speaking and in this manner be doing, namely, as those who are about to be judged by a law of liberty, for the judgment will be without mercy to the person who did not show mercy; mercy exults in triumph over judgment.

14-17   What profit is there, my brethren, if a person is saying, I am in possession of faith, and he is not in possession of works? The aforementioned faith [namely, that faith which does not result in good works] is not able to save him, is it? If a brother [Christian] or a sister [in Christ] have been poorly dressed for a long time and are lacking in daily food, and one of you says to them, Be going away in peace, be warming yourselves and be feeding yourselves to your utter satisfaction, and you do not give them the things needful for the body, what profit is there? Thus also, the aforementioned faith, if it does not keep on having works, is dead in its very constituent elements.

18-20   But a person will say, As for you, you have faith, and I have works. Prove to me [your actual possession of] the faith you [profess to] possess apart from any accompanying works, and I will prove to you my [actual possession of] faith by my works. As for you, you give credence to [the doctrine] that God is one. You are doing well. The demons also give credence [to that fact] and shudder. But, do you desire to come to know, O senseless man! that the aforementioned faith [that exists] apart from works is unproductive?

Was not our father Abraham vindicated by works   21-23
[justified as to his claim to a living faith] in that he offered his son Isaac on the altar of sacrifice? You see that the aforementioned faith was co-operating and working with his works [and thereby was responsible for their production], and by his works was this faith brought to completion in a well-rounded whole. And the scripture was actually and fully realized [brought into operation] which said, And Abraham believed God, and it [his act of faith] was put to his account for righteousness. And a friend of God he was called.

You see that by works a man is justified and not by   24-26
faith alone. Now, similarly, was not Rahab the prostitute also vindicated [justified as to her possession of a living faith] in that she entertained as guests the messengers and thrust them forth by means of a different way [from that by which they entered the city]? For even as the body apart from breath is dead, so also the aforementioned faith apart from works is dead.

Stop becoming many teachers, my brethren, knowing   1-4
that we shall receive a more severe sentence of condemnation, for with reference to many things everybody stumbles [makes a mistake, goes astray, sins]. If anyone does not stumble in what he says, this one is a spiritually mature man, able to hold in check also his entire body. Now if, as is the case, we put bridles in the mouths of the horses in order that they may be obeying us, we also guide their entire body. Behold also the ships, though they are so large and are driven by strong winds, are guided by a very small rudder wherever the impulse of the steersman leads him.

Even so the tongue also is a small member [of the   5-8
human body] and boasts great things. Behold, how great

a forest a little fire sets ablaze. And the tongue is a fire, the sum total of iniquity. The tongue is so constituted in our members that it defiles the entire body and sets on fire the round of existence and is constantly being set on fire by Gehenna [hell]. For every creature, quadrupeds and birds and reptiles and marine life, is controlled and has been controlled by mankind. But the tongue no one in the human race is able to control. It is a restless, unstable evil, full of lethal poison.

9-12   By means of it we eulogize the Lord, even the Father, and by means of it we curse men who have been made in the image of God. Out of the same mouth there proceeds eulogies and cursings. My brethren, these things ought not thus inappropriately to keep on taking place. The spring does not pour forth out of the same opening the sweet and the bitter [water], does it? A fig tree, my brethren, is not able to produce olives, is it, or a vine, figs? Neither is salt water able to produce sweet water.

13-16   Who is wise and well informed among you? Let him demonstrate from the source of a good and beautiful manner of life his works in meekness, which [meekness] is characterized by wisdom. But if, as is the case, you are having bitter jealousy and contentiousness in your heart, stop boasting and lying against the truth. This wisdom is not the wisdom which comes down from above, but is earthly, unspiritual [having to do with the natural, physical existence as over against the spiritual world of the supernatural], demonic; for where jealousy and contentiousness are, there, in that place, are restlessness and instability and every base deed.

17, 18   But the wisdom which is from above is essentially pure, then peaceable, sweetly reasonable, satisfied with less than its due, compliant, full of mercy and good fruits, impartial, free from insincerity. And the fruit of righteousness is sown in peace for those who make peace.

1-4   From what source do quarrels and conflicts among you come? Do they not come from this source, namely, from your inordinate passions which are struggling with

544

one another in your members? You have a passionate
desire and are not realizing its fulfillment; you murder.
And you covet and are filled with jealousy, and you are
not able to obtain. You engage in conflicts and quarrel.
You do not have because you are not praying for something to be given you. You pray for something to be
given you and do not receive because you pray with evil
intent in order that you may use it [for self-gratification]
in your inordinate passions. O, [spiritual] adulteresses
[untrue to God your husband, O.T. relation of Israel to
God], do you not know that your friendship with the
world is enmity with God? Whoever therefore would desire after mature consideration to be a friend of the
world is [thereby] constituted an enemy of God.

Or, do you think that the scripture says in an empty   5, 6
manner and to no purpose, The Spirit [Holy Spirit] who
has been caused to make His permanent home in us has
a passionate desire [to control us] to the point of envy
[of any control indwelling sin may have over us]? Moreover, He [the Holy Spirit] gives greater grace. For this
reason [in conformity with this] He [the Holy Spirit]
says, God sets himself in battle array against the arrogant
and haughty but gives grace to the humble and lowly.

Be subject with implicit obedience to God at once and   7-12
once for all. Stand immovable against the onset of the
devil and he will flee from you. Draw near to God and
He will draw near to you. Cleanse [your] hands, O
sinners, and purify [your] hearts, O double-minded. Be
sorrowful and distressed and grieve and weep audibly
[over your sins]. Let your laughter be turned to sad-
ness and your joy to gloominess. Permit yourselves to
be humbled in the Lord's presence and He will exalt
you. Stop defaming one another, brethren. He who
defames his brother [Christian] or passes a condemnatory judgment upon his brother [Christian], defames
the law and passes a condemnatory judgment upon the
law. Now, if you pass a condemnatory judgment upon
the law, you are not a doer of the law but a judge. One
only is a lawgiver and a judge, He who is able to save

and to destroy. But as for you, who are you who passes a condemnatory judgment upon your fellow-man?

13-17   Come now, you who are saying, Today or tomorrow we shall proceed to this city and we shall spend a year there and buy and sell and make a profit. You are of the class [of men] that does not know what shall be tomorrow [and] of what character is your life. For you are a mist which appears for a little time and then disappears — instead of your saying, If the Lord so desires it, we shall both live and do this or that. But now you are glorying in your self-deceived and groundless trust in the stability of your life and possessions. All such glorying is pernicious. Therefore, to the person who knows how to be doing good and is not doing it, to him it is sin.

1-6   Come now, O rich men, burst into audible weeping, wailing, and crying aloud, because of your miseries which are coming upon you. Your wealth has rotted away and your garments have become moth-eaten. Your gold and your silver have become completely tarnished and corroded, and their rust shall be for a witness against you, and shall eat your flesh like fire. You stored up treasure in the last days. Behold, the pay of the laborers who mowed your fields which has been withheld by you cries out. And the cries of those who reaped have entered the ears of the Lord of hosts. You spent a luxurious life upon the earth and lived voluptuously. You fattened your hearts in a day of slaughter. You condemned, you murdered the just and upright person, and he does not resist you.

7, 8   Be long-suffering, patiently enduring the mistreatment of others, restraining your soul from the passion of anger, therefore, brethren, until the coming of the Lord. Consider this. The farmer waits with expectation for the precious produce of the earth, patiently waiting, longing and hoping over it, until [that time in which] it [the earth] may receive an early and a late rain. As for you, you also be long-suffering, patiently enduring the mistreatment of others, restraining your soul from the passion of anger. Stabilize your hearts, because the coming of the Lord has drawn near and is imminent.

Stop complaining, brethren, about one another, in order that you may not be judged. Consider this. The judge has taken His stand before the doors. Take the prophets who spoke in the Name of the Lord, brethren, as an example of suffering and of patience under the mistreatment of others. Put your thought upon this. We consider those who patiently remain under their trials spiritually prosperous and fortunate. You heard of the patience of Job, how he patiently remained under the trials to which he was subjected, and you saw the consummation [of those trials] brought about by the Lord, that the Lord is compassionate and merciful.

9-11

But especially, my brethren, stop the practice of putting yourselves under oath, neither by the heaven, nor by the earth, nor by any other oath, but be letting your Yes be Yes and your No be No in order that you may not fall under judgment.

12

Is anyone among you suffering misfortune? Let him keep on constantly praying. Is anyone cheerful? Let him keep on singing praises. Is anyone among you ill? Let him call at once the elders of the [local] assembly, and let them pray over him, having massaged him [with olive oil] in the Name of the Lord. And the prayer offered in faith shall make the sick person well, and the Lord shall raise him up. And if he is in a state of having committed sin [i.e., under the moral or physical consequences of having sinned], it shall be forgiven him. Be confessing therefore your sins to one another for your own benefit, and be praying for one another that you may be healed. A prayer of a righteous person is able to do much as it operates.

13-16

Elijah was a human being of like nature and constitution to us. And he prayed fervently that it might not rain, and it did not rain upon the earth for three years and six months. And he prayed again and the heaven gave rain, and the earth produced its fruit.

17, 18

19, 20   My brethren, if any one among you wanders away from the truth and anyone brings him back, let him be knowing that he who has turned a sinner from the error of his way shall save his soul from death and shall cover up a large number of sins.

Peter, an ambassador of Jesus Christ, to those who have settled down alongside of a pagan population, sown as seed throughout Pontus, Galatia, Cappadocia, Asia, and Bithynia, chosen-out ones, this choice having been determined by the foreordination of God the Father, those chosen out to be recipients of the setting-apart work of the Spirit resulting in obedience [of faith] and [this resulting] in the sprinkling of the blood of Jesus Christ. [Sanctifying] grace to you, and [tranquilizing] peace be multiplied.

1, 2

Let the God and Father of our Lord Jesus Christ be eulogized, who impelled by His abundant mercy caused us to be born again so that we have a hope which is alive, this living hope having been made actual through the intermediate instrumentality of the resurrection of Jesus Christ out from among those who are dead, resulting in an inheritance, imperishable and undefiled, and that does not fade away, which inheritance has been laid up and is now kept guarded in safe deposit in heaven for you who are constantly being kept guarded by the power of God through faith for a salvation ready to be revealed in a last season which is epochal and strategic in its significance.

3-5

In which last season you are to be constantly rejoicing with a joy that expresses itself in a triumphant exuberance, although for a little while at the present time if perchance there is need for it, you have been made sorrowful in the midst of many different kinds of testings in order that the approval of your faith, which faith was examined by testing for the purpose of being approved, that approval being much more precious than the approval of gold which perishes, even though that gold be approved by fire-testing, may be discovered after scrutiny to result in praise and glory and honor at the time of the revelation of Jesus Christ; whom not having seen, you love because of His preciousness, in whom now not seeing yet believing you are to be rejoicing with an inexpressible and glorified joy upon the occasion of your receiving the promised consummation of your faith which is the [final] salvation of your souls.

6-9

10-12   Concerning which salvation prophets conducted an exhaustive inquiry and search, those who prophesied concerning the particular grace destined for you, searching as to what season or character of season the Spirit of Christ who was in them was making plain when He was testifying beforehand concerning the sufferings of Christ and the glories which would come after these sufferings; to whom it was revealed that not for themselves were they ministering these things which now have been reported to you through those who have announced the glad tidings to you by the Holy Spirit who was sent down on a commission from heaven, which things angels have a passionate desire to stoop way down and look into [like the cherubim above the mercy seat who gazed at the sprinkled blood and wondered at its meaning].

13-16   Wherefore, having put out of the way once for all everything that would impede the free action of your mind, be calm and collected in spirit, and set your hope perfectly, wholly, and unchangeably, without doubt and despondency, upon the grace that is being brought to you upon the occasion of the revelation of Jesus Christ; as obedient children, not assuming an outward expression which does not come from your inner being [as a child of God] and is not representative of it, an expression patterned after that expression which you formerly had in the ignorance of your passionate desires, but after the pattern of the One who called you, the Holy One, you yourselves also become holy persons in every kind of behavior, because it has been written and is on record, You be holy individuals, because, as for myself, I am holy.

17-21   And in view of the fact that you call on as Father Him who judges, not with a partiality based upon mere outward appearance, but with an impartiality in accordance with each individual's work, with a wholesome, serious caution order your behavior during the time of your residence as a foreigner [a citizen of heaven living for the time being amongst the unsaved on this earth, which is foreign territory governed by the god of this world], knowing as you do, that not by means of perishable things, little coins of silver and gold, were you set free

once for all by the payment of ransom money, out of and
away from your futile manner of life handed down from
generation to generation, but with costly blood, highly
honored, blood as of a lamb that is without blemish and
spotless, the blood of Christ, who indeed was foreordained
before the foundation of the universe was laid, but was
visibly manifested at the closing years of the times for
your sake who through Him are believers in God, the
One who raised Him out from among those who are dead
and gave Him glory, so that your faith and hope might
be in God.

Having purified your souls by means of your obedi-   **22-25**
ence to the truth, resulting in not an assumed but a
genuine affection and fondness for the brethren, an affection and fondness that springs from your hearts by reason of the pleasure you take in them; from the heart love
each other with an intense reciprocal love that springs
from your hearts because of your estimation of the preciousness of the brethren, and which is divinely self-sacrificial in its essence, having been begotten again not of
perishable seed but of imperishable, through the word of
God which lives and abides; for every kind of flesh is as
grass, and its every kind of glory is as the flower of grass.
The grass was caused to wither away, and the flower fell
off, but the word of the Lord abides forever. And this
is the Word which in the declaration of the good news
was preached to you.

Wherefore, having put away once for all every wick-   **1-5**
edness and every craftiness, and hypocrisies and envies,
and all slanderings, as newborn infants do, intensely yearn
for the unadulterated spiritual milk in order that by it
you may be nourished and make progress in [your] salvation in view of the fact that you tasted that the Lord
is kind, loving, and benevolent; toward whom we are constantly drawing near, himself in character a Living Stone,
indeed by men repudiated after they had tested Him for
the purpose of approving Him, in which investigation
they found Him to be that which did not meet their specifications, but in the sight of God a chosen-out One and
highly honored and precious. And you yourselves also as

living stones are being built up a spiritual house to be a priesthood that is holy, bringing up to God's altars spiritual sacrifices which are acceptable to God through the mediatorship of Jesus Christ.

6-10   Because of this it is contained in scripture, Behold, I lay in Zion a Stone, one chosen out, a Cornerstone, highly honored and precious, and the one who rests his faith on Him shall positively not be disappointed. For you therefore who are believers is the honor and the preciousness [of the Living Stone], but to those who are disbelievers, the Stone which the builders repudiated after they had tested Him for the purpose of approving Him, finding Him to be that which did not meet their specifications, this Stone became a Head Cornerstone, and an obstacle stone against which one cuts, and a rock which trips one, even to those who because they are non-persuasible, stumble up against the Word, to which [action of stumbling] they were indeed appointed. But as for you, you are a race chosen out, king-priests, a set-apart nation, a people formed for [God's own] possession, in order that you might proclaim abroad the excellencies of the One who out of darkness called you into participation in His marvelous light, who at one time were not a people but now are God's people; who were not subjects of mercy, but now have become objects of mercy.

11, 12   Divinely loved ones [loved by God], I beg of you, please, as aliens and those who have settled down alongside of pagan [unsaved] people should, be constantly holding yourselves back from the passionate cravings which are fleshly by nature [fleshly in that they come from the totally depraved nature], cravings of such a nature that, like an army carrying on a military campaign, they are waging war, hurling themselves down upon your soul; holding your manner of life among the unsaved steadily beautiful in its goodness, in order that in the thing in which they defame you as those who do evil [namely, your Christianity], because of your works beautiful in their goodness which they are constantly, carefully, and attentively watching, they may glorify God in the day of His overseeing care.

Put yourselves in the attitude of submission to, thus **13-17**
giving yourselves to the implicit obedience of, every
human regulation for the sake of the Lord, whether to a
king as one who is supereminent, or to governors as those
sent by him to inflict punishment upon those who do evil,
and to give praise to those who do good; for so is the will
of God, that by doing good you might be reducing to
silence the ignorance of men who are unreflecting and
unintelligent; doing all this as those who have their liberty,
and not as those who are holding their liberty as a cloak
of wickedness, but as those who are God's bondmen. Pay
honor to all, be loving the brotherhood, be fearing God,
be paying honor to the king.

Household slaves, put yourselves in constant subjec- **18-20**
tion with every fear in implicit obedience to your absolute lords and masters; not only to those who are good at
heart and sweetly reasonable, satisfied with less than
their due, but also to those who are against you; for this
subjection to those who are against you is something
which is beyond the ordinary course of what might be
expected and is therefore commendable, namely, when
a person because of the conscious sense of his relation
to God bears up under pain, suffering unjustly. For what
sort of fame is it when you fall short of the mark and
are pummeled with the fist, you endure this patiently?
But when you are in the habit of doing good and then
suffer constantly for it, and this you patiently endure,
this is an unusual and not-to-be-expected action, and
therefore commendable in the sight of God.

For to this very thing were you called [namely, to **21-25**
patient endurance in the case of unjust punishment], because Christ also suffered on your behalf, leaving behind
for you a model to imitate, in order that by close appli-
cation you might follow in His footprints; who never in
a single instance committed a sin, and in whose mouth,
after careful scrutiny, there was found not even craftiness; who when His heart was being wounded with an
accursed sting, and when He was being made the object
of harsh rebuke and biting, never retaliated, and who
while suffering never threatened, but rather kept on de-

livering all into the keeping of the One who judges righteously; who himself carried up to the Cross our sins in His body and offered himself there as on an altar, doing this in order that we, having died with respect to our sins, might live with respect to righteousness, by means of whose bleeding stripe [the word "stripe" is in the singular here; a picture of our Lord's back after the scourging, one mass of raw, quivering flesh with no skin remaining, trickling with blood] you were healed, for you were as sheep that are going astray and are wandering about, but now have been turned back to the Shepherd and [spiritual] Overseer of your souls.

1-4   In like manner, wives, put yourselves in subjection to your own husbands with implicit obedience, in order that even though certain ones obstinately refuse to be persuaded by the Word and are therefore disobedient to it, they may through the manner of life of the wives without a word [from the wives] be gained, having viewed attentively your pure manner of life which is accompanied by a reverential fear; let your adornment not be that adornment which is from without and merely external, namely, an elaborate gathering of the hair into knots, and a lavish display of gold ornaments, or the donning of apparel, but let that adornment be the hidden personality in the heart, imperishable in quality, the adornment of a meek and quiet disposition, which is in the sight of God very costly.

5-7   For thus formerly also the holy women, the ones whose hope is directed to and rests in God, were accustomed to adorn themselves, putting themselves in subjection with implicit obedience to their own husbands, as Sarah was in the habit of rendering obedience to Abraham, calling him lord, whose children [namely, Sarah's] you become if the whole course of your life is in the doing of good, and you are not being caused to fear by even one particle of terror. Husbands, in like manner, let your home life with them be governed by the dictates of knowledge, they being the weaker instrument, the feminine, holding in reserve for them particularly honor as to those who are also fellow-inheritors with you of the grace of life, and this, in order that no [Satanic] inroads be made into your prayers.

Now, to come to a conclusion. Be all of you like-minded. Be sympathetic. Have a brotherly affection for one another. Be tender-hearted. Be humble-minded, not giving back evil in exchange for evil, or verbal abuse in exchange for verbal abuse, but instead, on the contrary, be constantly blessing, since for this very purpose you were called, that you might inherit a blessing. For he who desires to be loving life and to see good days, let him stop the natural tendency of his tongue from evil, and the natural tendency of his lips to the end that they speak no craftiness, but let him rather at once and once for all turn away from evil and let him do good. Let him seek peace and pursue it, because the Lord's eyes are directed in a favorable attitude towards the righteous, and His ears are inclined unto their petitions, but the Lord's face is against those who practice evil things.

And who is he that will do you evil if you become zealots of the good? But if even you should perchance suffer for the sake of righteousness, you are spiritually prosperous ones. Moreover, do not be affected with fear of them by the fear which they strive to inspire in you, neither become agitated, but set apart Christ as Lord in your hearts, always being those who are ready to present a verbal defense to everyone who asks you for a logical explanation concerning the hope which is in all of you, but doing this with meekness and a wholesome serious caution, having a conscience unimpaired, in order that in the very thing in which they defame you, they may be put to shame, those who spitefully abuse, insult, and traduce your good behavior which is in Christ; for it is better when doing good, if perchance it be the will of God that you be suffering, rather than when doing evil.

Because Christ also died once for all in relation to sins, a just One on behalf of unjust ones, in order that He might provide you with an entree into the presence of God, having in fact been put to death with respect to the flesh [His human body], but made alive with respect to the spirit [His human spirit], by which [human spirit] also having proceeded, He made a proclamation to the imprisoned spirits who were at one time rebels when the long-suffering of God waited out to the end in the days of Noah while the ark was being made ready; in which eight souls were brought safely through [the time of the deluge] by means of the intermediate agency of water, which [water] also as a counterpart now saves you, [namely] baptism; not a putting off of filth of flesh, but the witness of a good conscience toward God, through the resurrection of Jesus Christ who is at the right hand of God, having proceeded into heaven, there having been made subject to Him, angels, and authorities, and powers.

1-6   Therefore, in view of the fact that Christ suffered with respect to the flesh, you also yourselves put on as armor the same mind, because the one who has suffered with respect to the flesh has done with sin, with a view to his no longer living the rest of his time while in his physical body in the sphere of the cravings of men, but in the sphere of the will of God. For adequate has been the time that is now past and done with for you to have carried to its ultimate conclusion the counsel of the pagans [the unsaved], conducting yourselves as you have done in disgusting sensualities, in cravings, in wine-guzzlings, in carousals, in drinking bouts, and in unlawful idolatries, in which they think it a thing alien to you that you do not run in a troop like a band of revelers with them in the same slough of dissoluteness, speaking evil of you, who [namely, the unsaved] shall give an account to the One who is holding himself in readiness to judge the living and the dead. For, for this purpose also to those who are [now] dead was the good news preached, in order that they might be judged according to men with respect to their physical existence, but live according to God with respect to their spirit existence.

7-11   But of all things the end has come near. Be of sound mind therefore, and be calm and collected in spirit with a view to [giving yourselves to] prayer; before all things in order of importance, having fervent love among yourselves, because love hides a multitude of sins. Show hospitality to one another without murmuring. In whatever quality or quantity each one has received a gift, be ministering it among yourselves as good stewards of the variegated grace of God. If anyone speaks, as utterances of God let them be. If anyone ministers, let him minister as out of the strength which God supplies, in order that in all things God may be glorified through Jesus Christ, in whom there is the glory and the power forever and ever. Amen.

12-14 Divinely loved ones [divinely loved by God], stop thinking that the smelting process which is [operating] among you and which has come to you for the purpose of testing [you], is a thing alien to you, but insofar as you share in common with the sufferings of Christ, be rejoicing, in order that also at the time of the unveiling of His glory, you may rejoice exultingly. In view of the fact that you have cast in your teeth, as it were, revilings because of the Name of Christ, spiritually prosperous [are you], because the Spirit of the Glory, even the Spirit of God, is resting with refreshing power upon you.

15-19 Now, let no one of you continue to be suffering [reproach] as a murderer or a thief or an evildoer or as a self-appointed overseer in other men's matters. But if he suffer [reproach] as a Christian, let him not continue to be ashamed, but let him be glorifying God because of this name, for the time is now, of the judgment beginning at the house of God. But if it start first with us, what shall be the end of those who are not obeying the good news of God? And if he who is righteous is with difficulty being saved, he that is impious and a sinner, where shall he appear? Therefore, also let those who are suffering according to the will of God be constantly committing the safekeeping of their souls by a continuance in the doing of good to a faithful Creator.

1-5 Elders therefore who are among you, I exhort, I who am your fellow elder, and one who saw the sufferings of the Christ and who has been retained as a witness to bear testimony concerning them, who also am a fellow partaker of the glory which is about to be unveiled;

shepherd the flock of God which is among you, doing so not by reason of constraint put upon you, but willingly according to God; not in fondness for dishonest gain but freely, nor yet as lording it in a high-handed manner over the portions of the flock assigned to you, but as becoming patterns for the flock. And when the Chief Shepherd appears, you shall receive the victor's unfading crown of glory. Likewise, younger ones, be in subjection to the elders.

5-14   Moreover, all of you, clothe yourselves with humility toward one another, because God opposes himself to those who set themselves above others, but gives grace to those who are lowly. Permit yourselves therefore to be humbled under the mighty hand of God, in order that you He may exalt in an appropriate season, having deposited with Him once for all the whole of your worry, because to Him it is a matter of concern respecting you. Be of a sober mind, be watchful. Your adversary who is a slanderer, namely, the devil, as a lion roaring in fierce hunger, is constantly walking about, always seeking someone to be devouring. Stand immovable against his onset, solid as a rock in your faith, knowing that the same kind of sufferings are being accomplished in your brotherhood which is in the world. But the God of every grace, the One who summoned you in Christ with a view to His eternal glory, after you have suffered a little while, shall himself make you complete, shall establish you firmly, shall strengthen you, shall ground you as on a foundation. To Him let there be ascribed this power forever and forever. Amen. Through Silvanus, the faithful brother, which is my estimate of him, briefly I am writing to you, exhorting and testifying that this is the true grace of God, in which stand. The [church] in Babylon, chosen out with you, sends greetings; also Mark, my son. Greet one another with a kiss of love. Peace be with you all who are in Christ.

Simon Peter, a bondslave and an ambassador of Jesus Christ, to those who have been divinely allotted like precious faith with us by the equitable treatment of our God and Saviour, Jesus Christ. [Sanctifying] grace to you and [tranquilizing] peace be multiplied in the sphere of and by the experiential knowledge [which the believer has] of God, even Jesus, our Lord. Seeing that all things to us His divine power has generously given, the things which pertain to life and godliness, through the experiential knowledge [which the believer has] of the One who called us [into salvation] by means of His own glory and virtue, by means of which [glory and virtue] there have been generously given to us the precious and exceedingly great promises in order that through these you might become partakers of the divine nature, having escaped by flight the corruption which is in the world in the sphere of passionate cravings. **1-4**

And for this very cause, having added on your part every intense effort, provide lavishly in your faith the aforementioned virtue, and in the virtue experiential knowledge, and in the experiential knowledge self-control, and in the self-control patience, and in the patience godliness, and in the godliness an affection for the brethren, and in the affection for the brethren the divine love; for if these things are your natural and rightful possession, and are in superabundance, they so constitute you that you are not idle nor unfruitful in the experiential knowledge of our Lord Jesus Christ, for he to whom these things are not present is blind, being short-sighted, having taken forgetfulness of the cleansing of his old sins. **5-9**

Wherefore, brethren, exert yourselves the more, and bend every effort to make for yourselves your divine call [into salvation] and your divine selection [for salvation] things that have been confirmed, for doing these things, you will never stumble, for in this way the entrance shall be richly provided for you into the eternal kingdom of our Lord Jesus Christ. **10, 11**

Wherefore, I intend always to be reminding you concerning these things even though you know them and have **12-14** become firmly established in the truth which is present with you. Indeed, I consider it due you as long as I am in this tent to keep on arousing you by means of a reminder, knowing that very soon there is the putting off of my tent, even as also our Lord Jesus Christ gave me to understand.

15-18   Indeed, I will do my best also that on each occasion when you have need after my departure you will be able to call these things to remembrance, for we did not follow out to their termination cleverly devised myths when we made known to you the power and personal coming of our Lord Jesus Christ, but became spectators of that One's magnificence. For having received from the presence of God the Father honor and glory, there was borne along by the sublime glory such a voice, My Son, the beloved One, this One is, in whom I am well pleased. And this voice we heard borne along, out from heaven, when we were with Him in the holy mountain.

19-21   And we have the prophetic word as a surer foundation, to which you are doing well to pay attention as to a lamp which is shining in a squalid place, until day dawns and a morning star arises in your hearts; knowing this first, that every prophecy of scripture does not originate from any private explanation [held by the writer], for not by the desire of man did prophecy come aforetime, but being carried along by the Holy Spirit men spoke words from God who is the ultimate source [of what they spoke].

1-9   But there arose also false prophets among the people, even as also among you there shall be false teachers, who will be of such a character as to bring in alongside [of true doctrine] destructive heresies, even denying the Lord who purchased them, bringing upon themselves swift destruction. And many will follow their licentious conduct to its consummation, on account of whom the way of the truth will be reviled. And in the sphere of covetousness, with fabricated words they will exploit you, for whom from ancient times their judgment has not been idle [i.e., it is being prepared], and their destruction is not sleeping. For, in view of the fact that God did not spare angels who sinned, but having thrust them down into Tartarus, committed them to pits of nether-world gloom, being reserved for judgment, and did not spare the ancient world, but preserved Noah as the eighth person [to be preserved], a proclaimer of righteousness, having let loose the deluge upon the world of those who were destitute of reverential awe towards God, and the cities of Sodom and Gomorrha having reduced to ashes, He condemned them to destruction, having constituted them a permanent example to the ungodly of things about to come; and righteous Lot, completely worn down by the manner of life of the lawless in the sphere of unbridled lust He delivered, for, in seeing and hearing, the aforementioned righteous one, having settled down permanently among them, day in, day out, tormented his righteous soul with their lawless works. The Lord knows how to be delivering the godly out of testing and temptation but to be reserving the unrighteous for the day of judgment to be punished.

But [He knows how to reserve for the day of judgment to be punished] especially those who proceed on their way, hot in pursuit of the flesh [the totally depraved nature] in the sphere of the passionate desire of that which defiles, and who disdain authority. Presumptuous, arrogant, they do not tremble when defaming those in exalted positions. Whereas angels, being greater in power and might, are not bringing against them from the presence of the Lord reproachful judgment. But these, as irrational creatures, having been born as creatures of instinct, [destined] for capture and destruction, uttering blasphemies in the sphere of those things concerning which they are ignorant, shall in their [acts of] destroying surely be destroyed, receiving unrighteousness as the hire for unrighteousness, deeming luxurious living in the daytime a pleasure; moral blemishes and disgraceful blots, reveling in their deceitful cravings while they are feasting with you [at the Christian love-feasts], having eyes full of an adulteress and which are unable to cease from sin, catching unstable souls with bait, having a heart completely exercised in covetousness, children of a curse.

10-16

Abandoning the straight road, they went astray, having followed assiduously the road of Balaam, the son of Bosor, who set a high value upon and thus came to love the hire of unrighteousness, but was the recipient of an effectual rebuke for his own lawlessness; the inarticulate beast of burden, having spoken in a man's voice, restrained the insanity of the prophet.

17-19   These are springs without water, and mists driven by a tempest, for whom the blackness of the darkness has been reserved. For when they are uttering extravagant things that are in their character futile, they are alluring by means of the cravings of the flesh [the totally depraved nature], by means of wanton acts, those who are just about escaping from those who are ordering their behavior in the sphere of error. While they are promising them liberty, they themselves are slaves of corruption. For by whom a person has been overcome with the result that he is in a state of subjugation, to this one has he been enslaved with the result that he is in a state of slavery.

20-22   For if, having escaped the pollutions of the world by an experiential knowledge of the Lord and Saviour Jesus Christ, in these moreover again being entangled, they have been overcome with the result that they are in a state of subjugation, the last things have become to them worse than the first ones; for it were better for them not to have known the way of righteousness than, having known it, to turn back from the holy commandment which was delivered to them. But it has happened to them according to the true saying: a dog returns to his own vomit, and a sow, having been bathed, to its rolling in mire.

1-4   This already, divinely loved ones, is a second letter I am writing to you, in which I am stirring up your unsullied mind by way of remembrance, that you should remember the words spoken previously by the holy prophets and the commandment of the Lord and Saviour spoken by your apostles; knowing this first, that there shall come in the last of the days mockers with mockery, ordering their manner of life according to their own personal desires, and saying, Where is the promise of His coming? For since the fathers fell asleep, all things are remaining permanently in that state in which they were since the beginning of the creation.

For concerning this they willfully forget that heavens existed from ancient times, and land [standing] out of water, and by means of water cohering by the word of God, through which the ordered world of that time, having been deluged by water, was ruined. But the present heavens and the earth by the same word have been stored with fire, being kept so guarded with a view to the day of judgment and misery of men destitute of reverential awe towards God.

5-7

But this one thing, stop allowing it to be hidden from you, divinely loved ones, that one day in the sight of the Lord is as a thousand years, and a thousand years as one day. The Lord is not tardy with regard to the appointed time of His promise, as certain consider tardiness, but is long-suffering toward us, not having it as His considered will that certain should perish, but that all should come to repentance.

8, 9

But there will come the day of the Lord as a thief, in which the heavens with a rushing noise will be dissolved, and the elements being scorched will be dissolved, and the earth also and the works in it will be burned up. All these things in this manner being in process of dissolution, what exotic persons is it necessary in the nature of the case for you to be in the sphere of holy behaviors and pieties, looking for and hastening the coming of the day of God, on account of which [day] heavens being on fire shall be dissolved and elements burning up are being melted.

10-12

But heavens new in quality and an earth new in quality according to His promise we are looking for, in which righteousness is permanently at home. On which account, divinely loved ones, since you are looking for these things, do your best to be found with reference to Him irreproachable and unblamable, in peace. And the long-suf-

13-16

fering of our Lord, consider it as salvation, just as our beloved brother Paul according to the wisdom given to him, wrote to you, as also in all his letters, speaking in them concerning these things, in which letters are certain things difficult of being understood which those who are unlearned and lacking stability distort [from their proper meaning] as also the rest of the scriptures to their own destruction.

17, 18   As for you, therefore, divinely loved ones, knowing [these things] beforehand, be constantly on your guard, lest having been carried away by the error of unprincipled men, you fall from your own steadfastness. But be constantly growing in the sphere of grace and an experiential knowledge of our Lord and Saviour Jesus Christ. To Him be glory both now and to the day of eternity.

That which was from the beginning, that which we have heard with the present result that it is ringing in our ears, that which we have discerningly seen with our eyes with the present result that it is in our mind's eye, that which we gazed upon as a spectacle, and our hands handled with a view to investigation, that which is concerning the Word of the life — and this aforementioned life was made visible, and we have seen it with discernment and have it in our mind's eye, and are bearing witness and bringing back to you a message concerning the life, the eternal life, which is of such a nature as to have been in fellowship with the Father and was made visible to us.

That which we have seen with discernment and at present is in our mind's eye, and that which we have heard and at present is ringing in our ears, we are reporting also to you, in order that as for you also, you may be participating jointly in common with us [in our first-hand knowledge of the life of our Lord]. And the fellowship indeed which is ours, is with the Father and with His Son, Jesus Christ. And these things, as for us, we are writing in order that our joy, having been filled completely full in times past may persist in that state of fullness through present time.

And it is this message which we have heard from Him and at present is ringing in our ears and we are bringing back tidings to you, that God as to His nature is light, and darkness in Him does not exist, not even one particle. If we say that things in common we are having with Him, and thus fellowship, and in the sphere of the aforementioned darkness are habitually ordering our behavior, we are lying, and we are not doing the truth. But if within the sphere of the light we are habitually ordering our behavior as He himself is in the light, things in common and thus fellowship we [the believer and God] are having with one another, and the blood of Jesus His Son keeps continually cleansing us from every sin.

If we say that [indwelling] sin we are not having, ourselves we are leading astray [nobody else], and the truth is not in us. If we continue to confess our sins, faithful is He and just to forgive us our sins and to cleanse us from every unrighteousness. If we say that we have not sinned and are now in a state where we do not sin, a liar we are making Him, and His word is not in us.

1, 2   My little children [born-ones, bairns], these things I am writing to you in order that you may not commit an act of sin. And if anyone commits an act of sin, One who pleads our cause we constantly have facing the Father, Jesus Christ the righteous One. And He himself is an expiatory satisfaction for our sins, and not only for ours but also for the whole world.

3-6   And in this we know experientially that we have come to know Him experientially and are in that state at present, if we are continually having a solicitous, watchful care in safeguarding His precepts by obeying them. He who keeps on saying, I have come to know Him experientially and as a present result am in that state, and His precepts is not habitually safeguarding with solicitous care, is a liar, and in this one the truth does not exist. But whoever habitually with a solicitous care is keeping His word, truly, in this one the love of God has been brought to its completion with the present result that it is in that state of completion. In this we have an experiential knowledge that in Him we are. He who is constantly saying that he as a habit of life is living in close fellowship with and dependence upon Him is morally obligated just as that One conducted himself, also himself in the manner spoken of to be conducting himself.

7, 8   Divinely loved ones, no commandment new in quality am I writing to you, but a commandment, an old one, which you have had constantly from the beginning. The commandment, the old one, is the Word which you heard. Again, a commandment, one new in quality, I am writing to you, which fact is true in Him and in you, because the darkness is being caused to pass away, and the light, the genuine light, already is shining.

He who is saying that in the light he is, and is habitually hating his brother [Christian] is in the darkness up to this moment. He who is habitually loving his brother [Christian] in the light is abiding, and a stumbling block in him there is not. But he who as a habit of life hates his brother [Christian] is in the darkness, and in the sphere of the darkness is habitually ordering his behavior, and he does not know where he is going, because the darkness blinded his eyes.

I am writing to you, little children [born-ones, bairns], because your sins have been put away for you permanently because of His Name. I am writing to you, fathers, because you have come to know experientially the One who is from the beginning, and as a present result are possessors of that knowledge. I am writing to you, young men, because you have gained the victory over the Pernicious One and as a present result are victorious over him. I write to you, little children under instruction, because you have come to know the Father experientially, with the present result that you are possessors of that knowledge. I write to you, fathers, because you have come to know experientally the One who is from the beginning, and are as a present result possessors of that knowledge. I write to you, young men, because you are strong with endowed strength and the word of God in you is abiding, and you have gained the victory over the Pernicious One, and as a present result are victorious over him.

Stop considering the world precious with the result that you love it, and the things in the world. If anyone as a habit of life is considering the world precious and is therefore loving it, there does not exist the Father's love [i.e., the love possessed by the Father] in him. Because everything which is in the world, the passionate desire of the flesh [the totally depraved nature], and the passionate desire of the eyes, and the insolent and empty assurance which trusts in the things that serve the creature life, is not from the Father as a source but is from the world as a source. And the world is being caused to pass away, and its passionate desire. But the one who keeps on habitually doing the will of God abides forever.

18, 19   Little children under instruction, it is a last hour in character. And even as you heard that Antichrist comes, even now, antichrists, many of them, have arisen and are here; from which fact we know by experience that it is a last hour in character. Out from us they departed [doctrinally], but they did not belong to us as a source. For if they had belonged to us, they would in that case have remained with us. But they departed in order that they might be plainly recognized, that all do not belong to us as a source.

20, 21   But as for you [in contradistinction to the antichrists], an anointing you have from the holy One, and all of you have the capacity to know [spiritual truth]. I am not writing to you because you do not know the truth, but because you know it, and because every lie is not out of the truth as a source.

22, 23   Who is the liar if not the one who is denying that Jesus is the Christ? This one is the antichrist, the one who is denying the Father and the Son. Everyone who denies the Son, not even does he have the Father. The one who confesses the Son also has the Father.

24-27   As for you, that which you heard from the beginning, in you let it be constantly abiding. If in you there abides that which from the beginning you heard, both in the Son and in the Father you will abide. And this is the promise which He himself promised us, the life, the eternal life. These things I am writing to you concerning those who are leading you astray. But as for you, the anointing which you received from Him remains in you. And no need are you constantly having that anyone be constantly teaching you. But even as His anointing teaches you concerning all things, and is true and is not a lie, and even as He [the Holy Spirit, the anointing] taught you, be constantly abiding in Him.

28, 29   And now, little children [born-ones, bairns], be continually abiding in Him, in order that whenever He is made visible, we may have instant freedom of speech and not be made to shrink away from Him in shame at His coming and personal presence. If you know in an absolute manner that He is righteous, you know experientially that everyone who habitually does this aforementioned righteousness [which God is], out from Him has been born, with the present result that that one is a born-one.

Behold what exotic [foreign to the human heart] love **1-3** the Father has permanently bestowed upon us, to the end that we may be named children [born-ones, bairns] of God. And we are. On this account the world does not have an experiential knowledge of us, because it has not come into an experiential knowledge of Him. Divinely loved ones, now born-ones of God we are. And not yet has it been made visible what we shall be. We know absolutely that whenever it is made visible, like ones to Him we shall be, because we shall see Him just as He is. And everyone who has this hope continually set on Him is constantly purifying himself just as that One is pure.

Everyone who habitually commits sin, also habitually **4-8** commits lawlessness; and sin is lawlessness. And you know absolutely that that One was manifested in order that He might take away our sins; and sin in Him does not exist. Everyone who in Him is constantly abiding is not habitually sinning. Everyone who is constantly sinning has not with discernment seen Him, nor has he known Him, with the result that that condition is true of him at present. Little born-ones, stop allowing anyone to be leading you astray. The one who habitually does righteousness is righteous, just as that One is righteous. The one who is habitually committing sin is out of the devil as a source, because from the beginning the devil has been sinning. For this purpose there was manifested the Son of God, in order that He might bring to naught the works of the devil.

Everyone who has been born out of God with the **9, 10** present result that he is a born-one of God does not habitually commit sin because His seed remains in him. And he is not able habitually to sin, because out of God he has been born with the present result that he is a born-one of God. In this is apparent who are the born-ones of God and the born-ones of the devil. Everyone who is not habitually doing righteousness is not of God, also the one who is not habitually loving his brother [Christian] with a divine and self-sacrificial love.

11-15   Because this is the message which you heard from the beginning, namely, We should habitually be loving one another with a divine and self-sacrificial love; not even as Cain [who] was out of the Pernicious One, and killed his brother by severing his jugular vein. And on what account did he kill him? Because his works were pernicious and those of his brother righteous. Stop marveling, brethren, if, as is the case, the world hates you. As for us, we know absolutely that we have passed over permanently out of the death into the life, because we are habitually loving the brethren with a divine and self-sacrificial love. The one who is not habitually loving in this manner is abiding in the sphere of the death. Everyone who habitually is hating his brother [Christian] is a manslayer. And you know absolutely that no manslayer has life eternal abiding in him.

16-22   In this we have come to know by experience the aforementioned love, because that One on behalf of us laid down His soul. And, as for us, we have a moral obligation on behalf of our brethren to lay down our souls. But whoever has as a constant possession the necessities of life, and deliberately keeps on contemplating his brother constantly having need, and snaps shut his heart from him, how is it possible that the love of God is abiding in him? Little born-ones, let us not be loving in the sphere of word, nor even in the sphere of the tongue, but in the sphere of deed and truth. In this we shall know experientially that we are out of the truth, and in His presence shall tranquilize our hearts in whatever our hearts condemn us, because greater is God than our hearts and knows all things. Divinely loved ones, if our hearts are not condemning us, a fearless confidence we constantly have facing God the Father, and whatever we are habitually asking we keep on receiving from Him, because His commandments we are habitually keeping with solicitous care, and the things which are pleasing in His penetrating gaze we are habitually doing.

And this is His commandment, namely, We should **23, 24** believe the Name of His Son Jesus Christ, and be habitually loving one another even as He gave a commandment to us. And the one who as a habit of life exercises a solicitous care in keeping His commandments, in Him is abiding, and He himself is abiding in him. And in this we know experientially that He is abiding in us, from the Spirit as a source whom He gave to us.

Divinely loved ones, stop believing every spirit. But **1-3** put the spirits to the test to see whether they are of God and for the purpose of approving them if they are, and finding that they meet the specifications laid down [as to orthodoxy in doctrine], put your approval upon them, because many false prophets are gone out into the world. In this you know experientially the Spirit of God. Every spirit who agrees [to the doctrinal statement] that Jesus Christ has come in the sphere of the flesh [i.e., in incarnation] and still remains incarnate [in human form] is of God; and every spirit who does not confess this aforementioned Jesus [agree to the above teaching concerning Him] is not of God. And this is the spirit of the Antichrist which you have heard that it comes, and now is already in the world.

As for you, out of God you are, little born-ones, and **4-6** you have gained a complete victory over them and are still victors, because greater is He who is in you than he who is in the world. They themselves are out of the world as a source. On this account out of the world as a source they are constantly speaking, and the world listens to them. As for us, out of God we are. The one who is knowing God in an experiential way is listening to us. He who is not out of God is not listening to us. From this we know experientially the Spirit of the truth and the spirit of the error.

7-10   Divinely loved ones, let us be habitually loving one another with a divine and self-sacrificial love, because this aforementioned love is out of God as a source; and everyone who is in this manner habitually loving, out of God has been born with the present result that he is regenerated and knows God in an experiential way. The one who is not habitually loving in this manner has not come to know God, because God as to His nature is love. In this was clearly shown the love of God in our case, because His Son, the uniquely begotten One, God sent off into the world on a mission in order that we may live through Him. In this is the love, not that we have loved God, but that He himself loved us, and sent off His Son, an expiatory satisfaction concerning our sins.

11-16   Divinely loved ones, since in that manner and to that extent did God love us, also, as for us, we are under moral obligation to be constantly loving one another. God in His [invisible] essence no one has ever yet beheld, with the result that no one has the capacity to behold Him. If we habitually are loving one another, God in us is abiding, and His love has been brought to its fullness in us and exists in that state of fullness. In this we know experientially that in Him we are dwelling and He himself in us, because He has given us from His Spirit as a source [spiritual gifts and their operation] as a permanent gift. And as for us, we have deliberately and steadfastly contemplated, and we are testifying that the Father has sent off the Son as Saviour of the world. Whoever agrees with the statement that Jesus is the Son of God, God in him dwells and he himself in God. And as for us, we have known experientially the love which God has in our case, and have that knowledge at present, and we have believed and at present maintain that attitude. God is, as to His nature, love, and he who dwells in the aforementioned love in God is dwelling, and God in him is dwelling.

17-21   In this has been brought to completion the aforementioned love which is in us [produced by the Holy Spirit], which love exists in its completed state, resulting in our having unreservedness of speech at the day of the

judgment, because just as that One is, also, as for us, we
are in this world. Fear does not exist in the sphere of the
aforementioned love. Certainly, this aforementioned love
which exists in its completed state throws fear outside,
because this fear has a penalty, and the one who fears
has not been brought to completion in the sphere of this
love, and is not in that state at present. As for us, let us
be constantly loving, because He himself first loved us.
If anyone says, I am constantly loving God, and is
as constantly hating his brother [Christian], he is a liar.
For the one who is not constantly loving his brother
[Christian] whom he has seen with discernment and at
present has within the range of his vision, God whom he
has not seen with discernment and at present does not
have within the range of his vision he is not able to be
loving. And this commandment we have from him,
[namely], The one who is constantly loving God should
constantly be loving also his brother [Christian].

Everyone who believes that Jesus is the Christ, out 1-5
from God has been born and as a result is His child.
And everyone who loves the One who begot loves the one
who has been begotten out from Him. In this we know
experientially that we are habitually loving the born-ones
of God, whenever God we are habitually loving and His
commandments are habitually obeying. For this is the
love of God, namely, that we are habitually and with
solicitous care guarding and observing His commandments. And His commandments are not burdensome,
because everything that has been born of God is constantly coming off victorious over the world. And this is
the victory that has come off victorious over the world,
our faith. Who is he who is constantly coming off victorious over the world but the one who believes that Jesus
is the Son of God?

This is the One who came through the instrumentality 6, 8
of water and blood, Jesus Christ; not in the sphere of the
water only, but in the sphere of the water and the blood.
And the Spirit is the One who is constantly bearing
witness, because the Spirit is the truth. Because three
there are that are constantly bearing testimony, the Spirit

and the water and the blood. And the aforementioned three concur in the one thing.

9-12   Since the testimony of men we are habitually receiving, the testimony of God is greater, because this is the testimony of God, [namely], that He has borne testimony concerning His Son, and this testimony is on record. The one who believes on the Son of God has the testimony in himself. The one who does not believe God has made Him a liar, and as a result considers Him to be such because he has not believed the testimony which God has given concerning His Son, which testimony is on record, with the result that he is in a settled state of unbelief. And this is the testimony, that life eternal God gave us. And this life is in His Son. The one who has the Son has the life. The one who does not have the Son of God the life he does not have.

13-15   These things I write to you in order that you may know with an absolute knowledge that life you are having, eternal life, to you who believe on the Name of the Son of God. And this is the assurance which we are having toward Him, that if we keep on asking anything for ourselves, [which is] according to His will, He hears us. And if we know with an absolute knowledge that He hears us, whatever we are asking for ourselves, we know with an absolute knowledge that we have the things which we have asked from Him.

16-21   If anyone sees his brother sinning a sin which is not in its tendency towards death, he should ask, and He will give him life, to those who are sinning not with a tendency towards death. There is a sin which tends towards death. Not concerning that one [sin] do I say that he should ask. Every unrighteousness is sin. And there is a sin which does not tend towards death. We know absolutely that everyone who has been born of God and as a result is a regenerated individual does not keep on habitually sinning. But He who was born of God maintains a watchful guardianship over him, and the Pernicious One does not lay hold of him. We know with an absolute knowledge that out of God we are, and the whole world is lying in the Pernicious One. We know with an absolute knowledge that the Son of God has come and is here, and that He has given us a permanent understanding in order that we may be knowing in an experiential way the One who is genuine. And we are in the Genuine One, in His Son, Jesus Christ. This is the genuine God and life eternal. Little children [born-ones, bairns], guard yourselves from the idols.

The Elder, to the selected-out Lady, [selected out by sovereign grace for salvation], and to her born-ones, whom, as for myself, I love in the sphere of the truth [with a love in Christ ministered by the Holy Spirit], and not only I, but also all who have come to know experientially the truth and at present possess a knowledge of it, [whom I love] because of the truth which is continuously dwelling in us, and with us shall be forever. There shall be with us grace, mercy, peace, from the presence of God the Father, and from the presence of Jesus Christ, the Son of the Father, in the sphere of truth and love.

1-3

I rejoice greatly that I have found some of your born-ones conducting themselves in the sphere of the truth, even as a commandment we received from the presence of the Father. And now I entreat you, Lady, not as writing a commandment to you which is new in quality, but that commandment which we have been having continually from the beginning, namely, that we should be habitually loving one another with a divine love sacrificial in its essence. And this is the aforementioned love, namely, that we should be ordering our behavior dominated by His commandments. This is the commandment, just as you heard from the beginning, namely, that in its sphere you should be ordering your behavior. Because many deceivers went forth into the world, those who do not agree [with the teaching] that Jehoshua, [the] Anointed One, sphere of flesh. This one is the deceiver and the antichrist.

4-7

Ever be keeping a watchful eye upon yourselves in order that you do not lose the things we accomplished, but that you receive a full reward. Everyone who goes beyond the limits [of true doctrine] and does not remain in the aforementioned teaching with reference to the Christ does not possess God. The one who remains in the aforementioned teaching, this one possesses both the Father and the Son. If, as is the case, a certain one comes to you and this teaching is not bearing, stop receiving him into your house. And stop giving him greet-

8-11

ing. For the one who gives him greeting is a partner in his works which are pernicious.

12, 13   Having many things to be writing to you, I did not, after giving the matter mature consideration, desire to do so with pen and ink, but I am hoping to be present with you and to speak face to face, in order that our joy, having been filled completely full, might persist in that state of fullness through present time.   There greet you the born-ones of your sister, the selected-out one.

The Elder, to Gaius, the beloved, whom, as for my-self, I love in the sphere of the truth. Beloved, in all things I am praying that you will be prospering, and that you will be continually having good health just as your soul is prospering. For I rejoiced greatly when brethren were constantly coming and bearing witness of your truth, just as, as for you, in the sphere of the truth you are conducting yourself. Greater joy than this I do not have, namely, that I am hearing that my own children are habitually ordering their behavior in the sphere of the truth.

1-4

Beloved, you are doing a work of faith, whatever you are performing for the brethren, and this for strangers, those who bore testimony of your love before the assembly, whom you are doing well to provide with the necessities of travel [assuming the responsibility for their expenses] on their journey in a manner worthy of God; because, for the sake of the Name they went forth, taking not even one thing from the pagans. Therefore, as for us, we ought as a moral obligation to underwrite such as these, in order that we may become fellow workers with the truth.

5-8

I wrote something to the assembly. But the one who is fond of being the pre-eminent one among them, Diotrephes, [the name means "nourished by Zeus," the chief god of the Greeks], is not accepting us. On this account, if I should come, I shall bring to remembrance his works which he has been constantly doing, prating against us with pernicious words, and not being content with these things, neither does he himself accept the brethren; and those who after mature consideration desire to do so, he prevents, and out of the assembly he throws them. Beloved, do not have the habit of imitating the evil, but the good. The one who is in the habit of doing good is out of God. The one who is in the habit of doing evil has not seen God.

9-11

To Demetrius there has been borne testimony by all, and by the truth itself, and this testimony still holds true. And, as for us, moreover, we are bearing testimony. And

12-14

I know positively that our testimony is true. I have been having many things to write to you, but I do not desire to be writing to you with ink and pen. But I am hoping shortly to see you, and face to face we shall speak. Peace be to you. The friends send greeting to you. Be greeting the friends by name.

JUDE

Jude, a bondslave of Jesus Christ and brother of James, to those who by God the Father have been loved and are the permanent objects of His love, and who for Jesus Christ have been guarded and are in a position of being carefully guarded, to those who were divinely summoned [into salvation] individuals. Mercy to you and peace and love be multiplied.

1, 2

Divinely loved ones, when giving every diligence to be writing to you concerning the salvation possessed in common by all of us, I had constraint laid upon me to write to you, beseeching you to contend with intensity and determination for the Faith once for all entrusted into the safe-keeping of the saints. For certain men entered surreptitiously who were of old predicted with reference to this judgment, men destitute of reverential awe towards God, perverting the grace of our God into moral anarchy and lack of self-restraint, and denying the only absolute Master, even our Lord Jesus Christ.

3, 4

Moreover, after mature consideration I desire to remind you, though you know all things once for all, that the Lord, having saved the people out of the land of Egypt, then destroyed those who did not believe. And angels who did not carefully keep inviolate their original position of pre-eminent dignity but abandoned once for all their own private dwelling place, with a view to the judgment of the great day, in everlasting bonds under darkness He has placed under careful guard. Just as Sodom and Gomorrha and the cities about them, in like manner to these [the angels of verse 6], having given themselves over with a complete abandon to fornication, and having gone after a different kind of flesh [from their own, cohabiting with beings of a different nature], are being set forth as an exhibit, undergoing the punishment of everlasting fire.

5-7

In the same manner nevertheless, also these who have visions in dreams [metaphorically, those who are beguiled with sensual images and carried away to an impious course of conduct], defile indeed the flesh, and set at naught authority, and defame pre-eminence. Yet Michael,

8-10

the archangel, when disputing with the devil, arguing concerning the body of Moses, dared not bring a sentence of judgment that would impugn his [original] dignity, but said, May the Lord rebuke you. But these, on the one hand, revile as many things concerning which they do not have absolute knowledge, and, on the other hand, revile as many things by instinct like the unreasoning animals, which they understand, by these they are being brought to ruin.

11-13 Woe to them, because in the way of Cain they took their way, and to the error of Balaam they abandoned themselves for a reward, and in the gainsaying of Kore they perished. These are those individuals who are hidden rocks in your love feasts, sumptuously feasting with you without fear, as shepherds leading themselves to pasture, waterless clouds carried along by winds, autumn trees without fruit, having died twice, rooted up, wild, untamed sea waves, foaming up their own shames, wandering meteors, for whom the blackness of the darkness has been reserved forever.

14-16 And there prophesied also with respect to these the seventh from Adam, Enoch, saying, Behold, there comes the Lord with His holy myriads to execute judgment against all and to effectually convict all those who are destitute of a reverential awe towards God, concerning all their works of impiety which they impiously performed and concerning all the harsh things which impious sinners spoke against Him. These are murmurers, complaining against their lot, ordering their course of conduct in accordance with their own passionate cravings, and their mouth speaks immoderate, extravagant things, catering to personalities for the sake of advantage.

17-19 But, as for you, divinely loved ones, remember the words which were spoken previously by the apostles of our Lord Jesus Christ, that they were saying to you, In the last time there shall be mockers ordering their course of conduct in accordance with their own passionate cravings which are destitute of reverential awe towards God. These are those individuals who cause divisions, egocentric, not holding the spirit [the human spirit, that is, being egocentric, they ignore their human spirit which has to do with the spiritual, religious part of a person's life].

But, as for you, divinely loved ones, building your- **20, 21** selves up constantly in the sphere of and by means of your most holy Faith, and as constantly praying in the sphere of and by means of the Holy Spirit, with watchful care keep yourselves within the sphere of God's love, expectantly looking for the mercy of our Lord Jesus Christ resulting in life eternal.

And on some, on the one hand, be showing mercy, **22, 23** on those who are in doubt; be saving them, snatching them out of the fire; to others, on the other hand, be showing mercy in fear, hating even the undergarment completely defiled by the flesh.

Now, to the One who is able to guard you from stum- **24, 25** bling and to place you before the presence of His glory faultless in great rejoicing, to the only God our Saviour, through Jesus Christ our Lord, be glory, majesty, might, and authority before all time, both now and forever. Amen.

THE BOOK OF REVELATION

A revelation possessed by Jesus Christ, which God [the Father] gave to Him for the purpose of making known to His bondslaves things which in the nature of the case necessarily must come to pass in their entirety shortly. And He made them known, having sent them through the agency of His messenger to His bondslave, John, who is now declaring [in writing] the word of God and the testimony given by Jesus Christ, as many things as he saw. Spiritually prosperous is he who reads in the worship assembly of the local church and spiritually prosperous are those who hear the words of this prophecy and observe the things which in it have been written and are on record, for the strategic, epochal season is imminent.

1-3

John [writing] to the seven assemblies, the ones in Asia. [Sanctifying] grace to you and [tranquilizing] peace, from Him who is and who was and who is coming, and from the seven spirits which are before His throne, and from Jesus Christ, the trustworthy, dependable witness, the first-born of the dead, and the ruler of the kings of the earth. To Him who loves us and set us free from our sins by means of His blood, and who constituted us a kingdom, priests to His God and Father, to Him is the glory and the power forever and forever. Amen.

4-6

Consider this. He comes with the clouds, and every eye shall observe Him with recognition and understanding, also those who were such that they pierced Him. And all the people of the earth shall beat their breasts in anguish because of Him. So is it to be. Amen.

7

As for myself, I am the Alpha and the Omega, says the Lord God, the One who is and who was and who is coming, the Omnipotent One.

8

As for myself, I, John, your brother and fellow-participant in the tribulation and kingdom and patience which are in Jesus, came to be in the island called Patmos because of the word of God and the testimony concerning Jesus [to which I bore witness]. I entered into a different experience in the sphere of the Spirit [His absolute control] on the Lord's day, and heard behind me a voice, a

9-11

great one, like a trumpet, saying, That which you see, write at once in a book and send it directly to the seven [local] assemblies; to Ephesus and to Smyrna and to Pergamos and to Thyatira and to Sardis and to Philadelphia and to Laodicea.

12-16   And I turned around for the purpose of seeing the voice, of what sort it was, that was engaging me in conversation. And having turned around, I saw seven golden lampstands, and in the midst of the lampstands one like a son of man [i.e., human], clothed with a garment reaching to the feet, and a gold belt around Him at the breasts. And His head and His hair were as white wool, white as snow. And His eyes were like a flame of fire. And His feet were like burnished brass when it has been refined in a smelter. And His voice was like a sound of many waters. And He has in His right hand seven stars. And out of His mouth there proceeds a sword, double-edged, sharp. And His face was like the sun when it shines in its strength.

17, 18   And when I saw Him, I fell at His feet like a dead man. And He laid His right hand upon me, saying, Stop fearing. As for myself, I am the first and the last and the living One, and I became dead, and consider this, I am alive forever and forever. And I have the keys of death and of the Unseen.

19   Write at once, therefore, the things you saw, and the things which are, and the things which are destined to take place after these aforementioned things.

20   The mystery of the seven stars which you saw upon my right hand, and the seven golden lampstands. The seven stars are the messengers of the seven assemblies, and the seven lampstands are the seven assemblies.

1-3   To the messenger of the assembly in Ephesus write at once: These things says He who is holding fast the seven stars in His right hand, He who is walking about in the midst of the seven golden lampstands. I know with absolute clearness your works and toil and steadfast endurance and fortitude under trials, and that you are not able to endure evil men, and you have put to the test those who say they are apostles and are not, and you found them to be false. And you have steadfast endurance and fortitude under trials, and you endured [persecution] because of my Name, and you have not become weary.

But I have [this] against you. Your love [for me], that earliest love, you abandoned. Be remembering, therefore, from where you have fallen, and at once have a change of mind, and the early works perform directly — or else I am coming to you and will remove your lampstand out of its place unless you have a change of mind. **4, 5**

But this you do have. You hate the works of the Nicolaitanes which [works] I also hate. He who has ears, let him hear at once what the Spirit is saying to the assemblies. To the person who gains the victory, I will give to him [the right] to eat of the tree of the life which is in the paradise of God. **6, 7**

And to the messenger of the assembly in Smyrna write at once: These things says the First and the Last, He who became dead and lived again. I know with absolute clearness your tribulation and poverty. But you are wealthy. And I know with absolute clearness the slander [against believers] that emanates from those who say they are Jews and are not, but are a synagogue of Satan. Stop being afraid of the things which you are about to be suffering. Consider this. The devil is about to be throwing some of you into prison in order that you may be tested for the purpose of determining what good or evil there may be in you. And you shall have tribulation ten days. Be becoming [increasingly] faithful [through these repeated testings] to the extent of [suffering a martyr's] death, and I will give you the victor's crown pertaining to the life [eternal life]. He who has ears, let him hear at once what the Spirit is saying to the assemblies. He who gains the victory shall positively not be harmed by the second death. **8-11**

12, 13   And to the messenger of the assembly in Pergamos write at once: These things says He who has the sharp, two-edged sword. I know with absolute clearness where you settled down and have your dwelling place: where the throne of Satan is located. Yet you are holding fast my Name and did not deny your faith in me even in the days of Antipas, my witness, my faithful one, who was murdered among you, where Satan settled down and has his dwelling place.

14-16   But I have a few things against you, because you have in that place men holding the teaching of Balaam who taught Balac to place an enticement to sin before the sons of Israel, to eat things sacrificed to idols and to commit fornication. Thus, as for you, you also have men who are holding the teaching likewise of the Nicolaitanes. Therefore, have a change of mind at once. But if you do not, I am coming to you quickly and will war against them with the sword of my mouth.

17   He who has an ear, let him hear at once what the Spirit is saying to the assemblies. To the person who gains the victory, I will give to him the manna, the manna which has been hidden, and I will give him a white stone, and on the stone a name which has been permanently inscribed, new in quality, a name which no individual knows with absolute clearness except the person who receives it.

18, 19   And to the messenger of the assembly in Thyatira write at once: These things says the Son of God, He who has eyes like a flame of fire, and whose feet are like burnished brass. I know with absolute clearness your works and love and faithfulness and ministration and steadfast endurance and fortitude under trials, and your works, which last ones are more than the first.

20-23   But I have this against you. You are tolerating the woman Jezebel who calls herself a prophetess and who teaches and seduces my bondslaves to commit fornication and to eat things sacrificed to idols. And I gave her a respite in order that she might have a change of mind. And she is not desirous of changing her mind so as to

come out of and escape from her [sin of] fornication.
Consider this. I am throwing her into a bed [of tribulation which she will have instead of her bed of fornication]; also those who together with her are participants in the same sin, that of fornication, I am throwing into great tribulation, if they do not have a change of mind so as to come out of and escape from her deeds. Also her children I will kill with death. And all the assemblies shall come to know experientially that, as for myself, I am He who searches minds and hearts. I will give to each of you in accordance with your works.

But to you I am saying, to the rest who are in Thyatira, as many as are not holding this teaching, who are of such a character that they did not come to know experientially the deep things of Satan, as they say; I am not placing upon you another burden. However, that [burden] which you have, hold fast until that time whenever I may come. And he who gains the victory and safeguards my works from violation by performing them until the end [when I come], I will give to him authority over the nations, and he shall shepherd them with an iron scepter; as vessels made of clay they are shattered, as I also have received from the presence of my Father. And I will give him the star, the star of the morning. He who has ears, let him hear at once what the Spirit is saying to the assemblies. 24-29

And to the messenger of the assembly in Sardis write at once: These things says He who has the seven Spirits of God and the seven stars. I know with absolute clearness your works, that you have a reputation that you are alive. And yet you are dead. Be becoming watchful and alert, and stabilize at once the remaining things which were about to die, for I have found no works of yours that have been brought to a state of completeness in the sight of my God. Be remembering, therefore, in what way you have received [the truth as a permanent deposit] and in what way you heard [it], and be safeguarding [it], and have a change of mind at once. If then you do not watch, I will come like a thief, and you will by no means know what kind of an hour I will come upon you. 1-3

4-6   But you have a few names in Sardis who did not defile their garments. And they shall walk [in fellowship] with me in white [garments] because they are worthy. He who gains the victory shall in that manner be arrayed in white garments. And I will positively not erase his name from the scroll of the life. And I will openly confess his name before my Father and before His angels. He who has ears, let him hear at once what the Spirit is saying to the assemblies.

7-9   And to the messenger of the assembly in Philadelphia write at once: These things says the Holy One, He who is genuine, He who has the key of David, He who opens and no one shall shut, and who shuts and no one opens. I know with absolute clearness your works. Consider this. I have given [you] as a permanent possession a door which has been permanently opened, which no one is able to close; because you have but a small amount of power, and you safeguarded my word by carefully observing it, and you did not deny my Name. Consider this. I give [to you] certain ones of the synagogue of Satan, certain ones of those who profess to be Jews and are not, but are lying. Consider this. I will make them that they shall come and prostrate themselves at your feet and offer you their homage and humble respect. And they shall come to know experientially that, as for myself, I loved you.

10   Because you safeguarded the Word by observing it, which to observe requires the endurance which is mine, as for myself, I also will safeguard you from the hour of the trial which is destined to be coming upon the entire inhabited earth to put to the test those who dwell upon the earth.

11-13   I am coming quickly. Be holding fast that which you have in order that no one takes your victor's crown. The one who gains the victory, I will make him a pillar in the inner sanctuary of my God. And he shall by no means go out any more. And I will write upon him the Name of my God and the name of the city of my God, the Jerusalem new in quality which comes down out of heaven from my God, also my Name, the one new in quality. He who

has ears, let him hear at once what the Spirit is saying
to the assemblies.

And to the messenger of the assembly in Laodicea   14-16
write at once: These things says the Amen, the witness
who is trustworthy and dependable, the originating source
of the creation of God. I know with absolute clearness
your works, that you are neither cold nor hot. Would
that you were cold or hot. Thus, because you are luke-
warm and neither hot nor cold, I am about to vomit you
out of my mouth.

Because you are saying, I am wealthy [in this world's   17, 18
goods] and have gotten [spiritual] riches and have need
of not even one thing, and because you do not have a
clear and absolute knowledge of the fact that, as for you,
you are the wretched one and an object of pity, and are
poverty-stricken and blind and naked, I counsel you to
buy from me gold refined in the fire in order that you
may be wealthy, and white garments in order that you
may clothe yourself and in order that your shameful
nakedness may not be made manifest, and eye-salve to
rub on your eyes in order that you may be seeing.

As for myself, as many as I am fond of, I reprove   19-22
so as to bring out conviction and confession, and I
discipline, correct, and guide. Be constantly zealous, therefore, and have a change of mind at once. Consider this.
I have taken my stand at the door and am politely knocking. If anyone hears my voice and opens the door, I will
come in to him, and I will dine with him and he himself
will dine with me. The one who gains the victory, I will
give to him [the privilege and honor] of sitting with me
on my throne, as I gained the victory and sat down with
my Father on His throne. He who has ears, let him hear
at once what the Spirit is saying to the assemblies.

After these things I saw, and consider this, a door in   1-3
heaven that had been opened and now stood open, and the
voice, the first one that I heard, which was like a trumpet,
breaking silence and engaging me in conversation, saying,
Come up here at once, and I will show you things which

must of the necessity in the nature of the case take place after these things. Immediately I found myself to be in [the absolute control of] the Spirit [a continuation of the experience into which John was brought in 1:10]. And consider this. A throne was there in heaven. And there was One seated on the throne. And He who was seated was in appearance like a jasper stone and a carnelian. And encircling the throne there was a ring of light which was like an emerald in appearance.

4, 5 And encircling the throne there were twenty-four thrones, and upon the twenty-four thrones, elders sitting, clothed in white garments, and upon their heads golden crowns of victory. And out from the throne there are proceeding lightnings and voices and thunders. And seven blazing torches are burning before the throne which are the seven Spirits of God.

6-8 And before the throne there was as it were a glassy sea like crystal. And in the midst of the throne and encircling the throne there were four living beings full of eyes in front and in back. And the first living being was like a lion, and the second living being like a calf, and the third living being has the face like that of a man, and the fourth living being was like an eagle when it is flying. And the four living beings have, each one of them, six wings apiece, and are full of eyes round about and within. And rest they do not have day and night, saying, Holy, holy, holy, Lord God, the Omnipotent, He who was and He who is, and He who is coming.

9-11 And whenever the living beings give glory and honor and thanksgiving to the One who is seated on the throne, to Him who lives forever and forever, the twenty-four elders fall down before the One seated on the throne and worship Him who lives forever and forever. And they place their crowns of victory before the throne saying, Worthy are you, our Lord and our God, to receive the glory and the honor and the power, because, as for you, you created all things, and because you willed it, they existed and were created.

And I saw upon the right hand of the One seated on   1-4
the throne a scroll which was inscribed on both sides and
sealed shut with seven seals. And I saw an angel, a
strong one, proclaiming with a great voice, Who is worthy
to open the scroll and to break its seals? And no one was
able in heaven nor even upon earth nor even under the
earth to open the scroll nor so much as to be looking upon
it. And I kept on weeping audibly and profusely because
no one was found worthy to open the scroll and to be
looking upon it.

And one of the elders says to me, Stop weeping. Con-   5, 6
sider this. The Lion of the tribe of Judah, the Scion of
David, gained the victory [and thus is able] to open the
scroll and its seven seals. And I saw in the midst of the
throne and of the four living beings and in the midst of
the elders, a Lamb standing, [in appearance] like a lamb
that has been slain [bearing the wounds of the Cross in
His glorified body], having seven horns and seven eyes
which [eyes] are the seven Spirits of God that have been
sent forth on a commission into all the earth.

And He came, and He has taken the scroll out of the   7-10
right hand of Him who is seated on the throne. And when
He took the scroll, the four living beings and the twenty-
four elders fell down before the Lamb, each one holding
a harp and golden bowls full of incense which are the
prayers of the saints. And they sing a song new in
quality, saying, You are worthy to take the scroll and to
open its seals, because you were slain and you redeemed
to God through your blood [men] out of every tribe and
language and people and nation, and constituted them to
our God a kingdom and priests, and they shall reign as
kings on the earth.

And I saw, and I heard a voice of many angels who   11-14
encircled the throne and a voice of the living beings and
of the elders — and their number was ten thousand times
ten thousand and thousands of thousands — saying with
a great voice, Worthy is the Lamb who has been slain to
receive power and riches and wisdom and might and
honor and glory and eulogy. And every created thing

which is in the heaven and upon the earth and under the earth and upon the sea and all the things that are in them, I heard saying, To Him who sits upon the throne and to the Lamb be the eulogy and the honor and the glory and the power forever and forever. And the four living beings kept on saying, Amen. And the elders fell down and worshipped.

1-4   And I saw when the Lamb opened one of the seven seals. And I heard one of the four living beings saying in a voice like [the sound of] thunder, Be coming. And I saw, and consider this, a white horse. And he who is seated upon it has a bow [but no arrows]. And there was given to him a victor's crown. And he came forth conquering and in order to conquer. And when he opened the second seal I heard the second living being saying, Be coming. And there came forth another horse, flame-colored, blood-red. And to the one seated upon it there was granted [permission] to take the peace from the earth, and that they shall slaughter one another. And there was given to him a great sword.

5-8   And when he opened the third seal, I heard the third living being saying, Be coming. And I saw, and consider this, a black horse. And the one seated on it had a pair of scales in his hand. And I heard as it were a voice in the midst of the four living beings, saying, A choenix of wheat for a denarius, and three of barley for a denarius. And do not begin to damage the olive oil and the wine. And when he opened the fourth seal, I heard the voice of the fourth living being, saying, Be coming. And I saw, and consider this, a pallid horse, greenish-yellow in color. And the one who is seated upon it was named The Death. And the Unseen kept on following with him. And there was given to them authority over one fourth of the earth, to kill with the sword and with famine and with pestilence and by means of the wild beasts of the earth.

9-11   And when he opened the fifth seal I saw under the altar the souls of those who were slain because of the word of God and because of the testimony which they were maintaining. And they cried with a great voice, saying, How long, O Master, the holy One and the dependable One, are you not judging and exacting vengeance for our blood from those who dwell upon the earth? And there was given to each one of them a white robe. And it was told them that they should rest yet for a little time until there shall also be fulfilled [the martyrdom] of their fellow bondslaves and their brethren who were destined to be killed as they themselves also were killed.

And I saw when he opened the sixth seal. And there **12-14** occurred an earthquake, a great one. And the sun became black as sackcloth made of hair. And the entire moon became as blood. And the meteors of the heaven fell to the earth as a fig tree casts its unripe figs when it is being shaken by a strong wind. And the heaven was removed like a scroll when it is rolled up. And every mountain and island were moved out of their places.

And the kings of the earth and the princes and the **15-17** chiliarchs and the rich men and the strong men and every slave and freeman hid themselves in the caves and in the rocks of the mountains, and they say to the mountains and to the rocks, Fall on us at once, and hide us quickly from the presence of Him who is seated upon the throne and from the wrath of the Lamb, because the day, the great day of their wrath has come, and who is able to stand?

After this I saw four angels standing on the four **1-3** corners of the earth, firmly holding the four winds of the earth lest the wind keep on blowing upon the land or upon the sea or upon any tree. And I saw another angel ascending from the rising of the sun, having a seal of the living God. And he cried with a great voice to the four angels to whom there was given [authority] to injure the land and the sea, saying, Do not begin to injure the land nor the sea nor the trees until we shall have sealed the bondslaves of our God upon their foreheads.

And I heard the number of those who were sealed; **4-8** one hundred forty-four thousand were sealed out of every tribe of the sons of Israel. From the tribe of Judah were sealed twelve thousand, from the tribe of Reuben twelve thousand, from the tribe of Gad twelve thousand, from the tribe of Asher twelve thousand, from the tribe of Naphtali twelve thousand, from the tribe of Manasseh twelve thousand, from the tribe of Simeon twelve thousand, from the tribe of Levi twelve thousand, from the tribe of Issachar twelve thousand, from the tribe of Zebulon twelve thousand, from the tribe of Joseph twelve thousand, from the tribe of Benjamin there was sealed twelve thousand.

9-12   After these things I saw, and consider this, a great multitude which no one was able to count, out of every nation and tribe and people and language, standing before the throne and before the Lamb, clothed with white robes, and [having] palm branches in their hands. And they cry out with a great voice, saying, The salvation [is to be ascribed] to our God who is seated upon the throne and to the Lamb. And all the angels were standing in a circle around the throne and the elders and the four living beings. And they fell down before the throne upon their faces and worshipped God, saying, Amen. The eulogy and the glory and the wisdom and the thanksgiving and the honor and the power and the might be to our God forever and forever. Amen.

13-17   And one of the elders answered, saying to me, These who are clothed in the white robes, who are they and from where did they come? And I said to him, My lord, as for you, you know. And he said to me, These are they who come out of the tribulation, the great one, and they washed their robes and made them white in the blood of the Lamb. Because of this are they before the throne of God and render sacred service to Him day and night in His inner sanctuary. And He who is seated upon the throne shall spread a tent over them [to shelter them]. They shall no longer hunger nor even shall they thirst any longer, nor shall the sun nor any scorching heat strike upon them, positively not, because the Lamb in the midst of the throne shall shepherd them and shall lead them to springs of water of life. And God shall wipe away every tear out of their eyes.

And when he opened the seventh seal there came a 1-6
silence in heaven for about one half hour. And I saw the
seven angels who had taken a stand before God and who
were standing there. And there was given to them seven
trumpets. And another angel came and stood over the
altar, holding a golden censer. And there was given to
him much incense in order that he might add it to the
prayers of all the saints upon the golden altar which is
before the throne. And the smoke of the incense went up
together with the prayers of the saints out of the hand
of the angel before God. And the angel has taken the
censer. And he filled it with [the burning coals] out of
the fire on the altar, and he threw them [the burning contents of the censer] into the earth. And there followed
thunders and voices and lightnings and an earthquake.
And the seven angels who have the seven trumpets prepared themselves for the purpose of sounding their
trumpets.

And the first sounded his trumpet, and there followed 7
hail and fire mixed together in [a shower of] blood, and
they were thrown into the earth. And the third part of
the earth was burnt up, and the third part of the trees
was burnt up, and all green grass was burnt up.

And the second angel sounded his trumpet. And [a 8, 9
mass] as large as a great mountain burning with fire was
thrown into the sea. And the third part of the sea became
blood. And the third part of the creatures which were in
the sea died, the ones having life. And the third part of
the ships was destroyed.

And the third angel sounded his trumpet. And there 10, 11
fell out of the heaven a great meteor blazing like a torch.
And it fell upon the third part of the rivers and upon the
springs of the waters. And the name of the meteor is The
Wormwood. And the third part of the waters became
wormwood. And many of the men died by reason of the
waters because they had become bitter.

And the fourth angel sounded his trumpet. And the 12
third part of the sun was dealt a blow, also the third

part of the moon, also the third part of the stars, in order that the third part of these might be darkened, and to the end that the day might not be illuminated for a third part of its duration, and in like manner the night.

13   And I saw, and I heard an eagle flying in mid-heaven, saying with a great voice, Woe, woe, woe to those who are dwelling on the earth because of the remaining voices of the trumpet of the three angels who are about to be sounding their trumpets.

1-4   And the fifth angel sounded his trumpet. And I saw a meteor of the heaven which had fallen into the earth. And to him there was given the key of the shaft leading down to the bottomless place. And he opened the shaft of the bottomless place. And there arose smoke out of the shaft like smoke of a great furnace. And the sun and the lower atmosphere were darkened by reason of the smoke of the shaft. And out of the smoke there came grasshoppers into the earth. And there was given to them power like the power which the scorpions of the earth possess. And it was told them that they should not injure the grass of the earth nor any green [vegetation] nor any tree, only such men as do not have the seal of God on their foreheads.

5, 6   And to them there was given [a charge] that they should not kill them but that they should be tortured five months. And their torture is like the torture of a scorpion when it strikes a man. And in those days the men shall seek death and shall by no means find it. And they shall long to die, and death flees from them.

7-9   And the resemblances of the grasshoppers were similar to those of horses which have been prepared for war. And upon their heads were as it were victor's crowns which resembled gold. And their faces were like the faces possessed by men. And they were having hair like the hair of women. And their teeth were like those of lions. And they were having a breastplate like a breastplate of iron. And the sound of their wings was like the sound of moving chariots, of many horses running into battle.

And they have tails like those of scorpions, and **10-12**
stings. And in their tails there resides the power to injure
the men five months. They have over them as king the
angel of the bottomless place. His name in Hebrew is
Abaddon [the destroyer], and in Greek he has a name,
Apollyon [the destroyer]. The one woe has past. Consider
this. There comes yet a second woe after these things.

And the sixth angel sounded his trumpet. And I **13-16**
heard a voice out of the four horns of the golden altar
which is before God saying to the sixth angel who has
the trumpet, Set free at once the four angels who have
been bound at the river, the great river, the Euphrates.
And the four angels were set free who had been kept in
readiness for the hour and day and month and year in
order that they should kill the third part of the men. And
the number of the armies of the horsemen was two hundred million. I heard the number of them.

And after this manner I saw the horses in my vision, **17-19**
and those seated upon them having breastplates of fire
and of jacinth and of brimstone. And the heads of the
horses were like the heads of lions. And out of their
mouths there proceeds fire and smoke and brimstone. By
these three plagues there was killed the third part of the
men, by the fire and the smoke and the brimstone which
proceed out of their mouths. For the power of the horses
is in their mouths and in their tails. For their tails were
like snakes, having heads. And by means of them they
cause injury.

And the rest of the men, those who were not killed by **20, 21**
these plagues, did not have a change of mind which would
cause them to abandon the work of their hands with the
result that they would not worship the demons and the
idols of gold and silver and brass and stone and wood
which are not able to be seeing nor to be hearing nor to
be walking. Neither did they have a change of mind regarding their murders nor their magical arts nor their
fornications nor their thefts which would cause them to
abandon them.

1-4   And I saw another angel, a powerful one, descending out of the heaven, clothed with a cloud. And the colored halo, shining with a radiance, was over his head. And his face was like the sun. And his feet were like pillars of fire. And he has in his hand a little scroll which was unrolled. And he placed his foot, the right one, upon the sea, and the left one upon the land. And he cried with a great voice just as a lion roars. And when he cried, the seven thunders uttered their own voices. And when the seven thunders uttered [their voices] I was about to begin to be writing. And I heard a voice out of the heaven saying, Place a seal at once upon the things which the seven thunders said, and do not begin to write them.

5-7   And the angel whom I saw standing on the sea and on the land raised his right hand to heaven and placed himself under oath, swearing by the One who lives forever and forever, who created the heaven and the things in it and the earth and the things in it and the sea and the things in it, that there should be no longer any delay or respite, but in the days of the voice of the seventh angel when he is about to begin to be sounding his trumpet, then the mystery of God has been fulfilled, even as He proclaimed [this mystery] as good news to His own bondslaves, the prophets.

8-11   And the voice which I heard out of the heaven I heard again speaking with me and saying, Be going and take at once the scroll, the one that has been opened, which is in the hand of the angel who is standing on the sea and on the land. And I went off to the angel, saying to him that he should give me at once the little scroll. And he says to me, Take it at once and eat it up, and it shall make your stomach bitter, but in your mouth it shall be sweet as honey. And I took the little scroll out of the hand of the angel and ate it up. And it was in my mouth like honey, sweet. And when I ate it, my stomach was made bitter. And they say to me, It is a necessity in the nature of the case for you again to prophesy concerning peoples and nations and languages and many kings.

And there was given to me a reed like a stick, and one said, Be arising and measure at once the inner sanctuary of God [the Holy Place and the Holy of Holies], and the altar, and those who are worshiping in it. But the court which is outside of the inner sanctuary leave out [of your calculations] and do not begin to measure it, because it was given to the nations. And the city, the city set apart for the worship and service of God, they shall trample in contempt and disdain forty-two months. **1, 2**

And I will give [authority] to my two witnesses, and they shall prophesy one thousand two hundred and sixty days, clothed in sackcloth. These are the two olive trees and the two lampstands who have taken their stand before the Lord of the earth. And if, as is the case, anyone desires to injure them, fire proceeds out of their mouth and consumes their enemies. And if, as is the case, anyone shall desire to injure them, in this manner it is a necessity in the nature of the case for him to be killed. These have authority to shut the heaven to the end that no rain may be falling during the days of their prophecy. And they possess authority over the waters to be transforming them to blood and to strike the land with every plague as often as they shall desire. **3-6**

And whenever they finish their testimony, the Wild Beast, the one who ascends out of the bottomless place, shall make war with them and gain the victory over them and shall kill them. And their dead bodies [shall lie] upon the street of the city, the great one, which is of such a character that it is called allegorically Sodom and Egypt, where also their Lord was crucified. And they of the people and tribes and languages and nations keep looking at their dead bodies three days and one-half. And they do not permit their dead bodies to be laid in a tomb. And those who dwell on the earth rejoice over them and make merry. And gifts they shall send to one another, because these two prophets tormented those who live upon the earth. And after three and one half days the breath of life from God entered them, and they stood on their feet. And a fear, a great one, fell upon those who were observ- **7-12** ing them with interest and purpose. And they heard a voice, a great one, out of heaven, saying to them, Come up here at once. And they ascended to heaven in the cloud. And their enemies viewed them with interest and purpose.

13, 14   And at the same hour there occurred an earthquake, a great one. And the tenth part of the city fell. And there were killed in the earthquake seven thousand persons. And the rest became terror-stricken and gave glory to the God of heaven. The second woe is past. Consider this. The third woe is coming shortly.

15-19   And the seventh angel sounded his trumpet. And it came to pass that there were voices, great ones, in the heaven, saying, The kingdom of the world has come into the possession of our Lord and His Christ. And He shall reign as king forever and forever. And the twenty-four elders who are before God, seated on their thrones, fell upon their faces and worshipped God, saying, We give thanks to you, O Lord God, the Omnipotent One, the One who is and who was, because you assumed your great power and reigned as King. And the nations became angry, and your wrath has come, and the time of the dead to be judged, and to give reward to your bondslaves the prophets and to the saints and to those who fear your Name, to the small and to the great, and to destroy those who are destroying the earth. And the inner sanctuary of God, the one in heaven, was opened, and the ark of His testament was seen in His inner sanctuary, and there came lightnings and voices and thunders and an earthquake and a hailstorm, a great one.

1, 2   And there became visible a miraculous portent, a great one in the heaven: a woman arrayed with the sun. And the moon [was] under her feet, and upon her head [was] a victor's crown of twelve stars. And she was with child. And she cried out, suffering birth pangs, in pain to give birth.

3, 4   And there became visible another miraculous portent in the heaven; and consider this, a Dragon, a red one, a great one, having seven heads and ten horns, and upon his heads seven royal crowns. And his tail sweeps away the third of the stars of the heaven, dragging them away by force. And he threw them into the earth. And the Dragon took his stand before the woman about to give birth in order that whenever she would give birth he might destroy her child.

And she gave birth to a son, a male child [i.e., with **5, 6** the peculiar qualities of masculinity-power and vigor], who is destined to be shepherding all the nations with a scepter of iron. And her child was snatched up to God and to His throne. And the woman fled into the uninhabited region where she has there a place which is in a state of readiness, having been so prepared by God, in order that there they might be providing her with food one thousand two hundred and sixty days.

And there arose a war in the heaven. Michael and **7-9** his angels went forth to do battle with the Dragon. And the Dragon fought, and his angels. Yet they did not have the power to win out. Neither was there found any longer place for them in the heaven. And the Dragon, the great one, was thrown down once for all, the snake, the ancient snake, the one called the Devil [slanderer] and the Satan [the adversary], he who deceives the entire inhabited earth. He was thrown into the earth, and his angels were thrown down with him.

And I heard a voice, a great one, in the heaven, saying, **10, 11** Now there has come to pass the salvation and the power and the kingdom of our God and the authority of His Christ, because he who accuses our brethren has been thrown down once for all, he who accuses them before our God day and night. And they themselves gained the victory over him through the blood of the Lamb and through the word of their testimony. And they did not consider their lives precious, and thus come to love them, to the extent of death [they were willing to die a martyr's death].

12   Because of this, be rejoicing, O heavens, and those who are dwelling in them. Woe to the land and the sea, because the Devil went down to you having wrath, a great wrath, knowing that he has [but] a little time.

13-   And when the Dragon saw that he was thrown into
XIII 1 the earth, he persecuted the woman who gave birth to the male child. And there was given to the woman the two wings of the great eagle, in order that she might be flying into the uninhabited region into her place, where she is being provided with food there a time and times and one half a time, [safe] from the presence of the snake. And the snake threw water like a river out of his mouth after the woman in order that he might sweep her away with the river. And the earth went to the help of the woman, and the earth opened its mouth and swallowed up the river which the Dragon threw out of his mouth. And the Dragon was angry with the woman and went off to wage war with the rest of her children, those who keep the commandments of God and have the testimony of [concerning] Jesus. And he stood upon the sand of the sea.

1, 2   And I saw a Wild Beast coming up out of the sea, having ten horns and seven heads, and upon his horns ten royal crowns and upon his heads names, the essence of which is impious and reproachful speech injurious to the divine majesty of deity. And the Wild Beast whom I saw resembled a leopard. And his feet were like those of a bear. And his mouth resembled a lion's mouth. And the Dragon gave him his [the Dragon's] miraculous power and his throne and great authority.

3, 4   And one of his heads appeared to have been mortally wounded, the throat having been slashed. And his death-stroke was healed. And the whole earth followed after the Wild Beast in amazement. And they worshipped the Dragon because he gave the authority to the Wild Beast. And they worshipped the Wild Beast, saying, Who is like the Wild Beast, and who is able to go to war with him?

And there was given to him a mouth speaking great things and things injurious and reproachful to the divine majesty of deity. And there was given him authority to operate forty-two months. And he opened his mouth in a slanderous attack against God, to His face, to defame His Name and His dwelling place, [and] those who dwell in heaven.

5, 6

And there was given to him [permission] to make war with the saints and to gain the victory over them. And there was given to him authority over every tribe and people and language and nation. And they shall worship him, all who dwell upon the earth, [everyone] whose name does not stand written in the scroll of the life [the scroll] belonging to the Lamb who has been slain [in the mind and purpose of God] since the time when the foundations of the universe were laid, and who is looked upon [by God] as the slain Lamb at present.

7, 8

If, as is the case, anyone has ears, let him hear at once. If, as is the case, anyone leads [others] into captivity, he goes into captivity. If, as is the case, anyone kills with a sword, it is a necessity in the nature of the case for him to be put to death by a sword. Here is the endurance and fidelity of the saints.

9, 10

And I saw another wild beast of the same character coming up out of the earth. And he was having two horns like a lamb, but he was hissing like a dragon. And the authority of the first Wild Beast, all of it, he exercises in his sight. And he causes the earth and those who dwell on it to worship the Wild Beast, the first one, whose death-stroke was healed. And he performs great miracles the purpose of which is to attest the divine source of the words uttered by the one performing the miracle, even to the extent that he causes fire to be descending out of the heaven into the earth in the sight of the men. And he deceives those dwelling on the earth by means of the miracles which it was given him to perform in the sight of the Wild Beast, saying to those who are dwelling on the earth that they should make an image of the Wild Beast derived from his likeness, [the Wild Beast] who

11-14

has [scars of] the death-stroke made by the sword and [yet] who came to life [note — he was actually dead].

15-17 And there was given to him [the ability] to give animation to the image of the Wild Beast, to the end that also the image of the Wild Beast should utter words, and that it should cause as many as do not worship the image of the Wild Beast to be put to death. And he causes all, those who are lowly in station and those who are great, and those who are wealthy and those who are poverty-stricken, and those who are freemen and those who are slaves, to be given a mark of identification upon their hand, the right one, or upon their forehead, to the end that no one should be able to buy or sell except he who has the mark of identification consisting of the name of the Wild Beast or the number which stands for his name.

18 Here is wisdom. He who has understanding, let him calculate at once the number of the Wild Beast, for the number is that of man [the human race]. And his number is six hundred sixty-six.

1-5 And I saw, and consider this, the Lamb standing on the hill of Zion, and with Him one hundred forty-four thousand having His Name and the Name of His Father permanently inscribed on their foreheads. And I heard a voice out of the heaven like a sound of many waters and like a sound of great thunder. And the sound which I heard was like that of harpists playing upon their harps. And they are singing a song new in quality before the throne and before the four living beings and the elders. And no one was able to learn the song except the one hundred forty-four thousand, those who had been redeemed out from the earth. These are they who were not defiled with women [in any illicit way], for they are chaste individuals. These are they who follow with the Lamb wherever He may be going. These were redeemed from among men, first fruits to God and the Lamb. And in their mouth was not found a lie. They are without blemish.

And I saw another angel flying in mid-heaven, having a message of good news eternal in its character to proclaim as glad tidings to those who live upon the earth, and to every nation and tribe and language and people, saying with a great voice, Fear God at once and at once give Him glory, because the hour of His judgment has come, and worship Him at once who made the heaven and the earth and sea and springs of waters. And another angel, a second one, followed, saying, It has fallen, it has fallen, Babylon the Great, which has caused all the nations to drink of the wine of her fornication and the wrath [of God which accompanies it as its retribution].

6-8

And another angel, a third one, followed them, saying with a great voice, If, as is the case, anyone worships the Wild Beast and his image, and receives a mark of identification upon his forehead or upon his hand, he shall also himself drink of the wine of the wrath of God which has been poured out unmixed in the cup of His anger. And he shall be tormented with fire and brimstone in the presence of holy angels and in the presence of the Lamb. And the smoke of [connected with] their torment ascends forever and forever. And they do not have rest day and night, those who worship the Wild Beast and his image, also, as is the case, if anyone receives the mark of identification which consists of his name. Here is the endurance of the saints, [namely] those who keep the commandments of God and the faith [which they have] in Jesus. And I heard a voice out of the heaven saying, Write at once, Spiritually prosperous are the dead who die in the Lord from this time forth; Yes, says the Spirit, to the end that they may rest from their labors, for their works accompany them.

9-13

And I saw, and consider this, a cloud, a white one, and upon the cloud one sitting, in appearance like a son of man [i.e., human in appearance], having upon His head a crown of victory, a golden one, and in His hand a sickle, a sharp one. And another angel came out of the inner sanctuary, crying with a great voice to Him who is seated on the cloud, Thrust in your sickle at once and reap quickly, because the hour to reap has come, for the

14-16

reason that the harvest of the earth has become dry and thus perfectly ripe. And He who is seated on the cloud thrust His sickle upon the earth, and the earth was reaped.

17-20   And another angel came out of the inner sanctuary, the sanctuary in heaven, having also himself a sickle, a sharp one. And another angel came out of the altar who has authority over the fire. And he cried with a great voice to the one who has the sharp sickle, saying, Thrust in your sharp sickle at once and gather at once the bunches of grapes of the vine of the earth, for its bunches of grapes have become ripe. And the angel thrust his sickle into the earth, and he gathered the vintage of the earth and threw it into the wine press of the wrath of God, the great wine press. And the wine press was trodden outside of the city. And there came out of the wine press blood as far as to the bridles of the horses, to a distance of one thousand six hundred stades.

1, 2   And I saw another supernatural portent, an attesting miracle, in the heaven, a great and marvelous one; seven angels having seven plagues, the final ones, final, because in them has been brought to its intended end the wrath of God. And I saw something resembling a glassy sea mingled with fire, and those who have come off triumphantly out of the [meshes] of the Wild Beast and his image and the number which signifies his name, standing on the glassy sea, having harps of God.

3, 4   And they are singing the song of Moses, the bond-slave of God, and the song of the Lamb, saying, Great and marvelous are your works, O Lord God, Omnipotent. Just and dependable are your ways, O King of the nations. Who shall not fear, O Lord, and glorify your Name? because you only are holy, for all the nations shall come and worship before you, for your judicial acts characterized by righteousness have been shown openly.

5-8   And after these things I saw, and there was opened the inner sanctuary of the tent of the testimony in heaven. And there came out of the inner sanctuary the seven angels, the ones having the seven plagues, arrayed in linen, clean, shining, and girded around the breasts with golden girdles. And one of the four living beings gave to the seven angels seven golden bowls filled with the wrath of God who lives forever and forever. And the inner sanctuary was filled with the smoke [arising] from the glory of God and from His might. And no one was able to enter the inner sanctuary until the seven plagues of the seven angels should be brought to an end.

And I heard a great voice out of the inner sanctuary **1-7** saying to the seven angels, Be going on your ways and be pouring out the seven bowls of the wrath of God into the earth. And the first went off and poured out his bowl into the earth. And there came a foul and pernicious suppurated sore upon the men who have the mark of identification of the Wild Beast and who worship his image. And the second poured out his bowl into the sea. And it became blood like that of a corpse. And every living creature died, the things in the sea. And the third poured out his bowl into the rivers and springs of the waters. And they became blood. And I heard the angel of the waters saying, You are just, [you who are] the One who is and who was, the Holy One, because you administered justice in the case of these things, for they poured out saints' and prophets' blood, and blood to them you have given to drink. They are those who deserve this. And I heard the altar saying, Yes, O Lord God, Omnipotent, dependable and just are your judgments.

And the fourth poured out his bowl upon the sun. **8-12** And there was given to him [the power] to burn the men with fire. And the men were burned with a great scorching heat. And they reviled the Name of the God who has the power over these plagues, reviling Him with impious and reproachful speech injurious to His divine majesty. And they did not have a change of mind with the result that they would give Him glory. And the fifth poured out his bowl upon the throne of the Wild Beast. And it came to pass that his kingdom was darkened, and they chewed their tongues because of the pain. And they reviled the God of heaven because of their pains and because of their sores with impious and reproachful speech injurious to His divine majesty, and did not have a change of mind with reference to their works which would cause them to abandon them. And the sixth poured out his bowl upon the river, the great Euphrates. And its water was dried up in order that the road of the kings from the sunrising might be prepared.

13-16 And I saw [come] out of the mouth of the Dragon and out of the mouth of the Wild Beast and out of the mouth of the False Prophet, spirits [free moral intelligences without a physical body], three of them, unclean, [in appearance] like frogs, for they are spirits of demons performing attesting miracles, which [spirits] go out to the kings of the whole inhabited earth for the purpose of gathering them together for the war of the great day of God, the Omnipotent. Consider this. I come like a thief. Spiritually prosperous is he who is on the alert and who keeps his garments lest he be walking about unclad and they be observing his shame. And they gathered them together to the place which is called in Hebrew, Armageddon.

17, 18 And the seventh poured his bowl upon the lower atmosphere. And there came out a great voice out of the inner sanctuary from the throne saying, It has come to pass and is now an accomplished fact. And there came lightnings and voices and thunders, and there came an earthquake, a great one of such a nature that an earthquake of that kind has not occurred since the time man came to be upon the earth, so mighty an earthquake, so great.

19-21 And the city, the great one, was divided into three parts. And the cities of the nations fell. And Babylon the Great was remembered before God for the purpose of giving her the cup of the wine of the fury of His wrath. And every island vanished. And mountains were not found. And a hail, a great one, [each hailstone] having the weight of a talent descends out of heaven upon the men. And the men reviled God with impious and reproachful speech injurious to the divine majesty of deity because of the plague of the hail, for the blow [it inflicted] is great, very great.

And there came one of the seven angels who have the seven bowls. And he spoke with me, saying, Come here. I will show you the condemnation and punishment of the prostitute, the great one, who is sitting on many waters, with whom the kings of the earth committed fornication; and those who dwell on the earth were made drunken by the wine of her fornication. And he carried me away into an uninhabited place in [my] spirit. And I saw a woman sitting on a Wild Beast, a scarlet one, filled with names reproachful and injurious to the divine majesty of deity, having seven heads and ten horns. And the woman was arrayed in purple and scarlet, and was adorned with gold and precious stone and pearls, having a golden cup in her hand filled with abominations and the unclean things of her fornication. And on her forehead a name has been written in a permanent inscription, Mystery, Babylon the Great, the Mother of Prostitutes and of the Abominations of the Earth. **1-5**

And I saw the woman intoxicated, the source of her intoxication being the blood of the saints and the blood of the martyrs of Jesus. And I wondered, seeing the woman, with a great wonder. And the angel said to me, Why did you wonder? As for myself, I will tell you the mystery of the woman and of the Wild Beast who is carrying her who [the Wild Beast] has the seven heads and the ten horns. The Wild Beast whom you saw was, and is not, and is destined to be ascending out of the bottomless place, and he goes off into perdition. And those who dwell on the earth shall wonder, whose names have not been permanently inscribed upon the scroll of the life from the time of the foundation of the universe, when they see the Wild Beast, how that he was and is not and shall come. **6-8**

Here is the intelligence that has wisdom. The seven heads are seven hills. The woman is seated upon them. **9, 10**

And there are seven kings. The five fell. The one is. The other one has not yet come. And whenever he comes it is a necessity in the nature of the case for him to continue for a brief time.

11-14   And the Wild Beast who was and is not is himself also an eighth [king], and is out of the seven as a source. And into perdition he goes off. And the ten horns which you saw are ten kings of the kind which did not yet receive royal power, but they will receive authority as kings one hour with the Wild Beast. These have one purpose and they give their power and authority to the Wild Beast. These shall make war with the Lamb, and the Lamb shall gain the victory over them because He is Lord of lords and King of kings, and they shall also gain the victory who are with Him, the called and the chosen and the faithful.

15-18   And he says to me, The waters which you saw, where the prostitute is sitting, are peoples and multitudes and nations and languages. And the ten horns which you saw and the Wild Beast, these shall hate the prostitute and shall make her a ruin and reduce her to nakedness. And her flesh they shall eat. And they shall consume her with fire, for God did put it into their hearts to do that which was in His mind, and to come to one mind and to give their [royal] power to the Wild Beast until the words of God should be accomplished. And the woman whom you saw is the city, the great one, which possesses [imperial] power over the kings of the earth.

1-3   After these things I saw another angel coming down out of heaven having great authority. And the earth was illuminated by his glory. And he cried with a mighty voice, saying, It has fallen, it has fallen, Babylon the Great, and it has become a dwelling place of demons and a haunt of every unclean spirit and a haunt of every unclean bird, and the object of detestation, because as a result of the wine of the wrath [that fell upon her], because of her fornication all the nations have fallen. And the kings of the earth committed fornication with her.

And the merchants of the earth as a result of her power and luxury became wealthy.

And I heard another voice out of the heaven, saying, **4-8** Come out of her at once, my people, in order that you may not be a joint-participant with her in her sins, and in order that you may not receive of her plagues, for her sins have piled up in a coherent mass so that they touch the heaven [i.e., the sky]. And God remembered her crimes. Render to her at once as she herself also rendered [to others], and pay back double according to her works. In the cup in which she mixed, mix for her at once a double [allotment]. In the measure in which she glorified herself and lived in luxury, in that measure render to her torment and sorrow, because in her heart she is saying, I am enthroned as a queen, and am not a widow, and sorrow I shall positively not see. Because of this in one day shall her plagues come, death and sorrow and famine, and in fire she shall be completely consumed, for mighty is the Lord God who has handed her over for judicial punishment.

And they shall weep audibly and beat their breasts **9-13** in grief over her, the kings of the earth who with her committed fornication and lived in luxury, when they are looking upon the smoke of her burning, standing at a distance because of the fear of her torment, saying, Woe, woe, the city, the great city, Babylon, the city which is mighty, because in one hour your judicial punishment has come. And the merchants of the earth weep audibly and are grieved over her, because their cargo no one any longer buys in the market, a cargo of gold and silver and precious stone and pearls and fine linen and purple cloth and silk and scarlet cloth and every kind of citron wood and every kind of an article made of ivory and every kind of an article made of most costly wood and of brass and of iron and of marble; and cinnamon and spice and incense and perfume and frankincense and wine and olive oil and the finest grade of wheat flour and grain and cattle and sheep and horses and four-wheeled carriages and persons of individuals and souls of men.

14-19   And the fruit which your soul longed after has departed from you. And all the luxurious things and the brightly shining things have perished from you, and no longer will you see them at all. The merchants who dealt in these things, those who became wealthy by her, shall stand at a distance because of the fear of her torment, weeping audibly and grieving, saying, Woe, woe, the city, the great city, the city arrayed in fine linen and purple and scarlet garments, adorned with gold and precious stone and pearl, because in one hour such great wealth has been ruined. And every sailing-master and everyone who sails to a place and mariners and as many as earn their living by the sea, stood at a distance and kept on crying out, seeing the smoke of her burning, saying, What city is like the city, the great city? And they threw dust upon their heads and kept on crying out, weeping audibly and grieving, saying, Woe, woe, the city, the great one, in which all those who have ships on the sea were made wealthy by reason of her abundance of costly things, because in one hour she was ruined.

20, 21   Be rejoicing over her, O heaven, and you saints and apostles and prophets, because God pronounced judgment for you against her. And one angel, a mighty one, took up a stone like a great millstone and hurled it into the sea, saying, In this manner, with a violent rush, shall Babylon, the great city, be thrown down and shall never again be found.

22-24   And a sound of harpers and musicians and flute players and of trumpet players shall never again be heard in you. And every craftsman of every craft shall never again be found in you. And the sound of a millstone shall never again be heard in you. And the light of a lamp shall never again shine in you. And a voice of a bridegroom and a bride shall never again be heard in you; because your merchants were the great men of the earth, because with your magical arts all the nations were led astray. And in her there was found blood of prophets and saints and of all those who have been slain on the earth.

After these things I heard a great sound like that of **1-3**
a great multitude in heaven, saying, Hallelujah [Praise
the Lord]. The salvation and the glory and the power
belong to our God, because dependable and righteous are
His judgments, for He administered justice upon the
prostitute, the great one, who is of such a character that
she corrupted the earth with her fornication, and He has
exacted a penalty from her because of the blood of His
bondslaves. And a second time they said, Hallelujah.
And her smoke ascends forever and forever.

And the twenty-four elders and the four living beings **4-10**
fell down and worshipped God who is seated upon the
throne, saying, Amen. Hallelujah. And there came out
a voice from the throne, saying, Be giving praise to our
God, all those who are His bondslaves, those who fear
Him, those who are of a lowly station in life and those
who are great. And I heard a sound like the voice of
a great multitude and like the sound of many waters and
like the sound of mighty thunders, saying, Hallelujah, because the Lord our God, the Omnipotent, has assumed His
royal authority. Let us be rejoicing and let us be glad. And
let us give the glory to Him at once, because the wedding
of the Lamb has come, and His bride has made herself
ready. And it was given to her that she should array herself in fine linen, shining, bright, clean, for the fine linen is
the righteous acts of the saints. And he says to me, Write
at once. Spiritually prosperous and fortunate are those
who have been invited to the banquet of the wedding of
the Lamb. And he says to me, These are the dependable
words of God. And I fell at his feet to worship him. And
he says to me, See to it that you do not do so. I am a
fellow bondslave of yours and of your brethren who hold
the testimony of [concerning] Jesus. Worship God. For
the testimony of [concerning] Jesus is the spirit [the disposition or characteristic] of prophecy [the forth-telling of
God's word].

And I saw the opened heaven. And consider this. A **11-13**
horse, a white one, and He who is seated upon it who is
called Faithful and Dependable. And in righteousness

He administers justice and makes war. And His eyes were a flame of fire. And upon His head there were royal crowns, many of them. He has a name which has been written which no one knows except He himself. And He is clothed with a garment which has been stained with blood. And His name has been called, and the name is on record, The Word of God.

14-16 And the armies which are in heaven kept on following Him [in a steady procession, rank after rank] upon white horses, clothed in fine linen, shining, bright, clean. And out of His mouth there proceeds a sword, a sharp one, in order that with it He should strike down the nations. And He himself shall shepherd them with an iron scepter. And He himself treads the wine press of the wine of the wrath of the anger of God, the Omnipotent. And He has upon His garment and upon His thigh a name which has been written, King of kings and Lord of lords.

17, 18 And I saw an angel standing in the sun. And he cried out with a great voice, saying to all the birds that fly in mid-heaven, Come. Be gathered together to the banquet, the great one of God, in order that you may eat the flesh of kings and the flesh of chiliarchs and the flesh of mighty men and the flesh of horses and of those who sit on them, and the flesh of freemen and also of slaves and of small and great.

19-21 And I saw the Wild Beast and the kings of the earth and their troops gathered together for the purpose of engaging in battle with Him who is seated on the horse and with His army. And the Wild Beast was seized and with him the False Prophet who performed the attesting miracles before him by which he deceived those who received the mark of identification of the Wild Beast and those who worship his image. The two were thrown alive into the lake of fire burning with brimstone. And the rest were killed with the sword of Him who is seated upon the horse, which sword proceeded out of His mouth. And all the birds gorged themselves with their flesh.

And I saw an angel coming down out of heaven having   1-3
the key of the bottomless place and a great chain upon his
hand. And he seized the Dragon in one fell swoop, the
snake, the ancient snake who is the Devil and the Satan,
and bound him for one thousand years. And he threw
him into the bottomless place and locked and sealed it over
him in order that he should not deceive the nations any
longer until the thousand years have been brought to an
end. After these things it is a necessity in the nature of
the case for him to be set free for a brief period.

And I saw thrones, and they sat upon them, and au-   4-6
thority to administer justice was given them. And I saw
the souls of those who had been beheaded because of the
testimony [they bore to] of Jesus and because of the
word of God. And I saw those who were such that they
did not worship the Wild Beast nor his image and did
not receive his mark of identification upon their forehead
and hand. And they lived and reigned as kings with the
Christ one thousand years. The rest of the dead did not
live until the thousand years were brought to a close.
This is the resurrection, the first one. Spiritually prosperous and holy is he who has a share in the first resurrection. Over these the second death does not have authority. But they shall be priests of God and of the
Christ. And they shall reign as kings with Him one
thousand years.

And whenever the thousand years are finished the   7-10
Satan shall be set free from his prison and shall go forth
to deceive the nations which are in the four corners of
the earth, Gog and Magog, to gather them together for
the war, their number being as the sand of the sea. And
they went up over the breadth of the earth, and encircled
the camp of the saints and the city, the beloved one. And
fire came down out of the heaven and consumed them.
And the Devil, the one who deceives them, was thrown
into the lake of fire and brimstone where both the Wild
Beast and the False Prophet [are]. And they shall be
tormented day and night forever and forever.

11-15   And I saw a throne, a great white one, and Him who is seated on it, from whose face the earth and the heaven fled. And place was not found for them. And I saw the dead, the great and the small, standing before the throne. And the scrolls were opened. And another scroll was opened which is the scroll of the life. And the dead were judged on the basis of the things that stand written in the scrolls according to their works. And the sea gave up the dead who were in it. And death and the Unseen gave up the dead who were in them. And each one was judged according to their works. And death and the Unseen were thrown into the lake of fire. This is the second death, the lake of fire. And whoever was not found recorded in the book of the life was cast into the lake of fire.

1, 2   And I saw a heaven new in quality and an earth new in quality, for the first heaven and the first earth passed away. And the sea does not exist any longer. And the city, the holy city, Jerusalem, the one new in quality, I saw coming down out of heaven from God, having been prepared as a bride who has been adorned for her groom.

3, 4   And I heard a voice, a great one, out of the throne, saying, Consider this. The tent of God [the glorified body of the Lord Jesus in which He lives] is with men. And He shall live in a tent with them. And they themselves shall be His people, and God himself shall be with them, and shall wipe out every tear from their eyes. And death shall be no more. Neither shall there be any longer mourning nor crying nor pain, for the former things passed away.

5-8   And He who is seated upon the throne said, Consider this. I make all things new in quality. And He says, Write at once, because these words are trustworthy and dependable. And He said to me, They have come to pass and stand accomplished. As for myself, I am the Alpha and the Omega, the originating cause and the One who brings things to their consummation. As for myself, I will give to him who is thirsty out of the spring of the water of the life as an undeserved gift. He who gains the victory shall inherit these things. And I will be his God and he himself will be my son. But the cowardly and the unbelievers and those defiled with that which is abominable and murderers and prostitutes and those who practice magical arts and idolaters and all liars shall have their part in the lake which burns with fire and brimstone, which is the second death.

And there came one of the seven angels who have the seven bowls filled with the seven plagues, the final ones, and spoke with me, saying, Come. I will show you the bride, the wife of the Lamb. And he carried me off in [my] spirit to a mountain, great and lofty, and showed me the holy city, Jerusalem, coming down out of heaven from God, having the glory of God. Its splendor and radiance as a luminary, a light-giving body, was like a stone which is most precious, like a stone of crystal-clear jasper, having a wall, great and high, having twelve large gates, and at the gates twelve angels, and names written upon them which are the names of the twelve sons of Israel; on the east three gates, on the north three gates, on the south three gates, and on the west three gates. And the wall of the city has twelve foundations, and upon them twelve names of the twelve apostles of the Lamb. **9-14**

And he who is speaking with me was having as a measuring instrument a golden reed, in order that he might measure the city and its gates and its wall. And the city is laid out in the form of a square, and its length is equal to the breadth. And he measured the city with the reed, fifteen hundred miles [on each side]. Its length and breadth and height are equal. And he measured its wall, two hundred and sixteen feet [in height], using the measuring system of mankind, which was that used by the angel. And the material of which its wall was composed was jasper. And the city was pure gold like clear crystal. **15-18**

The foundations of the wall of the city have been adorned with every kind of precious stone. The first foundation was jasper, the second sapphire, the third a chalcedony, the fourth an emerald, the fifth sardonyx, the sixth sardius, the seventh chrysolite, the eighth beryl, the ninth a topaz, the tenth a chrysoprasus, the eleventh **19-22** a jacinth, the twelfth an amethyst. And the twelve gates were twelve pearls. Each one of the several gates was one pearl. And the broad avenue of the city was pure gold like transparent glass. And an inner sanctuary I did not see in it, for the Lord God, the Omnipotent, is its inner sanctuary, and the Lamb.

23-27   And the city has no need of the sun nor of the moon to illuminate it, for the glory of God illuminated it, and its lamp is the Lamb. And the nations shall walk by means of its light. And the kings of the earth bring their glory into it. And its gates shall by no means be locked during the day, for night shall not be there. And they shall bring the glory and the honor of the nations into it. And there shall positively not enter it anything unclean and he who makes an abomination and a lie, except those written in the scroll of the life of the Lamb.

1, 2   And he showed me a river of water of life, sparkling like crystal, proceeding out of the throne of God and of the Lamb. In the midst of its [the city's] broad avenue and on this side and on that side of the river was a tree of life bearing twelve fruits, yielding its fruit each month. And the leaves of the tree were for the health of the nations.

3-7   And every curse shall exist no longer. And the throne of God and of the Lamb shall be in it. And His bondslaves shall render Him sacred service. And they shall see His face. And His Name shall be on their foreheads. And there shall be night no longer. And they do not have need of the light of a lamp nor of the sun because the Lord God shall shed light upon them. And they shall reign as kings forever and forever.

And he said to me, These words are trustworthy and dependable. And the Lord God of the spirits [their human spirits as informed by the Holy Spirit] of the prophets sent His messenger on a commission to show to His bondslaves things which of necessity must come to pass shortly. And consider this. I am coming soon. Spiritually prosperous is he who keeps the words of the prophecy of this scroll.

And I, John, am he who is hearing and seeing these things. And when I heard and saw, I fell down to worship before the feet of the angel who was showing me these things. And he says to me, See to it that you do not do so. I am a fellow bondslave of yours and of your brethren the prophets and of those who are keeping the words of this scroll. Worship God. **8, 9**

And he says to me, Do not begin to seal up the words of the prophecy of this scroll, for the strategic, epochal time is imminent. He who is unrighteous, let him practice unrighteousness still. And he who is [morally] polluted, let him pollute himself still. And he who is righteous, let him practice righteousness still. And he who is holy, let him be made holy still. **10, 11**

Consider this. I am coming soon. And my reward is with me, to render to each one according to his work. As for myself, I am the Alpha and the Omega, the First and the Last, the originating cause and the One who brings to completion. Spiritually prosperous are those who wash their robes in order that theirs shall be the authority over the tree of the life and in order that they may go through the gates into the city. Outside are the dogs and those who practice magical arts, and the fornicators and the murderers and the idolaters and everyone who is fond of and practices falsehood. **12-15**

I, Jesus, sent my messenger to testify these things to you in the [local] assemblies. As for myself, I am the root and the offspring of David, the star, the bright one, the morning star. And the Spirit and the bride are saying, Be coming. And he who hears, let him say, Be coming. And he who is thirsty, let him be coming. He who is desirous, let him take at once the water of life gratis. It is I who am testifying to everyone who hears the words of the prophecy of this scroll; if anyone adds to them, God shall add to him the plagues which stand written in this scroll. And if anyone shall take away from the words of the scroll of [containing] this prophecy, God shall take away his portion from the tree of the life and from **16-19**

the holy city, from the things which stand written in
this scroll.

21   He who testifies these things says, Surely, I am coming soon. Amen [So let it be]. Be coming, Lord Jesus.

20   The grace of the Lord Jesus be with all.